TOWARD A LITERARY HISTORY OF BLACK WOMEN

"If there is a single distinguishing feature of the literature of black women—and this accounts for their lack of recognition—it is this: their literature is about black women; it takes the trouble to record the thoughts, words, feelings and deeds of black women, experiences that make the realities of being black in America look very different from what men have written."

—from Mary Helen Washington's essay
in *Reading Black, Reading Feminist*

From the literary tradition of the slave narrative to the poetry of Maya Angelou and the prize-winning fiction of Alice Walker and Gloria Naylor, this unique collection offers a piercing look at an important group of writers, some of whom have been heretofore absent from official black histories and literary criticism. Here is a unique new perspective on women's writing that is both black and feminist, providing a running commentary on the collective experience of black women in the United States.

HENRY LOUIS GATES, JR. is one of the most active and visible scholars in the field of African-American Studies. He has taught at Yale and Cornell and is currently the John Spencer Bassett Professor of English at Duke University. In 1981 Gates was awarded a MacArthur Foundation "genius" grant, and his book *The Signifying Monkey: A Theory of Afro-American Literary Criticism* won an American Book Award in 1989.

READING BLACK, READING FEMINIST

A Critical Anthology

Edited by
Henry Louis Gates, Jr.

A MERIDIAN BOOK

For Ruth Simmons and Eleanor Traylor

MERIDIAN
Published by the Penguin Group
Penguin Books USA Inc., 375 Hudson Street, New York, New York 10014, U.S.A.
Penguin Books Ltd, 27 Wrights Lane, London W8 5TZ, England
Penguin Books Australia Ltd, Ringwood, Victoria, Australia
Penguin Books Canada Ltd, 2801 John Street, Markham, Ontario, Canada L3R 1B4
Penguin Books (N.Z.) Ltd, 182-190 Wairau Road, Auckland 10, New Zealand

Penguin Books Ltd, Registered Offices: Harmondsworth, Middlesex, England

First published by Meridian, an imprint of New American Library,
a division of Penguin Books USA Inc.
Published simultaneously in Canada.

First Printing, October, 1990
10   9   8   7   6   5   4   3   2

REGISTERED TRADEMARK—MARCA REGISTRADA

LIBRARY OF CONGRESS CATALOGING IN PUBLICATION DATA

Reading black, reading feminist : a critical anthology / edited by
    Henry Louis Gates, Jr.
        p.   cm.
    ISBN 0-452-01045-4
    1. American literature—Afro-American authors—History and
criticism.   2. Feminism and literature—United States—History—20th
century.   3. Women and literature—United States—History—20th century.
4. American literature—Women authors—History and criticism.   5. American
literature—20th century—History and criticism.   6. Afro-American
women in literature.   7. Afro-Americans in literature.   I. Gates, Henry Louis.
PS153.N5R38   1990
810.9'352042—dc20
                                                            90-35286
                                                            CIP

Printed in the United States of America
Set in Palatino
Designed by Nissa Knuth

Contents

Reading Black, Reading Feminist

Interviews

Introduction

Henry Louis Gates, Jr.

Obviously we will have to learn to read the Afro-American literary tradition in new ways, for continuing on in the old way is impossible . . . The making of a literary history in which black women are fully represented is a search for full vision to create a circle where now we have but a segment.

—Mary Helen Washington

I

Anna Julia Cooper, a prototypical black feminist whose 1892 book of essays, *A Voice from the South*, is considered to be one of the founding texts of the black feminist movement, argued eloquently for the recognition of the black woman's literary tradition:

One muffled strain in the Silent South, a jarring chord and a vague and uncomprehended cadenza has been and still is the Negro. And of that muffled chord, the one mute and voiceless note has been the sadly expectant Black Woman . . . The "other side" has not been represented by one who "lives there." And not many can more sensibly realize and more accurately tell the weight and fret of the "long dull pain" than the open-eyed but hitherto voiceless Black Woman of America . . . [just] as our Caucasian barristers are not to blame if they cannot *quite* put themselves in the dark man's place, neither should the dark man be wholly expected fully and adequately to reproduce the exact Voice of the Black Woman.

Cooper's claim of the especial authority of the black woman's voice, and her explicit challenge to black male authors who until quite recently felt no apparent ambivalence at all when claiming to speak for "the Negro" or representing "the Negro" as a man, has taken three quarters of a century to manifest itself in a literary tradition of its own. Since 1970, with the publication of those monuments of this tradition, Toni Morrison's *The Bluest Eye*, Alice Walker's *The Third Life of Grange Copeland*, and Maya Angelou's *I Know Why the Caged Bird Sings*, and of Toni Cade Bambara's anthology, *The Black Woman*, black women writers have come to the forefront of Afro-American literary creativity.

Much has been made—too much—of the supposed social animosities between black men and women and the relation between the commercial success of the black women's literary movement and the depiction of black male sexism. Perhaps some media commentators have been titillated by the notion of a primal black fratricide–sororicide. But the popularity of black women's literature has nothing to do with anti–black male conspiracies—as is occasionally charged. Rather, it stems from the compelling blend of realistic and lyrical narrative modes, as demonstrated, for example, in the so-called "magical realism" of Toni Morrison's *Song of Solomon* and *Beloved*. It is as if the best of Richard Wright's prose and the best of Ralph Ellison's prose had fused into a new literary language. Added to this is the sheer energy that accompanies the utterance of a new subject matter, a formalized breaking of the silence of black women as authors. In doing so, they have generated a resoundingly new voice, one that is at once black *and* female, replete with its own shadings and timbres, topoi and tropes.

But no literary movement can be understood apart from the institutional and demographic facts of reading and writing that sustain—or fail to sustain—the author and her audience. This tradition within a tradition is often related to, yet stands independent of, the black male tradition and its triangle of influence, Richard Wright, James Baldwin, and Ralph Ellison. Yet contemporary black women writers have generated collectively a loyal and devoted readership more cosmopolitan and integrated (by race *and* by gender) than the customary market for black male writing has been. The phenomenal sales figures of works by Morrison and Walker, for instance, and the sheer level of production of novels and books of poems in less than two decades—works by Paule Marshall, Toni Cade Bambara, Gloria Naylor, Jamaica Kincaid, Andrea Lee, Lucille Clifton, Sherley Anne Williams, Ann Shockley, Ntozake Shange, Adrienne Kennedy, Alexis Deveaux, Kristin Hunter, Gayl Jones, Octavia Butler, Terry Macmillan, Thulani Davis, Maya Angelou, Michele Cliff, Marita Golden, June Jordan, Sonia Sanchez, Audre Lorde, Rita Dove, Gwendolyn Brooks, and several others—attest to the vitality and consistency both of this new readership and of the movement itself. As feminist critic Hortense Spillers put it, "The community of black women writing in the United States now can be regarded as a vivid new fact of national life." Nor is this merely an American phenomenon: As critic Selwyn Cudjoe recently noted, black women writers in the Caribbean have published over thirty novels since 1970. Clearly, we are in the midst of a major international literary movement.

Octavia Butler has published nine novels, Toni Morrison has published five, and Walker has published four. Morrison was also a powerful and imaginative editor at Random House when the movement began, and her role in its generation was key. Publishing such formidable figures as Toni Cade Bambara, Gayl Jones, and Angela Davis; inspiring by her own example a younger generation of writers, especially Gloria Naylor; and writing several best-selling novels herself, Morrison demonstrated to publishing houses that a new and identifiable readership eager for a "woman-oriented" content would handily sustain even more publications by black women. Her productivity, vision, and craft established the movement's pace; hers has been a role similar to that of Alain Locke in the Harlem Renaissance and Amiri Baraka in the Black Arts movement.

The black women's literary movement, it seems safe to say, already has taken its place as a distinct period in Afro-American literary history, and could very well prove to be one of the most productive and sustained. Certainly it has features that make it anomalous in black literary history. Despite the very public and bitter rows about the political implications of black women writing about black male sexism, this movement has not promoted itself as bombastically or as self-consciously as, say, did the Harlem Renaissance or the Black Arts movement. And whereas most older black male writers deny any black influence at all—or eagerly claim a white paternity—black female authors often claim descent from other black women literary ancestors, such as Zora Neale Hurston and Ann Petry. To an unparalleled extent, the writers in this movement have been intent upon bonding with other women. And the "patricide" which characterized Baldwin's and Ellison's declarations of independence from Wright has no matricidal counterpart. Indeed, Morrison's generous stewardship has served as a model for the creation of a literary sisterhood that seems to take it for granted that good writing will find a publisher. Black women writers are free of the anxiety that only one black writer can emerge from the group, in splendid commercial isolation, as "the" black writer of the decade.

In part, this movement is an extension of the Black Arts movement, as well as its repudiation. While several authors have bridged both movements (Brooks, Sanchez, Marshall, Morrison), black women's writings since 1970 represent worlds in which the Black Goddess/Black Queen stereotypes of the Black Arts movement—and the corresponding Black Warrior/Black Prince stereotypes for men—are rejected as cardboard stereotypes just as pernicious as the Sambo–Mammy types of the white racist plantation tradition. In this sense, the writing of black women is "political," indeed, but it takes its craft too seriously to be dismissed as merely propaganda.

What effect has the explosion of black women's writing had upon scholarship? The growing institutionalization of Afro-American literature in traditional English departments has been concomitant with the growth of black women's literature. Afro-American Studies and Women's Studies share a common terrain and a common discourse in the criticism of black women's writings: As Houston Baker put the matter recently, "The convergence of feminist and Afro-American theoretical formulations offers the most challenging nexus for scholarship in the coming years . . . One aspect of that development will be the continued reshaping of the literary canon as forgotten, neglected, or suppressed texts are rediscovered."

A split, or doubled readership, one both black and female, has created a market larger and more consistent than that enjoyed by black authors since perhaps the abolitionist movement. The production of works of criticism by and about black women's writing has kept pace with the production of texts by black women creative artists. Critical works by—among others—Barbara Christian, Hazel Carby, Mari Evans, Valerie Smith, Gloria Hull, Trudier Harris, Thadious Davis, Mae Henderson, Hortense Spillers, Gloria Watkins, Barbara Johnson, Deborah McDowell, Frances Foster, Susan Willis, Barbara Smith, Houston Baker, Nellie McKay, Elizabeth Ammons, Michael Awkward, and even Harold Bloom, have either recently been published or are scheduled to appear soon. The launching of several reprint series, including the Beacon Black Women Writers Series, Rutgers's American Women Writers Series, and the Oxford-Schomburg forty-volume Library of 19th Century Black Women's Writings are signs of this movement's expanding and voracious readership.

Several important anthologies, such as Mary Helen Washington's *Invented Lives*, Mari Evans's *The Black Woman Writer* and *But Some of Us Are Brave*, edited by Gloria Hull, Patricia Bell Scott, and Barbara Smith, have played a pivotal role in the institutionalization of black women in literature in the university curriculum. Every anthology defines a canon and thereby serves to preserve a tradition in what is designated as its most representative parts. In black letters, anthologies have *carried* a literary inheritance along from generation to generation, protecting an author's works from loss. Some black women writers' works, especially in the first half of this century, exist *only* in anthologies. Many, however, were not so fortunately preserved.

Above all, the writers collected here are concerned with tradition and its construction. "Tradition. Now there's a word that nags the feminist critic," Mary Helen Washington writes.

A word that has so often been used to exclude or misrepresent women . . . Why is the fugitive slave, the fiery orator, the political activist, the abolitionist always represented as a black *man*? How does the heroic voice and heroic image of the black woman get suppressed in a culture that depended on her heroism for its survival?

The clarity of Washington's answer disturbs:

What we have to recognize is that the creation of the fiction of tradition is a matter of power, not justice, and

that that power has always been in the hands of men—
mostly white but some black. Women are the disinherited. Our "ritual journeys," our "articulate voices," our
"symbolic spaces" are rarely the same as men's . . . The
appropriation by men of power to define tradition accounts for women's absence from our records.

By and large, black women have been absent from official
black histories and literary criticism. We are only just recover-
ing, piece by piece, the parts of black women's literary past.
But Mary Helen Washington's reference to the "fiction of
tradition" is a clue to the way in which this organizing concept has itself been criticized and reconstructed. Because "tradition" has served as a powerful heuristic term, we are always
in danger of reifying it, treating it as literary structure that
exists independently of the narratives we construct about it,
independently of the social practices of reading. Nor can we
conflate tradition as it conditions the contemporary act of
reading and tradition as it conditions the historic act of writing; this is simply a failure to appreciate the distinct social and
historical positioning of reader and writer. That an ideology of
tradition *can* tend toward a naive organicism, however, need
not vitiate its value for the self-conscious critic, as a generation
of black feminist critics have demonstrated. If it is a fiction, it
remains a necessary fiction.
The mixed blessing of the scholar of this body of texts is
that we must resurrect it even before we can analyze it. As
Spillers put it cogently, with the exception of a handful of
autobiographical narratives from the nineteenth-century, the
black woman's

realities are virtually suppressed until the period of the
Harlem Renaissance and later. Essentially the black woman
as artist, as intellectual spokesperson for her own cultural
apprenticeship, has not existed before, for anyone. At the
source of her own symbol-making task, this community
of writers confronts, therefore, a tradition of work that is
quite recent, its continuities, broken and sporadic.

Reading Black, Reading Feminist is just one effort in the larger
project to resurrect, explicate, and canonize the Afro-American

women's literary heritage. In reading these texts, we overhear a black woman *testifying* about what the twin scourges of sexism and racism, merged into one oppressive entity, actually *do* to a human being, how the combination confines the imagination, perplexes the will, and delimits free choice. What unites these texts, what makes them cohere into that imaginary metatext we call a tradition, is their shared structures and common themes. As Washington argues,

> Their literature is about black women; it takes the trouble to record the thoughts, words, feelings, and deeds of black women, experiences that make the realities of being black in America look very different from what men have written. There are no women in this tradition hibernating in dark holes contemplating their invisibility; there are no women dismembering the bodies or crushing the skulls of either women or men; and few, if any, women in the literature of black women succeed in heroic quests without the support of other women or men in their communities. Women talk to other women in this tradition.

The essays in this collection seek to demonstrate explicitly how the texts of black women configure into a tradition, both thematically and structurally, in which black women's texts are set in conversation. Literary works are in dialogue not because of some mystical collective unconscious determined by the biology of race or gender, but because writers read other writers and *ground* their representations of experience in models of language provided largely by other writers to whom they feel akin. It is through this mode of literary revision, amply evident in the *texts* themselves—in formal echoes, recast metaphors, even in parody—that a "tradition" emerges and is defined.

But such formal bonding is only one dimension of the larger project of literary history. And to appreciate this means not to ignore the claims of experience, of history itself: When sexuality, race, and gender are both the condition and the basis of personal identity, they must shape the very possibility of expressive culture.

It is hardly surprising, therefore, that these critics have brought home the importance of attending to one's own positionality, a move that has often emerged in what Houston Baker calls the "black autobiographical moment." Few are inclined to stake out any Olympian perch; few profess a disinterested gaze. Criticism, for them, is as local, provisional, and context bound as the literature on which it comments. And as scholars, they retain the historical sense that the black woman subject—or, for that matter, the white male subject—does not arrive already constituted upon the historical stage. Studies of those formative eighteenth- and nineteenth-century discourses have acquainted us with the ways in which gender has become racialized, and race gendered. But to point out that such categories have always been fluid is only to say that they have, from the beginning, named sites for contestation and negotiation.

Perhaps they have learned from some of the early missteps of both the black nationalist and women's movements. In any event, having been excluded from representational authority for so long, black feminists have declined to respond with a counter-politics of exclusion. They have never been obsessed with arriving at any singular self-image; or legislating who may or may not speak on the subject; or policing boundaries between "us" and "them." And of course, it is just such an embracive politics of inclusion that has made this book possible.

Inspirited by the important work of such activist-intellectuals as Barbara Smith and Angela Davis, black feminist criticism has been empowering for a whole community of critics; almost all worthwhile criticism of black literature written in the past decade has been profoundly informed by its insights and perspectives. And for all its current diversity, it has taken Davis's warnings about the perils of narrowly interest-based politics to heart. Again, rather than attempt to construct a monolith of "the" black woman's experience, black feminists have sought to chart the multiplicity of experiences and perspectives. Perhaps, then, the contradictions that *Reading Black, Reading Feminist* contains (and is contained by) will themselves prove instructive. And it is very much my hope that the heteroglossia that Mae Henderson explores as characteristic of black women's literature may find a correlate in the polyphony of voices—female and male, black and white, gay and straight—that this collection seeks to present.

II

It is fitting that the collection begin with an unpublished essay by Zora Neale Hurston, whose work and career more than those of any other black woman writer, have become the symbols of a reclaimed literary tradition. Hurston wrote the essay, dated January 13, 1938, while working on a volume about "The Negro in Florida" for the Federal Writers Project, under the supervision of Stetson Kennedy, who is responsible for the essay's survival and its publication here. Kennedy's introduction provides the context for the essay's origins, and offers a unique interpretation of Hurston during this period in her career. It is not surprising that the essay was not published, for it serves as a bold critique of certain conventions of representation within the African-American literary tradition, conventions utilized in the main by black male authors, conventions under which Hurston obviously felt constrained. These conventions, Hurston argues, have "precluded originality and denied creation in the arts," producing a literature characterized by "the same old theme, the same old phrases." A thinly veiled critique of W.E.B. Du Bois and Richard Wright, among others, the essay is also noteworthy for what it reveals about Hurston's understanding of the import of her own novels—especially *Jonah's Gourd Vine*—in relation to the black male conventions of "Race Champions," and her belief that she had, as she puts it, "for the first time" written "a Negro story . . . without special pleading. The characters [in *Jonah's Gourd Vine*] are seen in relation to themselves and not in relation to the whites as has been the rule. To watch these people one would conclude that there are no white people in the world." Hurston concludes her third-person account of her own significance by arguing that "the author is an artist that will go far." Hurston's brief for what she calls "a growing taste for literature," rather than propaganda or protest—stated here for the first time in such explicit terms— is of enormous significance to the contemporary black women's literary movement, especially because it is this aspect of Hurston's art that has proved to be compelling for writers such as Toni Cade Bambara, Toni Morrison, and Alice Walker.

Mary Helen Washington occupies a unique place in the renascence of interest in black women's literature; these "Notes

Toward a Literary History of Black Women" come from one of the most distinguished practitioners of such literary history. To reject and transcend the male-centered literary history of the past, Washington points out, "is an act of enlightenment, not simply repudiation." She transumes an image from Anna Julia Cooper's *A Voice from the South* to figure her own literary endeavor, "a search for full vision, to create a circle where now we have but a segment."

In "The High's and the Low's," Barbara Christian, the first scholar to write a book about the black women's literary tradition, offers a spirited critique of the uncritical reappropriation of the values and language of so-called "high" academic culture by black feminists, and urges them instead simultaneously to "retrieve the low ground," the very grounds of ritual and the vernacular upon which the Black Women's literary tradition is founded.

Michele Wallace, whose *Black Macho and the Myth of the Superwoman* proved to be a signal intervention in the generation of the contemporary black woman's literary movement, explores "the revolutionary challenge black feminist creativity could pose to white male cultural hegemony." Wallace critiques the binary oppositions of "the discourse of the dominant culture [which] tends to automatically erase black female subjectivity." Positing the black woman as "the 'other' of the 'other,' " Wallace argues persuasively that "radical negation, or doubling or tripling the difference," could very well offer a means by which "to reformulate the problem of black female subjectivity and black female participation in culture," in a critical discourse created by black women themselves.

Sherley Anne Williams, a distinguished novelist and critic, argues that a "womanist" perspective can help illuminate our understanding of the black man under patriarchy as well as the black woman, and briefly surveys the changing representation of the black man in nineteenth- and twentieth-century literature. Williams cites a conception of engaged (*bolekaja*) criticism from the Nigerian Leavisite, Chinweizu, as a possible model for a womanist theory of reading that will promote both community and dialogue.

Hazel Carby's essay explores the issue of representation in black writing, bringing in proximity its distinct political and discursive senses. Carby reads Nella Larsen's *Quicksands* as a representation of an alienated individual "embedded within capitalist social relations," and contrasts Larsen with Jessie Fauset. Fauset, Carby argues, "adapted but did not transcend the form of the romance," whereas Nella Larsen refused to provide a resolution on the level of a narrative of contradictions in the social real. Wary of the retreat from realism represented by the rural idyll, Carby also questions the tendency to fetishize the rural *Lebenswelt* over the proletarian urban life.

Deborah McDowell's contribution focuses on the shift from a public (exemplary) to a private (and self-expressive) narrative, and counterposes the didacticism of Frances E. W. Harper's *Iola LeRoy* (1892) to the overt psychologism of Alice Walker's *The Color Purple*. "Each writer writes the missing parts to the other writer's story," Alice Walker insists. "And the whole story is what I'm after." Precisely what is or is not missing, and why, is McDowell's concern in this essay.

Mae Henderson brings to bear linguistic insights of Mikhail Bakhtin in tracing the interplay of glossolalia and heteroglossia from the Old and New Testaments to twentieth-century Afro-American women's literature. Henderson advances a truly critical stance that would resist monisms of all sorts, and that insists on plural subject-positions, and on a dialogic subjectivity that is radical to both race and gender, as she explores Sherley Anne Williams's *Dessa Rose* and Zora Neale Hurston's *Their Eyes Were Watching God*.

III

Barbara Johnson's essay on Richard Wright's *Native Son* implicitly responds to Sherley Anne Williams's challenge to employ feminist insights to reread the representations of the black male in the Afro-American canon. The strategic importance of Johnson's intervention, indeed a feminist rereading of the archetypal black male author, poses the question, "Where, in Richard Wright, does the black woman stand with respect to the black man's *writing*?" Johnson cunningly elicits the story of the black female reader in the text, locating the reader—and the reading—Richard Wright must face.

Starting with a conception of picture making as a kind of world making, Timothy Murray centers on dramas by Ntozake

Shange and Adrienne Kennedy that are, in some sense, about visual representation. Given an ideology of the visible, Murray asks if we can move toward the specificity of "a *black* corporeal presence." As he explores the possibilities of a "technologically stressed aesthetic commitment," Murray shows how the works of Shange and Kennedy eschew the prospect of any transcendental point of view as they carry out a project of "redemption, retrieval, and reclamation of the literary page and visual space."

Examining the history of black women's self-representation, Elizabeth Fox-Genovese finds that the "identity of the self remains hostage to the history of the collectivity." Reading the autobiographical mode in Harriet Jacobs (Linda Brent), Harriet Wilson, and Zora Neale Hurston, she shows how a distrust or ambivalence toward the reader cannot always be divorced from an author's struggle against those structures of oppression that help to confer on her a social and political identity.

Barbara Johnson returns with a very brief consideration of the first black American poet, a figure more often adulated, anathematized, or allegorized than *read*. She examines the strategy of "excessive compliance" by which Phillis Wheatley exposed the contradictions inherent in her own situation, and, Johnson suggests, in white liberalism more generally.

Valerie Smith's reading of Harriet Jacobs's classic *Incidents in the Life of a Slave Girl* shows that its confinement to the idiom of the sentimental novel does not prevent it from developing that narrative space as a literary loophole of retreat—as a space of liberation. Straining the form's generic limits, she can speak of its inadequacies through her silences; even as she casts herself as a character in a sentimental romance, she can still make mayhem.

Nellie McKay, herself a distinguished practitioner of the biographer's art, proposes the idea of *feminist* autobiography that would not cover public, intellectual achievements at the expense of one's more inward, emotional life; that would, indeed, break down this opposition between public and private spheres. In a sympathetic reading of W.E.B. Du Bois, McKay suggests that his *Darkwater* carries a feminist critique, that its author hates the South for injuring black womanhood. Surveying the role of black women in his life, McKay further suggests that Du Bois understood the politics of gender far better than he is usually given credit for, and she argues that "it was in the souls of black women folk that he touched the chords in himself that brought him closest to an understanding of just what [feminist autobiography] might mean."

Hortense Spillers's discussion of Gwendolyn Brooks and the nature of the feminine raises broader questions of critical methodology. Maud Martha, Brooks wrote, "wanted to found— tradition. She had wanted to shape . . . a set of falterless customs. She had wanted stone." Yet this "shimmering form" is neither stone nor falterless; nor, as Spillers observes, is it "a dead letter, or a reliquary of ancestral ghosts." Combining theoretical inquiry with formal analysis, Spillers moves toward a provisional redefinition of the "feminine," arguing that "woman-freedom" in the novel is found in the fact that "the text itself that has no centrality, no force, no sticking-point other than the imaginative nuances of the subject's consciousness."

Selwyn Cudjoe surveys the autobiographical trajectory of Maya Angelou and offers individual assessments of its varied installments. For Angelou, Cudjoe argues, "the pain and suffering of black women flow like tributaries into the rivers of our general pain, with the poignant demand that the black male be cognizant of their special pains. Theirs is a pain that possesses its own particularities . . . It is well that we listen and learn."

The distinguished poet Jewelle Gomez offers a very personal tribute to Lorraine Hansberry as cultural worker and dramatist, commending her as an uncommon warrior against sexual and racial subjugation. In a day when the work of this playwright is often patronized as too mainstream and middle-brow, Gomez locates her subversive core with respect to the hegemonic sexual politics of her time, and ours as well.

Taking up the sounding kinesthetics of "renaissancism," Houston Baker establishes the importance of Sonia Sanchez through a critique of the black aesthetic movement and of the black nationalism of the 1960s and 1970s, which remained, he argues, entrapped within the structures and assumptions of repression. In the multiple modes of Sonia Sanchez, Baker finds a more promising prospect for a revolutionary art. At the same time, he shows how a revolutionary black feminist needs to be on guard against, for example, homophobia, as in the earlier specimens of Sanchez's "revolutionary didacticism"

he examines and finds transcended in her later work. Surveying the poetry of her maturity, Baker argues that "[i]f the
notion of a black renaissance may be assumed to imply communal leadership and a response among black people themselves—a self-direction, selection, and empowerment that do
not recreate bourgeois forms for private gain and white
acknowledgment—then Sonia Sanchez and her audience clearly
mark a new, postmodern, and dynamically sounding renaissancism." In short, "Sonia Sanchez *sounds* a new day."

Barbara Christian examines Gloria Naylor's recent novels in
the context of other black feminist works concerned with "a
distinct Afro-American middle class," and finds that she has
read deeply, and learned much, from Afro-American wom-
en's literature. Naylor's—and Christian's—concern is with the
historical dimension, the ways in which communities are made,
or fail to be made. As an instance of the failure of community,
Christian finds that the character of Lorraine in *The Women of
Brewster Place*—who, as a lesbian, is rejected by her Brewster
Place neighbors—illustrates how "the effects of racism on this
black community exacerbate the homophobia so rampant in
the outer world." The more readily allegorical *Linden Hills*
starkly shows that "the repression of women's herstory is
necessary to the maintenance of patriarchy, and why it is that
History is so exclusively male." But Christian finds the focus
on community in black women's literature easily explained:
"Because of their origins and history, Afro-American women
could lay claim to a viable tradition in which they had been
strong central persons in their families and communities, not
solely because of their relationship to men, but because they
themselves had bonded together to ensure survival of their
children, their communities, the race."

In a close and insightful reading of Rita Dove's *Thomas and
Beulah*, one of the major achievements in contemporary poetry
by black women, John Shoptaw reminds us that it is for its
language that we read (and reread) poetry. He focuses on
Dove's depiction of the ordinary, the quotidian, as she renders a quiet story of unrecovered loss and unfulfilled promise.
"Strong poems omit their linkages," he notes, and these are
indeed poems whose resonance depends upon omission, on
what is not said.

Françoise Lionnet-McCumber squarely addresses a vexing

aspect of Hurston's legacy: her resolute commitment to individualism over the communal or communitarian ideals of race solidarity (or, by the same token, feminism). She sees *Dust Tracks* as, quite precisely, "autoethnography"—"the process of defining one's subjective ethnicity as mediated through language, history, and ethnographical analysis," a " 'figural anthropology' of the self." But if Hurston is the ultimate participant-observer, hers is an "orphan-text which attempts to create its own genealogy by simultaneously appealing to, and debunking, the cultural traditions it helps to define." And Lionnet-McCumber seeks to adopt such a Hurstonian approach to Hurston's text, exploring her resistance toward race as a basis for human solidarity; her aversion to ressentiment; her bold use of Greek and Egyptian mythology to figure her own liminality.

Marianne Hirsch discusses the way in which feminist readings have customarily treated the mother as object rather than subject of representation, so that feminism as a "daughterly" discourse occludes the uncomfortable possibilities of maternal agency. Her probing account of Toni Morrison's *Sula* shows it to thematize such ambivalences about maternal discourse, while *Beloved* can be seen as registering and representing the maternal voices usually muted.

From the perspective of radical critique, Bell Hooks assays the ideological contours of Alice Walker's *The Color Purple*. On the one hand, Hooks finds the novel's feminism curiously undercut by the normative "success story" paradigm that it seems to follow; on the other hand, she also finds a moment of liberation within Walker's "womanist" imagination, and within its powers of self-fashioning and reinvention. For Hooks, Walker's narrative inscribes the tensions that beset any project of emancipation, illustrating the difficulties of ever escaping entirely the confines of patriarchal discourse.

Dorothy Allison provides a detailed close reading of the nine novels of Octavia Butler, a central figure among contemporary science fiction novelists, exploring Butler's critiques of "human sexual relations and what it means to be other" through her themes of surrender and adjustment. From her first novel, *Patternmaster* (1976), through her most recent novel, *Imago* (1989), Allison traces Butler's depictions of women "not as dispassionate historical constructs, overlaid with political slogans and psychological reinterpretations, but as real women caught in impossible situations." Above all else, Allison concludes, Butler is concerned with exploring the intricacies and ironies of the family bond, and the forces that threaten to rend it asunder.

Molly Hite's essay returns us to the twin touchstones of Walker's *The Color Purple* and Hurston's *Their Eyes Were Watching God*. Hite views these narratives as examples of romance against the Shakespearian paradigms, and allows them to critique the centrality—and adequacy—of that paradigm in literary criticism. While conventional romance entertains hierarchic reversals so long as order is restored at closure, these narratives will destabilize relations of margin and center with no such commitment to oppressive norms, even to the extent of shifting and recirculating the role of motherhood itself. As Hite argues, "By treating the marginal as central and thereby unsettling the hierarchical relations that structure 'mainstream' genres, Walker and Hurston manage to handle very well the conventions that threaten to enslave them in a system of representation not of their own making."

In a way, that is a universal condition: The means of our representations are not of our own devising; they are, to be sure, of no one's devising. And in that respect at least, the self is always, as Fox-Genovese says, hostage to the collectivity. But black women today *are* making history, in every sense, even if not in circumstances of their own choosing. As never before, we are being asked as readers to reflect upon our own positionality, and to meld our formalisms to the discontinuous function that is history lived. As the essays in this collection suggest, part of what distinguishes black women's writing in the contemporary scene is a sense of historical community and its peculiarities—sometimes antic, sometimes grim, but never quite reducible to a master plot of victim and victimizer. At their best, these texts are porous to history and propose an articulation of power that is more decentered and nuanced than most of us are accustomed to. And if we as critics help in reading this literature, perhaps it is as repayment for a literature that has helped show us what it means to read.

The collection ends with two conversations, one between Rita Dove and Helen Vendler, the other between Jamaica Kincaid and Donna Perry. Both interviews provide fascinating glimpses into these two writers' ideas of influence and the complexity of their own multiple traditions or literary heritages, crucial biographical data, and careful and illuminating discussions of individual works of art, through carefully constructed encounters between two major critics and two major authors. Vendler, our most perceptive critic of poetry, and Perry, a champion of contemporary women writers outside the white, middle-class mainstream, have structured exchanges that illuminate the work of Dove and Kincaid in the most rewarding manner. Kincaid, a novelist and essayist, and Dove, whose *Thomas and Beulah* won the Pulitzer Prize for poetry, represent two of the most compelling younger voices in the African-American women's tradition, and their works suggest something of the new directions that tradition is assuming in the 1990s.

CONSTRUCTING A TRADITION

tremendous importance no matter which way you look at it. What went on inside the Negro was of more importance than the turbulent doings going on external of him. This post-war generation time was a matrix from which certain ideas came that have seriously affected art creation as well as every other form of Negro expression, including the economic.

Out of this period of sound and emotion came the Race Man and Race Woman; that great horde of individuals known as "Race Champions." The great Frederick Douglass was the original pattern, no doubt, for these people who went up and down the land making speeches so fixed in type as to become a folk pattern. But Douglass had the combination of a great cause and the propitious moment as a setting for his talents and he became a famous man. These others had the wish to be heard and a set of phrases so they became "Race" Men or Women as the case might be. It was the era of tongue and lung. The "leaders" loved to speak and the new-freed field hands loved gatherings and brave words, so the tribe increased.

It was so easy to become a Race Leader in those days. So few Negroes knew how to read and write that any black man who was proficient in these arts was something to be wondered at. What had been looked upon as something that only the brains of the master-kind could cope with was done by a black person! Astonishing! He must be exceptional to do all that! He was a leader, and went north to his life work of talking the race problem. He could and did teach school like white folks. If he was not "called to preach" he most certainly was made a teacher and either of these positions made him a local leader. The idea grew and traveled. When the first Negroes entered northern colleges even the northern whites were tremendously impressed. It was apparent that while setting the slaves free they had declared the equality of men, they did not actually believe any such thing except as voting power. To see a Negro enter Yale to attempt to master the same courses as the whites was something to marvel over. To see one actually take a degree at Harvard, let us say, was a miracle. The phenomenon was made over and pampered. He was told so often that his mentality stood him alone among his kind and that it was a tragic accident that made him a Negro that he came to believe it himself and struck the tragic pose. Naturally he became a leader. Any Negro who graduated from a white school automatically became a national leader and as such could give opinions on anything at all in which the word Negro occurred. But it had to be sad. Any Negro who had all that brains to be taking a degree at a white college was bound to know every thought and feeling of every other Negro in America, however remote from him, and he was bound to feel sad. It was assumed that no Negro brain could ever grasp the curriculum of a white college, so the black man who did had come by some white folk's brain by accident and there was bound to be conflict between his dark body and his white mind. Hence the stultifying doctrine that has not altogether been laughed out of existence at the present. In spite of the thousands and thousands of Negro graduates of good colleges, in spite of hundreds of graduates of New England and Western Colleges, there are gray-haired graduates of New England colleges still clutching at the vapors of uniqueness. Despite the fact that Negroes have distinguished themselves in every major field of activity in the nation some of the left-overs still grab at the mantle of "Race Leader." Just let them hear that white people have curiosity about some activity among Negroes, and these "leaders" will not let their shirt-tails touch them (i.e. sit down) until they have rushed forward and offered themselves as an authority on the subject whether they have ever heard of it before or not. In the very face of a situation as different from the 1880s as chalk is from cheese, they stand around and mouth the same trite phrases, and try their practised-best to look sad. They call spirituals "Our Sorrow Songs" and other such tom-foolery in an effort to get into the spotlight if possible without having ever done anything to improve education, industry, invention, art and never having uttered a quotable line. Though he is being jostled about these days and paid scant attention, the Race Man is still with us—he and his Reconstruction pulings. His job today is to rush around seeking for something he can "resent."

How has this Race attitude affected the Arts in Florida? In Florida as elsewhere in America this background has worked the mind of the creator. Can the black poet sing a song to the morning? Upsprings the song to his lips but it is fought back. He says to himself, "Ah this is a beautiful song inside me. I feel the morning star in my throat. I will sing of the star and the morning." Then his background thrusts itself between his lips and the star and he mutters, "Ought I not to be singing of our sorrows? That is what is expected of me and I shall be considered forgetful of our past and present. If I do not some will even call me a coward. The one subject for a Negro is the Race and its sufferings and so the song of the morning must be choked back. I will write of a lynching instead." So the same old theme, the same old phrases get done again to the detriment of art. To him no Negro exists as an individual—he exists only as another tragic unit of the Race. This in spite of the obvious fact that Negroes love and hate and fight and play and strive and travel and have a thousand and one interests in life like other humans. When his baby cuts a new tooth he brags as shamelessly as anyone else without once weeping over the prospect of some Klansman knocking it out when and if the child ever gets grown. The Negro artist knows all this but he conceives that a Negro can do nothing but weave something in his particular art form about the Race problem. The writer thinks that he has been brave in following in the groove of the Race champions, when the truth is, it is the line of least resistance and least originality—certain to be approved of by the "champions" who want to hear the same thing over and over again even though they already know it by heart, and certain to be unread by everybody else. It is the same thing as waving the American flag in a poorly constructed play. Anyway, the effect of the whole period has been to fix activities in a mold that precluded originality and denied creation in the arts.

Results:

In painting one artist, O. Richard Reid of Fernandina who at one time created a stir in New York Art Circles with his portraits of Fannie Hurst, John Barrymore and H. L. Mencken. Of his recent works we hear nothing.

In sculpture, Augusta Savage of Green Cove Springs is making greater and greater contributions to what is significant in American Art. Her subjects are Negroid for the most part but any sort of preachment is absent from her art. She seems striving to reach out to the rimbones of nothing and in so doing she touches a responsive chord in the universe and grows in stature. [Here, Hurston intended to add names of Savage's most important work.—ed.]

The world of music has been enriched by the talents of J. Rosamond Johnson, a Jacksonville Negro. His range has been from light and frivolous tunes of musical comedy designed to merely entertain to some beautiful arrangements of spirituals which have been sung all over the world in concert halls. His truly great composition is the air which accompanies the words of the so-called "Negro National Anthem." The bitter-sweet poem is by his brother James Weldon Johnson.

Though it is not widely known, there is a house in Fernandina, Florida whose interior is beautifully decorated in original wood-carving. It is the work of the late Brooks Thompson who was born a slave. Without ever having known anything about African Art, he has achieved something very close to African concepts on the walls, doors and ceilings of three rooms. His doors are things of wondrous beauty. The greater part of the work was done after he was in his seventies. "The feeling just came and I did it," is his explanation of how the carpenter turned wood-carver in his old age.

In literature Florida has two names: James Weldon Johnson, of many talents and Zora Neale Hurston. As a poet Johnson wrote scattered bits of verse, and he wrote lyrics for the music of his brother Rosamond. Then he wrote the campaign song for Theodore Roosevelt's campaign. "You're Alright Teddy" which swept the nation. After Theodore Roosevelt was safe in the White House he appointed the poet as Consul to Venezuela. The time came when Johnson published volumes of verse and collected a volume of Negro sermons which he published under the title of *God's Trombones*. Among his most noted prose works are "The Autobiography of an Ex-Colored Man," *Black Manhattan* and his story of his own life, *Along This Way*.

Zora Neale Hurston won critical acclaim for two new things in Negro fiction. The first was an objective point of view. The subjective view was so universal that it had come to be taken for granted. When her first book, *Jonah's Gourd Vine*, a novel, appeared in 1934, the critics announced across the nation, "Here at last is a Negro story without bias. The characters live and move. The story is about Negroes but it could be anybody. It is the first time that a Negro story has been offered without special pleading. The characters in the story are seen in relation to themselves and not in relation to the whites as has been the rule. To watch these people one would conclude that there were no white people in the world. The author is an artist that will go far."

The second element that attracted attention was the telling of the story in the idiom—not the dialect—of the Negro. The Negro's poetical flow of language, his thinking in images and figures was called to the attention of the outside world. It gave verisimilitude to the narrative by stewing the subject in its own juice.

Zora Hurston is the author of three other books, "Mules and Men," "Their Eyes Were Watching God" (published also in England; translated into the Italian by Ada Prospero and published in Rome), and "Tell My Horse."

It is not to be concluded from these meager offerings in the arts that Negro talent is lacking. There has been a cruel waste of genius during the long generations of slavery. There has been a squandering of genius during the three generations since Surrender on Race. So the Negro begins feeling with his fingers to find himself in the plastic arts. He is well established in music, but still a long way to go to overtake his possibilities. In literature the first writings have been little more than the putting into writing the sayings of the Race Men and Women and champions of "Race Consciousness." So that what was produced was a self-conscious document lacking in drama, analysis, characterization and the universal oneness necessary to literature. But the idea was not to produce literature—it was to "champion the Race." The Fourteenth and Fifteenth Amendments got some pretty hard wear and that sentence "You have made the *greatest* progress in so and so many years" was all the art in the literature in the purpose and period.

But one finds on all hands the weakening of race consciousness, impatience with Race Champions and a growing taste for literature as such. The wedge has entered the great inert mass and one may expect some noble things from the Florida Negro in Art in the next decade.

Postscript: The Mark of Zora

Stetson Kennedy

When the preceding essay, "Art and Such," landed on my desk, postmarked "Eatonville, Fla., January 13, 1938," I knew that it had come from none other than Zora Neale Hurston. I was at the time serving as state director of folklore, life history, and social-ethnic studies for the WPA Florida Writers Project, and Zora had penned the piece with intent that it be published, anonymously, in a projected volume of the FWP, *The Florida Negro.* Being "free, white, and [precisely] twenty-one" (as folksay put it at the time), I presumed to shelve "Art and Such," and there it has remained these three score years before being published here and now.

It was in May of that year that Dr. Carita Doggett Corse, state director of the FWP, had summoned her half dozen lily-white state editors into her office and informed us that the "Negro novelist" Zora Neale Hurston had signed on, and would be paying us a state visit. Zora had been lionized by New York literary circles, Dr. Corse said, and had therefore put on certain airs, among them the smoking of cigarettes in the presence of white folks, so we would all have to make allowances.

And so Zora came, and Zora smoked, and we made allowances . . . .

Prior to Zora's coming on board, it had been bruited about in correspondence between the national office in Washington and state office in Jacksonville that she could serve both as

supervisor of our "Negro Unit" and editor of *The Florida Negro*.
To the best of my knowledge and the archival evidence, she
never did either.

Hurston's biographer, Robert Hemenway, is quite right in
asserting that she "never had a desk" during her eighteen-
month tenure on the FWP, working for the most part out of
her residence in Eatonville. Like rather many of our "field
workers" (myself included when I began in that category), her
production was sporadic. Dr. Corse would pop out of her
office and ask, "Anybody heard from Zora?" When we looked
blank, she would ask "How long has it been?" "Several weeks,"
was my frequent reply, whereupon Dr. Corse would say,
"Better write her a letter and jog her up!" I would do so, and
by return mail we always received a thick packet of the most
fabulous folk stuff imaginable. We cared not a whit where and
when she had collected it, but hastened to sprinkle it about in
The Florida Guide manuscript for seasoning.

The authorized strength of the Florida project when launched
in the fall of 1935 had been two hundred, of which ten slots
were set aside for a "Negro Unit," which was ensconced in
the Eartha White Mission, a soup kitchen in the heart of
Jacksonville's black ghetto. We had no idea what any of them
looked like, our only visual contact being with the messenger
they sent over every two weeks to pick up their checks.

Zora's actual job title was "Junior Interviewer," and she
was paid the prevailing "P&T" (Professional & Technical)
WPA wage scale for Orange County, $67.20 per month. Ironi-
cally, Ruth Bolton, the clerical worker attached to the Negro
Unit, was paid a bit more, by virtue of the higher cost-of-
living index in Jacksonville.

During the two and a half years Before Zora, the staff of the
Negro Unit had produced thousands of pages of superbly
researched and written copy on the life and history of African-
Americans in Florida. By the time I was promoted from Junior
Interviewer to a State Editor in the spring of 1937, the editorial
staff had gone through this wealth of material, and come up
with a 167-page white-written version of *The Florida Negro*,
consisting in the main of chapters on such subjects as Hoodoo, Superstitions, Spirituals, Diversions, Bolita, Unusual Communities, and the like. It contained not a word, of course,
about segregation, discrimination, illiteracy, infant mortality,

substandard housing, disfranchisement, chain gangs, sweat-boxes, lynching, or the Ku Klux Klan.

This was the manuscript that was ostensibly tossed into Zora's lap, and for which she wrote "Art and Such."

"The Darkened Eye Restored":

Notes Toward a Literary History of Black Women

Mary Helen Washington

When Gwendolyn Brooks won the Pulitzer prize for her second book of poems, *Annie Allen*, in 1950, *Negro Digest* sent a male reporter who covered the story and wrote a brief "homey" article about the life of a Pulitzer-prize-winning poet. The article begins with a list of people who didn't believe Brooks had won the prize—her son, her mother, her husband, friends—even the poet herself. It then catalogs all the negative experiences Brooks had after winning the prize—phones ringing, people dropping in, work interrupted, the family overwhelmed. It mentions her husband, Henry Blakely, as a poet who devotes only occasional time to poetry because "he feels no one family can support two poets." We also learn that the poet was "shy and self conscious" (her terms) until she married Blakely, who helped her to lose some of her "social backwardness" (the reporter's terms). The last paragraph of the article, devoted to the poet's nine-year-old son, includes one of the boy's poems (but not a line from the poet who has just won the Pulitzer!) and ends with the son's rejection of his mother's fame because it has upset his life: "All the attention is wearing off now and I sure am glad. I don't like to be so famous. You have too many people talking to you. You never have any peace."[1] The entire article was an act of sabotage, situating Brooks in a domestic milieu where her "proper" role as wife and mother could be asserted and her role as serious artist—a role this reporter obviously found too threatening to even consider—could be undercut.

Three years later when Brooks published her first—and still her only novel—*Maud Martha* (1953), a novel about a woman's anger, repressions, and silences, the critical reviews were equally condescending and dismissive. Despite Brooks's stature as a Pulitzer-prize-winning poet, the reviews were short, ranging in length from one hundred and sixty to six hundred words, and many were unsigned. Here is a novel that deals with the most compelling themes in contemporary literature: the struggle to sustain one's identity against a racist and sexist society, the silences that result from repressed anger, the need to assert a creative life. Had *Maud Martha* been written by a man about a man's experience, it would have been considered a brilliant modernist text. But these reviewers, unable to place *Maud Martha* in any literary context, chose instead to concentrate on female cheerfulness, calling Maud Martha "a spunky and sophisticated Negro girl" who, they said, had a marvelous "ability to turn unhappiness and anger into a joke."[2]

Consider the way Ralph Ellison's first novel, *Invisible Man*, was received the year before *Maud Martha* when Ellison was still relatively unknown. *The New Republic, Crisis, The Nation, The New Yorker*, and *The Atlantic* published lengthy and signed reviews, ranging in length from six hundred to twenty-one hundred words. Wright Morris and Irving Howe were called in to write serious critical assessments for the *Times* and *The Nation*. Although Brooks's protagonist was never compared to any other literary character, Ellison's nameless hero was considered not only "the embodiment of the Negro race" but the "conscience of all races." The titles of Ellison's reviews—"Black & Blue," "Underground Notes," "Brother Betrayed," "Black Man's Burdens"—suggest the universality of the invisible man's struggle. The title of Brooks's reviews—"Young Girl Growing Up" and "Daydreams of Flight," beside being misleading, deny any relationship between the protagonist's personal experiences and the historical experiences of her people. Ellison himself was compared to Richard Wright, Dostoyevski, and Faulkner; Brooks, only to the unspecified "imagists." Most critically, Ellison's work was placed in a tradition; it was described as an example of the "picaresque" tradition and the pilgrim/journey tradition by all reviews. (Later it would be considered a descendant of the slave narrative tradition.) *Maud Martha*, the reviewers said, "stood alone."[3]

Reading these reviews I was struck not only by their resistance to the deeper meaning in *Maud Martha* but by their absolute refusal to see Brooks's novel as part of any tradition in Afro-American or mainstream American literature. Is this because few critics could picture the questing figure, the powerful articulate voice in the tradition as a plain, dark-skinned housewife living in a kitchenette apartment on the south side of Chicago? As I have written earlier, I realize that the supreme confidence of the Ellison text—its epic sweep, its eloquent flow of words, its conscious manipulation of historical situations—invites its greater critical acceptance. By comparison, the *Maud Martha* text is hesitant, self-doubting, retentive, mute. Maud is restricted, for a good part of the novel, to a domestic life that seems narrow and limited—even to her. And, yet, if the terms *invisibility, double-consciousness, the black mask* have any meaning at all for the Afro-American literary tradition, then *Maud Martha*, whose protagonist is more intimately acquainted with the meanings of those words than any male character, belongs unquestionably to that tradition.

Tradition. Now there's a word that nags the feminist critic. A word that has so often been used to exclude or misrepresent women. It is always something of a shock to see black women, sharing equally (and sometimes more than equally) in the labor and strife of black people, expunged from the text when that history becomes shaped into what we call tradition. Why is the fugitive slave, the fiery orator, the political activist, the abolitionist always represented as a black *man*?[4] How does the heroic voice and heroic image of the black woman get suppressed in a culture that depended on her heroism for its survival? What we have to recognize is that the creation of the fiction of tradition is a matter of power, not justice, and that that power has always been in the hands of men—mostly white but some black. Women are the disinherited. Our "ritual journeys," our "articulate voices," our "symbolic spaces" are rarely the same as men's. Those differences and the assumption that those differences make women inherently inferior, plus the appropriation by men of the power to define tradition, account for women's absence from our written records.

In the early 1890s when a number of leading black intellectuals decided to form "an organization of Colored authors, scholars, and artists," with the expressed intent of raising "the standard of intellectual endeavor among American Negroes," one of the invited members wrote to declare himself "decidedly opposed to the admission of women to membership" because "literary matters and social matters do not mix." He need not have concerned himself since the distinguished luminaries, among them Alexander Crummell, Francis Grimké, and W.E.B. Du Bois, proposed from the beginning that the American Negro Academy—a kind of think tank for that intellectual black elite called the Talented Tenth—be open only to "*men* of African descent."[5] Imagine, if you can, black women intellectuals and activists, who in the 1890s had taken on such issues as the moral integrity of black women, lynching, and the education of black youth, being considered social decorations. I mention this egregious example of sexism in the black intellectual community—which by and large was and still is far more egalitarian than their white counterparts—because it underscores an attitude toward black women that has helped to maintain and perpetuate a male-dominated literary and critical tradition. Women have worked assiduously in this tradition as writers, as editors, sometimes, though rarely, as critics, and yet every study of Afro-American narrative, every anthology of *the* Afro-American literary tradition has set forth a model of literary paternity in which each male author vies with his predecessor for greater authenticity, greater control over *his* voice, thus fulfilling the mission his *forefathers* left unfinished.

Women in this model are sometimes granted a place as a stepdaughter who prefigures and directs us to the real heirs (like Ellison and Wright) but they do not influence and determine the direction and shape of the literary canon.[6] Women's writing is considered singular and anomalous, not universal and representative, and for some mysterious reason, writing about black women is not considered as racially significant as writing about black men. Zora Neale Hurston was chastised by critic Benjamin Brawley because "Her interest . . . is not in solving problems, the chief concern being with individuals."[7] And, in his now-famous contemptuous review of Hurston's *Their Eyes Were Watching God*, Richard Wright objects to her novel because her characters (unlike his) live in a "safe and narrow orbit . . . between laughter and tears."[8] Male critics go to great lengths to explain the political naïveté or racial ambivalence of male writers while they harshly criticize women writers for the same kinds of shortcomings. In Wright's essay, "Literature of the Negro of the United States," he forgives George Moses Horton, an early black poet, for being "a split man," trapped in a culture of which he was not really a part; but Phillis Wheatley, he says, is fully culpable. She was, Wright claims, so fully at one with white colonial culture that she developed "innocently," free "to give utterance to what she felt without the humiliating pressure of the color line."[9]

Banished to the "nigger pews" in the Christian churches of Colonial Boston, deprived of the companionship of other blacks, totally under the control of whites, "torn by contrary instincts," Phillis Wheatley was never "at one with her culture." As a new generation of critics, led by William Robinson, Alice Walker, and Merle A. Richmond, has shown us, Phillis Wheatley was a young slave woman whose choice to be an artist in the repressive, racist era of Colonial America represents "the triumph of the artist amid catastrophe."[10]

> With the exception of a handful of autobiographical narratives from the nineteenth century, the black woman's realities are virtually suppressed until the period of the Harlem Renaissance and later. Essentially the black woman as artist, as intellectual spokesperson for her own cultural apprenticeship, has not existed before, for anyone. At the source of her own symbol-making task, this community of writers confronts, therefore, a tradition of work that is quite recent, its continuities, broken and sporadic.[11]

Without exception Afro-American women writers have been dismissed by Afro-American literary critics until they were rediscovered and reevaluated by feminist critics. Examples: Linda Brent's slave narrative, *Incidents in the Life of a Slave Girl* (1860), was judged by male historians to be inauthentic because her story was "too melodramatic" and not "representative."[12] Contemporary feminist critics have documented Brent's life as not only entirely authentic but "representative" of the experience of many slave women. Except for Barbara Christian's *Black Women Novelists* and other texts that specifically deal with women writers, critical texts have never considered Frances Harper and Pauline Hopkins makers of early black literary traditions. Like many white women writers of the nineteenth century, they were dismissed as "sentimentalists," even though their male counterparts wrote similarly sentimental novels. Zora Hurston's *Their Eyes Were Watching God* was declared by Richard Wright to be a novel that carried "no theme, no message, no thought," and during the thirty years that Wright dominated the black literary scene, Hurston's novel was out of print.[13] Nella Larsen was also out of print for many years and was not until recently considered a major Harlem Renaissance writer. Ann Petry is usually analyzed as a disciple of Wright's school of social protest fiction, and Dorothy West has not been written about seriously since Robert Bone's *The Negro Novel in America* in 1965. Brooks's novel, *Maud Martha*, though it perfectly expresses the race alienation of the 1950s, was totally eclipsed by Ellison's *Invisible Man* and never considered a vital part of the Afro-American canon.

If there is a single distinguishing feature of the literature of black women—and this accounts for their lack of recognition—it is this: their literature is about black women; it takes the trouble to record the thoughts, words, feelings, and deeds of black women, experiences that make the realities of being black in America look very different from what men have written. There are no women in this tradition hibernating in dark holes contemplating their invisibility; there are no women dismembering the bodies or crushing the skulls of either women or men; and few, if any, women in the literature of black women succeed in heroic quests without the support of other women or men in their communities. Women talk to other women in this tradition, and their friendships with other women— mothers, sisters, grandmothers, friends, lovers—are vital to their growth and well-being. A common scene recurring in at least five of the eight fiction writers in this collection is one in which women (usually two) gather together in a small room to share intimacies that can be trusted only to a kindred female spirit. That intimacy is a tool, allowing women writers to represent women more fully. The friendship between Sappho and Dora in *Contending Forces*, Janie and Pheoby in *Their Eyes Were Watching God*, Linda and her grandmother in *Incidents in the Life of a Slave Girl*, Helga and Mrs. Hayes-Rore in *Quicksand*, Cleo and her sisters in *The Living Is Easy* emphasize this

concern with female bonding and suggest that female relationships are an essential aspect of self-definition for women.

I do not want these writers to be misrepresented as apolitical because of their deep concern for the personal lives of their
characters. All of these texts are clearly involved with issues of
social justice: the rape of black women, the lynching of black
men, slavery and Reconstruction, class distinctions among
blacks, and all forms of discrimination against black people.
No romantic heroines, all of these women work, and in nearly
every one of these eight selections women experience discrimination against them in the workplace, a subject that almost
never surfaces in the writings of men. At the beginning of
Contending Forces, Sappho Clark brings her stenography work
home with her because blacks are not allowed in the office.
Iola Leroy is twice dismissed from jobs when her coworkers
discover her race. The educated Helga Crane seeks work as a
domestic in Chicago because black women are barred from the
professions and from clerical work. Maud Martha also finds
work as a domestic where she encounters the brutal conde-
scension of her white employers. These examples have a special meaning for me because in the 1920s my mother and my
five aunts migrated to Cleveland, Ohio, from Indianapolis
and, in spite of their many talents, they found every door
except the kitchen door closed to them. My youngest aunt
was trained as a bookkeeper and was so good at her work that
her white employer at Guardian Savings of Indianapolis allowed her to work at the branch in a black area. The Cleveland Trust Company was not so liberal, however, so in
Cleveland (as Toni Morrison asks, "What could go wrong in
Ohio?") she went to work in what is known in the black
community as "private family." Her thwarted career is not
simply a narrow personal tragedy. As these texts make clear
to us—and they are the only texts that tell this story—several
generations of competent and talented black women, all of
whom *had* to work, were denied access to the most ordinary
kind of jobs and therefore to any kind of economic freedom.

Women's sexuality is another subject treated very differently by women and men writers. In the male slave narrative,
for example, sexuality is nearly always avoided, and when it
does surface it is to report the sexual abuse of female slaves.
The male slave narrator was under no compulsion to discuss

his own sexuality nor that of other men. As far as we know, the only slave narrator forced to admit a sexual life was Linda Brent, who bore two children as a single woman rather than submit to forced concubinage. Her reluctance to publish *Incidents* because it was not the life of "a Heroine with no degradation associated with it" shows that sexuality literally made a woman an unfit subject for literature. In Harlem Renaissance literature, as Barbara Christian reminds us, only male writers felt free to celebrate exoticized sexuality: "The garb of uninhibited passion wears better on a male, who after all, does not have to carry the burden of the race's morality or lack of it."[14] In Renaissance literature, Nella Larsen does represent Helga as a sexual being but that treatment of sex is never celebratory. Helga's sexuality is constantly thwarted, ending as Hazel Carby notes, not in exotic passion but in biological entrapment. In *The Living Is Easy*, Cleo connects sexuality to women's repression and refuses any kind of sexual life, preferring instead emotional intimacy with her sisters and their children. The only woman in these excerpts who revels in her sexuality is Janie Crawford in *Their Eyes Were Watching God*, and, significantly, even in this seemingly idyllic treatment of erotic love, female sexuality is always associated with violence. Janie's mother and grandmother are sexually exploited and Janie is beaten by her glorious lover, Tea Cake, so that he can prove his superiority to other men. What do these stories say about female sexuality? It seems to me that all of them point to the fundamental issue of whether or not women can exert control over their sexuality. Helga Crane, for example, fights against the sexual attraction she feels for Dr. Anderson because that attraction makes her feel out of control. Cleo, who is controlled by her husband in all other aspects of her life, controls him by refusing sex. In *Contending Forces*, Sappho forces her lover to undergo a series of tests in order to determine the constancy of his love. And surely the clearest statement of women's anxiety about sexuality and the need for control over one's female body is made by Linda Brent when she tries to explain to her white female audience why she deliberately chose to bear two children outside of marriage to a white man who was not her owner: "It seems less degrading to give one's self, than to submit to compulsion. There is something akin to freedom in having a lover *who has no control over you*, [emphasis mine] except that which he gains by kindness and attachment."[15] Given this deep alienation from and anxiety about heterosexual relationships, we might wonder if any of these women considered taking women as lovers. If they did, they wrote about such affairs in private places—letters, journals, diaries, poetry—if they wrote about them at all. In a diary, which she kept in the 1920s and 1930s, Alice Dunbar-Nelson is more explicit about sexual intimacy among black women than any writer of that period that I know, but even her revelations are quite guarded: "And Fay, lovely little Fay. One day we saw each other, *one day*, and a year has passed. And still we cannot meet again . . ."[16]

The anxiety of black women writers over the representation of sexuality goes back to the nineteenth century and the prescription for womanly "virtues" which made slave women automatically immoral and less "feminine than white women," but that anxiety is evident even in contemporary texts, many of which avoid any kind of sexual vulnerability or project the most extreme forms of sexual vulnerability onto children and poor women. Once again the issue is control, and control is bought by cordoning off those aspects of sexuality that threaten to make women feel powerless. If pleasure and danger are concomitant aspects of sexuality, it seems clear to me that black women writers have, out of historical necessity, registered far more of the latter than the former.

> For a woman to write, she must experiment with "altering and adapting the current shape of her thought without crushing or distorting it."[17]

Although many writers in some way challenge conventional notions of what is possible for women characters, "dissenting" from traditions that demand female subordination, I want to single out Zora Neale Hurston and Gwendolyn Brooks for creating narrative strategies whose major concern is the empowerment of women. Both Hurston and Brooks enter fiction through a side door: Hurston was a folklorist and anthropologist; Brooks is primarily a poet. As outsiders both were freer to experiment with fictional forms, the result being that they were able to choose forms that resist female entrapment. Janie Crawford's quest in *Their Eyes Were Watching God* is to recover her own voice and her own sense of autonomy. By framing the story with Janie telling her tale to her friend Pheoby, Hurston makes Janie's self-conscious reflections on her life the central narrative concern. Though Hurston often denies this quest story in favor of the romantic plot, her interest in Janie's heroic potential is unmistakable. In *Maud Martha* Brooks also dislodges the romance plot, first by inventing a woman who does not fit the profile of a romantic heroine and then by making the death of romance essential to Maud's growth. Being a wife, "in every way considering and replenishing him," is in conflict with Maud's own desire for what she vaguely terms "more life." And finally the narrative form itself, as it enacts Maud's rage, her muteness, her indirection, places narrative emphasis on the unsparing, meticulous, courageous consciousness of Maud Martha, making that female consciousness the heroic center of the text. The text that was so arrogantly dismissed in 1953 returns, subversively, in the 1980s, with its rejection of male power, as a critique of the very patriarchal authority that sought its dismissal.

Obviously we will have to learn to read the Afro-American literary tradition in new ways, for continuing on in the old way is impossible. In the past ten or fifteen years the crucial task of reconstruction has been carried on by a number of scholars whose work has made it possible to document black women as artists, as intellectuals, as symbol makers. The continuities of this tradition, as Hortense Spillers tells us, are broken and sporadic, but the knitting together of these fragments has begun. As I look around at my own library shelves I see the texts that have helped to make my recent book, *Invented Lives*, possible. First those pioneering studies undertaken to pave the way for the rest of us: Barbara Christian's, *Black Women Novelists, The Development of a Tradition, 1892–1976;* the invaluable sourcebook, *All the Women Are White, All the Blacks Are Men, But Some of Us Are Brave,* edited by Gloria L. Hull, Patricia Bell Scott, and Barbara Smith; Marilyn Richardson's bibliography, *Black Women and Religion;* Ora Williams's bibliography, *American Black Women:* those early anthologies of black women's literature, *The Black Woman,* edited by Toni Cade Bambara; Pat Crutchfield Exum's *Keeping the Faith;* and *Sturdy Black Bridges; Visions of Black Women in Literature,* edited by Beverly Guy-Sheftall, Roseann P. Bell, and Bettye J. Parker.

Robert Hemenway's biography, *Zora Neale Hurston: A Literary Biography*, and Alice Walker's *I Love Myself When I Am Laughing . . . And Then Again When I Am Looking Mean and Impressive: A Zora Neale Hurston Reader* are the major scholarly works that allowed us to reclaim Hurston. Two books on black women's spiritual autobiography, Jean McMahon Humez's *Gifts of Power*, an edition of the writings of Rebecca Jackson Cox, as well as William Andrews's *Sisters of the Spirit* have reclaimed a unique part of black women's early literary tradition. Gloria Hull's edition of Alice Dunbar-Nelson's diary, *Give Us Each Day*, and Dorothy Sterling's *We Are Your Sisters*, a documentary portrayal of nineteenth-century black women, provide evidence of the rich cultural history of black women that is to be found in nontraditional sources. Paula Giddings's history of black women, *When and Where I Enter: The Impact of Black Women on Race and Sex in America*, documents the political, social, and literary work of black women.

Deborah E. McDowell's Beacon Press series on black women's fiction has already reissued a number of out-of-print novels, for example, *The Street, Like One of the Family*, and *Iola Leroy*. Rutgers University Press has reissued *Quicksand* and *Passing*. In 1987 a number of important works on black women were published: Jean Fagan Yellin's definitive edition of Harriet Jacobs's *Incidents in the Life of a Slave Girl* and Hazel Carby's ground-breaking work on black women's narrative tradition: *Reconstructing Womanhood: The Emergence of the Afro-American Woman Novelist*.

As we continue the work of reconstructing a literary history that insists on black women as central to that history, as we reject the old male-dominated accounts of history, refusing to be cramped into the little spaces men have allotted women, we should be aware that this is an act of enlightenment, not simply repudiation. In her 1892 text on black women, *A Voice from the South*, Anna Julia Cooper says that a world in which the female is made subordinate is like a body with one eye bandaged. When the bandage is removed, the body is filled with light: "It sees a circle where before it saw a segment. The darkened eye restored, every member rejoices with it."[18] The making of a literary history in which black women are fully represented is a search for full vision, to create a circle where now we have but a segment.

NOTES

1. Frank Harriott, "The Life of a Pulitzer Poet," *Negro Digest* (August 1950): 14–16.
2. 1953 reviews of *Maud Martha: The New Yorker* (October 10, 1953), unsigned, 160 words; Hubert Creekmore, "Daydreams in Flight," *New York Times Book Review* (October 4, 1953), 400 words; Nicolas Monjo, "Young Girl Growing up," *Saturday Review* (October 31, 1953), 140 words; and Coleman Rosenberger, New York *Herald Tribune* (October 18, 1953), 600 words.
3. 1952 reviews of *Invisible Man:* George Mayberry, "Underground Notes," *The New Republic* (April 21, 1952), 600 words; Irving Howe, "A Negro in America," *The Nation* (May 10, 1952), 950 words; Anthony West, "Black Man's Burden," *The New Yorker* (May 31, 1952), 2,100 words: C. J. Rolo, "Candide in Harlem," *The Atlantic* (July 1952), 450 words; Wright Morris, "The World Below," *New York Times Book Review* (April 13, 1952), 900 words; "Black & Blue," *Time* (April 14, 1952), 850 words; and J. E. Cassidy "A Brother Betrayed," *Commonweal* (May 2, 1952), 850 words.
   1953 reviews of Maud Martha: *The New Yorker* (October 10, 1953), unsigned 160 words; Hubert Creekmore, "Daydreams in Flight," *New York Times Book Review* (October 4, 1953), 400 words; Nicolas Monjo "Young Girl Growing Up," *Saturday Review* (October 31, 1953), 140 words; and Coleman Rosenberger, New York *Herald Tribune* (October 18, 1953), 600 words.
   The diction of the reviews, too, is revealing. The tone of *Invisible Man* was defined as "vigorous, imaginative, violently humorous and quietly tragic" (*New Republic*), "searing and exalted" (*The Nation*); while *Maud Martha* drew "freshness, warm cheerfulness . . . [and]) vitality" (*New York Times*), "ingratiating" (*Saturday Review*). Several reviews of Ellison used "gusto," for Brooks, "liveliness." Brooks's "Negro heroine" (*New York Times*), was characterized as a "young colored woman" (*Saturday Review*) and a "spunky and sophisticated Negro girl" (*New York Times*); Ellison's character as a "hero" and "pilgrim" (*New Republic*).
   Matters of style received mixed response in both novels, *Maud Martha*'s "impressionistic style" was deemed "not quite sharp or firm enough" and her "remarkable gift" was seen (in the same review) as "mimicry" and an "ability to turn unhappiness and anger into a joke"—a gift that her style did not engender (*New York Times*). The *Saturday Review* said: "Its form is no more than a random narration of loosely assembled incidents" and called its "framework . . . somewhat ramshackle." Only the *New York Times* noticed a significance in her style, and likened the "flashes . . . of sensitive lightness" to Imagist poetics, as well as commenting on the "finer qualities of insight and rhythm."
   Both authors are criticized along the same lines concerning form and style, but in the reviews of Brooks, her style is the topic that draws the most attention, and the review is favorable or unfavorable depending upon whether or not the reviewer is personally attracted to "impressionism." Ellison's novel is treated more seriously than Brooks's because his novel is seen as addressing a broader range of issues, despite his sometimes "hysterical" style.
   This position is most apparent in Howe's review in *The Nation*. Howe asks serious questions about traditional literary devices, such as narrative stance and voice, and method of characterization, despite the book's lack of "finish." (Ellison's first-person narration is discussed by all reviewers, while Brooks's narrative style is hardly mentioned in any review.) Implicit in Howe's stance toward *Invisible Man* is an assumption that this is a serious novel to be investigated rigorously in accordance with the (high) standards of the academy. Despite those qualities of tone and style that Howe criticizes it for, *Invisible Man* is important, finally, because it fits into the literary tradition of the epic journey of discovery. Howe calls it a "searing and exalted record

of a Negro's journey toward contemporary America in search of success, companionship, and finally himself."

4. The extent to which black men are considered representative of the race was suggested to me most emphatically in *Black Women in Nineteenth-Century American Life: Their Words, Their Thoughts, Their Feelings,* ed. Bert James Loewenberg and Ruth Bogin (University Park: Pennsylvania State University Press, 1976). In their introduction, "Women, Blacks, History," the editors make this comment: "Not only do black women seldom appear in treatments of black history, but historians have been content to permit the male to represent the female in almost every significant category. Thus it is the male who is the representative abolitionist, fugitive slave, or political activist. The black male is the leader, the entrepreneur, the politician, the man of thought. When historians discuss black abolitionist writers and lecturers, they are men. David Walker, Charles Lenox Remond, and a procession of male stalwarts preempt the list in conventional accounts. Particularly later when black history was consciously written, it was the male, not the female, who recorded it. Women are conspicuous by their silence." (p. 4)

5. Alfred A. Moss, Jr., *The American Negro Academy: Voice of the Talented Tenth* (Baton Rouge: Louisiana State University Press, 1981). According to Moss, The American Negro Academy, the first major black American learned society, was founded March 5, 1897 in Washington, D.C. The constitution of the ANA defined it as "an organization of authors, scholars, artists, and those distinguished in other walks of life, men of African descent, for the promotion of Letters, Science, and Art." While Dubois argued for a more democratic membership "because we find men who are not distinguished in science or literature or art are just the men we want," he did not, apparently, argue for women. Theophilus G. Steward, one of the invited members, was the only one who specifically declared himself opposed to the admission of women. (pp. 38, 42)

6. Nearly every Afro-American literary history reads the tradition as primarily a male tradition, beginning with the male slave narrative as the source which generates the essential texts in the canon. With absolute predictability the Frederick Douglass 1845 *Narrative* is the text that issues the call, and the response comes back loud and clear from W. E. B. Du Bois, James Weldon Johnson, Richard Wright, James Baldwin, and Ralph Ellison. So firmly established is this male hegemony that even men's arguments with one another (Wright, Baldwin, Elllison) get written into the tradition as a way of interpreting its development. As most feminist critics have noted, women writers cannot simply be inserted into the gaps, or be used to prefigure male writers, the tradition has to be conceptualized from a feminist viewpoint.

7. Benjamin Brawley, *The Negro Genius: A New Appraisal of the Achievement of the American Negro in Literature and the Fine Arts* (New York: Bibb and Tannen, 1969), 258. Of the thirteen portraits of writers and artists in this book, only two are of women.

8. Richard Wright, "Between Laughter and Tears," *New Masses 5* (October 1937): 25–26.

9. Richard Wright, "The Literature of the Negro of the United States," in *White Man Listen!* (Garden City, N.Y.: Doubleday & Company, 1964), 76.

10. William Robinson, *Phillis Wheatley in the Black American Beginnings* (Detroit: Broadside Press, 1976); Alice Walker, "In Search of Our Mothers' Gardens," in *In Search of Our Mothers' Gardens: Womanist Prose* (New York: Harcourt Brace Jovanovich, 1983), 231–43; and M. A. Richmond, *Bid the Vassal Soar: Interpretive Essays on the Life and Poetry of Phillis Wheatley and George Moses Horton* (Washington, D.C.: Howard University Press, 1974).

11. Hortense J. Spillers, "A Hateful Passion, A Lost Love," *Feminist Studies* 9, no. 2 (Summer 1983): 297.

12. In *Reconstructing Womanhood: The Emergence of the Afro-American Woman Novelist* (New York: Oxford University Press, 1987). Hazel Carby discusses this dismissal of the Brent narrative by John Blassingame in *The Slave Community: Plantation Life in the Antebellum South* (New York: Oxford University Press, 1979).

13. Wright, " 'Beyond Laughter and Tears.' "

14. Barbara Christian, *Black Women Novelists: The Development of a Tradition 1892–1976* (Westport, Conn.: Greenwood Press, 1980). 40.

15. Linda Brent, *Incidents in the Life of a Slave Girl*, ed. L. Maria Child (New York: Harcourt Brace Jovanovich, 1973), 55.

16. Gloria T. Hull, ed., *Give Us Each Day: The Diary of Alice Dunbar-Nelson* (New York: W. W. Norton & Company, 1984) 421–22.

17. In *Writing Beyond the Ending: Narrative Strategies of Twentieth-Century Women Writers* (Bloomington: Indiana University Press, 1985), p. 32. Rachel Blau DuPlessis quotes Virginia Woolf's prescription for women's writing, "Women and Fiction," in *Granite and Rainbow* (New York: Harcourt Brace and Company, 1958), 80.

18. Anna J. Cooper, *A Voice from the South by a Black Woman of the South* (Xenia, Oh.: Aldine Printing House, 1892), 123.

The Highs and the Lows of
Black Feminist Criticism

Barbara Christian

In her essay, "In Search of Our Mothers' Gardens," Alice
Walker asked the questions, "What is *my* literary tradition?
Who are the black women artists who preceded me? Do I have
a ground to stand on?" Confronted by centuries of Afro-
American women who, but for an exceptional few, lived under conditions antithetical to the creation of Art as it was then
defined, how could she claim a creative legacy of foremothers,
women who after all had no access to the pen, to paints, or to
clay? If American cultural history was accurate, singing was
the only art form in which black women participated.

But Walker turned the *idea* of Art on its head. Instead of
looking high, she suggested, we should look low. On that low
ground she found a multitude of artist-mothers—the women
who'd transformed the material to which they'd had access
into their conception of Beauty: cooking, gardening, quilting,
storytelling. In retrieving that low ground, Walker not only
reclaimed her foremothers, she pointed to a critical approach.
For she reminded us that Art, and the thought and sense of
beauty on which it is based, is the province not only of those
with a room of their own, or of those in libraries, universities
and literary Renaissances—that *creating* is necessary to those
who work in kitchens and factories, nurture children and
adorn homes, sweep streets or harvest crops, type in offices
or manage them.

In the early seventies, when anyone asked me, "What do
you think you're doing anyway? What is this Black Feminist

Literary Critic thing you're trying to become?" I would immediately think of Alice's essay.

Like any other critic, my personal history has much to do with what I hear when I read. Perhaps because I am from the Caribbean, Alice's *high* and *low* struck chords in me. I'd grown up with a sharp division between the "high" thought, language, behavior expected in school and in church, and the "low" language that persisted at home and in the yards and the streets.

In school: Proper English, Romanesque sentences, Western philosophy, jargon and exegesis; boys always before girls, lines and lines; *My Country 'Tis of Thee*, the authority of the teacher.

In church: Unintelligible Latin and Greek, the canon, the text; the Virgin Mary and the nuclear family; priests always before nuns; Gregorian chant and tiptoeing.

At home: Bad English, raunchy sayings and stories, the intoning of toasts; women in the kitchen, the parlor *and* the market; kallaloo, loud supper talk, cousins, father, aunts, godmothers.

In the yards: Sashaying and bodies, sweat, calypso, long talk and plenty voices; women and men bantering, bad words, politics and bambooshaying.

What was real? The high, though endured, was valued. The low, though enjoyed, was denigrated even by the lowest of the low.

As I read *Jane Eyre*, I wondered what women dreamt as they gazed at men and at the sea. I knew that women as well as men gazed. My mother and aunts constantly assessed men's bodies, the sea's rhythm. But Charlotte Brontë was in print. She had a language across time and space. I could not find my mother's language, far less her attitude, in any books, despite the fact that her phrasing was as complex and as subtle as Charlotte's.

Because of the 1950s (which for me was not the Eisenhower years but rather the Civil Rights movement, rhythm 'n' blues, and the works of James Baldwin), because of the 1960s (which for me was not the Free Speech Movement and the Weathermen, but rather SNCC, SEEK, the Black Muslims, Aretha and

the Black Arts Movement), the *low* began to be valued by
some of us. Yet there remained the high and the low for many
black women. Camouflaged by the rhetoric of the period, we
were, on high ground, a monolithic Harriet Tubman or a
silent Queen of Africa; on low ground, we were screaming
sapphires or bourgeois bitches.

But what were *we* saying, writing? By the early seventies, I
knew some black women had written. I'd read Phillis Wheatley,
Gwendolyn Brooks, and Lorraine Hansberry. I'd heard poets
like Nikki Giovanni and June Jordan read. I'd known women
in my childhood and adolescence who'd written stories. Yet I
had never, in my years of formal schooling from kindergarten
in the black Virgin Islands through a Ph.D. at white Columbia,
heard even the name of *one* black woman writer. That women
writers were studied, I knew. I'd had courses in which Jane
Austen, George Elliot, Emily Dickinson, and Virginia Woolf
appeared like fleeting phantoms. I knew the university knew
that black male writers existed. My professors bristled at the
names of Richard Wright and James Baldwin and barely acknowledged Langston Hughes and Ralph Ellison.

But what of black women writers? No phantoms, no
bristlings—not even a mention. Few of us knew they wrote;
fewer of us cared. In fact, who even perceived of us, as late as
the early 1970s, as writers, artists, thinkers? Why should anyone want to know what we thought or imagined? What could
we tell others, far less show them, that they did not already
know? After all, weren't we, as Mister taunts Celie, "black"
"pore," woman, and therefore "nothing at all?"

Of course we were telling stories, playing with language,
speculating and specifying, reaching for wisdom, transforming the universe in our image.

Who but us could end a harrowing tale with these words to
her tormentors?

Frado has passed from their memories as Joseph from the
butler's but she will never cease to track them *till* beyond
mortal vision. (Harriet Wilson, *Our Nig*)

Who but us could use the image of a Plum Bun for the
intersection of racism and sexism in this country? (Jessie Fauset,
Plum Bun)

Who but us could begin her story with this comment?

Now, women forget all those things they don't want to remember and remember everything they don't want to forget. The dream is the truth. Then they act and do things accordingly. (Zora Neale Hurston, *Their Eyes Were Watching God*)

Who but us could lovingly present women poets in the kitchen? (Paule Marshall, *Poets in the Kitchen*)

Who but us could tell how it was possible to clean the blood off [our]) beaten men and yet receive abuse from the victim? (Toni Morrison, *The Bluest Eye*)
Who but us could chant:

momma/momma/mammy/nanny/granny/
woman/mistress/sista luv
(June Jordan, Trying to Get Over)

But who knew that we knew? Even those of us who were telling stories or writing did not always see ourselves as artists of the word. And those of us who did know our genius were so rejected, unheard that we sometimes became crazy women crying in the wind or silenced scarecrows. Who could answer us but us?

For us did need us if only to validate that which we knew, we knew. The publications of first novels, Toni Morrison's *The Bluest Eye*, Alice Walker's *The Third Life of Grange Copeland*, June Jordan's *His Own Where*, heralded the decade of the seventies. While their novels were barely acknowledged in 1970, the movement of women all over the world was highlighted by American women who had some access to the Big Capital Media. Inspired, though sometimes disappointed, by movements of people of color, of blacks in the United States, of liberation struggles of "underdeveloped" nations, some American women began to seek themselves as women and to protest the truncated definition of woman in this society. In this context the literature of women, the critical responses of women were published as never before during a decade when many others were asserting that *The* Movement was dead.

For those of us who came out of the sixties, the vision of women moving all over the world was not solely a claiming of our rights but also the rights of all those who had been denied their humanity. In the space created for us by our foremothers, by our sisters in the streets, the houses, the factories, the schools, we were now able to speak and to listen to each other, to hear our own language, to refine and critique it across time and space, through the written word. For me that dialogue *is* the kernel of what a black feminist literary critic tries to do. We listen to those of us who speak, write, read, to those who have written, to those who may write. We write to those who write, read, speak, may write, and we try to hear the voiceless. We are participants in a many-voiced palaver of thought/feeling, image/language that moves us to *move*—toward a world where, like Alice Walker's revolutionary petunias, all of us can bloom.

We found that in order to move beyond prescribed categories we had to "rememory"—reconstruct our past. But in the literary church of the sixties, such an appeal to history was anathema. Presiding at the altar were the new critic priests, for whom the text was God, unstained by history, politics, experience, the world. Art for them was artifact. So, for example, the literature of blacks could not be literature, tainted as it was by what they called sociology. To the side of the altar were the pretenders, the political revolutionaries and new philosophers for whom creative works were primarily a pretext to expound their own ideas, their world programs. For both groups, women were neither the word nor the world, though sometimes we could be dots on some i's, muses or furies in the service of the text or the idea.

We found that we could not talk to either group unless we talked their talk, which was specialized, abstract—on high ground. So we learned their language only to find that its character had a profound effect on the questions we thought, the images we evoked, and that such thinking recalled a tradition beyond which we had to move if *we* were to be included in any authentic dialogue.

Because language is one (though not the only) way to express what one knows/feels even when one doesn't know one knows it, because storytelling *is* a dynamic form of remem-

bering/recreating, we found that it was often in the relationship between literatures and the world that re-visioning
occurred. It is often in the poem, the story, the play, rather
than in Western philosophical theorizing, that feminist thought/
feeling evolves, challenges and renews itself. So our Sister-
bonding was presented and celebrated in novels like *Sula*, our
body/spirit/erotic in works like *The Color Purple*, our revision of
biography in works like *Zami*. It has often been through our
literatures that women have renamed critical areas of human
life: mothering, sexuality, bodies, friendship, spirituality, economics, the process of literature itself. And it was to these
expressions that many of us turned in order to turn to ourselves as situated in a dynamic rather than a fixed world. For
many of us such a turning led us to universities where words,
ideas, are, were supposed to be nurtured and valued.

And—ah, here's the rub.

As a result of that gravitation, we *have* moved to excavate
the past and restore to ourselves the words of many of our
foremothers who were buried in the rumble of distorted history. We have questioned the idea of great works of literature,
preferences clearly determined by a powerful elite. We have
asked why some forms are not considered literature—for example, the diary, the journal, the letter. We have built journals and presses through which the works of women might be
published. We have developed women's studies programs.
Using our stories and images, we have taught our daughters
and sons about ourselves, our sisters, brothers, and lovers
about our desires. And some of us have shared a palaver with
our writers/readers that prompts us all to re-vision ourselves.

Yet even as we moved, the high, the low persisted, in fact
moved further and further apart. For we now confronted the
revelation we always knew, that there is both a She and there
are many she's. And that sometimes, in our work we seemed
to reduce the *both-and* to *either-or*. That revelation made itself
strongly felt in the exclusion that women of color protested
when Woman was defined, in the rejection that many working-
class women experienced when Woman was described. The
awareness that we too seek to homogenize the world of our
Sisters, to fix ourselves in boxes and categories through jargon, theory, abstraction, is upon us.

Why so? Has our training led us back to the high ground

that had rejected us, our education to the very language that masked our existence? So often feminist literary discussion seems riveted on defining Woman in much the same way that Western medieval scholars tried to define God. Why is it that rather than acknowledging that we are both-and, we persist in seeking the either-or. Might that be because the either-or construction, the either-or deconstruction, is so embedded in our education? Might it be because that language, whether it moves us anywhere or not, is recognized, rewarded as brilliant, intellectual, high, in contrast to the low, vulgar, ordinary language of most creative writers and readers? Is it that we too are drawn to the power that resides on the high ground?

Even as we turned to our literatures, in which language is not merely an object but is always situated in a context, in which the pleasure and emotion of language are as important as its meaning, we have gravitated toward a critical language that is riddled with abstraction and is as distanced as possible from the creative work, and from pleasure. I sometimes wonder if we critics read stories and poems, or, if as our language indicates, our reading fare is primarily that of other critics and philosophers? Do we know our own literatures? Why, for example, does it appear that white feminist critics have abandoned their contemporary novelists? Where is the palaver among them? Or are Freud, Lacan, Barthes, Foucault, Derrida inevitably more appealing? Why are we so riveted on male thinkers, preferably dead or European? Why is it that in refuting essence, we become so fixed on essence? To whom are we writing when we write? Have we turned so far round that we have completed our circle? Is it that we no longer see any connections between the emotion/knowing language of women's literature, the many-voiced sounds of our own language and the re-visioning we seek?

Now when I think of Alice's *high* and *low*, I feel a new meaning. Because I am a black literary/feminist critic, I live in a sharp distinction between the high world of lit crit books, journals, and conferences, the middle world of classrooms and graduate students, and the low world of bookstores, kitchens, communities, and creative writers.

In the high world:	Discourse, theory, the canon, the body, the boys (preferably Lacan, Derrida, and Foucault) before the girls; linguistics, the authority of the critic, the exclusion of creative writings.
In the middle world:	Reading the texts, sometimes of creative writers; negotiating between advancement and appreciation; tropes, research, discourse; now I understand my mother; narrative strategies. What does it mean? The race for theory.
In the low world:	Stories, poems, plays. The language of the folk. Many bodies—the feeling as one with June, Alice, Toni. I sure know what she's talking about. I don't want to hear that. Her words move me. That poem changed my life.

I dream like that.
That's really disturbing.
God—that's beautiful.
Perhaps I'm not so crazy after all.
I want to write too.
Say what?

Much, of course, can be learned by all of us from all of us who speak, read, write, including those of us who look high. But as we look high, we might also look low, lest we devalue women in the world even as we define *Woman*. In ignoring their voices, we may not only truncate our movement but we may also limit our own process until our voices no longer sound like women's voices to anyone.

Variations on Negation and the Heresy of Black Feminist Creativity

Michele Wallace

In short, the image of black women writing in isolation, across time and space, is conduced toward radical revision. The room of one's own explodes its four walls to embrace the classroom, the library, and the various mechanisms of institutional and media life, including conferences, the lecture platform, the television talk show, the publishing house, the 'best seller,' and collections of critical essays.

—*Hortense Spiller*, "Cross-currents,
Discontinuities: Black Womens' Fiction"[1]

In the past seventeen years, or more, black women writers have begun to produce a literature that transcends its intrinsic political boundaries of invisibility to address the world. Yet despite the commercial success of some books by some black women writers, most black women writers are not well known. Their creativity—especially if it doesn't fit the Book-of-the-Month Club/*NY Times* Best-Seller mold—continues to suffer the fate of marginality. Perhaps the most persuasive evidence of this predicament is the way black feminist interpretation has been all but extinguished in mainstream and academic discourses, despite the omnipresent mechanical reproduction of interpretation through electronic media. Meanwhile, the highly visible success of a few works—including my own *Black Macho and the Myth of the Superwoman* in 1979—sometimes obscures the revolutionary challenge black feminist creativity could pose to white male cultural hegemony.

Sadder still is that nobody in particular and everybody in

general seems responsible for this situation. Universities, museums, and publishing houses, what Ishmael Reed calls "cultural detention centers," run by white men and their surrogates, remain the unrelenting arbiters of cultural standards, which exclude or erase the diverse creativity of nonelite populations. Post-modernists, new historicists, deconstructionists, Marxists, Afro-Americanists, feminists, and even some black female academics, for the most part, fail to challenge the exclusionary parlor games of knowledge production.

While I will focus on black women writers, my overall concern is with black feminist creativity in general and with the manner in which, in fields like popular music, opera, and modeling, media visibility may be allowed to substitute for black female economic and political power, whereas in more politically articulate fields such as film, theatre, and TV news commentary, black feminist creativity is routinely gagged and "disappeared."

From the black woman whose face is featured on the cover of *Vogue* to the recordings of black female rappers to Sue Simmons interviewing rhythm n' blues singer "Wicked" Wilson Pickett on the New York TV talk show *Live At Five*, at some level, all black feminist creativity wants to make the world a place that will be safe for women of color, their men, and their children. Nevertheless, I will refer to black feminist creativity at its most profound—in the novels and poetry of writers like Toni Morrison, Alice Walker, and Ntozake Shange; in the performances of singers like Nina Simone, Miriam Makeba, and Betty Carter; and in the work of artists like Faith Ringgold (my mother) and Bettye Saar—as the "incommensurable," or "variations on negation," in order to characterize the precarious dialectic of a creative project that is forced to be "other" to the creativity of white women and black men, who are "other" themselves.[2] You've probably heard a great deal of talk about the "other"—lately the problem of choice in culture and politics. The question being posed here concerns the "other" of the "other" in public discourse: the culture's potential for the Rainbow Coalition in general, black feminist creativity in particular.

For Marxist historian Hayden White, the tropological—or the tendency of all written argument to rely on figurative language to persuade—is a good name for the perpetual gaps in that discourse which ordinarily describes itself as rational, logical, and therefore universally true. I would add that these tropes or gaps in the dominant discourse become a kind of road map of where the bodies—the bodies of those who have been ignored or negated—are buried. "There is no document of civilization which is not at the same time a document of barbarism," Walter Benjamin once pointed out. Moreover, as feminist philosopher Alison Jagger has said, "the myth of dispassionate investigation bolsters the epistemic authority of white men," a procedure that results in their "emotional hegemony." Therefore, in a subversive critical process, "outlaw emotions become a primary motivation for investigation," which is another way of saying that the personal becomes political yet again.[3]

In this light, what interests me is the problem of a black female cultural perspective, which for the most part is not allowed to become written in a society in which writing is the primary currency of knowledge. How then does black feminist creativity finally surface as writing? Moreover, can it be self-critical?

Hayden White uses the tropological to diagnose the discontinuities in white male cultural hegemony, while reconsolidating precisely the same hegemony. (This move is habitual among white male theorists, which continues to be the problem in using their work to other ends.) In *Blues, Ideology and Afro-American Literature*, Afro-American literary critic Houston Baker borrows the tropological from White to construct a black male cultural hegemony. Neither White nor Baker is concerned to read into the apparent gaps the disorderliness of sexuality.

Baker's key trope in describing the work of Richard Wright is a black hole, an area in which gravitation is so intense that no light can escape. Contrary to what we might expect, black holes are full not empty. They are unimaginably dense stars. "They are surrounded by an 'event horizon,' a membrane that prevents the unaltered escape of anything which passes through," Baker writes. "Light shone into a black hole disappears," it converts energy into mass that is infinitely compressed, and "all objects are 'squeezed' to zero volume."[4]

But a feminist physics major at the University of Oklahoma told me something else about black holes. Physicists now believe black holes may give access to other dimensions. An object or energy enters the black hole and is infinitely compressed to zero volume, as Baker reports; then it passes through to another dimension, whereupon the object and/or energy reassumes volume, mass, form, direction, velocity—all the properties of visibility and concreteness, but in another dimension. The idea of a black hole as a process—as a progression that appears differently, or not at all, from various perspectives—seems a useful way of illustrating how I conceive of incommensurability, or variations on negation, as characteristic of black feminist creativity.

The point in using the analogy of the black hole is not simply the obvious sexual one—nor even that if you add up all the cases of successful creative black women, you'll arrive at only a small fraction of black women engaged in creative acts—but rather that even successful creative black women have next to nothing to say about the nature of commentary and interpretation in their respective fields. So to the extent that the arts exist as a byproduct of diverse acts of interpretation and analysis, black feminist creativity is virtually nonexistent. Moreover, it is nonexistent precisely because everybody (including many black women) agrees that black women have no interest in criticism, interpretation, and theoretical analysis, and no capacity for it.

In other words, the black hole represents the dense accumulation, without explanation or inventory, of black feminist creativity. Prevented from assuming a commensurable role in critical theory and the production of knowledge by a combination of external and internal pressures, it is confined to the aesthetic and the commercial. To compensate for ghettoization, black feminist creativity's concentration in music and now literature has become provocatively intense. And yet it is still difficult, even for those who study this music and literature, to apprehend black feminist creativity as a continuous and coherent discourse.

What most people see of the black woman is a void, a black hole that appears empty, not full. The outsider sees black feminist creativity as a dark hole from which nothing worthwhile can emerge and in which everything is forced to assume the zero volume of nothingness, the invisibility, that results from the intense pressure of race, class, and sex.

Even when a media production is passed off as a translation of black feminist creativity—as in Steven Spielberg's translation of Alice Walker's *The Color Purple*—it is crucial to speak of its inadequacies and failures. To those of us hypnotized by the dominant discourse, as Ntozake Shange put it in *For Colored Girls Who Have Considered Suicide When the Rainbow Is Enuf*, black feminist creativity sounds like "half-notes scattered/ without rhythm/no tune."[5]

When I wrote "The Myth of the Superwoman" in 1977–1978, I tried to subsume a lot of smaller, historically specific cultural myths about the strength of the black woman—such stereotypes as "mammy," "Sapphire," "matriarch," "Aunt Jemima" —under the rubric of one large, all-purpose myth. In the process, of course, I was defeating the very purpose of myth, which is to obscure contradiction and drown out history and the dialectical in a superficial (marketable) binary opposition. But that was not the way I saw things then.

It seemed to me that the evidence was everywhere in American culture that precisely because of their profound political and economic disadvantages, black women were considered to have a peculiar advantage. Not only did this premise seem basic to representations of black women in the dominant discourse, it was also becoming characteristic of a lot of Afro-American discourse.

No doubt, as Alice Walker said in her essay "To the Black Scholar,"[6] I thought my ideas were more original than they were. Moreover, while my role models for cultural criticism in 1978 were Tom Wolfe, Norman Mailer, Hunter Thompson, Joan Didion, and James Baldwin, an emergent feminist cultural studies approach has been instrumental in persuading me that style, or strategies of public address, has profound political implications in dealing with material concerning women of color because of their limited access to mainstream, academic, and "avant-garde" discourses.

Specifically, few black critics understood the rhetorical imperative—imposed by the combination of "white" media/ marketplace and "black" audience—which produced *Black Macho and the Myth of the Superwoman*. A black woman writer who wants to write seriously about contemporary cultural issues and how they are socially constructed is faced with an almost

insurmountable communication problem: if she takes a scholarly approach, she will be virtually ignored because black
women have no power in that context; if she takes a colloquial
"entertainment" approach—as I did in *Black Macho*—then she
will be read, but she will be attacked and ostracized. Either
way can cut the possibility of constructive commentary—in
the work itself or in the criticism of that work—down to zero.[7]
The trick may be to fall somewhere in between the academic and the entertaining, as did Walker in *In Search of Our
Mothers' Gardens*. Yet her plain-spoken, "commonsense" style
has its limits as well.

As for Walker's discussion of "The Myth of the Superwoman," she does not significantly disagree with my general thesis in her essay, originally written in 1979 as a letter
to *The Black Scholar*. This issue of *The Black Scholar* responded
to the controversy over the publication of my book and the
connection between it and Shange's *For Colored Girls*, which
was then on Broadway. Briefly, the controversy had to do with
the problem of black images, and whether or not my work
and Shange's work helped to perpetuate stereotypical images
of the race. In a short prologue to the essay, Walker says
that *The Black Scholar* refused to publish it because they considered the tone too "personal" and "hysterical."

What Walker takes exception to is my assertion that "the
myth of the superwoman" is "unquestioned even by the occasional black woman writer or politician." " 'It is a lie,' " she
reports having written to my publishers. " 'I can't speak for
politicians but I can certainly speak for myself. I've been hack-
ing away at that stereotype for years, and so have a good
many other black women writers.' I thought not simply of Meridian, but of Janie Crawford, of Pecola, of Sula and Nell,
of Edith Jackson, even of Iola Leroy and Medga, for God's
sake. (Characters of black women writers Ms. Wallace is un-
acquainted with; an ignorance that is acceptable only in someone not writing a book about black women.)"[8]

I agree. But it wasn't true that I hadn't read Walker's second
novel *Meridian* or Toni Morrison's *Sula* or Zora Neale Hurston's
Their Eyes Were Watching God, although Frances Harper's *Iola
Leroy* wasn't generally available then (and Megda and Edith
Jackson I still don't know). Like many other black women of
my generation, I eagerly awaited the publication or reissue of

black women's books. But as a young black woman who was
in search of feminist solidarity *and* a writing career, I wanted
something very specific from the black women writers I read.
I had grown up in Harlem, not in the rural South. My family
had lived in Harlem for three generations. To me, the South
these writers recollected was fragmented and nostalgic. My
mother Faith Ringgold was an artist, my grandmother Willi
Posey was a fashion designer, and I had been the beneficiary
of a private school education, purchased with greater difficulty than I was then capable of understanding—an education
that had acquainted me with the extent to which black women
were customarily denied cultural participation. I felt rebuffed
by the unwillingness of black women writers to deal with a
contemporary urban context. Moreover, I wanted them to
deal with the problem of being a black woman writer, which
seemed to me overwhelming, and I wanted them to do so
immediately and explicitly, to cease their endless deflecting in
their lyrical way about a rural Afro-American purity forever
lost.

Of course, this view was unfair in that it did not take into
account the work of Louise Meriweather, Ann Petry, Toni
Cade Bambara, and Paule Marshall, although I had read the
black feminist anthology *The Black Woman* from cover to cover
when it was published in 1971, and I had also read Petry's *The
Street*, Meriweather's *Daddy Was a Numbers Runner*, and some
of Bambara's short stories.[9] Yet none of this work had any
particular impact on my misgivings about black women's fiction, because I saw this work, as well, as fundamentally continuous with the kind of mysticism about the power of "roots"
that characterized their fictions in rural settings.

I read *Mules and Men* and *Their Eyes Were Watching God* by
Zora Neale Hurston in 1971 and 1972, while I was a student
majoring in English and writing at the City College of New
York. Fascinated as much by Jane Austen and George Eliot as
by Hurston, and already thinking of myself as a "black feminist" thanks to the encouragement and support of an actively
feminist mother, I was in the front row of the first Women's
Studies classes at City College.

I read *The Bluest Eye* in 1974, while working as a secretary at
Random House, where Toni Morrison was then an editor. That
summer Angela Davis often came to see Morrison to work on

her autobiography. When it was published in 1975, I read it
immediately. In 1975 I also attended the first conference of the
National Black Feminist Organization in New York, at which
Shirley Chisholm, Eleanor Holmes Norton, and Florynce Kennedy were keynote speakers. Alice Walker led a workshop
discussion together with Faith, my mother, on black women
in the arts.

It was around this time that I read Walker's first book of
short stories, *In Love and Trouble*, as well as the essay "In
Search of Our Mothers' Gardens," which immediately became
essential reading for black feminists, but which struck me
then as afflicted by the same nostalgia for and valorization of
the rural and the anonymity of the unlettered that I considered so problematic in the work of black women novelists. In
particular, the premise of the article—that black women writers should speak for previous generations of silenced black
women—posed certain conceptual difficulties for me. First, no
one can really speak *for* anybody else. Inevitably, we silence
others that we may speak at all. This is particularly true of
"speaking" in print. Second, there was an implicit denial of
the necessity for generational conflict and critical dialectic,
which I found totally paralyzing. Anyhow, my mother was a
prominent artist, well educated and active in the Women's
Movement. So how could I pursue Walker's proposal? Moreover, didn't it imply that black women writers would always
"speak" from the platform of a silenced past?

Faith was then (and still is) involved on a daily basis in
making a politically engaged black feminist art out of quilting,
soft sculpture, sewing, painting, lettering, and performance.
My interest in visual art and art criticism—which was shaped
by Faith's involvement with artists on the left organizing to
protest the Vietnam War and the racism and sexism of establishment museums—was perhaps the largest influence on my
notion of what black feminist creativity could mean at that
point.

So when I completed the manuscript of my book in 1978,
my decision to make the statement that black women writers
were reinforcing "the myth of the superwoman" was no accidental afterthought, nor was it made because I didn't think art
was important, or because I didn't know of Pecola, Meridian,
and Janie Crawford. Now I realize that I was reading too

narrowly. My sense of these matters has changed mostly because of black feminist reinterpretations of Hurston's *Their Eyes Were Watching God* that foreground Janie's ascension to the posture of articulate storyteller, despite the obstacle of a twisted sexism coming from a black community besieged by racism.[10]

Moreover, the interpretation of deconstructivist critic Barbara Johnson makes the point that polar or binary oppositions are crucial to the logic of our culture's rhetoric about race and sex. That Hurston occupied the wrong end of each of these oppositions made inevitable the continuous splitting of the difference (it's sometimes called "waffling" in Baldwin's work) that marked Hurston's narrative and expositional style. Johnson divides the field of the dominant discourse into four realms: white men make statements of universality; white women make statements of "complementarity"; black men make statements of "the other"; and black female discourse is identified only by the lowercase "x" of radical negation. "The black woman is both invisible and ubiquitous," Johnson writes of the often paltry efforts of black men, white men, and white women to include her in their progressive political formulations, "never seen in her own right but forever appropriated by the others for their own ends."[11]

While Johnson's thesis is meant to be illuminating and suggestive rather than precisely sociological, there is no question in my mind that the unrelenting logic of dualism, or polar oppositions—such as black and white, good and evil, male and female—is basic to the discourse of the dominant culture and tends to automatically erase black female subjectivity. The "on the one hand/on the other hand" logic of most rational argumentation works out fine if you happen to fit neatly into one of the following categories: (1) the unified, universalizing subject, usually claimed by white men, or (2) the "other," usually spoken for by white women or men of color. But if you happen to have more than one feature disqualifying you from participation in the dominant discourse—if you are black and a woman, and perhaps lesbian and poor, as well—and you insist on writing about it, you're in danger of not making any sense, because you are attempting speech from the dangerously unspeakable posture of the "other" of the "other."

It was my view that black women writers were verifying

"the myth of the superwoman" by creating perverse characterizations, which displayed inordinate strengths and abilities
as the inevitable booby prize of a romanticized marginality.
The problem with the myth of the superwoman, as I saw and
still see it, is that it seems designed to cover up an inexorable
process of black female disenfranchisement, exploitation, oppression, and despair. Even more important than whether
black women believe the myth or whether some black women
engage in superlative accomplishments (which they obviously
do) is the way the dominant culture perpetuates the myth, not
to celebrate the black woman but as a weapon against her.
"She is already liberated" becomes an excuse for placing her
needs last on every shopping list in town. Also very important is the way in which otherwise liberal or marginal constituencies, such as white progressives, white feminists, and
ordinarily enlightened black male intellectuals, benignly consent to or actively conspire with the dominant discourse in
this process.

The "other" of the "other," or incommensurability, is another approach to the same problem. Whereas the myth of the
superwoman was a concept designed to describe the culture's
general misapprehension about black women, the "other" of
the "other" is an attempt to diagnose the black woman's
relationship to the dominant discourse. It is more important to
talk about the "other" of the "other" at this point, not because
there is no longer a problem of myths (or stereotypes), but
because myths are not dispelled by revelation. Rather the
revelation of myth simply continues the process of myth. Or,
as Claude Lévi-Strauss's reading of Freud's encounter with
the Oedipus myth would imply,[12] the "revelation" becomes
yet another version of the myth by not focusing on the politics
of who speaks and who doesn't, which ultimately determines
the power of knowledge and the knowledge thus derived of
the world. At the same time, the "other" of the "other" is
resistant to theoretical articulation—hence the black feminist
fear of theory, the invisibility of black feminist interpretation
in the realm of the dominant discourse, and the way black
feminist literature prioritizes variations on negation.

Another way of describing variations on negation would be to
call them "negative images." But I prefer the phrase "varia-

tions on negation" because "negation" seems indispensable to a dialectical critical process. My liking for the term "variations" is more whimsical, based on an idea of musical performance. To me, "variations" suggest experimental approaches that delay closure almost indefinitely. Billie Holiday used to sing "The difficult I'll do right now, the impossible will take a little while." Variations on negation confront "the impossible," the radical being and not-being of women of color.

The capacity for rendering the negative substantial and dialectical has been a particular strength of fiction by black women writers—a point that Barbara Smith, Deborah McDowell, and other black feminist critics, in their pursuit of programmatic concerns, have minimized.[13] The way these variations on negation occur is twofold, as can be seen in Toni Morrison's *Sula*. On the level of content, the reader can't help but notice that the black community, called "The Bottom," comes to dislike Sula, even as Sula's best friend rejects her for "stealing her man." Neither Sula, nor her mother Hannah, nor her grandmother Eva fits anybody's notion of a good guy. But Nel, her mother Helene, and her grandmother are hardly positive images either. Rather, their characterizations seem a direct response to the imbalances of Sula, Hannah, and Eva, which bears upon the second way of reading variations on negation.

It is the relationship (or gaps) between items in the text—description, character, plot, dialogue—that gives this book its force. The book's power lies in its willingness to contradict itself. In particular, one must look for moments that directly oppose one another in their construction of "reality."

The various oppositions of race, class, and sex only support the paramount opposition between Sula—the epitome of the "negative being," who will not marry or settle down and who breaks all the conventions of adult behavior by living, unhypo-critically, for pleasure—and the "Bottom," whose sentiments are ultimately personified by Nel, who marries and settles down while Sula goes off to college. The tension between Sula and Nel is the level at which Morrison is problematizing issues of black feminist creativity. Sula's and Nel's individual characterizations are less important than the roles they play in the novel's larger problem of working out how black feminist creativity will become written.

Certainly, the undermining of facile dualisms or binary oppositions of class, race, and sex is a priority in fiction by black
women. One intriguing possibility is that there may be a
systematic disorder within language itself, which helps to
explain the perpetual invisibility of women of color to the
dominant discourse. Another provocative possibility is that
the very process of radical negation, or doubling and tripling
the difference, may provide a way to reformulate the problem
of black female subjectivity and black female participation in
culture.

Perhaps the most important book to look at in this regard is
Morrison's *The Bluest Eye*. When I first read this book, I was
deeply troubled by Pecola's characterization as a victim of
incest and by her subsequent loss of the ability to communicate rationally. It seemed to me such a story was hopelessly
negative, not transformational or transcendent in a manner I
considered essential to creative acts. Now, however, I think
that in the relationship between Pecola and Claudia, who serves
as narrator for much of the book, we find a problematization
of the conditions that plague the discourse of the "other" of
the "other."

Pecola illustrates the path of those who will never recover,
the ultimate victim who will never be able to speak for herself.
Claudia is the survivor, who sees color and variety even in the
somber, severe circumstances of her childhood. Her narration
moves smoothly from childhood reminiscence to the occasional adult/editorial reflection of "the author," incorporating
the pain and victimization of Pecola as a crucial factor in her
need to be articulate, or to write. In the end—which is also
where the book begins—Pecola is living on the edge of town,
permanently isolated from the black community by her inability to rise above the crimes committed against her.

Without Claudia's and Morrison's storytelling, Pecola's
marginalization and social death become a distinct possibility
for anyone who challenges the present invisibility of black
feminist interpretation by speaking the unspeakable hell of
Pecola's real-life counterparts. Yet there isn't a character in *The
Bluest Eye* who doesn't have more psychological resources
than Pecola in combatting an internalization of self-hatred that
might be considered routine in the black community.

Indeed, as much as this book is about the plight of the

individual incest victim, it is also about the collective internalization of self-hatred, the cultural erasure of a people and
their mostly unconscious battle with what Western civilization
calls "madness." That political, economic, and cultural process of negation, which the sociologist Orlando Patterson calls
"social death," and which we date from slavery, is where *The
Bluest Eye* starts. It is announced by Morrison's use of the
"Dick and Jane" primer text:

> Here is the House. It is green and white. It has a red
> door. It is very pretty. Here is the family. Mother, Father,
> Dick, and Jane live in the green-and-white house. They
> are very happy. See Jane. She has a red dress. She wants
> to play. Who will play with Jane?[14]

Countless American children have encountered this text—which
lays out the world as classless, lily-white, sexually stratified
but sexless, timeless and without history—as the single path
to learning, to the achievement of knowledge. Morrison announces that the meaninglessness of this official text (and
perhaps all unitary models) will be a primary focus in *The
Bluest Eye* by repeating it a second time without punctuation—
the law of the Father, or dominant discourse—and a third time
without space between the words, undercutting the very basis
of the alphabet's power to signify. In the process, Morrison
suggests that Pecola's madness originates less in her individual psyche or the psyche of anyone else in the ghetto; rather,
it is socially and linguistically constructed by the dominant
discourse. The book then details the social construction of that
"otherness" to Dick and Jane's world by systematically contrasting houses, families, mothers, fathers, siblings, and play
in Pecola's community. Pecola's family is extremely dysfunc-
tional; Claudia's family is much better. And there are other
examples, although all belie the reality of the Dick and Jane
model. Yet, everyone and everything is powerless to protect
Pecola from tragedy.

Through Soaphead Church, Morrison designates one culprit
as the European Judeo-Christian patriarchal tradition. When
he takes God's place by pretending to grant Pecola blue eyes—
the book's symbol of whiteness, safety, and madness—Morrison
seems to be saying that Soaphead Church is all the God that

one can expect in a world that believes in binary oppositions.

At the same time, I haven't done justice to the compositional complexity of *The Bluest Eye* if I've given the impression that this novel explicitly advocates black feminist creativity as a corrective for what ails the black community. The richness of its variations on negation lies precisely in its unwillingness to advocate anything but the circular progress of its own logic. Perhaps the difficulty of identifying the novel's opinion of feminist engagement is clearest in the depiction of Marie, Poland, and China, the three prostitutes who live over the storefront occupied by Pecola's family. In distinct contrast to the variety of maternal images in the book, these women neither nurture nor protect children. They engage in (mostly pointless) resistances to local male authority, yet fail to understand victimization or the fact that Pecola is in danger. Their inclusion in the text seems to question the self-involvement of traditional modes of black female creativity, as well as posing a general critique of more recent feminist strategies of "man-hating" and self-love.

I now see that like many other people who read *The Bluest Eye* and other books by black women writers, I focused too much on the extent to which they mirrored certain obvious sociological realities.[15] This, too, is part of invisibility and the peculiar limitations of the "other" of the "other." From the perspective of dominance, a woman of color who insists on functioning as a speaking (writing) subject threatens the status of Truth itself. The indirection of fiction that seems essential to override reader resistance is, in fact, the shortest distance between two ideological points. Thus the Afro-American woman's talent for fictional narrative is steeped in what Susan Willis has called "the changes wrought by history."[16] As she suggests, black women writers show an uncanny ability for rendering a collective black history of migration, poverty, segregation, and exploitation singular and readable.

Further, black women writers not only make it possible to understand how a convergence of racism, sexism, and class antagonism marks the Third World woman's peculiar position in discourse, but their work calls into question the truth value of any unitary or dualistic apprehension of the world. Not only is it necessary that we focus on difference rather than sameness or universality, but also, at every conceivable moment, we must choose and take responsibility for what we will emphasize in ourselves and others. And we must respond to Michel Foucault's question "What matter who's speaking?" with the recognition that it matters mostly because there's no variety.

I was struck by these issues most forcefully when I attended a performance of Lorraine Hansberry's *A Raisin in the Sun* about two years ago. The first time I saw *A Raisin in the Sun*—indeed, the first time I saw evidence that black women were capable of literature—was when I saw the movie in 1961. I was nine years old and I remember it well because my entire family went to the theatre together. Like the movie of *The Color Purple*, it was a historic occasion.

Every time I see *A Raisin in the Sun* my attention is drawn to how the female characters—the mother, Walter Lee's wife, and Beneatha—represent more thoroughly than most other works of American literature the archetypal choices available to black women (except lesbians) in this culture, as well as the nature of those obstacles blocking critical self-expression. And it is interesting to me that what critics have considered inherent shortcomings in Hansberry's attempts to re-create Chicago tenement life realistically really have to do with her depicting her own complex relation to American intellectual and cultural life. In a family drama, and therefore conventionally, Hansberry explores the myriad tensions of race, class, and sex that plague the black community.

Nevertheless, there's no question that conventional form and conventional gender roles are a handicap in Hansberry's attempt to grapple with who Beneatha is/can be, and that conventionality, in general, limits black feminist explorations. I am also well aware that I lay myself open to the charge of elitism when I proceed as though cultural criticism were as crucial as health, the law, politics, economics, and the family to the condition of black women. But I am convinced that the major battle for the "other" of the "other" will be to achieve a voice, or voices, thus inevitably transforming the basic relations of dominant discourse. Only with those voices—written, published, televised, taped, filmed, staged, crossindexed, and footnoted—will we approach control over our own lives.

NOTES

1. Marjorie Pryse and Hortense Spiller, eds., *Conjuring: Black Women, Fiction and Literary Tradition* (Bloomington: Indiana University Press, 1985), 250.

2. See Michele Wallace, "Female Troubles: Ishmael Reed's Tunnel Vision," *Voice Literary Supplement* (December 1986), 10–11.

3. See Hayden White, *Tropics of Discourse: Essays in Cultural Criticism* (Baltimore: Johns Hopkins University Press, 1978); Walter Benjamin, *Illuminations* (New York: Schocken Books [1955] 1968), 256; Alison Jaggar, "Love & Knowledge: Emotions as an Epistemic Resource for Feminism," delivered at SUNY-Buffalo, November 11, 1987.

4. Houston Baker, *Blues, Ideology and Afro-American Literature* (Chicago: University of Chicago Press, 1984), 145.

5. See Michele Wallace, " 'The Color Purple': Blues for Mr. Spielberg," *Village Voice*, March 18, 1986) 21–24, 26; Ntozake Shange, *For Colored Girls Who Have Considered Suicide When the Rainbow Is Enuf* (New York: Bantam [1976] 1980), 1.

6. Alice Walker, *In Search of Our Mothers' Gardens* (New York: Harcourt Brace/Jovanovich, 1983), 322.

7. Obviously, this is too broad a generalization and black women have engaged in constructive written commentary before. One could point to June Jordan's *Civil Wars*, Audre Lorde's *Sister Outsideer*, Barbara Christian's *Black Feminist Criticism*, Bell Hook's *Ain't I a Woman* and *Feminist Theory*, but this work remains marginal to every academic establishment except Women's Studies.

8. Walker, *In Search of Our Mothers' Gardens*, 324–25.

9. Toni Cade Bambara, ed., *The Black Woman* (New York: Fawcett, 1971); *Gorilla, My Love* (New York: Random House, 1972); Paule Marshall, *Brown Girls, Brownstones* (Boston: Beacon, 1960)

10. See Michele Wallace, "Who Owns Zora Neale Hurston? Critics Carve Up the Legend," *Village Voice Literary Supplement*, 64 (April 1988), 18–21.

11. Barbara Johnson, *A World of Difference* (Baltimore: Johns Hopkins University Press, 1987), 166–71.

12. Claude Lévi-Strauss, "The Structural Study of Myth," in *The Structuralists from Marx to Lévi-Strauss*, ed. Richard and Fernande DeGeorge (New York: Doubleday Anchor, 1972), 181.

13. Barbara Smith, "Toward a Black Feminist Criticism," 168– 85; Deborah E. McDowell, "New Directions for Black Feminist Criticism," 186–99, in *The New Feminist Criticism: Essays on Women, Literature & Theory*, ed. Elaine Showalter (New York: Pantheon, 1985).

14. Toni Morrison, *The Bluest Eye* (New York: Holt, Rinhart and Winston, 1970), 1.

15. Sociological misreadings of black women writers are legend. See, for instance, Mel Watkins, "Sexism, Racism and Black Women Writers," *New York Times Book Review* (June 15, 1986), 1, 35–36; Darryl Pinckney, "Black Victims, Black Villains," *New York Review of Books* (January 29, 1987), 17–20; Marlaine Gicksman, "Lee's Way," *Film* (October 1986), 46–49; Stanley Crouche, "Aunt Meda," *New Republic*, (October 1987), 38–43.

16. Susan Willis, *Specifying: Black Women Writing the American Experience* (Madison: University of Wisconsin Press, 1987), 3.

Some Implications of Womanist Theory*

Sherley Anne Williams

I am an Afro-Americanist and enough of an Africanist to know something of the enormous differences between African literatures and Afro-American literature, and something, too, of the remarkable parallels and similarities between them. We do in English, after all, trace our literary roots back to the same foreparents, the Senegalese-American, Phillis Wheatley and the Nigerian-American, Gustavas Vassa or Olaudah Equiano, the African. So you must make your own analogies with what follows here; I am assuming that feminist criticism receives much the same reception it has met with among Afro-American critics, male and female. Often, feminist concerns are seen as a divisive, white importation that further fragments an already divided and embattled race, as trivial mind games unworthy of response while black people everywhere confront massive economic and social problems. I don't deny feminism's potential for divisiveness, but the concerns of women are neither trivial nor petty. The relation between male and female is the very foundation of human society. If black men refuse to engage the unease at the race's heart, they cannot speak or even see truthfully anywhere else.

Feminist readings can lead to misapprehensions of particular texts or even of a whole tradition, but certain of its formulations offer us a vocabulary that can be made meaningful in terms of our own experience. Feminist theory, like black aes-

* Presented at the African Literature Association Conference, April 17, 1986

thetics, offers us not only the possibility of changing one's *reading* of the world, but of changing the world itself. And like black aesthetics, it is far more egalitarian than the prevailing mode. What follows, then, is both a critique of feminist theory and an application of that branch of it Alice Walker has called "womanist."[1] It is as much *bolekaja* criticism as "feminist" theory, for black women writers have been urging black men not so much to "come down [and] fight," as to come down and talk, even before Chinweizu, Jemie, and Madubuike coined a critical term to describe our challenge.[2]

Feminist criticism, to paraphrase Elaine Showalter's words in the "Introduction" to *The New Feminist Criticism*,[3] challenges the fundamental theoretical assumptions of literary history and criticism by demanding a radical rethinking and revisioning of the conceptual grounds of literary study that have been based almost entirely on male literary experiences. Some of the implications of this radical revisioning have already been realized in Afro-American literature. The works of forgotten black women writers are being resurrected and critics are at work revising the slighting, often misinformed critical opinions of their works. We have a fuller understanding of these writers because feminist criticism has begun to eliminate much of the phallocentrism from our readings of their work and to recover the female aesthetics said to distinguish female creativity from male. We can see the results of this inquiry in the numerous monographs and articles that have appeared in the nine years since the publication of Barbara Smith's groundbreaking essay, "Towards a Black Feminist Criticism" and in the fact that some black male critics are now numbered among the ranks of feminist critics.

Much of the present interest in black feminist criticism is rooted in the fact that black women writers are among the most exciting writers on the contemporary American literary scene, but the interest began in the confrontation of black women readers in the early seventies with black female portraiture (or its lack) in fiction by black male writers. Deborah E. McDowell, in "New Directions for Black Feminist Theory,"[4] values these pioneering studies of negative and derogatory female portraiture as an impetus to early black feminist inquiry and acknowledges that a black feminist criticism must do more than "merely focus on how black men have treated black women in literature." McDowell's major concern is with encouraging the development of theories that will help us to properly see and understand the themes, motifs, and idioms used by black women writers, but she raises other important issues as well. She touches upon one of the most disturbing aspects of current black feminist criticism, its separatism—its tendency to see not only a *distinct* black female culture but to see that culture as a separate cultural form having more in common with white female experience than with the facticity of Afro-American life. This proposition is problematic, even as a theoretical conjecture, especially since even its adherents have conceded that, until quite recently, black women's literary experiences were excluded from consideration in the literature of white feminists. For this reason, I prefer Alice Walker's term, *womanist*, as the referent for what I attempt here. Womanist theory is, by definition, "committed to the survival and wholeness of entire people," female *and* male, as well as to a valorization of women's works in all their varieties and multitudes. That commitment places it squarely within the challenge of engagement implicit in *bolekaja* criticism.

McDowell also calls for black feminist critics to turn their attention to the "challenging and necessary task" of a thoroughgoing examination of the works of black male writers, and suggests a line of inquiry that implicitly affirms kinship among Afro-American writers, "the countless thematic, stylistic, and imagistic parallels between black male and black female writing." Her call, however, does not go far enough. By limiting the studies of writings by black males to efforts "to determine the ways in which these commonalities are manifested differently in black women's writings and the ways in which they coincide with writings by black men," she seems to imply that feminist inquiry can only illuminate works by women and works that include female portraiture, that our rereadings of female image will not also change our readings of men. Womanist inquiry, on the other hand, assumes that it can talk both effectively and productively about men. This is a necessary assumption because the negative, stereotyped images of black women are only a part of the problem of phallocentric writings by black males. In order to understand that problem more fully, we must turn to what black men have written about themselves.

Much literature, classic and popular, by white American males valorizes the white patriarchal ideals of physical aggression, heroic conquest, and intellectual domination. A conventional feminist reading of black male literature, recognizing that a difference in actual circumstances forced distinguishing and different characteristics on would-be black patriarchs, would see these ideals only partially "encoded" in writings by black American males. Even so, such ideals would be the desired ones and deviation from them taken as signs of diminished masculine self-esteem. That is, explicit social protest about racial prohibitions that restrict black men from exercising patriarchal authority is part of their "heroic quest" because they don't possess all the privileges of white men. Such a reading, of course, tends to reduce the black struggle for justice and equal opportunity to the right to beat one's wife and daughter. Many black men refused to exercise such "rights" and many black women resisted those who tried.[5] Nor was physical aggression really a value in the literature of black males before 1940. Physical force, even when used by non-heroic black men, was almost always defensive, especially against white people, and, when used against other blacks, generally symbolized the corruption wrought by slavery. The initial *formulation*, however, does serve to illuminate some instances of black male self-portraiture, particularly in nineteenth-century narrative and fiction.

Nineteenth-century black men, confronted with the impossibility of being the (white) patriarch, began to subvert certain of patriarchy's ideals and values to conform to their own images. Thus, the degree to which, and the basis on which, the hero avoids physical aggression was one means of establishing the hero's noble stature and contributed to the hero's intellectual equality with—not dominance over—the collective white man. Frederick Douglass's 1845 autobiography, *Narrative of the Life of Frederick Douglass, An American Slave*,[6] offers several instances of this subversion and redefinition of white patriarchal ideals. I focus on what he will later call "The Fight."[7] Douglass, an "uppity" slave, is hired out to Covey, a "nigger-breaker," to have his spirit curbed. Douglass's "fight" with Covey marks the turning point in his development from slave to free man. In the instant he refuses to be whipped, Douglass ceases "to be a slave in fact." Yet Douglass is not the aggres-

sor. Douglass seizes Covey by the throat when the latter tries
to tie him up and holds him "uneasy"; though Douglass does
draw Covey's blood, he actually touches him only with the
ends of his fingers. Douglass brings the white man to the
ground but never lays violent hands on him; rather, he "seizes
him by the collar." Douglass is thus able to dominate Covey
by his own self-restraint and self-control rather than by *force
major*. Douglass takes a great delight in having bested Covey
while conforming to a semblance of the master–slave relationship. In the later retelling of the episode he returns "a polite,
'Yes, sir,' " to Covey's outraged, "Are you going to continue
to resist?" and concludes, "I was victorious because my aim
had not been to injure him but to prevent his injuring me."

Robert B. Stepto, in *From Behind the Veil*[8] (itself a brilliant
example of the use to which genre studies can be put), details
the brilliant strokes by which "Douglass reinforces his posture
as an articulate hero"—that is, the intellectual equal of the
white men who introduce and thus vouch for the authenticity
of Douglass and his narrative before the white world. In
"supplant[ing the white men] as the definitive historian[s] of
his past," Douglass self-consciously reverses the usual patterns of authentication in black texts; this manifestation of his
intellectual independence is characterized by the same restraint and subtlety as his description of his successful psychological rite of passage.

The pattern of self-restraint, of physical self-control as an
avenue to moral superiority and intellectual equality vis-a-vis
white society, dominates male self-portraiture in the nineteenth century, where achieving heroic stature is most often
the means by which the black male hero also assumes the
mantle of the "patriarch." But the black patriarch in the nineteenth century has more to do with providing for and protecting his "dependents" than with wielding authority or exploiting
their dependency so as to achieve his own privilege. Once
free, Douglass marries, takes a job, becomes a leader in the
struggle for the abolition of slavery; Josiah Henson, the model
for Harriet Beecher Stowe's *Uncle Tom*,[9] escapes from slavery
with his wife beside him and two children on his back, works
on the Underground Railroad, and founds a black township in
Canada. Dr. Miller, the hero of Charles Chesnutt's turn-of-the-
century novel, *The Marrow of Tradition*,[10] is a husband, father,

son, and founder of a hospital and school for blacks. Black male heroic stature was most often achieved within the context of marriage, family, and black community—all of which depend on a relationship with, if not a black woman, at least other black people.

The nature of the black male character's heroic quest and the means by which the hero achieves intellectual parity begin to change in the twentieth century. The heroic quest through the early thirties was a largely introspective one whose goal was the reintegration of the educated hero with the unlettered black masses who symbolized his negro-ness.[11] But the valuation of black community and black family (often an extended family) continues until 1940. Richard Wright's *Native Son* began a period in which the black heroic quest was increasingly externalized. A perceptive, though not necessarily articulate or educated, protagonist seeks recognition from the white power structure and in the process comes to recognize—and realize—himself. By the mid 1960s, white society was typically characterized by physically frail and cowardly, morally weak, sexually impotent, effeminate white men and super-feminine white women who personified the official standard of feminine beauty—delicate, dainty, sexually inhibited until liberated by a hyperpotent black man.[12] The goal of the black hero's quest was to dominate the one and marry the other. Black community, once the object of heroic quest, was, in these works, an impediment to its success; black female portraiture, when present, was often no more than demeaning stereotypes used to justify what even the hero sometimes recognized as a pathological obsession with the white woman. This kind of heroic quest is a dominant feature in some important contemporary texts; however, black male self-portraiture, by the late 1970s, was presented within a broader spectrum of themes—patriarchal responsibility, sibling relations, and male bonding—that were self-questioning rather than self-satisfied or self-righteous.[13] These few texts can be construed as a positive response to the black feminist criticism of the early seventies. Yet they are largely neglected by the Afro-American critical establishment which, by and large, leaves to *The New York Times* the task of canonizing our literature. The present interest in black women's writing arose outside that hegemony, as had the interest in black poetry in the late sixties.

And, like the black aesthetics that arose as a response to black arts poetry, black feminist criticism runs the risk of being narrowly proscriptive rather than broadly analytic.

Michele Wallace, using a combination of fiction and nonfiction prose—the novels of Richard Wright, Ralph Ellison, and James Baldwin, the essays of Baldwin, Norman Mailer, and Eldridge Cleaver—suggests, in *Black Macho and the Myth of the Superwoman*,[14] a black feminist reading of the development of modern black male self-image that is similar to what I have said here. Wallace was roundly damned and told by sister feminists "to read it again," as though we ourselves had not suspected, even suggested, these things before. And no one has quite dared since then to hold up the record black men have written of themselves. Rather, since black men gave little evidence of talking to us, we talked to each other.

Having confronted what black men have said about us, it is now time for black feminist critics to confront black male writers with what they have said about themselves. What is needed is a thoroughgoing examination of male images in the works of black male writers. This is a necessary step in ending the separatist tendency in Afro-American criticism and in achieving in Afro-American literature feminist's theory's avowed aim of "challenging the fundamental theoretical assumptions of traditional literary history and criticism." Black women as readers and writers have been kept out of literary endeavor, so we had, and have, a lot to say. But to focus solely on ourselves is to fall into the same hole The Brother has dug for himself—narcissism, isolation, inarticulation, obscurity. Of course we must keep talking to and about ourselves, but literature, as Chinweizu and Walker remind us, is about community and dialogue; theories or ways of reading ought actively to promote the enlargement of both.

NOTES

1. Alice Walker, *In Search of Our Mothers' Gardens* (San Diego: Harcourt Brace/Jovanovich, 1984), xi.
2. Onwuchekwa Jemie, Chinweizu, Ihechukwu Madbuike, *Toward the Decolonization of African Literature* (Washington: Howard University Press, 1983), xii.
3. Elaine Showalter, ed. *The New Feminist Criticism: Essays on Women, Literature and Theory* (New York: Pantheon Books, 1985), 8.
4. Deborah McDowell, "New Directions for Black Feminist Criticism," *op. cit.*, 196.

5. Further research in both traditional and contemporary Afro-American orature just might document that the community valued going "upside" anyone's head as a *last*, rather than the first, resort at least as much as they admired the ability or will to do so.

6. Frederick Douglass, *Narrative of the Life of an American Slave Written by Himself*, ed. Benjamin Quarles (1845; reprint, Cambridge, Mass.: Harvard University Press, 1960), 103–104.

7. Federick Douglass, *My Bondage and My Freedom* 1855; (reprint, New York: Arno Press, 1969), 243.

8. Robert B. Stepto, *From Behind the Veil* (Urbana, Ill.: 1979), 16–26.

9. Josiah Henson, *Father Henson's Own Story* (reprint, Upper Saddle River, N.J.: 1849; Literature House rep, 1970).

10. Charles Chesnutt, *The Marrow of Tradition* (1901; reprint, Ann Arbor, Mich. University of Michigan Press, 1969).

11. The key texts include James Weldon Johnson's *The Autobiography of an Ex-Colored Man* (1912), Jean Toomer's *Cane* (1923), and Langston Hughes's *Not Without Laughter* (1930).

12. The terminology is drawn from Eldridge Cleaver's *Soul on Ice* (New York: McGraw-Hill, Inc., 1968), but the portrayal can be found in the works of black male writers from Richard Wright and Ralph Ellison to Ishmael Reed.

13. Ernest J. Gaines's *In My Father's House* (New York: W.W. Norton Co., 1978) and Wesley Brown's *Tragic Magic* (New York: Random House, 1978) come most readily to mind; however, the works of William Melvin Kelley, John McCluskey, and John A. Williams present a range of black male characters that still awaits close discussion.

14. Michelle Wallace, *Black Macho and the Myth of the Superwoman* (New York: The Dial Press, 1978).

The Quicksands of Representation:

Rethinking Black Cultural Politics

Hazel V. Carby

The term "renaissance" in Afro-American cultural history has been almost exclusively applied to the literary and artistic production of intellectuals in Harlem in the years between the end of the World War I and the Depression.[1] But definitions of the Harlem Renaissance are notoriously elusive; descriptions of it as a moment of intense literary and artistic production, or as an intellectual awakening, or as the period of the self-proclaimed "New Negro" are concepts that are not applicable only to Harlem or to the twenties.[2] This particular cultural moment has come to dominate Afro-American cultural history and overshadow earlier attempts of black intellectuals to assert their collective presence. However, the more assertive we try to be as cultural critics and cultural historians about what the Harlem Renaissance was, what it was not, and when it occurred, the less sure we become about what made this moment of Afro-American cultural history unique. The staff of the *Colored American Magazine* considered their journal as a tool in the creation of a black renaissance, an inspiration for "Theologians, Artists [and] Scientists whose theories had grown dormant for lack of a channel of communication,"[3] but no comparative cultural study has been undertaken to reveal the relation between the intellectual activity of the city of Boston at the turn of the century and Harlem in the twenties. Indeed, the Harlem Renaissance is frequently conceived as a unique, intellectually cohesive and homogeneous historical moment, a mythology which has disguised the contradictory

This essay has previously appeared in *Reconstructing Womenhood: The Emergence of the African American Woman Novelist* (New York: Oxford University Press, 1987)

impulses of the Harlem intellectuals. I do not intend to argue
the case that the Harlem Renaissance is purely an invention of
the literary and cultural historian, although to a large extent
this is the case. Rather I want to indicate the shift in concerns
of the intellectuals of the twenties as opposed to those of the
previous two decades by stressing the discontinuities and
contradictions surrounding issues of representation.

I use the word representation in two distinct but related
ways: as it is formally understood in relation to art and creative practices, and as it applies to intellectuals who understand themselves to be responsible for the representation of
"the race," defining and constructing in their art its representative members and situating themselves as representative
members of an oppressed social group. The relation of the
black intellectual elite to the majority of black people changed
drastically as a result of the migration north of southern blacks.
Before World War I, the overwhelming majority of blacks
lived in the South, at a vast physical and metaphorical distance from the intellectuals who represented the interests of
the race. After the war, black intellectuals had to confront the
black masses on the streets of their cities and they responded
in a variety of ways.

At the turn of the century in Boston, Pauline Hopkins and
the staff of the *Colored American Magazine* assumed that their
relation to the majority of black people was entirely unproblematic
and unmediated. The *Colored American Magazine* unashamedly asserted that it could speak for and represent the unique historical experience of "the black people" and addressed them in
these all-encompassing terms. These intellectuals did not doubt
or question their position of leadership as members of the
"Talented Tenth" speaking from the North to the majority of
blacks who lived outside of it. But after World War I, the
large-scale movement of black people into the cities of the
North meant that intellectual leadership and its constituencies
fragmented. No longer was it possible to mobilize an undiffer-
entiated address to "the black people" once an urban black
working class was established.

This movement of masses of rural black southern workers
destined to become an urban proletariat was not immediately
represented in fiction, but there was a distinct shift in who
were represented as "the people." One possibility, in fiction,

was that "the people" were represented as a metaphorical "folk," which in its rural connotations avoided and ignored the implication of the presence of black city workers. Zora Neale Hurston, for example, who felt concerned that whites just did not know who blacks were, chose to reconstruct figures of "the folk" in her novels. Most literary criticism acknowledges this representation of the folk as "the people" but does not question the historical significance of Hurston's choice. On the contrary, the representation of "the folk" is usually regarded as an ahistorical literary convention that is a natural expression of the Afro-American experience.[4] But we need to recognize that the "folk" was neither an inevitable nor a natural selection. Many intellectuals, including Jessie Fauset, registered the gap between the immediate and disconcerting presence of the black masses and membership in the black elite by representing this difference in class terms.

The concept of the "New Negro" of the Harlem Renaissance has become a conventional way of referring to these literary and artistic intellectuals, but this limited contemporary application has emptied the term of its radical working-class meaning, established by the group of intellectuals, leaders, organizations, and journals that were devoted to "economic radicalism." For radical intellectuals like Asa Philip Randolph and Chandler Owen, editors of the *Messenger*, the "New" Negro was "the product of the same worldwide forces that have brought into being the great liberal and radical movements that are now seizing the reins of political, economic, and social power in all the civilized countries of the world."[5] The editorial continued to assert that the " 'New' Negro 'unlike the old Negro' was not to be 'lulled into a false sense of security with political spoils and patronage.' "[6]

This issue of patronage provides another point of contrast between the literary intellectuals of the twenties and their predecessors in Boston. The young black artists in the Harlem of the twenties were acutely aware of a high degree of reliance on the patronage of white individuals and organizations.[7] But the staff of the *Colored American Magazine*, like the economic radicals of the twenties, made specific attempts to avoid such a situation of dependency. As they stated after the first year in print, "There has been no attempt to seek the aid of philanthropists, although we feel that there have been many less deserving projects which have been lavishly supported in that way."[8] The issue of the acceptability of patronage and its role in defining and limiting what could be represented was of intense concern to the intellectuals of both cultural moments. But what differentiated most clearly the crisis of representation of the twenties from the intellectual assurance of the turn of the century was the relation of the intellectual to "the people."

In 1900, Pauline Hopkins and the staff of the *Colored American Magazine* assumed a hegemonic position as representatives of black people, calling themselves "the mouth-piece and inspiration of the Negro race throughout not only this country, but the world."[9] After World War I and the migration, the role of intellectuals became problematic in two ways: There was no longer a unitary "people" who could be represented and the variety of intellectual practice—literary, political, and cultural— became increasingly separated. The Colored Co-operative Publishing Company was a collective attempt to hold together the practices of literature, art, and political agitation for social change. But by the twenties, black writers sought artistic autonomy for their cultural practices and products and separated themselves from the task of writing for the uplift of the race as a whole. The urban black worker in the twenties could look toward a range of other representatives that included black union organizations, economic radicals, or Marcus Garvey and the Universal Negro Improvement Association.

It is within this increasingly fragmented discourse of "the people" and intellectual leadership that I want to situate an analysis of Nella Larsen's *Quicksand*, published in 1928.[10] Traditional Afro-American literary and cultural criticism has failed to adequately consider the significance of the work of Larsen and Fauset.[11] Both writers have at times been dismissed as minor figures, mere background to a major event, the Harlem Renaissance. In contrast, Zora Neale Hurston has been seen as a distinct literary figure.[12] Hurston, as I have indicated, epitomized the intellectual who represented "the people" through a reconstruction of "the folk," avoiding the class confrontation of the northern cities. Fauset and Larsen, however, wrote more directly out of this urban confrontation, though each developed strategies of fictional representation that indicated their very different responses to their class, racial, and sexual position as black female intellectuals.

Fauset responded to an emerging black, urban working class by a mediation of her authorial position as a class perspective. She represented in her fiction a middle-class code of morality and behavior that structured the existence of her characters and worked as a code of appropriate social behavior for her readers.[13] Fauset's intellectual contribution was the development of an ideology that would establish the emerging black middle class as acceptably urbane and civilized and distinguish it from the rural influx.[14] Unlike earlier women novelists, Fauset did not consider the aftermath of slavery and the failure of Reconstruction a sufficient source of echoes and foreshadowings for her representation of the emergent black middle class, who needed a new relation to history. Fauset represented this new history through a generational difference, a difference figured as a recognition of the need for the protagonists to revise the irrelevant history of their parents, a history tied to the consequences of slavery.

Deborah McDowell, in her introduction to the new edition of Fauset's *Plum Bun*, pleads for a sympathetic consideration of the progressive aspects of Fauset's novels, especially in relation to her implicit critique of the structures of women's romance.[15] However, I would argue that ultimately the conservatism of Fauset's ideology dominates her texts. In *The Chinaberry Tree*, for example, which focused on two women, the movement of the text is away from the figures of isolated unmarried mothers and daughters supporting themselves through their own labor, toward the articulation of a new morality and community in which black women were lifted from the abyss of scandal and gossip that threatened to overwhelm them by professional black men, who reinserted the women into a newly formed and respectable community as dependent wives. The individual and collective pasts of the female characters led them to flounder in the waters of misdirected desires; their history was anarchic and self-destructive. The future, within which the women could survive, was secured when they were grounded, protected, and wrapped around by decent men. In order to represent a new, emergent social group, Fauset by necessity had to sever ties with the past; the characteristics of the new class were those of individual success and triumph over ties to and previous interpretations of history. To signal the depth of this new fictional strategy, consider Pauline Hopkins's use of history to raise questions of inheritance and heritage that were crucial to her political perception. Who Hopkins's characters were and what they were to become was to be understood in relation to their ancestors. The quality of these ancestors and the nature of their past actions had specific ramifications for the present: The consequences of history were Hopkins's fictional future. In stark contrast, in *The Chinaberry Tree*, Fauset constructed a chaotic and irrelevant history to which the heroes, not the heroines, brought a new order and meaning. The new middle class both emerged from and changed previous history and its interpretations; the forces of previous history alone could not provide a basis for its future. Fauset adapted but did not transcend the form of the romance. It is important that her work did reveal many of the contradictory aspects of romantic conventions of womanhood, but her imaginary resolutions to what were social contradictions confirmed that women ultimately had to be saved from the consequences of their independence and become wives.

In stark contrast, Nella Larsen in *Quicksand* refused the resolutions offered by this developing code of black middle-class morality at the same time she launched a severe critique against the earlier but still influential ideology of racial uplift. The *Quicksand* of 1928 did not just explore the contradictory terrain of women and romance but its sexual politics tore apart the very fabric of the romance form.

At the beginning of the novel, Helga Crane, the protagonist, was a teacher at Naxos, a black school in the South, which appeared to be a combination of Atlanta, Fisk, and Tuskegee. Dissatisfied with what she saw as a process of repression, the stunting of intellectual growth and creativity, Helga resigned her job in a stormy interview with the new president, Dr. Anderson. She returned to Chicago, where she had grown up, but was unable to find a job and eventually traveled to Harlem as secretary to a famous "spokeswoman for the race." In Harlem she lived with a woman called Anne Grey, worked in a black insurance company, and was an observer of the Renaissance. Helga was disdainful of the ideology of racial uplift, critical of Anne's continual preoccupation with the problems of the race, and disparaging of the hypocrisy of the emerging black middle class. This class, she felt, condemned white racism while imitating white middle-class behavior and adopting their values and moral codes. Feeling that she was again being stifled, Helga determined to leave Harlem, using a legacy from a white uncle to visit her Danish aunt in Copenhagen. For two years, Helga lived in Europe, where the appreciation she had so desired was lavished upon her. However, though pampered, Helga realized that she was being treated like an exotic object, admired only as a representative of the primitive and sensual. Experiencing a desperate need to be again among black people, she sailed to Harlem for the wedding of Anne and Dr. Anderson, intending only a temporary visit but staying long after the wedding. Helga recognized a long-repressed sexual attraction for Anderson and in response to his encouragement determined to finally acknowledge her sexuality and sleep with him. Anderson's awkward rebuff shattered Helga's new acceptance of her sexual self and when she accidently met a hedonistic southern preacher in a storefront church she slept with him. She returned to the South as the wife of the Rev. Mr. Pleasant Green, blind to everything but the sensual aspect of their relationship. Helga planned to uplift the women and instruct the children of this community of southern folk but instead constant childbirth degraded and oppressed her. She nearly died giving birth to her fourth child and the novel ends with her fifth pregnancy, for her a certain death.

In *Quicksand* Larsen embodied the major aspects of what I have referred to as the crisis of representation of the period. She was unable to romanticize "the people" as the folk or to accept the world view of the new black middle class. Helga Crane explored the contradictions of her racial, sexual, and class position by being both inside and outside these perspectives. Larsen was able to represent such duality by making her protagonist an alienated heroine who was, at various points in the text, alienated from her sex, her race, and her class. Alienation is often represented as a state of consciousness, as a frame of mind. Implied in this definition is the assumption that alienation can be eliminated or replaced by another state of consciousness; a purely individual transformation unrelated to necessary social or historical change. Helga Crane did question the possibility that her recurrent dissatisfaction with her life could be due to her state of mind, wondering if a change in her attitudes could make her happy. But against this view Larsen placed an alternate reading of Helga's progress—that her alienation, produced by existing forms of social relations, could be eliminated only by a change in those social relations. That Larsen incorporated this alternate definition of alienation in her text has political significance, for the representation of alienation as only a state of mind reduces history to an act of thought and leads to a political conservatism. For if people can change not their conditions but the way they feel about them, they can only legitimize and approve the status quo, and social criticism becomes irrelevant.

Quicksand, however, represented the full complexity of the modern alienated individual and is the first text by a black woman to be a conscious narrative of a woman embedded within capitalist social relations. In the opening pages, Helga Crane was represented as an isolated figure but a consumer, a character initially defined through the objects that surrounded her. Though Larsen made Helga a teacher and described a school, she utilized the language of the factory and the ideology of Taylorism in her creation of Naxos. Alienated from her work, Helga experienced no emotional or intellectual sustenance from her teaching. Like a small insignificant part in a big machine, Helga made no difference and felt that an essential part of her and the students' humanity was denied in favor of the production of uniformity. Naxos

> had grown into a machine. It was now a show place in the black belt, exemplification of the white man's magnanimity, refutation of the black man's inefficiency. Life had died out of it. It was . . . only a big knife . . . cutting all to a pattern, the white man's pattern. Teachers as well as students were subjected to the paring process, for it tolerated no innovations, no individualisms (9).

Students were described as products, as automatons who goose-stepped in massed phalanxes (28). Consciously created as subject to an industrial time and discipline, the dullness of the outward appearance of everyone at Naxos was represented as symbolic of the acceptance of their oppressed social condition. Within this order, Helga was an expression of powerlessness, the alienated individual who could not change her social condition and felt only a sense of individual failure.

The critique of Naxos as a black college was a critique of the policy of racial uplift and of black intellectual leadership. As a product of Fisk herself, Larsen was directing a bitter attack toward black educators as race representatives. She detached her protagonist from their narrow-minded adherence to the dictates of white southern expectations of Negro passivity and separated her from their class perspective. For Helga had neither a community nor a network of black kinship. She had no black family and thus lacked the connections that Larsen condemned for being so important to the black middle-class society that Larsen represented to be as exclusive as its white counterpart. This critique of the black middle class was continued in the section of the novel set in Harlem. In direct contrast to Jessie Fauset, Larsen did not feel that the middle class were the guardians of civilized behavior and moral values. She criticized Harlem intellectuals for two major acts of hypocrisy—their announced hatred for white people and deprecation of any contact with white society while imitating their clothes, manners, and ways of life; and their proclamation of the undiluted good of all things Negro that disguised a disdain, contempt, and amusement for the actual culture and behavior of the majority of black people. Larsen used Helga, a black intellectual and a member of the middle class who stood outside of both groups, as a figure who could question the limits of middle-class intellectual pretension.

Larsen augmented this questioning of the representative nature of a black elite and accentuated Helga's social displacement by her particular use of the figure of the mulatto. The mulatto is most usefully regarded as a convention of Afro-American literature that enabled the exploration in fiction of relations that were socially proscribed. The mulatto figure is a narrative device of mediation, allowing a fictional exploration of the relation between the races while offering an imaginary expression of the relation between them. One mode of representing this social tension is the passing novel, where the protagonist pretends to be white, as in Fauset's *Plum Bun* and Larsen's second novel, *Passing*.[16] But in *Quicksand* this option was refused. Larsen's particular use of the mulatto figure allowed her protagonist to be both inside and outside contemporary race issues. Helga was at once critical of what she regarded as an all-pervasive concern with race problems while at the same time was subject to racism. The section of the novel set in Copenhagen confronted directly the question of the representation of blacks by whites. Helga's portrait was painted by a leading Danish artist, who created an animalistic, sensuous creature on his canvas. Larsen displaced to Europe an issue of central concern to the intellectuals of the Harlem Renaissance—white fascination with the "exotic" and the "primitive." Outside of the black community, Helga became a mere object for white consumption.

Social relations that objectified the body permeate the text. Helga herself was represented as a consumer, a woman who defined a self through the acquisition of commercial products, consumer goods, and commodities. As a woman she was at the center of a complex process of exchange. Money was crucial to Larsen's narrative, structuring power relations, controlling social movement, and defining the boundaries of Helga's environment. Money replaced kinship as the prime mediator of social relations: Helga's white uncle sent her money as he could not afford to acknowledge her relation to him. This money allowed her social movement; she bought her way out of a Jim Crow car and eventually out of Harlem. In Chicago, Helga spent money, buying and consuming rather than facing her desperate conditions. While the possession of money disguised her real social predicament, the lack of money forced degradation and the recognition that in the job market her social position as black woman was narrowly defined as domestic worker.

While money grants Helga the power of movement within the text, the locations between which she moves displace the tensions of migration through a structure of oppositions between country and city. Helga's first movement in the text was from South to North, from the rural outskirts of Atlanta to industrial Chicago. Immediately upon arrival in Chicago, Helga became one of a crowd. Her initial identification was with the anonymity of the city, which offered her the appearance of freedom but no actual home or friends. This anonymity brought brief satisfaction and content and allowed her to maintain her position as consumer, but she discovered her vulnerability as an object of exchange when her money ran out. Larsen represented the city as a conglomeration of strangers in which social relations were structured through the consumption of both objects and people. The imagery of commerce and this process of exchange dominates the text as it moves to New York and Copenhagen. This polarity between the rural and urban experience frames the text when, in the closing pages, all cities are finally abandoned and Helga was metaphorically and, the reader is led to assume, literally, buried in the rural South.

Helga was a consumer but as a woman she was also potentially a consumable object. Larsen's representation of sexual politics delineated the dilemma of the woman's body as a commercialized object. Helga's sexuality was not only objectified in relation to art, but when she failed to get a job as a maid in Chicago, she had offers of money for sexual services. Helga, as an unmarried woman, was brought to a recognition of her exchange value, which denied her humanity while cementing her fragile dependence on money. Larsen represented the ideologies of consumerism, capitalism, and sexuality as being intimately connected. In the process of this critique Larsen not only revealed the inability of the structure of the romance to adequately express the experience of women but also posed a challenge to the readers' expectations of the form of the novel.

Larsen stressed the contradictory nature of the search for a female self by refusing the romance and structuring the relation of the individual to the social formation through the interconnection of sexual, racial, and class identity. The conclusion of the text offered no imaginary resolutions to the contradictions Larsen raised. As readers, we are left meditating the problematic nature of alternative possibilities of a social self. Consider the metaphor of quicksand: In it, individual struggle and isolated effort are doomed to failure. Helga's search led to the burial, not the discovery, of the self. The only way out of quicksand is by external help; isolated individual struggle ensured only that Helga would sink deeper into the quagmire. The question that remains is to what social group does Helga attach herself in order to be saved? Unlike Jessie Fauset, whom I have described as an ideologue for an emergent middle class, Larsen found it impossible to represent the experience of the black middle class as representative of the race. The black bourgeoisie was attacked on many levels—for its hypocrisy, its articulation of the race "problem," and its moral and aesthetic code.

But Larsen did not consider the crisis of representation facing Harlem intellectuals only in terms of class. Her particular use of the figure of the mulatto allowed Larsen to negotiate issues of race as they were articulated by both white and black. However, Larsen's representation of both race and class is structured through a prism of black female sexuality. Larsen recognized that the repression of the sensual in Afro-American fiction, in response to the long history of the exploitation of black sexuality, led to the repression of passion and to the repression or denial of female sexuality and desire. Of course the representation of black female sexuality meant risking that it be defined as primitive and exotic within a racist society. Larsen attempted to embody, but could not hope to resolve, these contradictions in her representation of Helga as sexual being, making Helga the first truly sexual black female protagonist in Afro-American fiction. Racist sexual ideologies proclaimed the black woman to be a rampant sexual being; in response, black women writers either focused on defending their morality or on displacing sexuality onto another terrain. Larsen confronted this denial directly in her fiction. Helga consistently attempted to deny her sensuality and repress her sexual desires and the result was tragedy. Each of the crises of the text center upon sexual desire until the conclusion of the novel, where Helga's control over her body was denied and her sexuality was reduced to its biological capacity to bear children. Helga's four children represented her entrapment as she was unable to desert them; her fifth child represented her certain death.

Larsen offered her readers few avenues of resolution. Liberation through money, allowing Helga to explore Europe, the "Old World," white "civilization," as an alternative to the United States, was rejected as a viable alternative. The figure of the mulatto allowed Larsen's protagonist to ask why her future should be yoked to a despised social group, but living in a white world was no alternative. Readers are left with the unresolvable. Harlem was simultaneously represented as a black city that appeared to allow for the unfettered possibili-

ties of black cultural expression, and as a cage or ghetto. The
novel closes with a representation of "the folk," but not as a
positive alternative to the black urban elite. The rural community was bound together through its allegiance to the black
preacher, Helga's husband, who appeared as an Old Testament patriarch. Unlike Hurston's folk, who were represented
as embodying in their culture and language the unique "truth"
of the Afro-American experience, Larsen represented the folk
as deluded. Their religion, the core of their existence, was the
great illusion that robbed them of the crudest truths. In a
passage of bitter denunciation, Helga concluded that religion

> ailed the whole Negro race in America, this fatuous belief
> in the white man's God, this childlike trust in full com-
> pensation for all woes and privations in "kingdom come"
> . . . [It] Bound them to slavery, then to poverty and
> insult, and made them bear it unresistingly, uncomplain-
> ingly almost, by sweet promises of mansions in the sky
> by and by (297).

In the country, among the folk, Helga felt only suffocation
and a great loathing. It was the moment of her greatest oppression and degradation. Chained to her children, the quicksand engulfed her while she dreamt of "freedom and cities."

It is important that Larsen returned her readership to the
urban landscape and refused a romantic evocation of the folk,
for in this movement she stands as precurser not only to
Richard Wright and Ralph Ellison but to a neglected strand of
Afro-American women's fiction. In the search for a tradition
of black women writers of fiction, a pattern has been established from Alice Walker back through Zora Neale Hurston,
which represents the rural folk as bearers of Afro-American
history and preservers of Afro-American culture. This construction of a tradition of black women writing has effectively
marginalized the fictional urban confrontation of race, class,
and sexuality that was to follow *Quicksand*: Ann Petry's *The
Street* (1946); Dorothy West's *The Living Is Easy* (1948); Gwendolyn Brooks's *Maud Martha* (1953); and the works of Toni
Morrison.[17] Afro-American cultural and literary history should
not create and glorify a limited vision that, in its romantic
evocation of the rural and the folk, avoids some of the most

crucial and urgent issues of cultural struggle—a struggle that Larsen, Petry, West, Brooks, and Morrison recognized would have to be faced in the cities, the home of the black working class.

NOTES

1. The three major contemporary texts are Jervis Anderson, *This Was Harlem: A Cultural Portrait, 1900–1950* (New York: Farrar Straus Giroux, 1982); Nathan Irvin Huggins, *Harlem Renaissance* (New York: Oxford University Press, 1971); David Levering Lewis, *When Harlem Was in Vogue* (New York: Vintage, 1982). The term has recently been used to describe contemporary black cultural production, particularly of black women novelists who are linked to this first Renaissance by the figure of Zora Neale Hurston: "A second black literary Renaissance, in which women are taking a significant part, seems well under way." Mary V. Dearborn, *Pocahontas's Daughters: Gender and Ethnicity in American Culture* (New York: Oxford University Press, 1986), 61.
2. Alain Locke, ed., *The New Negro* (New York: Albert & Charles Boni, Inc., 1925; New York: Atheneum, 1970).
3. "Announcement," *Colored American Magazine* 1 (May 1900): 2.
4. For the best account of the relation between the various intellectual attitudes toward black culture during this period, see John Brown Childs, "Afro-American Intellectuals and the People's Culture," *Theory and Society* 13 (1984): 69–90, an informative and stimulating analysis of the vanguardism inherent in concepts of intellectuals as the "Talented Tenth," in Alain Locke's and Charles Johnson's approach to folk culture, and in Chandler Owen's and A. Philip Randolph's socialist "New" Negro. See Notes 2 and 5.
5. The *Messenger* (August 1920), 73, quoted in Sterling D. Spero and Abram L. Harris, *The Black Worker* (New York: Antheneum, 1969), 389. See also Jervis Anderson, *A. Philip Randolph: A Biographical Portrait* (New York: Harcourt Brace Jovanovich, 1972), 98; William H. Harris, *Keeping the Faith: A. Philip Randolph, Milton P. Webster, and the Brotherhood of Sleeping Car Porters, 1925–37* (Urbana: University of Illinois Press, 1977), 21, 98; an Theodore G. Vincent, ed., *Voices of a Black Nation: Political Journalism in the Harlem Renaissance* (San Francisco: Ramparts Press, 1973).
6. The *Messenger* (August 1920), 73, quoted in Spero and Harris, *The Black Worker*, 389–390.
7. See, for examples of the conflicts over patronage, the second edition of Zora Neale Hurston's *Dust Tracks on a Road: An Autobiography*, ed. Robert E. Hemenway (Urbana: University of Illinois Press, 1984); Claude McKay, *A Long Way From Home: An Autobiography* (1937; New York: Harcourt, Brace & World, 1970); and Langston Hughes, *The Big Sea: An Autobiography* (1940; New York: Hill and Wang, 1963). His second autobiography, *I Wonder As I Wander: An Autobiographical Journey* (1956; New York: Hill and Wang, 1964), opens with the acknowledgement of the loss of his patron.
8. R. S. Elliot, "The Story of Our Magazine," *Colored American Magazine* 3 (May 1901): 44. The journal did eventually have a black patron, Colonel William H. Dupress, to whom it was sold for debt. See Walter C. Daniel, ed., *Black Journals of the United States* (Westport, Ct.: Greenwood Press, 1982), 125.
9. Elliot, "The Story," 44.
10. Nella Larsen, *Quicksand* (New York: Alfred A. Knopf, 1928; Westport, Ct.: Negro Universities Press, 1969). Page references to this edition will be given parenthetically in the text.
11. Compare the responses of Robert Bone, *The Negro Novel in America* (New Haven: Yale University Press, 1958); Arthur P. Davis, *From the Dark Tower: Afro-American Writers 1900–1960* (1974; Washington, D.C.: Howard University Press, 1981); Addison Gayle, Jr., *The Way of the New World: The Black Novel in America* (Garden City, N.Y.:

Anchor Press, 1976); with the black feminist critique of Barbara Christian, *Black Women Novelists: The Development of a Tradition, 1892–1976* (Westport, Ct.: Greenwood Press, 1980) and the recent reconsideration of their position as ethnic writers in Dearborn, *Pocahontas's Daughters.*

12. And as the "founder of the tradition of contemporary black women writers." She is considered by all the critics cited in note 11, but the two people most responsible for the critical acclaim accorded Hurston's work were Robert Hemenway, *Zora Neale Hurston: A Literary Biography* (Urbana: University of Illinois Press, 1977) and Alice Walker, who wrote the foreword to Hemenway's text and edited *I Love Myself When I am Laughing . . .: A Zora Neale Hurston Reader* (Old Westbury, N.Y.: The Feminist Press, 1979). Zora Neale Hurston, *Jonah's Gourd Vine* (Philadelphia: J.B. Lippincott, 1934); *Mules and Men* (Philadelphia: J. B. Lippincott, 1935); *Their Eyes Were Watching God* (Philadelphia: J.B. Lippincott, 1937); *Tell My Horse* (Philadelphia: J.B. Lippincott, 1938); *Moses, Man of the Mountain* (Philadelphia: J.B. Lippincott, 1939); *Dust Tracks on a Road: An Autobiography* (Philadelphia: J.B. Lippincott, 1942); *Polk County, a Comedy of Negro Life on a Sawmill Camp* (unpublished, 1944); *Seraph on the Suwanee* (New York: Charles Scribner's Sons, 1948).

13. Jessie Redmond Fauset, *There is Confusion* (New York: Boni & Liveright, 1924); *Plum Bun* (New York: Frederick A. Stokes, 1928); *The Chinaberry Tree* (New York: Frederick A. Stokes, 1931); *Comedy, American Style* (New York: Frederick A. Stokes, 1933).

14. Fauset's middle-class code, however, was not merely imitative of white middle-class behavior of which she could be extremely critical. Rather, she tried to describe a particularly black middle-class ideology that was more moral and more civilized than the white racist society in which it existed.

15. Deborah E. McDowell, "Introduction: A Question of Power or the Rear Guard Faces Front," in Fauset, *Plum Bun* (1929; London: Routledge Kegan Paul, 1985), ix–xxiv.

16. Larsen, *Passing* (New York: Alfred A. Knopf, 1929).

17. Ann Petry, *The Street* (Boston: Houghton Mifflin, 1946); Dorothy West, *The Living is Easy* (1948; Old Westbury, N.Y.: Feminist Press, 1982); Gwendolyn Brooks, *Maud Martha* (1951; New York: Harper & Brothers, 1953); Toni Morrison, *The Bluest Eye* (New York: Simon and Schuster, 1972); *Sula* (New York: Alfred A. Knopf, 1973); *Song of Solomon* (New York: New American Library, 1977).

"The Changing Same:"[1]

Generational Connections and Black Women Novelists*

Deborah E. McDowell

As Iola finished, there was a ring of triumph in her voice, as if she were reviewing a path she had trodden with bleeding feet, and seen it change to lines of living light. Her soul seemed to be flashing through the rare loveliness of her face and etherealizing its beauty.

Everyone was spell-bound. Dr. Latimer was entranced, and, turning to Hon. Dugdale, said, in a low voice and with deep-drawn breath, "She is angelic! . . . She is strangely beautiful! . . . The tones of her voice are like benedictions of peace; her words a call to higher service and nobler life."[2]

As soon as dinner over, Shug push back her chair and light a cigarette. Now is come the time to tell yall, she say.

Tell us what? Harpo ast.

Us leaving, she say.

Yeah? say Harpo, looking round for the coffee. And then looking over at Grady.

Us leaving, Shug say again. Mr.———— look struck, like he always look when Shug say she going anywhere. He

*This is a revision of a colloquium at the Mary Ingraham Bunting Institute, Radcliffe College, March 1984. I am deeply grateful to the following people for their thoughtful comments and suggestions: Elizabeth Ammons, Bettina Friedl, Nathan Huggins, Susan Kirschner, Susan Lanser, Nan Bauer Maglin, Nellie McKay, and Marilyn Richardson. It is reprinted here from *New Literary History* 18 (Winter 1987), 281–302.

reach down and rub his stomach, look off side her head like nothing been said. . . .

Celie is coming with us, say Shug. . . .

Over my dead body, Mr.——— say.

You satisfied that what you want, Shug say, cool as clabber.

Mr.——— start up from his seat, look at Shug, plop back down again. He look over at me. I thought you was finally happy, he say. What wrong now?

You a lowdown dog is what's wrong, I say. It's time to leave you and enter in the Creation. And your dead body just the welcome mat I need.[3]

The character being *spoken about* in the first passage is Iola Leroy, the heroine of Frances E. W. Harper's 1892 novel of the same name. A group of men are giving their approval of an impromptu speech that Iola has just delivered on the ennobling effects of suffering and the necessity for Christian service. They lay stress, simultaneously, on her physical beauty and saintliness.

In the second passage, from Alice Walker's 1982 novel *The Color Purple*, Celie, the novel's central character, *is speaking*, along with her spirit guide and lover, the itinerant blues singer Shug Avery. Celie's, unlike Iola's, is an audience of hostile, disapproving men; nevertheless, with force and resoluteness, Celie announces her plans to move on in search of personal fulfillment and spiritual growth.

I cite these two passages as examples of two strikingly different images of black female character in black women's fiction—one "exceptional" and outer-directed, the other "ordinary" and inner-directed; two different approaches to characterization, one external, the other internal; and finally, two different narrative voices, one strained, stilted, genteel and inhibited, the other, spontaneous, immediate, fresh, and authoritative.[4]

Although the passages are different, the novels from which they are excerpted share important basic patterns. Both novels recount the problems of familial separation and reunion, of lost and found identities. More significantly, however, these novels represent the two most salient paradigms in the black female literary tradition in the novel. Although manipulated differently, depending on the author, these paradigms derive from a common center in black women's novels. Both revisionist in impulse, they are revealed, most graphically, in the depiction of black female characters. Borrowing from Susan Lanser's *The Narrative Act*, I call these paradigms, simply, public and private narrative fiction. I see them posed respectively and most dramatically in Frances E. W. Harper's *Iola Leroy* and Alice Walker's *The Color Purple*.[5]

Of necessity, I use these terms not literally but metaphorically, for as Lanser notes correctly, "obviously all fictional narration is 'public' in the sense that it was written to be published and read by an audience. What I am distinguishing here are fictional narrative acts designed for an apparently public readership [or one 'outside' the text] and those narratives designed for reception only by other characters and textual figures."[6]

In the following discussion, I would like to adapt and modify Lanser's distinction between public and private point of view to posit a provisional distinction between public and private narrative fiction.[7] I wish to distinguish here between those novels by black women that seem to imply a public readership, or one outside the black cultural community, and those that imply a private readership, or one within that cultural matrix.[8]

Given the complexity and ambiguity inherent in questions of audience, one can only speculate about the audience for whom a specific text seems intended. To be certain, authors cannot determine conclusively who their actual readers are. Nevertheless, all writers begin by fictionalizing or imagining an audience. As Peter Rabinowitz and other audience-oriented critics have argued, authors "cannot make artistic decisions without prior assumptions (conscious or unconscious) [stated or implied] about their audience's beliefs, knowledge, and familiarity with conventions," literary and/or social.[9] Each text, then, selects, encodes, and images its targeted audience—what Wolfgang Iser calls its "implied reader"—through the style, language, and strategies it employs. (That does not preclude, of course, its being read by those outside the targeted reading group.)

I have chosen character as a springboard for examining these paradigms even though the current wave of literary/theoretical sophistication calls into question "naive commonsense categories of 'character,' 'protagonist,' or 'hero' "[10] and rejects the "prevalent conception of character in the novel" which assumes that "the most successful and 'living' characters are richly delineated autonomous wholes."[11] For, despite such positions, imaging the black woman as a "whole" character or "self" has been a consistent preoccupation of black female novelists throughout their literary history.[12] That they frequently use the *Bildungsroman*—a genre that focuses primarily on the gradual growth and development of a "self" from childhood to adulthood—attests strongly to this preoccupation. It seems appropriate, therefore, to allow the critical concerns of black women's novels to emerge organically from those texts, rather than to allow current critical fashion to dictate what those concerns should be.

In considering character in black women's fiction as a reflection of the central paradigms in their tradition, other critical questions arise. Although the scope of this essay does not permit me to explore them in full and equal detail, the following interlocking questions are implied in my consideration of characterization. In that one of the most challenging aspects of characterization for any writer is the authentic representation of speech, what is the relationship between race/gender and literary voice? In turn, what is the relationship between author and audience, for that relationship largely determines and explains, not only narrative voice, but also a range of artistic strategies and choices. What do the configurations and variations of character in black women's fiction reveal about patterns of literary influence among black women writers, about their literary history?[13] In other words, a study of how black women writers depict black female characters raises both aesthetic and sociological questions, illuminating vividly the intricate connections between the two.

I

Largely because degraded images of black women have persisted throughout history, both in and out of literature, black women novelists have assumed throughout their tradition a revisionist mission aimed at substituting reality for stereotype.[14] Frances E. W. Harper and her female contemporaries Pauline Hopkins and Emma Dunham Kelley epitomized this revisionist mission, yoking it to a larger and related mission: to elevate the image of the entire black race. In so doing, they naively believed, they could eliminate caste injustices. They would manifest in literature the movement of racial uplift led by a widespread network of black club women of the nineteenth century whose motto was "Lifting as We Climb."[15]

The impulse is at once the greatest strength and the greatest weakness of these early texts, for it results without exception in the creation of static, disembodied, larger-than-life characters. These early black heroines are invariably exemplary, characterized by their self-sacrifice and by their tireless labor for the collective good. But probably their most cherished and enduring mark is their chastity, a quality that black club women also struggled to defend in the uplift cause. To counter the widespread assumption that black women were sexually immoral, these club women "wanted to be remembered as upholders of puritan morality," hence, much of their work involved "encourag[ing] . . . masses of black women to accept the sexual morality of the Victorian bourgeoisie."[16] Ironically, despite the early writers' efforts to revise homogenized literary images, they succeeded merely, and inevitably, in offering alternative homogenization; they traded myth for countermyth, an exchange consistent with their public mission.

The countermyth dominates *Iola Leroy*. It is most striking in Iola's conscious choice to glorify the virtues of motherhood and domesticity, the mainstays of the mid–nineteenth-century cult of true womanhood.[17] Although this ideology of domesticity was the veritable antithesis of the black woman's reality, Harper, like the majority of black writers of her era—both men and women—ironically accommodated her "new" model image of black womanhood to its contours. As Barbara Christian observes, "Since positive female qualities were all attributed to the white lady," black writers of the nineteenth century "based their counterimage on her ideal qualities, more than on [those] of any real black women." The image of the Lady combined and conflated physical appearance with character traits. Immortalized particularly in the southern antebellum novel, the image required "physical beauty [i.e., fair skin] . . .

fragility, refinement and helplessness." "The closest black women could come to such an ideal, at least physically," Christian continues, "would . . . have to be the mulatta, quadroon, or octoroon."[18] Iola fulfills this physical requirement. "My! but she's putty," says the slave through whose eyes we first see her. "Beautiful long hair comes way down her back; putty blue eyes, an' jis' ez white ez anybody's in dis place" (38). This ideal dominates novels by black women in the nineteenth century, due, as Alice Walker argues reasonably, to a predominately white readership "who could identify human feeling, humanness, only if it came in a white or near-white body." She concludes, " 'Fairness' was and is the standard of Euro-American femininity."[19]

By giving Iola a role to play in the larger struggle for racial uplift, Harper modified the image of the southern lady, but it is important to note that Iola's role in the struggle is enacted within the boundaries of the traditional expectations of women as mothers and nurturers, expectations that form the cornerstone of the cult of true womanhood. According to Iola, "a great amount of sin and misery springs from the weakness and inefficiency of women." In "The Education of Mothers," one of the two public speeches she gives in the novel (public speaking being largely reserved for men in the text), she appeals for "a union of women with the warmest hearts and clearest brains to help in the moral education of the race" (254).[20]

Not only does the content of such speeches contribute to Iola's exemplary image, the style and language do also. Ordinary or black folk speech has been historically devalued by the standard (white) English-speaking community, a devaluation that, as John Wideman maintains, "implies a linguistic hierarchy, the dominance of one version of reality over others."[21] That devaluation and all that it implies was especially pervasive in Harper's era. Arlene Elder points out that "Blacks were ridiculed in white plantation and Reconstruction humor for the rough rhythms, slurred words, malapropisms, and quaint images in their language. In order to escape this degrading image, [early] Black novelists sped to the other extreme of creating cultured mulattoes"[22] who used the elegant, elaborate, and artificial language found in much of the popular fiction of their day. At every point that Iola speaks in the novel, it is in the form of a carefully reasoned oration, in defense either of her virtue or of some moral or social ideal. Even in conversations at home with family and friends, Iola expounds, as in the following example: "To be . . . the leader of a race to higher planes of thought and action, to teach men clearer views of life and duty, and to inspire their souls with loftier aims, is a far greater privilege than it is to open the gates of material prosperity and fill every home with sensuous enjoyment" (219).

In significant contrast to Iola's formal oratory is the more authentic folk speech of the novel's secondary characters, captured particularly well in the opening chapter entitled "Mystery of Market Speech and Prayer Meeting." The chapter describes the slaves' masterful invention of a coded language to convey secretly information to each other about battles won and lost during the Civil War. Their rich and imaginative language is self-consciously mediated in this chapter and throughout the novel by the stilted and pedantic voices of the narrator and the novel's major character. Nowhere is this pattern more strikingly illustrated in the novel than in the passage that describes the reunion between Iola's uncle, Robert, and his mother, from whom he was separated as a child. "Well, I'se got one chile, an' I means to keep on prayin' tell I fine my daughter," says Robert's mother. "I'm *so* happy! I feels like a new woman!" (183). In contrast Robert responds: "My dear mother . . . now that I have found you, I mean to hold you fast just as long as you live. . . . I want you to see joy according to all the days wherein you have seen sorrow" (183).

In *Iola Leroy*, the propaganda motive, the hallmark of public discourse, largely explains these extreme differences of speech styles between the principal characters—all educated mulattoes—and the minor characters, all illiterate and visibly black servants and workers. The implications of such differentiations are clear: the speech of these secondary characters (which Iola finds "quaint," "interesting," and "amusing") must be mediated and legitimated in white terms by the more accepted language of the major characters.

In the course of *Iola Leroy*, as Iola fulfills her role as exemplary black woman she comes to resemble a human being less and less and a saint more and more. We learn very little about her thoughts, her inner life. Nothing about her is individual-ized, nor does this seem to be Harper's chief concern, for she is creating an exemplary type who is always part of some larger framework. That larger framework is moral and social in *Iola Leroy*, and every aspect of the text, especially character, must be carefully selected to serve its purpose. All of the novel's characters are trapped in an ideological schema that predetermines their identities. Every detail of Iola's life, down to the most personal experiences of family life, is stripped of its intimate implications and invested with social and mythical implications. It is significant that of all the Old Testament types, she identifies with Moses and Nehemiah, for "they were willing to put aside their own advantages for their race and country" (265).

Iola's role as social and moral exemplar is paralleled by the novel's role as exemplum. Like its title character, *Iola Leroy* is on trial before the world. It aims for a favorable verdict by choosing its models carefully. Harper's most visible model is Harriet Beecher Stowe's *Uncle Tom's Cabin*, the most popular novel of the mid-nineteenth century in America. Space does not permit me to detail the striking similarities of plot, theme, style, and characterization between the two novels. Although Harper makes slight modifications, echoes of the most salient episodes of *Uncle Tom's Cabin* are present throughout *Iola Leroy*.[23]

Harper's choice of *Uncle Tom's Cabin* as model is a logical and appropriate one, given the polemical and public role that she expected her novel to play, a role that Stowe's novel had played to unrivaled success with an audience comprised mainly of northern white Christians. Harper addresses and appeals to this audience directly in the afternote of the novel: "From threads of fact and fiction I have woven a story whose mission will not be in vain if it awaken in the hearts of our country-men a stronger sense of justice and a more Christlike human-ity in behalf of those whom the fortunes of war threw, homeless, ignorant and poor, upon the threshold of a new era" (282). Those northern whites might be more inclined to lend their assistance to this homeless and displaced lot if the images of black life that Harper and her black contemporaries valued and affirmed accorded with that audience's horizon of social and literary expectations. In this respect, *Iola Leroy* is in company with a number of novels by black writers of its era, all dedicated to a public mission, all foundering on the shoals of two contradictory attempts: "to conform to the accepted social [and] literary . . . standards of their day and their almost antithetical need to portray their own people with honesty and imagination."[24]

II

The need to portray their people with honesty and imagination has been paramount for contemporary black women novelists. For many—Alice Walker, Toni Morrison, Gayl Jones, among others—that need has compelled them to transform the black female literary ideal inherited from their nineteenth-century predecessors. Although these recent writers have preserved the revisionist mission that inspired that ideal, they have liberated their own characters from the burden of being exemplary standard-bearers in an enterprise to uplift the race. The result is not only greater complexity and possibility for their heroines, but also greater complexity and artistic possibility for themselves as writers. Alice Walker is a good example of this paradigm shift.[25]

In "Beyond the Peacock," an essay in her recent collection *In Search of Our Mothers' Gardens*, Walker writes, "each writer writes the missing parts to the other writer's story. And the whole story is what I'm after."[26] To Walker, a major if not *the* major missing part is the story of what she calls the "black black" heroine, described in the essay "If the Present Looks Like the Past." Unlike Iola Leroy and the other nineteenth-century black women characters that Walker surveys in the essay, the black black heroine cannot pass for white and is not protected by class privilege. While Walker isn't the only black female novelist to attempt an alternative to the Iola Leroy type,[27] she has made a particularly skillful revision in the Celie letters of *The Color Purple*. These letters can be read as Walker's effort to write the missing parts of *Iola Leroy* and other black women's texts in its tradition. In other words, Celie is a revision of a revision of black female character, rendered, for the most part, with the honesty and imagination lacking in *Iola Leroy*.

Whereas Iola Leroy as character is largely indistinguishable from the southern Lady and is devoted to the mission of middle-class racial "uplift," Celie is a poor, visibly black, barely literate drudge devoted simply to avoiding and surviving the brutalities inflicted on her by every man with whom she comes into contact. Unlike Iola, no ornate and elevated speeches come trippingly to Celie's tongue. She speaks in black folk English, and, unlike Harper, Alice Walker provides none of the self-conscious assurances to the reader—apostrophes, contractions, corrections from more "well-spoken" characters—that she knows the standard.

But perhaps Celie's most striking difference from Iola is her sexual experience. Unlike Iola, Celie has been unable to fend off attacks on her virtue by predatory men as her very first letter makes starkly clear: "You gonna do what your mammy wouldn't. First he put his thing up against my hip and sort of wiggle it around. Then he grab hold my titties. Then he push his thing inside my pussy" (11). Although Celie's introduction to sexuality is rape, as her narrative unfolds, she, unlike Iola, discovers how vital healthy sexual experiences are to the development of her self-esteem and her creative powers. Significantly, the only form of sexuality that aids that process is expressed with a woman, one of the few lesbian relationships explored in black women's literature.[28]

Iola and Celie reflect their authors' divergent approaches to characterization as well. Whereas Harper approaches Iola's character largely from the outside through her physical characteristics and through what others say about her, Walker reveals Celie's character completely from the inside. Everything we learn about Celie is filtered through her own consciousness and rendered in her own voice.

In Iola Leroy the creation of a distinct self is sacrificed to the collective mission, and the result is a static symbol rather than a dynamic character. In The Color Purple, the collective mission, as imaged by Harper, is sacrificed to the self, and the result is the creation of a character in process, one more complex and thoroughly realized than Iola Leroy.[29] Iola's energy is invariably directed outside of herself, and the narrative's action is, correspondingly, social and public in emphasis. Celie's energy, on the other hand, is primarily directed inward, and the narrative action of The Color Purple is correspondingly psychological, personal, and intimate in emphasis.

Unlike *Iola Leroy*, *The Color Purple* fits primarily into the private paradigm, suggested by its choice of the epistolary mode—by definition personal and private—and the finite focus of the Celie letters. One of their most striking features is the conspicuous absence of any reference to the "outside" world. Except for an occasional reference to Macon, Memphis, and one to World War I, the world is shut out.[30] Instead, like epistolary novels generically, *The Color Purple* emphasizes the psychological development of character.

Celie begins her story at age fourteen in the form of letters to God, the only one who can hear her, she thinks. Feeling isolated and ashamed, she tells Him of her life of brutality and exploitation at the hands of men. Writing is all-important to Celie; her last resounding word to her sister Nettie before they separate is "Write" (26).

While Celie's letters are an attempt to communicate with someone outside herself, they also reveal a process of self-examination and self-discovery in much the same way the letter functioned for the protagonists in Richardson's *Clarissa* and *Pamela*. In other words, Celie's growth is chartable through her letters to God, which are essentially letters of self-exploration, enabling her to become connected to her thoughts and feelings. That connection eventually liberates her from a belief in a God outside herself, whom she has always imagined as "Big and old and tall and graybearded and white" (176). and acquaints her with the God inside herself.

The spiritual dimension of Celie's discovery of the God-in-self has striking implications for her experience as a writer—for a writer she is, first and foremost. A self-reflexive novel, *The Color Purple* explicitly allegorizes much about the process and problematics of writing for the black woman. For example, the process by which Celie comes to shift her addressee from God to Nettie suggests much about the relationship between writer and audience and its effect on narrative authority and autonomy, to forceful voice. *The Color Purple* makes clear that the black woman writer has written primarily without an audience capable of accepting and appreciating that the full, raw, unmediated range of the black woman's story could be appropriate subject matter for art.[31]

The Celie letters addressed to God indicate that she is a

writer without an audience, without a hearing, a predicament she recognizes only after discovering that her husband has intercepted and hidden in a trunk letters her sister Nettie has written to her from Africa over a thirty-year period. As Celie recovers from the shock, she announces to Shug that she has ceased to write to God, now realizing that ". . . the God I been praying and writing to is a man, and just like all the others mens I know. Trifling, forgitful, and low-down." When Shug cautions Celie to be quiet, lest God hear her, Celie responds defiantly, "Let 'im hear me, I say. If he ever listened to poor colored women the world would be a different place" (175).

Celie's decision to cease writing to God and to begin writing to her sister Nettie marks a critical point in both her psychological development and in her development as a writer. Significantly, before Celie discovers that God is not listening, her letters to him record passive resignation, silence, and blind faith in his benevolence. She can suffer abuses in this life, she confides to Sofia, because "[it] soon be over . . . Heaven last all ways" (47). In these letters, she identifies with Squeak, who speaks in a "little teenouncy voice" (83). She "stutters," "mutters"; her "throat closes" (86), and "nothing come[s] out but a little burp" (115). Celie admits that she "can't fix [her] mouth to say how [she] feel[s]" (88). Appropriately, these letters record a distinct split between what she thinks and what she feels and says. For example, when Nettie leaves for Africa, she expresses sadness at leaving Celie to be buried by the burden of caring for Mr.——— and his children. Celie writes, "It's worse than that, I think. If I was buried, I wouldn't have to work. But I just say, Never mine, never mine, long as I can spell G-o-d I got somebody along" (26). Similarly, when Celie thinks she sees her daughter Olivia at the drygoods store in town, she strikes up a conversation with the woman who has custody of the child. The woman makes a joke about the child's name, and Celie writes: "I git it and laugh. It feel like to split my face" (24). The image of the split functions here, as in so many novels by women, as a sign of the character's tenuous sense of self, of identity, if you will.[32] The image objectifies the split between Celie's outer and inner selves that will ultimately be made whole as the novel develops.

It is further significant that none of the letters addressed to God is signed. In their anonymity, their namelessness, the letters further underscore Celie's lack of individuality. When she begins to write to Nettie, however, her inner and outer selves become connected. Her thoughts are fused with her feelings, her actions, her words, and the letters assume a quality of force and authority, at times of prophecy, as seen in Celie's conversation with Mr.——— before she leaves for Memphis:

> Until you do right by me, everything you touch will crumble.
>   He laugh. Who you think you is? he say. You can't curse nobody. Look at you. You black, you pore, you ugly, you a woman. Goddam, he say, you nothing at all.
>   Until you do right by me, I say, everything you even dream about will fail (187).

Celie concludes: "I'm pore, I'm black, I may be ugly and can't cook. . . . But I'm here" (187). Thus these letters addressed to Nettie are alternately signed "Your sister, Celie" and "Amen," expressions of ratification, of approval, of assertion, of validation. The suggestion is clear: Celie is now ratifying, asserting, and validating her own words, her own worth, and the authority of her own experience. Celie's validation of her linguistic experience is especially important, for it is so critical to the establishment of her own literary voice.

Celie's story underscores sharply, as Iola's does not, the argument of many students of language that "ordinary" discourse can be continuous with "poetic," or "literary" discourse, and that any assumed distinctions between the two are unsupported by linguistic research.[33] For considerations of Afro-American literature that argument is especially critical, for if both forms of discourse can be continuous with each other, the need for an external and legitimating filter is eliminated.[34] Jerene and Darlene, Celie's helpers in her Folkspants, Unlimited enterprise, in wanting to teach her to "talk correctly," imply the popular belief that ordinary black speech must be "corrected" in order to have literate status, but Celie comes to understand that "only a fool would want you to talk in a way that feel peculiar to your mind" (194).

The narrative links Celie's refusal to talk in a manner peculiar to her mind with a change of audience. That refusal—the
mark of psychic wholeness as well as of narrative authority
and autonomy—is licensed and buttressed by the sympathetic
audience she imagines. Significantly, Celie directs her letters
away from God, a "public" and alien audience outside herself
and toward her sister Nettie, a private, familial, familiar, and
receptive audience. The qualitative differences between the
letters to God and those to Nettie imply a causal connection
between a receptive audience (imaged as one with "kinship"
ties to the writer) and the emergence of a forceful, authoritative, and self-validating narrative voice.[35]

III

The question which immediately arises, however, is: Given
this connection, what explains the comparative lack of force
and authority in Nettie's letters? How do they serve the narrative? Early reviewers of *The Color Purple* rightly saw Nettie's
letters as lackluster and unengaging compared to Celie's. While
they advance the narrative line, they disrupt the immediacy
and momentum of Celie's letters. That notwithstanding, Nettie's letters do function to unify the narrative by repeating its
central images and concerns. Most significantly, they continue
and expand its commentary on the act of writing and the role
that context and circumstances play in the creative process.

But the Nettie letters have perhaps the most striking and
intriguing implications for Alice Walker as a writer, for her
discovery of her own voice. For Walker, as for so many women
writers, the process of that discovery begins with thinking
back through and reclaiming her female ancestors. While much
has been made (with Walker's encouragement) of Walker's
obvious debt to Zora Neale Hurston, there has been virtually
no acknowledgment that she owes an equal though different
debt to black women writers before Hurston. In "Saving the
Life That Is Your Own: The Importance of Models in the
Artist's Life," Walker admits that her need to know the oral
stories *told* by her female ancestors, stories which Hurston
transcribed in her folklore and writing, was equal to her need

to know the stories *written* by nineteenth-century black women.[36] Even if they had to be transformed or rejected altogether, the experiences that these earlier writers recorded were crucial to Walker's development as a writer.

Walker notes in an interview with Gloria Steinem that "writing *The Color Purple* was writing in my first language," in its "natural, flowing way."[37] In the novel, that language is Celie's, not Nettie's, indicating that Walker identifies her own writing voice with Celie's. However, that identification does not require that she reject Nettie's. Both the oral and the literate are parts of her literary ancestry, and she conjoins them in the Celie and Nettie letters, respectively, reinforcing one of the novel's central themes: female bonding. Together their letters form a study of converging contrasts that are homologous with the relationship between Frances Harper and Alice Walker.

As their letters reveal, the correspondences between the sisters' experiences are striking, even strained and over-determined. Much of what Nettie writes to Celie describing the situation in Africa—the breakdown of male/female relationships, the power of male domination, and the bonding between women—is replicated in Celie's experiences in the rural South. Nettie writes to Celie of the paved roads in Africa; Celie, to her, of those in Georgia. Nettie describes her round and windowless African hut; Celie, Shug's difficulty including windows in her plans for a round house in Memphis.

While the sisters' experiences converge at these critical points, they diverge at others, perhaps most importantly in the voice, content, and style of their epistles. While Celie's letters are written in black folk English and record her personal trials and near defeat, Nettie's, written in more formal language, record the trials and decimation of a people and their culture. Nettie's personal relationships with Samuel, Corinne, and their children seem dwarfed and insignificant compared to the destruction of the Olinka culture. In other words, while the majority of Celie's letters can be said to represent the private paradigm of the Afro-American female tradition in the novel, the majority of Nettie's letters can be said to represent the public paradigm. I say "majority" because Nettie's letters to Celie are, significantly, in two distinct linguistic registers. Her first letters to Celie focus on personal matters and are largely indistinguishable from Celie's letters:

> Dear Celie, *the first letter say,*
>   You've got to fight and get away from Albert. He ain't no good.
>   When I left you all's house, walking, he followed me on his horse. When we was well out of sight of the house, he caught up with me and started trying to talk. You know how he do . . . (119).

The next letter reads: "I keep thinking it's too soon to look for a letter from you. And I know how busy you is with all Mr.——— children . . ." (120). Shortly after these letters, Nettie writes to Celie of the events leading to her decision to go to Africa as a missionary, explaining her agreement to help build a school in exchange for furthering her education. That letter reads: ". . . When Corinne and Samuel asked me if I would come with them and help them build a school . . . I said yes. But only if they would teach me everything they knew to make me useful as a missionary. . . . They agreed to this condition, and my real education began at that time" (124). From this point on, Nettie's letters shift from the personal to the social, the political, the historical. They assume the quality of lecture and oration, losing the intimacy more appropriate in correspondence to a sister. Nettie's has become an educated imagination, shaped by the context within which she moves as well as by her function as a missionary in a colonizing enterprise.

Although Celie and Nettie are separated by a continent, by their lifestyles—one ordinary, the other exceptional—and by the style of their epistles—oral and literate—these separate realities become integrated in the novel and held in sustained equilibrium. Each sister is allowed to exist as an independent entity; each, through her letters, allowed to speak in her own voice without apology, mediation, or derision.

While one might expect it, there is no apology, mediation, or derision on Walker's part for her predecessor Frances Harper, the impulses of whose work she incorporates in the voice and experiences of Nettie. Reminiscent of Iola, Nettie guards her virginity. Her self-conscious and ambiguous description of her developing passion for Samuel brings to mind Iola's reticence about sexuality. In one letter Nettie recounts to Celie her "forward behavior" with Samuel. As she and Samuel embrace, Nettie writes, "concern and passion soon ran away with us," and "I was transported by ecstasy in Samuel's arms" (210–11).

But the more important resemblance between Nettie and Iola is their sacrifice of personal needs and wishes for a larger social purpose. Nettie is swept up in a social movement and energized by its unofficial motto: "OUR COMMUNITY COVERS THE WORLD" (208). She is, in her words, working for the "uplift of black people everywhere" (127). The concept of racial uplift, of corporate mission, so central to *Iola Leroy*, is explicit in Nettie's letters and acts as counterpoint to Celie's more private and personal concerns. Further, together these letters objectify the pattern of intertextual relations among black women writers, a pattern which departs from what Harold Bloom describes in *The Anxiety of Influence* and *A Map of Misreading*.[38] Bloom's linear theory of the oedipal war between literary fathers and sons does not obtain among black women writers, many of whom reverently acknowledge their debts to their literary foremothers. Unlike Bloom, I see literary influence, to borrow from Julia Kristeva, in the intertextual sense, each text in dialogue with all previous texts, transforming and retaining narrative patterns and strategies in endless possibility.[39]

This pattern of literary influence from Harper to Walker is also distinct from that among black men.[40] Henry Louis Gates's description of intertextuality in his discussion of Richard Wright, Ralph Ellison, and Ishmael Reed, for example, characterizes the formal relations between them as largely adversarial and parodic.[41] While there is certainly much to parody in Harper's *Iola Leroy*—most notably, the stilted language that accompanied the uplift concept—Walker refrains from doing so, and perhaps therein lies a fundamental distinction between Afro-American male and female literary relations. We might argue that Walker has transformed and updated the concept of "uplift" associated almost exclusively with Harper and her generation, for a kind of uplift functions metaphorically in *The Color Purple*. The novel elevates the folk forms of rural and southern blacks to the status of art. In a similar fashion, it elevates the tradition of letters and diaries, commonly considered a "female" tradition (and therefore inferior), from the category of "non-art" to art.

IV

But while Walker retains uplift as metaphor in *The Color Purple*, she rejects the burden it imposes on the writer, a burden that black writers have shouldered to excess throughout their literary history in fulfillment of a corporate mission. Certainly a major consequence of that mission for the writers of Harper's generation was a homogenized literary era that inhibited the writers' discovery of their unique voices.

The Color Purple is rich with images of voice, of singing, that complement and comment upon the novel's controlling metaphor of writing as seen in Celie's description of an exchange between Shug and Mary Agnes, aka Squeak:

> Shug say to Squeak, I mean, Mary Agnes, You ought to sing in public.
>
> Mary Agnes say, *Naw*. She think cause she don't sing big and broad like Shug nobody want to hear her. But Shug say she wrong.
>
> What about all them funny voices you hear singing in church? Shug say. What about all them sounds that sound good but they not the sounds you thought folks could make? What bout that? (111)

Mary Agnes does go on to become a blues singer in her own right, singing in her own unimitative voice. Moreover, the narrative clearly implies that she can sing in public only when she discovers her own name (Mary Agnes, not Squeak) and her own "private," unique voice.

The Color Purple implies the regrettable fact that black writers have not been permitted the freedom to discover and then to speak in their unique voices largely because they have been compelled to use their art for mainly propagandistic (public) purposes. Ntozake Shange makes that point in her collection of poems *nappy edges*: "We, as a people, or as a literary cult, or a literary culture / have not demanded singularity from our writers. we could all sound the same, come from the same region. be the same gender. born the same year." She adds, "we assume a musical solo is a personal statement / we think the poet is speakin for the world, there's something wrong there, a writer's first commitment is to the piece itself," then comes the political commitment.[42]

The work of Frances Harper implies no such choice. Her age demanded the reverse. The morality of black women was being rampantly impugned, black people were being lynched in numbers and were suffering rank injustices. Unarguably, the writer lifted the pen to uplift the race.

Walker sacrifices the impulse to uplift the race, although hers is no less than Harper's a project whose aim is cultural transformation. She envisions a new world—at times utopian in dimension—in which power relations between men and women, between the colonizers and the colonized are reconfigured to eliminate domination and promote cooperation. Further, in the structural arrangement of the letters—Celie's first, then Nettie's, then alternation of the two—she shows that self-development and corporate mission are not mutually exclusive but can be consonant with each other.

The Color Purple reflects Walker's awareness that the literary manifestations of racial uplift (or any social movement for that matter) are explained, in part, by the relationship between writer and audience. Unlike Harper, Walker could choose to ignore the fact that her audience was predominantly white, a choice strongly influenced, as was Harper's, by the social realities and literary circumstances of her place and time. We might pinpoint specifically the emergence of black nationalism in the 1960s and 70s and the rise of the women's movement that followed closely on its heels. During this period, the writers and critics who formed the cultural arm of the larger political movement became convinced, as Houston Baker notes, that "their real audience, like the nation to come, was black." Accordingly, they directed "their energies to the creation of a new nation and their voices to an audience radically different from any [they] had ever conceived of," a black audience which would include, as never before, ordinary blacks from ghetto communities.[43] They fashioned a critical methodology termed the "black aesthetic," a "system of isolating and evalu-

ating the artistic works of black people which reflect the special character and imperatives of black experience."[44]

Like the black aestheticians, those women in the vanguard
of the women's movement's second wave called for women's
release from unreal and oppressive loyalties. Feminist criticism
became one literary manifestation of that political stance. Similar in spirit and methodology to the largely male-dominated
black aesthetic movement, feminist critics likewise repudiated
and subverted what they considered alien, male-created literary standards, and began to describe and analyze a female
aesthetic which reflected women's unique culture.

It is necessary to note that, ironically, in their earliest formulations, the objectives and practices of both the black aesthetic and feminist criticism often came dangerously close to
insisting on a different and no less rigid set of creative standards. Despite their own prescriptive leanings, however, these
two modes of critical inquiry must be credited with opening
up unprecedented possibilities for black and women writers.
In isolating and affirming the particulars of black and female
experience, they inspired and authorized writers from those
cultures to sing in their different voices and to imagine an
audience that could hear the song.

The narrative strongly implies that that audience is comprised mainly of Walker's "sisters," other black women. Its
structure and plot—two black sisters writing to each other—
lend support. It is not that Walker can or even desires to
exclude writers outside this group; it is simply that she addresses her letters to them.

I am all too aware that the theoretical argument that Alice
Walker addresses her letters first to black women raises at
least two glaring empirical paradoxes: the novel has been
enormously successful with a very diverse readership, a large
part of which is white and often criticized by those to whom it
seems addressed.[45] However, the premise is recommended
and supported by a major thread in the novel's plot: the act of
reading letters that are written and intended for other eyes.

Just as the novel's letters lend themselves to Walker's reflexive depiction of the act of writing, they simultaneously lend
themselves to her reflexive depiction of the act of reading.
They offer a compelling model of the relationship Walker implies between herself and her readers, her own correspon-

dents, her audience of "kissin' friends" who enter by the "intimate gate," to borrow from Zora Neale Hurston. In choosing them as her auditors and their experiences as her story, she has made the private public, and in the process created a new literary space for the black and the female idiom against and within a traditionally Eurocentric and androcentric literary history.

NOTES

1. I borrow the title and its underlying premise from Leroi Jones's (aka Amiri Baraka) "The Changing Same (R & B and New Black Music)" in *The Black Aesthetic*, ed. Addison Gayle, Jr. (New York, 1971), 112–25. In this essay, Jones traces the continuities in the black musical tradition, which he argues has its roots in African religion and spirit worship. He submits that even as it has changed, in both vocal and instrumental forms, black music has remained the same, continuing patterns and impulses that originated in Africa and were transplanted and "Christianized" in America—shouts, hollers, call and response (lead and chorus), for example. Analogously, we can observe continuities in black women's fiction from the nineteenth century forward, even as the tradition changes.
2. Frances E. W. Harper, *Iola Leroy or Shadows Uplifted* (1892: report. College Park, Md., 1969), 257; hereafter cited in text.
3. Alice Walker, *The Color Purple* (New York, 1982), 181; hereafter cited in text.
4. Throughout this discussion I will refer to the black female literary tradition in the novel, but the reference is restricted to Afro-American women novelists.
5. Although these two texts best exemplify my concerns here, I might also have chosen Harriet Wilson's *Our Nig* (1859), Emma Dunham Kelley's *Megda* (1892), or Pauline Hopkins's *Contending Forces* (1900) to represent the public paradigm as seen in nineteenth-century novelists. To represent the private paradigm characteristic almost exclusively of late–twentieth-century black women novelists, I might have chosen either Gwendolyn Brooks's *Maud Martha* (1953: reprint. New York, 1979), Toni Morrison's *Sula* (New York, 1974), Gayl Jones's *Corregidora* (New York, 1975) or her *Eva's Man* (New York, 1976), Toni Cade Bambara's *The Salt Eaters* (New York, 1980), Ntozake Shange's *Sassafras, Cypress & Indigo: A Novel* (New York, 1982), or Gloria Naylor's *The Women of Brewster Place* (New York, 1982).
6. Susan Lanser, *The Narrative Act* (Princeton, 1981), 137–38. Although Lanser refers specifically to point of view in narrative, her use of "public" and "private" can be applied more broadly to other narrative structures, models, and genres.
7. Throughout the following discussion, my use of "public" and "private" will ring familiar to students of Afro-American literature, who will notice the similarity between the terms I use and other dichotomies used to describe Afro-American literature. For example, in his essay "The Literature of the Negro in the United States," included in his *White Man, Listen!* (Garden City, N.Y., 1964), Richard Wright distinguishes between what he calls the "Narcissistic Level" and "The Forms of Things Unknown." The former is characterized by formal, self-conscious, and imitative writing indicting racist attitudes and institutions. The latter is spontaneous, expressive writing deriving from black folk forms. In *The Negro Novel in America* (New Haven, 1958), Robert Bone sees the same stylistic patterns in the Afro-American novel that Wright described in his essay. Bone simply renames the categories "assimilationism/integrationism" and "Negro nationalism." I have chosen "public" and "private" instead, in an attempt at greater terminological simplicity than Wright employs and in an attempt to avoid the value judgments and political overtones of Bone's distinc-

tions. Finally, more than either Wright's or Bone's terms, "public" and "private" are flexible as descriptive paradigms, their implications and resonances more suggestive for the questions about narrative voice and literary audience that this discussion raises. I should hasten to add that, like any literary taxonomy, mine cannot be strictly applied to every novel written by an Afro-American woman. That would grossly oversimplify a very rich and complex tradition. Further, there is overlap between the public and private modes, sometimes within a single text, as evidenced in *The Color Purple*. I intend these terms merely as convenient points of entry into individual texts rather than as substitutions for the subtle distinctions that those texts require.

8. In the case of *The Color Purple*, the public/private distinction requires a finer and more precise definition that includes gender as well as cultural specificities. As I will discuss later, for example, in tone, texture, gesture, and strategy, the narrative strongly implies a female addressee. Deciding that "God must be sleep" or "glorying in being deaf," Celie begins to address her letters to her sister Nettie. Likewise, Celie, and not Mr.———, is the intended recipient of Nettie's letters.

9. Peter Rabinowitz, " 'What's Hecuba to Us?' The Audience's Experience of Literary Borrowing," in *The Reader in the Text: Essays on Audience and Interpretation*, ed. Susan Suleiman and Inge Crosman (Princeton, 1980), 243. See also Wolfgang Iser, *The Implied Reader* (Baltimore, 1974); *Reader-Response Criticism*, ed. Jane P. Tompkins (Baltimore, 1980); and Walter J. Ong, S. J., "The Writer's Audience is Always a Fiction," *PMLA*, 90 (1975), 9–21.

10. Fredric Jameson, *The Political Unconscious: Narrative as a Socially Symbolic Act* (Ithaca, 1981), 153.

11. Jonathan Culler, *Structuralist Poetics* (Ithaca, 1975), 230.

12. Mary Helen Washington notes correctly that "one of the main preoccupations of the black woman writer has been the black woman herself . . ." See *Black-Eyed Susans* (New York, 1975), x. This preoccupation with fashioning a self is not peculiar to black women writers. As Henry Louis Gates notes accurately, "the single most pervasive and consistent assumption of all black writing since the eighteenth century has been that there exists an unassailable, integral, black self . . . whole . . . knowable, retrievable [and] recuperable . . ." See "Frederick Douglass and the Language of the Self," *The Yale Review*, 70 (1981), 604.

13. Attempting to chart these variations by examining two texts from different periods might seem a curious strategy, but as students of literary history have begun to observe, juxtaposing works from diverse periods can reveal as much if not more about historical continuities and discontinuities than can a strict chronological narrative. See Herbert Lindenberger, "Toward a New History in Literary Study," *Profession 84*, 16–22.

14. Since readers are undoubtedly familiar with them, I need not rehearse these stereotypes, nor offer explanations for the cultural function they have served throughout history. Paule Marshall has identified the two extremes of these cliched images as the "nigger wench" and the mammy. See "The Negro Woman in American Literature," *Freedomways*, 6, No. 1 (1966), 20.

15. See Paula Giddings, *When and Where I Enter: The Impact of Black Women on Race and Sex in America* (New York, 1984) and Elizabeth Davis, *Lifting As They Climb: The National Association of Colored Women* (n.p., 1933).

16. Wilson J. Moses, *The Golden Age of Black Nationalism, 1850–1925* (Hamden, Conn., 1978), 122–31.

17. For a discussion of "the cult of true womanhood," see Barbara Welter's article of the same name in *American Quarterly*, 18 (1966), 151–74. For a discussion of the "cult of domesticity," see Aileen Kraditor's *Up From the Pedestal* (Chicago, 1968). Nancy Cott combines the two concepts in her treatment of "women's sphere" in New England in *The Bonds of Womanhood* (New Haven, 1977). According to Cott, the "cult of true womanhood" was a northern bourgeois tradition which "prescribed a role of utility, not leisure, decoration, or helplessness for women." The image of the lady, on the other hand, was southern and "belonged more directly to the historical tradition immortalizing the [idle] aristocratic lady." Though they began as separate, indigenous traditions, the "Southern tradition influences Northern conceptions of women's roles more than vice versa," adds Cott, which explains why "by mid-[nineteenth] century

Northern rhetoric on women's roles sounded increasingly like Southern" (p.11). Harper seems to have combined elements of both the northern and southern traditions in her portrait of Iola Leroy.

18. Barbara Christian, *Black Women Novelists: The Development of a Tradition* (Westport, Conn., 1980), 22.

19. Alice Walker, "If the Present Looks Like the Past, What Does the Future Look Like?" in her *In Search of Our Mothers' Gardens* (New York, 1983), 301.

20. I am grateful to Elizabeth Ammons for suggesting that the glorification of motherhood as woman's heroic work was "modern" at the turn of the century. It was part of the attempt to elevate women's traditional work into a modern, disciplined, even scientific calling. It is possible, then, to see Iola Leroy as a part of that movement. Significantly, she lectures on and teaches the objectives of the "domestic science" movement, which attempted to make women's work a highly developed skill, a step up and forward, not backward. See her essay "Stowe's Dream of the Mother-Savior: *Uncle Tom's Cabin* and American Women Writers Before the 1920's" in *New Essays on Uncle Tom's Cabin*, ed. Eric Sundquist (Cambridge, 1986).

21. John Wideman, "Defining the Black Voice in Fiction," *Black American Literature Forum*, 11 (1977), 81.

22. Arlene Elder, *The 'Hindered Hand': Cultural Implications of Early African-American Fiction* (Westport, Conn., 1978), 16.

23. Allow a few examples to suffice. Iola, like Stowe's Cassy, does not discover she is a slave until her white father dies and she is then sold into slavery. Before she is remanded to slavery, however, Iola ardently defends the institution to a black schoolmate, arguing the classic plantation line: slaves are content with their lot. Her friend responds, "I do not think that that slave mother who took her four children, crossed the Ohio River on the ice, killed one of the children and attempted the lives of the other two, was a contented slave" (98). Although in this speech Harper has made slight modifications in Stowe's plot, the reminiscences of Eliza's famous trek across the ice to escape slave hunters and Cassy's administration of laudanum to her child are all strong. (Incidentally, Harper's poem "Eliza Harris" dramatizes Eliza's escape.) Finally, the death of Iola's young sister Grace is modelled directly on the death of Stowe's Little Eva. "Swiftly the tidings went through the house that Gracie was dying. The servants gathered around her with tearful eyes, as she bade them all good-bye. When she had finished and Mammy had lowered the pillow, an unwonted radiance lit up her eye and an expression of ineffable gladness overspread her face, as she murmured: 'It is beautiful, so beautiful!' " (108).

24. Elder, xiv.

25. Although my aim here is not to trace the linear development of character in black women's fiction, it is useful to provide at least a sketch of the tradition between Harper and Walker. Harper's legacy continues in the novels of Jessie Fauset and Nella Larsen in the 1920s and 30s, which focus on middle-class, upwardly mobile heroines. The heroines' motivations shift, however, from a concern for racial uplift and corporate mission to a frequently destructive obsession with material security and social status. See Fauset's four novels—*There is Confusion* (1924; report. New York, 1929); *Plum Bun* (London, 1928); *The Chinaberry Tree* (New York, 1931); *Comedy, American Style* (New York, 1933)—and Larsen's *Quicksand* (New York and London, 1928) and *Passing* (New York and London, 1929). Zora Neale Hurston can be regarded as a transitional figure between the nineteenth-century tradition, represented by Harper and continued by Fauset and Larsen, and the contemporary tradition, represented by Alice Walker and her black female contemporaries. She shifts away from the public conception of character and art to one more private, more culturally self-contained, one seemingly indifferent to public example and approval. The best example of this shift is her novel *Their Eyes Were Watching God* (London, 1937; report. Urbana, Ill., 1978).

26. Walker, *In Search of Our Mothers' Gardens*, 49.

27. Among the black female novelists to depict the "ordinary" black heroine are Ann Petry in *The Street* (Boston, 1948); Gwendolyn Brooks in *Maud Martha* (New York, 1953); and Sarah E. Wright in *This Child's Gonna Live* (New York, 1969).

28. Before the 1970s there are noticeably few lesbian relationships in black women's

fiction. Nella Larsen flirts with the possibility of such a relationship in her novel *Passing* (1929). For a discussion of that aspect of the novel see my introduction to the reprint of Larsen's *Passing* and *Quicksand* (New Brunswick, N.J., 1986). Other such relationships in black women's novels include those in Gloria Naylor's *The Women of Brewster Place* (New York, 1982); Ntozake Shange's *Sassafras, Cypress & Indigo*; Ann Allen Shockley's *Loving Her* (1974; report. New York, 1978) and *Say Jesus and Come to Me* (New York, 1982); and Rosa Guy's *Ruby* (New York, 1976).

29. It is useful to note that in creating Celie, Alice Walker has not only revised nineteenth-century prototypes, but also previous characters of her own creation. E.g., the title character of Walker's second novel, *Meridian* (New York, 1976), is depicted in images that resemble these early heroines. She is mythical, spiritual, described in Christlike images, and sacrifices all personal gain for a larger social good.

30. The following conversation between Shug, Tobias, and Celie reinforces the point:

> 'All womens not alike, Tobias, she [Shug] say.
> Believe it or not. Oh, I believe it, he say.
> Just can't prove it to the world.'
> First time I think about world, [says Celie].
> What the world got to do with anything, I think. (52)

31. As Alice Walker reminds us, "The majority of black women who tried to express themselves by writing and who tried to make a living doing so, died in obscurity and poverty usually before their time. . . . Phillis Wheatley died, along with her three children, of malnutrition, in a cheap boardinghouse where she worked as a drudge. Nella Larsen died in almost complete obscurity after turning her back on her writing in order to become a practical nurse, an occupation that would at least buy food . . . and a place to sleep. And Zora Neale Hurston . . . died in poverty in the swamps of Florida, where she was again working as a housemaid," and was buried in an unmarked grave. See "A Talk: Convocation 1972," in *In Search of Our Mothers' Gardens*, 35.

32. It is reminiscent, e.g., of Janie in Zora Neale Hurston's *Their Eyes Were Watching God* (1937), a novel that Walker freely admits has influenced her own work. Before Janie gains her full voice, she describes being split in two. For this image in other works by women, see Charlotte Perkins Gilman, *The Yellow Wallpaper* (1899; report. New York, 1973); Sylvia Plath's *The Bell Jar* (New York, 1971); Margaret Atwood's *Surfacing* (Toronto, 1972); and Rita Mae Brown's *Rubyfruit Jungle* (1973; report. New York, 1983).

33. See Susan Lanser, *The Narrative Act*; Mary Louise Pratt, "The 'Poetic Language' Fallacy" and "Natural Narrative: What is 'Ordinary Language' Really Like?" in her *Toward a Speech Act Theory of Literary Discourse* (Bloomington, 1977); and Stanley Fish, "How Ordinary Is Ordinary Language?" *New Literary History*, 5, No. 1 (Autumn 1973), 41–54.

34. See John Wideman's "Defining the Black Voice in Fiction" for a discussion of such legitimating filters in Afro-American literature.

35. The same is implied in Hurston's *Their Eyes Were Watching God*. The authority that Janie's story has is due to her intimate and receptive audience, again a woman, her friend Phoeby. They have been "kissin' friends" for twenty years, and when Phoeby comes to hear Janie's epic story, she enters by the "intimate gate."

36. Walker, "Saving the Life That Is Your Own" in *In Search of Our Mothers' Gardens*, 3–14.

37. Gloria Steinem, "Do You Know This Woman? She Knows You: A Portrait of Alice Walker," *Ms.*, June 1982, 35–37, 89–94.

38. Harold Bloom, *The Anxiety of Influence* (New York, 1973) and *A Map of Misreading* (New York, 1975). In her excellent essay "A Hateful Passion, a Lost Love," *Feminist Studies*, 9 (1983), 293–323, Hortense Spillers makes a similar point about the nature of literary influence among black women writers.

39. Although Kristeva does not use the term "intertextuality" in conjunction with discussions of influence, it is possible to use the concept in such discussions without

violating the integrity of Kristeva's original definition. In formulating her definition, Kristeva borrows from Mikhail Bakhtin's "conception of the 'literary word' as an intersection of textual surfaces . . . as a dialogue among several writings . . . [A]ny text is constructed as a mosaic of quotations; any text is the absorption and transformation of another." See "The Bounded Text" and "Word, Dialogue, and Novel" in Julia Kristeva, *Desire in Language; A Semiotic Approach to Literature and Art*, ed. Leon S. Roudiez, tr. Thomas Gora, Alice Jardine, and Leon S. Roudiez (New York, 1980), 64–66.

40. Both Robert Stepto (*From Behind the Veil* [Urbana, 1979]) and Henry Louis Gates ("The 'Blackness of Blackness': A Critique of the Sign and the Signifying Monkey," *Critical Inquiry*, 9 [1983], 685–723) have provided excellent adaptations of the theory of intertextuality in their readings of certain Afro-American texts. While they go far toward defining the Afro-American narrative tradition, neither examines, in any thoroughgoing way, the place of Afro-American female writers in the tradition as they define it.

41. Gates, "The 'Blackness of Blackness,' " 696–97.

42. Ntozake Shange, *nappy edges* (New York, 1978), 4–5, 11.

43. Houston A. Baker, Jr., *The Journey Back* (Chicago, 1980), 109.

44. Gayle, Jr. See the other essays on the subject in that collection.

45. For a discussion of *The Color Purple*'s popularity see Trudier Harris, "On *The Color Purple*, Stereotypes, and Silence," *Black American Literature Forum*, 18 (Winter 1984), 155–61. The film adaptation of the novel has been the subject of intense and heated debate. Much of the criticism has been waged by black men who see the novel and the film as alike in their degrading depiction of black men.

Speaking in Tongues:

Dialogics, Dialectics, and the Black Woman Writer's Literary Tradition

Mae Gwendolyn Henderson

I am who I am, doing what I came to do, acting
upon you like a drug or a chisel to remind you of your me-ness, as
I discover you in myself.
　　　　　　　　—*Audre Lorde*, Sister Outsider (*emphasis mine*)

> *There's a noisy feelin' near the cracks*
> *crowdin' me . . . slips into those long, loopin' "B's"*
> *There's a noisy feelin' near the cracks*
> *crowdin' me . . . slips into those long, loopin' "B's"*
> *of Miss Garrison's handwritin' class;*
> *they become the wire hoops I must jump through.*
> *It spooks my alley, it spooks my play,*
> *more nosey now than noisy,*
> *　　lookin' for a tongue*
> *　　lookin' for a tongue*
> *　　to get holy in.*
> *Who can tell this feelin' where to set up church?*
> *Who can tell this noise where to go?*
> *A root woman workin' . . . a mo-jo,*
> *Just to the left of my ear.*
> 　　　　　　　　—*Cherry Muhanji*, Tight Spaces

Some years ago, three black feminist critics and scholars edited an anthology entitled *All the Women Are White, All the Blacks Are Men, But Some of Us Are Brave*,[1] suggesting in the title the unique and peculiar dilemma of black women. Since then it has perhaps become almost commonplace for literary critics, male and female, black and white, to note that black women have been discounted or unaccounted for in the "traditions" of black, women's, and American literature as well as in the contemporary literary-critical dialogue. More recently, black women writers have begun to receive token recognition as they are subsumed under the category of woman in the feminist critique and the category of black in the racial critique. Certainly these "gendered" and "racial" decodings of black women authors present strong and revisionary methods of reading, focusing as they do on literary discourses regarded as marginal to the dominant literary-critical tradition. Yet the "critical insights" of one reading might well become the "blind spots" of another reading. That is, by privileging one category of analysis at the expense of the other, each of these methods risks setting up what Fredric Jameson describes as "strategies of containment," which restrict or repress different or alternative readings.[2] More specifically, blindness to what Nancy Fraser describes as "the gender subtext" can be just as occluding as blindness to *the racial subtext* in the works of black women writers.[3]

Such approaches can result in exclusion at worst and, at best, a reading of part of the text as the whole—a strategy that threatens to replicate (if not valorize) the reification against which black women struggle in life and literature. What I propose is a theory of interpretation based on what I refer to as the "simultaneity of discourse," a term inspired by Barbara Smith's seminal work on black feminist criticism.[4] This concept is meant to signify a mode of reading which examines the ways in which the perspectives of race and gender, and their interrelationships, structure the discourse of black women writers. Such an approach is intended to acknowledge and overcome the limitations imposed by assumptions of internal identity (homogeneity) and the repression of internal differences (heterogeneity) in racial and gendered readings of works by black women writers. In other words, I propose a model that seeks to account for racial difference within gender identity and gender difference within racial identity. This approach represents my effort to avoid what one critic describes as the presumed "absolute and self-sufficient" *otherness* of the critical stance in order to allow the complex representations of black women writers to steer us away from "a simple and reductive paradigm of 'otherness.' "[5]

DISCURSIVE DIVERSITY: SPEAKING IN TONGUES

What is at once characteristic and suggestive about black wom-
en's writing is its interlocutory, or dialogic, character, reflecting not only a relationship with the "other(s)," but an internal
dialogue with the plural aspects of self that constitute the
matrix of black female subjectivity. The interlocutory character
of black women's writings is, thus, not only a consequence of
a dialogic relationship with an imaginary or "generalized
Other," but a dialogue with the aspects of "otherness" within
the self. The complex situatedness of the black woman as not
only the "Other" of the Same, but also as the "other" of the
other(s) implies, as we shall see, a relationship of difference
and identification with the "other(s)."

It is Mikhail Bakhtin's notion of dialogism and consciousness that provides the primary model for this approach. According to Bakhtin, each social group speaks in its own "social
dialect"—possesses its own unique language—expressing
shared values, perspectives, ideology, and norms. These social dialects become the "languages" of heteroglossia "intersect[ing] with each other in many different ways . . . As such
they all may be juxtaposed to one another, mutually supplement one another, contradict one another and be interrelated
dialogically."[6] Yet if language, for Bakhtin, is an expression of
social identity, then subjectivity (subjecthood) is constituted
as a social entity through the "role of [the] word as medium of
consciousness." Consciousness, then, like language, is shaped
by the social environment. ("Consciousness becomes consciousness only . . . in the process of social interaction.") Moreover,
"the semiotic material of the psyche is preeminently the word—
inner speech." Bakhtin in fact defines the relationship between
consciousness and inner speech even more precisely: "Analysis would show that the units of which inner speech is constituted are certain *whole entities . . . [resembling] the alternating
lines of a dialogue*. There was good reason why thinkers in
ancient times should have conceived of inner speech as *inner
dialogue*."[7] Thus consciousness becomes a kind of "inner speech"
reflecting "the outer word" in a process that links the psyche,
language, and social interaction.

It is the process by which these heteroglossic voices of the
other(s) "encounter one another and coexist in the conscious-

ness of real people—first and foremost in the creative consciousness of people who write novels,"[8] that speaks to the situation of black women writers in particular, "privileged" by a social positionality that enables them to speak in dialogically racial and gendered voices to the other(s) both within and without. If the psyche functions as an internalization of heterogeneous social voices, black women's speech/writing becomes at once a dialogue between self and society and between self and psyche. Writing as inner speech, then, becomes what Bakhtin would describe as "a unique form of collaboration with oneself" in the works of these writers.[9]

Revising and expanding Teresa de Lauretis's formulation of the "social subject and the relations of subjectivity to sociality," I propose a model that is intended not only to address "a subject en-gendered in the experiencing of race," but also what I submit is *a subject "racialized" in the experiencing of gender*.[10] Speaking both to and from the position of the other(s), black women writers must, in the words of Audre Lorde, deal not only with "the external manifestations of racism and sexism," but also "with the results of those distortions internalized within our consciousness of ourselves and one another."[11]

What distinguishes black women's writing, then, is the privileging (rather than repressing) of "the other in ourselves." Writing of Lorde's notion of self and otherness, black feminist critic Barbara Christian observes of Lorde what I argue is true to a greater or lesser degree in the discourse of black women writers: "As a black, lesbian, feminist, poet, mother, Lorde has, in her own life, had to search long and hard for *her* people. In responding to each of these audiences, in which a part of her identity lies, she refuses to give up her differences. In fact she uses them, as woman to man, black to white, lesbian to heterosexual, as a means of conducting creative dialogue."[12]

If black women speak from a multiple and complex social, historical, and cultural positionality which, in effect, constitutes black female subjectivity, Christian's term "creative dialogue" then refers to the expression of a multiple *dialogic of differences* based on this complex subjectivity. At the same time, however, black women enter into a *dialectic of identity* with those aspects of self shared with others. It is Hans-Georg Gadamer's "dialectical model of conversation," rather than

Bakhtin's dialogics of discourse, that provides an appropriate model for articulating a relation of mutuality and reciprocity with the "Thou"—or intimate other(s). Whatever the critic thinks of Gadamer's views concerning history, tradition, and the like, one can still find Gadamer's emphases—especially as they complement Bakhtin's—to be useful and productive. If the Bakhtinian model is primarily adversarial, assuming that verbal communication (and social interaction) is characterized by contestation with the other(s), then the Gadamerian model presupposes as its goal a language of consensus, communality, and even identification, in which "one claims to express the other's claim and even to understand the other better than the other understands [him or herself]." In the "I–Thou" relationship proposed by Gadamer, "the important thing is . . . to experience the 'Thou' truly as a 'Thou,' that is, not to overlook [the other's] claim and to listen to what [s/he] has to say to us." Gadamer's dialectic, based on a typology of the "hermeneutical experience," privileges tradition as "a genuine partner in communication, with which we have fellowship as does the 'I' with a 'Thou.'" For black and women writers, such an avowal of tradition in the subdominant order, of course, constitutes an operative challenge to the dominant order. It is this rereading of the notion of tradition within a field of gender and ethnicity that supports and enables the notion of community among those who share a common history, language, and culture. If Bakhtin's dialogic engagement with the Other signifies conflict, Gadamer's monologic acknowledgment of the Thou signifies the potential of agreement. If the Bakhtinian dialogic model speaks to the other within, then Gadamer's speaks to *the same within*. Thus, "the [dialectic] understanding of the [Thou]" (like the dialogic understanding of the other[s]) becomes "a form of self-relatedness."[13]

It is this notion of discursive difference and identity underlying the simultaneity of discourse which typically characterizes black women's writing. Through the multiple voices that enunciate her complex subjectivity, the black woman writer not only speaks familiarly in the discourse of the other(s), but as Other she is in contestorial dialogue with the hegemonic dominant and subdominant or "ambiguously (non)hegemonic" discourses.[14] These writers enter simultaneously into familial,

or *testimonial* and public, or *competitive* discourses—discourses
that both affirm and challenge the values and expectations of
the reader. As such, black women writers enter into testimonial discourse with black men as blacks, with white women as
women, and with black women as black women.[15] At the
same time, they enter into a competitive discourse with black
men as women, with white women as blacks, and with white
men as black women. If black women speak a discourse of
racial and gendered difference in the dominant or hegemonic
discursive order, they speak a discourse of racial and gender
identity and difference in the subdominant discursive order.
This dialogic of difference and dialectic of identity characterize
both black women's subjectivity and black women's discourse.
It is the complexity of these simultaneously homogeneous and
heterogeneous social and discursive domains out of which
black women write and construct themselves (as blacks and
women and, often, as poor, black women) that enables black
women writers authoritatively to speak to and engage both
hegemonic and ambiguously (non)hegemonic discourse.

Janie, the protagonist in Zora Neale Hurston's *Their Eyes
Were Watching God*, demonstrates how the dialectics/dialogics
of black and female subjectivity structure black women's
discourse.[16] Combining personal and public forms of discourse
in the court scene where she is on trial and fighting not only
for her life but against "lying thoughts" and "misunderstand-
ing," Janie addresses the judge, a jury composed of "twelve
more white men," and spectators ("eight or ten white women"
and "all the Negroes [men] for miles around" [274]). The
challenge of Hurston's character is that of the black woman
writer—to speak at once to a diverse audience about her
experience in a racist and sexist society where to be black and
female is to be, so to speak, "on trial." Janie not only speaks
in a discourse of gender and racial difference to the white
male judge and jurors, but also in a discourse of gender
difference (and racial identity) to the black male spectators
and a discourse of racial difference (and gender identity) to
the white women spectators. Significantly, it is the white men
who constitute both judge and jury, and, by virtue of their
control of power and discourse, possess the authority of life
and death over the black woman. In contrast, the black men
(who are convinced that the "nigger [woman] kin kill . . . jus'

as many niggers as she please") and white women (who "didn't seem too mad") read and witness/oppose a situation over which they exercise neither power nor discourse (225, 280).

Janie's courtroom discourse also emblematizes the way in which the categories of public and private break down in black women's discourse. In the context of Janie's courtroom scene, testimonial discourse takes on an expanded meaning, referring to both juridical, public, and dominant discourse as well as familial, private, and nondominant discourse. Testimonial, in this sense, derives its meaning from both "testimony" as an official discursive mode and "testifying," defined by Geneva Smitherman as "a ritualized form of . . . communication in which the speaker gives verbal witness to the efficacy, truth, and power of some experience in which [the group has] shared." The latter connotation suggests an additional meaning in the context of theological discourse where testifying refers to a "spontaneous expression to the church community [by whomever) feels the spirit."[17]

Like Janie, black women must speak in a plurality of voices as well as in a multiplicity of discourses. This discursive diversity, or simultaneity of discourse, I call "speaking in tongues." Significantly, glossolalia, or speaking in tongues, is a practice associated with black women in the Pentecostal Holiness church, the church of my childhood and the church of my mother. In the Holiness church (or as we called it, the Sanctified church), speaking unknown tongues (tongues known only to God) is in fact a sign of election, or holiness. As a trope it is also intended to remind us of Alice Walker's characterization of black women as artists, as "Creators," intensely rich in that spirituality which Walker sees as "the basis of Art."[18]

Glossolalia is perhaps the meaning most frequently associated with speaking in tongues. It is this connotation which emphasizes the particular, private, closed, and privileged communication between the congregant and the divinity. Inaccessible to the general congregation, this mode of communication is outside the realm of public discourse and foreign to the known tongues of humankind.

But there is a second connotation to the notion of speaking in tongues—one that suggests not glossolalia, but heteroglossia, the ability to speak in diverse known languages. While glossolalia refers to the ability to "utter the mysteries of the spirit," heteroglossia describes the ability to speak in the multiple languages of public discourse. If glossolalia suggests private, nonmediated, nondifferentiated univocality, heteroglossia connotes public, differentiated, social, mediated, dialogic discourse. Returning from the trope to the act of reading, perhaps we can say that speaking in tongues connotes both the semiotic, presymbolic babble (baby talk), as between mother and child— which Julia Kristeva postulates as the "mother tongue"—as well as the diversity of voices, discourses, and languages described by Mikhail Bakhtin.

Speaking in tongues, my trope for both glossolalia and heteroglossia, has a precise genealogical evolution in the Scriptures. In Genesis 11, God confounded the world's language when the city of Babel built a tower in an attempt to reach the heavens. Speaking in many and different tongues, the dwellers of Babel, unable to understand each other, fell into confusion, discord, and strife, and had to abandon the project. Etymologically, the name of the city Babel sounds much like the Hebrew word for "babble"—meaning confused, as in baby talk. Babel, then, suggests the two related, but distinctly different, meanings of speaking in tongues, meanings borne out in other parts of the Scriptures. The most common is that implied in 1 Corinthians 14—the ability to speak in unknown tongues. According to this interpretation, speaking in tongues suggests the ability to speak in and through the spirit. Associated with glossolalia—speech in unknown tongues—it is ecstatic, rapturous, inspired speech, based on a relation of intimacy and identification between the individual and God.

If Genesis tells of the disempowerment of a people by the introduction of different tongues, then Acts 2 suggests the empowerment of the disciples who, assembled on the day of Pentecost in the upper room of the temple in Jerusalem, "were filled with the Holy Spirit and began to speak in other tongues." Although the people thought the disciples had "imbibed a strange and unknown wine," it was the Holy Spirit which had driven them, filled with ecstasy, from the upper room to speak among the five thousand Jews surrounding the temple. The Scriptures tell us that the tribes of Israel all understood them, each in his own tongue. The Old Testament, then, suggests the dialogics of difference in its diversity of discourse, while the New Testament, in its unifying language of the spirit, suggests the dialectics of identity. If the Bakhtinian model suggests the multiplicity of speech as suggested in the dialogics of difference, then Gadamer's model moves toward a unity of understanding in its dialectics of identity.

It is the first as well as the second meaning which we privilege in speaking of black women writers: the first connoting polyphony, multivocality, and plurality of voices, and the second signifying intimate, private, inspired utterances. Through their intimacy with the discourse of the other(s), black women writers weave into their work competing and complementary discourses—discourses that seek both to adjudicate competing claims and witness common concerns.[19]

Also interesting is the link between the gift of tongues, the gift of prophecy, and the gift of interpretation. While distinguishing between these three gifts, the Scriptures frequently conflate or conjoin them. If to speak in tongues is to utter mysteries in and through the Spirit, to prophesy is to speak to others in a (diversity of) language(s) which the congregation can understand. The Scriptures would suggest that the disciples were able to perform both. I propose, at this juncture, an enabling critical fiction—that it is black women writers who are the modern-day apostles, empowered by experience to speak as poets and prophets in many tongues. With this critical gesture, I also intend to signify a deliberate intervention by black women writers into the canonic tradition of sacred/literary texts.[20]

A DISCURSIVE DILEMMA

In their works, black women writers have encoded oppression as a discursive dilemma, that is, their works have consistently raised the problem of the black woman's relationship to power and discourse. Silence is an important element of this code. The classic black woman's text *Their Eyes Were Watching God* charts the female protagonist's development from voicelessness to voice, from silence to tongues. Yet this movement does not exist without intervention by the other(s)—who speak for and about black women. In other words, it is not that black women, in the past, have had nothing to say, but rather that they have had no say. The absence of black female voices has allowed others to inscribe, or write, and ascribe to, or read, them. The notion of speaking in tongues, however, leads us away from an examination of how the Other has written/read black women and toward an examination of how black women have written the other(s)' writing/reading black women.

Using the notion of "speaking in tongues" as our model, let us offer a kind of paradigmatic reading of two works which encode and resist the material and discursive dilemma of the black woman writer. Sherley Anne Williams's *Dessa Rose* and Toni Morrison's *Sula* are novels that emphasize respectively the *inter*cultural/racial and *intra*cultural/racial sites from which black women speak, as well as the signs under which they speak in both these milieus.[21] Artificial though this separation may be—since, as we have seen, black women are located simultaneously within both these discursive domains—such a distinction makes possible an examination of black women's literary relations to both dominant and subdominant discourse. These works also allow us to compare the suppression of the black female voice in the dominant discourse with its repression in the subdominant discourse.[22] Finally, they provide models for the disruption of the dominant and subdominant discourse by black and female expression, as well as for the appropriation and transformation of these discourses.

The heroine of Sherley Anne Williams's first novel, *Dessa Rose*, is a fugitive slave woman introduced to the reader as "the Darky" by Adam Nehemiah, a white male writer interviewing her in preparation for a forthcoming book, *The Roots of Rebellion in the Slave Population and Some Means of Eradicating Them* (or, more simply, *The Work*). The opening section of the novel is structured primarily by notations from Nehemiah's journal, based on his interactions with the slave woman during her confinement in a root cellar while awaiting her fate at the gallows. The latter section, describing her adventures as a fugitive involved in a scam against unsuspecting slaveholders and traders, is narrated primarily in the voice of Dessa (as the slave woman calls herself) after she has managed, with the assistance of fellow slaves, to escape the root cellar. At the end of the novel, the writer-interviewer, Adam Nehemiah, still carrying around his notes for *The Work*, espies the fugitive Dessa.

Brandishing a poster advertising a reward for her recapture, and a physical description of her identifying markings (an R branded on the thigh and whip-scarred hips), Adam Nehemiah coerces the local sheriff into detaining Dessa for identification. Significantly, Adam Nehemiah, named after his precursor— the archetypal white male namer, creator, and interpreter— attempts not only to remand Dessa into slavery but to inscribe her experiences as a slave woman through a discourse that suppresses her voice. Like the Adam of Genesis, Nehemiah asserts the right of ownership through the privilege of naming. Not only is his claim of discursive and material power held together symbolically in his name, but his acts and his words conflate: Nehemiah not only wishes to capture Odessa (as he calls her) in words that are instructive in the preservation of slavery, but he wishes to confine her in material slavery. Just as the biblical Nehemiah constructed the wall to protect the Israelites against attack by their enemies, so Williams's Nehemiah sets out to write a manual designed to protect the American South against insurrection by the slaves. Ironically, the character of Nehemiah, a patriot and leader of the Jews after the years of Babylonian captivity, is reread in the context of the Old South as a racist and expert on the "sound management" of the slaves.[23]

Dessa fears that exposure of her scars/branding will confirm her slave status. As she awaits the arrival of Ruth, the white woman who abets in the perpetration of the scam, Dessa thinks to herself, "I could feel everyone of them scars, the one roped partway to my navel that the waist of my draws itched, the corduroyed welts across my hips, and R on my thighs" (223). What interests me here is the literal inscription of Dessa's body, signified by the whip marks and, more specifically, the branded R, as well as the white male writer-cum-reader's attempt to exercise discursive domination over Dessa. Seeking to inscribe black female subjectivity, the white male, in effect, relegates the black woman to the status of discursive object, or spoken subject. The location of the inscriptions—in the area of the genitalia—moreover, signals an attempt to inscribe the sign *slave* in an area that marks her as *woman* ("Scar tissue plowed through her pubic region so no hair would ever grow there again"[154]). The effect is to attempt to deprive the slave woman of her femininity and render the surface of her skin a parchment upon which meaning is etched by the whip (pen) of white patriarchal authority and sealed by the firebrand. Together, these inscriptions produce the meaning of black female subjectivity in the discursive domain of slavery.[24] Importantly, the literal inscription of the flesh emphasizes what Monique Wittig, insisting on "the *material* oppression of individuals by discourses," describes as the "unrelenting tyranny that [male discourses] exert upon our *physical* and *mental* selves" (emphasis mine).[25] Dessa is ordered by the sheriff to lift her skirt so that these inscriptions can be "read" by her potential captors. (Perhaps we should read the R on Dessa's thigh as part of an acrostic for *Read*.) The signifying function of her scars is reinforced when Dessa recognizes that "[Nehemiah] wouldn't have to say nothing. Sheriff would see [i.e., read] that for himself"(223). Her remarks also suggest the mortal consequence of such a reading, or misreading:[26] "This [the scars] was what would betray me . . . these white mens would kill me"(223).

If Williams's *Dessa Rose* contains a representation of the inscription of *black female* in the dominative white and male discourse, then Morrison's *Sula* contains a representation of *female* ascription in black subdominative discourse. If in the context of the white community's discourse Dessa is suppressed as woman *and* black, in the discourse of the black community she is repressed as woman.

Like Dessa, Sula is marked. Unlike Dessa, Sula is marked from birth. Hers is a mark of nativity—a biological rather than cultural inscription, appropriate in this instance because it functions to mark her as a "naturally" inferior female within the black community.[27] The birthmark, "spread[ing] from the middle of the lid toward the eyebrow" (45), is associated with a series of images. For her mother, Hannah, Sula's birthmark "looked more and more like a stem and a rose" (64). Although in European and Eurocentric culture the rose is the gift of love as well as the traditional romantic symbol of female beauty and innocence (lily-white skin and rose blush), it is a symbol that has been appropriated by black women writers from Frances Harper, who uses it as a symbol of romantic love, to Alice Walker, who associates it with sexual love.[28]

Jude, the husband of Nel, Sula's best friend, refers to the birthmark as a "copperhead" and, later, as "the rattlesnake over her eye." If the image of the rose suggests female romantic love and sexuality, then the snake evokes the archetypal Garden and the story of Eve's seduction by the serpent.[29] The association is significant in light of the subsequent seduction scene between Jude and Sula, for it is Jude's perception of the snake imagery which structures his relationship with Sula, suggesting not only that the meaning he ascribes to the birthmark reflects the potential of his relationship with her, but that, on a broader level, it is the "male gaze" which constitutes female subjectivity. At the same time, Morrison redeploys the role of Other in a way that suggests how the black woman as Other is used to constitute (black) male subjectivity.

The community, "clearing up," as it thought, "the meaning of the birthmark over her eye," tells the reader that "it was not a stemmed rose, or a snake, it was Hannah's ashes marking Sula from the very beginning" (99). (That Sula had watched her mother burn to death was her grandmother's contention and the community gossip.) If Jude represents the subject constituted in relation to the black woman as Other, the community represents a culture constituted in relation to the black woman as Other:

> Their conviction of Sula's evil changed them in accountable yet mysterious ways. Once the source of their personal misfortune was identified, they had leave to protect and love one another. They began to cherish their husbands and wives, protect their children, repair their homes and in general band together against the devil in their midst (102).

Sula signifies, for the community, the chaos and evil against which it must define and protect itself. Convinced that she bears the mark of the devil because of her association with Shadrack, the town reprobate, the community closes ranks against one who transgresses the boundaries prescribed for women.

For Shadrack, the shell-shocked World War I veteran who has become the community pariah, Sula's birthmark represents "the mark of the fish he loved"—the tadpole (134). A symbol of the primordial beginnings of life in the sea, the tadpole represents potential, transformation, and rebirth. Such an image contrasts with the apocalyptic ending of life by fire suggested by the community's perception of Hannah's ashes.[30] As an amphibious creature, the tadpole has the capacity to live both terrestrially and aquatically. Etymologically, Sula's name is derived from the designation of a genus of seabird, again an image associated with a dual environment—aquatic and ariel. These contrasts suggestively position Sula at the crossroads or intersection of life and death, land and sea, earth and air. Thus both the mark and the designation are particularly appropriate for the black woman as one situated within two social domains (black and female) and, as such, implicated in both a racial and gendered discourse.

But it is the black community—the Bottom—which provides the setting for the action in Morrison's novel, and it is the men who have the final say in the community: "It was the men," writes the narrator, "who gave [Sula] the final label, who *fingerprinted* her for all time" (emphasis mine; 197). The men in the community speak a racial discourse that reduces Sula finally to her sexuality: "The word was passed around" that "Sula slept with *white* men" (emphasis mine; 97). It is thus her sexuality, read through the race relation, which structures her subjectivity within the male-dominated discourse of the black community.

The power of male discourse and naming is also suggested in the epithet directed to the twelve-year-old Sula as she, along with her friend Nel, saunters by Edna Finch's ice cream parlor one afternoon, passing the old and young men of the Bottom:

Pig meat. The words were in all their minds. And one of them, one of the young ones, said it aloud. . . . His name was Ajax, a twenty-one-year-old pool haunt of sinister beauty. Graceful and economical in every movement, he held a place of envy with men of all ages for his magnificently foul mouth. In fact he seldom cursed, and the epithets he chose were dull, even harmless. His reputation was derived from the way he handled the words. When he said "hell" he hit the *h* with his lungs and the impact was greater than the achievement of the most

imaginative foul mouth in the town. He could say "shit"
with a nastiness impossible to imitate (43).

Not only does the language itself take on a special potency
when exercised by males, but the epithet "pigmeat" which
Ajax confers on Sula still has a powerful hold on her seventeen years later, when at twenty-nine, having traveled across
the country and returned to the Bottom, she is greeted by the
now thirty-eight-year-old Ajax at her screen door: "Sula . . .
was curious. She knew nothing about him except the word he
had called out to her years ago and the feeling he had excited
in her then" (110).

The images associated with Sula's birthmark connote, as we
have seen, a plurality of meanings. These images become not
only symbols of opposition and ambiguity associated with the
stemmed rose, snake, fire, and tadpole, but they evoke the
qualities of permanence and mutability (nature and culture)
inherent in the sign of the birthmark, the meaning and va-
lence of which changes with the reading and the reader. At
one point, Nel, Sula's complement in the novel, describes her
as one who "helped others define themselves," that is, one
who takes on the complementary aspect of the Other in the
process of constituting subjectivity. As if to underscore Sula's
signifying function as absence or mutability, Sula is described
as having "no center" and "no ego," "no speck around which
to grow" (103). The plurality and flux of meaning ascribed to
the birthmark share some of the characteristics of the Sign or,
perhaps more precisely, the Signifier. Sula's association with
the birthmark gradually evolves, through synecdoche, into an
identification between the subject/object and the Sign. Thus
her entry into the subdominative discursive order confers on
her the status of "a free-floating signifier," open to diverse
interpretations.

The inscription (writing) of Dessa and the ascription (reading) of Sula together encode the discursive dilemma of black
women in hegemonic and ambiguously (non)hegemonic discursive contexts. However, these works also embody a code
of resistance to the discursive and material dominance of
black women. To different degrees and in different ways,
Williams and Morrison fashion a counterdiscourse within their
texts.

DISRUPTION AND REVISION

In negotiating the discursive dilemma of their characters, these writers accomplish two objectives: the self-inscription of black womanhood, and the establishment of a dialogue of discourses with the other(s). The self-inscription of black women requires disruption, rereading and rewriting the conventional and canonical stories, as well as revising the conventional generic forms that convey these stories. Through this interventionist, intertextual, and revisionary activity, black women writers enter into dialogue with the discourses of the other(s). Disruption—the initial response to hegemonic and ambiguously (non)hegemonic discourse—and revision (rewriting or rereading) together suggest a model for reading black and female literary expression.

Dessa's continued rejection of Adam Nehemiah's inscription suggests that we must read with some measure of credence her claims of being mis-recognized. ("I don't even know this master, Mistress," she says. "They mistook me for another Dessa, Mistress" [226–227].) Ultimately, Dessa's insistence on *meconnaissance* is vindicated in the failure of Nehemiah's attempts either to *con*fine her in the social system or *de*fine her in the dominant discourse.

Dessa not only succeeds in rupturing the narrator's discourse at the outset of the novel through a series of interventionist acts—singing, evasion, silence, nonacquiescence, and dissemblance—but she employs these strategies to effect her escape and seize discursive control of the story.[31] Moreover, Dessa's repeated use of the word *track* (a term connoting both pursuit and inscription) in reference to Nehemiah takes on added significance in the context of both her inscription and revision. Tracking becomes the object of her reflections: "Why this white man *track* me down like he owned me, like a bloodhound on my *trail*," and later, "crazy white man, *tracking* me all cross the country like he owned me" (emphasis mine; 225). In other words, Nehemiah *tracks* Dessa in an attempt to establish ownership—that is, the colonization—of her body. Yet tracking also suggests that Dessa's flight becomes a text that she writes and Nehemiah reads. His tracking (i.e., reading of Dessa's text) thus becomes the means by which he

attempts to capture her (i.e., suppress her voice in the production of his own text).

If the pursuit/flight pattern emblematizes a strategic engagement for discursive control, Dessa's tracks also mark her emergence as narrator of her own story. It is her escape—loosely
speaking, her "making tracks"—that precludes the closure/
completion of Nehemiah's book. The story of Dessa's successful revolt and escape, in effect, prefigures the rewriting of *The
Work*—Nehemiah's projected treatise on the control of slaves
and the prevention of slave revolts. The latter part of the
novel, recounted from Dessa's perspective and in her own
voice, establishes her as the successful author of her own
narrative. Tracking thus becomes a metaphor for writing/reading
from the white male narrator's perspective, and a metaphor
for revision (*re*writing/*re*reading) from Dessa's. Creating her
own track therefore corresponds to Dessa's assumption of
discursive control of the novel, that is, the telling of her own
story. In flight, then, Dessa challenges the material and discursive elements of her oppression and, at the same time,
provides a model for writing as struggle.

Nehemiah's inability to capture Dessa in print is paralleled,
finally, in his failure to secure her recapture. As Dessa walks
out of the sheriff's office, Nehemiah cries: "I know it's her . . .
I got her down here in my book." Leaving, Dessa tells the
reader, "And he reach and took out that little black-bound
pad he wrote in the whole time I knowed him" (231). But the
futility of his efforts is represented in the reactions of the
onlookers to the unbound pages of Nehemiah's notebook as
they tumble and scatter to the floor:

> [Sheriff] Nemi, ain't nothing but some scribbling on
> here. . . . Can't no one read this.
>
> [Ruth] And these [pages] is blank, sheriff (232).

Finally, in two dramatic acts of self-entitlement, Dessa reaf-
firms her ability to name herself and her own experience. In
the first instance, she challenges Nehemiah's efforts to capture her—in person and in print: "Why, he didn't even know
how to call my name—talking about *Odessa*" (emphasis mine;
225). And in the second, after her release she informs Ruth,

her white accomplice and alleged mistress, "My name Dessa, Dessa Rose. Ain't no *O* to it" (232). She is, of course, distinguishing between Odessa, an ascription by the white, male slave master and used by both Nehemiah and Ruth, and Dessa, her entitlement proper. Her rejection of the *O* signifies her rejection of the inscription of her body by the other(s). In other words, Dessa's repudiation of the *O* (Otherness?) signifies her always already presence—what Ralph Ellison describes as the unquestioned humanity of the slave. She deletes nothing—except the white, male other's inscription/ascription.[32]

At the conclusion of the novel, Dessa once again affirms the importance of writing oneself and one's own history. It is a responsibility that devolves upon the next generation, privileged with a literacy Dessa herself has been denied: "My mind wanders. This is why I have it wrote down, why I has the child say it back. I never will forget Nemi trying to read [and write] me, knowing I had put myself in his hands. Well, *this* the childrens have heard from our own lips" (236). Yet, as Walker might say, the story bears the mother's signature.[33]

While Dessa, through interventions and rewriting, rejects white, male attempts to write and read black female subjectivity, Sula, through disruption and rereading, repudiates black male readings of black female subjectivity. (Significantly, black males, like white females, lack the power to *write*, but not the power to *read* black women.) If it is her sexuality which structures Sula within the confines of black (male) discourse, it is also her sexuality which creates a rupture in that discourse. It is through the act of sexual intercourse that Sula discovers "the center of . . . silence" and a "loneliness so profound *the word itself had no meaning*" (emphasis mine; 106). The "desperate terrain" which she reaches, the "high silence of orgasm" (112), is a nodal point that locates Sula in the interstices of the closed system of (black) male signification. She has, in effect, "[leapt] from the edge" of discourse "into soundlessness" and "[gone] down howling" (106). Howling, a unary movement of nondifferentiated sound, contrasts with the phonic differentiation on which the closed system of language is based. Like the birthmark, which is the symbolic sign of life, the howl is the first sound of life—not yet broken down and differentiated to emerge as intersubjective communication, or discourse. The howl, signifying a prediscursive mode, thus becomes an act of self-reconstitution as well as an act of subversion or resistance to the "network of signification" represented by the symbolic order. The "high silence of orgasm" and the howl allow temporary retreats from or breaks in the dominant discourse. Like Dessa's evasions and interventions, Sula's silences and howls serve to disrupt or subvert the "symbolic function of the language." It is precisely these violations or transgressions of the symbolic order that allow for the expression of the suppressed or repressed aspects of black female subjectivity. The reconstitutive function of Sula's sexuality is suggested in the image of the "post-coital privateness in which she met herself, welcomed herself, and joined herself in matchless harmony" (107). The image is that of symbiosis and fusion—a stage or condition represented in psychoanalysis as pre-Oedipal and anterior to the acquisition of language or entry into the symbolic order.[34]

It is through the howl of orgasm that Sula discovers a prediscursive center of experience that positions her at a vantage point outside of the dominant discursive order. The howl is a form of speaking in tongues and a linguistic disruption that serves as the precondition for Sula's entry into language. Unless she breaks the conventional structures and associations of the dominant discourse, Sula cannot enter through the interstices.[35] (This reading of *Sula*, in effect, reverses the biblical movement from contestorial, public discourse to intimate, familial discourse.)

In contrast to the howl, of course, is the stunning language of poetic metaphor with which Sula represents her lover and the act of love:

If I take a chamois and rub real hard on the bone, right on the ledge of your cheek bone, some of the black will disappear. It will flake away into the chamois and underneath there will be gold leaf . . . And if I take a nail file or even Eva's old paring knife . . . and scrape away at the gold, it will fall away and there will be alabaster . . . Then I can take a chisel and small tap hammer and tap away at the alabaster. It will crack then like ice under the pick, and through the breaks I will see the [fertile] loam (112).

It is an eloquent passage—not of self-representation, however, but of representation of the male other. If Sula cannot
find the language, the trope, the form, to embody her own
"experimental" life, she "engage[s] her tremendous curiosity
and her gift for metaphor" in the delineation of her lover. The
poetic penetration of her lover through the layers of black,
gold leaf, alabaster, and loam signals that her assumption of a
"masculine" role parallels the appropriation of the male voice,
prerequisite for her entry into the symbolic order. (Such an
appropriation is, of course, earlier signaled by the association
of the birthmark with the stemmed rose, the snake, the
tadpole—a series of phallic images.)

I propose, however, in the spirit of the metaphor, to take it
one step further and suggest that the imagery and mode of
the prose poem form a kind of model for the deconstructive
function of black feminist literary criticism—and to the extent
that literature itself is always an act of interpretation, a model
for the deconstructive function of black women's writing—that
is, to interpret or interpenetrate the signifying structures of
the dominant and subdominant discourse in order to formulate a critique and, ultimately, a transformation of the hegemonic white and male symbolic order.

If Williams's primary emphasis is on the act of rewriting,
then Morrison's is on the act of rereading. Perhaps the best
example of Sula's deconstructive rereading of the black male
text is exemplified in her reformulation of Jude's "whiny tale"
describing his victimization as a black man in a world that the
"white man running":

I don't know what the fuss is about. I mean, everything
in the world loves you. White men love you. They spend
so much time worrying about your penis they forget their
own. The only thing they want to do is cut off a nigger's
privates. And if that ain't love and respect I don't know
what is. And white women? They chase you all to every
corner of the earth, feel for you under every bed . . .
Now ain't that love? They think rape soon's they see you,
and if they don't get the rape they looking for, they
scream it anyway just so the search won't be in vain.
Colored women worry themselves into bad health just
trying to hang on to your cuffs. Even little children—

white and black, boys and girls—spend all their childhood eating their hearts out 'cause they think you don't
love them. And if that ain't enough, you love yourselves.
Nothing in this world loves a black man more than another black man (89).

Adrienne Munich points out that "Jude's real difficulties allow
him to maintain his male identity, to exploit women, and not
to examine himself." Sula, she argues, turns "Jude's story of
powerlessness into a tale of power." Through a deconstructive
reading of his story, Sula's interpretation demonstrates how
Jude uses "racial politics [to mask] sexual politics."[36]
If Sula's silences and howls represent breaks in the symbolic
order, then her magnificent prose poem looks to the possibilities of appropriating the male voice as a prerequisite for entry
into that order. Dessa similarly moves from intervention to
appropriation and revision of the dominant discourse. As the
author of her own story, Dessa writes herself into the dominant discourse and, in the process, transforms it. What these
two works suggest in variable, but interchangeable, strategies
is that, in both dominant and subdominant discourses, the
initial expression of a marginal presence takes the form of
disruption—a departure or a break with conventional semantics and/or phonetics. This rupture is followed by a rewriting or
rereading of the dominant story, resulting in a "delegitimation"
of the prior story or a "displacement" which shifts attention
"to the other side of the story."[37] Disruption—the initial response to hegemonic and ambiguously (non)hegemonic discourse—and the subsequent response, revision (rewriting or
rereading), together represent a progressive model for black
and female utterance. I propose, in an appropriation of a
current critical paradigm, that Sula's primal scream constitutes
a "womblike matrix" in which soundlessness can be transformed into utterance, unity into diversity, formlessness into
form, chaos into art, silence into tongues, and glossolalia into
heteroglossia.
It is this quality of speaking in tongues, that is, multivocality,
I further propose, that accounts in part for the current popularity and critical success of black women's writing. The engagement of multiple others broadens the audience for black
women's writing, for like the disciples of Pentecost who spoke

in diverse tongues, black women, speaking out of the specificity of their racial and gender experiences, are able to communicate in a diversity of discourses. If the ability to communicate
accounts for the popularity of black women writers, it also
explains much of the controversy surrounding some of this
writing. Black women's writing speaks with what Mikhail
Bakhtin would describe as heterological or "centrifugal force"
but (in a sense somewhat different from that which Bakhtin
intended) also unifying or "centripetal force."[38] This literature speaks as much to the notion of commonality and universalism as it does to the sense of difference and diversity.

Yet the objective of these writers is not, as some critics
suggest, to move from margin to center, but to remain on
the borders of discourse, speaking from the vantage point of the
insider/outsider. As Bakhtin further suggests, fusion with
the (dominant) Other can only duplicate the tragedy or mis-
fortune of the Other's dilemma. On the other hand, as Gadamer
makes clear, "there is a kind of experience of the 'Thou' that
seeks to discover things that are typical in the behaviour of
[the other] and is able to make predictions concerning another
person on the basis of [a commonality] of experience."[39] To
maintain this insider/outsider position, or perhaps what Myra
Jehlen calls the "extra-terrestrial fulcrum" that Archimedes
never acquired, is to see the other, but also to see what the
other cannot see, and to use this insight to enrich both our
own and the other's understanding.[40]

As gendered and racial subjects, black women speak/write
in multiple voices—not all simultaneously or with equal weight,
but with various and changing degrees of intensity, privileging one *parole* and then another. One discovers in these writers a kind of internal dialogue reflecting an *intrasubjective*
engagement with the *intersubjective* aspects of self, a dialectic
neither repressing difference nor, for that matter, privileging
identity, but rather expressing engagement with the social
aspects of self ("the other[s] in ourselves"). It is this subjective
plurality (rather than the notion of the cohesive or fractured
subject) that, finally, allows the black woman to become an
expressive site for a dialectics/dialogics of identity and difference.

Unlike Bloom's "anxiety of influence" model configuring a
white male poetic tradition shaped by an adversarial dialogue
between literary fathers and sons (as well as the appropriation

of this model by Joseph Skerrett and others to discuss black male writers), and unlike Gilbert and Gubar's "anxiety of authorship" model informed by the white women writer's sense of "dis-ease" within a white patriarchal tradition, the present model configures a tradition of black women writers generated less by neurotic anxiety or dis-ease than by an emancipatory impulse which freely engages both hegemonic and ambiguously (non)hegemonic discourse.[41] Summarizing Morrison's perspectives, Andrea Stuart perhaps best expresses this notion:

> I think you [Morrison] summed up the appeal of black women writers when you said that white men, quite naturally, wrote about themselves and their world; white women tended to write about white men because they were so close to them as husbands, lovers and sons; and black men wrote about white men as the oppressor or the yardstick against which they measured themselves. Only black women writers were not interested in writing about white men and therefore they freed literature to take on other concerns.[42]

In conclusion, I return to the gifts of the Holy Spirit: 1 Corinthians 12 tells us that "the [one] who speaks in tongues should pray that [s/he] may interpret what [s/he] says." Yet the Scriptures also speak to interpretation as a separate gift—the ninth and final gift of the Spirit. Might I suggest that if black women writers speak in tongues, then it is we black feminist critics who are charged with the hermeneutical task of interpreting tongues?

NOTES

1. Gloria Hull, Patricia Bell Scott, and Barbara Smith, eds., *All the Women Are White, All the Blacks Are Men, But Some of Us Are Brave* (Old Westbury, N.Y.: Feminist Press, 1982).
2. Fredric Jameson, *The Political Unconscious: Narrative as a Socially Symbolic Act* (Ithaca, N.Y.: Cornell University Press, 1981), 53.
3. The phrase "gender subtext" is used by Nancy Fraser (and attributed to Dorothy Smith) in Fraser's critique of Habermas in Nancy Fraser, "What's Critical about Critical Theory?" in Seyla Benehabib and Drucilla Cornell, eds., *Feminism as Critique* (Minneapolis: University of Minnesota Press, 1987), 42.

4. See Barbara Smith, ed., *Home Girls: A Black Feminist Anthology* (New York: Kitchen Table: Women of Color Press, 1983), xxxii.

5. John Carlos Rowe, "To Live Outside the Law, You Must Be Honest: The Authority of the Margin in Contemporary Theory," *Cultural Critique* I (2): 67–68.

6. Mikhail Bakhtin, "Discourse in the Novel," reprinted in Michael Holquist, ed., *The Dialogic Imagination: Four Essays by M. M. Bakhtin* (Austin: University of Texas Press, 1981), 292. Bakhtin's social groups are designated according to class, religion, generation, region, and profession. The interpretative model I propose extends and rereads Bakhtin's theory from the standpoint of race and gender, categories absent in Bakhtin's original system of social and linguistic stratification.

7. V. N. Volosinov [Mikhail Bakhtin], *Marxism and the Philosophy of Language* (New York: Seminar Press, 1973), 11, 29, 38. Originally published in Russian as *Marksizm I Filosofija Jazyka* (Leningrad, 1930). Notably, this concept of the "subjective psyche" constituted primarily as a "social entity" distinguishes the Bakhtinian notion of self from the Freudian notion of identity.

8. Bakhtin, "Discourse in the Novel," 292.

9. According to Bakhtin, "The processes that basically define the content of the psyche occur not inside but outside the individual organism . . . Moreover, the psyche enjoys extraterritorial status . . . [as] a social entity that penetrates inside the organism of the individual personal" (*Marxism and the Philosophy of Language* 25, 39). Explicating Caryl Emerson's position on Bakhtin, Gary Saul Morson argues that selfhood "derives from an internalization of the voices a person has heard, and each of these voices is saturated with social and ideological values." "Thought itself," he writes, "is but 'inner speech,' and inner speech is outer speech that we have learned to 'speak' in our heads while retaining the full register of conflicting social values." See Gary Saul Morson, "Dialogue, Monologue, and the Social: A Reply to Ken Hirshkop," in Morson, ed., *Bakhtin: Essays and Dialogues on His Work* (Chicago: University of Chicago Press, 1986), 85.

10. Teresa de Lauretis, *Technologies of Gender* (Bloomington: Indiana University Press, 1987), 2.

11. Audre Lorde, "Eye to Eye," included in *Sister Outsider* (Tramansburg, N.Y.: Crossing Press, 1984), 147.

12. Barbara Christian, "The Dynamics of Difference: Book Review of Audre Lorde's *Sister Outsider*," in *Black Feminist Criticism: Perspectives in Black Women Writers* (New York: Pergamon Press, 1985), 209.

13. While acknowledging the importance of historicism, I can only agree with Frank Lentricchia's conclusion that in some respects Gadamer's "historicist argument begs more questions than it answers. If we can applaud the generous intention, virtually unknown in structuralist quarters, of recapturing history for textual interpetation, then we can only be stunned by the implication of what he has uncritically to say about authority, the power of tradition, knowledge, our institutions, and our attitudes." See Frank Lentricchia, *After the New Criticism* (Chicago: University of Chicago Press, 1980), 153. Certainly, Gadamer's model privileges the individual's relation to history and tradition in a way that might seem problematic in formulating a discursive model for the "noncanonical" or marginalized writer. However, just as the above model of dialogics is meant to extend Bakhtin's notion of class difference to encompass gender and race, so the present model revises and limits Gadamer's notion of tradition. See Hans-Georg Gadamer, *Truth and Method* (New York: Seabury Press, 1975), 321– 325. My introduction to the significance of Gadamer's work for my own reading of black women writers was first suggested by Don Bialostosky's excellent paper entitled "Dialectic and Anti-Dialectic: A Bakhtinian Critique of Gadamer's Dialectical Model of Conversation," delivered at the International Association of Philosophy and Literature in May 1989 at Emory University in Atlanta, Georgia.

14. I extend Rachel Blau DuPlessis's term designating white women as a group privileged by race and oppressed by gender to black men as a group privileged by gender and oppressed by race. In this instance, I use "ambiguously (non)hegemonic" to signify the discursive status of both these groups.

15. Black women enter into dialogue with other black women in a discourse that I would characterize as primarily testimonial, resulting from a similar discursive and

social positionality. It is this commonality of history, culture, and language which, finally, constitutes the basis of a tradition of black women's expressive culture. In terms of actual literary dialogue among black women, I would suggest a relatively modern provenance of such a tradition, but again, one based primarily on a dialogue of affirmation rather than contestation. As I see it, this dialogue begins with Alice Walker's response to Zora Neale Hurston. Although the present article is devoted primarily to contestorial function of black women's writing, my forthcoming work (of which the present essay constitutes only a part) deals extensively with the relationships among black women writers.

16. Zora Neale Hurston, *Their Eyes Were Watching God* (1937; report., Urbana: University of Illinois Press, 1978). All subsequent references in the text.

17. Geneva Smitherman, *Talkin and Testifyin: The Language of Black America* (Detroit: Wayne State University Press, 1986), 58.

18. Alice Walker, "In Search of Our Mothers' Gardens," in *In Search of Our Mothers' Gardens: Womanist Prose* (New York: Harcourt Brace Jovanovich, 1984), 232.

19. Not only does such an approach problematize conventional categories and boundaries of discourse, but, most importantly, it signals the collapse of the unifying consensus posited by the discourse of universalism and reconstructs the concept of unity in diversity implicit in the discourse of difference.

20. The arrogant and misogynistic Paul tells us, "I thank God that I speak in tongues more than all of you. But in church I would rather speak five intelligible words to instruct others [i.e., to prophesy] than ten thousand words in a tongue." Even though we are perhaps most familiar with Paul's injunction to women in the church to keep silent, the prophet Joel, in the Old Testament, speaks to a diversity of voices that includes women: "In the last days, God says, I will pour out my Spirit on all people. Your sons and *daughters* will prophesy . . . Even on my servants, both men and *women*, I will pour out my Spirit in those days, and they will prophesy" (emphasis mine). I am grateful to the Rev. Joseph Stephens whose vast scriptural knowledge helped guide me through these and other revelations.

21. Sherley Anne Williams, *Dessa Rose* (New York; William Morrow, 1986), and Toni Morrison, *Sula* (New York: Alfred A. Knopf, 1973; report., Bantam, 1975). Page references for these two works are given in the text.

22. I draw on the distinction between the political connotation of *supression* and the psychological connotation of *repression*. Suppression results from external pressures and censorship imposed by the dominant culture, while repression refers to the internal self-censorship and silencing emanating from the subdominative community.

23. Nehemiah, a minor prophet in the Old Testament, is best remembered for rebuilding the walls around Jerusalem in order to fortify the city against invasion by hostile neighbors of Israel. Under his governorship, Ezra and the Levites instructed the people in the law of Moses "which the Lord had commanded for Israel." He is represented as a reformer who restored the ancient ordinances regarding proper observance of the Sabbath and the collection of the tithes; he also enforced bans against intermarriage with the Gentiles. He is perhaps most noted for the reply he sent, while rebuilding the walls, to a request from his enemies, Sanballat and Gesham, to meet with him: "I am doing a great *work* and cannot go down" (emphasis mine). Williams's Nehemiah, like his prototype, is devoted to the completion of a project he calls *The Work*—in this instance a book entitled *The Roots of Rebellion in the Slave Population and Some Means of Eradicating Them*. Significantly, the name of Williams's character, Adam Nehemiah, reverses the name of Nehemiah Adams, author of *A South-side View of Slavery* (1854), and a Boston minister who wrote an account of his experiences in the South from a point of view apostate to the northern antislavery cause.

24. The mark of the whip inscribes Dessa as a slave while she remains within the discursive domain of slavery—a domain architecturally figured by the prison from which she escapes, but also a domain legally and more discursively defined by the Fugitive Slave Act, the runaway ads, and the courts and depositions of the nation. Note, however, that within the northern lecture halls and the slave narratives—the spatial and discursive domains of abolitionism—the marks do not identify an individual, but signify upon the character and nature of the institution of slavery.

25. Monique Wittig, "The Straight Mind," *Feminist Issues* 1 (Summer 1980): 105–106.

26. Although the status of slave is not a "misreading" within the discursive domain of slavery, it is clearly a misreading according to Dessa's self-identification.

27. One might describe Sula's birthmark as an iconicized representation rather than, strictly speaking, an inscription. For our purposes, however, it has the force of a sign marking her birth or entry into black discourse.

28. Morrison's epigram to the novel highlights the cultural significance of the birthmark by quoting from Tennessee Williams's *The Rose Tattoo*: "Nobody knew my rose of the world but me . . . I had too much glory. They don't want glory like that in nobody's heart." In "The Mission of the Flowers," Harper describes the rose as "a thing of joy and beauty" whose mission is to "lay her fairest buds and flowers upon the altars of love." Walker's protagonist Celie compares her own sex to the "inside of a wet rose." See Frances E. W. Harper, *Idylls of the Bible* (Philadelphia: George S. Ferguson, 1901), quoted in Erlene Stetson, ed., *Black Sister* (Bloomington: Indiana University Press, 1981), 34–6, and Alice Walker, *The Color Purple* (New York: Harcourt Brace Jovanovich, 1982), 69. In naming her own character Dessa *Rose*, Williams not only plays on the above connotations, but links them, at the same time, to the transcendence implicit in "arising" and the insurgence suggested in "uprising."

29. Signifying perhaps on Hawthorne's short story "The Birthmark," Sula's mark can be reread as a sign of human imperfection and mortality, a consequence of Eve's seduction by the serpent in the Garden.

30. The fire and water image, associated with the tadpole and ashes, respectively complement and contrast with that of the snake—a symbol of death and renewal—and that of the stemmed rose—an image suggesting not only love and sexuality, but the beauty and brevity of life as a temporal experience.

31. I do not develop here the interviewer's misreadings of Dessa in the early part of the novel, nor the specific insurgent strategies with which Dessa continually outwits him. These details are treated extensively, however, in my article on Williams's "Meditations on History," the short story on which the novel is based. It appears in Linda Kauffman, ed., *Gender and Theory: A Dialogue between the Sexes*, vol. 2 (London: Basil Blackwell, 1989).

32. Williams also uses onomastics to signify upon a less rebellious female heroine, somewhat more complicitous with female ascription by the Other. See Kaja Silverman's excellent discussion of Pauline Reage's *The Story of O*, in her article "Histoire d'O: The Construction of a Female Subject," in Carole S. Vance, ed., *Pleasure and Danger: Exploring Female Sexuality* (Boston: Routledge and Kegan Paul, 1984).

33. Williams, in her earlier version of this story, "Meditations on History," privileges orality (rather than writing)—as I attempt to demonstrate in my article "W(R)iting *The Work* and working the Rites," in Kauffman, *Gender and Theory*, vol. 2.

34. Positing a kind of "mother tongue," Julia Kristeva argues that "language as symbolic function constitutes itself at the cost of repressing instinctual drive and continuous relation to the mother." This order of expression, she contends, is presymbolic and linked with the mother tongue. According to Nelly Furman's interpretation, the existence of this order "does not refute the symbolic but is anterior to it, and associated with the maternal aspects of language. This order, which [Kristeva] calls 'semiotic,' is not a separate entity from the symbolic, on the contrary, it is the system which supports symbolic coherence." Continuing, Furman quotes Josette Feral in establishing a dialogical relationship between the semiotic and symbolic orders "which places the semiotic *inside* the symbolic as a condition of the symbolic, while positing the symbolic as a condition of the semiotic and founded on its repression. Now it happens that the Name-of-the-Father, in order to establish itself, needs the repression of the mother. It needs this otherness in order to reassure itself about its unity and identity, but is unwittingly affected by this otherness that is working within it." Nelly Furman, "The Politics of Language: Beyond the Gender Principle?" in Gayle Greene and Coppelia Kahn, eds., *Making A Difference: Feminist Literary Criticism* (London and New York: Methuen, 1985), 72–73.

35. In contrast to Dessa, who disrupts the dominant discourse, Sula would seem to disrupt not only discourse but, indeed, language itself.

36. Adrienne Munich, "Feminist Criticism and Literary Tradition," in Greene and Kahn, *Making a Difference*, 245–254.

37. Rachel Blau DuPlessis uses these terms to describe the "tactics of revisionary mythopoesis" created by women poets whose purpose is to "attack cultural hegemony." "Narrative displacement is like breaking the sentence," writes DuPlessis, "because it offers the possibility of speech to the female in the case, giving voice to the muted. Narrative delegitimation 'breaks the sequence'; a realignment that puts the last first and the first last has always ruptured conventional morality, politics, and narrative." Rachel Blau DuPlessis, *Writing Beyond the Ending* (Bloomington: Indiana University Press, 1985), 108.

38. Bakhtin, "Discourse in the Novel," 271–272.

39. Gadamer, *Truth and Method*, 321.

40. Myra Jehlen, "Archimedes and the Paradox of Feminist Criticism," reprinted in Elizabeth Abel and Emily K. Abel, eds., *The Signs Reader: Women, Gender and Scholarship* (Chicago: University of Chicago Press, 1983).

41. See Harold Bloom, *The Anxiety of Influence: A Theory of Poetry* (New York: Oxford University Press, 1973); Sandra M. Gilbert and Susan Gubar, eds., *The Madwoman in the Attic: The Woman Writer and the Nineteenth-Century Literary Imagination* (New Haven: Yale University Press, 1979); and Joseph T. Skerret, "The Wright Interpretation: Ralph Ellison and the Anxiety of Influence," *Massachusetts Review* 21 (Spring 1980): 196–212.

42. Andrea Stuart in an interview with Toni Morrison, "Telling Our Story," *Sparerib* (April 1988): 12–15.

Reading Black, Reading Feminist

The Re(a)d and the Black

Barbara E. Johnson

It is not surprising that this novel plumbs blacker depths of human experience than American literature has yet had.

—*Dorothy Canfield Fisher*

In the fall of 1937, Richard Wright published an essay entitled "Blueprint for Negro Writing" in *New Challenge*, a little left-wing magazine he was helping Marian Minus and Dorothy West edit. In that essay he characterized previous Negro writing as "humble novels, poems, and plays, prim and decorous ambassadors who went a-begging to white America."[1] He urged Negro writers to abandon the posture of humility and the bourgeois path of "individual achievement," and to develop a collective voice of social consciousness, both nationalist and Marxist. "The Negro writer must realize within the area of his own personal experience those impulses which, when prefigured in terms of broad social movements, constitute the stuff of nationalism . . . It is through a Marxist conception of reality and society that the maximum degree of freedom in thought and feeling can be gained for the Negro writer" (43, 44). Negro writing, in other words, could fulfill itself only by becoming at once black and red.

Three years later, Wright published a novel that seemed to carry out this design, one that transformed the avuncular diminutions of previous Negro writing (including his own) into a larger and bolder form of assertion, changing the uncle, Tom, into a bigger Thomas. *Native Son* presents a new social

archetype of American hunger, one that attempts to view the
distorted strength of the black folk hero through the lens of a
communist defense. Yet the merger between the red and the
black is as problematic in the novel as it came to be for
Richard Wright in life. What the communist lawyer, Max,
cannot hear is precisely Bigger's "I am," his ascension to the
status of speaking subject:

> Bigger saw Max back away from him with compressed
> lips. But he felt he had to make Max understand how he
> saw things now.
> "I didn't want to kill!" Bigger shouted. "But what I
> killed for, I *am*! It must've been pretty deep in me to
> make me kill! I must have felt it awful hard to murder . . ."
> Max lifted his hand to touch Bigger, but did not.
> "No; no; no . . . Bigger, not that . . ." Max pleaded
> despairingly.[2]

What is it about Bigger that cannot be re(a)d within the perspective of Ma(r)x?

Max's understanding of Bigger's two murders places them
squarely within the perspective of economic determinism. As
Max tells the court, Bigger kills because other channels of
self-expression are closed to him:

> Listen: what Bigger Thomas did early that Sunday morn-
> ing in the Dalton home and what he did that Sunday
> night in that empty building was but a tiny aspect of
> what he had been doing all his life long! He was *living*,
> only as he knew how, and as we have forced him to live.
> The actions that resulted in the death of those two women
> were as instinctive and inevitable as breathing or blinking
> one's eyes. It was an act of *creation*! (366)

It has often been assumed that Bigger's crimes can therefore
be seen as that which, in the novel, stands in the place of *art*.
Bigger is an artist with no medium to work in other than
violence.

But is this actually the case? It will be my contention that
there is in fact, within the novel itself, another sort of "Blueprint for Negro Writing," one that complicates the notion of a

creativity "as instinctive and inevitable as breathing or blinking one's eyes" (indeed, one that makes even breathing and blinking the eyes into signifying acts that are not merely instinctual).

For Bigger, in fact, does not merely kill. He also writes. He writes a ransom note to the father of the white woman he has inadvertently killed. That note, and the scene of its writing, can be read in a way that exceeds its contextual function. And the reception of that text turns out to be as telling as its creation.

The scene of writing (166–167) begins with the silencing of Bessie, the black woman whose involvement with Bigger will soon prove fatal to her.

> "I ain't asking you but once more to shut up!" he said, pushing the knife out of the way so he could write.

Substituting the pencil for the knife, Bigger performs an elaborate ritual of concealment, self-protection, and disguise:

> He put on the gloves and took up the pencil in a trembling hand and held it poised over the paper. He should disguise his handwriting. He changed the pencil from his right to his left hand. He would not write it; he would print it. He swallowed with dry throat.

Bigger's writing is designed to betray no trace of origin or signature. He is then faced with the question of pronoun: is his writing to be individual or collective? This is indeed the question Richard Wright has put before the Negro writer who wishes to write on the "left."

> Now, what would be the best kind of note? He thought, I want you to put ten thousand . . . Naw; that would not do. Not "I." It would be better to say "we."

Instead of proceeding directly to his demand ("I want you to put ten thousand . . ."), Bigger now makes up a story for the benefit of the addressee, the white male reader, leading with what he knows to be Mr. Dalton's concern:

We got your daughter, he printed slowly in big round letters. That was better. He ought to say something to let Mr. Dalton think that Mary was still alive. He wrote: *She is safe.* Now, tell him not to go to the police. No! Say something about Mary first! He bent and wrote: *She wants to come home.*

As he continues the note, he makes a crucial textual revision:

Now, tell him not to go to the police. *Don't go to the police if you want your daughter back safe.* Naw; that ain't good. His scalp tingled with excitement; it seemed that he could . feel each strand of hair upon his head. He read the line over and crossed out "safe" and wrote "alive."

What Bigger's visceral reaction demonstrates is his knowledge that his own fate is bound to the way in which his writing is linked, in the implied reader's mind, with the fate of a white woman. It is precisely Bigger's belief in the white father's inability to think his daughter safe that has led to her not being alive in the first place. Bigger implicitly feels the significance of his revision and all that needs to be revised behind it:

For a moment he was frozen, still. There was in his stomach a slow, cold, vast rising movement, as though he held within the embrace of his bowels the swing of planets through space. He was giddy. He caught hold of himself, focused his attention to write again.

The details of the ransom drop follow. The only part of the note he pronounces "good" comes to him from another text:

Now, about the money. How much? Yes; make it ten thousand. *Get ten thousand in 5 and 10 bills and put it in a shoe box . . .* That's good. He had read that somewhere *. . . and tomorrow night ride your car up and down Michigan Avenue from 35th Street to 40th Street.* That would make it hard for anybody to tell just where Bessie would be hiding. He wrote: *Blink your headlights some. When you see a light in a window blink three times throw the box in the snow and drive off. Do what this letter say.* Now, he would sign it.

But how? It should be signed in some way that would throw them off the trail. Oh, yes! Sign it "Red." He printed, *Red*.

Like Richard Wright himself in 1940, Bigger is compelled to sign his writing "Red." Yet the note is signed "Black" as well: *"Do what this letter say."* Hidden behind the letter's detour through communism is the unmistakable stylistic trace of its black authorship. Yet no one in the novel seems to be able to read it. In passing under the signature "Red," the text's blackness is precisely what goes un-read. Bigger is in fact present at the scene of the letter's reception, but he remains unseen, "nobody."

> The door swung in violently. Bigger started in fright. Mr. Dalton came into the kitchen, his face ashy. He stared at Peggy and Peggy, holding a dish towel in her hand, stared at him. In Mr. Dalton's hand was the letter, opened.
> "What's the matter, Mr. Dalton?"
> "Who . . . Where did . . . Who gave you this?"
> "What?"
> "This *letter*."
> "Why, nobody. I got it from the door."
> "When?"
> "A few minutes ago. Anything wrong?"
> Mr. Dalton looked round the entire kitchen, not at anything in particular, but just round the entire stretch of four walls, his eyes wide and unseeing (177).

Like Poe's purloined letter, the identity of the author of the note remains invisible because the detectives do not know how to read what is plainly there before them. Behind the sentence *"Do what this letter say"* lies the possibility—and the invisibility—of a whole vernacular literature.

If Bigger's ransom note represents in some sense black vernacular literature, does this mean that in the writing of black men the life and death of white womanhood is at stake? It is clear that this is the story the white fathers will listen to. Indeed, whatever the facts, it seems that this is the *only* story they will hear. This is what Bigger believes as he stands over the bed of the intoxicated Mary, watching the blind Mrs. Dalton approach. What *must not happen* is that he be caught alone in the bedroom of a white woman. He forces a pillow over Mary's face in order to prevent her from betraying his presence. Like Oedipus, it is through his efforts to *avoid* enacting the forbidden story that he inevitably enacts it. Like Oedipus, he participates in a primal scene of, and with, blindness.

The name of the forbidden story in America is "rape." In an essay entitled "How 'Bigger' was Born," Wright describes his growing awareness of the character type he wished to portray. As for the plot, it was already scripted by American society:

> Any Negro who has lived in the North or the South knows that times without number he has heard of some Negro boy being picked up on the streets and carted off to jail and charged with "rape." This thing happens so often that to my mind it had become a representative symbol of the Negro's uncertain position in America. Never for a second was I in doubt as to what kind of social reality or dramatic situation I'd put Bigger in, what kind of test-tube life I'd set up to evoke his deepest reactions. Life had made the plot over and over again, to the extent that I knew it by heart (*Native Son*, xxviii).

As many commentators have noted, the myth of the black rapist is an inversion of historical fact—the frequent rape of black slave women by their white owners. Yet Bigger Thomas does not rape Mary Dalton; he kills her because he thinks that the only possible interpretation of his presence in her room is "rape." It is not surprising that the first edition of *Native Son* should have been preceded by an introduction written by Dorothy Canfield Fisher. The envelope of Wright's letter had to be made to say "The white woman is safe."

To the extent that the rape of Mary Dalton does not occur, the "rape" plot in *Native Son* may be read in terms of racist overdetermination. But what can be said about the fate of Bessie Mears, the black woman who *is* raped by Bigger, and whose murder is far from accidental? Is the rape and murder of a black woman somehow a correlative to the black man's quest for manhood, a figure for the defeminization Wright

calls for in his blueprint for a literature that would no longer
go "curtsying to show that the Negro was not inferior" (*Blueprint*, 37)? If the novel makes a plea for Bigger's victimization,
does it implicitly excuse his treatment of the black woman?
Does racism explain away the novel's careless misogyny?

It would be easy to attack Richard Wright for placing violence, as James Baldwin puts it, in the space where sex should
be.[3] It would be easy to read *Native Son*'s depiction of the
relations between black men and black women as unhealably
troubled; indeed, to read the novel as itself an act of violence
against black women. I would like to shift the ground of this
interpretation slightly in order to ask: Where, in Richard Wright,
does the black woman stand with respect to the black man's
writing?

As we have seen, Bessie Mears is a silent (silenced) presence in the scene in which Bigger Thomas writes. As Bigger
completes the ransom note, he lifts his eyes and sees Bessie
standing behind him. She has read the note over his shoulder
and guessed the truth. "She looked straight into his eyes and
whispered, 'Bigger, did you kill that girl?' " Bigger denies that
she has interpreted his writing correctly, but he formulates a
plan to kill her to prevent her from saying what she knows.
The black woman, then, is a reader whose reading is both
accurate and threatening.

Bigger's ransom note is not the only example in Richard
Wright's work of a paradigmatic scene of writing in which
what is at stake is the death of a nonblack woman. To this
scene I would like to juxtapose a scene from Wright's autobiography, *Black Boy*. One of his earliest attempts at writing, he
tells us, was the story of a beautiful Indian maiden.

> I remembered a series of volumes of Indian history I had
> read the year before. Yes, I knew what I would do; I
> would write a story about the Indians . . . But what
> about them? Well, an Indian girl . . . I wrote of an Indian
> maiden, beautiful and reserved, who sat alone upon the
> bank of a still stream, surrounded by eternal twilight and
> ancient trees, waiting . . . The girl was keeping some
> vow which I could not describe and, not knowing how to
> develop the story, I resolved that the girl had to die. She
> rose slowly and walked toward the dark stream, her face

stately and cold; she entered the water and walked on until the water reached her shoulders, her chin; then it covered her. Not a murmur or a gasp came from her, even in dying.[4]

Writing in the illustrious tradition of Hawthorne, Poe, Wordsworth, Lamartine, and hundreds of other white men of letters, Wright has no difficulty seeing the death of an idealized woman as a significant literary subject. Not all male writers are candid enough, however, to admit that their heroine's untimely death is the result of a failure of imagination. "Not knowing how to develop the story, I resolved that the girl had to die." One wonders whether this might explain the early demise of Lucy or Annabel Lee—or even of Edna Pontellier.

But dead women are not the only women present in these scenes of writing, and in both cases the "other woman" is a black female reader whose reading cannot be mastered by the writer. As we have seen, Bessie reads Bigger's ransom note and begins to suspect that he has killed Mary Dalton. Later, his scheme thwarted, Bigger first rapes, then kills Bessie in order to prevent her from talking, in order to gain total control over a story that has been out of his control from the beginning. In the case of the Indian maiden, Wright excitedly decides to read his literary creation to a young woman who lives next door.

> I interrupted her as she was washing dishes and, swearing her to secrecy, I read the composition aloud. When I finished she smiled at me oddly, her eyes baffled and astonished.
> "What's that for?" she asked.
> "Nothing," I said.
> "But why did you write it?"
> "I just wanted to."
> "Where did you get the idea?"
> I wagged my head, pulled down the corners of my mouth, stuffed my manuscript into my pocket and looked at her in a cocky manner that said: Oh, it's nothing at all. I write stuff like this all the time. It's easy, if you know how. But I merely said in an humble, quiet voice:
> "Oh, I don't know. I just thought it up."

"What're you going to do with it?"

"Nothing."

God only knows what she thought. My environment contained nothing more alien than writing or the desire to express one's self in writing. But I never forgot the look of astonishment and bewilderment on the young woman's face when I had finished reading and glanced at her. Her inability to grasp what I had done or was trying to do somehow gratified me. Afterwards whenever I thought of her reaction I smiled happily for some unaccountable reason (133–134).

It would be hard to imagine a scene of reading in which less was understood. It is entirely possible that the woman was indeed wondering why Wright was writing at all. It is also possible that she was wondering why he was writing about the death of a woman. It is even possible that she was wondering why *he* wasn't wondering that.

What Wright's writing demonstrates again and again is the deadly effect both of overdetermination and of underdetermination in storytelling. It is because the "rape" plot is so overdetermined that Bigger becomes a murderer. It is because there are so few available models for the plots of Indian maidens that Wright's heroine "has to die." And it is because the "rape" plot about white women or the "idealization" plot about Indian women are so overdetermined that the plot about black women remains muffled beyond recognition. When the black woman does attempt to take control of her own plot in Wright's short story, "Long Black Song," the black man dies in an apocalyptic fire. The unavailability of new plots is deadly. As Wright says of his Indian maiden composition, "I was excited; I read it over and saw that there was a yawning void in it. There was no plot, no action, nothing save atmosphere and longing and death" (133).

Yet even when a black woman's story *is* available, there is no guarantee that it will be recognized. Upon reading Zora Neale Hurston's *Their Eyes Were Watching God*, Wright was able to see only red, not black; male, not female. "The sensory sweep of her novel," he wrote, "carries no theme, no message, no thought."[5] The black woman's story can remain invisible no matter how visible it is, like the black vernacular origin of Bigger's ransom note. No reader has a monopoly on blindness. But Wright's blindness here is far from simple.

In a surprising and fascinating passage in Wright's essay, "How Bigger Was Born," we encounter the announcement of a novel that was never to reach completion: "I am launching out upon another novel, this time about the status of women in American society." The desire to tell a woman's story seems to infuse Wright's writing from the beginning. Yet however aborted the plots of his women protagonists, the figure of the black woman as *reader* in his work is fundamental. Silent, baffled, or filled with a dangerous insight, Wright consistently sees the black woman as the reader his writing must face. *Native Son*, indeed, is dedicated to Wright's own paralyzed mother.

NOTES

1. Reprinted in *The Richard Wright Reader*, *ed*. Ellen Wright and Michel Fabre (New York: Harper & Row, 1978), 37.
2. Richard Wright, *Native Son* (New York: Harper & Row, 1940), 391–392.
3. James Baldwin, "Alas, Poor Richard," in *Nobody Knows My Name* (New York: Laurel, 1961), 151.
4. Richard Wright, *Black Boy* (New York: Harper & Row, 1945), 132–133.
5. Richard Wright, review of *Their Eyes Were Watching God* by Zora Neale Hurston, *New Masses* (October 5, 1937), 26.

Facing the Camera's Eye:

Black and White Terrain in Women's Drama*

Timothy Murray

The fundamental event of the modern age is the conquest of the world as picture. The word "picture" [Bild] now means the structured image [Gebild] that is the creature of man's producing which represents and sets before. In such producing, man contends for the position in which he can be that particular being who gives the measure and draws up the guidelines for everything that is. Because this position secures, organizes, and articulates itself as a world view, the modern relationship to that which is, is one that becomes, in its decisive unfolding, a confrontation of world views . . . For the sake of this struggle of world views and in keeping with its meaning, man brings into play his unlimited power for the calculating, planning, and molding of all things.
　　　　　—Martin Heidegger, "The Age of the World Picture"

A desire for the possibilities of the uncolonized black female body occupies a utopian space; it is the false hope of Sappho Clark's pretend history. Black feminists understood that the struggle would have to take place on the terrain of the previously colonized: the struggle was to be characterized by redemption, retrieval, and reclamation.
　　　　　—Hazel V. Carby, " 'On the Threshold of Woman's Era' "

When framed by Hazel Carby's appeal for the reclamation of usurped female terrain, Martin Heidegger's reflections on technology expose modern man's pictorial productions as scopic and colonial.[1] In the light of today's feminist discussions of film theory, psychoanalysis, and contemporary art, Heidegger's earlier analyses of questions concerning technology leave contemporary critics (especially those of us inheriting the world

* This essay appeared, in a different version, in *Modern Drama*, 28, No. 1 (March, 1985), 110–124.

view of the "white male") with the burden of acknowledging the ideological weight of complicity with technological machines of communication. This relation is grounded in what Heidegger depicts as the *twofold* fiber constituting the contemporary (technological) image as both a structure of representation and a device or apparatus [tool and *épistèmé*] lending itself naturally to colonial struggles for unlimited power and authority. To speak of contemporary artistic performance in view of the technological image is to raise the specter of man bringing "into play [this] unlimited power for the calculating, planning, and molding of all things."

Carby's alternative suggestion that black feminist efforts need "take place on" (re-situate/ re-cite/ re-sight) previously colonized terrain calls to mind recent collaborative artistic and literary attempts to probe the relation of the technological to gender, race, and representation. Exemplary of such efforts are the 1983 traveling exhibition, "Art contre/against Apartheid," the essays and art projects comprising the New Museum of Contemporary Art's 1985 exhibition, "Difference: On Representation and Sexuality," and the special 1985 edition of *Critical Inquiry* on *"Race," Writing, and Difference.*[2] Many striking pieces in these projects redress the technological image with the aesthetic and ideological fabrics of confrontational strategy and revolutionary enactment.

While the scope and collaborative nature of these artistic and literary ventures have resulted in wide publicity and critical acclaim, similar individual and isolated representations in the theatre have received far less attention from theorists of gender, race, and representation. Especially in contemporary black American women's drama, the complexity of technological manipulation and subsequent theatrical confrontation has been developed with particular care and theoretical concern. In the serious play world of black American theatre, mixed-media pieces by women playwrights unveil how the marvelous technicolors of the camera have yet to escape from their white against black fundamentals.

A CAST OF CAMERAS

"A photograph is like a fingerprint/ it stays & stays forever/ we cd have something forever/ just how we want it. give me a camera," boasts the aspiring photographer, Sean, in Ntozake Shange's *a photograph: lovers in motion*, "& i cd get you anything you wanted/ breeze/ a wad of money/ madness/ women on back porches kneading bread/ stars falling/ ice cream & drunks & forever/ i cd give you forever in a night sky/ michael/ i cd give you love/ pure & full/ in a photograph."[3] Sean's unspoken assertion here is that the objects of desire and excess, from money to ice cream, from madness to intoxication, from breeze to eternity, are unrealizable on a stage lying outside of the realm of the camera, outside of the world of the picture. His hopeful, and yet clearly desperate, position suggests that desire can be permanently fulfilled only as a picture, as a copy, as a supplement. Of course, Sean's trust in the essence of pictorial representation ("my photographs are the contours of life unnoticed")[4] is not a new or merely technological belief, but rather one common to the conceptual history of drama. It would not be that difficult to extend Sean's hope in photographic mimesis to the historical depiction of theatre as imitative *pharmakon*, as a curative experience of the world.[5] Yet Ntozake Shange directs the audience to suspect the authenticity of any pictorial catharsis in the world of her play "which has no cures for our 'condition' save those we afford ourselves."[6] Even Sean's best photos seem dull and lifeless when compared to the fluid movements of the dancer, Michael, who maintains her own private visions of a fantasy love, of whom "i never even saw a picture/ but not far from me never far from me/ i've kept a lover who waznt all-american/ who didnt believe/ wdnt straighten up."[7] In the shadow of the now-implausible cure of traditional, mimetic notions of theatre and visual arts, Shange displays most effectively the sickly "condition" of hope in an all-american world picture nurtured mainly by the veil of visual presence.

As Heidegger explained as early as 1938, this is a blighted condition, untreatable by (partially because it might stem from) Aristotle's notion of mimetic, curative drama:

> With the word "picture" we think first of all of a copy of something. Accordingly, the world picture would be a painting, so to speak, of what is as a whole. But "world picture" means more than this. We mean by it the world itself, the world as such, what is, in its entirety, just as it is normative and binding for us . . . Hence world picture, when understood essentially, does not mean a picture of the world but the world conceived and grasped as picture. What is, in its entirety, is now taken in such a way that it first is in being and only is in being to the extent that it is set up by man, who represents and sets forth.[8]

The stage in this context is not a picture of the world but the world as picture, the world, say, of Sean's *photographic construction* in Shange's play. "i've got it all there in that frame. i gotta whole dynamic of centuries/ in a two-dimensional plane."[9] What makes modern drama's alliance with the world as 9picture decisively different from the staged world of Aristotelian poetics is that the technological apparatus of the camera now urges man to fortify through mechanical reproduction his position as, according to Heidegger, "the representative of that which is, in the sense of that which has the character of object. . . . What is decisive," Heidegger adds, "is that man himself expressly takes up this position as one constituted by himself, that he intentionally maintains it as that taken up by himself, and that he makes it secure as the solid footing for a possible development of humanity."[10] We need but listen again to the photog rapher Sean to appreciate how the modern love affair with the camera can turn unformulated desires into formulaic phantasms of creative potency: "i gotta world i'm making in my image/ i got something for a change/ lil sean david who never got over on nothing but bitches/ is building a world in his image."[11] The photographic process allows Sean to objectify the world around him, to stabilize the fluid and changeable referents around him, and to arrange the world according "to a point of view which endows it with a recognizable meaning."[12] To Sean, most significantly, this imagistic constancy provides the frame for the objectification of his own (masculine) self, the reproduction of "my image" into "his image." Such an object building through the genius of mechanical reproduction allows Sean, as Jean-François Lyotard puts it, "to arrive easily at the consciousness of his own identity as well as the approval he thereby receives from others—since such structures of images and sequences constitute a communication code among all of them."[13] As Sean puts it, "i'm a genius for unravelling the mysteries of the darker races."[14]

Yet Shange's play does not permit Sean to receive easy approval from his interlocutors. Although his female counterpart, Michael, has little difficulty acknowledging Sean's desire to conceive the world as picture, she does not let him forget that his self-esteem as a maker of both pictures and women is always already mediated on the stage of the world by the presence of a technological character, the camera. "You tell em straight out," she taunts Sean, "that you are/ osiris returned & yr camera has been the missing organ in our forsaken land."[15] As Michael dismissively interprets Sean's phallic antidote for the diseased condition of black American culture, hope lies less in the subjective (im)potency of its voyeuristic user than in the idealized character of the camera.

In perusing contemporary black American women's drama, readers come across a domineering cast of cameras posing as the technological hope and strength of their users, who tend, curiously enough, to be male. Sean's camera in *a photograph* performs a role similar to that of Martin's camera in *Toe Jam*, a script written by the sensitive playwright, Elaine Jackson. In this text, the photographic machine provides the material condition for Xenith's misdirected hope that her newly objectified image will launch her black face into fame as "the new look." "I'm gonna get me a real tough photographer," she boasts, "like tough Martin, to get me in all the magazines—make me the 'in' look and . . . these sweet, big, juicy lips will be the new lip-line for 19."[16] To her surprise, however, she finds that her look is not new but has been "made" and objectified many times before by Martin's secretive voyeurism aided and abetted by the masterful eye of his camera. This ideological formation of camera as phallic voyeur and shaper of the female "look," serving male desire, also surfaces in *a photograph* when Sean recounts how he has made pictures ever "since we cd hide neath mary susan's window in the projects & watch her undress."[17] In these instances, the fixating camera and the desirous male gaze come together in a performance of masculine entrapment as deeply oppressive as is the racism from which the characters all hope to escape.

This complicity of the controlling male gaze with deeper structures of black oppression also surfaces as the broad subject of Adrienne Kennedy's media play, *An Evening with Dead Essex*. Here, the cast of actors is supplemented by the erect figure of a slide projector, "slightly larger than reality and very black."[18] But any hope in this larger-than-real black character is diminished by Kennedy's introduction of its projectionist, the only white character in the play who arranges "his slides in the order He will use them."[19] The play itself presents actors in rehearsal who, with the aid of the manipulative projectionist, reconstruct the photos, stories, and abstract images surrounding and haunting the mind of black Mark Essex. A tragic victim of the massive conscription of American blacks in the campaign of genocide against the Vietnamese, Essex safely returns from the war only to be violently massacred by the New Orleans police in retaliation for his crazed but racially motivated sniping from a Howard Johnson's rooftop. The play is a subsequent attempt to recount the media's collaboration in creating Mark Essex's picture of the world, "that open American look—I guess innocence is the word." This is a mythical picture positioning black Mark Essex as its always-alien spectator. Joining his numerous innocent victims, Essex silently cries out as the bullet-ridden icon of that open American look, the one carefully nurtured for profit by the media's intruding cameras. (This is similar to a pattern in Amiri Baraka's play, *The Motion of History*. In this documentation of the history of black oppression, the television camera functions as the compromising device permitting Kenneth Clark, the keeper of white, cultural innocence, to discourse with the black militant, Malcolm X. Later in Baraka's play, Reggie speaks harshly of television's ultimate effect on black revolution: "You fall out in front of that television set like you crazy. TV set say, 'Look into my eyes. Now get up, go climb up on that ledge, now take a giant step . . . Sucker!' "[20]

What is striking about the overall role of the cast of cameras in these plays is its mesmerizing ability to nurture a hope in the dissemination of a liberating black image while, to recall Heidegger's distinction between image and representational function, always operating as a memory device of the ideological heritage of the camera. Consider, for instance, Sean's boast in *a photograph* that "these photographs are for them/ they are gonna see our faces/ the visage of the sons/ the sons who wdnt disappear niggahs who are still alive i'm gonna go ona rampage/ a raid on the sleeping settlers/ this camera's gonna get em."[21] This suggests a revolutionary trust in the camera while at the same time attributing that trust to the tainted memory of the device's past and present as a filial agent of cultural hegemony, recollective also of Baraka's rampaging Red Squad in *S-1*, the squad that specializes in raiding sleeping leftists.

THE VEIL OF VISIBLE CONSENSUS

This blatant identification of camera and Red Squad, particularly worrisome twenty years ago in North America and frightfully repressed today, is laden with a long history of increasingly complex ideological formations of technological and philosophical structures.[22] The French film theoreticians Marcelin Pleynet, Jean-Louis Baudry, and Jean-Louis Comolli have documented the abstract relationship of the development of the camera with the colonial history of Occidental humanism. Pleynet was first among them to insist that "the film camera is an ideological instrument in its own right, it expresses bourgeois ideology before expressing anything else . . . It produces a directly inherited code of perspective, built on the model of the scientific perspective of the Quattrocento. What needs to be shown is the meticulous way in which the construction of the camera is geared to 'rectify' any anomalies in perspective in order to reproduce in all its authority the visual code laid down by renaissant humanism."[23] In essence, the camera is an agent of the ideology of the visible, a belief that "the human eye is at the center of the system of representation, with that centrality at once excluding any other representative system, assuring the eye's domination over any other organ of the senses and putting the eye in a strictly divine place."[24] The philosophical corollary is, of course, transcendental subjectivity, which positions the gazing subject as the unifying agent. In terms of the relation of theatre and camera, this tradition encourages the spectator, according to Baudry, "to identify himself less with the represented, the spectacle itself, than with that which puts into play or dramatizes the spectacle; with that which is not visible but which shows, in the same movement as he, the spectator, sees—obligating the spectator to see what he sees, that is to say the function assured by the relaying space of the camera."[25] The ideological mechanism at work here is the concretization of the rapport between camera and subject, the maintenance of a dominant ideology of visibility sustaining the idealization of the representing subject—the power-laden subject conceiving and grasping the world as picture.

The complex relation of camera and transcendental philosophy remains as a prior horizon to contemporary theatre's casting of the camera as a character of visual knowledge and social advancement. Further reflection on this horizon in terms of its epistemological implications would encourage us to ponder the relation of the ideology of the visible to the ideology of cognitive agreement. This problematic has been the focus of much of Jean-François Lyotard's recent work, in which he analyzes how the mechanical "objects and the thoughts which originate in scientific knowledge and the capitalist economy convey with them one of the rules which supports their possibility; the rule that there is no reality unless testified by a consensus between partners over a certain knowledge and certain commitments."[26] The ideology of consensus operates according to the principle that we can agree on cognitive boundaries, allowing us to recognize what lies inside or outside reality, or similarly, in view of my attentiveness here to black American women's drama, that we can come to an agreement about or even mastery over what is white and what is black, or even what is male and what is female.

Thus we enter into the exceptionally complicated situation of contemporary drama operating in the material and cognitive world of the camera. From the horizon of philosophical knowledge stems the mechanism of control. The ideologies of visibility and consensus enshroud the stage and its dramatic characters, from Shange's Michael to Sean's camera, in the web of the hegemony of the eye (I). "The problem of theatre and of 'figurative' painting," Lyotard suggests, "is no longer posed as a problem of understanding or knowledge, or even of truth, but as a problem of force and power: force of creatures provisionally enslaved on the stage, power of the spectator–director who is master [*metteur en scène . . . metteur en cage*]."[27] Or, to situate Lyotard's point about art and theatre in a realm even more familiar to North American critical theorists, we need only recall Derrida's frequently cited statement regarding metaphysics and Artaud: "Directors or actors, enslaved interpreters . . . represent more or less directly the thought of the 'creator.' Interpreting slaves, faithfully executing the providential designs of the 'master.' "[28] Implied by these connections of spectators, authors, and directors is the final link in the hegemonic chain—the operation of dramatic spectatorship which, as I suggest elsewhere, is equally entrapped in the tradition of the ideologies of the visible and consensual.[29]

Our understanding of this collusion of vision and consensus by the audience as producer—itself a specialized product of technological reproduction—is indebted, of course, to the writings of Walter Benjamin. In the early years of the burgeoning film industry, Benjamin insightfully suggested that the film apparatus diminishes "the distinction between criticism and enjoyment by the public." This nurtures the positive force of public consensus at the expense of hierarchically elitist expressions of reception. "Mechanical reproduction of art," he writes, "changes the reaction of the masses toward art . . . With regard to the screen, the critical and the receptive attitudes of the public coincide. The decisive reason for this is that individual reactions are predetermined by the mass audience response they are about to produce, and this is nowhere more pronounced than in the film. The moment these responses become manifest they control each other."[30] But while Benjamin applauds the value of film's "distracted" spectatorship in contributing to "simultaneous collective experience," Max Horkheimer and Theodor Adorno focus on the false promises of the audience's coproduction of predictable forms of numbing entertainment. Through transformation of predetermined mass response into normative products, the culture industry benefits in profit and power from the public's newly acquired authority over technological culture. "This promise held out by the work of art that it will create truth by lending new shape to the conventional social forms is as necessary as it is hypocritical. . . . In the culture industry this imitation finally becomes absolute. Having ceased to be anything but style, it reveals the latter's secret: obedience to the social hierarchy. . . . Culture as a common denominator already contains in embryo that schematization and process of cataloguing and classification which bring culture within the sphere of administration."[31] Sustaining the comfortable mastery of coproduction, then, are the well-established ideologies of consensus and visibility, now accurately represented in black drama by the character of the camera.

In all fairness, however, I should point out that theatre practictioners and theoreticians have not absentmindedly accepted the argument that the veil of the camera's eye enshrouds the enterprise of theatre. Indeed, the predominant critical position has been to emphasize the fundamental difference between the institution of theatre and the entertainment industry most dependent on the apparatus of the camera, film. Even Benjamin was quick to stress "that there is no greater contrast than that of the stage play to the work of art that is completely subject to or, like the film, founded in, mechanical reproduction."[32] More recently this distinction has been made in regard to two significant, theoretical factors. First, Christian Metz emphasizes that theatre as an empirical activity does not share film's dependence on the camera as a transcendental subject. For what defines the scopic specificity of the camera work is the empirical fact of the *absence* of its objects of representation. As seen only on the screen, actors are not physically present in the movie house. Metz understands this absence, moreover, to compound the psychological potency of visual authority and scopic force. He contends that while the spectator's filmic vision in the darkened cinema may be psychologically "collective," it is not always "authorized" and "verifiable" as a shared public activity, thus positioning the filmic institution in the realm of forbidden sight—the primordial ground of the solitude of spectatorial experience.[33]

To provide a corollary from the plays discussed above, I might relate how the filmic spectator remains unknown to the work of art, unknown as the viewer of the sort of libidinal drama revealed by Martin to Xenith, the object of his gaze in *Toe Jam*:

> You didn't know me years ago when I used to watch you
> and Alice behind your fence when we lived over on

Canon Street . . . You didn't now how I used to climb up
on the roof of my house just to watch you play in your
backyard. You didn't know how I used to stand outside
your house just to watch your mother take you to school.
. . . I got tons of pictures of you that you don't even
know I took. It's like I was an undeveloped negative,
sweetheart.[34]

In so positioning the spectator as an undeveloped *negative* (as
something other than an ethically developed and socially positive force), film has been said to part from theatre by inscribing
itself psychologically as well as sociologically in the undiffer-
entiated (invisible/visible) space of globalizing representation.

In Herbert Blau's opinion, this inscription leads to a second
and even more empirically specific difference between film
and theatre. "The cinematic institution . . . shifts the locus of
vulnerability from the film, the art-object, or the actors in the
film (if there are actors)—the image of human agency in the
narrative—to its *representatives*."[35] According to this view, film
differs from theatre in that it provides a less immediate, perhaps even inauthentic, presentation of human agency. Bodily
presence, the fundamental phenomenological attribute of Being-
in-the World, is reduced by film to technological representatives, to undeveloped negatives. "So as regards the power of
a disappearing presence," Blau writes concerning the development of our acknowledgment of ideological representations,
"the theatre would appear to have the advantage, its very
corporeality being the basis of its most powerful illusion, that
something is substantially there, the thing itself, even as it
vanishes."[36] Whether or not it is always conceived as a picture, the body of the theatre actor is always *there (Da-sein)*,
thus differentiating itself in presence *and* in absence from its
spectatorial Other. It is this presentational fact of the body,
the fact of a body that can and does vanish in the sight of the
scopic eye, which Blau attributes to theatre as its contribution
to the demystification of hegemonic control. "What the theatre does, then, is to bring into presence what, without theatre,
cannot be present."[37] Such a stress on bodily presence, in and
of itself, might be grounds for renewed hope in a specifically
black American theatre, a drama of the presentation of *black*
corporeal presence.

From an empirical perspective, the arguments of both Metz and Blau concerning theatre's specificity are convincing and hopeful. They provoke recollection of "Evolution of a People's Theatre," the 1970 political tract by Woody King and Ron Milner requiring that black theatre "go home! If a new black theatre is to be born, sustain itself, and justify its own being, it must go home. Go home psychically, mentally, aesthetically, and, we think, physically."[38] Yet the preceding discussion of contemporary women's drama in the eye of the camera might be enough to advise against including theatre in an empirically privileged position lying outside of the penetrating gaze performed daily by the mechanical productions of film and television. Such legitimation of theatre on an empirical foundation might work merely to reinscribe contemporary drama in an idealism of essence and an ideology of consensus.[39] Black practitioners of drama might remind us that the empirical reduction of theatre's contemporary structures to the primacy of corporeal presence might endow too strong a trust in phenomenological relations. As Shange's actor, Alec, in *Spell #7*, warns us, black skin does not necessarily guarantee a black art free of the hegemonic structures encouraged by artistic tradition: "i'm not playing the fool or the black buck pimp circus/ i'm an actor not a stereotype . . . we arent gonna get anyplace/ by doin every bit part for a niggah that someone waves in fronta my face."[40] In contrast, a significant body of contemporary black women's theatre pieces, like Shange's text, subtitled "geechee jibara quik magic trance manual for technologically stressed third world people," work to question the efficacy, not to mention the possibility, of theatre's evasion of the mixture of visual and narrative structures of the visual media—the narrative structures with which the contemporary audience is familiar, and the visual codes which offer us so many technical options for staging and for interpretive representation.

FRAMING WORLD VIEWS

Shange's *a photograph: lovers in motion* provides us with a striking example of such a mixture of dramatic and filmic vision. The play opens with the disjunctive performances of two "struggling artists." One, Sean, struggles to control the female subjects of his photographic art. "How did you get her to do that," asks his friend, Earl, "pour jack daniels all over herself/ & get out the tub at the same time/ smiling/ how she does."[41] The other, Michael, turns to her inner world of dance and movement as a fluid expression of the psycho-economic struggle of "our lives/ our grandparents & their uncles/ it's how we came to be/ by taking our lives seriously/ we fight for every breath every goddamn day."[42] Michael's dances of rebellion, both inside and outside, for and against the hegemony characteristic of the age of the world picture, are what establish the conceptual framework of Shange's play. The dance is something Sean "cant have or return to/ something dim in memory/ barely articulated."[43] Always present among these *lovers in motion*, dance takes on the character of a cinematic memory, a memory of corporeal freedom in an age when technology increases both the stakes and the potential of hegemonism. And while Sean displays slides of the Muslim woman whose toiletry he secretly films from across the street, Michael describes her dance to Sean, as if reinforcing the memory in its most vulnerable state:

i am space & winds
like a soft rain or a torrent of dust/ i can move
be free in time/ a moment is mine always
i am not like a flower at all
tho i can bloom & be a wisp of sunlight
i'm a rustling of dead leaves
collections of ol women by the weddin
the legs of a cotton club queen
& so familiar with tears
alla this is mine/ so long as i breathe/ i'm gonna dance
for all of us/ everybody dead/ everybody busy
everybody too burdened to jump thru a nite
a hot & bluesy jump in the guts of ourselves
a dance is like a dream/ i can always remember
make it come again . . . i can make it come again.[44]

Through the mixture of oppressive photo clips and lively dances performing the memory of rebellion, the play blends

corporeal presence and technological image into one representational *filmic body*, a visual membrane depicting, to recall
Heidegger's words, "a confrontation of world views."

The two actors' differing commentary on how art takes up
life's "slack" positions the dramatic image as more than a
merely phenomenological hope or vision, as something more
than the aesthetic object of theatrical performance. The coalition of photo and dance—the fusion of technology's representations and drama's human forms—produce a screen of artistic
struggle in which the crucial activity is less human agency
than its representatives, that is to say, its framings, its readings, its interpretations. Responding to Sean's claim that "i
thot art waz survival," Michael insists, "no. it's love. it's
fighting to give something/ it's giving yrself to someone/ who
loves you . . . lettin everybody in & giving up what is most
treasured."[45] As Shange's visionary of moving dreams, Michael confirms that her art is framed in pathos, in struggle, in
vulnerable openness. The clash of Shange's filmic bodies thus
provokes us to acknowledge, to read, the structural anxieties
and abstract relations enslaving art in the age of the white
against black, even male against female, world picture.

In Michael's view, the economies of race and gender are
emphatically intertwined in Sean's peculiar notion of artistic
survival. "i dont like thinking that you think yr dick means
more to me than yr work/ you dont give yrself anymore than
anyone is willing to give you."[46] By so revealing the photographer's sense of his eye (I), Shange confronts her spectators
with the acknowledgment of phallic visibility as dominant
ideology. This visibility is not a primary activity but a representative one within the frame of ideology: "a 'representation'
of the imaginary relationship of individuals to their real conditions of existence."[47] Any dramatic representation of the ideology of visibility, moreover, goes hand in hand (or eye in eye)
with the analysis of its structure and our particular *fictive*
relation to it. Shange's emotional dialogue indirectly deconstructs
the master relations of dramatic form and political content
sustaining the lasting Oedipal tradition of Western drama, one
blending castration anxiety with ritual and economic sacrifice
of the cultural Other. "For too long now," Shange writes of
her project, "afro-americans in theater have been duped by
the same artificial aesthetics that plague our white counterparts/

'the perfect play,' as we know it to be/ a truly european framework for european psychology/ cannot function efficiently for those of us from this hemisphere."[48]

Adrienne Kennedy, another creative innovator of black female aesthetics, not only structures *An Evening with Dead Essex* around a personal mixture of visual strategies and artistic philosophies, but also turns to narrative techniques refined particularly well by the visual media and its Brechtian counterparts on the stage.[49] This play's actors-in-rehearsal reconstruct the photos, stories, and abstract images surrounding and haunting the mind of black Mark Essex. The cast's difficult project of sifting randomly through the artifacts of this real character's tragedy expose on stage the false unities and connections underlying the media re-presentation of the history of Mark Essex. Actors, taped voice-overs, and audience re-play again and again the same mediating images and newspaper accounts of Vietnam, the evening of the death of Essex, and the tragedy of America's myth of unification, replete with the assassinations of Malcolm X, Martin Luther King, and the Kent State killings. Kennedy's drama performs a coming and going from one contemporary historical moment to another reminiscent of the irreverence for temporal order developed by the television news and the cinematic presentation of documentary film clips. In this context, we might appreciate the play's production as a condensed collage of recent black American history. The stylized form of Kennedy's visual and verbal collage, moreover, asks its spectator to witness how its parts, enslaved by difference, produce a picture Other than the unified black and white photograph of progressive American history.[50]

Saying, "let's not get away from the idea of recounting what people said about Essex,"[51] the Director in *An Evening with Dead Essex* inscribes mediation and alienation into the fabric of narrative as collage. Underlying this troupe's attempt to arrive through rehearsal (répétition) at a reasonably harmonious image of Essex is the play's attentiveness to the deception inherent in the project of such narration. Referring to Nixon's "Peace Is At Hand Speech," the Director ironizes the fallacy of consensus underlying the rehearsal process: "I want the repetition of the coming of peace, the coming of peace, peace coming of peace. In all that repetition is deception—and

Essex was a man sensitive to deception . . . Yes we want that picture ['of Kissinger entering the peace talks again and again'] over and over entering and leaving, entering and leaving the peace talkings with peace at hand—smiling—all this happening around Essex—all appearing deception to him."[52] Appearance as deception—this is the fabric of Kennedy's play, with its dizzying collage-like effects always standing beside its larger-than-life black film projector. Framed by an even more dominating screen, "slightly bigger in scale than everything else," this projector emits "razor sharp" images continuously demystified by the fact that they "vary in focus."

Kennedy's play joins Shange's in reshaping the structures or laws of dramatic focus. We should note that it is conventional for the theatre or film documentary to provide us with a sharp overview of a world picture, an overview closely dependent on the ideology of the visible, that is to say, an overview contingent on the projection of a unified and objective (objectified) historical narrative. [53] When spectators look for razor sharpness in An Evening with Dead Essex, however, they will notice that the play lacks a narrator's eye or voice to put its picture into focus. Presenting the spectator with something resisting the transcendental point of view of documentary, the play turns aside from the frames and formulas of black-and-white clarity to enact the energetic friction of differing positions of plot and scenario. The structural laws underlying the play's ideological reality are dizzying, just like the temporal flux of the play. The characters' realities are as libidinal as they are historical, calling to mind the laws of condensation, displacement, figuration, and elaboration constituting the economies of representation—whether psychological or material.[54] These are the very unpredictable and unframeable structures confronting the fiction of a black-and-white world view.

The technologically stressed plays by Adrienne Kennedy and Ntozake Shange acknowledge the continual production of differing imaginative relations to real conditions that stimulate, unlike slavery's need to obscure, a confrontation of world views. "What is fascinating," Ntozake Shange writes about her own dramatic struggle for oppressed Third World people, "is the multiplicity of individual responses" to racial repression.[55] Differing strategies of confrontation within the realm of technological representation constitute the imaginative pharmakon of the black American reaction to art-as-technology. This response faces eye to eye the threats and advantages of technology in the age of the world picture. Shange's essay, "unrecovered losses/ black theater traditions," leaves us with an image of a living, breathing, but always fractured filmic body—poised to confront the potential losses of uniform trust in a transcendental eye:

> "Combat breathing" is the living response/ the drive to reconcile the irreconcilable/ the black & white of what we live n where. (unfortunately, this language doesnt allow me to broaden "black" & "white" to figurative terms/ which is criminal since the words are so much larger n richer than our culture allows.) i have lived with this for 31 years/ as my people have lived with cut-off lives n limbs. the three pieces in this collection are the throes of pain n sensation experienced by my characters responding to the involuntary constrictions n amputations of their humanity/ in the context of combat breathing.[56]

Shange's emphasis on her personal relation to the artistic enterprise introduces a final, if not an essential, aspect of contemporary black women's writing—that breathing precedes politics.

But isn't this to say that the breath of racial/sexual difference is in itself political as an ideological condition and assertion? Readers of either Shange's or Kennedy's prose frequently come across statements resituating the terrain of the political in these women's writings. At the core of their work lies an animated commitment to an interpersonalized autobiographical fiction. In Kennedy's words,

> Autobiographical work is the only thing that interests me, apparently because that is what I do best. I write about my family. In many ways I would like to break out of that, but I don't know how to break out of it. . . . I feel overwhelmed by family problems and family realities. I see my writing as being an outlet for inner, psychological confusion and questions stemming from childhood. I don't know any other way. It's really figuring out the "why" of things—that is, if that is even possible. I'm not sure you

can figure out the "why" of anything anymore. You try
to struggle with the material that is lodged in your unconscious, and try to bring it to the conscious level. You
try to remain as honest about that as possible, without
fear.[57]

Here the enigmatic implosions of autobiography frame (veil)
the visible explosions of social struggle. Shange makes a similar point when she speaks up for the "singularity" of black
writers. In "takin a solo/a poetic possibility/ a poetic imperative," she reinscribes ontological difference as the precondition of all political writing:

we assume a musical solo is a personal statement/ we
think the poet is speakin for the world/ there's something
wrong there, a writer's first commitment is to the piece,
itself. how the words fall & leap/ or if they dawdle & sit
down fannin themselves. writers are dealing with language/
not politics. that comes later. so much later. to think abt
the politics of a poem/ before we think abt the poem/ is to
put what is correct before the moment.[58]

Although the phallocentric tradition of "European psychology" might be quick to label such autobiography as apolitical
narcissism weighted down by penile envy,[59] the black female
playwright would be more inclined to understand it in the
agonistic context of being-together-differently.[60] Theirs is a
living struggle characterized by redemption, retrieval, and
reclamation of the literary page and visual space—a re-citing
of their own previously colonized breath.
    Such is the structural paradox of technologically stressed
aesthetic commitment. That to breathe is to live, differently; to
live is to act, politically; and yet to act is to dance, dreamily—on
the previously colonized familial terrain that always already
sets the political tone of the writer's solo voice. So stands the
dilemma of Ntosake Shange:

when i take my voice into a poem or a story/ i am trying
desperately to give that/ i am not trying to give you a
history of my family/ the struggle of black people all over
the world or the fight goin on upstairs tween susie &

matt/ i am giving you a moment/ like something isnt coming back/ a something particularly itself/ like an alto solo in december in nashville in 1937.[61]

NOTES

1. Martin Heidegger, "The Age of the World Picture," in *The Question Concerning Technology and Other Essays*, trans. William Lovitt (New York: Harper & Row, 1977), 3–35; Hazel V. Carby, " 'On the Threshold of Woman's Era': Lynching, Empire, and Sexuality in Black Feminist Theory," *Critical Inquiry*, 12, No. 1 (Autumn 1985), 262–277.
2. See Kate Linker and Jane Weinstock, guest curators, *Difference: On Representation and Sexuality* (New York: The New Museum of Contemporary Art, 1984); Henry Louis Gates, Jr., guest editor, *"Race," Writing, and Difference*, *Critical Inquiry*, 12, No. 1 (Autumn 1985). This volume also includes Jacques Derrida's essay, "Racism's Last Word," trans. Peggy Kamuf, 290–299, written for the catalogue of *Art contre/against Apartheid*.
3. *Ntozake Shange, a photograph: lovers in motion*, in *Three Pieces* (New York: Penguin, 1981), 77.
4. Shange, *a photograph*, 93, 108. In Act 2, Sean repeats this phrase almost as an autobiographical refrain.
5. Theatre's curative power as pharmakon underlies the well-known theories of the dramatic scapegoat developed separately by Kenneth Burke and René Girard. However, Jacques Derrida, in "La Pharmacie de Platon," in *La dissémination* (Paris: Éditions du Seuil, 1972), 69–197, discusses the illusory nature of such a cure, entrapped as it is within the larger world picture of an illusory metaphysics, what I will discuss below as the ideology of the visible. For a discussion of Burke's specific metaphysical entrapment, see Timothy Murray, "Kenneth Burke's Logology: A Mock Logomachy," in *Glyph 2* (Baltimore: Johns Hopkins University Press, 1977), 144–161.
6. Shange, "unrecovered losses/ black theatre traditions," *Three Pieces*, p. xiv.
7. Shange, *a photograph*, 63.
8. Heidegger, "The Age of the World Picture," 129–130.
9. Shange, *a photograph*, 76.
10. Heidegger, "The Age of the World Picture," 132.
11. Shange, *a photograph*, 79.
12. Jean-François Lyotard, "Answering the Question: What is Postmodernism?" trans. Régis Durand, in *Innovation/Renovation: New Perspectives on the Humanities*, eds. Ihab and Sally Hassan (Madison: University of Wisconsin Press, 1983), 333.
13. Ibid.
14. Shange, *a photograph*, 76–77.
15. Ibid., 93.
16. Elaine Jackson, *Toe Jam*, in *Black Drama Anthology*, eds. Woodie King and Ron Milner (New York: Signet), 649.
17. Shange, *a photograph*, 95. For acute discussions of the cinematic look and sexual politics, see Laura Mulvey, "Visual Pleasure and Narrative Cinema," and Kate Linker, "Representation and Sexuality," both included in Brian Wallis, ed., *Art After Modernism: Rethinking Representation* (New York: The New Museum of Contemporary Art/ Boston: David R. Godine, 1984), 361–89; 391–415.
18. Adrienne Kennedy, *An Evening with Dead Essex*, *Theater*, 9, No. 2 (Spring 1978), 71.
19. Ibid.
20. Amiri Baraka, *The Motion of History* (New York: William Morrow, 1978), 108. I discuss Baraka's work more fully in an earlier version of this essay, "Screening the Camera's Eye: Black and White Confrontations of Technological Representation," *Modern Drama*, 28, No. 1 (March 1985), 110–124. See Michael R. Winston, "Racial Consciousness and the Evolution of Mass Communications in the United States," *Daedalus*, "Print Culture and Video Culture," 111, No. 4 (Fall 1982), 171–182, for an

insightful discussion of the false hope in television as a racial consciousness raiser.

21. Shange, *a photograph*, 62.

22. This aside is especially pertinent given the recent increase of police surveillance of American anti-apartheid demonstrations. In the Summer of 1985, to cite one instance, Cornell University faculty picketers for divestment found themselves being secretly photographed by (male) University police agents peering out the windows of a (women's) bathroom—a sadly humorous example of the extent to which surveillance of race/gender becomes confused.

23. Marcelin Pleynet with Jean Thibaudeau, "Economique, idéologie, formel," *Cinéthique*, 3 (1969), 10, as cited by Jean-Louis Comolli in "Technique and Ideology: Camera, Perspective, Depth of Field," *Film Reader* 2 (1977), 129. For elaborations on film's relation to perspectival theory, see William C. Wees, "The Cinematic Image: As a Visualization of Sight," *Wide Angle*, 4, No.3, 28–37, and Serge Daney's "Sur Salador," *Cahiers du cinéma*, 222 (July 1970), 39, where he defines the ideology of the visible.

24. Jean-Louis Comolli, "Machines of the Visible," in *The Cinematic Apparatus*, eds. Teresa de Lauretis and Stephen Heath (London: Macmillan, 1980), 126.

25. Jean-Louis Baudry, *L'effet cinéma* (Paris: Éditions Albatros, 1978), 25. See also Christian Metz's comments on monocular perspective in *Le signifiant imaginaire: psychanalyse et cinéma* (Paris: 10/18, 1977), 70–71.

26. Lyotard, "Answering the Question," 335–336. For Lyotard's more complete discussion of the ideological role of consensus in postmodern culture, see *La condition postmoderne* (Paris: Éditions de Minuit, 1979).

27. Jean-François Lyotard, "Contribution des tableaux de Jacques Monory," in *Figurations 1960/1973*, ed. Bernard Lamarche-Vadel (Paris: 10/18, 1973), 156.

28. Jacques Derrida, *L'écriture et la différence* (Paris: Éditions du Seuil, 1967), 345.

29. Timothy Murray, "Patriarchal Panopticism, or The Seduction of a Bad Joke: *Getting Out* in Theory," *Theatre Journal*, 35, No. 3 (October 1983), 376–388.

30. Walter Benjamin, "The Work of Art in the Age of Mechanical Reproduction," in *Illuminations*, trans. Harry Zohn (New York: Schocken, 1969), 234.

31. Max Horkheimer and Theodor W. Adorno, *Dialectic of Enlightenment*, trans. John Cumming (New York: Continuum, 1982), 130–131.

32. Benjamin, "The Work of Art," 230.

33. Metz, *Le signifiant imaginaire*, 61–94.

34. Jackson, *Toe Jam*, 169–170.

35. Herbert Blau, *Blooded Thought: Occasions of Theatre* (New York: Performing Arts Journal Publications, 1982), 134.

36. Ibid., 132.

37. Ibid., 130. Blau is not alone in arguing for the representational specificity of the dramatic body. In "Signes et sens du corps dans le théâtre moderne," *Parachute* 27 (Summer 1982), 35, Wladimir Krysinski goes so far as to conclude that "the modern theatre is marked by the predominance of value systems favoring the body and putting it in relief . . . As a theatrical sign liberated from the constraining logos, the body lays the foundation of the symbolic fable."

38. Woodie King and Ron Milner, "Introduction: Evolution of a People's Theatre," in *Black Drama Anthology* (New York: Signet, 1971), viii.

39. In *For Marx*, trans. Ben Brewster (London: NLB, 1977), 228, Louis Althusser stresses that "an empiricism of the subject always corresponds to an idealism of the essence (or an empiricism of the essence to an idealism of the subject)."

40. Shange, *spell no. 7: geechee jibara quik magic trance for technologically stressed third world people*, in *Three Pieces*, 44–45. Shange, *a photograph*, 60.

42. Ibid., 80.

43. Ibid., 77.

44. Ibid.

45. Ibid., 85.

46. Ibid., 86.

47. Louis Althusser, "Ideology and Ideological State Apparatuses: Notes Towards an Investigation," trans. Ben Brewster, in *Lenin and Philosophy and Other Essays* (New York: Monthly Review Press, 1971), 162.

48. Shange, "foreword/ unrecovered losses/ black theater traditions," in *Three Pieces*, ix.

49. In "Lessons from Brecht," *Screen*, 15, No. 2 (Summer 1974), 111, Stephen Heath emphasizes how theatre and film can work together to achieve a Brechtian alienation effect, similar to Baraka's, in which "the aim is no longer to fix the spectator apart as receiver of a representation but to pull the audience into an activity of reading; far from separating the spectator, this is a step towards his inclusion in a process."

50. On the theory of collage and its practical applications, see the special issue of *Revue d'esthétique*, 3–4 (1978) on *Collages* (Paris: 10/18); Derrida's readings of the frames and margins of textuality—most pertinent to the concerns of this text is *La vérité en peinture* (Paris: Flammarion, 1978); and Gregory L. Ulmer's discussion of Heidegger, Derrida, and the pictures of montage in "The Object of Post-Criticism," in *The Anti-Aesthetic: Essays on Postmodern Culture*, ed. Hal Foster (Port Townsend, Wash.: Bay Press, 1983), 83–110.

51. Kennedy, *An Evening with Dead Essex*, 72.

52. Ibid., 71–72.

53. See Heath, "Lessons from Brecht," 110.

54. On the relation of libidinal economies to political and aesthetic economies, see Jean-François Lyotard, *Discours, figure* (Paris: Éditions Klincksieck, 1973) and *Économie libidinale* (Paris: Éditions de Minuit, 1974). In "The Place of Visual Illusions," in *The Cinematic Apparatus*, eds. de Lauretis and Heath, 143–150, Maureen Turim discusses the applicability of Lyotard's theories to discussions of the cinematic apparatus.

55. Shange, "unrecovered losses/ black theater traditions," foreword to *Three Pieces*, xv.

56. Ibid., xiii.

57. Kennedy, "A Growth of Images, *The Drama Review*, 21, No. 4 (December 1977), 42.

58. Shange, *See No Evil: Prefaces, Essays & Accounts, 1976–1983* (San Francisco: Momo's Press, 1984), 31.

59. On the Freudian notion of narcissism and its phallocratic entrapment of woman, see Luce Irigaray, *Speculum de l'autre femme* (Paris: Éditions de Minuit, 1974); and Julia Kristeva, *Pouvoirs de l'horreur: essai sur l'abjection* (Éditions du Seuil, 1980).

60. In the words of Henry Louis Gates, Jr., "Writing 'Race' and the Difference It Makes," *Critical Inquiry*, 12, No. 1 (Autumn 1985), 12, "Black writing, and especially the language of the slave [enslaved woman?], served not to obliterate the difference of race; rather, the inscription of the black voice in Western literatures has preserved those very cultural differences to be repeated, imitated, and revised in a separate Western literary tradition, a tradition of black difference." On the difference of black autobiography per se, see Roger Rosenblatt, "Black Autobiography: Life as the Death Weapon," in James Olney, ed., *Autobiography: Essays Theoretical and Critical* (Princeton: Princeton University Press, 1980), 169–180.

61. Shange, *See No Evil*, 32.

My Statue, My Self:

Autobiographical Writings of Afro-American Women

Elizabeth Fox-Genovese

Zora Neale Hurston, in her troubling autobiography *Dust Tracks on a Road*, unmistakably identifies the problematic relation between her private self and her self-representation: "I did not know then, as I know now, that people are prone to build a statue of the kind of person that it pleases them to be." Few people, she adds, "want to be forced to ask themselves, 'What if there is no me like my statue?' The thing to do is to grab the broom of anger and drive off the beast of fear" (34).

Hurston's statue has recently been rescued from the attics of marginal memory and received its deserved place in the museum of cultural history. But its rescuers have authenticated it in the name of values that Hurston herself might have found puzzling and perhaps would not even have entirely approved. While she might have been delighted to be acknowledged, finally, as the centerpiece of an Afro-American female literary tradition, she might also have been secretly disappointed to be acknowledged as only that. More than anything, she might have been surprised to see her multiple—and intentionally duplicitous—self-representations accepted as a progenitor of the new Afro-American female self. She might even have laughed before drawing herself up to look mean and impressive. For the rescue of Hurston's statue has been effected, at least in part, at the expense of the anger and the fear and of their consequences for the ways in which she chose publicly to represent her very private self.

The authentication of Hurston's statue cannot be divorced

from the authentication of the Afro-American female literary tradition as a whole. In the search for mothers' gardens, it is both central and pivotal.[1] For Hurston, as often as not, speaks in the language of everyday use. But what are we to make of her when she does not? What, especially, do we make of the autobiography in which she does not? Hurston continually challenges us to rethink our preconceptions, to forswear our fantasies. Attentively read, she reminds that more often than not the autobiographies of Afro-American women have been written from within the cage. Frequently they sing with the voice of freedom, but always they betray the confinement from which that freedom is wrested. Linda Brent, crouched in her grandmother's attic, knows more freedom than she knew as the prey of Dr. Flint's assaults, but the freedom of her soul cannot relieve the confinement of her body. The self, in other words, develops in opposition to, rather than as an articulation of, condition. Yet the condition remains as that against which the self is forged. And the condition, as much as the representations of self, constitutes an inescapable aspect of the Afro-American female literary tradition, especially of Afro-American women's autobiographies.

Hurston's statue, like that of her foremothers and successors, was fashioned of disparate materials. Uneasily poised between the discourses through which any writer represents the self and the conditions of gender, class, and race through which any personal experience is articulated, the statue embodies elements of both. But the combining of elements transforms them. Hurston does not simply "tell it like it is," does not write directly out of experience. The discourses through which she works—and presumably expects to be read—shape her presentation of experience even as her specific experience shapes the ways in which she locates herself in discourses.

Hurston, in fact, never explicitly describes her own statue, although internal evidence suggests that she, like other female autobiographers (notably Simone de Beauvoir), had set her sights on an ideal beyond the horizon of everyday life, beyond the boundaries of her immediate community, beyond the confines of her gender.[2] For Hurston, the statue figures as the ideal for the self or, in psychoanalytic language, the ego ideal. The challenge of the autobiography, then, is to relate the ideal self to the self of everyday life—the contingent self. In Hurston's

case, the statue might be said to consist primarily in a freedom
from the contingent self that would permit her access as an
equal to the republic of letters, the ideal interpretive community. Yet her picture of her contingent self emphasizes all the
attributes that would bar her from membership in that community: her gender, her race, her identification with place. It
also presents her progress towards her statue as, in large part,
a succession of dependencies. Like the fool of Shakespearian
drama, she fawns and flatters, reserving to herself the right to
speak difficult truths that her demeanor and role appear to
belie. Like the trickster of Afro-American folk culture, she
speaks with a double tongue. Like the exile, she re-creates her
own previous life as a function of her nostalgia. How, in the
midst of this deliberate evasiveness that borders on willful
duplicity, are we to locate the core of her self-representation?
And how are we to locate it in relation to black women's
tradition of autobiography?

A literary tradition, even an autobiographical tradition, constitutes something more than a running, unmediated account
of the experience of a particular group. The coherence of such
a tradition consists as much in unfolding strategies of representation as in experience itself. Some would even argue that
the coherence of a tradition is only to be sought in the strategies of representation; the self is a function of discourse—a
textual construct—not of experience at all. Others, including
many black feminist critics, would emphasize black women's
writing as personal testimony to oppression, thus emphasizing experience at the expense of text. Neither extreme will do.
The coherence of black women's autobiographical discourse
does incontrovertibly derive from black women's experience,
although less from experience in the narrow empirical sense
than from condition—the condition or interlocking structures
of gender, class, and race. But it derives even more from the
tension between condition and discourse, from the changing
ways in which black women writers have attempted to represent a personal experience of condition through available discourses and in interaction with imagined readers.

Autobiographies of black women, each of which is necessarily personal and unique, constitute a running commentary on
the collective experience of black women in the United States.
They are inescapably grounded in the experience of slavery

and the literary tradition of the slave narratives. Their common denominator, which establishes their integrity as a subgenre, derives not from the general categories of race or sex, but from the historical experience of being black and female in a specific society at a specific moment and over succeeding generations.[3] Black women's autobiographies resist reduction to either political or critical pieties and resist even more firmly reduction to mindless empiricism. In short, they command an attention to theory and method that respects their distinctiveness as a discourse and their relation to other discourses.

In what sense can black women's autobiographies be read as constituting a distinct discourse? Why should they not be lumped with those of black men or those of white women? Politics justifies the differentiation, but its introduction disputes what some would see as the self-referential nature of the autobiographical text. To categorize autobiographies according to the race and gender of those who write them is to acknowledge some relation, however problematical, between the text and its author and, more, between the text and its author's experience. And to acknowledge this relation is to dispute prevailing theories of the multiple deaths of the subject, the self, and the author. Much contemporary theory has found the relations between politics—understood broadly as collective human experience—and the text problematic. These autobiographies defy any apolitical reading of texts, even—perhaps especially—when they seem to invite it.

To accept the ruling pieties about double oppression will not do. Simple addition does not amount to a new theoretical category. Sex assigns black women to the same category as white women; race assigns them to the same category as black men. Both feminist and black-nationalist critics consider their particular claims prior and decisive. Neither group shows much interest in class relations in particular or social relations in general. In all fairness, sex and race more readily lend themselves to symbolization than does class, and thus they also more readily lend themselves to representation, fabulation, and myth. Sex and race more obviously define what we intuitively perceive ourselves to be: male or female, white or black. But even these basic self-perceptions are socially learned and result from acts of (re)cognition. The question thus remains: Why do we find it so much more acceptable to perceive ourselves as members of a sex or a race than as members of a gender or, even more, of a class?[4]

Americans, as a people, do not like fences. Yet as a people we have spent most of our history in raising them. Our open lands lie carved, parceled, and constructed. Our landscape features barriers. Gender and class transform sex and race into barriers, transform the forms of their exclusion into positive social values. To argue for the centrality of gender and class to any analysis of women's self-representation is not to deny the overpowering force of the racism and sexism that stalk women's experience. It is, rather, to argue that if we focus exclusively on sexism and racism we remain mired in the myths we are trying to dissipate.

In theory, it is possible to write about black women's autobiographies as so many discrete cases of the genre "autobiography." Like other autobiographers, black women construct prose portraits of themselves as histories of their lives or of the salient aspects of their lives. The special relation between the autobiographer and the final text outshines all other considerations, especially referential considerations, and reduces specific aspects of the individual history to accidents. There is no theoretical distinction to be made between Jean-Jacques Rousseau's *Confessions* and Zora Neale Hurston's *Dust Tracks*.[5]

Feminist critics, like critics of Afro-American and Third World literatures, are beginning to refuse the implied blackmail of Western, white, male criticism. The death of the subject and of the author may accurately reflect the perceived crisis of Western culture and the bottomless anxieties of its most privileged subjects—the white male authors who had presumed to define it. Those subjects and those authors may, as it were, be dying, but it remains to be demonstrated that their deaths constitute the collective or generic death of subject and author. There remain plenty of subjects and authors who, never having had much opportunity to write in their own names or the names of their kind, much less in the name of the culture as a whole, are eager to seize the abandoned podium. The white male cultural elite has not in fact abandoned the podium; it has merely insisted that the podium cannot be claimed in the name of any particular personal experience. And it has been busily trying to convince the world that intellectual excellence requires depersonalization and abstraction. The virtuosity, born of centuries of privilege, with which these ghosts of authors make their case demands that others, who have something else to say, meet the ghosts' standards of pyrotechnics.[6]

Rejection of the prevailing pyrotechnics does not guarantee their replacement by something better. The theoretical challenge lies in bringing sophisticated skills to the service of a politically informed reading of texts. To read well, to read fully, is inescapably to read politically, but to foreground the politics, as if these could somehow be distinguished from the reading itself, is to render the reading suspect. Political and social considerations inform any reading, for all readers are political and social beings. To deny the applicability of political or social considerations is to take a political position. The reading of black women's autobiographies forcefully exposes the extent to which the tools of criticism are shaped by the politics that guide them. Wole Soyinka insists upon the bourgeois character of "culture"—its origins, its finality, and its instruments—but he also insists that the dismissal of all "culture" on the grounds of bourgeois contamination ends in "the destruction of all discourse" (55).

Black women's autobiography, as a category, requires justification, and justification requires classification and the delineation of principles and practices of reading.[7] The classification of black women's autobiography forces careful consideration of extratextual conditions. Some current critical tendencies reject the relevance of the extratextual and insist, in a manner reminiscent of the once New Criticism, on evaluating the text on its aesthetic merits, free of such extraneous influences as the experience of the author. These days, evaluating the autobiographical text on its merits is further seen to expose as romanticism and humanism any concern with the self as in some way prior to the text. These views embody a sharp and understandable reaction against the more sentimental manifestations of bourgeois individualism, but they hardly provide adequate critical standards for the classification of black women's autobiography as a distinct subgenre.

To take the text on its merits legitimates Mattie Griffith's *Autobiography of a Slave Girl* as the autobiography of an Afro-American slave—which it was not. As Robert Stepto has tellingly argued, authentication of the author as author of his or her own text ranked as an important concern for the authors of slave narratives. Stepto proposes a categorization of slave narratives according to the relation between plot or narrative and legitimation in the text as a whole.[8] Although Stepto does not discuss the earliest known prose writings by Afro-American women, both Harriet Jacobs's *Incidents in the Life of a Slave Girl* and Harriet Wilson's *Our Nig* contain legitimating documentation that different readers may perceive as more or less integral parts of the texts. But both Harriet Jacobs, who wrote under a pseudonym, and Harriet Wilson, who did not, felt impelled if not obliged to provide verification of their being both themselves and worthy women. These tactical maneuvers to authenticate the black woman's authorship oblige modern readers to respect these authors' concern for the relation between their texts and their experience. They do not oblige us to take any of the history offered in the texts at face value. Rather, we should be prepared merely to accept the text as bearing some (possibly distorted) relation to reality.

The principles of classification must begin with history. Barbara Christian insists upon the significance of periodization for understanding the development of black women's fiction during the twentieth century. Gwendolyn Brooks, who organized her own autobiography around the historical sea change of the emergence of a new form of black consciousness in the 1960s, forcefully emphasizes the relation between history and consciousness. "There is indeed," she wrote in 1972 in *Report from Part One*, "a new black today. He is different from any the world has known . . . And he is understood by no white." And, she adds: "I have hopes for myself."[9] For Christian, Brooks, and other critics of and participants in black women's culture, the relevant history concerns the coming to consciousness of Afro-Americans during the second half of the twentieth century, and perhaps the growth of American women's consciousness during the same period. The black movement and the feminist movement, with all their internal currents and tensions, have presided over the recent developments in Afro-American women's political and self-consciousness. Both have contributed to the growing emphasis on varieties of Pan-Africanism, including Pan-African feminism, and the repudiation of slavery as a significant contributor to contemporary black consciousness. In this general respect, race is taken to transcend class in the forging of Afro-American identities. Notwithstanding these long, tempestuous, and unresolvable debates, a specific case can be made for the autobiographies of black women.

Nikki Giovanni has, with special force, made the case for the relation of black women's autobiographies to changing political conditions. She attacks the assumption "that the self is not part of the body politic," insisting, "there's no separation" (Tate 62). Giovanni believes that literature, to be worthy of its claims, must reflect and seek to change reality. And the reality black people have known has left much to be desired: "It's very difficult to gauge what we have done as a people when we have been systematically subjected to the whims of other people" (Tate 63). According to Giovanni, this collective subjection to the whims of others has resulted in the alienation of black Americans from other Americans. For as black Americans "living in a foreign nation we are, as the wandering Jew, both myth and reality." Giovanni believes that black Americans will always be "strangers. But our alienation is our greatest strength" (Tate 70). She does not believe that the alienation, or the collective history that produced it, makes black experience or writing incomprehensible to others. "I have not created a totally unique, incomprehensible feat. I can understand Milton and T. S. Eliot, so the critic can understand me. That's the critic's job" (Tate 64).

Personal experience must be understood in social context. Its representation is susceptible to the critic's reading, regardless of whether he or she shares the personal experience. Giovanni rejects the claim that black writing should be the exclusive preserve of black critics—that it is qualitatively different from white writing, immune to any common principles of analysis, and thus severed from any common discourse. There is no argument about the ways in which the common discourse has treated black writing, especially the writing of black women: shamefully, outrageously, contemptuously, and silently. The argument concerns who can read black texts and the principles of the reading. For, as Soyinka said, if the denial of bourgeois culture ends in the destruction of discourse, the refusal of critical distance ends in the acceptance of an exceptionalism that portends extreme political danger.

Giovanni explicitly and implicitly makes the main points: the identity of the self remains hostage to the history of the collectivity; the representation of the self in prose or verse invites the critical scrutiny of the culture. Both points undercut the myth of the unique individual and force a fresh look at the autobiographies of black women.

Selwyn R. Cudjoe, writing of Maya Angelou, has insisted that Afro-American autobiography "as a form tends to be bereft of any *excessive subjectivism* and *mindless* egotism." Rather, Afro-American autobiographies present the experience of the individual "as reflecting a much more *im-personal* condition, the autobiographical subject emerging as an almost random member of the group, selected to tell his/her tale." Accordingly, he views Afro-American autobiography as "a *public* rather than a *private* gesture, *me-ism* gives way to *our-ism* and superficial concerns about *individual subject* usually give way to the *collective subjection* of the group" (9). Cudjoe contends that these characteristics establish black autobiography as objective and realistic. In so arguing, he is extending significantly the tradition of the slave narratives that sought to provide living, firsthand accounts of the evils of "that demon slavery" for a northern audience.[10]

The genre of black autobiography contains an important strand that could be subsumed under the general rubric of "report from the war zone." Brooks uses "report" in her title, *Report From Part One.* Giovanni's *Gemini* features a rather staccato, journalistic style. Both depict the author's "self" indirectly, obliquely, through reports of actions more than through discussions of states of mind. The responsibility to report on experience even more clearly shapes such autobiographies as those of Ida B. Wells and Era Bell Thompson. In their representations of a specific life, the autobiographical writings of many black women, like those of many black men, do bear witness to a collective experience—to black powers of survival and creativity as well as to white oppression. Much of the autobiographical writing of black women eschews the confessional mode—the examinations of personal motives, the searchings of the soul—that white women autobiographers so frequently adopt. Black women's autobiographies seem torn between exhibitionism and secrecy, between self-display and self-concealment. The same is true of all autobiographies, but the proportions differ from text to text, perhaps from group to group of autobiographers. And the emotions and events displayed or concealed also differ.

All autobiographers confront the problem of readers, the audience to whom their self-representation is addressed. Black female autobiographers confront the problem in especially acute form—or so their texts suggest.[11] Harriet Jacobs and Harriet Wilson seem to have assumed that most of their readers would be white abolitionists or potential abolitionists. Both, especially Harriet Jacobs, also seem to have addressed themselves especially to white, middle-class women. Neither Jacobs nor Wilson identified with those likely readers, but both sought to interest them. And in both cases, the professed reason for seeking that interest was to instruct white women in the special horrors of slavery for women and the ways in which the tentacles of slavery reached into the interstices of northern society. Both texts reveal that their authors harbored deep bitterness toward northern society in general and northern white women in particular, even though they frequently expressed it indirectly. And that bitterness inescapably spills over into their imagined relations to their readers, into the ways in which they present themselves and their histories.

There is little evidence that black women autobiographers assumed that any significant number of other black women would read their work. To the extent that they have, until very recently, written for other black women, they seem to have written for younger women, for daughters, for those who would come after. Black women's autobiographies abound with evidence of or references to the love that black female autobiographers felt for and felt from their female elders: mothers, aunts, grandmothers. For the most part, those female elders are represented as rural in identification and origin, if not always in current location; immersed in folk communities; deeply religious; and the privileged custodians of the values and, especially, of the highest standards of their people. They are not necessarily literate, and those who are literate are unlikely to spend money on any books except the Bible.

From Harriet Jacobs and Harriet Wilson onward, black female autobiographers wrote to be read by those who might influence the course of public events, might pay money for

their books, or might authenticate them as authors. Neither
Jacobs nor Wilson wrote primarily, much less exclusively, for
members of the slave community. How could they have?
Subsequent black women autobiographers, many of whom
have been writers or professional women, have also tended to
write as much for white readers, or for black male intellectuals, as for other black women. Their focus has been changing
recently with the explosion of Afro-American women's fiction
in the work of Toni Morrison, Alice Walker, Ntozake Shange,
Gloria Naylor, and many others.[12] But regardless of the present circumstances, it is difficult to find evidence for the emergence of a distinctive Afro-American domestic literary tradition
or women's culture during the nineteenth and even the first
half of the twentieth century.

Afro-American women have written of themselves as persons and as women under special conditions of colonization.
In this respect, their writings cry out for comparison with
those of white women. Prevailing opinion insists upon the
special tradition of white American women's writing during
the nineteenth and early twentieth centuries. Despite frequently
sharp differences among feminist critics, there remains a general consensus that white women wrote themselves out of
their domestic tradition in both senses of the phrase: they
wrote from the experience, and they wrote to subvert the
constraints it imposed upon them. It is not fashionable to
insist upon the colonization of the imagination of white women
writers, but it, too, has existed. For white women did suffer
exclusion from the dominant cultural traditions and frequently
from the educations and careers that provided the institutional foundations for equal participation in those traditions.
That is a different problem, but it deserves mention as a way
of locating the experience of black women in relation to the
complexities of American culture as a system. It has been
possible for feminist critics to pass briefly over white women's
relation to the "high culture" of their period, in part, because
of the general agreement about women's identification with
literary domesticity. White women largely accepted the limitations of their sphere, sometimes turning the limitations to
their advantage, and wrote either as representatives of its
values, or for its other members, or both. However one as-
sesses the value of their efforts and of their contributions

(neglected, silenced) to American culture, it remains beyond dispute that they self-consciously wrote as women, as the representatives of a gender.[13]

For white American women, the self comes wrapped in gender, or rather, gender constitutes the invisible, seamless wrapping of the self. Such is the point of gender in a stable society. For in stable societies gender, in the sense of society's prescriptions for how to grow up as a man or as a woman, is inculcated in tandem with and indissolubly bound to the child's growing sense of "who I am." To be an "I" at all, to be a self, is to belong to a gender. Any society contains individuals who, for whatever reason, find their gender identification problematic. During the nineteenth and twentieth centuries, many American women began to question the attributes of or limitations on their gender. But, at least until World War II, most white American women apparently accepted their society's view of gender as in some deep way related to the persons they perceived themselves to be. For gender, understood as the social construction of sexuality, mediates between sexual identity and social identity—it binds the former to the latter and roots the latter in the former.

Under unstable social conditions, it is possible for gender, as a normative model of being male or female, to come unstuck from sexuality. Once the gaps between sexuality and gender begin to appear, men and women can begin to question whether gender flows naturally from sexuality, whether social demands on the individual are biologically determined. Gender identities derive from a system of gender relations. How to be a woman is defined in relation to how to be a man and the reverse. Neither masculinity nor femininity exists as an absolute.

In a society and culture like that of the United States, a dominant gender system or model of gender relations wrestles with various subsystems or alternate systems. But from at least the beginnings of the nineteenth century and the consolidation of the special American version of the ideology of separate spheres, the dominant model of gender relations has exercised hegemony, in part because of its importance as an alternative to class relations as a system of social classification, and in part because of its invitation to different groups of immigrants who brought with them one or another version of separate male and female spheres and a commitment to one or another form of male dominance. The hegemony of that gender system has influenced the ways in which most American women have written about themselves and their lives, and it especially has influenced their sense of their readers.

The experience and writings of Afro-American women have departed significantly from this model. For the experience of Afro-American women has left them simultaneously alienated from and bound to the dominant models in ways that sharply differentiate their experience from that of white women. There is no reason to believe that Afro-American women experienced gender as the seamless wrapping of their selves. Slavery bequeathed to Afro-American women a double view of gender relations that fully exposed the artificial or problematic aspects of gender identification. Slavery stripped black men of the social attributes of manhood in general and fatherhood in particular. As a result, black women had no satisfactory social definition of themselves as women. This social "unmanning" of the men, with its negative consequences for the women, should not be confused with the personal emasculation upon which some historians have erroneously insisted.[14] Sojourner Truth captured the contradictions in her address "Ar'n't I a Woman?" In effect Truth was insisting on her own femaleness and then querying the relation between her experience of being female and the white, middle-class experience of being a woman. She may not have put it quite that way, and she may not fully have elaborated the depths of the pain and the contradictions, but she exposed the main aspect of the problem: black slave women had suffered the pain of childbirth and the sorrow of losing children and had labored like men. Were they or were they not women?[15]

Truth's query has been widely recognized as a challenge to the possible self-satisfaction of middle-class men and women with respect to black slave women, who were not normally helped over puddles or wrapped in protective coverings. It has been recognized less widely as a challenge to assumptions about the nature of the links between femaleness and self-perception or identity in Afro-American women. Truth effectively chided white men and women for their racism—for not welcoming black women into the sisterhood of womanhood. But there is more to the story.

Truth counterposed "I"—the self—and "woman" in her hostile challenge to her white audience. Black female autobiographers have done the same, although not always with such open defiance. The tension at the heart of black women's autobiography derives in large part from the chasm between an autobiographer's intuitive sense of herself and her attitude toward her probable readers. Imagined readers shape the ways in which an autobiographer constructs the narrative of her life. Harriet Jacobs, in *Incidents in the Life of a Slave Girl*, left no doubt about the audience for whom she thought she was writing: "O, you happy free women, contrast *your* New Year's day with that of the poor bond-woman!" (14).

Jacobs wrote, at least in part, to introduce the world to the special horrors of slavery for women. To achieve her goal, she sought to touch the hearts of northern white women and, accordingly, wrote as far as possible in their idiom. She so doggedly followed the model of sentimental domestic fiction that for a long time it was assumed that her editor, Lydia Maria Child, had written the book. Jacobs's surviving correspondence proves that she, not Child, wrote her own story, as she claimed in its subtitle: "written by herself."[16] And Jacobs's text differs significantly in tone and content from other examples of domestic fiction. In particular, her withering indictment of slavery portrays the institution as a violation of womanhood. Time and again she not merely asserts but demonstrates that if slavery is bad for men, it is worse for women. Thinking that she understands the northern, middle-class female audience, she specifically relates the horrors of slavery for women to assaults upon female chastity and conjugal domesticity.

Linda Brent, Jacobs's self in the narrative, grows up in the shadow of her master's determination to possess her sexually. She claims to fend off his advances as an affront to her chastity. Ultimately, her determination to avoid him leads her, after her master has prohibited her sale and marriage to the free black man she loves, to accept another white man as a lover and to bear him two children. One important strand of her story concerns the ways in which she atones for this "fall" and, especially, regains the respect and love of her own daughter. In some sense Jacobs attempts to present her resistance to her master as a defense of her virtue, even though that defense leads her into a loss of "virtue" by another route. Jacobs does not fully resolve the contradictions in her behavior and principles at this level of discourse, however hard she tries. Ultimately, she throws herself on the pity—and guilt—of her readers, as she threw herself on the pity of her daughter. But Jacobs's text also invites another reading or, to put it differently, conceals another text.

Jacobs begins her narrative: "I was born a slave; but I never knew it till six years of happy childhood had passed away" (3). The claim not to have recognized one's condition—of race or of enslavement—until six or seven years of age is common among Afro-American authors.[17] For Jacobs, that opening sentence underscores the difference between condition and consciousness and thereby distances the self from the condition. But Jacobs never suggests that the condition does not, in some measure, influence the self. She insists that her father "had more of the feelings of a freeman than is common among slaves," thereby implicitly acknowledging the difference between slavery and freedom in the development of an independent self. In the same passage she reveals how heavily slavery could weigh upon the slave's sense of manhood. On one occasion Jacobs's father and mistress both happened to call her brother at the same moment. The boy, after a moment's hesitation, went to the mistress. The father sharply reproved him: "You are *my* child . . . and when I call you, you should come immediately, if you have to pass through fire and water" (7). The father's desire to command the primary obedience of his own child flows from his feelings of being a free man and contradicts the harshest realities of slavery. Slavery stripped men of fatherhood. Even a free father could not unambiguously call his child by a slave wife his own, for the child, following the condition of the mother, remained a slave. Jacobs is, surely not by accident, depicting a spirit of manliness and an instinctive grasp of the virtues of freedom in her father as the introduction to her own story of resistance.

Jacobs's narrative embodies every conceivable element of fantasy and ambiguity. Her father and mother were mulattoes who lived in a model of conjugal domesticity. Her maternal grandmother was the daughter of a South Carolina planter who apparently has inherited the lowcountry, slaveholding elite's own sense of honor—more than could be said for her owners. Jacobs, in other words, endows herself with a pedigree of physical, mental, and moral comeliness. She is not like the other slaves among whom she lives. She has the capacity to rise above her condition. Her sense of herself in relation to the other slaves leaves something to be desired for an opponent of slavery; worse, it reflects either her assimilation of "white" values or her determination to play to the prejudices of her audience. Jacobs offers a confused picture of the relation between the identity and behavior of Afro-Americans, including herself, and the effects of slavery. If slavery is evil, it has evil consequences. If those evil consequences include a breaking of the spirit of the enslaved, then how can slaves be credited with character and will? The questions circle on and on, admitting of no easy answers. Clearly they plague Jacobs.

These difficult questions do not seriously cloud Jacobs's sense of self. They do affect her sense of how best to present that self to others, her sense of the relation between her self and her gender, and her sense of the relation between self and social condition. The awareness of white readers deeply influences the ways in which she depicts life under slavery. But under, or woven through, the discourse for the readers runs a discourse for herself. For Jacobs herself, the primary issue between her and her master was not one of virtue, chastity, sexuality, or any of the rest. It was the conflict of two wills. Having described her master's foul intentions toward her, she adds that he had told her "I was made for his use, made to obey his command in *every* thing; that I was nothing but a slave, whose will must and should surrender to his" (16). The words make her "puny" arm feel stronger than it ever had: "The war of my life had begun; and though one of God's most powerless creatures, I resolved never to be conquered. Alas, for me!" (17). The "alas for me" should not be read as regret about her determination or as any acknowledgement that such willful feelings might be inappropriate for a woman, but as a confirmation that everything that follows stems directly from her determination not to be conquered.

Jacobs's narrative of her successful flight from slavery can be read as a journey or progress from her initial state of innocence; through the mires of her struggle against her social condition; to a prolonged period of ritual, or mythic, conceal-ment; on to the flight itself; and finally to the state of knowl-edge that accompanies her ultimate acquisition of freedom. The myth or metaphor of the journey to selfhood is as old as culture, although it has carried a special resonance for West-ern Christian, notably Protestant, culture. Jacobs, in some respects like Harriet Wilson, registers the end of the journey as a somewhat bleak dawn on a troubled landscape. Here is no pot of gold at the end of the rainbow. The accrued self-knowledge consists above all in the recognition that there is no resting place for the fugitive. The struggle for the dignity of the self persists. Insults and injuries abound in freedom as under slavery, albeit in different forms. Life remains a war. But the focused struggle of wills with the master has given way to a more generalized struggle to affirm the self in a hostile, or indifferent, environment.

Significantly, Harriet Wilson, whose narrative unfolds en-tirely in freedom, portrays the primary enemy as a woman rather than a man. To explore the respective cultural roles of men and women as heads of households in slave and free society would take us far afield. But the difference should be noted, not least because Wilson's enemy represents the world of female domesticity and, inescapably, underscores the possi-ble adversarial relation between the Afro-American female autobiographer and her readers.[18] Wilson's narrative remains even more problematical as autobiography than Jacobs's, for it is cast as a fiction—and it remains, overall, far more disturb-ing. I can only note in passing that its structure commands close attention, especially Wilson's purpose in beginning with the story of her white mother, Mag Smith, who, as the only alternative to starvation, married a black man who loves her.

Taken together, Jacobs's and Wilson's narratives establish some important characteristics of black women's autobiograph-ical writing. Both use the metaphor of the journey. Both betray mixed emotions toward their probable and intended (white, female) readers. Both embrace some of the rhetoric and conventions of literary domesticity even as they challenge the reigning pieties of its discourse. Both subvert the prom-ised candor toward those readers.

The problem of readers, of those for whom one writes,

persists in the autobiographical writing of black women, although it assumes a variety of forms. Writing in the late
1960s, Maya Angelou noted in an apparent aside in the first
volume of her own autobiography: "If you ask a negro where
he's been, he'll tell you where he's going" (86). Her observation should be appreciated in the context of Zora Neale
Hurston's calling storytelling "lying"—and then offering the
world her own demonstrably inaccurate autobiography.[19]

Hurston's autobiography poignantly captures the dilemmas
that seemed to confront black women writers—or intellectuals
—of her generation. *Dust Tracks on a Road* inimitably combines
all the best and worst of Hurston's intellect and imagination.
Critics and scholars have demonstrated that it does not pass
muster as a factual account of her life, beginning with its
inaccurate recording of her date of birth. Theoretically, that
mere inaccuracy should not matter to modern critics of the
text-in-itself: take the text on its merits and to hell with the
facts. But Hurston's deceptions in *Dust Tracks* may exceed
mere facts. She embellishes the text with a series of observations on contemporary politics and race relations that have
seriously disturbed some of her most devoted would-be ad-
mirers. Finally, although Hurston wrote much more in the
idiom of Afro-American culture, even of folk culture, than
Jacobs or Wilson, her text does not inspire confidence in the
"authenticity" of her self-revelation. In most respects, *Dust
Tracks* constitutes a marvel of self-concealment. Hurston, like
the storytellers on the porch whom she celebrated in *Mules
and Men*, delighted in "lying."

As the single most important link between the different
phases in black women's autobiographies, Hurston's autobiography commands at least a preliminary assessment.[20] Hurston
should be understood as a woman who was, regarding her
self-representation, concerned primarily with a "self" uncon-
strained by gender in particular and condition in general. Her
life made her an expert on anger and fear. Determined to
become a respected person, to become someone, she wrestled—
not always gracefully or successfully—with the expectations of
those around her. In mediating between the world of Eatonville
from which she came and the worlds of Baltimore, Washington, and New York to which she moved, she functioned as a
translator. In fact, Hurston used her acquired skills as an

anthropologist to describe the world of her childhood. Her uncommon gift for language brought that world to life in her pages, but her obsession with self-concealment led her to veil the nature of her identification with her origins. Hurston's narrator is her statue—the amused observer she wished to become.

Hurston's autobiography singularly lacks any convincing picture of her own feelings. Her little essay on "love," which purports to convey her adult feelings toward men, reads like the amused and balanced memories of a perfectly successful individual. Men are presented as having loved her even more than she loved them. Love is portrayed as having invariably treated her well. She gives no hint of bitter disappointment, longing, or crippling loss. Maybe she suffered none, although extratextual sources invite skepticism. But the passage itself looks more like a screen than a window. There is nothing in *Dust Tracks* to suggest that Hurston trusted her readers. She never precisely identifies them, although she cultivates an arresting mixture of the urbane intellectual and the *enfant terrible*. Presumably she expected to be read by New York intellectuals, black and white. And, presumably, she was not about to trust them with her private self.

Hurston provides clues about where she wants to go, what kind of statue she wants to build. She resoundingly repudiates any possible connection between slavery and her own life or self-representation. Slavery, however unfortunate, belongs to a past that has left no relevant legacy: "I have no personal memory of those times, and no responsibility for them" (282). Above all, she fears the debilitating effects of bitterness; to be bitter is to become dependent, crippled, humiliated. She appears to have forgotten her own earlier evocation of the "broom of anger," appears not to want to explore the place of righteous anger in her responses. The purpose of the broom of anger was to sweep away fear, and she is no longer acknowledging fear. By collapsing anger into bitterness and repudiating bitterness as, in some way, an unclean emotion, she is denying the need for anger. Facing the white reader, she prefers to deny the relevance of previous oppression to her sense of herself. Just as clearly as Jacobs, she expects "you" (her reader) to be white: "So I give you all my right hand of fellowship and love . . . In my eyesight, you lose nothing by

not looking just like me . . . Let us all be kissing-friends"
(286).

Hurston also refuses to attribute any significance to race.
Having been bombarded with the problem of race for years,
she saw the light when she "realized that I did not have to
consider any racial group as a whole. God made them duck
by duck and that was the only way I could see them" (235).
She learned that the color of the skin provided no measure of
the person inside, even though she acerbically points out that
blacks, like whites, rank blacks according to the degree of
lightness of their skin. She then reminds her readers that she
is of mixed race. Finally, with deep ambiguity, she asserts: "I
maintain that I have been a Negro three times—a Negro baby,
a Negro girl and a Negro woman." Yet she knows not what
"the Negro in America is like" (237). The Negro does not
exist. Independent of its political problems—and Hurston's
politics were nothing if not complex—this statement creates
considerable doubt about her identification as a woman. If the
Negro does not exist, and the only times that she has been a
Negro included the times at which she was a girl and a
woman, then what? The reader is left to complete the syllogism.

Dust Tracks constitutes only one panel in the triptych of
Hurston's autobiography. The second can be found in her
extraordinary novel, Their Eyes Were Watching God, and the
third in her collections of black folklore, notably Mules and
Men. Hurston's collections of folklore provide a way for her to
appropriate the collective history of the community to which
she belongs. Their Eyes Were Watching God, which is widely
recognized as an autobiographical novel, offers her most sustained attempt to provide some representations of her own
emotional life. Here, evoking the novel as an indispensable
counterpoint to Dust Tracks, I would emphasize one theme. In
the book's most famous passage, the protagonist Janie's grandmother says: "Honey, de white man is de ruler of everything
as fur as Ah been able tuh find out." There may be some place
"way off in de ocean" in which the black man rules, "but we
don't know nothin' but what we see." The white man throws
down his load and forces the black man to pick it up. "He
pick it up because he have to, but he don't tote it. He hand it
to his womenfolks. De nigger woman is de mule uh de world
so fur as Ah can see" (29). Janie's grandmother has been

praying that things will be different with her. Hurston portrays the answer to that prayer as Janie's relations with Tea Cake—a mutual delight in shared sexuality.

The world that Hurston depicts in *Their Eyes Were Watching God* closely resembles Maya Angelou's Stamps, Arkansas. Hurston does not emphasize the oppressive weight of the neighboring white community as much as Angelou does, but she does not shy away from its influence on the possible conditions of black lives, even in an entirely black community. And her plot mercilessly reveals the burdens that a legacy of slavery and racism impose on black people. In particular she subtly, almost deceptively, offers hints of her real feelings about what it means to be a black woman. She reveals the extent to which the black community—or black men—have embraced the gender conventions of white bourgeois society. Black men seek to transfer their burdens to black women by forcing those women into domestic corsets. A woman like Janie resists. She retains her commitment to equality and partnership with the man she loves. Above all, she retains a commitment to the possible joy of love and sexuality. But even at her moment of greatest success, the legacy of the social features of black manhood leads Teacake into a terrible battle. At the novel's close, which is also its beginning, she is returning home to other black women—alone and childless. Mules. Are they metaphors or reality? Mules abound in Hurston's work. Is she inviting us to understand black women like herself as being of mixed ancestry and incapable of reproduction? Is she inviting us—as she seems to be—to recognize both the richness and the dead-endedness of black women's own traditions? To attempt a clear answer would seem to be premature, but the elements of the puzzle should not be denied.

Throughout *Dust Tracks*, Hurston provides numerous clues that her primary identification, her primary sense of herself, transcends gender. Most dramatically, in a passage reminiscent of other tales of mythic births on mythically stormy nights, she relates that at her birth her mother was unprepared and without assistance.[21] Fate intervened by sending "a white man of many acres and things" to "granny" for her mother—to fill in for the missing midwife, Aunt Judy. It is a tale of wonderful reversals: Zora was brought into the world by a man rather than a woman, by a white rather than a black. The chapter in which she relates her birth concludes with a passage about her mother's alarm that at an early age Zora manifested a clear tendency to keep on walking toward the horizon. The mother explained this behavior by blaming "a woman who was an enemy of hers" for sprinkling " 'travel dust' around the doorstep the day I was born." Zora wonders at her mother's acceptance of such an explanation. "I don't know why it never occurred to her to connect my tendency with my father, who didn't have a thing on his mind but this town and the next one." She might have taken a hint from his wanderlust. "Some children are just bound to take after their fathers in spite of women's prayers" (32).

Hurston vacillates among sympathy, scorn, and amused tolerance in her discussion of the women of the black community from which she springs. She movingly depicts her grief and guilt at her own inability to carry out her dying mother's instructions due to the opposition of the other members of the black community. And she clearly links her own departure from the world of her childhood with her mother's death. She shows flashes of tenderness. But her identification with other black women remains shaky. She refuses the double role of victim and warrior that Jacobs constructs for herself. For Hurston to admit the conditions or causes of her possible victimization is to belittle herself. But her goals for herself—her statue—remain shaped by that refusal: she aspires, in some way, to transcend the constraints of group identification. By insisting on being a self independent of history, race, and gender, she comes close to insisting on being a self independent of body.

Hurston wrote under the influence of the Harlem Renaissance and the increasingly successful attempts of Afro-American men to establish a model of cultural respectability, and she wrote under the shadow of emerging professional successes for some middle-class white women. That is, she sought to carve a compelling statue for herself at a particular historical moment. Much like Harriet Jacobs, she pictured herself at war with the world in her attempt to defend her integrity. Much like Harriet Jacobs, she refused the limitations of gender and cultivated what she took to be the language of her readers only to subvert—or manipulate—their values. But where Jacobs warred with slavery, Hurston warred with a dominant bourgeois culture in which she sought acceptance as an equal. No less than Jacobs, Hurston warred with the legacy of slavery for black women. But changing times had made it difficult for her to name that war. And, unable or unwilling to name it, she spun web upon web of deception so that her statue of herself would appear to be standing in clouds.

Those who came after—especially Angelou, Giovanni, and Brooks—would find new names for the war and a new acceptance of their own black female bodies. But they would also benefit from the slow emergence of black women readers. And even they would remain at odds with the gender identifications of white society. The gap between black women and the dominant model of womanhood continues to add richness and mystery to black women's writing. The account of origins remains, at least in part, a map of "where I'm bound." The account of the black woman's self cannot be divorced from the history of that self or the history of the people among whom it took shape. It also cannot be divorced from the language through which it is represented, or from the readers of other classes and races who not only lay claim to it but who have helped to shape it. To write the account of one's self is to inscribe it in a culture that for each of us is only partially our own. For black women autobiographers, the gap between the self and the language in which it is inscribed looms especially large and remains fraught with struggle.

Above all, black women's autobiographies suggest a tension in black women's relations to various dominant discourses. Jacobs and Wilson both self-consciously sought to work within bourgeois women's domestic discourse, even as they subverted its deepest premises about the relations between the female self and gender. Their concern for discursive respectability persisted in the works of many black women from Reconstruction to the 1920s and flowered in the works of Jessie Fauset and Nella Larsen. This concern should be understood in the context of black people's struggle for respect within the confines of dominant American bourgeois conventions, even if the female embodiments of the tradition invariably, if covertly, challenged its stereotypical views of gender relations and gender identity. Hurston makes explicit two contradictory and submerged elements of that tradition: First, and most visibly, she restores funkiness and folk roots to black women's discourse; second, and no less important, she dares to articulate black women's craving for independent recognition in the republic of letters. Recent critics have reminded us that Harriet Beecher Stowe and Susan Warner deserve considerably more respect than the dominant (male) tradition chose to accord them.[22] But Hurston also had her eyes on the pinnacles of the prestigious tradition of Western letters, on Shakespeare and his canonized successors. Even her representation of black women's private selves was informed with this ambition. Her difficulty in clearly depicting her own statue resulted at least in part from the deadlock between her commitment to her roots as a black woman in a black community and her commitment to transcending all social and gender roots in her craft. In her fictional and anthropological writings, she could distance herself as artist—as translator—from the immediacy of her material. When she came to depict herself, the strategy faltered. How could she bear to lay bare that private self for which the canon allowed no position of respect? Nevertheless, the best clue to the essence of that private self lies in the troubling autobiography, which, more than all the other writings, reveals the struggles that wracked the self, even if it does not directly testify to them—does not, as it were, confess.

Few have written more movingly or with greater anger of the toll extracted by cultural colonization than Frantz Fanon. Fanon, in particular, walked the narrow boundary between recording the dreadful impact of specific instances of colonization and raising the concept of colonization to the status of a metaphor for the dependent status of all subgroups in a dominant culture. The autobiographies of Afro-American women similarly delineate a specific history of colonization and offer a compelling metaphor for the human spirit's dependency on the communities and forms of expression to which it belongs. Black women like Jacobs and Wilson insisted on their right to an independent self under conditions in which they could counterpoise the self to enslavement. Since emancipation, black women have been torn between their independent relation to the dominant culture and their people's relation to it. In complex ways, their self-perceptions retain a characteristically uneasy relation to the wrappings of gender. Is the black woman writer first a self, a solitary statue? Or is she first a woman—

and if so, in relation to whom? No dilemma could more clearly expose the condition of any self as hostage to society, politics, and language.

NOTES

1. See Walker, *In Search of Our Mothers' Gardens*. On new directions in black feminist criticism, see Smith; McDowell.
2. See Miller.
3. Black women's "autobiographies," as used here, includes some autobiographical fiction as well as formal autobiographies, both streams of which have sourcès in a rich oral Afro-American culture.
4. I am using *gender* to mean the social construction of sexuality.
5. For my own views on autobiography as a genre, see Fox-Genovese, *Autobiography of Du Pont de Nemours*, 38–51. Among the many other recent works on autobiography, see Olney, *Autobiography*; Weintraub; Lejeune; Gunn; Stone; and—for a review of recent critical trends—Lang, "Autobiography in the Aftermath of Romanticism."
6. The quintessential statement of the position remains Michel Foucault, "Qu'est-ce un auteur?" For a feminist defense of deconstruction in terms of the Third World, see Spivak, " 'Draupadi,' " but for a defense of the claims of gender and race, see her "Politics of Interpretation."
7. On the general problem of black women's autobiography, see Blackburn.
8. See Stepto. This article was apparently reprinted in the Davis collection from Stepto's *From Behind the Veil: A Study of Afro-American Narrative* (Urbana: University of Illinois Press, 1979).
9. Brooks's autobiography should be read in conjunction with her autobiographical novel, *Maud Martha*. See also Washington; Christian, *Black Literature and Literary Theory* and *Black Feminist Criticism*.
10. The phrase "demon slavery" is from Harriet Wilson, *Our Nig*.
11. See Tompkins, *Reader-Response Criticism*; Flynn and Schweickart, *Gender and Reading*.
12. See Christian, *Black Women Novelists*, for a preliminary periodization. For a sharp assessment of the relation between one black novelist and her readers, see Harris.
13. The work on white women's writing, in sharp contrast to that on black women's writing, has grown extensive. Among many, see Baym, Kelley, and Kolodny.
14. See Elkins, in particular. Elkins has not significantly revised his position in the two subsequent editions of *Slavery*. See, for instance, Lane. For alternate views on the effect of slavery on Afro-American men, see Harding and Genovese.
15. For a recent overview of women's position under slavery, see White.
16. See Yellin, "Texts and Contexts" and "Written by Herself." Henceforth, Yellin's edition of *Incidents* will be the standard, but it did not appear in time for me to use it in this essay. For Jacobs's account of her experience and authorship, see her correspondence in the Post family papers, University of Rochester Library. Dorothy Sterling has reprinted some of Jacobs's letters in her excellent anthology, *We Are Your Sisters*. On the general tradition of the slave narrative, see, among many, Starling; Sekora and Turner; Olney, " 'I Was Born' "; Baker; and Davis, "The Slave Narrative." As a rule, treatments of slave narratives take little or no account of any female perception, in part because so few women either escaped or wrote narratives.
17. See, among many, Hurston's *Their Eyes Were Watching God*: "Ah was wid dem white chillun so much till Ah didn't know Ah wuzn't white till Ah was round six years old" (21).
18. See Gates's introduction to *Our Nig*. He offers a preliminary exploration of the role of white women in the novel but does not discuss the problem of Wilson's attitude toward her readers. For a fuller discussion of the differences between women's roles in northern and southern households, see Fox-Genovese, *Within the Plantation Household*.

19. On the facts of Hurston's life and the variants of the text, see Hemmenway's introduction to *Dust Tracks*; see also his comprehensive study of her life and work, *Zora Neale Hurston*. For a composite picture of Hurston culled from her own writings, see Walker, *I Love Myself When I am Laughing*. See also Walker's essay on Hurston in *In Search of Our Mothers' Gardens*; Johnson, "Metaphor, Metonymy, and Voice"; Hurston, *Tell My Horse*.

20. On the successive phases of Afro-American women's writing, see McCaskill. The generation of Afro-American women writers that preceded Hurston, including Frances Ellen Watkins Harper, Amanda Smith, Julia Foote, Elizabeth Keckley, and Bethany Veney, focused on racial uplift and on proving the respectability of Afro-American womanhood.

21. Black women writers' use of African and Western myths deserves more attention than it has yet received. Angelou, for example, in *Gather Together in My Name*, reworks the Persephone myth for her own purposes. Jacobs, in the account of her period of concealment and flight, draws on African mythology. Gates's concept of the "signifying monkey" opens the discussion but does not pay special attention to the blending of cultures in Afro-American women's imaginations (see his "The 'Blackness of Blackness' " and *The Signifying Monkey*). For a sensitive discussion of Afro-American culture, see Levine.

22. See Tompkins; and Ann Douglas's introduction to Stowe.

WORKS CITED

Angelou, Maya. *I Know Why the Caged Bird Sings*. New York: Random House, 1969.
———.*Gather Together in My Name*. New York: Random House, 1974.
Baker, Houston A., Jr. "Autobiographical Acts and the Voice of the Southern Slave." In Davis, 242–61.
Baym, Nina. *Woman's Fiction: A Guide to Novels by and about Women in America 1820–1870*. Ithaca: Cornell University Press, 1978.
Blackburn, Regina. "In Search of the Black Female Self: African-American Women's Autobiographies and Ethnicity." In Jelinek, 133–48.
Brooks, Gwendolyn, *Maud Martha*. Boston: Atlantic Monthly Press, 1953.
———. *Report from Part One*. Detroit: Broadside Press, 1972.
Christian, Barbara. *Black Feminist Criticism: Perspectives on Black Women Writers*. New York: Pergamon Press, 1985.
———. *Black Women Novelists: The Development of a Tradition, 1892–1976*. Westport: Greenwood Press, 1980.
———. *Perspectives on Black Women Writers*. New York: Pergamon Press, 1985.
Cudjoe, Selwyn R. "Maya Angelou and the Autobiographical Statement." In Evans, 6–24.
Davis, Charles T. "The Slave Narrative: First Major Art Form in an Emerging Black Tradition." In Davis and Gates, 83–119.
———. *Black Is the Color of the Cosmos: Essays on Afro-American Literature and Culture, 1942–1981*. Ed. Henry Louis Gates. New York: Garland Publishing, 1982.
Davis, Charles T., and Henry Louis Gates, eds. *The Slave's Narrative*. New York; Oxford University Press, 1985.
Elkins, Stanley. *Slavery: A Problem in American Institutional and Intellectual Life*. Chicago: University of Chicago Press, 1959.
Evans, Mari. *Black Women Writers (1950–1980)*. Garden City: Anchor Books, 1984.
Flynn, Elizabeth A., and Patrocinio P. Schweickart. *Gender and Reading: Essays on Readers, Texts, and Contexts*. Baltimore: Johns Hopkins University Press, 1986.
Foucault, Michel. "Qu'est-ce un auteur?" *Bulletin de la Société Française de Philosophie* 63.3 (1969): 75–104.
Fox-Genovese, Elizabeth. *Within the Plantation Household: Black and White Women of the Old South*. Chapel Hill: University of North Carolina Press, 1988.
———, ed. and trans. *The Autobiography of Du Pont de Nemours*. Wilmington: Scholarly Resources Press, 1984.

Gates, Henry Louis, Jr. "The 'Blackness of Blackness': A Critique of the Sign and the Signifying Monkey." *Critical Inquiry* 9.4 (1983): 685–724.

———, ed. *Black Literature and Literary Theory*. New York: Methuen, 1984.

Genovese, Eugene D. *Roll, Jordan, Roll: The World the Slaves Made*. New York: Pantheon, 1974.

Gilbert, Olive, comp. *Narrative of Sojourner Truth: A Bondswoman of Olden Time*. 1878. New York: Arno Press, 1968.

Giovanni, Nikki, *Gemini: An Extended Autobiographical Statement on My First Twenty-Five Years of Being a Black Poet*. Indianapolis: Bobbs-Merrill, 1971.

Griffiths, Mattie. *Autobiography of a Female Slave*. 1857. Miami: Mnemosyne, 1969.

Gunn, Janet Varner. *Autobiography: Toward a Poetics of Experience*. Philadelphia; University of Pennsylvania Press, 1982.

Harding, Vincent. *There is a River: The Black Struggle for Freedom in America*. New York: Harcourt Brace Jovanovich, 1981.

Harris, Trudier. "On *The Color Purple*, Stereotypes, and Silence." *Black American Literature Forum* 18.4 (1984): 155–61.

Hemenway, Robert. *Zora Neale Hurston: A Literary Biography*. Urbana: University of Illinois Press, 1977.

Hurston, Zora Neale. *Dust Tracks on a Road: An Autobiography*. 1942. Ed. Robert Hemenway. 2d ed. Urbana: University of Illinois Press, 1984.

———. *Mules and Men*. 1935. New York: Harper and Row, 1970.

———. *Tell My Horse*. 1938. Berkeley: Turtle Island, 1981.

———. *Their Eyes Were Watching God*. 1937. Urbana: University of Illinois Press, 1978.

Jacobs, Harriet [Linda Brent]. *Incidents in the Life of a Slave Girl, Written by Herself*. Ed. Lydia Maria Child,. 1861. New ed. Walter Teller. New York: Harcourt Brace Jovanovich, 1973.

———. *Incidents in the Life of a Slave Girl, Written by Herself*. Ed. Jean Fagan Yellin. Cambridge: Harvard University Press, 1987.

Jelinek, Estelle, ed. *Women's Autobiography: Essays in Criticism*. Bloomington: Indiana University Press, 1980.

Johnson, Barbara. "Metaphor, Metonymy and Voice in *Their Eyes Were Watching God*." In Gates, *Black Literature*, 205–20.

Kelley, Mary. *Private Woman, Public Stage: Literary Domesticity in Nineteenth-Century America*. New York:: Oxford University Press, 1984.

Kolodny, Annette. *The Land Before Her: Fantasy and Experience of the American Frontiers, 1630–1860*. Chapel Hill: University of North Carolina Press, 1984.

Lane, Ann J., ed. *The Debate over Slavery: Stanley Elkins and His Critics*. Urbana: University of Illinois Press, 1971.

Lang, Candace. "Autobiography in the Aftermath of Romanticism." *Diacritics* 12 (Winter 1982): 2–16.

Lejeune, Philippe. *Le pacte autobiographique*. Paris: Editions du Seuil, 1975.

Levine, Lawrence W. *Black Culture and Black Consciousness: Afro-American Folk Thought from Slavery to Freedom*. New York: Oxford University Press, 1977.

McCaskill, Barbara. "Eternity for Telling: Topological Traditions in Afro-American Women's Literature." Ph.D. diss., Emory University, 1988.

McConnell-Ginet, Sally, Ruth Borker, and Nelly Furman, eds. *Women and Language in Literature and Society*. New York: Praeger, 1980.

McDowell, Deborah E. "New Directions for Black Feminist Criticism." In Showalter, 186–99.

Miller, Nancy K. "Women's Autobiography in France: For a Dialectics of Identification." In McConnell-Ginet et al., 258–73.

Olney, James. *Autobiography: Essays Theoretical and Critical*. Princeton: Princeton University Press, 1980.

———. " 'I Was Born': Slave Narratives. Their Status as Autobiography and as Literature." In Davis and Gates, 148–75.

Sekora, John, and Darwin T. Turner, eds. *The Art of Slave Narrative*. Macomb: Northern Illinois University Press, 1982.

Showalter, Elaine, ed. *Feminist Criticism: Essays on Women, Literature, Theory*. New York: Pantheon, 1985.

Smith, Barbara. "Toward a Black Feminist Criticism." In Showalter, 168–85.

Soyinka, Wole. "The Critic and Society: Barthes, Leftocracy and Other Mythologies." In Gates, *Black Literature*, 27–58.

Spivak, Gayatri Chakravorty. " 'Drapaudi' by Mahasveta Devi." *Critical Inquiry* 8.2 (1981): 381–402.

———. "The Politics of Interpretation." *Critical Inquiry* 9.1 (1982): 259–78.

Starling, Marion Wilson. *The Slave Narrative: Its Place in History*. Boston: G. K. Hall, 1981.

Stepto, Robert Burns. "I Rose and Found My Voice: Narration, Authentication, and Authorial Control in Four Slave Narratives." In Davis and Gates, 225–41.

Sterling, Dorothy, ed. *We Are Your Sisters: Black Women in the Nineteenth Century*. New York: Norton, 1984.

Stone, Albert E. *Autobiographical Occasions and Original Acts*. Philadelphia: University of Pennsylvania Press, 1982.

Stowe, Harriet Beecher. *Uncle Tom's Cabin or, Life among the Lowly*. 1852. New York: Penguin, 1981.

Tate, Claudia, ed. *Black Women Writers at Work*. New York: Continuum, 1983.

Thompson, Era Bell. *American Daughter*. Rev. ed. Chicago: University of Chicago Press, 1967.

Tompkins, Jane P., ed. *Reader-Response Criticism: From Formalism to Post-Structuralism*. Baltimore: Johns Hopkins University Press, 1980.

———. *Sensational Designs: The Cultural Work of American Fiction 1790–1860*. New York: Oxford University Press, 1985.

Walker, Alice. *In Search of Our Mothers' Gardens: Womanist Prose*. New York: Harcourt Brace Jovanovich, 1983.

———. "Looking for Zora." In Walker, *In Search of Our Mothers' Gardens*.

———. "Zora Neale Hurston: A Cautionary Tale and a Partisan View." In Walker, *In Search of Our Mothers' Gardens*.

———, ed. *I Love Myself When I Am Laughing . . . and Then Again When I Am Looking Mean and Impressive: A Zora Neale Hurston Reader*. Old Westbury: Feminist Press, 1979.

Washington, Mary Helen. " 'Taming All That Anger Down': Rage and Silence in Gwendolyn Brooks's *Maud Martha*." In Gates, *Black Literature*, 249–62.

Weintraub, Karl H. *The Value of the Individual: Self and Circumstance in Autobiography*. Chicago: University of Chicago Press, 1978.

Wells, Ida B. *The Autobiography of Ida B. Wells*. Ed. Alfred M. Duster. Chicago: University of Chicago Press, 1970.

White, Deborah G. *Ar'n't I a Woman: Female Slaves in the Plantation South*. New York: Norton, 1985.

Wilson, Harriet E. *Our Nig: Or, Stretches from the Life of a Free Black, in a Two-Story White House, North. Showing That Slavery's Shadows Fall Even There. By "Our Nig."* Ed. Henry Louis Gates. New York: Vintage, 1983.

Yellin, Jean Fagan. "Texts and Contexts of Harriet Jacobs' *Incidents in the Life of a Slave Girl: Written by Herself*." In Davis and Gates, 262–82.

———. "Written By Herself: *Harriet Jacobs' Slave Narrative*." *American Literature* 53.3 (1981): 479–86.

Euphemism, Understatement, and the Passive Voice:

A Genealogy of Afro-American Poetry

Barbara E. Johnson

In his well-known essay of 1937, "Blueprint for Negro Writing," Richard Wright expresses an ambivalence toward his precursors that has been shared by many subsequent Afro-American writers. "Generally speaking," he writes:

> Negro writing in the past has been confined to humble novels, poems, and plays, prim and decorous ambassadors who went a-begging to white America. They entered the Court of American Public Opinion dressed in the knee-pants of servility, curtsying to show that the Negro was not inferior, that he was human, and that he had a life comparable to that of other people. For the most part these artistic ambassadors were received as though they were French poodles who do clever tricks.[1]

In this paper I would like to examine some of the more covert strategies of protest implicit in the writings of some of the ambassadors Wright might have had in mind: James Weldon Johnson, Countee Cullen, and, most particularly, Phillis Wheatley, whose 1773 volume was the first book of poems published by a black American. While decorousness may in some ways have been disabling, I will try to show that these writers nevertheless set up conditions of utterance in which the French poodle could sometimes function as a Trojan horse.

In 1921, at the start of what has come to be known as the Harlem Renaissance, James Weldon Johnson edited what he hoped would be a major anthology of Afro-American poetry. The collection was designed to remedy what he called a "lack of information" on the part of "the public." Nothing could be less inflammatory than the desire to supply information that is lacking. Through a carefully calculated use of the passive voice, an avoidance of black/white binary oppositions, and the elaboration of a seemingly syllogistic logic, Johnson attempts nothing less than to convince the world to acknowledge the greatness of the Negro people:

> There is, perhaps, a better excuse for giving an Anthology of American Negro Poetry to the public than can be offered for many of the anthologies that have recently been issued. The public, generally speaking, does not know that there are American Negro poets—to supply this lack of information is, alone, a work worthy of somebody's effort.
>
> Moreover, the matter of Negro poets and the production of literature by the colored people in this country involves more than supplying information that is lacking. It is a matter which has a direct bearing on the most vital of American problems.
>
> A people may become great through many means, but there is only one measure by which its greatness is recognized and acknowledged. The final measure of the greatness of all peoples is the amount and standard of the literature and art they have produced. The world does not know that a people is great until that people produces great literature and art. No people that has produced great literature and art has ever been looked upon by the world as distinctly inferior.
>
> The status of the Negro in the United States is more a question of national mental attitude toward the race than of actual conditions. And nothing will do more to change that mental attitude and raise his status than a demonstration of intellectual parity by the Negro through the production of literature and art.[2]

Johnson goes on to assert that the Negro has already contributed to American culture the only artistic productions "the world" (that is, Europe) acknowledges as distinctively Ameri-

can: Uncle Remus stories, spirituals, the cakewalk, and rag-
time. Again, Johnson uses the passive voice as a cover for
unspecified (here, all-conquering) agency:

> As for Ragtime, I go straight to the statement that it is the
> one artistic production by which America is known the
> world over. It has been all-conquering. Everywhere it is
> hailed as "American music" (11).

Through his use of ellipsis, understatement, unspecified agency,
and non-binarity, Johnson is thus attempting to bring about a
change in the status of the Negro without explicitly acknowledging or processing conflict and dispossession. When such
rhetorical strategies are used by a dominant discourse, the
reason for the avoidance of conflict is the avoidance of change.
But when acknowledging the conflict may mean granting it a
legitimacy it does not deserve, when processing difference
might seem to involve accepting the premises of racial in-
equality, then the bootstrap operation of passivity and euphemism may well begin to set the stage for an unimpeded and
newly empowered affirmation.

Moving from music to poetry, Johnson continues to employ
euphemism and the passive voice to describe the previous
history of the Afro-American lyric. The list, he writes, begins
with Phillis Wheatley. It soon becomes clear, however, that
Johnson's own history, therefore, begins with ambivalence.
The passive voice he uses in speaking about Wheatley expresses both an avoidance of conflict and an avoidance of
change—that is, both an opposition to and an identification
with dominant discourse:

> Phillis Wheatley has never been given her rightful place
> in American literature. By some sort of conspiracy she is
> kept out of most of the books, especially the text-books
> on literature used in the schools. Of course, she is not a
> *great* American poet—and in her day there were no great
> American poets—but she is an important American poet.
> Her importance, if for no other reason, rests on the fact
> that, save one, she is the first in order of time of all the
> women poets of America. And she is among the first of
> all American poets to issue a volume (23).

Johnson, too, does not grant Phillis Wheatley her rightful place at the head of the list, but rather confines her to the space of his preface, the place of prehistory. She is the ancestor half acknowledged, half obscured. Johnson wishes to combat the injustice of her exclusion, yet cannot quite bring himself to place her first. Is this mere misogyny? Mere identification with male hegemony? Perhaps. Indeed, Wright's scorn for the curtsying ambassadors is also a resistance to the feminine as ancestor. But what Johnson holds against Wheatley is her avoidance of passionate personal utterance: "One looks in vain for some outburst or even some complaint against the bondage of her people, for some agonising cry about her native land . . . In the poem addressed to the Earl of Dartmouth, she speaks of freedom and makes a reference to the parents from whom she was taken as child, a reference which cannot but strike the reader as rather unimpassioned" (28, 29). In other words, what Johnson holds against Wheatley is precisely the stylistic avoidance of conflict and outcry that characterizes his own writing in this preface. Could one not, for instance, characterize as "unimpassioned" Johnson's own use of words like "curious" and "strange," as in the following sentence:

> It seems *strange* that the books generally give space to a mention of Urian Oakes, President of Harvard College, and to quotations from the crude and lengthy elegy which he published in 1667 . . . and yet deny a place to Phillis Wheatley (23).

Johnson's use of "strange" here echoes Countee Cullen's use of "curious" in what Johnson himself calls "the two most poignant lines in American literature":

> Yet do I marvel at this curious thing—
> To make a poet black and bid him sing. (231)

Johnson's sense of the poignancy of these lines may well stem from his own knowledge of all that a word like "curious" can conceal. Euphemism may be a way of avoiding conflict, but it also functions as an X marking a spot where later, perhaps, a poet will be able to say more. Protest may not yet be voiced, but at least the spot has been marked.

Countee Cullen himself is a master of the marked spot. In his poem "Heritage," he manages to keep the question "What is Africa to me?" in perfect suspension between a rhetorical and a real question. The question itself, like the poem's speaker, "plays a double part," as does the repeated phrase "so I lie," which carries the ambiguity the poem enacts between language and the body, between legend and unconscious desire. Africa may be only a book, says the poem, but nevertheless what is repressed can return. Another of the poem's ploys is its strategic use of the bad rhyme:

> Quaint, outlandish heathen gods
> Black men fashion out of rods,
> Clay, and brittle bits of stone,
> In a likeness like their own,
> My conversion came high-priced;
> I belong to Jesus Christ,
> Preacher of humility;
> Heathen gods are naught to me. (224)

The wince produced by rhyming "Christ" with "priced" soon gives way, I think, to a recognition of its rightness, of all that is condensed behind that rhyme. The Christianization of Africans was indeed accomplished through their transformation into human commodities. Why should a conversion brought about by enslavement produce a *good* rhyme? The seemingly innocuous forcing of the rhyme euphemistically marks the barbarity of the historical process itself.

The art of forcing a rhyme between conversion and enslavement has its origins in the 1773 volume of poetry written by Phillis Wheatley. The eighteen-year-old slave girl from Boston stands indeed as the inventor of a whole tradition of protest through excessive compliance.

Wheatley's poetry repeatedly describes several analogous processes of transformation: death, conversion, and the American struggle for independence. These are usually described in terms of travel from one location to another. In her numerous elegies, Wheatley describes the dead as winging their way to a happier place:

Ere yet the morn its lovely blushes spread,
See Sewell numbered with the happy dead.
Hail, holy man, arriv'd th' immortal shore,
Though we shall hear thy warning voice no more.
Come, let us all behold with wistful eyes
The saint ascending to his native skies.[3]

In her poem "On being brought from Africa to America," she
writes:

'Twas mercy brought me from my Pagan land,
Taught my benighted soul to understand
That there's a God, that there's a Saviour too:
Once I redemption neither sought nor knew. (53)

(This, as June Jordan remarks, is also a way of saying: "Once I
existed on other than your terms.")[4] And finally, in her pro-
revolutionary poem to the Earl of Dartmouth, she writes:

No more, America, in mournful strain
Of wrongs, and grievance unredress'd complain,
No longer shalt thou dread the iron chain,
Which wanton Tyranny with lawless hand
Had made, and with it meant t' enslave the land. (83)

Then she goes on:

Should you, my lord, while you peruse my song,
Wonder from whence my love of Freedom sprung,
Whence flow these wishes for the common good,
By feeling hearts alone best understood,
I, young in life, by seeming cruel fate
Was snatched from Afric's fancy'd happy seat:
What pangs excruciating must molest,
What sorrows labour in my parent's breast?
Steel'd was that soul and by no misery mov'd
That from a father seiz'd his babe belov'd:
Such, such my case. And can I then but pray
Others may never feel tyrannic sway? (83)

By simply repeating the ideology she has learned, Wheatley
exposes a glaring contradiction. She presents us with some-

thing like the schoolbook exercise: "What's wrong with this picture?" While the voyage from life to death, from paganism to Christianity, and from English rule to American rule might be seen to involve a passage from bondage to freedom, the voyage from Africa to America has clearly gone the other way. Under Wheatley's pen, the lessons she has learned so well self-deconstruct. That she knew exactly what she was doing is evident from a letter she wrote to the Indian minister Samson Occom, which she published a number of times in 1774, several months after she obtained her freedom:

In every human Breast, God has implanted a Principle, which we call Love of Freedom; it is impatient of oppression, and pants for Deliverance; and by the Leave of our modern Egyptians I will assert that the same Principle lives in us. God grant Deliverance in his own Way and Time, and get him honour upon all those whose Avarice impels them to countenance and help forward the Calamities of their fellow Creatures. This I desire not for their Hurt, but to convince them of the *strange* [emphasis mine-B.J.] Absurdity of their conduct whose Words and Actions are so diametrically opposite. How well the Cry for Liberty, and the reverse Disposition for the exercise of oppressive Power over others agree,—I humbly think it does not require the Penetration of a Philosopher to determine. (204)

By making explicit her history and her status, Wheatley in a sense wrote her way to freedom simply by letting the contradictions in her master's position speak for themselves.

In the preface to her volume of poems, Wheatley speaks of her own enslavement in the following terms:

As to the Disadvantages she has labored under, with Regard to Learning, nothing needs to be offered, as her Master's Letter in the following Page will sufficiently show the Difficulties in this Respect she had to encounter. (46)

There follows a letter from "the author's master" detailing Wheatley's prodigious accomplishments as a slave in his household. The *fact* of that letter speaks for itself. Wheatley has placed in her master's hand the boomerang of her compliance. While the Wheatleys send her book into the world as an ambassador of their own benevolence, it comes back with the response from English readers it was meant to impress: "Why is she still a slave?" John and Susannah Wheatley, caught in the trap of their own self-image, grant Phillis her freedom upon her return from England. And Phillis Wheatley thus becomes the first in a long line of successful manipulators and demystifiers of the narcissism inherent in white liberalism.

NOTES

1. Reprinted in *The Richard Wright Reader*, ed. Ellen Wright and Michel Fabre (New York: Harper & Row, 1978), 37.
2. James Weldon Johnson, *The Book of American Negro Poetry* (New York: Harcourt Brace Jovanovich, reprint 1969), 9.
3. Julian D. Mason, Jr., ed., *The Poems of Phillis Wheatley* (1773; reprint, Chapel Hill: The University of North Carolina Press, 1989), 54.
4. June Jordan, "The Difficult Miracle of Black Poetry in America or Something Like a Sonnet for Phillis Wheatley," in her *On Call* (Boston: South End Press, 1985), 91.

"Loopholes of Retreat":

Architecture and Ideology in Harriet Jacobs's
Incidents in the Life of a Slave Girl

Valerie Smith

In *Incidents in the Life of a Slave Girl*, the account of her life as a slave and escape to freedom, Harriet Jacobs refers to the crawl space in which she concealed herself for seven years as a "loophole of retreat."[1] The phrase calls attention both to the closeness of her hiding place—three feet high, nine feet long, seven feet wide—and the passivity that even voluntary confinement imposes. For if the combined weight of racism and sexism already placed inexorable restrictions upon her as a black female slave in the antebellum South, her options seem even narrower after she conceals herself in the garret, where just to speak to her loved ones jeopardizes her own and their welfare.

And yet Jacobs's phrase, "the loophole of retreat," possesses an ambiguity of meaning that extends to the literal loophole as well. For if a loophole signifies for Jacobs a place of withdrawal, it signifies in common parlance an avenue of escape. Likewise, the garret, a place of confinement, also— perhaps more importantly—renders the narrator spiritually independent of her master, and makes possible her ultimate escape to freedom. It is thus hardly surprising that Jacobs finds her imprisonment, however uncomfortable, an improvement over "[her] lot as a slave" (117). As her statement implies, she dates her emancipation from the time she entered her loophole, even though she did not cross over into the free states until seven years later. Given the constraints that framed her ordinary life, even the act of choosing her own mode of confinement constituted an exercise of will, an indirect assault against her master's domination.[2]

The plot of Jacobs's narrative, her journey from slavery to freedom, is punctuated by a series of similar structures of confinement, both literal and figurative. Not only does she spend much of her time in tiny rooms (her grandmother's garret, closets in the homes of two friends), but she seems as well to have been hemmed in by the importunities of Dr. Flint, her master:

> My master met me at every turn, reminding me that I belonged to him, and swearing by heaven and earth that he would compel me to submit to him. If I went out for a breath of fresh air, after a day of unwearied toil, his footsteps dogged me. If I knelt by my mother's grave, his dark shadow fell on me even there (27).

Repeatedly, she escapes overwhelming persecutions only by choosing her own space of confinement: the stigma of unwed motherhood over sexual submission to her master; conceal- ment in one friend's home, another friend's closet, and her grandmother's garret over her own and her children's en- slavement on a plantation; Jim Crowism and the threat of the Fugitive Slave Law in the North over institutionalized slavery at home. As my discussion of *Incidents* will demonstrate, how- ever, each moment of apparent enclosure actually empowers Jacobs to redirect her own and her children's destiny. To borrow Elaine Showalter's formulation, she inscribes a subver- sive plot of empowerment beneath the more orthodox, public plot of weakness and vulnerability.[3]

I would suggest further that these metaphoric loopholes provide a figure in terms of which we may read her relation to the literary forms that shape her story. Restricted by the conventions and rhetoric of the slave narrative—a genre that presupposes a range of options more available to men than to women—Jacobs borrows heavily from the rhetoric of the sen- timental novel. This latter form imposed upon her restrictions of its own. Yet she seized authority over her literary restraints in much the same way that she seized power in life. From within her ellipses and ironies—linguistic narrow spaces— she expresses the complexity of her experience as a black woman.

It is not surprising that both literal and figurative enclosures proliferate in Jacobs's narrative. As a nineteenth-century black woman, former slave, and writer, she labored under myriad social and literary restrictions that shaped the art she produced. Feminist scholarship has shown that, in general, women's writing in the nineteenth and twentieth centuries has been strongly marked by imagery of confinement—a pattern of imagery that reflects the limited cultural options available to the authors because of their gender and chosen profession. Sandra Gilbert and Susan Gubar, for instance, describe the prodigious restraints imposed historically upon women that led to the recurrence of structures of concealment and evasion in their literature.[4] Not only were they denied access to the professions, civic responsibilities, and higher education, but their secular and religious instruction alike encouraged them from childhood in the "feminine," passive virtues of "submissiveness, modesty, self-lessness."[5] Taken to its extreme, such an idealization of female weakness and self-effacement contributed to what Ann Douglas has called a "domestication of death" characterized by the prevalence in literature of a hagiography of dying women and children, and the predilection in life for dietary, sartorial, and medical practices that led to actual or illusory weakness and illness.[6]

Literary women confronted additional restraints, given the widespread cultural identification of creativity with maleness. As Gubar argues elsewhere, "[our] culture is steeped in . . . myths of male primacy in theological, artistic, and scientific creativity," myths that image women as art objects perhaps, but never as creators.[7] These ideological restraints, made concrete by inhospitable editors, publishers, and reviewers, and by disapproving relatives and friends, have (as Gilbert and Gubar demonstrate) traditionally invaded women's literary undertakings with all manner of tensions. The most obvious sign of the nineteenth-century women writers' anxiety about their vocation (one which, however, might also be attributed to the demands of the literary marketplace) is the frequency with which they published either anonymously or under male pseudonyms. Their sense of engagement in an improper enterprise is evidenced as well by their tendency both to disparage their own accomplishments in autobiographical remarks, and to inscribe deprecations of women's creativity within their fictions. Moreover, they found themselves in a curious relation to the implements of their own craft. The literary conventions they received from genres dominated by male authors perpetuated reductive, destructive images of women that cried out to be revised. Yet the nature of the women writers' socialization precluded their confronting problematic stereotypes directly. Instead, as Patricia Spacks, Carolyn Heilbrun, and Catharine Stimpson, as well as Showalter, and Gilbert and Gubar, have shown, the most significant women writers secreted either within or behind the more accessible content of their work revisions of received plots and assumptions.[8]

Jacobs describes her escape as a progression from one small space to another. Indeed, as if to underscore her helplessness and vulnerability, she indicates that although she ran alone to her first friend's home, she left each of her hiding places only with the aid of someone else. In fact, when she goes to her second and third hiding places, she is entirely at the mercy of her companion, for she is kept ignorant of her destination. Yet each closet, while at one level a prison, is also a station on her journey to freedom. Moreover, from the garret of her seven-year imprisonment, she uses to her advantage all the power of the voyeur—the person who sees but remains herself unseen. When she learns that Sands is about to leave town, she descends from her hiding place and, partly because she catches him unawares, she secures his promise to free her children. In addition, she prevents her own capture not merely by remaining concealed, but more importantly, by embroiling her master in an elaborate plot that deflects his attention. Fearing that he suspects her whereabouts, she writes him letters that she then has postmarked in Boston and New York to send him off in hot pursuit in the wrong direction. Despite her grandmother's trepidation, Jacobs clearly delights in exerting some influence over the man who has tried to control her.

Indeed, I would argue that if the architectural close places are at once prisons and exits, then her relationship to Sands is both as well. She suggests that when she decides to take him as her lover, she's caught between Scylla and Charybdis. Forbidden to marry the freedman she loves, she knows that by becoming Sands's mistress she will compromise her virtue and reputation. But, she remarks, given that her alternative is the master she loathes, she has no choice but to have relations with Sands. As she writes: "It seems less degrading to give one's self, than to submit to compulsion. There is something akin to freedom in having a lover who has no control over you, except that which he gains by kindness and attachment (55)."

One might argue that Jacobs's dilemma encapsulates the slave woman's sexual victimization and vulnerability. But while I do not mean to impugn that reading, I would suggest that her relation to Sands provides her with a measure of power. Out of his consideration for her, he purchases her children and her brother from Flint. William, her brother, eventually escapes from slavery on his own, but Sands frees the children in accordance with their mother's wishes. In a system that allowed the buying and selling of people as if they were animals, Jacobs's influence is clearly minimal. Yet even at the moments when she seems most vulnerable, she manipulates some degree of control.

As the writer of a slave narrative, Jacobs's freedom to reconstruct her life was limited by a genre that suppressed subjective experience in favor of abolitionist polemics. But if slave narrators in general were restricted by the antislavery agenda, Jacobs was doubly bound by the form in which she wrote, for it contained a plot more compatible with received notions of masculinity than with those of womanhood. Like the archetypal hero of the bildungsroman or the adventure tale, the representative hero of the slave narrative moves from the idyllic life of childhood ignorance in the country into a metaphoric wilderness, in this case the recognition of his status as a slave. His struggle for survival requires him to overcome numerous obstacles, but through his own talents (and some Providential assistance), he finds the Promised Land of a responsible social position, a job, and a wife. The slave narrative typically extols the hero's stalwart individuality. And the narratives of male slaves often link the escape to freedom to the act of physically subduing the master. Frederick Douglass writes, for example, that once he had overpowered the man whose job it was to break him, then he knew that he would soon be free.[9]

Like the prototypical bildungsroman plot, the plot of the slave narrative does not adequately accommodate differences in male and female development.[10] Jacobs's tale is not the classic story of the triumph of the individual will; rather, it is more a story of a triumphant self-in-relation.[11] With the notable exception of the narrative of William and Ellen Craft, most of the narratives by men represent the life in slavery and the escape as essentially solitary journeys. This is not to suggest that male slaves were more isolated than their female counterparts, but they were attempting to prove their equality, their manhood, in terms acceptable to their white, middle-class readers.

Under different, equally restrictive injunctions, Jacobs readily acknowledges the support and assistance she received, as the description of her escape makes clear. Not only does she diminish her own role in her escape, but she is quick to recognize the care and generosity of her family in the South and her friends in the North. The opening chapter of her account focuses not on the solitary "I" of so many narratives, but on Jacobs's relatives. And she associates her own desire for freedom with her desire to provide opportunities for her children.

By mythologizing rugged individuality, physical strength, and geographical mobility, the narratives enshrine cultural definitions of masculinity.[12] The plot of the standard narrative may thus be seen not only as the journey from slavery to freedom, but also as the journey from slavehood to manhood. Indeed, that rhetoric explicitly informs some of the best-known and most influential narratives. In the key scene in William Wells Brown's account, for example, a Quaker friend and supporter names the protagonist because, "Since thee has got out of slavery, thee has become a man, and men always have two names."[13] Douglass also explicitly contrasts slavehood and manhood, for he argues that learning to read made him a man, but being beaten made him a slave. Only by overpowering his overseer was he able to be a man—or free—again.

Simply by underscoring her reliance upon other people, Jacobs reveals another way that the story of slavery and escape might be written. But in at least one place in the narrative she makes obvious her problematic relation to the rhetoric she uses. The fourth chapter, "The Slave Who Dared to Feel Like a Man," bears a title reminiscent of one of the most familiar lines from Frederick Douglass's 1845 *Narrative*. Here, Jacobs links three anecdotes that illustrate the fact that indepen-

dence of mind is incompatible with the demands of life as a
slave. She begins with a scene in which her grandmother
urges her family to content themselves with their lot as slaves,
but her son and grandchildren, however, cannot help resent-
ing her admonitions. The chapter then centers on the story of
her Uncle Ben, a slave who retaliates when his master tries to
beat him, and who eventually escapes to the North.

The chapter title thus refers explicitly to Ben, the slave who,
by defending himself, dared to feel like a man. And yet, it
might also refer to the other two stories included in the chapter. In the first, Jacobs's brother William refuses to capitulate
to his master's authority. In the second, Jacobs describes her
own earliest resolution to resist her master's advances. Although the situation does not yet require her to fight back,
she does say that her young arm never felt half so strong. Like
her uncle and brother, she determines to remain unconquered.

The chapter foregrounds Ben's story, then, but it indicates
also that his niece and nephew resisted authority. Its title
might therefore refer to either of them as well. As Jacobs
suggests by indirection, as long as the rhetoric of the genre
identifies the black man's freedom and independence of thought
with manhood, it lacks a category for describing the achievements of the tenacious black woman.

As L. Maria Child's "Introduction," the author's "Preface,"
and the numerous asides in the narrative make clear, Jacobs
wrote for an audience of northern white women, a readership
that by mid-century had grown increasingly leisured, middle-
class, and accustomed to the conventions of the novel of
domestic sentiment. Under the auspices of Child, herself an
editor and writer of sentimental fiction, Jacobs constructed the
story of her life in terms that her reader would find familiar.
Certainly Jacobs's *Incidents* contains conventional apostrophes
that explicitly call attention to the interests she shares with her
readers. But as an additional strategy for enlisting their sympathy, she couches her story in the rhetoric and structures of
popular fiction.

As Annette Niemtzow has suggested, Jacobs may well have
been drawn to the genre because it provided her with a way
of talking about her vulnerability to the constant threat of
rape.[14] Indeed, the details of the narrator's life that made her
experience as a slave more comfortable than most are pre-

cisely those that render her story particularly amenable to the conventions and assumptions of the sentimental novel. Slave narratives often begin with an absence, the narrator announcing from the first that he has no idea where or when he was born, or who his parents were. But Jacobs was fortunate enough to have been born into a stable family at once nuclear and extended. Although both of her parents died young, she nurtures vivid, pleasant memories of them. Moreover, she remains close to her grandmother, an emancipated, self-supporting, property-owning black woman, and to her uncles and aunts, until she escapes to the North.

Jacobs's class affiliation, and the fact that she was subjected to relatively minor forms of abuse as a slave, enable her to locate a point of identification both with her readers and with the protagonists of sentimental fiction. Like them, she aspires to chastity and piety as consummate feminine virtues, and hopes that marriage and family would be her earthly reward. Her master, for some reason reluctant to force her to submit sexually, harasses, pleads with, and tries to bribe her into capitulating, in the manner of an importunate suitor like Richardson's seducer. He tells her, for example, that he would be within his right to kill her or have her imprisoned for resisting his advances, but he wishes to make her happy and thus will be lenient towards her. She likens his behavior to that of a jealous lover on the occasion that he becomes violent with her son. And he repeatedly offers to make a lady of her, volunteering to set her up in a cottage of her own where she can raise her children if she will grant him her favors.

By pointing up the similarities between her own story and those plots with which her readers would have been familiar, she could thus expect her readers to identify with her suffering. Moreover, this technique would enable them to appreciate the ways that slavery converts into liabilities the very qualities of virtue and beauty that women were taught to cultivate. This tactic has serious limitations, however. As is always the case when one attempts to universalize a specific political point, Jacobs here trivializes the complexity of her situation when she likens it to a familiar paradigm. Like Richardson's Pamela, Jacobs is servant to her pursuer. But Pamela is free to escape, if she chooses, to the refuge of her parents' home. As Dr. Flint's property, Jacobs's options are severely limited. Moreover, Mr. B., in the terms the novel constructs, can redeem his importunities by marrying Pamela and elevating her and their progeny to his position. No such possibility exists for Jacobs and her master. Indeed, the system of slavery, conflating as it does the categories of property and sexuality, ensures that her posterity will become his material possessions.

For other reasons as well, the genre seems inappropriate for Jacobs's purposes. As the prefatory documents imply, Jacobs's readers are accustomed to novels of propriety and circumlocution. In keeping with cultural injunctions against women's assertiveness and directness in speech, the literature they wrote and read tended to be "exercises in euphemism" that excluded certain subjects from the purview of fiction.[15] Jacobs's purpose, in contrast, is to celebrate her freedom to express what she has undergone, and to engender additional abolitionist support. Child and Jacobs both recognize that Jacobs's story may well violate the rules of decorum in the genre. Their opening statements express the tension between the content of the narrative and the form in which it appears.

Child's introduction performs the function conventional to the slave narrative of establishing the reliability of the accompanying narrative and the narrator's veracity. What is unusual about her introduction, however, is the basis of her authenticating statement; she establishes her faith in Jacobs's story upon the correctness and delicacy of the author's manner:

> The author of the following autobiography is personally known to me, and her conversation and manners inspire me with confidence. During the last seventeen years, she has lived the greater part of the time with a distinguished family in New York, and has so deported herself as to be highly esteemed by them. This fact is sufficient, without further credentials of her character. I believe those who know her will not be disposed to doubt her veracity, though some incidents in her story are more romantic than fiction (xi).

This paragraph attempts to equate contradictory notions; Child implies not only that Jacobs is both truthful and a model of decorous behavior, but also that her propriety ensures her veracity. Child's assumption is troublesome, since ordinarily, decorousness connotes the opposite of candor—one equates propriety not with openness, but with concealment in the interest of taste.

Indeed, later in her introduction Child seems to recognize that an explicit political imperative may well be completely incompatible with bourgeois notions of propriety. While in the first paragraph she suggests that Jacobs's manner guarantees her veracity, by the last she has begun to ask if questions of delicacy have any place at all in discussions of human injustice. In the last paragraph, for example, she writes, "I am well aware that many will accuse me of indecorum for presenting these pages to the public." Here, rather than equating truthfulness with propriety, she acknowledges somewhat apologetically that candor about her chosen subject may well violate common rules of decorum. From this point, she proceeds tactfully but firmly to dismantle the usefulness of delicacy as a category where subjects of urgency are concerned. She remarks, for instance, that "the experiences of this intelligent and much-injured woman belong to a class which some call delicate subjects, and others indelicate." By pointing to the fact that one might identify Jacobs's story as either delicate or its opposite, she acknowledges the superfluity of this particular label.

In the third and fourth sentences of this paragraph, Child offers her most substantive critique of delicacy, for she suggests that it allows the reader an excuse for insensitivity and self-involvement. The third sentence reads as follows: "This peculiar phase of slavery has generally been kept veiled; but the public ought to be made acquainted with its monstrous features, and I willingly take the responsibility of presenting them with the veil withdrawn." Here, she invokes and reverses the traditional symbol of feminine modesty. A veil (read euphemism) is ordinarily understood to protect the wearer (read reader) from the ravages of a threatening world. Child suggests, however, that a veil (or euphemism) may also work the other way, to conceal the hideous countenance of truth from those who choose ignorance above discomfort.

In the fourth sentence, she pursues further the implication that considerations of decorum may well excuse the reader's self-involvement. She writes: "I do this for the sake of my sisters in bondage, who are suffering wrongs so foul, that our ears are too delicate to listen to them." The structure of this sentence is especially revealing, for it provides a figure for the narcissism of which she implicitly accuses the reader. A sentence that begins, as Child's does, "I do this for the sake of my sisters in bondage, who suffering wrongs so foul that . . ." would ordinarily conclude with some reference to the "sisters" or wrongs they endure. We would thus expect the sentence to read something like, "I do this for the sake of my sisters in bondage, who are suffering wrongs so foul that they must soon take up arms against their master," or "that they no longer believe in a moral order." Instead, Child's sentence rather awkwardly imposes the reader in the precise grammatical location where the slave woman ought to be. This usurpation of linguistic space parallels the potential for narcissism of which Child suggests her reader is guilty.

Child, the editor, the voice of form and convention in the narrative—the one who revised, condensed, and ordered the manuscript and "pruned [its] excrescences"—thus prepares the reader for its straightforwardness. Jacobs, whose life provides the narrative subject, in apparent contradiction of Child calls attention in her preface to her book's silences. Rather conventionally, she admits to concealing the names of places and people to protect those who aided in her escape. And, one might be tempted to say that rather conventionally she apologizes for the inadequacy of her literary skills. But in fact, when Jacobs asserts that her narrative is not fiction, that her adventures may seem incredible but they are nevertheless true, and that only experience can reveal the abomination of slavery, she underscores the inability of her form adequately to capture her experience.

Although Child and Jacobs are aware of the limitations of genre, the account often rings false. Characters speak like literate, middle-class workers out of a romance. Moreover, the form only allows Jacobs to talk about her sexual experiences when they are the result of her victimization. She becomes curiously silent about the fact that her relations with Sands continue even after Flint seems no longer a threat.

I would argue that its ideological assumptions are the most serious problem the form presents. Jacobs invokes a plot initiated by Richardson's *Pamela* and recapitulated in nineteenth-century American sentimental novels. In this plot, a persistent male of elevated social rank seeks to seduce a woman of a lower class. Through her resistance and piety, however, she educates her would-be seducer into an awareness of his own depravity and his capacity for true honorable love. In the manner of Pamela's Mr. B., the reformed villain rewards the heroine's virtue by marrying her.

As is the case with popular literature generally, this paradigm affirms the dominant ideology, in this instance the power of patriarchy. As Tania Modleski and Janice Radway have shown, the seduction plot typically encodes pursuit or harassment as love, allowing the protagonist and reader alike to interpret the male's abusiveness as a sign of his inability to express his profound love for the heroine.[16] The problem is one that Ann Douglas attributes to sentimentalism as a mode of discourse, one that never challenges fundamental assumptions and structures:

> Sentimentalism is a complex phenomenon. It asserts that the values a society's activity denies are precisely the ones it cherishes; it attempts to deal with the phenomenon of cultural bifurcation by the manipulation of nostalgia. Sentimentalism provides a way to protest a power to which one has already in part capitulated.[17]

Capitulation is certainly not what Jacobs intends, especially since the patriarchy is, for her, synonymous with slavocracy. But to invoke that plot is, I would suggest, to invoke the clusters of associations and assumptions that surround it.

As Jacobs exercised authority over the limits of the male narrative, however, she triumphs as well over the limits of the sentimental novel, a genre more suited to the experience of her white, middle-class reader than it was to her own. From at least three narrative spaces, analogs to the garret in which she concealed herself, she displays her power over the forms at her disposal.

In the much-quoted line from the last paragraph of her account, she writes: "Reader, my story ends with freedom, not in the usual way, with marriage (207)." In this sentence, she calls attention to the space between the traditional happy ending of the novel of domestic sentiment and the ending of her story. She acknowledges that however much her story may resemble superficially the story of the sentimental heroine, as a black woman she plays for different stakes; marriage is not the ultimate reward she seeks.

Another gap occurs at the point when she announces her second pregnancy. She describes her initial involvement with Sands as a conundrum. The brutality of neighboring masters, the indifference of the legal system, and her own master's harassment force her to take a white man as her lover. Both in the way she leads up to this revelation, and in the explicit apostrophes to the reader, she presents it as a situation in which she has no choice. Her explanation for taking Sands as her lover is accompanied by the appropriate regret and chagrin, and then followed by two general chapters about slave religion and the local response to the Nat Turner rebellion. When we return to Jacobs's story, she remarks that Flint's harassment persists, and then announces her second pregnancy by saying simply, "When Dr. Flint learned that I was again to be a mother, he was exasperated beyond measure (79)." Her continued relations with Sands and her own response to her second pregnancy are submerged in the subtext of the two previous chapters and in the space between paragraphs. By consigning to the narrative silences those aspects of her own sexuality for which the genre does not allow, Jacobs points to an inadequacy in the form.

The third such gap occurs a bit later, just before she leaves the plantation. Her master's great-aunt, Miss Fanny, a kindhearted, elderly woman who is a great favorite with Jacobs's grandmother, comes to visit. Jacobs is clearly fond of this woman, but as she tells the story she admits that she resents the old woman's attempts to sentimentalize her situation. As Jacobs tells it, Miss Fanny remarks at one point that she "wished that I and all my grandmother's family were at rest in our graves, for not until then should she feel any peace about us (91)." Jacobs then reflects privately that "The good old soul did not dream that I was planning to bestow peace upon her, with regard to myself and my children; not by death, but by securing our freedom." Here, Jacobs resists becoming the object of someone else's sentimentality, and calls attention to the inappropriateness of this response. Although she certainly draws on the conventions of sentimentalism when they suit her purposes, she is also capable of replacing the self-indulgent mythification of death with the more practical solution of freedom.

The work of Barbara Smith, Paula Giddings, Angela Davis, and Elizabeth Spelman has shown that the complex experience of the black woman has eluded analyses and theories that focus on any one of the variables of race, class, and gender alone.[18] As Barbara Smith has remarked, the effect of the multiple oppression of race, class, and gender is not merely arithmetic. That is, one cannot say only that in addition to racism, black women have had to confront the problem of sexism. Rather, we must recognize that issues of class and race alter one's experience of gender, just as gender alters one's experience of class and race. Whatever the limitations of her narrative, Jacobs anticipates these recent developments in class, race, and gender analysis. Her account indicates that the story of a black woman does not emerge from the superimposition of a slave narrative on a sentimental novel. Rather, in the ironies and silences and spaces of her book, she makes not-quite-adequate forms more truly her own.

NOTES

1. Linda Brent [Harriet Jacobs], *Incidents in the Life of a Slave Girl* (New York: Harcourt Brace Jovanovich, 1973), 117. Subsequent references will be to this edition.
2. As I completed revisions of this discussion, I read Houston Baker's *Blues, Ideology, and Afro-American Literature* (Chicago: University of Chicago Press, 1984). He too considers the centrality of this image to Jacobs's account, but he focuses on Jacobs's ability to transform the economics of her oppression, while I concentrate on her use of received literary conventions.
3. Elaine Showalter, "Review Essay," *Signs* 1 (1975), 435.
4. Sandra M. Gilbert and Susan Gubar, *The Madwoman in the Attic* (New Haven: Yale University Press, 1979). 3–104 *passim*.
5. Ibid., 23.
6. Ann Douglas, *The Feminization of American Culture* (New York: Avon Books, 1977), 240–73 *passim*.
7. Susan Gubar, " 'The Blank Page' and the Issues of Female Creativity," in Elizabeth Abel, ed., *Writing and Sexual Difference* (Chicago: University of Chicago Press, 1982), 74.
8. See Showalter, Gilbert and Gubar, *op.cit.* See also Patricia Meyer Spacks, *The Female Imagination* (New York: Knopf, 1975), 317, and Carolyn Heilbrun and Catharine Stimpson, "Theories of Feminist Criticism: A Dialogue," in Josephine Donovan, ed., *Feminist Literary Criticism* (Lexington: University Press of Kentucky, 1975), 62.
9. Frederick Douglass, *Narrative of the Life of Frederick Douglass, An American Slave, Written by Himself* (Cambridge: Harvard University Press, 1973), 104–105.
10. See Elizabeth Abel, Marianne Hirsch, and Elizabeth Langland, eds., *The Voyage In: Fictions of Female Development* (University Press of New England, 1983), 3–19.

11. I draw here on the vocabulary of recent feminist psychoanalytic theory that revises traditional accounts of female psychosexual development. See Jean Baker Miller, *Toward A New Psychology of Women* (Boston: Beacon Press, 1976); Nancy Chodorow, *The Reproduction of Mothering: Psychoanalysis and the Sociology of Gender* (Berkeley: University of California Press, 1978); Carol Gilligan, *In a Different Voice* (Cambridge: Harvard University Press, 1982).

12. I acknowledge here my gratitude to Mary Helen Washington for helping me to recognize this characteristic of the narratives.

13. William Wells Brown, *Narrative of William W. Brown* (Boston: The Anti-Slavery Office, 1847; New York: Arno Press, 1968), 105.

14. Annette Niemtzow, "The Problematic of Self in Autobiography: The Example of the Slave Narrative," in *The Art of the Slave Narrative: Original Essays in Criticism and Theory,* ed. John Sekora and Darwin T. Turner (Macomb: Western Illinois University Press, 1982), 105–106.

15. See Douglas, *op. cit,* 72.

16. See Tania Modleski, *Loving With a Vengeance: Mass-Produced Fantasies for Women* (New York: Archon Books, 1982), 17; Janice Radway, *Reading the Romance: Women, Patriarchy, and Popular Literature* (Chapel Hill: University of North Carolina Press, 1984), 75.

17. See Douglas, *op.cit.,* 12.

18. See Barbara Smith, "Notes For Yet Another Paper on Black Feminism, Or Will the Real Enemy Please Stand Up," *Conditions 5,* 123–132.; Paula Giddings, *When And Where I Enter: The Impact of Black Women on Race and Sex in America* (New York: William Morrow and Company, 1984); Angela Davis, *Women, Race, and Class* (New York: Vintage Books, 1983); Elizabeth V. Spelman, "Theories of Race and Gender: The Erasure of Black Women," *Quest 5* (1979), 36–62.

come to realize that the public/private, intellectual/emotional, rational/intuitive (spiritual), mind/body split that dominates much of the portrayal of experience in literature and history is intimately related to long-standing socially accepted notions of differences in gender roles, and elitist patriarchal biases toward what constitutes the important aspects of the individual life. We note, for instance, that what is left out of the autobiographies of most men, and even some women, is almost exclusively related to the affairs of women, children (especially girls), home, and family. Generally perceived as the domestic and private areas of reality, and associated with the emotional and spiritual responses to experience, these affairs belong to the province of women and children. Unfortunately, the major paradigms in western autobiography have developed from models set in this exclusionary mode. For example, in American autobiography, whether we look at the writings of Benjamin Franklin or Frederick Douglass, clearly, what they considered most valuable to set down excluded what occurred in the private spheres of their lives, although we can be reasonably sure that family and family relationships determined much of their public successes. To give a concrete example is to point to the most glaring gap in the narratives of Frederick Douglass. It is with no thanks to him that we know that the unsung free southern black woman named Anna Murray was sufficiently important to the life of the young Frederick Bailey that she was the most instrumental person in his escape from slavery; and if he repaid her by marrying her soon after, that importance to him continued until her death. Throughout her entire life in the North she was the source of the family, economic, and emotional strength that enabled him to achieve the greatness for which, as male, he was presumably destined. Does the life of Anna Douglass have meaning in the nineteenth-century struggle for black freedom? Certainly not in the memoirs of the man who knew it best. In hundreds of pages of narrative—three volumes to be exact—her life receives one reference at the point at which she joined him shortly after his escape to freedom: "My intended wife came . . . and we were married" (*My Bondage*, 341). Yet, critics of Douglass's otherwise memorable, exciting, and astonishingly brilliant autobiographies do not raise the issue of the silence surrounding the existence of Anna Douglass, without whom we may never have had the historical presence of Frederick Douglass.[2]

I begin this essay on "The Souls of Black Women Folk in W.E.B. Du Bois's Writings" on this note because, in the conversation with my friend, Du Bois immediately came to mind as an exception to the rule, if the idea of feminist autobiography indicates an inclusionary process by which a writer acknowledges the important connections between many aspects of her/his existence, and brings them together to present a more realistic image of that life. I thought that while it is true that Du Bois's autobiographies are about "ideas" and do not represent the archetypal "journey" of the man, the extent to which he includes the influences of women's experiences, and especially those of black women, on his thinking; his recognition of gender oppression; and his acceptance of the worth of his emotional and spiritual feelings makes his works distinctive. More than any other black man in our history, his three autobiographies demonstrate that black women have been central to the development of his intellectual thought. In his old age he would say that he had always had more friends among black women than among black men; that he was less attracted to relationships with the men of the race because many of them "imitated an American culture which [he] did not share" (*Autobiography*, 279). Using the criteria of inclusiveness of experience, and an awareness of race and gender oppression as aspects of the composition of feminist autobiography, Du Bois comes closer to consciously repudiating the intellectual/emotional, mind/body split than many other writers of intellectual autobiography.

To begin at the beginning, we know that Du Bois had a perception that black folk have "souls" that not only understand the problems of the Veil, but also embody peculiarly transcending sensibilities that enhance their humanity. We also know that he was aware that the folk were not all men. If anything can be said about his views on the souls of black women folk, it is that he felt that they had struggled through to an even higher plane than black men had. He was not afraid to acknowledge his own spiritual–emotional feelings, and he was not afraid to acknowledge their manifestations in the lives of others, including women. In like manner, he was not afraid to recognize the more concrete elements of human experience. It is this kind of inclusive perspective on experience that makes his autobiographies stand out for me. I suspect, for instance, that were he still alive, Du Bois's commentary on the current debate surrounding the writings of contemporary black women artists would be controversial. On the other hand, the fact that so little has been written about Du Bois's more creative, less sociological works, where most of his thoughts on women and his own fundamental spirituality are expressed, may be no accident of the critical imagination. Take, for instance, his most widely read book, *The Souls of Black Folk*, which combines autobiography, history, fiction, and sociology. For three quarters of a century the public discussion of this much-recognized classic centered predominantly around the Du Bois/ Washington controversy, and it was not until Arnold Rampersad's 1977 biography of Du Bois that we had a major critic commenting substantially on the magnificent spiritual insights in "Of the Coming of John," or of the new image of black women in the character of Josie in "Of the Meaning of Progress," or on the femalelike outpouring of personal grief in "Of the Passing of the Firstborn," all of which are chapters in *The Souls of Black Folk*.[3] We might well ask the question: Why has this been so?

There is little doubt that the souls of black women folk were close to Du Bois's consciousness throughout his life—that is, that the importance of women, beyond their socially defined roles of subordination to men, was a matter that he took seriously. On the other hand, to best understand his autobiographies we must also read the life as a metaphor of one facet of the black experience. And Du Bois's perceptions of the "souls of black folk"—that spiritual essence that made survival and transcendence possible for an entire race in spite of indescribable oppression, was most obvious in his discourse on black women. Interestingly, these perceptions—themselves a spiritual comprehension—seem to have been shared and captured adequately by only one other writer, who also traveled from North to South before he too understood the meaning of the term. As Alice Walker writes:

> When the poet Jean Toomer walked through the South in the early twenties, he discovered a curious thing: black women whose spirituality was so intense, so deep, so

unconscious, that they were themselves unaware of the richness they held . . . In the still heat of the post-Reconstruction South . . . they seemed to Jean Toomer: exquisite butterflies trapped in an evil honey, toiling away their lives in an era, a century, that did not acknowledge them (*In Search of Our Mothers' Gardens*, 231–232).

And as I have written elsewhere, what Jean Toomer recognized in the women whom he described in his own masterpiece, *Cane*, was the representative sustaining quality of the souls of black folk—of its women and its men—but he could describe this best through the essence of black women.[4]

As noted above, much of Du Bois's discourse on women and the emotional feelings that prompted this discourse were expressed in his creative works—his autobiographies and fiction. While the former have served historians and sociologists as markers for the progress of this writer's social and political thought, the latter has fared less well, and in fact has been almost universally ignored. Few people, even those who have spent years reading and studying Du Bois, know that he wrote five novels and published a volume of poetry. As Rampersad notes in his very good biography, many reputations in belles lettres have been made on much less of an output, but this does not alter the case in point.

No one, not even the staunchest Du Bois supporter (of whom I consider myself one), would argue that he was a great literateur. However, one can argue that his creative work deserves attention, especially in its relationship to his entire body of writings. For many of the political ideas that surface in the later writings appear first in his fiction. And in his contemplation of his personal life and the development of his political philosophy, he never lost sight of the value of the imaginative dimension. That is, Du Bois, in viewing his own life, did not de-privilege his feelings in favor of his purely intellectual ideas, and in the majority of instances where this surfaces in his writings, the relationship is to women in his life or to the experiences of women in general. This essay focuses on "the souls of black women folk" in his three volumes of autobiography: *Darkwater: Voices From Behind the Veil* (1920), *Dusk of Dawn: An Essay Toward An Autobiography of a Race Concept* (1940), and *The Autobiography of W.E.B. Du Bois:*

A Soliloquy on Viewing My Life from the Last Decade of Its First Century (1968), edited by Herbert Aptheker and published posthumously. I will also refer to examples from *The Souls of Black Folk* (1903).

Looking at the black autobiographical tradition backward from Du Bois, we face the slave narrative as the preeminent form in the nineteenth-century tradition. Writers in this time, including the most well known—Frederick Douglass and Booker T. Washington—assure us that the most devastating aspect of the slave child's life was that of the unstable family—the missing immediate parent or parents, and the absence of a sense of lineage. Where mothers are known (fathers are generally even more problematic), if even for a short time (as in the case of both Douglass and Washington), and grandparents (as in the case of Douglass), they are spoken of with the highest regard. In making public the stories of their lives in slavery, and their trials to overcome the effects of that institution on them even after they became free, ex–slave narrators are extremely articulate in their condemnation of the destruction of the fabric of black family life wrought by the many atrocities of servitude. There is, however, a clear line that separates the slave narratives of men and women regarding the influences that women, particularly mothers, grandmothers, and other relatives, have on their later lives. For men, the emphasis falls on the deprivations caused by the absence of childhood nurturing that unstable family situations creates for them; while women find ways to pattern their own lives after the heroism they perceive in their female elders. For women, there is always a strong female bond that exists with forebears, and this invests them with the power to resist, survive, and transcend their own oppression.

William Edward Burghardt Du Bois had very strong links with some of the women in his family, and it is from them that he derived his early sense of self. In converse to nineteenth-century black autobiographers in the slave South, his was a childhood of privilege that began in 1868 "by a golden river and in the shadow of two great hills," far removed from the slavocracy, in the town of Great Barrington, Massachusetts. His family had lived in the area for close to two hundred years (*Dusk of Dawn* 8). (A similar description is given in *Darkwater* [5] and *Autobiography* [61].) The setting was pastoral: "A boy's

paradise . . . mountains to climb and rivers to wade and
swim; lakes to freeze and hills for coasting . . . all of it apparently the property of the children of the town" (*Dusk of Dawn*
13). Besides, the atrocities of slavery had not touched his
family for many generations. And while innocence lasted, for
a long time he was unconscious of the knowledge that the
living was not easy for the woman who raised him.

In addition, unlike the slave narrators, he must have gained
a sense of emotional strength from his good fortune in being
able to trace a good deal of his family tree. "The black
Burghardts were a group of African Negroes descended from
Tom, who was born in West Africa about 1730" (*Autobiography*
62). As a child, Tom was stolen from his home by Dutch slave
traders and brought to America, where he grew up in the
valley of the Hudson with a Dutch family, whose name he
inherited (one cannot but think of the similarity of this story
with that of Phillis Wheatley's, which occurred in the same
time). Later Tom moved with his "owner" to the "howling
wilderness" of the Massachusetts Berkshires. His early status
is somewhat unclear, for Du Bois tells us he was not "legally"
a slave. In any case, he seems to have gained his freedom
before the Massachusetts Bill of Rights ending slavery in the
state became law in 1780, by enlisting in the Revolutionary
War for three years. The story continues that Tom's wife or
mother—and again Du Bois is unclear about the relationship (I
suspect that she was his wife)—was a "little black Bantu
woman, who never became reconciled to this strange land"
(*Autobiography* 62). Tom died around 1787, leaving many sons,
among them Jack, who with his wife Violet were the parents
of a "mighty family, splendidly named," which included
Du Bois's grandfather, Othello. The nameless little Bantu
woman, unlike Tom, left more to her sons and daughters and
their sons and daughters than the heritage of continuing her
line in utter despair—she left to her generations a link that
was a lifeline from their cultural past. According to her illustrious great-great-grandson, in her sorrow she refused to be
comforted, and instead she "clasped her knees and rocked
and crooned" a song in her native tongue. This song was
handed down through the family through the years until
Du Bois's own time. The words were unintelligible to those
who had never known the mother tongue, but the music was

not. When as a young man Du Bois heard the Negro spirituals—
the sorrow songs—in the South, he needed no one to tell him
from whence they originated. "They that walked in darkness
sang songs in the olden days," he writes in *The Souls of Black
Folk*, "the songs are indeed the siftings of centuries; the music
is far more ancient than the words." He recalls the troubled
croonings of his unhappy ancestor as he traces the American
development of that music which helped to define the souls of
black folk (264, 267).

Although his mother's parents had ten or more children,
the immediate family in which Du Bois grew up consisted of
his grandfather, Othello, his grandmother, Sally, his mother,
Mary Silvina, his aunts Lucinda and Minerva, and an uncle,
Jim. He also recalls several female cousins. His father, an
outsider to Great Barrington and openly disliked by the
Burghardt clan, perhaps from fear that he would take Mary
Burghardt away from them, disappeared long before his son
was old enough to form an opinion of him. As for the men in
his family, Du Bois remembers most prominently his "strong-
voiced and redolent with tobacco" grandfather, who sat in a
"great high chair" because his hip was broken. He was "good-
natured," but there was no "energy" in him, Du Bois writes.
On the other hand, he recalls his grandmother as "thin, tall,
yellow and hawk-faced . . . efficient and managing in her
age."

Only later does Du Bois realize how delicately balanced were
the economic and emotional threads that held his childhood
in place. By the time of his birth, the Burghardts, who had
made a comfortable living as farmers in the eighteenth and
early nineteenth centuries, were in financial decline. In his
earliest years, both of his grandparents were part of his household until their respective deaths. Then his mother became ill.
After many years of depression, seemingly the result of both
an unhappy love affair when she was very young and the
failure of her alliance with Alfred Du Bois, whom she had
married when she was thirty-five years old, Du Bois's mother
suffered a paralytic stroke that left her lame, though not
crippled, for the rest of her life. She died in 1884 at the age of
fifty-four, shortly before her son left home for college.

In spite of the precariousness of her financial and emotional
situation, Mary Burghardt Du Bois provided a stable home life

for her son. "We lived in simple comfort," he writes, "yet as I look back I cannot see how mother did it" (*Autobiography* 73). Apparently, the other members of the family and kind neighbors augmented her meagre earnings from the occasional housework she did for more affluent families in the community. It had to have been an enormous strain on her, and must have required Herculean efforts on her part not to reveal her burden to her son, who would write:

> My mother and myself must often have been near the edge of poverty. Yet I was not hungry or in lack of suitable clothing and shoes, or made to feel unfortunate in the company of my fellow students . . . When special expenditures were called for, new shoes or school books, the money often came from my uncle or aunts or less frequently from white families, long closely connected with the Burghardts. There may have been other gifts but they were never conspicuous. I never wore cast-off clothes (*Autobiography* 73).

His situation was no doubt less noticeable to him because most of the white children with whom he associated in school came from families that were equally indigent financially, and the contrast in living standards between the town's wealthier and less fortunate families was not very great. But if he did not fully understand the nature of his family's financial situation, his feelings for his mother were clear. Mother and son shared a warm and trusting relationship, to which he credits his deep and abiding respect for black women.

Du Bois, the "only colored student" in his class, graduated from high school in the summer of 1884, shortly before his mother's death. Having previously decided on a college career, his "grief was a challenge" to him, and it prompted him to love her in death with "a fierce sense of personal loss" (*Darkwater* 163), as well as to follow his plans for college because she had so desperately wanted him to succeed. He remained in his hometown for a year, working and otherwise receiving comfort and financial assistance from his Aunt Minerva. To the dismay of the Burghardts, in 1885 he left Great Barrington for Fisk University, and never returned to live there again. But the meaning of the years of his childhood in that place, surrounded by the love, protection, and the heritage of black women who, in the words of novelist Toni Morrison, "made a way when there was none," remained with him throughout his life. The lives and sacrifices of these women, and Du Bois's spiritual connection to the place in which he knew them, appear in each of his autobiographies, as well as in several other writings, including *The Souls of Black Folk*. He buried his infant son, his firstborn, in the Berkshires, in the bosom of the Burghardt clan.

The images of black women that appear in Du Bois's first book, *The Souls of Black Folk*, in two separate chapters, one autobiographical, the other fictional, confirm the claims I have so far been making for his connection and appreciation of the group as a whole. In "Of the Meaning of Progress," a recollection of his college-years summer teaching experiences in back-country Tennessee, through the failure and death of a young woman, he demonstrates the enormity of the problem of trying to educate rural blacks in the antebellum South. His attention is on Josie, in years barely a woman, who understands the value of education and finds her efforts to advance herself and the other members of her family and community stymied by ignorance and economic difficulties. The account of Josie, whose death comes out of her sense of the futility of her vision, pays tribute to the ambitions, faith, strength, and resourcefulness of black women, on behalf of racial progress, and in the face of insurmountable odds.

In the second illustration, a fictional account turns on a white/black male racial confrontation that originates in the sexual oppression of a young black girl. A young white male makes unwanted advances to the young black girl. The brother of the child challenges the assailant and there is a double death in the face of a lynching. Black oppression and tragedy take on transcendence and future hope in the young girl's awakening to the possibilities of knowledge and a sense of self-worth as weapons against racism. At a time when black male writers concentrated their efforts on the social, economic, and educational advancement of black men as the "leaders" of the race, Du Bois is something of an anomaly in his recognition that black women were equal partners in the struggle to claim the human dignity all black people were seeking.

One of his most moving discourses on the plight of black

women is "The Damnation of Women," a chapter in *Darkwater*. In this two-tiered essay, Du Bois first does a feminist critique of his recollections of the lives of the women who were important to him in his early years in Great Barrington, then generalizes from their experiences to the larger arena of the social, economic, and sexual oppression of all black women in America. Noting that his mother and three of his female cousins "represented the problem of the widow, the wife, the maiden, and the outcast," he vents anger that each in turn existed not for herself, but was "named" for the man to whom she was related, not "after the fashion of [her] own soul" (*Darkwater* 162). In commending the work of black women on behalf of the entire race, he writes:

> Despite the more spectacular advance of my brothers, I instinctively feel and know that it is the five million women of my race who really count. Black women . . . are today furnishing our teachers; they are the main pillars of those social settlements which we call churches (179).

He goes on to note that the accumulated assets of the black community were "wrung [largely] from the hearts of servant girls and washer women" who "toil hard" and have their value "trod under the feet of men" (*Darkwater* 179, 182).

Du Bois may well have read Maria Stewart or Anna Julia Cooper, nineteenth-century black women activists who articulated these concepts before he did. Stewart, a fiery speaker who published her speeches, began her career as feminist, abolitionist, and promoter of temperance on the lecture circuit in 1832, while Cooper's *A Voice From the South by a Black Woman of the South* carries the tradition into the later years of the century. On the other hand, Virginia Woolf may well have read "The Damnation of Women" or Stewart or Cooper, or any combination of them before she published *A Room of One's Own* in 1928. But regardless of who read whose work and borrowed from it, in his writings specifically about the plight of black women in 1920, Du Bois takes a radical feminist position and waxes eloquent in calling for their economic and work independence, and for their individual right to choose or reject motherhood. It "is the damnation of women," he writes, that "only at the sacrifice of intelligence and the chance to do their best work can the majority of modern women bear children" (*Darkwater* 164), and he warns that

> the future woman must have a life work and economic independence. She must have knowledge. She must have the right of motherhood at her own discretion (*Darkwater* 164).

In addition, he defends the beauty of black women against the "defective eyesight" of the white world, sings the praises of such heroines as Sojourner Truth and Harriet Tubman, and announces his intentions of never forgiving the South, "neither in this world nor the world to come: its wanton and continued and persistent insulting of the black womanhood which it sought and seeks to prostitute to its lust" (*Darkwater* 172). "The Damnation of Women" establishes that Du Bois, far from simply holding romantic notions about the beauty and strength of black women, independently understood the politics of race and gender decades before the majority of black women were able to make themselves heard on these issues by the rest of the society.

Studies of Du Bois's life have, for good reason, focused essentially on his intellectual and political thought and development. Most would agree he remains the premier black thinker of this century, and his writings of the early 1900s continue to engage our minds in challenging ways. All of his writings, including the autobiographies, generate and explore ideas, so that even now, as questions surface of his relationships with and to women in his writings, they must be examined for their intellectual as well as their personal/emotional content. So far, I have been doing the former, and I will now take a look at the latter.

For all of his intellectuality, Du Bois's autobiographies break out of standard patriarchal paradigms and offer a model that enlarges the boundaries of the form through their content and the method of their presentation. Also, given the nature of these works, they demonstrate that the intellectual integrity of the text need not be compromised by the dissolution of the rigid public/private split that feminist critics would like to achieve. Having made a case for Du Bois's very personal spiritual connection to the souls of black women folk in his childhood family, and his understanding of the political impact of gender on the lives of black women in America, beginning when he was a young man, I am also concerned with how what he tells us about at least one woman who shared his more private life contributes to the idea of what I have called feminist autobiography.

Du Bois, we know, married twice—once in 1897 while he was a very young man, and again when he was very old, following the death of his first wife, more than fifty years later. It is reasonable to say that his second marriage, to Shirley Graham, a woman well known in her own right long before that marriage, and more than forty years his junior, was a result of the deep respect they had for each other over the entire period of her life, one that came from the compatibility of their intellectual interests and their political goals. It is then his first marriage that concerns me most.

There are no references to Du Bois's adult private life in either *Darkwater* or *Dusk of Dawn*, and only in the final autobiography does he shed some light on his personal relationships. On the other hand, one of the most intimate pieces of his writing, in which he reveals his greatest vulnerability, "Of the Passing of the First-Born," appears in *The Souls of Black Folk*. This selection weaves his grief surrounding that event with his respect for the process of childbearing in general, and his love for the mother of his own child in particular. In *The Autobiography*, more than half a century later, he would say that he never fully recovered from the death of his eighteen-month-old infant son.

Nature and religious imagery dominate the essay. The miracle of childbirth and the emotional impact of motherhood, functions of women's bodies and minds, overwhelm Du Bois. Clearly, as he sees them, they defy male intellectual abstractions. His long years of formal education had not prepared him for the danger and the beauty they presented. His description of his initial reactions to the birth of his son—his reverence and his sense of wonder—are sheer poetry: "Up the stairs I ran to the wan mother and whimpering babe, to the sanctuary on whose altar a life at my bidding had offered itself to win a life and won" (*Souls* 227). Although at first he does not know how to love "this tiny formless thing," and could only handle it "curiously," and watch its movements with perplexity, he has no difficulty understanding the changes it would make in the life and psyche of his wife. Of her he says: "But her I loved, my girl-mother, she whom now I saw unfolding like the glory of the morning—the transfigured woman" (*Souls* 227). Through her he comes to love the "wee thing . . . as its little soul unfolded itself in cry and half-formed word, and its eyes caught the gleam and flash of life" (*Souls* 227). Later there is a hint of jealousy in his description of mother/child relationship:

> Her own life builded and molded itself upon the child; he tinged her every dream and idealized her every effort. No hands but hers must touch and garnish those little limbs; no dress or frill must touch them that had not wearied her fingers; no voice but hers could coax him off to Dreamland, and she and he together spoke some soft and unknown tongue and in it held communion (*Souls* 228).

Together the young parents plan for their child, they dream for him and "heard in his baby voice the voice of the Prophet that was to rise within the Veil" (*Souls*, 228). In the face of sudden and unexpected death, their dreams shatter:

> He died at eventide, when the sun lay like a brooding sorrow above the western hills, veiling its face; when the winds spoke not, and the trees, the great green trees he loved, stood motionless (*Souls*, 229).

Du Bois tries to console himself: the child had escaped the problems of the color line—he would never know the Veil, although it shadowed him. But there is little comfort in that thought, and besides, the child might have dealt with the burdens of race better than his parents. At the end of the essay the young father remains in great pain—which perhaps enables him to reveal to his readers the extent to which he feels completely vulnerable to the larger forces of life and death over which he has no control. "Of the Passing of the First-Born" permits us a privileged and seldom-glimpsed view of Du Bois—the young husband and young father—the private

man who in these intensely private moments acknowledges
and embraces the grief that defines the common humanity of
kings and beggars alike. As an excellent example of the "un-
split" self, "Of the Passing of the First-Born," in the language
of poetry and pathos, makes use of an intensely personal/
emotional experience to illustrate the intellectual human struggle to find spiritual meaning in the existential meaninglessness
of life and death.

The brief description of Du Bois's first marriage, in the final
volume of autobiography, can best be described as the bru-
tally honest musings of an old man who, sitting "high on the
ramparts of this blistering hell of life . . . [sees] the Truth . . .
[looks] it full in the face . . . and will not lie about it, neither
to [himself] . . . nor to the world" (*Autobiography* 415). For the
old man, there is acceptance (of its successes and failures),
self-praise (for what he thinks he did right), and self-censure
(assuming responsibility for his part in his failures); but more
to the point of this paper, we are able to participate in his
efforts to understand how the weaknesses and strengths of
this marriage indicate the powers of internal consent (autonomy) and of external compulsion (social conditions and
pressures).

The Du Boises lived together for more than half a century.
They had a second child, a daughter, who lived to full adulthood. But the marriage was never a union of equals. We do
not know what prompted her to accept him as her husband in
the first place, but we do know that he was attracted to her
because of "her rare beauty and excellent household training"
(the ability to be a good housekeeper), which she learned
from her mother. The fact that she was an orphan, and still
only a very young woman, may well have influenced her
decision at the time. On the other hand, for a young man with
Du Bois's training and ambitions around the turn of the century, and especially for one who describes himself as "lusty
with all normal appetites . . . [who] loved 'Wine, Women,
and Song,' " a beautiful wife who was also a good housekeeper must certainly have been a prize of great value. But we
can hardly escape the irony in his revelation when he tells us
that while she occupied herself with "marketing, sweeping
and cleaning" and a "few" women friends whose lives mirrored her own, his "main work was out in the world . . .

[where he] wandered . . . to wider and higher goals . . . with women [like Mary Church Terrell and Ida Wells Barnett, women] of brains and great effort, to work on the highest scale" (*Autobiography* 281–282). From his account, the death of their infant son heralds a major breakdown in their ability to communicate with each other: "it tore their lives in two." He is able to ease his sense of pain and loss by increased involvement in his work; for her, "the reason for living left [her] . . . soul [and she] . . . never forgave God for the unhealable wound" (*Autobiography* 281). The text indicates that he recognizes the major weaknesses in their relationship early on—"a difference in aim and function between its partners." However, his training, sense of responsibility, and perhaps even his genuine affection for this woman dictate not only that the marriage continue, but that he provide for his family to the best of his ability. This he does unflinchingly. As we know, he also spent an enormous amount of time away from home, completely immersed in the work of the "race." He is aware that for his wife, the years of her life are filled with loneliness of many kinds.

Du Bois's reflections on the strengths and weaknesses of the marriage in which he spent the major part of his life do not constitute a confession and plea for forgiveness from an understanding public. Setting them down here was a part of his effort, in this final volume of autobiography, to interpret, for us, his life and actions in the context of Western culture in the twentieth century. At the beginning of his illustrious career, he had made the stirring remark that the century's most pressing problem was the color line, and his words had proved prophetic. But Du Bois knew well that even as he lived constrained inside that line, there was a reciprocity of influence that had occurred—he had influenced as much as he had been influenced. He was also responsible for his times. So he was not apologizing for his weaknesses and failures—they had happened because he had been born and would die in the bosom of a civilization which accounted for his frailties. He had spent his life seeking Truth and Beauty for himself and others, and he had often found ugliness and hate. His power to change the world had been minuscule, but he also had to believe that his life had had meaning. How much? Posterity would be the judge of that, but in the meantime he could set it down as he remembered it, considering the task a "duty to contribute whatever enlightenment" he might to the world in which he had lived. And so in the *Soliloquy* he returns to review his boyhood in Great Barrington; his academic career; the effects of the Depression on the black community; his fifteen trips abroad; his sentiments about China and Russia; his life as an activist in the cause of race and world peace; and the mostly-shortcomings of fifty-three years of marriage. Feminist autobiography? Perhaps not quite, but one thing is clear: It was in the souls of black women folk that he touched the chords in himself that brought him closest to an understanding of just what that term might mean.

NOTES

1. In a conversation with historian Nell Irvin Painter. The discussion focused on contemporary autobiographies, including some by historians.
2. Although scholars in history and literature have written extensively on the life of Frederick Douglass, very little is still known of Anna Murray Douglass. Her life remains outside of the interests that continue to make her husband a topic of continuing inquiry.

WORKS CITED

Cooper, Anna Julia. *A Voice From the South by a Black Woman of the South.* Xenia, Ohio: Aldine Printers, 1892.
Douglass, Frederick. *My Bondage and My Freedom.* New York: Miller, Orton & Mulligan, 1855.
Du Bois, W.E.B. *The Autobiography of W.E.B. Du Bois: A Soliloquy on Viewing My Life From the Last Decade of its First Century.* Ed. Herbert Aptheker. New York: International Publishers, 1968.
———*DarkWater: Voices From Behind the Veil.* New York: Schocken Books, 1920.
———*Dusk of Dawn: An Essay Toward An Autobiography of a Race Concept.* New York: Harcourt, Brace, 1940.
———*The Souls of Black Folk.* Chicago: A.C. McClurg, 1903.
Stewart, Maria. *America's First Black Woman Political Writer: Essays and Speeches.* Ed. Marilyn Richardson. Bloomington and Indianapolis: Indiana University Press, 1987.
Walker, Alice. *In Search of Our Mothers' Gardens.* San Diego, New York, London: Harcourt Brace Jovanovich, 1983.

"An Order of Constancy":

Notes on Brooks and the Feminine*

Hortense J. Spillers

The adopted procedure for this essay is neither fish nor fowl and, as such, breathes in the impure air of literary interpretation, verging on social theory. It assumes for the moment a sort of critically illegitimate stance—the literary text *does* point outside itself—in the primary interest of leading the reader back inside the universe of the apparently self-contained artifact. With some luck, we hope to negotiate between two different kinds of related critical inquiry: What does the writer teach us, or illuminate in us, concerning situations for which we need a name,[1] in this case, the "feminine," whose very conjuring broaches more confusion than we can comfortably settle in the course of a workday? What does the writer take with her from "experience" to the transmuting work itself?

I

The stage of interaction that arises between an audience and the visible aspects of a public performance sketches a paradigm for understanding the social dimensions of an aesthetic act, but it also brings into focus the most acute aspects of consciousness—to perceive, to be perceived. On the one hand the subject is acting; on the other, acted upon. The distance

*A version of this essay was published under the same title in *The Centennial Review*, Vol. XXIX, No. 2 (Spring, 1985).

between these related grammatical properties, mobilized by a single term, is precisely the difference and overlap between subjects and objects of interrogation, neither of which can be split off from the other with integrity. To the extent that the writer and the artistic process that she or he engages are neither wholly autonomous nor dependent, but, rather, interdependent, suspended between opposing yet mutually coexistent means, both writer and process approach the "feminine," whose elusive claims escape not only precise definition but also decided terrain. Gwendolyn Brooks's "feminine" across the poet's writing career is a nominative of many facets. About this still center, modifiers shift, lose and gain emphases alternately, but there is an "order of constancy" here whose active paradoxes throw light on the paradox of the "feminine."

There are few things riskier at the moment than defining the "feminine" in a way that does not offend what, until yesterday, we thought of as its primary subject—"woman herself." Is this complex of traits gender related and, therefore, a locus of attributions culturally conferred, biologically sustained? Can we count on its disappearance when the "revolution" comes? Is the "feminine" yet one other heterosexist hoax whose genuinely fraudulent character will be revealed as such in the figurative "new world" of widened sexualities presently upon us?[2] According to the editors of a fairly recent work on feminist theory,[3] feminine consciousness is only a single aspect of woman-consciousness (whatever we decide that is), but it seems difficult to specify the boundaries of either, except insofar as "woman-consciousness" and "feminine" inscribe the absence of "male" and "masculine." *Feminist Theory: A Critique of Ideology* attempts to correct and revise our negative perspective on ideas regarding the "feminine." For feminist theoreticians, the "feminine" is often, ironically enough, an "object of analysis rather than a source of insight."[4] Insofar as the subject is the "object of attention of another," we might have anticipated that the "feminine" arises "from the sensation of being looked at,"[5] and involves, relatedly, the dialectical tensions at work in the "double consciousness."[6] Simone de Beauvoir in *The Second Sex* describes an existential correspondence between "feminine" and "other" so that both might be seen as a negation of ego (read "male"). We would intrude on this accumulated calculus of power a point of view too often short-shrifted: I would say that the "feminine" and "other" are subjectivities who experience their being from a posture of affirmation. We would regard the exception as aberrance. A theory that maintains the aberrant at the center of its interests might answer the needs of public policy, or unwittingly serve the requirements of the dominant myth, but its responsive capacity to the living situations of the social subject is, at times, embarrassingly limited.

Trapped between the Scylla of feminist mandates on the one hand and the Charybdis of dominative and patriarchal modes of power on the other, the subject of "feminine attributes" is apparently abandoned to a useless set of traits, not unlike a sixth toe or finger in some phase of human evolution. Exactly what it is that women in history are asked to abdicate in order to achieve authentic consciousness has the elusive subtleties of a Steuben glass or a cymbidium orchid and is invested with about as much actively negotiable and comparative power, except we know when we have seen either and that it is difficult for us to say now *why* we'd *prefer* not to be without access, real or imagined, to either. The "feminine" evades definition, perhaps, because it is both ubiquitous and shadowy on the world's body:

> The nuances of sensitivity to appearances, the fine distinctions in the observance of one's behavior and that of others, the silent exploration of the consciousness in which one functions as an "other" deserve our attention as means toward understanding human motivation and psychology as well as our condemnations as the product of asymmetrical power.[7]

For Keohane and the other editors of *A Critique of Ideology*, the "feminine" locates a disposition in the eyes of a gazer, female and male, but if the angle of seeing is obverted, how does the gazed upon see itself, see out?

For Julia Kristeva, the female body, specifically, the "maternal body" takes us to the limen of "nature/culture": The "not-sayable," the body of the mother escapes signification, meaning, sense because the "mother-woman" is rather a strange "fold" (*pli*) which turns nature into culture, and the "speaking subject" (*le parlant*) into biology. Although it affects each woman's body, this heterogeneity, which cannot be subsumed by the signifier, literally explodes with pregnancy—the dividing line between nature and culture—and with the arrival of the child—which frees a woman from uniqueness and gives her a chance, albeit not a certainty, of access to the other, to the ethical. These peculiarities of the maternal body make a woman a creature of folds, a catastrophe of being that cannot be subsumed by the dialectic of the trinity or its supplements.[8]

I am not entirely certain that the "feminine" and "female body" may be taken as synonymous constructs, but it does appear that the space of overlap between them is so broad that we cannot imagine one without deploying the other. For theorists of an "écriture feminine," of which Kristeva is said to be one, the "feminine" has little to do with women in history. In fact Alice Jardine's *Gynesis* ("woman-process")[9] concentrates on male writers in "modernity" and their reinstitution of the female body at a fundamental level of writing: 1) the subversion of the idea of a unified speaking subject; 2) the undermining of all authority; and 3) the figurative use of the female genitalia as a mode of decentering and deconstructing the text. The "fold," or "pli," the "hole," the "gap," or "interstice" become items of a revised critical lexis that is designed—we are led to believe—to engender a radically different ideology and practice of writing, focusing "feminine" and "female body" at the center of altered positions and dispositions.

In Jardine's view, these changes on the textual surface of male-writing (Derrida, Lacan, Deleuze, Guattari, of *Anti Oedipus*, specifically) invite a direct response from feminist investigation/theory, lest the latter find itself isolated from the contemporary intellectual scene. What seems to me a fairly complete breach between matters of feminist social theory and feminist metatheory appears beyond repair. If Susan Suleiman is correct, then "the cultural significance of the female body is not only (not even first and foremost) that of a flesh-and-blood entity, but that of a *symbolic construct*."[10] [Emphasis Suleiman's.]

To see the issue otherwise, Suleiman thinks, is to pursue the anachronistic. The "programmatic and polemical aspect" of *The Female Body in Western Culture* is to claim for the "feminine," more pointedly, the "female body," a status of contemporaneity: "Not everything we see and hear today deserves to be called contemporary . . . it is not enough to be *of* our time in order to be *with* our time."[11]

Risking an anachronism, with no hope at all of doing "my bit" here to rejoin "theory and practice," I would offer that the "flesh-and-blood entity" of the female body lends itself to historical enactment—I cannot imagine a more forceful example than the "mother-woman"—whose dimensions are *symbolic* at those points of contact where communities of women *live out* the symbolicities. If we concede that *discursivity* manifests a worrisome element of translation, then I see no reason why we might feel compelled to jettison the terrible flesh and blood. Though I am primarily concerned here with the specific uses of a cultural construct we would designate "feminine" in the case of a particular writer/poet, it is not beyond me to imagine what practical turn a theory *might* take.

The stipulative definition that I would offer for the "feminine" trait of human personality takes us back to Keohane's "Introduction" and an inquiry into the connotations of "everywhereness" and shadow. To the degree that "body" in reference to the "feminine" might be analogously read with Blake's Tharmas,[12] the principle that contains the rational will, the creative powers, the affective dispositions, the erotic centers, I mean "body" alongside the preceding terms—ubiquity, shadow. We might think of all three terms under the head of "surface" and "extensivity," meaning by both the definition that Schiller offers in "Letters on the Aesthetic Education of Man"[13] (sic). If "maximum changeability" and "maximum extensivity" stand here for the "feminine," then we would urge a sense of its application along more than a single line of stress, since neither the "feminine" nor receptivity to phenomena is alien to the masculine potential. Though Brooks's "feminine" refers primarily to the female, the resonance of the former is not at all unlike Woolf's "incandescence,"[14] which is not gender-rigid in its artistic practice and inspiration. My aim in trying to free up the "feminine" from its wonted vocation is not to generate an hermaphroditic wonder and lose women/

woman in a figurative replication of naive liberalist gestures, but to suggest that we replace our weapon in our holsters until an enemy has clearly shown itself: The idea (if it ever was) is not to be rid of the "feminine," whose details have yet to be fully elaborated, say nothing of exhausted, but, rather, to purge the world for a wider display of its powers. According to Jardine, at least *some* "men" might agree. More precisely, we wish to know what the "feminine" can do from its own vantage point, and such inquiry is "gynocritical" in its profoundest impulses.[15]

II

Gwendolyn Brooks's feminine landscape is clearly demarcated as heterosexual territory. Males are never far away from its female centers of attention, even when the male presence is overwhelmingly implicit and memorial, as it is in "The Anniad" and various other poems in the volume, "Annie Allen."[16] The poet's particular address to communities of women in her audience is persistent in the canon across four decades of work, reflecting the storm and stress of this period of African-American women's political consciousness with the 1981 publication, *Primer for Blacks: Three Preachments*, "To Those of My Sisters Who Kept Their Naturals."[17] Brooks's work interweaves the female and her distinctive feelings into a delicate tissue of poetic response to the human situation, defined by a particular historical order—the African-American personality among the urban poor in the city of Chicago between World War II and the present of the poem.[18] Within this body of work, the female voice, for all its poignant insistence, is a modified noun of vocality, danced through a range of appetite and desire that does not stand isolated from a masculine complement. If poetry is our teacher in this instance, not entirely estranged from theory, but subsuming it, then the "feminine" is manifest as an emphasis, neither hostile to "masculine" nor silenced by it. We are rather reminded now of an image of Jungian resolution with the circumferences of double circles overlapping to form an altered distance through the diameters of both.[19] It is only by virtue of a perversion in the seeing that the overlapping circles can de-

clare any independence whatsoever. They relinquish their imagined uniqueness to an enlarged order of circularity, as the
peripheries of both now involve us at the center of each.
Getting the point does not necessarily require that we embrace the idea, or the "man," but that we acknowledge it as a
viable figure in the universe of female and "feminine"
representability. This involved image of circularity renders a
geometry for poets, and those are the depths and surfaces
that claim our attention at the moment.

In Brooks's poetic order of things, the "feminine" is neither
cause for particular celebration nor certain despair, but near to
the "incandescent," it is analogous to that "wedged-shaped
core of darkness,"[20] through which vision we see things in
their fluid passage between dream and waking reality, as
multiple meanings impinge on a central event. The poet's
novelette *Maud Martha* does not exhaust Brooks's contemplation of the "feminine," but provides a point of illumination
and departure concerning an important phase of her long and
distinguished career as an American poet. If not chronologi-
cally central to the canon, *Maud Martha*, beside "The Anniad,"
is experienced by the reader as an "impression point."[21] In the
Harper and Row edition of her poetry, *Maud Martha* brings to
closure the poems in "A Street in Bronzeville" and "Annie
Allen," while it prepares the way for "The Bean Eaters" and,
from the sixties, the stunning poetry of *In the Mecca*.

Maud Martha was published in 1953.[22] The leading subject
and sole consciousness of the narrative, Maud Martha Brown,
comes of age during the Depression era. As the work is
broadly reflective of the social issues of two American decades, it might be read as the poet's version of a cultural
synthesis. By the end of World War II, Maud Martha is ex-
pecting her second child; her brother Harry returns home in
one piece from combat, and her first child Paulette grows up.
Paulette is old enough to recognize that the white "Santa
Claus" of a large department store in the city of Chicago does
not like little black girls. Somehow, the jolly creature cannot
even bring himself to *look* at the child, having hugged all the
blond ones, Paulette observes, to her mother's chagrin. The
instances that disclose racist sentiment in the text are so muted
and understated that they are rendered elements of background in which ambience the primary issues of the narrative

unfold: the extent to which the female can articulate her own values of sanctity and ritual, of aspiration and desire, of order and beauty in a hierarchically male-centered world, limited by the idioms of the literal.

Insofar as Maud Martha sustains heterosexual mating, she is "male-identified," but such identification is much less compelling than the imaginative integrity that keeps her alive and well. The woman reader of this text might well wonder how successfully Maud Martha would negotiate a sphere of influence broader than the domestic and the connubial. It is true that her talents are constrained by what we would now consider four narrow walls that provide her with neither a room of her own nor the time to miss it.[23] She is not a culture heroine, is not a woman's warrior, and the big bumbling immensities of the romantic and epic imagination—Rebellion, Bravery, Courage, Triumph, among them, those capitalized terms that Northrop Frye describes as "aureate"[24] and which Brooks's own "Strong Men Riding Horses" humorously debunks[25]—do not touch her identity in any remote way. And so we wind down into an arena of choices that take us to the heart of dailiness, of the mundane and the unglamorous, or the carefully circumscribed ambition. We protest—but isn't *this* the customary woman's place?

That the distaff is, from the point of view of the narrative and the world surrounding it, the peculiar custodial property of the female is not a conclusion. It is a beginning. Maud Martha commences with the raw elaborations of realism (read also "reality") and transforms them into a habitable space. This talent for the clean and well-lighted, however, is not only the central and embattled miracle of Maud Martha's world, but also a preeminent social value because it represents an actual living of what has been imagined, imagining what is known. We might think of Maud Martha's "miracle" as a gifted kind of "making" that turns the inner to the outer and redeems the room as an elaboration of the human and social body.[26]

If we look at the structurations of Maud Martha's character from her own place in the order of things, then we accord her special attention because of her highly developed powers *to play* and to play well within the framework of possibilities to which she has access. We can very well wish for her, imagine empathetically, a richer field of play; but the limitations imposed on her in no way mitigate her own considerable abilities to shape and define the world as she encounters it. In contrast to her husband, Paul Phillips, who occupies and rents space in his world, without an angle on it, or a critique of it, Maud Martha engages their common circumstance with an eye for the occasion. This looking through, for want of a better term, might be called a kind of displaced fable making so that Maud Martha might be seen as the "true poet" of the narrative and the writer herself the "imitator" of it. These functions come together under the guise of a central narrator, who speaks Maud Martha's script through a ventriloquized medium—the poet, assigning to the leading agent the primary powers of ordering.

The central thematics of the work are made explicit in the twenty-first and twenty-second episodes:

Could be nature, which had a seed, or root, or an element (what do you call it) of constancy, under all that system of change. Of course, to say "system" at all implied arrangement, and therefore some order of constancy (227).

What she had wanted was a solid. She had wanted shimmering form; warm, but hard as stone and as difficult to break. She wanted to found—tradition. She had wanted to shape, for their use, for hers, for his, for little Paulette's, a set of falterless customs. She had wanted stone (228).

A "stone," a "solid," as isolated lexical features, convey notions of the concrete and abstract at once. We can contemplate them on their own terms, apart from context to modify their function, but in relationship to "shimmering form," to "tradition," their meaning enriches to insinuate an indefinite specificity—a community of notions that range in weight and appeal from the architectural to the ingeniously diminutive object of decoration; from issues concerning values and aspirations to the specific questions and longings of desire. That the terms overlap on "falterless customs" and, by inference, the whole enterprise of shaping and preserving, foreshortened in the enumerated signs, renders Maud Martha a social "conservative," as "order of constancy" implies. But the wealth of connotative markers that the narrator achieves by mixing the metaphorical referents would suggest that Maud Martha's "conservatism" locates not only the preeminent force of intelligence at work in the narrative, but also the intelligence that tries things. I am assuming that Brooks's narrator does not intend irony or mockery when Maud Martha's consciousness speaks a desire for "stone," for "solid," or that she intends to say that Maud Martha is naive in wishing to establish "falterless customs." I would want to see the central figure's essentially experential character and lust for form as a necessary fable of paradox for living a life—in "literature," or "the streets"—that is sane and rewarding. For Maud Martha, "tradition" is not a dead letter, or a reliquary of ancestral ghosts. "Tradition" here would be "founded" the hard way, on the living, on a sort of frontier of immediacy, whose ready-to-hand objects might be invested with the only force for magic that there is—that which the imagination attributes to the event of neutral or indifferent meaning.

None of the items in Maud Martha's catalog of transmuted domestic objects can be regarded as esoteric: coffees, fruitcakes, plain shortbread, black walnut candy in "little flat white sheets," a dinner table spread with "white, white cloth . . . china . . . in cheerful dignity, firmly arranged, upon it" (232). Despite the availability of the scene at hand, we are compelled to consider it in a new light, seeing the details as "the plenitude of plan."[27] Maud Martha's "plan," however, is not so much a reflection of the arbitrary as it is a retrieving from chaos or oblivion the ordinary domestic object, much like poems cut "Out of air,/Night color, wind soprano, and such stuff."[28] If we perceive that the narrator is involving us in a romance of the diurnal, there is much to support the conclusion—the central artistic purpose of *Maud Martha* expresses the essentially "heroic" character of the "unheroic" by altering our opinion of "heroism" in the first place. Furthermore, "art" loses its remoteness and its claim to exclusion as Brooks imposes upon it a radically democratic context and purpose.

This capacity to draw the outer into oneself, retranslating it into an altered exterior, as though fields of force magnetized by an abiding centrality, locates the process that I would stipulate as the "feminine," finding in it the maximum exposure of surface to change. We will see shortly how the particular "epistemic habit of meaning"[29] in this narrative reenforces both the artistic energies of the piece and the function of the narrative itself as suggestive "equipment for living."[30]

In steady contrast to Maud Martha, there is a "husband," both a "real" one and the idea of "husband" in its limited masculine composition: "This man was not a lover of table-cloths, he could eat from a splintery board, he could eat from the earth" (232–233). The often sardonic quality of the writing and its persistently ironical force save the narrative from pathos as it challenges our sympathies to focus on specific detail in whimsical combinations. "Tablecloths" acquires metonymic value, as it defines the whole of Paul Phillips's inadequacies of imagination by humorously remarking a partial instance of it. Laughter here is usually ironically pointed so that antagonism to laughter falls into perspective rather than exaggeration or prominence. In that sense, the work evinces a tough-minded balance of tensions between the impinging extremes of Maud and Paul's "reality."

Maud Martha is herself as much an observer of her own scene as she is a participant in it, a maker of it. Alongside her dreamwork, she maintains the prerogatives of detachment so that at no point in the narrative—even when Maud Martha thinks the most harshly truthful things about herself and those around her—does the reader "feel sorry" for her. She will thrive not simply because she can bear to suffer—as traditional African-American female iconography valorizes beyond any practical use, beyond any probable endurance in the life of female progeny. Maud Martha thrives because she wills it through diverse acts of form, woven from the stuff of everyday life. Quite simply, she is smarter than Paul, who is not without desire, but rather, oppressed by the wrong ones.

Paul is not an adequate husband and lover precisely because he is lacking in "capable imagination." To use Alice Walker's terms for the particular etiology that blocks imaginative expansiveness in the man, Paul is a "racialist," with an overwhelming wish to have a liaison with a "light-skinned" female; the prize of "light-skin" would release in him the fruition of a range of fantasies so elusive to his grasp that they would thrill the analyst's heart and pocket. It is not an exaggeration to say that even now, at some years' remove from the passions, intensities, and commitments of the sixties' Black Nationalist movement in the United States, African-American men's community has yet, it seems, to come to terms with its profoundest impulses concerning African-American women and their "Africanity." The failure would appear ongoing, disquieting, repetitive, and disappointing. So close to the new century, this failure to grasp seems threatening in its political, cultural, and possibly genetic implications for an entire American community. From the vantage of the 1950s—since the tangle of issues to which I allude is not dated—the poet is not unaware of these charged and searching questions in their immediate impact on the ontological dimensions of her characters. Maud Martha is black skinned and, there but by the grace of a keen intelligence and generous affection, might have been undone by her world's sporadically obscene response to the color of her skin.

Paul's limitations are not solely determined by his interest in the "light-skinned" female. We can grant him whatever wishing his heart can stand, but that he sees no farther than the pointed recurrence of an imagistic symptom makes him ripe for a class of psychological subjects that we recognize as the obsessive-neurotic. That this heterosexual male would potentially love many women is not a serious crime, we finally decide, but Paul wants a figure of adoration to fill up his mind; he wants to fall into gyneolatrous[31] madness at the foot of a marvelous deception, male-engendered. There is more: Having no direct route of access to the originating inspiration of the European tradition of courtly love, embodied in "the female body in the West" (and "they" never mean "us,") Paul substitutes the fantasy's *next* best thing—the "high yaller" female hybrid of his community's peculiar American nightmare.

Two observations: First, Paul's low-order, low-key madness is decided not by the fictional context of his dreams but rather by their particular historical context. Traditionally, we are reminded that a lynching rope awaits the neck of the African-American male so bold as to approach his "it"—"the female body in the West." But we are reminded not by the local narrative before us but by the one that *haunts* it—his fate in approaching the woman/woman-body that is not "black."[32] This terroristic imagery is muted in the contemporary period but not at all forgotten. Therefore, the "white" female ac-

quires in Paul's eyes an altogether exaggerated status as object
of mimetic desire. Second, the amorous figures that surround
the characterizations of "black" are *historically* determined as
ideas and icons of "not freedom," of bindings and couplings,
of bondage and manipulation so complete that we can barely
imagine, for example, just what Paul and Maud Martha would
look like in a different universe of figuration. The liberation
project would release the character from the diseased "fix" of
static iconography just as surely as it would the African-
American community from the planned obsolescence of national policy and economic practice. While we must ultimately
encounter Maud and Paul on the terms that the story offers
and *for themselves*, we understand, unmistakably, that an aspect of "extra-territorial" narrative so decisively shadows their
tale that the genuinely agonized pairing here is not simply
"male" and "female," "feminine" and "masculine" (as though
they were simple), but these binary oppositions as they have
been orchestrated by the loudest and most persistent teleol-
ogy, "good" and "bad," and finally mediated, through the
very force of the language, by the most fateful of culturally
ascribed antinomies—"black" and "white." To that extent,
Paul is victim. We dislike him because, contrary to Maud
Martha, he doesn't *resist*; obeys no individual imperatives or
tested arrogance that would push through the accumulated
slime of a national history.

III

Chapter 19 of the narrative, "If You're Light and Have Long
Hair," brings home the particular social dynamics to which I
refer. Married for a time, Paul gets his first invitation to the
Foxy Cats' Annual Foxy Cats Dawn Ball. Though we recognize a persistent element of parody in the descriptive apparatus adapted to these scenes, we also acknowledge their quite
accurate conformity to a certain configuration of African-
American middle-class upward mobility. The Foxy Cats (who
resemble the undergraduate fraternity in its earnest and in-
genuous allegiance to fixed notions of proper behavior, sartorial style, and brainless imitation of what its members *think*
"class" is) bears the brunt of a well-deserved satirical com-

mentary. The wording of the invitation to the "Dawn Ball" is humorously, nervously redundant:

> He was to be present, in formal dress . . . No chances were taken. 'Top hat, white tie and tails,' hastily followed the 'Formal Dress,' and that elucidation was in bold type (205).

For Paul, the invitation represents "an honor of the first water, and . . . sufficient indication that he was, at last, a social somebody." This ironical vein is underscored and nourished in Maud Martha's thoughts by a brazen stroke of self-admission:

> My type is not a Foxy Cat favorite. But he can't avoid taking me—since he hasn't yet thought of words or ways strong enough, and at the same time soft enough—for he's kind: he doesn't like to injure—to carry across to me the news that he is not to be held permanently by my type, and that he can go on with this marriage only if I put no ropes or questions around him. Also, he'll want to humor me, now that I'm pregnant (207).

Days later, in the "main room of the Club 99," Maud and Paul join the other Foxy Cats and their "foxes" at the "Dawn Ball" itself. Paul, in effect, abandons Maud Martha shortly after their arrival, having escorted her to a bench by the wall, leaving her (211). Who he's left her for—"Maella"—is "red-haired and curved," of the "gold-spangled" bosomness. Rhetorically kin to a "sleek slit-eyed gypsy moan" of "The Anniad" and a "lemon-hued lynx/with sandwaves loving her brow" of the "Ballad of Chocolate Mabbie,"[33] "Maella" is not so much an embodied representation as she is a structure of emblematic traits that we recognize from other textual sources. The narrator needn't "explain." "Maella" need not speak, does not, nor can, since an entire secondary text speaks around her. In the maelstrom of emotions released by the appearance of this Idea, to whose bosom Paul salutes, we think of "gold-spangled" as a resonance of "star-spangled" and of Paul as locked in a veritable state of adoration. Maud Martha watches, thinking

not that they love each other. It oughta be that simple.
Then I could lick it. It oughta be that easy. But it's my
color that makes him mad. I try to shut my eyes to that,
but it's no good. What I am inside, what is really me, he
likes okay. But he keeps looking at my color, which is
like a wall. He has to jump over it in order to meet and
touch what I've got for him. He has to jump away up
high in order to see it. He gets awful tired of all that
jumping (214).

The narrator does not dwell on this aspect of the scene as
we will see, in time, a cluster of intricately differentiated
motives involved in it, nor is the painful resonance elaborated
here repeated. We understand its perspective against the whole.
My isolating it is intended to point an emphasis in suggesting
the nature of schismatic tendencies that divide Paul from
himself and those around him and to convey a sense of what
it is that Maud Martha strives to overcome as her own imagination projects it, as others impose it.

In psychological terms, we might say that Maud Martha
symbolizes a far more successfully "integrated" character than
Paul, and this fluency of response is primarily captivated by
narrative strategies that blend the advantages and benefits of
stream-of-consciousness and concealed narration in bringing
to light a character whom we know in the interstices of her
thought. The stage of action in *Maud Martha* is embedded in
none other than the landscape of its central consciousness,
and from this focal point—replete with particular biases and
allegiances—we come to know the "world" of the narrative.

What we discover through Maud Martha's perceptions unfolds in a rolling chronology. In other words, the narrator is
so selective in the detailing "spots of time" in reference to the
character that the work may be described as episodic, paratactic, and notational, or structured from peak points, of which
the Foxy Cats' Dawn Ball is a single example. This imitative
"autobiography" starts almost in the beginning, as we find
out that the subject liked "candy buttons, and books, and
painted music (deep blue, or delicate silver) and the west sky,
so altering, viewed from the steps of the back porch, and
dandelions" (127). The sentences are simple, tending toward
the fragmentary, and swift on the surface of the visual, tactile

world. We imagine not so much a structure of physical and physiological traits called "Maud Martha" as we do a profoundly active poetic sensibility, happily unbound in a world of marvelous color, of infinite allure.

Metaphors of painting seem especially apposite to narrative strategies here since the content of the opening episodes, in particular, is composed primarily of sensual imagery perceived through the brilliant color and texture often associated with impressionism.[34] To say that the "brush strokes" are light and decidedly whimsical is to insinuate the paratactic character of the writing: episodes, if not individual sentences, are self-contained units of perceptual activity. To speak of writing as painting (and somehow, the figure never goes the other way) metaphorizes either activity, but the narrator appears deliberately involved in the apparent crossing of arbitrary artistic boundaries in order to delineate character and movement in their initial urgency. To do so, the narrator adopts loose connections between things, weak or fairly discontinuous transitions from point to point. The agent is not a studied, or deliberative body, and the narrative, consequently, inscribes a deft movement of "symbol-making," as it starts up, we imagine, from the threshold of immediate feeling, of unchecked sensual response.

The painting metaphor further suggests the poet's attempt to invest the diurnal with vibrant color. Even the "grays" of this "universe" invite lyrical play, as Maud Martha roams her kitchenette for our benefit, building with a passionate eye for the unique angle in human and object relations. As a result of these self-conscious stylistic moves, the narrator intimates a confluence of thematic and strategic modes so thoroughgoing that Maud Martha stands in synecdochic relationship to the surround. Merging into into an untrammeled equality of means, agent and scenic device are reversible.

Though the episodes are arbitrarily connected, they are logically sequential: Narrative traces lead from childhood and early years at school through adolescence, to young womanhood and the adult years that follow. Maud Martha's first beaux, the death of her paternal grandmother, the quality of her dream life, the special nature of her relationship to her father and brother, the affective ambivalence that prevails among the women of the immediate family, for instance, become discrete moments of perception that take on even weight and intensity. Significant elements of the tale are, therefore, dispersed and accumulative, rather than dense and elaborated. In fact, the weakened copulatives create an aesthetic surface without "bulges"—the "peaks" and "valleys" of a schematic plot structure—or syntactic elements that do not adhere in a relationship of subordination and coordination. To that extent, the narrative voice speaks in the concisive rhythms of the contemporary poem. I have in mind symptoms of alignment rather than particular instances.

It doesn't matter, for instance, that the seeds of Maud Martha's troubled "femininity" are planted early on in her own awareness and, consequently, the reader's, because such information assumes no unusual or immediate focus: Two years older than Maud, sister Helen is "almost her own height and weight and thickness. But oh, the long lashes, the grace, the little ways with the hands and feet" (128–129). We will know more in time about Helen, the beautiful sister, but this clue, closing the inaugural scene, so casually intrudes itself that we register it only later as crucial. Even though the bulk of the narrative concerns Maud Martha's marriage and maternal career, these emphases fall into solid perspective with the whole. Relatedly, the narrative is unplotted (or not obviously plotted), pursues no climactic surprises, and resolves in syntactic and dramatic rhythms that evade rigid closure: "And in the meantime, she was going to have another baby. The weather was bidding her bon voyage" (306). The agreeable sense of an ending here could just as easily mark the beginnings of the next excursive phase of "autobiography," since pregnancy announces new life as well as the anticipation of one kind of finish; "bon voyage," analogously, situates a valedictory and salutatory marker. This strategic ambiguity, with its teasing abeyance of resolution, brings us back to questions concerning the "feminine."

IV

Virginia Woolf conjectured that the woman-text adapted to the rules of interruption—by the female writer's children, lovers, and general imperatives of caretaking; it was, then, of necessity, *short*. An "écriture feminine," apparently hinting the functions of the female body—with its fluidities, secret passageways and escape routes, or those convoluted folds along the uterus and vaginal vault—releases the "feminine," as a corporeality turned trope, onto a wider human path, not blocked by the specificities of female reproductive process. Once upon a time, in a cackle of rage, a Boston-not-so-lady declared to me what might well serve as a point of overlap between Woolf and latter-day theoreticians on the body writing: "Anything that takes more than nine months to bear is a joke!" She was talking about *novels*. But is it true that the vital, concentrated intensities of the pregnant body place on urgent notice the artist everywhere—"study long, study wrong"?

I would exercise the greatest caution in supporting a "feminine writing" as *practice*, if not as *theory*, however, since we presently have no acceptable name for the same individual writer—female or male—when she or he does *not* write in the suspension of authority, in the subversion of the hierarchical, in the shameless assertion of the vibrant mood. Is "Gwendolyn Brooks," for example, of "In the Mecca," the similar body that produced *Maud Martha*? No outer markings, or facings of the surface suggest it. And it is precisely this protocol of radically divergent aims that comes home in the singularity of an artist's career (or even *a* writing) that would challenge a rigorous notion of trophic determinism. There is in my reading of this novelette, however, symptoms of a program that I would designate "feminine," and it is embedded in the work's insistence on *self-involvement*; if this constant reference and return to the "inner" surrenders to figurative movement, then we might offer that female person's having to "listen" to her body and its cyclical rhythms dictates "stillness" as a redoubtable human and cultural value. This "serenity," replete with its own active turbulences through the whole being, recovers "invisibility," or the mental "calibrations," as a supremely *active* domain of the human. "Mrs. Ramsey" provides an insight:

> To be silent; to be alone. All the being and the doing, expansive, glittering, vocal, evaporated; and one shrunk, with a sense of solemnity, to being oneself, *a wedge-shaped core of darkness, something invisible to others*.[35] [Emphasis mine.]

I emphasize the latter half of the sentence in order to suggest that the "active"/"passive" split is as culpable in any
discussion of the "feminine" as the other patriarchal/patriarchist
oppositions that we already know too well to repeat. In a
remarkable episode from *Maud Martha*, the narrator provides
another example of what I would call a paradoxical nesting of
being-impulses—the personality drawn into the pluralities of
a self, "shrunk," as it were, opens, capably, outward: As a
young woman, Maud Martha essentially preserves her sense
of childhood wonder. Walking down a Chicago street, taking
in the rich scenes of store windows, she experiences so palpa-
bly the objects that she confronts that the reader is not completely sure (and no longer cares to be) if her body remains in
Chicago or actually goes off to New York:

> When she was out walking, and with grated iron swish a
> train whipped by, off, above, its passengers were always,
> for her comfort, New York bound. She sat inside with
> them. She leaned back in the plush. She sped, past farms,
> through tiny towns, where people slept, kissed, quar-
> reled, ate midnight snacks; unfortunate folk who were
> not New York bound and never would be (174).

This complex of desire, through which the encounters of
the subject are refracted, measured, considered, consumed, is
poised in brazen contrast to the "actual" world of Maud
Martha; that the "imagined" and the "real" abrade unrelent-
ingly is intended, because we gauge Maud Martha's internal
resources in even bolder relief against the brute "facts." We
could go so far as to say that the poet's insistence on the
narrative strategies of the piece and its rhetorical energies that
plumb the interior world of the character spares Maud Martha
the peculiar burdens of the "naturalistic" agent. In other words,
if *Maud Martha* were read through eyes not the character's
own, as would an omniscient voice, bent on imposing a content from the "outside," already made to order, then we
would not only lose Maud Martha's complexity, but would
also conclude that victimage alone determines her. By forcing
the reader, or inducing her, to confront Maud Martha as the
primary and central consciousness of the work, its subject *and*
object of gazing, speaking through the redoubled enuncia-

tions of her own stream-of-thought and a translation of it, the poet reclaims the territorial rights of an internal self and strikes for our mutual benefit a figure of autonomy. Despite her "blackness," her "femaleness," her poverty-line income, and perhaps *because* of these unalterable "facts" of mensuration, Maud Martha is allowed access to her own "moment of being," and the narrative renders its record.

It is beside the point that Maud Martha speaks few quoted or dramatic lines in the narrative, or that her private ways are quiet and unspectacular, or that she tolerates more of Paul than we think she ought; she is not a feminist, fifties' style. The demonstration, I believe, of woman-freedom is the text itself that has no centrality, no force, no sticking point other than the imaginative nuances of the subject's consciousness. Maud Martha's drama remains internal, and that interiority engenders the crucial aesthetic address of the work. We might want to alter drastically her "environment," change her clothes, where she lives, grant her a broader sphere of contact, but such is *our* fiction. In spite of it, we suspect that the character already has the capacity to disclose larger and even more refined versions of a fictional self *on her own terms.* Perhaps we could argue that the most impassioned attention to the drama of the interior self exposes the "feminine."

When young Maud Martha looks at magazines that say "New York," describing

> good objects there, wonderful people, recalled fine talk,
> the bristling or the creamy or the tactfully shimmering
> . . . her whole body become a hunger, she would pore
> over its pages (174).

That "looking" is governed here by "hunger" in the young Maud Martha reinforces the severe privacy of the perceptual act and provides a remarkable stroke of synaesthesia in the conflating tactile and visual sensation. The subject is not a mere looker, but looks with the entire ingestive range. Maud Martha's "good objects" are placed alongside objects of melancholy or objects of the nakedly furnished within a range of semantic valences that gain distinction solely by her capacity to imbue them with polyvalent meaning. We gather this stylistic trait on the basis of lexical items apparently chosen from two widely divergent arrays of things that operate in a kind of binary adhesion—those "good objects" of the above-quoted passage and those that belong with her kitchen sink, or the radiators in her parents' house, "high and hideous. And underneath the low sink-coiled unlovely pipes, that Helen said made her think of a careless woman's underwear, peeping out" (164). But then there are also natural objects that show the humble in special atmosphere and that persist as the contrapuntal assertion against the ravages of time. From two excerpts of the narrative: The house the Browns fear they might lose to the Home Owner's Loan Association, the one in which Maud Martha and her siblings have grown up, materializes an enamored object of the entire family, but for Maud Martha, "house" abstracts into an object of lyricism—of "writing":

> with the snake plant in the jardiniere in the southwest corner, and the obstinate slip from Aunt Eppie's magnificent Michigan fern at the left side of the friendly door . . . and the emphatic iron of the fence and . . . the poplar tree . . . Those shafts and pools of light, the tree, the graceful iron might soon be viewed possessively by different eyes (154–155).

From the ending:

> But the sun was shining, and some of the people in the world had been left alive, and it was doubtful whether the ridiculousness of man would ever completely succeed in destroying the world—or, in fact, the basic equanimity of the least and commonest flower: for would its kind not come up again in the spring? come up, if necessary, among, between, or out of—beastly inconvenient!—the smashed corpses lying in strict composure, in that hush infallible and sincere (305).

In the first instance, the vocabulary of natural objects so overwhelms the house of the living that the latter takes on a spirit of timelessness, enters a domain of the immutable. It is noteworthy that Maud Martha believes that the western sky acquires a certain unique aspect only from the back of this house: "the little line of white, somewhat ridged with smoked purple, and all that cream-shot saffron" (156). In the second instance, the natural objects—sun and earth—submerge the human deed in a grandly absurd and irresistible carnival of folly. In its concise reverberations of the strangely ridiculous and rhetorical questions of the disembodied voice from *The Waste Land*,[36] Brooks joins Eliot in adopting closural images from the iconic grotesquery of war—World War I for Eliot, World War II for Brooks. For both poets, the corpse loses its gothic and horrible magnificence as it is brought low, so to speak, into the stream of diachronous, even vegetal, being. This collapse of hierarchy in the poetic status of objects is entirely consonant with the principles of writing that order the whole of *Maud Martha*.

Whether or not the objects in Brooks's binary array are human contrivances or aspects of the natural order, both articulate and embody an impression of eternal forms. Their varied aspects and illuminations of the immanent would suggest not only the indeterminacy of their occurrence, but also the fluent nature of Maud Martha's stunning perceptual powers in the combinations, recombinations, and juxtapositions that the objects achieve on her site. A suggestion from the linguists as an insight into "making": If the objects that claim our attention are to the senses what words are to the vertical columns of the dictionary, then the stuff of seeing is the *lexis* of "experience"; their various combinations and laws of revision and recombination, its "syntax"; and the meanings and their arrangements, its "semantics." By calling the "feminine" a power that operates under concealment, I mean primarily the ability it grants us to stand still and see, or in one's perceptual place, await a content, arrange a consequence.

V

Returning momentarily to the scene of the Foxy Cats Ball will provide us, in a final example, with several crucial and interlocking points concerning the subject's consciousness and the study in subtleties that the "feminine" reveals as a theme of convergence between the beholder and the beheld. The rapidly alternating currents through which the reader watches the simultaneity of opposing rhetorical, aesthetic, and dramatic functions in this scene are translatable into the "feminine" beyond this text inasmuch as they express the intricacies of the "double consciousness." If Maud Martha cannot escape the implications of her mirror, or the pretexts that impinge on her, then she is fully capable of exploiting such captivity to the degree that the scene itself, the other agents on it, its purposes and motivations are reflected in her looking glass, whose thaumaturgic properties can bless or damn the occasion as the subject sees fit. Intent on neither, the voice of the interior monologue mobilizes a plenitude of terms that evoke the fundamental ambivalence at the core of consciousness itself.

We have already examined one of the decisive psychological components of this scene as Maud Martha, suddenly not unaware of her dark skin and its dubious social uses, fixes herself as subject and object of deeply embedded public and private motives. In other words, the extra-text that speaks loudly, even when none of the agents "mouth" it dramatically, and the text of Maud Martha's consciousness are interlarded threads cut cross the same bias. The "extra-text" to which I refer, examined at greater length in a progressive work, traces the historical implications of African-American women's community as a special instance of the "ungendered" female, as a vestibular subject of culture, and as an instance of the "flesh" as a primary, or first-level "body."[37] Because African-American women in their historic status represent the *only* community of American women *legally* denied the mother's access to her child, their relationship to the prerogatives of "gender" must be reexamined as the select strategem of an ethnic solidarity; of the dominant community's strict exploitation of the gender rule as an instrument of a "supremacist" program. This systematic unfolding of iconic and epistemic violence embattles Maud Martha, *without naming itself*, and discloses the central impoverishment of a public naming and imagining that have not yet discovered appropriate terms for this community of social subjects. In that sense, the "mulatta" —and we might assume that "Maella" is either proximate to, or appropriates, such status, figures into this calculus as the historic "alibi" that "shields" the African-American female from sight. The weight of *this* textuality, or a "symbolic construct" that *lives* itself out, or of a corporeality-turned-trope-returned "corporeality," *falls* on the historical and fictive subject with the convictions of steel. But the interconnections between "given" and "discovered" become the inseparable discretions of the tailor's herringbone. Or, to shift metaphors, an entire central nervous system is at work so that consciousness is perceived as the stunning poise in a dual and complicated awareness.

The paragraphs that inform us that Maud Martha is escorted to a bench and left—"she sat, trying not to show the inferiority she did not feel"—descries a single pattern in the fabric, intersecting others in an arrangement that the eye takes in at once. We are aware of an emphasis of weight, color, texture, mode of design. Just so, Maud Martha wholly experiences the rich implications of her "objectivity" and "subjectivity" in their yoked occurrence. If she is seen, she also sees, as the scene before us is rendered precisely demonstrative of perceptual activity as an occasion of mutually indulged gazing.

Despite the sharp satirical underpinnings of the scene, Maud Martha acknowledges that the "ball stirred her . . . made toys of her emotions." "The beautiful women in gorgeous attire, bustling and supercilious"; the overgallant young men; the drowsy lights and smell of food and flowers; the body perfumes and "sensuous heaviness of the wine-colored draperies at the many windows" conjure up notions of the sybaritic. The draped and gorgeous flesh, divided between female and male, suggests the tease of sexuality: We call it "glamour" and recognize in the scene the ritual of mating behind whose masks the actualities of lust are arrested. The scene's drama relies on the tensions set in motion between the arrested and the enacted. We are drawn to this moment (and moments like it in "real life") because it configures the vertical suspension of love-making as it leads, eventually, toward the bedroom, either *actively* or *fantastically*. But if "to die," to play a moment on the range of conventional literary meanings released in the infinitive, marks the final move of the love game as well, then the narrator cunningly exploits the ambiguities of intention by bringing together objects of decoration and gaiety that evoke shades of the mortal flesh, of death.

"Wine-colored drapery" also belongs to the funeral procession, as does the terrible satiety of flowers. Even the music of the ball runs a chordal progression that describes over the course of the evening the convoluted objectives of the moment: "now steamy and slow, now as clear and fragile as glass, now raging, passionate, now moaning and thickly gray" (210). The gallant young men, "who at other times unpleasantly blew their noses," master the required social proprieties of the occasion, but they are also the imagined subjects of promising toilet humor, darting "surreptitiously into alleys to relieve themselves" and the comedy of the private, unguarded self that sweats and swears at work and scratches its "more intimate parts." Maud Martha's dancing partner, another male, dispatched to entertain her while Paul celebrates the red arms of Maella, "*reeked* excitedly of tobacco, liquor, pinesoap, toilet water, and Sen, Sen." [Emphasis mine.] This aggregation of disparate olfactory sensations reinforces disparity in the mild tongue-twisting assonance of the second five-syllable grouping of the line—"tobacco"/"liquor." A deeper structural point obtains. The body, disguising from itself the deep knowledge of its own mortality, claims this scene for the grave as well as the bed. We could say that a careful consideration of the weave of the passage might suggest that their shared imagery of the horizontal posture collapses distinction. Just as the flesh is seen here in its various lights, *Maud Martha* dances the range of feeling in its complicated twists and turns.

VI

That the fictional subject disperses across an "inner" and "outer"—differing angles on a mutually concurrent process—fits well with coeval theories of reading that posit "division" at the center of knowing; *je est un autre*—there is no subject, only a "barred subject," in a constant oscillation of deferments. But reading counter to the current, we would claim for Maud Martha a subject's singularity that *contains* "division," in fact, generates it, through a female body, who, among social bodies, is the only one who can reproduce sameness and difference at once: The child resembles the begetters, "borrows" their tendencies, yet describes its own features of uniqueness. If we regard the "feminine," in the artistic instance, as a trope of the reproductive process, we might argue that it, like the female body, locates the convergence of anti-thetically destined properties—"female," "male," "mind," "body," "same," "other," "past," "future," "gazer," "gazed upon." Inscribing a notion of containment—in rooms, in the serene and vibrant spaces of the interior, in the intimacies that pass from lovers to enemies and back—the narrator suggests that the "feminine" constitutes the particular gifts of a *materialized* interior. Treating the text as a "strategy for encom-passing a situation,"[38] we think of it—in its brevity, in its fluent movement among textures of feeling—as a figure of the "feminine," writing itself into articulate motion.

NOTES

1. In discussing the social uses to which literature may be put, Kenneth Burke identifies the art work as a strategy for naming situations for which we need a name, "for selecting enemies and allies, for socializing losses, for warding off evil eye, for purification, propitiation, and desanctification, consolation and vengeance, admoni-tion and exhortation, implicit commands or instructions of one sort or another." In "Literature as Equipment for Living," *The Philosophy of Literary Form: Studies in Sym-bolic Action* (Berkeley: University of California Press, 1973), 304. The "feminine" as an embattled idea offers a single example of a mandate for strategy.

2. Adrienne Rich, "Compulsory Heterosexuality and Lesbian Experience," Catharine R. Stimpson and Ethel Spector Person, eds., *Women: Sex and Sexuality* (Chicago: University of Chicago Press, 1980). 62–92. Rich's article is addressed primarily to the experiences of lesbian women as they are refracted through the dominant cultural patterns of heterosexuality; implicit in her argument is the idea that the heterosexual synthesis represents an aspect of the oppression of women.

3. Nannerl O. Keohane, Michelle Z. Rosaldo, and Barbara C. Gelpi, eds., *Feminist Theory: A Critique of Ideology* (Chicago: University of Chicago Press, 1982).

4. *Ibid.*, ix.

5. *Ibid.*

6. For an American audience, Du Bois's concept of the "double consciousness" (*Souls of Black Folk*) in reference to African-American cultural apprenticeship remains the preeminent concept and icon for explicating the dual and conflicting character of the misplaced person "at home" in an alien context. Originally published three years after the turn of the century, this collection of essays has undergone a number of editions. (New York: Fawcett Publications, 1963).

7. Keohane *et al, Critique of Ideology*, ix.

8. Susan Rubin Suleiman, ed., *The Female Body in Western Culture: Contemporary Perspectives* (Cambridge: Harvard University Press, 1986); "Stabat Mater," 115.

9. Alice Jardine, *Gynesis* (Ithaca: Cornell University Press, 1985).

10. Suleiman, *The Female Body*, 2.

11. *Ibid.*

12. One of the poet's "prophetic books," *Vala, or the Four Zoas* offers a preromantic view of the "fall" of human society. "Tharmas," or the human body, represents one of four characters in Blake's work, suggesting the various ordering principles of the human personality. David V. Erdman, ed., *The Complete Poetry and Prose of William Blake* (Berkeley: University of California Press, 1982).

13. The excerpts from Schiller to which I refer are taken from his "Letters" in *Critical Theory Since Plato*, ed. Hazard Adams (New York: Harcourt Brace Jovanovich, 1972).

The distinction that Schiller draws between sensuality (the sensations) and form (the reason) in "Letter 13" and their mutual reconciliation and repose in the play-drive has been considerably influential on my own thinking about this topic.

Not wishing to confine "sensual/sensuality" to the "feminine" (since I believe that the "feminine" engenders its own forms and formalities), I have, nonetheless, been struck by the evidence of the "common sense" in speculating that the woman's intimate proximity to the theme of human continuance and nurture offers prime material for her cultural apprenticeship in the feelings and notions of receptivity. While I would agree with Dorothy Dinnerstein's position in *The Mermaid and the Minotaur* (New York: Harper Colophon Books, 1976) that the responsibility of human nurture must be shared by female and male, I shudder to think what might happen if the contest for "equal time" leads to women's abandonment of the site of the child, as has men's renunciation too often, and with absolutely fatal results.

14. Virginia Woolf, *A Room of One's Own* (New York: Harcourt, Brace and World, Inc., 1957). "Perhaps a mind that is purely masculine cannot create, any more than a mind that is purely feminine . . . Coleridge . . . meant, perhaps, that the androgynous mind is resonant and porous; that it transmits emotion without impediment;' that it is naturally creative, incandescent and undivided" (102).

15. Elaine Showalter, "Feminist Criticism in the Wilderness," in Elizabeth Abel, ed., *Writing and Sexual Difference* (Chicago: University of Chicago Press, 1982), 9–37. The displacing of male bias by various evidence of female experience generates the gynocritical enterprise that Showalter elaborates in this essay.

16. Gwendolyn Brooks, *The World of Gwendolyn Brooks* (New York: Harper & Row, 1971). During the 1970s, Brooks switched her publishing allegiance from the New York house to Detroit's Broadsides Press and, later on, to the Third World Press of Chicago as testimony to her commitment to the political ideas of the Black Nationalist movement. *Riot, Family Pictures, and Beckonings* were all volumes published under the Broadsides logo.

17. Gwendolyn Brooks, *Primer for Blacks: Three Preachments* (Chicago: Brooks Press, 1981). "Black Love," first published in *Ebony*, (August 1981), appeared in 1982 under the auspices of the Brooks Press.

18. Brooks, *The World of GB*, 125–307.

19. Showalter, "Feminist Criticism in the Wilderness," 30–31. Showalter's discussion and diagram of the work of British anthropologist Edwin Ardener poses a useful paradigm for perceiving the relationship between dominant and muted groups. The Ardener diagram is also a circle, reminiscent of a penumbra, in which case the y circle (muted) falls within the dominant circle x. The crescent of the y circle outside the dominant boundary might be called "wild." Showalter proposes that we can think of the "wild zone" of women's culture spatially, experientially, or metaphysically. Spatially, it stands for an area that is literally no-man's land.

In this imagined relationship between Brooks's "feminine" and "masculine," both circles bear crescents on their periphery. These equally "wild zones" are mutually exclusive, by inference, and we have no idea what the characters who live there utter. My guess is that their "wild" is a spiralling crescent to Ardener/Showalter's so that we would have to draw a far more elaborate configuration in order to address the realities of "color."

20. Woolf's central consciousness in *To the Lighthouse*, Mrs. Ramsay, provides an astonishing association for what I later explore here as a "severe privacy."

21. Frank Kermode, *The Genesis of Secrecy: On the Interpretation of Narrative* (Cambridge: Harvard University Press, 1979). From Dilthey, Kermode adopts this formulation to explain the hermeneutical relationship between interpreter and work. I borrow it here to offer that *Maud Martha* punctuates a significant period of work in the poet's career and that after it Brooks seems to turn increasingly toward the meditative poetry that we associate with *In the Mecca* and *After the Mecca*.

22. Brooks, The World of GB. (All references to *Maud Martha* come from this edition, page numbers noted in the text.)

23. For a full discussion of Brooks's projected sequel to *Maud Martha*, the reader should consult "Update on 'Part One': An Interview with Gwendolyn Brooks," by Gloria T. Hull and Posey Gallagher, *College Language Association Journal*, XXI, No. 1

(September 1977), 26–28. Brooks points out that the extant *Maud Martha* "has much autobiography though I've twisted things" (27).

For a complete autobiographical sketch, Brooks's *Report From Part One* (Detroit: Broadsides Press, 1973) is indispensable. The poet explains to Claudia Tate in a series of recent interviews that she is at work on a second volume of autobiography. Cf. *Black Women Writers at Work* (New York: Continuum, 1983), 39–48.

24. Northrop Frye, in a description of Emily Dickinson's poetic diction, takes the term "aureate" from medieval poetics: "big soft bumbling abstract words that absorb images into categories and ideas." *Fables of Identity: Studies in Poetic Mythology* (New York: Harcourt, Brace and World, 1963) 202.

25. Brooks, *The World of GB,* from "The Bean Eaters," 313.

26. A remarkable study of the human and social body as a site of *contracted* or *expanded* ground, Elaine Scarry's *Body in Pain* (New York: Oxford University Press, 1985) offers an unusual reading of aspects of Holy Scripture and excerpts from the Marxian canon as speculative inquiry into the principles of "making" and "unmaking."

27. From Gwendolyn Brooks, "The Womanhood: The Children of the Poor," *Selected Poems* (New York: Harper & Row, 1963), 53.

28. Brooks, "The Egg Boiler," *The World of GB,* 366.

29. Richard Ohmann's discussion of narrative/prose style as the writer's "epistemic choice" offers a richly suggestive study in the behavior of the rhetoric of fiction, in "Prolegomena to the Analysis of Prose Style," in *Essays in Stylistic Analysis,* ed. Howard S. Babb (New York: Harcourt Brace Jovanovich, 1972), 35–50.

30. Burke, "Literature as Equipment for Living," in *Philosophy of Literary Form,* 293–305.

31. The term is taken from W.J. Cash's classic study of the mythic operations of the "white male mind" of the South: *The Mind of the South* (New York: Alfred A. Knopf, 1941). It is not altogether surprising that "mind" in this case is confined to the male, while the female becomes the object of investigation.

32. I have placed these typically descriptive words for two American races in quotation marks here because the terms are often inadequate for what we actually mean. As we know, "color" in American is "washable" since "black" registers along a range of genetic traits, and so does "white," or the notion of "passing" would have no value whatsoever, either as an actual deed, or a trophic possibility. "Race" should be an anachronism, or dead, but it is neither. We await, in the meantime, a vocabulary that gets us through the complexities that we sometime observe.

33. Brooks, *The World of GB.*

34. Mary Helen Washington's "Plain, Black, and Decently Wild: The Heroic Possibilities of *Maud Martha*" in Elizabeth Abel, Marianne Hirsch, and Elizabeth Langland, eds. *The Voyage In: Fictions of Female Development,* (Hanover, New Hampshire: University Press of New England, 1983), 270–286 gives a good account of the coeval critical opinions of the work.

35. Compare with note 20.

36. "Stetson!/You who were with me in the ships at Mylae!/That corpse you planted last year in your garden,/Has it begun to sprout? Will it bloom this year?/Or has the sudden frost disturbed its bed?" from Valerie Eliot, ed., *A Facsimile and Transcript of the Original Drafts including the Annotations of Ezra Pound* (New York: Harcourt Brace Jovanovich, 1971), 136.

37. In two separate studies, I examine these historical/terministic issues with an eye to locating African-American women's community in relationship to questions of feminist investigation: "Mama's Baby, Papa's Maybe: An American Grammar Book" and " 'The Tragic Mulatta': Notes on an Alternative Model—Neither/Nor." These pieces anticipate a longer work that examines the rift between "the body" and "the flesh" as means of social and cultural production.

38. Burke, "Literature as Equipment for Living," in *Philosophy of Literary Form.*

Maya Angelou:

The Autobiographical Statement Updated

Selwyn R. Cudjoe

Everywhere there is a pure present. It is not a question of narration or description but of incantation . . . The incantation is at the same time transformation.
—Janheinz Jahn, Muntu

Slavery is terrible for men; but it is far more terrible for women. Superadded to the burden common to all, they have wrongs, and sufferings, and mortifications peculiarly their own.
—Linda Brent, Incidents in the Life of a Slave Girl

My people had used music to soothe slavery's torment or to propriate God, or to describe the sweetness of love and the distress of lovelessness, but I knew no race could sing and dance its way to freedom.
—Maya Angelou, The Heart of a Woman

BY WAY OF INTRODUCTION

The Afro-American autobiographical statement is the most Afro-American of all Afro-American literary pursuits. During the eighteenth century, thousands of narratives (the forerunner of the autobiography) were written by Afro-Americans to express their opposition to the evils of slavery and to effect their liberation. The autobiographical statement, up until the contemporary era, remains the quintessential (certainly the most predominant) literary genre for capturing the deep cadences of the Afro-American being, in which deepest aspirations are revealed and evolution and development under the impact of slavery and modern-day United States capitalism is traced.

In examining the social and political context out of which the Afro-American self evolved, it is important to note that in its most essential aspect, slavery did not differ very much from the "formal freedoms" that were granted to black people in the United States (the full and unencumbered franchise was not granted to Afro-Americans until the passage of the Civil Rights Act of 1965) and that slavery and its aftermath represented a system of organized and sustained violence, psychic and otherwise, against a subject people. While slavery enslaved the whole person, imperialism, under the illusion of granting full freedom to the individual, stole the labor of Afro-Americans just as savagely and limited their participation in the social and political affairs of the country to a minimal and peripheral degree. As a result, the entire social development of Afro-Americans has been conditioned by their struggle to liberate themselves from the crippling social and psychological effects of the dominant ideology and culture. To a large degree, this struggle manifested itself in the literature of Afro-American peoples, particularly in the autobiography. Since literature examines the manner in which ideology (ideas, values, and feelings) functions within the social totality, it is in these autobiographical statements that we begin to understand the manner in which the Afro-American person (self) evolved.[1] For Afro-American women, the violence, violation, and degradation possessed its own peculiarities and, as Linda Brent testifies in her autobiography, "Slavery is terrible for men; but it is far more terrible for women. Superadded to the burden common to all, *they* have wrongs, and sufferings, and mortifications peculiarly their own."[2] It is noteworthy that as early as the 1840s, Brent recognized the dual nature of her enslavement, having learned, as Angela Davis has noted in a similar context, that slave women had to "extract from the oppressive circumstances of their lives the strength needed to resist the daily humiliations of slavery."[3] It is even more remarkable that Brent recognized this duality long before the rise of the women's movement and at a time when Afro-American women were being particularly brutalized.[4]

In spite of this violence, the violation and degradation of the Afro-American woman remained largely ignored and seldomly discussed publicly. Her condition remained a closely guarded secret and few of the thousands of autobiographies that were published in the early years were concerned with her condition. This absence continued well into the contemporary era, leading to a situation in which one could speak about the autobiographical statement in Afro-American literature without really having to confront the Afro-American woman as black and as female; as a person and as a presence; as autonomous and as responsible. In the Afro-American autobiographical statement, the Afro-American woman remained an all-pervading absence until she was rescued by the literary activities of her black sisters in the latter part of the twentieth century.

CLEARING THE WAY

From its inception, the Afro-American autobiography has been subjected to the question of how authentic a statement it has been and whether or not the Afro-American had the ability or the capacity to make such a statement. When Phillis Wheatley ("an uncultivated barbarian from Africa," as she was called by some of her sponsors) published her poems in 1773, they were prefaced by a letter to the public that was signed by the governor and lieutenant governor of Massachusetts, seven clergymen, and nine gentlemen of standing in the community, who confirmed the authenticity of her poems.[5] When Gustavus Vassa wrote *The Interesting Narrative of the Life of Olaudah Equiano, or Gustavus Vassa, the African; Written by Himself*, the first narrative written by an African in English, questions about its authenticity also arose, and a reviewer of the narrative in *Monthly Review* in 1789, although not doubting "the general authenticity of this very intelligent African's interesting story," cautioned nonetheless,

It is not improbable that some English writer has assisted him in the complement, or, at least, the correction of his book: for it is sufficiently well written. The narrative wears an honest face: and we have conceived a good opinion of the man, from the artless manner in which he has detailed the variety of adventures and vicissitudes which have fallen to his lot.[6]

Such concerns for authenticity, though important, are not necessarily the most important aspect of the autobiography, for there is nothing in the autobiographical statement that makes it essentially different or signifies that it possesses a higher degree of authenticity than fiction except, perhaps, that which has been erected by convention. Michael Ryan, drawing on the observations of Jacques Derrida, has argued that inherent in the structure of the autobiographical statement is the necessary death of the author as a condition for the existence of the referential machinery. "The writing," he says, "must be capable, from the outset, of functioning independently of the subject. Strictly speaking, then, its referent is always 'ideal' or fictional—produced and sustained by convention." To the degree, however, that the referent is present in the autobiography (it being absent or "ideal" in fiction) "there is really nothing in the autobiography that guarantees that it will be read as fiction or vice-versa. The structural analogy between the two forms of writing can only be sundered by law."[7] As such, the question, "Is it really true?" that is almost always raised about the autobiography is not particularly relevant in that the Afro-American autobiography, a cultural act of self-reading, is meant to reflect a public concern rather than a private act of self-indulgence.[8] Even at this level, the "truth" of the autobiography must be confirmed by someone other than the referent (the subject); such "truth" being neither self-evident nor independent of extratextual confirmation.

In this sense, the autobiographical statement ought not to be seen as the exclusive creation of the author. Apart from its being a public gesture, the editors (as presumably all editors do) are called upon to add embellishments of their own to make the work more readable. For example, L. Maria Child, an ardent abolitionist and editor of *Incidents in the Life of a Slave Girl*, noted that she revised Brent's manuscript at the latter's request but the changes that she made were "mainly for purposes of condensation and orderly arrangement. I have not added any thing to the incidents, or changed the import of her very pertinent remarks. With trifling exceptions, both the ideas and the language are her own. *I pruned excrescences a little*, but otherwise I had no reason for changing her lively and dramatic way of telling her own story."[9]

On the other hand, James Weldon Johnson, in *The Autobiography of an Ex-Colored Man* (1912), a novel that attempts to look at the manner in which racism affects both races, presents quite opposite and different problems. Published anonymously so that it could have "passed" as an authentic autobiography, the author was intent on keeping his identity secret. Such a course of action was undertaken for well-defined literary purposes. He believed that "the story would gain in power if the reader believed [the incidents of the text] actually occurred" and wrote to his friend, George Towns, that when "the author is known, and known to be one who could not be the main character of the story, the book will fall flat."[10] Such caution did not seem to affect the reading of the work in any significant manner. The *Nashville Tennessean* called it a damned "lie" and an "insult to Southern womanhood," while the *New York Times* lauded its "calm judicial tone."[11]

To complicate matters further, Jessie Fauset, the well-known Afro-American woman author, reviewed the novel in *Crisis* and concluded that it was "an epitome of the race situation in the United States *told in the form of an autobiography*. The varied incidents, the numerous localities brought in, the setting forth in all its ramifications of our great and perplexing race problem, suggests a work of fiction founded on hard fact."[12] Eugene Levy claimed that Johnson used "the immediacy of the confession's first-person narrative to produce a largely didactic essay."[13] Thus it would seem that whether it is based on "hard facts" or not, the autobiographical acts of self-reading and self-writing are not only problematic but arbitrary as well. It is this complexity that led Ryan to argue that autobiography cannot be said "to dominate the field of writing as the superior pole of authenticity which places fictional writing in an inferior position because of its conventionality and arbitrarines; if autobiographical writing itself is normed by fiction, it cannot function authentically without itself being in a certain sense fictive."[14]

Thus, whether one reads *Incidents in the Life of a Slave Girl* or *The Autobiography of an Ex-Colored Man* as fact or fiction, it really matters little. They are both founded upon the reality of Afro-American life and culture and the position of the Afro-American subject within American society. Autobiography and fiction are simply different means of arriving at, or recognizing, the same truth: the manner in which and by which the Afro-American makes and is made by his historical, political, and social condition in the United States of America. Neither form of writing should be privileged over the other in our literary history. Each should be judged by its ability to speak honestly and perceptively about the experiences of the Afro-American in this land. The Afro-American autobiography must be seen as constructed, constituted, and formed by the specific practices and discourses of a specific people and their response to their time and place. It is not so much a unique statement of a particular individual but part of the signifying practices of an entire people.

THE IMPORTANCE OF THE AFRO-AMERICAN AUTOBIOGRAPHY

In terms of the Afro-American experience, the autobiography seems to signify in a very clear and urgent manner. Works such as the *Narrative of the Life of Frederick Douglass* (1845); *The Life of Josiah Henson* (1849), on which Harriet Beecher Stowe's *Uncle Tom's Cabin* (1853) was based; *Incidents in the Life of a Slave Girl* (1861); Booker T. Washington's *Up From Slavery* (1900); Zora Neale Hurston's *Dust Tracks on a Road* (1940); Richard Wright's *Black Boy* (1945); *The Autobiography of Malcolm X* (1964); *The Autobiography of W.E.B. Du Bois* (1968); and George Jackson's *Soledad Brothers* (1970) all seem to testify to the strength, consistency, and importance of this genre in Afro-American literature.

I will suggest three factors that account for the unique power and longevity of this genre in Afro-American writing and its specific permutations within the larger context of the genre. First, Afro-Americans attempt to control their own lives, leading to a concern for the personal; second, the word or "parole" plays an important part within the context of their lives; and third, the autobiography emphasizes the public rather than the private gesture of the group.

Hannah Nelson, a contemporary Afro-American woman, argues that "the most important thing about black people [in the United States] is that they don't control anything except their own persons. So that everything black people think and do has to be understood as very personal."[15] As a result, the inviolability of the Afro-American's personhood is so closely guarded that any assault or presumed assault upon his/her person is violently resisted. Such a response to their social reality always leads to complaints that blacks tend to be "too touchy" or "too sensitive" in most of their relationships with Euro-Americans.

Maya Angelou seems to have captured this position in her response to Mrs. Cullinan's inability to call her by her correct name; an attempt, as Angelou sees it, to deny her individuality. As Angelou notes, every person whom she knew "had a hellish horror of being 'called out of his name.' It was a dangerous practice to call a Negro anything that could be loosely construed as insulting because of the centuries of their having been called niggers, jigs, dinges, blackbirds, crows, boots and spooks."[16] In fact, the manner in which the Afro-American held the sanctity of the person and Mrs. Cullinan's reluctance to grant Maya Angelou her individuality leads to one of the most poignant moments in the text. In seeking revenge on Mrs. Cullinan's indifference and cruelty, Angelou drops one of Mrs. Cullinan's most treasured pieces of kitchenware (her casserole and green glass cups that had been passed down in the family) and thereby shocks Mrs. Cullinan into the re-cognition of her individuality. Recounting the incident, Angelou gives her side of the story:

Miss Glory came running in from the yard and the women from the porch crowded around. Miss Glory was almost as broken up as her mistress. "You mean to say she broke our Virginia dishes? What we gone do?"

Mrs. Cullinan cried louder, "That clumsy nigger. Clumsy little black nigger."

Old speckled-face leaned down and asked, "Who did it, Viola? Was it Mary? Who did it?"

Everything was happening so fast I can't remember whether her action preceded her words, but I know that Mrs. Cullinan said, "Her name's Margaret, goddamn it, her name's Margaret!" And she threw a wedge of the broken plate at me. It could have been the hysteria which put her aim off, but the flying crockery caught Miss Glory right over her ear and she started screaming.

I left the front door wide open so all the neighbors could hear.

Mrs. Cullinan was right about one thing. My name wasn't Mary (CB 93).

The realm of the personal and its violation are very important in Afro-American life.

In her discussion with Professor Gwaltney, Nelson goes on to make another important observation about the differences between Afro-American and European peoples, particularly in the capacity of the speech of the former to transmit experience. "Our speech," she says, "is most directly personal, and every other black person has a right to a personal opinion. In speaking of great matters, your personal experience is considered evidence. With us, distant statistics are certainly not as important as the actual experience of a sober person."[17] This tolerance for the ideas and practices of other persons is also recognized by Angelou when she notes the tolerance that the Afro-American community showed toward lesbians, long before it was fashionable in white, Protestant America: "The fact that the pimps and panderers didn't harass them, bespoke the tolerance in the black community for people who chose to lead lives different from the norm."[18] I believe that this spirit of tolerance was at work when the leaders of white America condemned the "racist" statements that Minister Louis Farrakhan, leader of the Nation of Islam, made during the 1984 presidential elections; they were very angry and disappointed when black leaders didn't follow their lead.

The speech of Afro-Americans and the sanctity of their personal opinions are accorded an unusually high degree of importance and suggest an arena in which one's personal and social liberation are realized and guarded in spite of (perhaps because of) all external pressure. In this context, the autobiographical statement can be perceived as one of the most important ways in which Afro-Americans negotiate their way out of their condition of enslavement as well as a means of expressing the intensity with which they experienced their violation and denigration as individual subjects. This capacity of speech or *parole* to convey their intensely lived experiences, and the closely guarded manner in which they hold the personal, give the Afro-American autobiography its special authority in Afro-American letters.

As a direct result of this condition, the Afro-American autobiographical statement is bereft of *excessive subjectivism* and *mindless egotism* and presents the Afro-American as reflecting a much more impersonal condition. The autobiographical subject thus emerges as an almost capricious member of the group, selected to tell his or her story and to explain the condition of the group rather than to assuage his or her egoistical concerns. As a consequence, the autobiographical statement emerges as a *public* rather than a *private* gesture, *me-ism* gives way to *our-ism* and superficial concerns with the *individual subject* (individualism) give way to the *collective subjection* of the group. Incidentally, this is one reason that the specific concerns of women at both the autobiographical and the fictional levels remained submerged so long, and why so many men find it so difficult to cope with the spate of works by Afro-American women writers that they interpret as violent attacks against them.[19]

The autobiography, then, is meant to serve the group rather than to glorify the individual's exploits. The concerns of the collective predominate and one's personal experiences are presumed to be the closest approximation of the group's experiences. Thus, statistical evidences and sociological treatises assume a secondary level of importance in trying to understand the concerns of the group. Vassa puts the contradictions best when he pleads for the abolition of the slave trade in the following manner:

Permit me, with the greatest deference and respect, to lay at your feet the following genuine narrative, the chief design of which is to excite in your august assemblies a sense of compassion for the miseries which the Slave-Trade has entailed on my unfortunate countrymen. By the horrors of that trade was I first torn away from all the tender connections that were naturally dear to my heart; but these, through the mysterious ways of Providence, I ought to regard as infinitely more than compensated by the introduction I have thence obtained to the knowledge of the Christian religion, and of a nation which, by its liberal sentiments, its humanity, the glorious freedom of its government, and its proficiency in arts and sciences, has exalted the dignity of human nature.[20]

Finally, it can be argued that the predominant place that the autobiographical statement assumes in Afro-American literature and the compelling images that it evokes have much of their origins in African religion, philosophy, and oral literary tradition. In another context, I have argued for the influence of African oral literature on the poems of Phillis Wheatley.[21] Janheinz Jahn, in his work, *Muntu*, argues for the centrality of the word in African thought and notes that "everything comes into being only through the word [or nommo]." Compared with the Christian concept of the logos, Jahn argues that

> Nommo does not stand above and beyond the earthly world. *Logos* becomes "flesh" everywhere. According to the apostle, *Logos* has made all things, once and for all, to become as they are, and since then all generated things remain as they are, and undergo no further transformation. Nommo, on the other hand, goes on unceasingly creating and procreating, creating even gods.[22]

Because the muntu (man or woman) speak the speech of the great rivers, command the world and go on ceaselessly reproducing the self and the world through the power of the word, the subject tends to establish a protective and familiar relationship with the word. The power that Aime Cesaire attributes to the word and the manner in which he evokes the world through the power of the word in his long poem, *Return to My Native Land*, seems to be a magnificent demonstration of the manner in which the nommo functions in African thought even in the New World.

In African thought the control over the word signified the African's possibility in this world. The notion that "the force, responsibility and commitment of the word, and the awareness that the word alone alters the world" seems to hark back to its origin in African culture.[23] The fact that Afro-Americans had to use the full power of the word when all other elements of resistance had ceased temporarily also helped to cement its magical importance in their cosmology. Stories of black people acting the fool when caught stealing or when implicated in other acts of malfeasance abound in the literature of Afro-American peoples. Tales of conjuration or the stereotype of the "Sambo" character seem to take their resonance and meaning from this notion of cultural resistance and survival.[24] To exist in America, particularly in the formative years of the country's development, necessitated the use of the word as a powerful and sensitive weapon for the survival of the Afro-American. Its transformative power in the changed historical conditions of America insured its use as a shield from the cruel reality of American life.

The capacity for speech (that is, the ability to "rap") assumed a primary place in the culture of Afro-Americans as a necessary, though not a sufficient, condition for liberation. Where other avenues of resistance were closed to Afro-Americans, they could use the nommo as an extended arena in which to continue to struggle for personal and social liberation. In both the metaphorical and literal sense, speech and language became instruments of liberation in Afro-American life, and the magical incantation of the word and its transformative power gave sustenance and hope to Afro-Americans even in their darkest hours. As an expression and signification of his/her experience, the autobiographical statement became an extension of the word, that strange ritual through which the complex consciousness and historical unfolding of a people revealed itself. It is of and from this experience that Maya Angelou speaks.

AFRO-AMERICAN WOMEN WRITERS OF THE 1970s

In an article entitled "What I Teach and Why," I suggested that the 1970s was an important decade for Afro-American literature because it was a time that saw the increased production of prose writings by Afro-American women writers who expressed themselves in the novel, the short story, and the autobiography.[25] A decade that began with Toni Morrison's *The Bluest Eye*, Louise Meriwether's *Daddy Was a Numbers Runner*, and Alice Walker's *The Third Life of Grange Copeland* ended with Michele Wallace's *Black Macho and the Myth of the Superwoman* (1979) and Mary Helen Washington's edited work, *Midnight Birds* (1980).

Throughout the decade, however, there was a subtle distancing of the Afro-American women writers from their male counterparts, particularly in the manner in which they treated the *subjectivity* of the major protagonists in their works (this would be true of the novel, the autobiography, and the short story); the manner in which these female protagonists were freed, not so much from the other but from their own men folk; the bold attempt to speak for the integrity of their selfhood and to define their being in their own terms; and the urgency with which they felt the need to speak about feminine concerns among themselves. Jeanne Nobles, in *Beautiful, Also, Are the Souls of My Black Sisters* (1978), argues that the black women writers of the 1970s "bypass[ed] the popular theme of black reactions to a racist society,"[26] while Gwendolyn Brooks confirms these sentiments when she claims that these black writers are "talking to themselves" rather than to others. Mary Helen Washington, in her introduction to the works of the black women writers of the seventies, celebrates the fact that their works represent "an open revolt against the ideologies and attitudes that impress [black] women into servitude."[27]

Such attitudes had a profound impact upon the direction and subsequent development of Afro-American literature. Because of certain limitations on the part of Afro-American male writers, black women characters never realized their essence as autonomous subjects within the mainstream of Afro-American literature. They were depicted as existing at the surface level of reality, mere appendages of black male life never really seeming to live important lives worthy of emulation. They always lived for others, be it for black men or white, black children or aged parents, bereft always, it would seem, of an autonomous self. This is not to suggest that black women were not writing seriously and sympathetically about their sisters and themselves prior to the seventies.[28] It is only meant to argue that the male writers were getting most of the literary play at the expense of the women writers.

The silence of these women also resulted partially from the manner in which the black male writers were manipulated by the white literary establishment. Chester Himes, in a very revealing moment in his autobiography, *The Quality of Hurt*, recounts a conversation between Richard Wright and James Baldwin that alluded to the tendency of the white literary establishment, until 1970, to allow only one black writer to emerge onto the literary scene. Mel Watkins, writing in *The New York Times* in February 1981, suggested that this tendency was beginning to rear its ugly head once more.[29] Because of this condition, the black male writers fought among themselves and remained at the mercy of white publishers to have their books published or to gain recognition.

Nor could the specific quality of the alienated lives of these women—the complete unraveling of the individual ego that we see in the works of the women writers of this decade—be depicted prior to the 1970s. Just as a Bigger Thomas, in spite of his limitations, could not be written before the influx of blacks into urban America in the 1920s, nor could black women of heroic proportions be depicted before the rise of black nationalism in the 1960s (see, for example, the manner in which Merle is depicted in Paule Marshall's *The Chosen Place, the Timeless People* [1969] or Vyry in Margaret Walker's *Jubilee* [1966]), neither could the complex and complicated lives of these black women be replicated before the seventies, no matter how hard black male or female writers tried. The decades prior to the seventies, quite simply, spoke to a different problem of the Afro-American being and this is one reason why Mel Watkins's argument that black women writers have placed themselves outside the traditional canons of black American literature is ahistorical and undialectical.[30]

It was the culmination of a number of factors at the end of the sixties that led to the outpouring of writings by Afro-American women. First, the inherent shortcomings of the nationalism of the Black Power movement; second, the increased social and economic pressures that led to the rapid deterioration of the urban centers of America; third, the rise of the feminist movement that made Afro-American women more conscious of their particularity; and, fourth, the increasing tensions in black male-female relations to which Michele Wallace addressed herself in *Black Macho and the Myth of the Superwoman*.[31] All of these factors led to a special kind of problematic to which the Afro-American woman had to address herself, adding a new and dynamic dimension to American literature. Watkins's contention that the white media exploited the rift between black men and women that this literature examined, leading subsequently to the popularity of black women writers, possesses some degree of truth.

It is out of these conditions and in response to these specific concerns that Maya Angelou offered her autobiographical statements: *I Know Why the Caged Bird Sings* (1970), *Gather Together in My Name* (1974), *Singin' and Swingin' and Gettin' Merry Like Christmas* (1976), *The Heart of a Woman* (1981), and *All God's Children Need Traveling Shoes* (1986). Although her last two works examine the manner in which the events of the sixties impacted upon her life, they were produced in a time when some of the social and political fervor of the 1970s had abated and thus allowed for a more sober assessment. Needless to say, the political currents of the time are more prominent in the last two segments of her statement. As a statement, Angelou presents a powerful, authentic, and profound signification of Afro-American life and the changing concerns of the Afro-American woman in her quest for personal autonomy, understanding, and love. Such a statement, because of the simple, forthright, and honest manner in which it is presented, is depicted against the larger struggle of Afro-American and African peoples for their liberation and triumphs. It is a celebration of the struggle, survival, and existence of Afro-American people.

I KNOW WHY THE CAGED BIRD SINGS

I Know Why the Caged Bird Sings is the story about what it means to grow up black and female in the American South during the second quarter of this century. It recounts the life of Maya Angelou from the age of three to the age of sixteen; the first ten years of which were lived in Stamps, Arkansas and the last three in Los Angeles and San Francisco. The world to which Angelou introduces us is embroidered with humiliation, violation, displacement, and loss. From the opening of the work, Angelou sounds the themes that engage our attention for the entire book when she announces that "if growing up is painful for the Southern Black girl, being aware of her displacement is the rust on the razor that threatens the throat. It is an unnecessary insult" (CB 3). From this point, she winds her way to a conclusion that asserts that the black woman is assaulted in her tender years "by all those common forces of nature at the same time that she is caught in the tripartite crossfire of masculine prejudice, white illogical hate and Black lack of power" (CB 231). The burden of the work, therefore, is to demonstrate the manner in which the black woman is violated by all of the forces above as well as by the unnecessary insults to which she is afflicted in her childhood and adolescence.

As Angelou demonstrates, the life of the South is one of harshness and brutality, exemplified by the conditions under which the workers of Stamps lived: the fear engendered by the Ku Klux Klan; the wanton murder of black folks (which led her grandmother, Mother Henderson, to send her and her brother, Bailey, to their mother in California); the racial separation of the town, and the innumerable incidents of denigration that made life in the South an abomination against God and man. The moments of happiness in her childhood life are rare and come, as Thomas Hardy characterized them in *The Mayor of Casterbridge*, as but "the occasional episode[s] in a general drama of pain."[32] Such cruelty leads to a well-defined pattern of behavior and the adoption of certain necessary codes of behavior to exist in that part of the country—the insults of the "powhitetrash" have to be accepted and the manner in which the whites try to debase the blacks have to be fended off at each moment.

The text charts Angelou's development from innocence to awareness, from childhood to an ever-quickening sense of adolescence. To maintain a relative sense of freedom and autonomy, Angelou overcomes certain ideological values that were inscribed within the social fabric. As she develops, she challenges and overcomes the pervasive and naturalizing tendencies of these values; this is the strength of this segment of her autobiography. The ability to subvert those institutional discourses and practices that were meant to ensure her mental enslavement become a very real part of her battle to survive in her world.

The heavyweight fight on June 25, 1935, between Joe Louis and Primo Carnera, intended to pacify, entertain, and demonstrate how far blacks had arrived in the society, turned out instead to be a tableau in which black America came face to face with white America and, in a strength of equals, the former triumphed even though only temporarily. Angelou describes the scene that takes place in her grandmother's store on the night of the fight as the real drama of American life played itself out in the boxing ring:[33]

Babies slid to the floor as women stood up and men leaned toward the radio.

"Here's the referee. He's counting. One, two, three, four, five, six, seven . . . Is the contender trying to get up again?"

All the men in the store shouted, "NO."

"-eight, nine, ten." There were a few sounds from the audience, but they seemed to be holding themselves in against tremendous pressure.

"The fight is all over, ladies and gentlemen. Let's get the microphone over to the referee . . . Here he is. He's got the Brown Bomber's hand, he's holding it up . . . Here he is . . ."

Then the voice, husky and familiar, came to wash over us—"The winnah, and still heavyweight champeen of the world . . . Joe Louis."

Champion of the world. A Black boy. Some Black mother's son. He was the strongest man in the world. People drank Coca-Colas like ambrosia and ate candy bars like Christmas. Some of the men went behind the Store and poured white lightning in their soft-drink bottles, and a few of the bigger boys followed them. Those who were not chased away came back blowing their breath in front of themselves like proud smokers.

It would take an hour or more before the people would leave the Store and head for home. Those who lived too far had made arrangements to stay in town. It wouldn't do for a Black man and his family to be caught on a lonely country road on a night when Joe Louis had proved that we were the strongest people in the world (CB 114–115).

Singing and perhaps swinging like Christmas, Angelou may have asked the forgiveness of the Italians for that act of celebration when she arrived in Italy some years later. As a girl in Arkansas, however, the struggle between the colors continued and the black people projected all of their pent-up emotions into that boxing match that came over that radio. Sports, as it were, became just another arena where the struggle for justice and liberation was carried on.

The most poignant moment of ideological unveilment comes when Angelou describes her 1940 graduation exercise at Lafayette County Training School. As she listens to the racist manner in which Edward Donleavy, the featured speaker, insults the intelligence of her class (with the approving "amens" of her elders), and the invidious comparisons he makes with the white school in the area (Central School), Angelou thinks how awful it is to have so little control over her life. "It was brutal to be young and already trained to sit quietly and listen to charges brought against my color with no chance of defense. We should all be dead. I thought I should like to see us all dead, one on top of the other" (CB 153).

Listening to Donleavy, Angelou shares in the collective malignment hurled against the group. In the impotence of childhood, there is little that she can do about it, but she does not forget the charges that have been brought against her group. It colors the texture of her world and she realizes the emptiness of the sentiments that are expressed in the valedictory address: "I am the master of my fate, I am the captain of my soul." Observing the inherent falsehood of the statement "To be, or not to be," she observes in ironic tones: "Hadn't he heard the whitefolks? We couldn't *be*, so the question was a waste of time" (CB 154). It is in Stamps, Arkansas, out of this web of reality, that she takes her first fumbling steps toward the articulation of her social self.

According to the text, then, the major crime of the dominant white society resides in its attempts to reduce all Negroes to a sense of impotence and nothingness. This is the internal "rust" that threatens the development of the personal identity of all black people in America. It is this inherent suicidal tendency of an oppressive and racist society that pushes these young people to the brink of spiritual waste and physical destruction. For Angelou, such a milieu becomes the point of departure from which she struggles to salvage a sense of dignity and personhood, the necessary prerequisite to expressing any sense of womanhood.

Like Linda Brent, Angelou understands that to be black and to be woman is to be faced with a special quality of violence and violation. This condition is brought into sharp focus when, at the age of eight, Angelou goes to St. Louis to live with her mother and is raped by her mother's boyfriend. Faced with this catastrophe, her first reaction is to withdraw into herself, but, more importantly, it is only because of the strength of her individual will that she is able to work herself back to a point where she can function in a seemingly productive manner in her social world. Yet the rape of this eight-year-old by an almost-impotent male who, it would seem, is unable to enjoy a relatively mature and respectful relationship with an adult black woman, can only be seen as symbolic of one aspect of this internal dimension of black life.

The brutality of this act suggests a new dimension in Afro-American autobiographical writing. Angelou implies that the same power, energy, and honesty that characterized our examination of our relationship with the oppressor class be now turned inward to examine some of the obstacles that have retarded our personal development and our social liberation. In other words, Afro-American liberation must contain both an internal and external dimension; the former must be our exclusive concern. It is this internal probing that characterizes this work and marks the writing of the contemporary Afro-American woman writer.

One ought not, however, simply read the shortcomings of black life into the text and forget the complicity of white capitalist society, the major cause of black denigration. On the larger canvas from which this life is drawn, the villain is a society that reduces men to impotence and women to lives of whoredom, and makes children the victims of their father's lust and impotence. In fact, the troubling question of what constitutes femininity and the beautiful lead Angelou into a sexual liaison that eventually results in an unwanted pregnancy. Certainly, at the age of sixteen, she was not prepared financially or emotionally to take care of a child.

To argue for the cruelty and brutality of the society is not to deny the episodes of beauty that relieve the monotony of life in Stamps. Nor can we deny the progressive tendency of the black church in Afro-American society. It is to argue, however, that the cruelty so overwhelms the sensibilities of the black person in the South that it makes her existence in the society so very difficult. For a black woman, her growth to

awareness in those circumstances is a very painful process. As
Angelou notes, "Without willing it, I had gone from being
ignorant of being ignorant to being aware of being aware.
And the worst part of my awareness was that I didn't know
what I was aware of" (CB 230). This awareness of her status
comes at a price: her subjection to the tripartite forces of the
masculine prejudice, the white illogical hate, and the black
powerlessness that shapes her existence in America.

In part, the shortcomings of the text revolve around the
manner in which the story is told from the point of view of an
adult who imposes the imagination, logic, and language of an
adult upon the work and thus prevents the reader from participating in the unfolding of childhood consciousness as it grows
into maturity. The even and repetitious tone of the work
causes it to be almost predictable in its development. The
rationalizations of later years almost destroy the flow of the
text and raise the question of the authenticity of her responses
to some of the incidents in her life.

Such an occasion occurs when Angelou offers what she
considers an ethical response to the dehumanization and exploitation of blacks. Speaking of the "black underground,"
she contends that she couldn't help but admire the criminals
in the black community and take pride in their achievements.
She continues:

> The needs of a society determine its ethics, and in the
> Black American ghettos the hero is that man who is
> offered only the crumbs from his country's table but by
> ingenuity and courage is able to take for himself a Lucullan
> feast. Hence the janitor who lives in one room but sports
> a robin's-egg-blue Cadillac is not laughed at but admired,
> and the domestic who buys forty-dollar shoes is not criti-
> cized but is appreciated. We know that they have to put
> to use their full mental and physical powers. Each single
> gain feeds into the gains of the body collective.
>
> Stories of law violations are weighted on a different set
> of scales in the Black mind than in the white. Petty
> crimes embarrass the community and many people
> wistfully wonder why Negroes don't rob more banks,
> embezzle more funds and employ graft in the unions.
> "We are the victims of the world's most comprehensive

robbery. Life demands a balance. It's all right if we do a little robbing now." This belief appeals particularly to one who is unable to compete legally with his fellow citizens (CB 190–191).

Such attitudes may extend to most members of the community since so few members can compete legally or equally with their white male counterparts, as far as finances are concerned. Perhaps the janitor ought to be laughed at. Yet what makes such an analysis untenable is the fact that ethical postulates in any society should transcend its mere "needs" if they lead to the reproduction of behavior patterns that are detrimental to the social development of the group. There is no demonstrable evidence that these people are in fact "heroic," since their activity tends to dehumanize, and produces people like Mr. Freeman, Angelou's mother's boyfriend, who raped the young girl. The inability to transcend the limits that are placed upon black society by the dominant culture can only lead to the reproduction of diminished persons. The criminal characters who are admired are certainly the mere extensions of Mr. Freeman.

The task of the autobiographical statement, then, is not the mere reproduction of naturalistic details. Because it involves the creative organization of ideas and situations and makes an ethical and moral statement about the lives it brings to life through *graphie* (writing), it must generate actions and activities that are purposeful and also signify our liberation. In fact, the "Principle of Reverse" of which Angelou speaks, may help an individual "to get over" initially, but, precisely because of its inherent characteristics, it follows that it can reverse itself and make the apparent victor its victim. Surely the "Principle of Reverse" may "pry open the door of rejection and [allow] . . . some revenge in the bargain" (CB 190); it certainly does not and cannot reverse a situation that makes the violation and denigration of the black woman possible in this society.

GATHER TOGETHER IN MY NAME

The intense solidity and moral center that we observe in *Caged Bird* is not to be found in *Gather Together in My Name*.

The dignified and ethical manner in which the black people of the rural South live is destroyed as they encounter the alienation and fragmentation that urban America engenders. These are the conditions that characterize the life of Maya Angelou as she seeks to situate herself in California from her sixteenth to her nineteenth years.

Gather Together introduces us to a world of prostitution and pimps, con men and street women, drug addiction and spiritual disintegration. Angelou manages to survive in that world but her life is without dignity and purpose and, at the end of the work, she concedes that she had no idea of what she was going to make of her life, "but I had given a promise and found my innocence" (CB 181). It is as though she had to go to the brink of destruction to realize herself—a striking demonstration of how capitalism always drives its victims to the end of endurance. One may either break down under the strains of society or work assiduously to salvage some dignity from the confusion of one's life.

Gather Together reveals a much more particular and selective vision of Afro-American life, in which Angelou's encounters are limited to the declassed elements of the society. She is a short-order cook, a waitress at a night club, a madam in charge of her own house of prostitution, a nightclub dancer, a prostitute, and the lover of a drug addict who steals dresses for a living. Her exploits as a madam and a prostitute take up approximately seventy-five of a one hundred eighty-page text; this emphasis differentiates this text from the others.

The violation that began in *Caged Bird* takes on a much sharper focus in *Gather Together*. To be sure, Angelou is still concerned with the questions of what it means to be black and female in America and exactly where she fits into the scheme of things. But her development is reflective of a particular type of black woman, located at a particular moment of history and subjected to certain social forces that assault the black woman with unusual ferocity. Thus, when Angelou arrives in Los Angeles she complains bitterly that her mother "hadn't the slightest idea that not only was I not a woman, but what passed for my mind was animal instinct. Like a tree or a river, I merely responded to the winds and the tides" (GT 23). In responding to her mother's indifference to her immaturity, she complains that "they were not equipped to understand that an eighteen-year-old mother is also an eighteen-year-old girl" (GT 27). It is from this angle of vision, that of a "tree in the wind" possessing mostly "animal instinct" to an "unequipped" eighteen-year-old young woman, that we must respond to the story that she tells.

Neither politically nor linguistically innocent, *Gather Together* reflects the imposition of values of a later period of the author's life. Undoubtedly, in organizing the incidents of the text and having recourse to memorization, the selection of incidents, the fictive principle, and so on come into full play. For example, it is difficult to believe that Angelou set out to organize the prostitution of Jonnie Mae and Beatrice because she wanted to revenge those "inconsiderate, stupid bitches" (GT 45).[34] Nor can we accept the fact that she "turned tricks" for L.D. because she believes that "there was nothing wrong with sex. I had no need for shame. Society dictated that sex was only licensed by marriage documents. Well, I didn't agree with that. Society is a conglomerate of human beings, and that's just what I was. A human being" (GT 142).

It rings hollow as a justification. Society is not a mere conglomerate of human beings. Society is a conglomeration of *social beings* whose acts make them *human* or *nonhuman*. To the degree that those acts affirm or negate our humanity they can be considered correct or incorrect. Such reasoning only keeps the argument within the context in which it is raised. The point is that one cannot justify the prostitution of one's body or that of others simply by asserting: "I didn't agree with that."

The importance of the text (its social significance, if you may) lies in its capacity to signify to and from a larger social context than that from which it originates. In spite of the imperial tone she sometimes adopts, Angelou is an extremely lonely young woman drifting through this phase of her life. She is more isolated in the bustle of California than she was in the rural quietude of Stamps. The kidnapping of her child, her most significant achievement so far, and her escape from a life of drugs (because of the generosity of Troubadour Martin) give her a new understanding of life, a rebirth into a higher level of dialectical understanding.

Yet, in a curious way, the book fails. Its lack of moral weight and absence of an ethical center deny it an organizing principle and rigor capable of keeping the work together. It is almost as though the incidents in the text were simply gathered together under the name of Maya Angelou but not so organized to achieve that complex level of signification that one expects in such a work. The absence of these qualities makes *Gather Together* conspicuously weak. The language of the text, more controlled, begins to loosen up—this is its saving grace. Where there were patches of beautiful writing in *Caged Bird*, here there is a much more consistent and sustained flow of eloquent and honey-dipped prose, while the simplicity of the speech patterns remains. The writing flows and shimmers with beauty, but the rigorous, coherent, and meaningful organization of experiences is missing.

SINGIN' AND SWINGIN' AND GETTIN' MERRY LIKE CHRISTMAS

The last scene of *Gather Together*, in which Angelou is taken to a room of drug addicts—the limits of chaos and destruction—can be contrasted to the opening scene of *Caged Bird*, a striking tableau of innocence in which Angelou identifies herself very strongly with all of the social and cultural notions that personify the "ideal" American life. The slide into iniquity that she experiences at the end of *Gather Together* can be interpreted as an indication of the discrepancy between the "ideal" and the "real" and the inability of the Afro-American to come anywhere close to achieving the former in American life. The horrifying last scene foreshadows the destruction that awaits those who attempt to achieve those ideals that America presents to her children.

The innocence that Angelou achieves at the end of *Gather Together* cannot be regarded in the same light as that which we found at the beginning of *Caged Bird*. It is the rediscovery of that primal innocence at a higher level of development that was lost in her original encounter with the American dream. The sinking into the slime of the American abyss represents the necessary condition of regeneration and rebirth that would make her a new and, one can hope, a more consciously liberated person, a position that *The Heart of a Woman* explores. If *Caged Bird* sets the stage for contextualizing the subject, then *Gather Together* presents itself as the necessary purgation that the initiate must undergo to recapture and re(de)fine the social self so as to function in a relatively rational and healthy manner.

Singin' and Swingin' and Gettin' Merry Like Christmas explores the adulthood of Angelou as she moves into and defines herself more centrally within the mainstream of the black experience. In this work, she encounters the white world in a much fuller and more sensuous manner, seeking to answer the major problem of her life: What does it mean to be black and female in America? In the final analysis, we see that this quest reduces itself to what it means to be a black person in America, the urgency of the former collapsing into the latter.[35] To achieve this end, the book is divided into two parts. In the first part, Angelou works out her relationship with the white world of the United States and in the second, she makes a statement about her own development through her encounter with Europe and Africa and her participation in the opera, *Porgy and Bess.*

Singin' and Swingin' opens with a scene of displacement in which Angelou feels "unanchored" as the family bonds of her youth are torn asunder under the impact of life in California. Under these new circumstances the author examines her feelings and her relationship with the larger white society as she encounters white people at an intimate and personal level for the first time in her life. Before she can do so, however, she must dispense with all of the stereotypical notions that she has about white people, many of which are punctured and eventually discarded. Her biggest test comes when she must decide whether or not to marry Tosh, a white man. As she notes, "Anger and guilt decided before my birth that Black was Black and white was white and although the two might share sex, they must never exchange love" (SS 27–28).

Angelou answers the question through a sort of evasion when she tells herself that Tosh "was Greek, not white American; therefore I needn't feel I had betrayed my race by marrying one of the enemy, nor could white Americans believe that I had so forgiven them the past that I was ready to love a member of their tribe" (SS 35). She is not entirely satisfied by the truce she has made with her blackness and for the rest of her marriage has to contend with the guilt that her marriage to a white male has created.

When her marriage ends, she is afraid that she will be cast into "a maelstrom of rootlessness" (SS 44) and be ridiculed by her people, who would see her as another victim of a "white man [who] had taken a Black woman's body and left her hopeless, helpless and alone" (SS 45). In spite of this failure, she feels better prepared to deal with her own life, having gained entrance into the white world while knowing the stubborn realities of her black life. The compromises that she makes to secure a stronger marriage (particularly the effacement of her being) cannot be seen only in the context of the *subjection* of a wife to her husband or a black woman to a white man, it can also be read as the subjection of the central values of the black world (and of the black woman) to the dominant values of the white world.

The tensions that keep the first section of the work together revolve around Angelou's yearning to be absorbed into the larger American culture while wanting to maintain her black identity. This antagonism leads to her first honest relationship with white people and causes her to note that "these whites were treating me as an equal as if I could do whatever they could do. They did not consider that race, height, or gender or lack of education might have crippled me and that I should be regarded as someone invalided" (SS 84). This relationship is significant to Angelou in that it allows her to grow and develop in new directions as a person.

As the second phase of her evolution into adulthood commences, she goes back to her southern origins to evaluate the major transformations that have taken place in her life. Enjoying the hospitality of her new friend, Yanko Varda, aboard his yacht, Angelou reflects upon her past life of hardships in Stamps, Arkansas, and contemplates her proposed trip to Europe, realizing that to achieve a level of maturity she has to fulfill "her motivations [and] her needs" (SS 145).

Her participation in *Porgy and Bess* brings her face to face with another dimension of her expanding self. It reveals the joyous plenitude of black life and takes her back to the roots of her people and their suffering. The empathy of the ordinary European with her people's suffering and their song, their immediate identification of her with Joe Louis, the enthusiastic manner in which they welcome her, lead to some of the most revealing moments of her life. Her recognition that "Europeans often made as clear a distinction between black and white Americans as did the most confirmed Southern bigot" (SS 164–165) raises Angelou's self-esteem and allows her to recognize her emerging place in the world. Her visit to Africa, particularly Egypt, adds to her self-esteem and gives a completion and roundness to her experiences that white America has tried to deny her. In Africa, she returns to her people literally and metaphorically.

Paradoxically, it is in Africa, amidst the beggars of Egypt, that she realizes the specific quality of her Americanness. "I was young, talented, well-dressed, and whether I take pride in the fact publicly or not, I was an American" (SS 230). Yet the manner in which she and her black colleagues resist the ostensible sights and practices of the enslavement of their fellow blacks in Egypt demonstrates an identity of common suffering and fraternity that bind them with the larger African community and its diaspora.

It is the success of *Porgy and Bess* that is paradigmatic of her evolution as an autonomous and fully liberated person. The pride that she takes in her company's professionalism, their discipline on stage and the well-spring of spirituality that the opera emotes parallel the organic harmony between her personal and social history. The triumph of *Porgy and Bess*, therefore, speaks not only to the dramatic success of a black company but also to the personal triumph of a remarkable black woman. *Singin' and Swingin'* is a wondrous celebration of that triumph.

THE HEART OF A WOMAN

The Heart of a Woman, the most political segment of Angelou's autobiographical statement, is set against the political upsurge of Afro-Americans and Africans between 1957 and 1962. From being peripheral to the political life of her people, Angelou etches herself more centrally into the rising civil rights movement and the African liberation struggle. Through her participation in them she becomes more of a person in the Platonic sense. As a result, the theme of this segment of her autobiography can be taken from the message that she heard Martin

Luther King, the great Afro-American freedom fighter, deliver in Harlem:

> We, the black people, the most displaced, the poorest, the most maligned and scourged, we had the glorious task of reclaiming the soul and saving the country. We, the most hated, must take hate into our hands and by the miracle of love, turn loathing into love. We, the most feared and apprehensive, must take fear and by love, change it into hope. We, who die daily in large and small ways, must take the demon death and turn it into Life.[36]

The Heart of a Woman, then, locates itself within the Afro-American and African struggle for liberation. It begins in Harlem in 1957 when Angelou joins the Harlem Writers Guild, and explores her involvement with the Southern Christian Leadership Conference in the "awakening summer of 1960," when "the entire country was in labor. Something wonderful was about to be born, and we were all going to be good parents to the welcome child. Its name was Freedom" (HOW 71). The book traces Angelou's growing consciousness as a woman ("I wanted to be a wife and to create a beautiful home to make my man happy, but there was more to life than being a diligent maid with a permanent pussy" [HOW 143]) and takes us to Ghana, where Kwame Nkrumah, the African hero, "had wedded Marxism to the innate African socialism, and was loved by black people all over the world as he was hated and feared by whites in power" (HOW 260). She recounts her meetings with Billie Holiday, Martin Luther King, Malcolm X, Oliver Tambo, leader of the African National Congress, as well as her friendship with his wife, her move from California to Harlem, her marriage to Vus (Vusumzi Make), an African freedom fighter, her subsequent involvement with the African liberation struggle, her living in Egypt, her work with the *Arab Observer*, and her move to Ghana, where her son, Guy, is admitted to university. While Angelou does not examine any of these concepts that arise in her work, they allow us to chart her development against a wider spectrum of social behavior and political practices.

In the process, two important intellectual reformulations occur in her statement. First, we observe the development of

Angelou and her son and the subtle change of emphasis from a purely nationalist to an internationalist perspective of black peoples' struggle. This changed dimension is emphasized when Guy comments to his mother on the meeting between Nikita Khrushchev, former general secretary of the Communist party of the Soviet Union, and Fidel Castro, president of Cuba: "To me, a black man, the meeting of Cuba and the Soviet Union in Harlem is the most important thing that could happen. It means that, in my time, I am seeing powerful forces get together to oppose capitalism. I don't know how it was in your time, the olden days, but in modern America this was something I had to see. It will influence my future" (HOW 97).

The second transformation occurs when Vus, in describing the significance of Jean Genet's play, *The Blacks*, to Angelou, brings to her attention the fact that blacks could behave just as cruelly as whites if their struggle does not adopt the correct ideological safeguards. He notes that there is nothing innately different in blacks. "Black people are human. No more, no less. Our backgrounds, our history make us act differently . . . [M]ost black revolutionaries, most black activists, do not really want change. They want exchange. This play points to that likelihood. And our people need to face the temptation" (HOW 175). Such dangers, he observes, have to be fought against. The Pan-Africanist vision of the work, its sense of a shared history and destiny, and the persistence of memory that binds all Africans and Afro-Americans together differentiate *The Heart of a Woman* from all of the other segments of her autobiography.

In this text, whites are noticeably peripheral to the central concerns. Black people have come into time and place and are the subjects of their own history. For the first time, they begin to create their own social selves; this is the strength of the statement. Where Angelou recognized her Americanness in *Singin' and Swingin'*, in this work she discovers that her Afro-Americanness is shaped inextricably by the currents of African history and culture. This explains the sadness that enraptures her soul when she leaves Egypt to go to Ghana:

> I had never felt that Egypt was really Africa, but now that our route had taken us across the Sahara, I could look down from my window seat and see trees, and

bushes, rivers and dense forest. It all began here. The
jumble of poverty-stricken children sleeping in rat-infested
tenements or abandoned cars. The terrifying moan of my
grandmother, "Bread of Heaven, Bread of Heaven, feed
me till I want no more." The drugged days and alcoholic
nights of men for whom hope had not been born. The
loneliness of women who would never know appreciation or a mite's share of honor. Here, there, along the
banks of that river, someone was taken, tied with ropes,
shackled with chains, forced to march for weeks carrying
the double burden of neck irons and abysmal fear. In that
large clump of trees, looking like wood moss from the
plane's great height, boys and girls had been hunted like
beasts, caught and tethered together. Sacrificial lambs on
the altar of greed. America's period of orgiastic lynchings
had begun on yonder broad savannah (HOW 257).

In a way, the text ends where it began, with Afro-America
(Harlem) reaching out to Africa (Ghana); from the urban disintegration of Harlem to the promised beginnings of recently
liberated Ghana, the first African country to be granted independence from the British colonial power. For many Afro-
Americans, the independence of Ghana coincides with their
rising nationalism and quest for liberation. Both of these concerns signify a new beginning and give Afro-Americans a new
pride in themselves. Such freedom causes Angelou to cast her
mind back to the plight of her brothers and sisters in America
and wonder what will happen to the little black children
who have to "walk between rows of cursing, spitting white
women and men, enroute to school [and] uniformed police
[who] sicked dogs on them just because they wanted to get to
class" (HOW 219).

For a moment, she would be protected by Africa. The entrance of Guy into the University of Ghana and his attempt to
wrest control of his life from his mother (that is, the mother
country, the dominant power, and so on) point to a new
social self. The movement of Africa suggests that inherent in
the formulation of the Afro-American self is the related African dimension that cannot be ignored as Afro-Americans try
to determine who they are and where they belong.

ALL GOD'S CHILDREN NEED TRAVELING SHOES

The promise of Africa, the part it plays in the construction of the Afro-American self, and the attempt to determine where the Afro-American belongs are the central concerns of *All God's Children*. To be sure, there is the recognition that "years of bondage, brutalities, the mixture of other bloods, customs and language had transformed us into an unrecognizable tribe"[37] or that "an airline ticket to Africa would [not] erase the past and open wide the gates to a perfect future" (AGC 41). Yet there is the major dilemma that many Afro-Americans faced in the 1960s: the recognition that they were cut off from the continuity of their past and hence were compelled to search for roots to supplement that loss. Angelou acknowledges her envy of those Africans who had remained on the continent and retained their culture intact. Even though they had been exploited by European colonialism they could still "reflect through their priests and chiefs on centuries of continuity. The lowliest could call the name of ancestors who lived centuries earlier. The land upon which they lived had been in their people's possession beyond remembered time. Despite political bondage and economic exploitation, they have retained an ineradicable innocence" (AGC 76). Once that quest for roots is exhausted, Angelou has to return to her homeland to participate in "her people's struggle" (AGC 194) for justice. Africa gives her "their affection and instructed [her] on the positive power of literally knowing one's place" (AGC 195). She needs that security to continue her work at home.

To the Afro-American, Africa remains a double-edged symbol, signifying the ancestral home and a sense of continuity, while America remains home, the site of a million humiliations. The physical sighting of Cape Coast Castle and Elmira Castle, holding forts for captured slaves who were taken to the Americas, troubles Angelou greatly and reminds her of the petrified past. Yet, curiously enough, when she sees the United States flag hoisted in that foreign land, "many of us had only begun to realize in Africa that the Stars and Stripes was our flag and our only flag, and that knowledge was almost too painful to bear . . . I shuddered to think that while we wanted that flag dragged into the mud and sullied beyond repair, we also wanted it pristine, its white stripes, summer

cloud white. Watching it wave in the breeze of a distance
made us nearly choke with emotion. It lifted us up with its
promise and broke our hearts with its denial" (AGC 127).

Against this double legacy and twined burden, the pro-
nouncements of Malcolm X are located strategically at the
center of the text. Having returned from his pilgrimage to
Mecca, he changed his opinions about many of his previous
concepts, most of all, those of racism. For Angelou, it is
Malcolm's challenge to return to the United States, where
there is much work to be done to free Afro-American people.
As she notes, Malcolm's "presence had elevated us, but with
his departure, we were what we had been before: a little
group of Black folks, looking for a home" (AGC 146). Such
melancholy brings home to Angelou with unusual clarity the
feeling that she is not "in the right place . . . I needed to get
away from Africa and its caché of subtle promises and at least
second-handed memories" (AGC 147–148).

Before Angelou can know where she belongs, she also has
to recognize the manner in which she differs from her African
brothers and sisters, and how her "native sassiness . . . had
been softened by contact with the respectfulness of Ghana-
ians, yet, unlike them I did not belong to a place from which I
could not be dislodged" (AGC 173–174). Although she does
not discover herself fully in Africa, her search has brought her
"closer to understanding myself and other human beings"
(AGC 196) and before she returns to America she is literally
claimed by Africans and acknowledged as one of their lost
sisters. As she says:

I had not consciously come to Ghana to find the roots
of my beginnings, but I had continually and accidentally
tripped over them or fallen upon them in my everyday
life. Once I had been taken for Bambara, and cared for
by other Africans as they would care for a Bambara
woman. Nana's family of Ahantas claimed me, crediting
my resemblance to a relative as proof of my Ahanta background. And here in my last days in Africa, descendants
of a pillaged past saw their history in my face and heard
their ancestors speak through my voice" (AGC206–207).

In the end, there is the affirmation of her Afro-American roots; her recognition that she and her people have withstood in the evil hour and hence her proclamation:

> The women wept and I wept. I too cried for the lost people, their ancestors and mine. But I was also weeping with a curious joy. Despite the murders, rapes and suicides, we had survived. The middle passage and the auction block had not erased us. Not humiliations nor lynchings, individual cruelties nor collective oppression had been able to eradicate us from the earth. We had come through despite our own ignorance and gullibility, and the ignorance and rapacious greed of our assailants.
>
> There was much to cry for, much to mourn, but in my heart I felt exalted knowing there was much to celebrate. Although separated from our languages, our families and customs, we had dared to continue to live. We had crossed the unknowable oceans in chains and had written its mysteries into "Deep River, my home is over Jordan." Through the centuries of despair and dislocation, we had been creative, because we faced down death by daring to hope (AGC 207).

Her statement is a celebration of hope, a paean to love, and a tribute to the magnificent spirit of her people overcoming downpression. Having glimpsed their strength, recognized that America is home in spite of all of its cruelties, she must return to her native land. As she notes, her first leave-taking from Africa was by force; this second one is by choice, since "my people had never completely left Africa. We had sung it in our blues, shouted it in our gospel and danced the continent in our breakdowns. As we carried it to Philadelphia, Boston and Birmingham we had changed its color, modified its rhythms, yet it was Africa which rode in the bulges of our high calves, shook in our protruding behinds and crackled in our wide open laughter" (AGC 208).

Her identification with Africa is complete and the link is made. A journey that began in Stamps, Arkansas has taken her to strange places in search of her self and a place that she can call home. It ends in Africa with the recognition that a person is not complete until she locates herself fully in her time (history) and her place (geography). The recognition of a self and the acceptance of one's place, no matter how grievous or repulsive its legacy, is the ultimate refuge of life—hence the celebration we encounter at the end of the text and the reason that God's children need traveling shoes.

CONTRAST AND CONCLUSION

In 1970, when Angelou and Toni Morrison produced their first books, they were concerned with what it meant to be black and female in America. By 1986, they had enlarged their concerns to ask what it meant to be a black person in America, given the social, political, and economic constraints which mitigate against such development. Morrison's *Tar Baby* suggests that the black presence in America functions to prick America's unconscious (a 1981 "Benito Cereno" updated) and, like Maya Angelou, really begins to attack the ideological structures that keep these inhuman relations in place. The relationship that takes place between Jadine and Son in the novel moves toward a recovery of the equilibrium between the Afro-American male and female that seem to be scuttled in most of the works of the 1970s and early eighties.

There is a clarity, truth, and beauty that inform the autobiographical statement of Angelou and the particularity of her experiences that are collapsed back into the general experiences of her people. Her search for roots, her involvement with the politics of her people in the United States and Africa, give her work a depth that is absent in many other such works. For Angelou, as for Morrison, the pain and suffering of black women flow like tributaries into the rivers of their general pain, with the poignant demand that the black male be cognizant of their special pains. Theirs is a pain that possesses its own particularities, a point that Brent made as early as 1861. It is well that we listen and learn.

NOTES

1. Terry Eagleton, in *Marxism and Literary Criticism* (Berkeley: University of California Press, 1976), notes that it is only in literature that certain ideas, values, and feelings are made available to us. See p. viii.

2. Linda Brent, *Incidents in the Life of a Slave Girl* (New York: Harcourt Brace Jovanovich, 1973), 79. In this essay, I contextualize the autobiographical statement of Maya Angelou with that of Linda Brent because her work represents one of the earliest statements of the Afro-American woman.

3. Angela Davis, *Women, Race and Class* (New York: Random House, 1981), 11.

4. See Davis, *Women, Race and Class* for a discussion of the black woman's dual role in slavery and the rise of the early women's movement and Theodore Weld, *American Slavery as It Is: Testimony of a Thousand Witnesses* (New York: Arno Press, 1968), for slaveholders' testimonies about the brutalities that were practiced against the slaves, particularly black women.

5. See Julian Mason, ed., *The Poems of Phillis Wheatley* (Chapel Hill: The University of North Carolina Press, 1966) and Paul Edwards and James Walvin, *Black Personalities in the Era of the Slave Trade* (London: Macmillian, 1983).

6. *Monthly Review,* 80 (June 1789), 551.

7. See Michael Ryan, "Self-Evidence," *Diacritics,* 10, No. 2 (Summer 1980), 6.

8. See Janet Gunn, *Autobiography: Toward a Poetics of Experience* (Philadelphia: University of Pennsylvania Press, 1982) for a discussion of the distinction between the autobiography as a cultural act of self-reading as opposed to the private act of self-writing.

9. *Ibid.,* xi.

10. Quoted in Eugene Levy, *James Weldon Johnson: Black Leader, Black Voice* (Chicago: University of Chicago Press, 1973), 126, 128. Levy discusses the fictional and autobiographical aspects of this text. See pp. 128–142.

11. *Ibid.,* 126.

12. Jessie Fauset, "What to Read," *Crisis,* 5, No. 1 (November 1912), 38. [Emphasis mine.]

13. Levy, *James Weldon Johnson,* 128.

14. Ryan, "Self-Evidence," 6.

15. Quoted in John Langston Gwaltney, *Drylonso: A Self-Portrait of Black America* (New York: Random House, 1980), 6.

16. Maya Angelou, *I Know Why the Caged Bird Sings* (New York: Random House, 1970), 91. Hereafter referred to as CB.

17. Gwaltney, *Drylonso,* 8.

18. Maya Angelou, *Gather Together in My Name* (New York: Random House, 1974), 34–35. Hereafter referred to as GT. See also Dudley Clendinen, "Brothers' Rift on Homosexuality Reflects a Division in Atlanta," *New York Times,* 12 October 1986, p. 12.

19. See in particular the response of black men to the writings of Alice Walker's *The Color Purple* (New York: Harcourt Brace Jovanovich, 1982), Ntozake Shange's *For colored girls who have considered suicide, when the rainbow is enuf* (New York: Bantam, 1980), and Michele Wallace's, *Black Macho: The Myth of the Superwoman* (New York: Dial, 1979). See also Mel Watkins, "Sexism, Racism and Black Women Writers," *New York Times Book Review,* 15 June 1986, pp. 1, 35–37, in which he advances a corrective vision to what he considers the excesses of black women writers.

20. Olaudah Equiano, *The Interesting Life of Olaudah Equiano or Gustavus Vassa, the African* (Leeds, England: printed for James Nichols; London: Cracock and Joy and W.H. Blackburn, 1814), iii–iv.

21. See Selwyn R. Cudjoe, "Criticism and the Neo-African Writer," *Black World,* 21, No. 2 (December 1971), 36–48.

22. Janheinz Jahn, Majorie Grene, trans. *Muntu: An Outline of New African Culture,* (New York: Grove Press, 1961), 132. See also John S. Mbiti, *African Religions and Philosophy* (New York: Praeger, 1961) for a discussion of the limitations of Jahn's ideas and a much more extensive discussion of African religions and philosophy.

23. Jahn, *Muntu*, 133.

24. See, for example, the conjure tales in Charles Chesnutt, *The Conjure Tales* (Ann Arbor: University of Michigan, 1969) and Stanley Elkins, *Slavery* (Chicago: University of Chicago Press, 1959) for a discussion of the Sambo stereotype.

25. See *Harvard Educational Review*, 50, No. 3 (August 1980).

26. Jeanne Nobles, *Beautiful, Also, Are the Souls of My Black Sisters* (Englewood Cliffs, New Jersey: Prentice-Hall, 1978) 188.

27. Mary Helen Washington, ed., *Midnight Birds* (New York: Anchor, 1980), xv.

28. See, for example, Zora Neale Hurston, *Dust Tracks on a Road: An Autobiography* (Philadelphia: J.P. Lippincott, 1942); Ann Petry, *The Street* (Boston: Houghton Mifflin, 1946); and Gwendolyn Brooks, *Maud Martha* (New York: Harper & Row, 1953).

29. See Chester Himes, *The Quality of Hurt* (New York: Doubleday, 1972), 201, and Mel Watkins, "Hard Times for Black Writers," *New York Times Book Review*, 22 February 1981.

30. See Watkins, "Sexism, Racism and Black Women Writers," 36.

31. See, for example, Claude Brown, *Manchild in the Promised Land* (New York: Macmillan, 1965) for a sense of the tremendous deterioration that was taking place in black urban communities. See also my comments on *Black Macho and the Myth of the Superwoman* in "What I Teach and Why."

32. Thomas Hardy, *The Mayor of Casterbridge* (London: Macmillan, 1931), 406.

33. This fight also possessed racial significance for white Americans, occurring as it did while tensions were brewing between Italy and Ethiopia. See Margery Miller, *Joe Louis: American* (New York: Current Books, A. A. Wyn, 1945), 45–46, for a discussion of this aspect of the fight.

34. When we arrive at Maya Angelou, *Singin' and Swingin' and Gettin' Merry Like Christmas* (New York: Random House, 1976) Angelou's response to this incident has changed. She notes that it was laid "over and over in my mind with forgiveness and a conscious affection of innocence" (10–11). It is obvious that with time, the perception of the subject has changed, which demonstrates that the autobiographical statement indicates one's attitudes toward the facts, rather than an objective presentation of those facts. The latter ought not to be perceived as given, final, and unalterable. Critics should pay more attention to those "attitudes toward the facts."

35. The works of Toni Morrison, for example, take this same line of development.

36. Maya Angelou, *The Heart of a Woman* (New York: Random House, 1986), 56. Hereafter referred to as HOW.

37. Maya Angelou, *All God's Children Need Traveling Shoes* (New York: Random House, 1986), 20. Hereafter referred to as AGC.

Lorraine Hansberry:

Uncommon Warrior

Jewelle L. Gomez

"I was born on the South Side of Chicago. I was born black and female. I was born in a depression after one world war, and came into my adolescence during another. While I was still in my teens the first atom bombs were dropped on human beings at Nagasaki and Hiroshima. And by the time I was twenty-three years old, my government and that of the Soviet Union had entered actively into the worst conflict of nerves in human history—the Cold War . . . I have, like all of you, on a thousand occasions seen indescribable displays of man's very real inhumanity to man, and I have come to maturity, as we all must, knowing that greed and malice and indifference to human misery and bigotry and corruption, brutality, and perhaps above all else, ignorance— the prime ancient and persistent enemy of man— abound in this world.

"I say all of this to say that one cannot live with sighted eyes and feeling heart and not know and react to the miseries which afflict this world."[1]

These words, from a speech Lorraine Hansberry made to a Black writers conference in New York City in 1959, could easily have been those of friends, others I know and work with or even my own. What is most familiar is the sense of disbelief at what we, as humanity, will do to each other, in the name of that same humanity.

These words provide a welcome opportunity to rediscover the depth and breadth of Hansberry's social and political concerns and to see how they are manifest in her work. I say rediscover because today one only need say *Raisin* and the world of her play, *A Raisin in the Sun*, springs fully realized to our minds. It is now easily recalled that she was the first black woman playwright to be produced on Broadway and the youngest ever to win the New York Critics Circle Award. These are statistical triumphs. But in 1959, we more clearly saw the political ramifications of every public black accomplishment. Today Hansberry has entered our consciousness and in some ways that casual acceptance of her success diminishes the social impact of those achievements and their lasting influence on our lives today.

I say rediscover because she was proud of being "young, gifted and Black" at a time when Black women were stereotyped as merely long-suffering matriarchs with sharp tongues. Hansberry's redefinition of black women as active and responsible participants in our political future was surprising in 1959 and remains so to some as we enter the 1990s. It is her pride and the scope of her vision that is the key to her uncommon consciousness. She was truly capable of being a warrior in what Barbara Smith has termed "the most expansive of revolutions."[2] This revolution resists the idea that "one for all and all for me" is a workable attitude. This revolution can no longer focus solely on the wrongs of the past as experienced by one group. That leaves too much room for us to solve our problems and then perpetuate misdeeds against some other group.

As a warrior in this expansive revolution, Hansberry realized that all acts of violence were connected and she did not feel so insecure that the freedom of others frightened her. In fact, she understood that our personal will, our fears, our joys would often be in conflict with our social and political concerns. She was prepared to explore her own insecurities and prejudices in order to confront the larger issues; to confront that system of thinking that had held Black people in subjugation long after slavery was abolished. In rediscovering this warrior waging this expansive revolution I reclaim her as my own. Like all of us, she was more than a snapshot or a bibliography. The legacy she left is that of not only a Black writer but also a political activist and a Black woman. I need her desperately and so should we all.

In the early 1900s actor-singer-minstrel Bert Williams made famous a song entitled "Nobody." It's clear that although the white theater establishment considered that word descriptive of Blacks, Bert Williams did not. He said, "It is no disgrace to be a Negro, but it is very inconvenient."[3] From the nineteenth-century melodramas and minstrel shows to the 1920s musicals like *Shuffle Along*, Black shows were constructed around one premise: Blacks are harmless, not always happy, but definitely as American as pizza pie. While theaters like the Lafayette lit up Harlem with Black stars such as Florence Mills and Charles Gilpin, white audiences were still intrigued by Ethyl Barrymore in blackface and O'Neill's rendition of the Black experience in *The Emperor Jones*.

Many musicals that originated in Harlem were moved downtown to the big time, making the Depression era one of the largest periods of employment of Black artists on Broadway. The country wanted singing and dancing even when it couldn't afford food! World War II put even greater emphasis on musicals and melodramas, for whites as well as Blacks.

Although the nicest thing that is usually said about the 1950s is that nothing happened, that, in fact, was not true. At the beginning of that decade the most well-known Black dramatic character was still the "mammy" figure embodied by Ethyl Waters in *A Member of the Wedding*, which opened on Broadway in 1950. Langston Hughes was adapting his tales of Semple for the stage; veteran Black actor Canada Lee had just died and his pal, Sidney Poitier, was running a rib joint on 7th Avenue and 131st Street.

Outside the theater, in the daylight, things were not much brighter, but things were happening. Segregation in public schools was being challenged in the courts; citizens were being hauled before the House Un-American Activities Committee (HUAC) and forced to betray their principles and their friends; Japanese-Americans were trying to rebuild their lives after being released from American concentration camps in the Midwest and, as Hansberry noted, the cold war was casting a chilly pall over everything.

It was into this broad arena of change that Lorraine Hansberry stepped. She arrived as an outsider, removed from, but certainly not unaware of, the helter-skelter of Harlem. The great thinkers of her day had been frequent visitors to her childhood home. Her family had lived through the integration of a white neighborhood and her father invested a good bit of his time and professional expertise winning them the right to live anywhere in Chicago that they chose.

Though an outsider, as a writer Hansberry was truly a descendant of the New York writers who came before her. She'd steeped herself in drama from the age of fourteen. She saw as much kinship with the Irish playwrights as with Langston Hughes. She understood the real element of truth in the tired axiom that "people are just people." She saw that in order for a great work to be truly universal it had to be painfully specific. The truth of Black lives had to be explored, not recast into imitations of white life, before Black theater would take its place in world drama. The beginning of the 1950s saw the revival of the 1921 musical hit, *Shuffle Along*, but the end of the decade saw questioning of this simplistic acceptance of Black characters who existed only in relationship to the white world.

> What happens to a dream deferred?
> Does it dry up
> like a raisin in the sun?
> Or fester like a sore—
> And then run?
> Does it stink like rotten meat?
> Or crust and sugar over—
> like a syrupy sweet?
> Maybe it just sags
> like a heavy load.
> Or does it explode?[4]

These questions posed by Langston Hughes were the same ones that Lorraine Hansberry began to address when her play, "A Raisin in the Sun," opened at the Barrymore Theatre in 1959. She wanted to explore the specifics of Black life; the ideas and urges that fueled our lives politically and personally. She began in a small room, examining it in detail, looking for the universal truth of dignity:

The Younger living room would be a comfortable and well ordered room if it were not for a number of indestructible contradictions to this state of being. Its furnishings are typical and undistinguished and their primary feature now is that they have clearly had to accommodate the living of too many people for too many years and they are tired . . . Weariness has, in fact, won in this room. Everything has been polished, washed, sat on, used, scrubbed too often. All pretenses but living itself have long since vanished from the very atmosphere of this room.[5]

She began in a small room with the simple story of a poor family trying to move into a better neighborhood. The family, much like her own in spirit, became a symbol of our aspirations. But as a writer, Hansberry's work is even bigger than that. She arrived at a pivotal point in the development of Black drama and Black thinking. She believed, as many were just beginning to, in probing the specifics of her characters by peeling back the generalities, whether those generalities were culture, ethnicity, gender or language. She was convinced that beneath any combination of these elements was a distinct human being who, given a voice, would make a valid statement about humankind.

Raisin opened up the questions of the validity of middle-class aspirations; the right of women to control their own bodies and their intellectual independence; the inherent conservatism of the underclasses; the myth of the Black matriarch; the connection between Africans and Afro-Americans; some of which were issues not being raised by Blacks in public. In the 1960s some implied Hansberry's inadequacy as a spokesperson for the Black revolution by saying she was too middle class, mistakenly assuming that socioeconomic status and personality are as immutable as race. It ignored the fact that many major social revolutionaries have risen from the middle classes: Gandhi, Marx, Ho Chi Minh, Nkrumah, Castro, King.

Hansberry was able to create substantial characters who lived and *grew*. The Younger family symbolized the opposing systems of thought that continue to tear this country apart, each character individually, and the family as a whole. It was not just a matter of house versus liquor store; Mama's dream versus Walter Lee's dream. The contest was also between the individual and the collective good. This was not a play simply about upward mobility or integration.

Many critics have neglected the full ramifications of Hansberry's life as a cultural worker. Her plays, the product of a young and diligent mind, work dramaturgically within the context of the drama of her day. When she arrived, American theater had fallen, head first, into the pit of naturalism, reducing plays from poetry to newspaper clippings. She was working in one medium (playwriting) which was taking its shape from another (fiction writing) and it was doing so poorly. Drama left the realm of wonder where it had begun: the church and the ritual that was its birthplace. It moved into an undefined arena where its artists were filled with self-consciousness about their craft. They sought legitimacy in staid presentations of "reality" rather than continuing the tradition of the transportation of the heart and soul.

Hansberry took that naturalistic style and deliberately infused it with an array of ideas, which other writers were consciously not doing. Beyond the message that Black is normal and good, there was no other dimension to the political and social concepts of Black drama. Hansberry was an intensely political person.

Once proclaimed the reigning queen of Black drama, Hansberry did not let up. In her next play, "The Sign in Sidney Brustein's Window," she had the audacity to make the central characters white! The play's production met scorn from both white and Black critics. This in spite of the fact that white people had been describing and defining Black people for centuries, not only on paper but in real life. The play also included a gay male character, but people were not interested in talking about him at all, much less demanding Hansberry's qualifications to describe him.

Lorraine Hansberry had many stories to tell. She did not feel the need to justify any one of them. She had strong concerns for many issues affecting this society and did not cower in the shadow of political repression that loomed over the 1950s. In 1957, Hansberry flew to a peace congress in Uruguay to deliver a speech in place of Paul Robeson, whose passport had been revoked. When she returned, the United States government revoked her passport.

In 1957, when the leader of the first gay male organization, The Mattachine Society, had already been called before the HUAC along with a number of "suspected" homosexuals, Hansberry still espoused human rights. At the same time she wrote a letter to *The Ladder*, the first journal published for lesbians in this country. She said: "It is time that 'half the human race' had something to say about the nature of its existence . . . In this kind of work there may be women to emerge who will be able to formulate a new and possible concept that homosexual persecution and condemnation has at its roots not only social ignorance but a philosophically active anti-feminist dogma."[6]

Anticipating the modern feminist movement, she wrote in 1957: "Woman, like the Negro, like the Jew, like colonial peoples, even in ignorance, is incapable of accepting the role with harmony. This is because it is an unnatural role. The station of woman is hardly one that she would assume by choice, any more than men would. It must necessarily be imposed on her by force . . . A status not freely chosen or entered into by an individual or group is necessarily one of oppression and the oppressed are by their nature . . . forever in ferment and agitation against their condition and what they understand to be their oppressors. If not by overt rebellion or revolution, then in the thousand and one ways they will devise with and without consciousness to alter their condition."[7]

Because Hansberry has been regarded only within the light of Black (mostly male) dramatists her larger context as a woman has been ignored. Discussion of *Raisin* is most often centered around Walter Lee and his frustrations or his conflict with his mother. The character frequently overlooked is Beneatha, Walter Lee's sister and the most autobiographical of Hansberry's characters. Early in *A Raisin in the Sun* Beneatha has this exchange with the African who is pushing her to marry him:

Beneatha: You never understood that there is more than one kind of feeling which can exist between a man and a woman—or, at least, there should be.
Asagai (Shaking his head negatively but gently): No. Between a man and a woman there need be only one kind of feeling. I have that for you . . .
Beneatha: I know—and by itself—it won't do. I can find that anywhere.
Asagai: For a woman it should be enough.
Beneatha: I know—because that's what it says in all the novels that men write. But it isn't.[8]

These words were not put in the mouth of Walter Lee's sister merely to show her as rebellious and troublesome. These were the political beliefs of Lorraine Hansberry. In some unpublished notes she examines the idea that "feminine" traits, such as love, compassion, and understanding are reserved for only woman's personality. She wrote: "This is the supreme insult against men. Is it only woman who truly possesses the most magnificent features of the human race—I a woman think not—and it is time men decided it is the great slander of the ages—to take our hands—truly—as comrades."[9]

As clearly as she understood the nature of relationships between women and men, she saw the relationships between nations. She foresaw that the betrayal of the Cuban Revolution would come from the U.S. Government, not from Fidel Castro, and said so in the *New York Times*.[10] She understood that colonialism was breaking the backs of people of color, not unlike herself, and said so in her play *Les Blancs*. She understood Zora Neale Hurston's comment that Black women are the mules of the world and she refused to be one and said so every opportunity she had.

Because we have not studied Hansberry as a cultural worker and thinker but only as a dramatist, we have lost touch with the urgency of her political message and the poetry of her writing, in particular her prose. In an essay for Broadway's *Playbill* magazine, she wrote:

> I remember being startled when I first saw my grandmother rocking away on her porch. All my life I had heard that she was a great beauty and no one had ever remarked that they meant a half century before. The woman I met was as wrinkled as a prune and could hardly hear and barely see and always seemed to be thinking of other times. But she could still rock and talk and even made wonderful cupcakes which were like cornbread only sweet. She died the next summer and that is all that I remember about her, except that she was born in slavery and had memories of it and they didn't sound anything like *Gone With the Wind*.[11]

Just as her grandmother's memories were able to shed light on the past and reshape her thinking about the Black reality,

Hansberry is able to look again at our lives as women and shine a light on them so we remember what it was really supposed to be about.

Hansberry's unfinished novel, *All the Dark and Beautiful Warriors*,[12] has not been published but it was excerpted in the *Village Voice*. The depth of her perception about women and men, their roles in society (Black and white), and the love with which she communicates this understanding are undeniable. The issues of class, sexism, and racism are addressed more adroitly in a few paragraphs of this unfinished work than in a good number of the volumes produced by the protests of the 1960s Black Nationalist movement.

There are several aspects to the tragedy of the loss of Lorraine Hansberry. She was not only a young woman, thirty-four years old, but a young writer. Her talent, her style, her ideas were being shaped by her just-beginning uncommon political consciousness. She was a young warrior in this "most expansive of revolutions." Yet she acknowledged that there is a unified system of thought that allows little Black girls to be blown to bits in Birmingham; that allows the flesh of Jews to be turned into lampshades; that allows generations of an indigenous people to be decimated in a place that is called the land of the free. It is a unified system of thinking that demands that women who have been raped justify their anger; that allows a man to do less time in prison than if he'd robbed a bank, although he's killed a public official. This system of thought decrees that this travesty is justice if the victim happens to be Jewish or gay.

Hansberry had considered all of these political issues and taken a solid position that their resolutions were interdependent. She would have been invaluable in the great divisive debate about whether or not Black women need feminism. In *Ebony* magazine in 1963 she wrote:

It is indeed a single march, a unified destiny and the prize is the future. In the ascent we shall want and need to lose some of the features of our collective personality for which we are justly ill-famed; but it is also to be hoped that we shall cling just as desperately to certain others for which we are not less harshly criticized. For above all, in behalf of an ailing world which sorely needs our defi-

ance, may we as Negroes or women never accept the
notion of—"our place."[13]

As a Black woman, a writer, and a lesbian-feminist, I need
Lorraine Hansberry so that her brilliant vision lights my path.
For by leaving us her notebooks and fragments of work, she
has created an invaluable wealth of energy and resources for
me as I search for the tradition of Black women writers and
thinkers into which I properly fit.

Etched on the marble stone of her grave are these words
from her play, *The Sign in Sidney Brustein's Window:* "I care. I
care about it all. It takes too much energy not to care . . . The
why of why we are here is an intrigue for adolescents; the how
is what must command the living. Which is why I have lately
become an insurgent again."[14]

She has lately become an insurgent again, inside of me. I
felt her moving me to action as I prepared this work. But she
predicted that, too. She knew that people/women would study
the specifics of her life and find the universal truths we needed
and that we would claim her. During her last days she dictated her feelings and ideas into a tape recorder. At the end
she said: "If anything should happen—before 'tis done—may
I trust that all commas and periods will be placed and someone will complete my thoughts—This last should be the least
difficult—since there are so many who think as I do."[15]

She was right, again.

NOTES

1. From a speech delivered at a Black writers' conference in 1959. Cited in *To Be
Young, Gifted, and Black,* adapted by Robert Nemiroff. (New York: New American
Library, 1969), 41.
2. Barbara Smith, "Toward a Black Feminist Criticism," *Conditions: Two* (October 1977)
42–47.
3. Loften Mitchell, *Black Drama* (New York: Hawthorne Books, 1967), 49.
4. Langston Hughes, "Montage of a Dream Deferred," in *Selected Poems/Langston
Hughes* (New York: Vintage Books, 1974), 268.
5. Lorraine Hansberry, *A Raisin in the Sun* (New York: New American Library of
World Literature, 1959), 11–12.
6. See Jonathan Katz, *Gay American History* (New York: Thomas Y. Crowell, 1976),
425.
7. See Adrienne Rich, "The Problem with Lorraine Hansberry," *Freedomways,* Vol. 19,
Number 4 (1979), 253.
8. Hansberry, *op. cit.,* 50.
9. Lorraine Hansberry's unpublished, untitled notes, New York City, November 16,

1955. As quoted in Margaret Wilkerson, "Lorraine Hansberry: The Complete Feminist," *Freedomways*, Vol. 19 (Number 4, 1979), 244.

10. Lorraine Hansberry, "Village Intellect Revealed," *New York Times*, 31 October 1964, section 2, 3.

11. Lorraine Hansberry, "On Summer," *Playbill* (June 27, 1960), 27.

12. Lorraine Hansberry, *All the Dark and Beautiful Warriors*, unpublished. Excerpted in the *Village Voice*, 16 August 1983, with introduction by Thulani Davis.

13. Lorraine Hansberry, "This Complex of Womanhood," *Ebony* (September 1963).

14. Lorraine Hansberry, *The Sign in Sidney Brustein's Window*, quoted in the preface to Anne Cheney, *Lorraine Hansberry* (Boston: Twayne Publishers, 1984).

15. *To Be Young, Gifted, and Black*, adapted by Robert Nemiroff (New York: New American Library, 1969), 265.

Our Lady:

Sonia Sanchez and the Writing of a Black Renaissance

Houston A. Baker, Jr.

for our lady
yeh.
billie.   if someone
had loved u like u
shud have been loved
ain't no tellen what
kinds of songs
     u would have swung
gainst this country's wite mind.
or what kinds of lyrics
          wud have pushed us from
our blue/nites.
          yeh.   billie.
if some blk/man
     had reallee
made u feel
     permanentlee warm.
ain't no tellen
     where the jazz of yo/songs
          wud have led us.

(from WE A BaddDD People)

I think it is very difficult when you talk about the Harlem Renaissance. I think it is a misnomer. Because I think the cords were still there—the connections to the white establishment—that made it impossible to have a clean birth.[1]

Models of literature, like models of literary criticism, are never products of pure creative or intellectual construction. There is always an element of the serendipitous involved in their emergence as illustrative or guiding paradigms. It is as though evidence and other preconditions gather out of sight, awaiting the arrival of the fortuitous moment that welds artist and form, critic and stunning example. On June 5, 1985, such a moment occurred at (of all unlikely places) the Horticultural Society of Philadelphia, when a group of generous and dedicated people honored the Afro-American writer Sonia Sanchez.

Ms. Sanchez has been a figure on the Afro-American expressive scene since the late 1960s, and her accomplishments were crowned in 1985 by receipt of an American Book Award from the Before Columbus Foundation of Berkeley, California for her volume of poetry entitled *Homegirls and Handgrenades*. The evening of June 5 was meant to mark the occasion of her award and was entitled "A Salute to Sonia Sanchez." In attendance were representatives of city and state governments; the executive director of the Philadelphia Mayor's Commission for Women; the president of Temple University (Ms. Sanchez's home institution); the director of PASCEP (a program for prison inmates); student representatives from Temple and from the Philadelphia Afro-American Historical and Cultural Museum, where Ms. Sanchez had recently conducted a poetry workshop and seminar; and "special presenters" from (among other places) Nigeria.

As tributes unfolded and plaques and citations were displayed, the model of a communal, authentic, and resoundingly liberating Black Expression was suddenly and resplendently at hand. If one thinks back to the 1920s and attempts to envision an evening like the salute to Sonia Sanchez, what comes immediately to mind are the magnificently orchestrated "Opportunity" dinners hosted by Charles Johnson.[2] But at the first such dinner attended by black Harlem Renaissance youth and proper white publishers, artists, and civic dignitaries, it would have been scandalous if a representative from that great space of Afro-American confinement—the American prison system—had stood to praise, say, Countee Cullen. Further, it is hard to envision a strong feminist constituency championing the work of anyone present at an Opportunity dinner or to think of state and local governments viewing

Afro-American writers as valued public resources. And a desperate act of fantasy is required to think of representatives of the Afro-American masses (whether people like Ms. Sanchez's students or a wider body implicit in the spectrum from black students to prison inmates to Nigerian artists considered as metonymic of global masses) acknowledging the liberating effects in their everyday lives of the work of Harlem Renaissance creators. But if the Sonia Sanchez salute was an anomaly by Harlem Renaissance standards, it was an anomaly that reveals itself as the very model latent in the general problematic of a black cultural/expressive "renaissance."

The creative and critical project of a black renaissance might more accurately be labeled the lasting Afro-American quest for revaluation. For, although various moments of transition in the African's New World existence in the United States have been marked by the sign "New Negro" or other such designations (from "Freedman" to "Buppy"), such moments have rarely been instances of radical and massive transformation.[3] The general rhythms and collective advantages of the black masses have remained constant. At the apex of the short and broad-based triangle that represents Afro-American social structure, a fraction of men and women moved during such instances into nontraditional (read: traditionally white) jobs and postures. But at the base, the blues remained representative of Afro-America's impoverishment by an economics of slavery.[4]

But if no essentially different black person has assumed mass representation at moments of transition, an altered sensibility has often permeated the masses, producing an altered axiology, or at least a rather generally held belief that an occasion for revaluation is at hand. What has varied in Afro-American transitional moments have been the suggested objects and criteria for evaluation. In the 1920s, for example, Alain Locke and others called for a revaluation of the "Negro" based on his artistic endowments and the expressive products of his culture. Since blacks were excluded by law and custom from virtually every form of responsible participation in the country's life (as David Lewis has so eloquently documented) Locke, Charles Johnson, James Weldon Johnson, and others who gave currency to the notion of an artistic renaissance in 1920s Harlem seized upon the creative/artistic domain as a region for a meeting of white judges and black contestants.

The idea was that Afro-Americans of the articulate, talented, college-bred variety (the Talented Tenth) would bring before evaluating white eyes the finest products (sometimes referred to as "gifts") of *The Negro*. Recognizing "how beautiful" these attainments were, whites would call blacks "out of the kitchen."[5] This summons from the sculleries would mark the beginning of a new, scientific, interracial collaboration leading to greater understanding and, presumably, basic civil rights.[6]

Of course Harlem Renaissance collaborators claimed that their program was a function of radical alterations in Afro-American personality. Empirically, there *were* more college-educated Afro-Americans than ever before. *Practically*, there was also poverty, repression, and despair *in extremis* in Afro-American life. Essentially, the southern agrarian black poor had shifted locale and become the northern urban black poor. If the city brother seemed, by all counts, slicker and less prone to tolerate the white man's nonsense, he was also, in many ways, infinitely more vulnerable in an urban world of family disintegration, unskilled wage labor, welfare economics, and bureaucratic indifference. If the country blues singer could always think of Hopping John and a few pounds of neckbone "on down the road," his corner-singing urban brother was more likely to bellow: "My shoes done got thin / I'm back on my feet again."

Locke and his talented cohort accurately noted a population shift, but they were overly sanguine about the *birth* of a fundamentally different man and the possibilities of a rebirth of wonder leading to Afro-American parity. A number of white publishers, writers, and critics were willing to try their hand at Negro matters. And in this respect, there was a "revaluation," a sudden and unpredictable hugging of black subjects to the American bosom. Carl Van Vechten, Vachel Lindsay, Witter Bynner, Eugene O'Neill, and Sherwood Anderson come to mind. The ironic characteristic of Talented Tenth propaganda and proselytizing, however, is its indisputably bourgeois cast.

All around the prime movers of the renaissance and burning in their ears—cooking and smoking—were the phonics of the blues. Hundreds of thousands of copies of new releases were selling each month, altering forever the generative conditions of American music. But scarcely one of the New Negroes checked out a bit of it. From Mamie Smith's recording of "Crazy Blues" for Okeh in 1920 until the end of the decade, the sound of American popular culture was the sound of blues.[7]

If Locke and others had observed the right places—blues clubs and resonant interstices of stated meaning and catchy phrases of blues songs themselves—the habitable spaces, as it were, of poetic blues images—they might well have begun to draw the outlines of a "new" Negro. No, it would be more exact here to say: They might well have found liberating material with which to begin the invention of a revolutionary black expressive project.

But while Locke's cohort had useful instincts and proclivities where "The folk" were concerned, they also had an insufferably overdetermined classicism with which to contend. Everything—education, saturation in Western culture, ideological orientation toward integration, white friendships and patronage—conspired to keep them on an elevated plane. Rather than getting down with the folk, they valorized the *folk* from academic studies and editorial offices, only suggesting black national possibilities—rarely *sounding* them. Finally, then, even the revaluation under their aegis was blind in one eye.

They evaluated a handful of books when there was a veritable quilt of invigorating sound wrapping America. The opportunity was present to begin demolition of a traditionally exclusive definition of *art* in the United States by opening up the axiological field surrounding American expression. Locke seemed to have a notion of such possibilities when he edited his monumental collection, *The New Negro* (1925). The work is a masterpiece of mutually supporting expressive forms, combining black-and-white and color graphics, African design motifs as floating signifiers, critical and creative prose, and drama, poetry, and analytical essays. And while there are no blues, there are repeated tributes to the spirituals. Locke himself wrote the centerpiece essay on the songs and included words and scores of spirituals at the very midpoint of his text. But *The New Negro* was a high point of Talented Tenth output, not the norm.

At the time of production, Locke's work was considered a compendium of middle-class sentiment meant to demonstrate that Negroes were ready, capable, and endowed to exist outside the kitchen. Its connection with a blues sensibility was certainly clouded by statements in the work, such as, "The multitude perhaps feels as yet only a strange relief and a new vague urge," or, "The articulate few" will carry a 'folk-gift' to the altitudes of "art." In truth, though, even if such statements had been absent, Locke's work and that of his cohort (with the magnificent exception of Langston Hughes) would never have been placed in a blues camp—by themselves, or by sympathetically revaluating whites.

The suggestion that a bourgeois orientation prevented the emergence of a "new" Negro is scarcely startling. The atmospheric conditions of the twenties are, in fact, constants of American race relations today. Freemen of color in the United States have seldom assumed their freedom as a birthright; they have always "felt compelled" (to appropriate a James Baldwin formula) to battle for their legitimacy according to brutal criteria bequeathed by the land of their birth.[8] Middle-class respectability, taste, and accomplishment have been the certified and adopted means of proving one has a right to be free. The irony of this bourgeois orientation, of course, is that it demands a loss of contact with both black metaphysical and corporeal moorings—thus leaving the *black* body and soul, awash in a flood of white behaviors. And what is lauded (or simply adjudged acceptable "black" accomplishment by white overseers) has little, finally, to do with the authentic state of Afro-American soul, or a blues body.

At the post–Civil War dawn of black freedom in America, the only lines of development that seemed available, according to W.E.B. Du Bois's brilliant analysis, were traditionally accepted and generally American ones of book learning and electoral politics. Obviously, no unique cultural figure signalled by the phrase the *New Negro*, could result from such strategies—contingent as they were upon white teachers, models, and candidates. As early as 1903, when *The Souls of Black Folk* was published, DuBois called Reconstruction and post–Reconstruction black ideals "the bright ideals of the past."[9] He went on to call for a new unique synthesis that would open up possibilities for a liberated Black America to bring forth stirring sounds and, ultimately, New World redemption.

By the twenties, however it was clear to everyone that America (a land of lynch law, restrictive covenants, and Jim

Crow) meant to deny blacks even the rudiments of education and politics. It was also clear that the country at large intended to keep Afro-America under terroristic threats of annihilation. (The "red summer" of 1919, for example, witnessed hundreds of lynchings and beatings.) While there were certainly non–middle-class efforts in the twenties, such as Garvey's *UNIA* and Chandler Owen's and A. Philip Randolph's socialism and labor organizing, the predominant cast of the decade was essentially like all decades before. It featured Negro "leaders" summoning middle-class norms and valorizing black products and behaviors that conformed to such norms.

Now the project of a *Black Renaissance*, when it is set against the backdrop just sketched, would seem virtually to have been accomplished during the recent decades of the 1960s and 1970s. For during these years, Afro-American spokespersons seemed to turn decisively away from a bourgeois orientation, condemning all white American "respectability" and shading off (toward the close of the "high nationalist" period) into revolutionary Marxist–Leninist–Mao-Tse-Tung–Lumpen–Proletarian socialism. Furthermore, in the *Black Arts, Black Aesthetic, Cultural Nationalist,* and *Revolutionary Nationalist* years, notions of selfhood seemed to shift dramatically. The black masses whom we saw walking arm-in-arm down southern streets toward courthouses to secure justice, or the blacks whom we saw occupying northern, urban corners clad in black berets and leather jackets appeared to be entirely new phenomena in our national history. The conversions brought about by the civil rights and black power movements seemed undeniably beneficial. And a genuinely "New Negro" seemed at hand.

Of course, the dismal tale of the demise of black nationalism and leftist political activism in the United States has been rehearsed too often to bear repeating here. But it is certainly worthwhile to note that black nationalist strategies—while they seemed to represent a decisive move beyond middle-class categories and constraints—were simply strident and vociferous manifestations of repression's subtle entrapment. For black nationalism during the 1960s and 1970s—as a function of the uncharacteristic openings allowed to blacks during these years—often fought battles in ways that were bone of the bone and flesh of the flesh of them who despised and wrongfully used Afro-America. What emerged from the nationalist camp was what might be termed a hermeneutics of overthrow.

The object of this interpretive enterprise was to summon various revered texts—whether literature, film, popular culture, or political, economic, or religious works—of white America. A fierce reexamination, revaluation, and reinterpretation were then begun as first steps toward the reversal of oppression.

What was absent in the hermeneutical moment of the sixties and seventies, however, was a distinctive Afro-American critical and creative vocabulary predicated upon authentic *sounds* (say, blues sounds) of our national life. What we witnessed, therefore, was black nationalist political scientists, literary critics, theologians, and political activists submitting—time and again—analyses that read and resonated to the rhythms and tonalities of a white American groove. For example, rather than rejecting out of hand the entire discursive field surrounding a deeply class-invested word like "aesthetic," black literary critics and artists merely readopted this field, proclaiming themselves *black aestheticians*. Of course, one cannot minimize the limited gains—the brief speaking space—achieved by such interpretive procedures.[10]

While black displeasure and suffering are made unequivocally clear by spokespersons at the apex, a resounding national (blues) identity remains a submerged content. What emerged from the sixties and seventies, therefore, was (as in the twenties) a declaration of the necessity for a revaluation. This declaration and its accompanying hermeneutics—from the viewpoint of scholarly, critical, or creative endeavors—left a legacy of broadly descriptive articles and monographs, interesting (if often flat-footed) writings and productions labeled *black art*, vague organizational strategies for community empowerment, and an overwhelming sense of frustration.

Perhaps the finest legacy, however, is the image of Afro-American masses engaged in liberating activity and Afro-American spokespersons *compelled* to tune their energies and voices to accord with such activity. Though it seems accurate to point out the absence of a decisive critical vocabulary and sound drawn from the masses as the governing mode among those at the apex of the triangle during recent decades, it also seems correct to assert that Afro-American *class* and *mass* came together more efficaciously than at any time in our national past. Black "popular" forms, fashions, and inclinations simply could not be ignored. And such mass manifestations were championed and adopted with a kind of startled passion. The dashiki-clad black academic or artist at an interracial dinner party speaking of black community empowerment and punctuating his discourse with an occasional "right on" may capture, at least, part of the paradoxical image I want to suggest.

Here, of course, was no *new negro*, but only an earnest Afro-American seeking revaluation, and, perhaps, also questing some culturally authentic "black" form that would please white folks—or, at least, be accepted and adjudged by such folks as "worthy" of consideration.

If the broad canvas I have sketched seems uniformly bleak, it is only because I have omitted all colorful exceptions in a general outline of "black renaissancism." Moments of transition have never simply *found* black men and women as passive ciphers waiting to be moved. Such moments have always, in fact, been energetically *founded* by black men and women intent on liberation. To wit: The Emancipation Proclamation was as deeply a function of black rebellion, abolitionism, flight, agitation, and general intractability under an exploitative system (a system rendered doubly inefficient by black resistance) as of any set of productive causes that might be entered into an analysis. Further, the moment of transition marked by the proclamation found Frederick Douglass in attendance, carrying forward an authentically national black sound in the same manner that the turn-of-the-century *new South* found the powerful voices of Booker T. Washington and W.E.B. Du Bois forcing black *national* interests and resonances into American consciousness. From the twenties, vernacular rhythms of Langston Hughes and Sterling Brown argue strongly against a despairing condemnation of early decades as *exclusively* bourgeois. And from recent decades, there is Sonia Sanchez.

What constitutes the distinguishing feature of our *founding* exceptions is their allegiance to the genuine, mass, black, national sounds and interests of an African presence in the New World. (If Washington seems an anomaly here, one must ask how many black people shared his effective commitment during his era to millions of blacks inhabiting the "country districts" of the South.) *Renaissancism*—most effectively and politically defined—consists, I believe, in efforts by Afro-Americans to articulate strategies for advancing a national *sound* and a national *sounding* of New World experience.

Phonics (a dedicated consideration of *sound*) is at the very heart of the matter. Similarly, the *processual* quality of the endeavor signaled by the suffix on sound is *de rigueur*. Drawing together sound and sounding is the sign, *cultural performance*. *Renaissancism* is a sounding kinesthetics—a cultural performative impulse and endeavor engaged by black spokespersons who know that it is only by bringing through a national sound that they can hope to achieve both reverberant expressive forms for their era and an ever-renewed and renewing sense of a brilliantly resilient African identity in America.

"Soul," "Frenzy," "Funk," or simply "Spirit" are terms that describe the essence of renaissancism. These signs all presuppose a *community* of interests. Beginning at a mass level of generation, the liberating spirit/sounds join in harmony with cries in South African townships and Salvadoran villages.

I never believe that we are put on this earth without any connective threads. I don't believe that I write and say: "Oh, yes, it is all *my* work." I clap at the same time as my audience at readings because I realize that poetry is subconscious conversation. It is the *joint* work of those who write it and those who also respond to it and are pushed by it.

What is paramount for renaissancism is not material instantiation at any given moment, but the efficacy of passage. The colloquial sign of successful passage in today's vernacular might be the phrase that greets a particularly stylish delivery of sound: "I *heard* that," or simpler still: "Word."

The riddle for the critic who would deal with the *sound* of Sonia Sanchez—the renaissancism of *her* transmission and passage of the word through a community of sharers—is how did an Alabama black child who turned away from the world surrounding her and found introspective refuge and psychological defense in stuttering move in her maturing years to achieve her own resonant articulation? When asked how she ceased stuttering, Ms. Sanchez tells of an act of will in which she simply decided to cure herself. When asked how she moved from introspection and moderate Americanism to active, nationalist cadences, she points to a moment on a Sunday evening in the sixties when she put aside a resolution to avoid Malcolm X's speeches and refused to be bound by an agreement among fellow workers in New York CORE that Malcolm was a racist to be shunned at all costs.

> Malcolm sent the word out that you could not have any kind of demonstration in Harlem unless he was a part of it. And so I remember saying to some people in the [CORE] office: "God, this man, he's nothing but a racist anyway. What is he gonna do?" Everytime he'd come to speak at demonstrations we were having, we'd walk back over to the office and go in there until he was finished and then come back for our part. But one day, a rainy day . . . I listened to Malcolm as the rain was drizzling . . . And I stood there with the rain hitting me and I kept looking and I kept listening . . . The danger of Malcolm and probably of Farakann, is that they . . . pull middle class people toward them . . . Our poems were almost direct results of how [Malcolm] presented things . . . always that strong line at the end—the kick at the end that people would repeat, repeat, and repeat, always a finely tuned phrase or line that people could remember.

Malcolm's speech, with its penetrating logic and obvious commitment, converted Sanchez forever. The vision that she seized on a rainy New York afternoon comes powerfully home in a characterization found in elegiac stanzas that she wrote for the brilliant Muslim leader:

> he was the sun that tagged
> the western sky and
> melted tiger-scholars
> while they searched for stripes.
> he said, "fuck you white
> man. we have been
> curled too long. nothing
> is sacred now. not your
> white faces nor any
> land that separates
> until some voices
> squat with spasms."[11]

The poem "malcolm" which appears in Ms. Sanchez's first volume, entitled *Home Coming* (1969), offers a fitting point of entry for a discussion of her poetry. I shall confine my discussion to poetry and will concentrate largely on her first and latest volumes of work, moving from *Home Coming* to the more vigorously titled *Homegirls and Handgrenades*. "Malcolm" is not only a fine point of entry because its political orientation is so clearly nationalist; it is also of interest because it suggests dominant structural features of Ms. Sanchez's early— indeed one might say "apprentice"—work. One notes, for example, the commitment to both spoken voice and colloquial vocabulary. Further, one notes in the poem a very personal, almost confessional, voice. "Malcolm" begins as follows:

> do not speak to me of martyrdom
> of men who die to be remembered
> on some parish day.
> i don't believe in dying
> though i too shall die
> and violets like castanets
> will echo me (15–16).

Elegiac conventions linking elegist and subject are preserved, and the conjunction between a sympathetic nature and mortal "Man" is summoned in the traditional manner. But also implicit in the opening "do not speak to me" is the muscular sanguinity that marks that standing classic of elegiac openings: "Tell me not in mournful numbers." There is, in short, a defiant tone that resists simple mourning. This resistance, I think, shades into another major feature of *Home Coming*— didacticism. The poem is not simply an elegy, but also a work of personal observation and implicit instruction. We clearly see this black instructionalism in the concluding verse paragraph:

> do not speak to me of living.
> life is obscene with crowds
> of white on black.
> death is my pulse.
> what might have been
> is not for him/or me

but what could have been
floods the womb until i drown (16).

Judgment of the universe is conditioned by the act of Malcolm's assassination. The speaker engages a double meaning (revenge and entropy) in the line "death is my pulse." The last quatrain witnesses a full merger of elegist and subject, suggesting the enormous loss of potential that American violence dictates.

Hence, the last stanza is ambiguous because it implies both accompanying loss and a clear and directed desire for vengeance, a loss of a prime black visionary, but also the receipt of vision by a suddenly bereft elegist. It is difficult to avoid thinking of "human voices" and drowning with the last line, as though T. S. Eliot's "Prufrock" is somehow the implicit sign and influence of a poetic barrenness that accompanies the loss of vital force such as Malcolm.

Home Coming, however, cannot be read simply as a "book" and analyzed exclusively in the way that I have explicated "malcolm." Rather than a coherent and seamless "book," the volume is a triple-voiced collection. It combines: graphemic records of revolutionary soundings meant for quick public delivery and consumption; experimental (disjunctive typography) personals in the mode of e. e. cummings and the Greenwich Village fifties; and lyrical confessionals that project an autobiographical speaker beset by American despair and stuttering loneliness. "To all sisters," as Ms. Sanchez recalls, was prompted by a young black woman's angry query during a black power rally at San Francisco State College.

It was a poem ["to all sisters"] that came from a student out at San Francisco State who was so angry that she lost her old man to one of the white women out there and we had all of these readings and conferences going on at the time and she jumped up and said: "What a white woman got 'cept her white pussy?!" . . . I wrote my poem in a fast, sassy way for the young sister. I read it at the next meeting we had. I remember reading it there. I can recall reading the poem and all of the black women getting up stomping their feet going: "YEAH!" And you talking about a DANCE! . . . YEAH! I mean the poetry reading didn't go on. I mean for five to ten minutes. It was just that kind of uproar. And the white women who were there were shocked because no one had said anything in such a fashion before.

Ms. Sanchez begins with the woman's query as the first line of her poem:

what a white woman got
  cept her white pussy
    always sucking after blk/ness
what a white woman got
  cept her straight hair
    covering her fucked up mind
what a white woman got
  cept her faggoty white man
    who goes to sleep in her
      without
        coming
what a white woman got
  cept money trying to buy up
    a blk/man?
      yeah.
what a white woman got? (27)

When the poem was read at a subsequent rally, the assembled audience, as Ms. Sanchez records, went wild. (One envisions Ms. Sanchez's performative presence in light of the photo on the back cover of *Home Coming*—refulgent Afro hairdo, bold-print African robing, striking jewelry as accoutrement.) People danced in the aisles, sent up hoots of approval, laughed/cried—went crazy. The meeting simply could not continue.

One imagines similar responses when any one of the other colloquial efforts in *Home Coming* was presented. The counterpart to "to all sisters" is "to all brothers" and commences:

yeah.
  they
hang you up
those grey chicks
parading their
tight asses
in front of you (10).

"To a jealous cat" similarly seeks to clear the air and prepare a space for successful black heterosexual relationships:

> my man.
>   don't try none
> of your jealous shit
> with me. don't you
> know where you
> at?
>   no one never told
> you that jealousy's
> a form of homo
> sexuality? (13)

Male suspiciousness is archly deconstructed as latent homosexuality. In "nigger," there is an instructive rap from the speaker on that word's outmodedness.

Such brief works as "poem," "to all sisters," and "definition for blk/children" are also examples from *Home Coming* of a revolutionary didacticism meant to inspire mass audiences. It is easy to view such efforts as oversimplifications, but in truth, their sentiments, issues, tone, and language fit them out ideally as addresses to an enormously complex situation in which few people speak in abstract syllables or demand wit, ambiguity, and refined tension. If the reception accorded "to all sisters" is exemplary, such didactic poems reveal Ms. Sanchez's genius for the vernacular. They also reveal her commitment to one of the most familiar cultural performances in the Afro-American community—"running it down."

In such performances, the single speaker puts into forceful language the wisdom of the tribe, stripping away pretense and, in almost shamanistic ways, colloquially exorcising demons of racism, sexism, and intraracial dissension. "Telling it like it 't'is" describes the process admirably, or, as Ralph Ellison's respondent says in *Invisible Man*: "We with you, Brother. You pitch 'em we catch 'em!"

When Ms. Sanchez had an opportunity to include "selected" poems from *Home Coming* in her 1978 volume, *I've Been A Woman*,[12] however, the poetic category that predominated was the personal/confessional. The force of "poem at thirty" suggests why this category assumes such presence in the poet's corpus:

> it is midnight
> no magical bewitching
> hour for me
> i know only that
> i am here waiting
> remembering that
> once as a child
> i walked two
> miles in my sleep.
> did i know
> then where i
> was going?
> traveling. i'm
> always traveling.
> i want to tell
> you about me
> about nights on a
> brown couch when
> i wrapped my
> bones in lint and
> refused to move.
> no one touches
> me anymore.
> father do not
> send me out
> among strangers.
> you you black man
> stretching scraping
> the mold from your body.
> here is my hand.
> i am not afraid
> of the night (10–11).

The words "no magical bewitching / hour for me" indicate that not only are fairy godmothers and carriage-and-pumpkin magic unavailable, but also any sign (insofar as witches are magical women who share the community of the coven) of sisterly community or female bonding. Life-in-death ("bones in lint") despair in an uneasy night of memory and futile apostrophe ("father") indicate stasis and vague expectation ("I am here waiting").

What gives energy to "poem at thirty" and provides possibilities of luminescent opening is an invited heterosexual bonding and collaborative journeying—"black man . . . here is my hand." Night is a familiar traveling space/time for the black blues cognizance that informs the poem—"once as a child / i walked two / miles in my sleep." Hence, there is no fear of darkness. Terror does not come from night per se, but from the realization of loneliness and alienation that accompany night. The possibility of conquering such isolation is hinted in the outstretched hand, and presumably, more productive apostrophe ("black man").

"Poem at thirty" is representative of a transpolitical group of efforts in *Home Coming* that includes "summary" and "personal letter no. 2." "Summary" is, in the poet's words: "a poem for the world / for the slow suicides / in seclusion" (14). Its theme is American despair *à la* Norman Mailer, or Amiri Baraka's universe of murderously materialistic "babblers and slow jivers" who must be eliminated if cleanliness and sanity are to rule the earth. Again, loneliness calls forth what might be defined as a blues moan:

    i am alone.
    one night of words
    will not change
    all that (15).

"Personal letter no. 2"—the concluding poem of *Home Coming*— rather than confirming the accuracy of the volume's title effort ("i have returned / leaving behind me / all those hide and / seek faces") echoes the blue aloneness of "poem at thirty":

    i speak skimpily to
    you about apartments i
    no longer dwell in
    and children who
    chant their dis
    obedience in choruses.
    if i were young

i wd stretch you
with my wild words
while our nights
run soft with hands.
but i am what i
am. woman. alone
amid all this noise (32).

A stutter is inscribed ("speak skimpily") in the poem's very opening just as a gap—a black space—rests between the articulations "home" and "coming" in the volume's title. Vacancy, absence, transience are concluding signs of the collection. Inhabited spaces ("apartments") have been abandoned. Heterosexual bonding is a tactile ideal that flickers for an instant but quickly gives way to "woman. alone."

Without engaging such typographically experimental efforts as "to CHuCK," I want to suggest that *Home Coming*'s three voices represent a stunning figuring forth of the Afro-American woman revolutionary performer. The demands of such a role in the 1960s and 1970s were awesome. The black masses called for a recognizably vernacular voice speaking the wisdom of the tribe and offering counsel for a liberated and empowered community. On the other hand, what was considered "revolutionary" by a "beat" artistic community was "concrete" lexical graphics seeking spatial and abstract aesthetics akin to painting. What was absolutely mandatory in a *black woman's emotive universe*—a world implicit in the interstices of Phillis Wheatley's polished heroic lyrics as well as in the rocky nocturnal spaces of Billie Holiday's blues—was a purgative rehearsal of loneliness "amid all this noise."

In the black womanly and womanist universe, there had to occur an optimistic extension of the hand to what a black woman could only hope was a redeemed black man. I want to suggest that the sound that virtually everyone took as Ms. Sanchez's authentically revolutionary voice was, in effect, merely the ephemeral stuff of political rallies. The Greenwich Village/e.e. cummings imitations were products of youthful mimesis. The black woman poems, by contrast, seem to me the truly *revolutionary* sound of resilient black survival motion—womanly blues filling nighttime air and converting "noise"—

transforming the noisy public moment into a traditional repetition and reworking of salvific wisdom.

> When I got up on stages of America and . . . opened my mouth I had to understand that I was opening my mouth for Moma and for those women who always opened their mouths and allowed us to hear . . . My grandmother [Moma] was a Deaconess in the AME Zion church and she and the other women of the church taught us—my sister and I lived in the church— empowerment, like "Don't never let nobody hit you more than once."

Ms. Sanchez's blues/autobiographical voice, in short, says that "home" ain't no easy place to come by if you are black, alone, a woman, and striving mightily for a *voiced* liberation. Rather than a homecoming in the manner of, say, the AME's special Sunday rituals, Ms. Sanchez's collection suggests a multivoiced attempt to bridge that space (seen in the work's title) between "coming" and (actually) arriving at "home."

Significantly, the figure depicted on the volume's cover is a young, black woman. Short hair, glimmering earrings, and bold-print robing, as well as the profile, indicate Africa. Feet and hands are in motion; in the right hand, a spear is poised. But the rhythmic motion implied by feet and hands gives a notion of dance and ceremony rather than of active warfare. There is, in other words, a feeling that the cover figure is engaged in a ritual performance rather than in murderous combat. It is a perfect icon, I think, for *Home Coming*, which has bold spears of colloquial wisdom to toss but is most sonorously effective in its deep-spirited womanly blues tonalities. Such tonalities lead not to hermenuetics of overthrow, but rather to a problematic of black self-love and Afro-American heterosexual bonding. There is in the volume a sense that even if the white West immediately capitulated, there would still be vital intraracial issues to be addressed by a blue/black magical woman singer.

The cultural performative mode that stands out most cogently when *Home Coming* is analyzed, then, is not "running it down" from a polemical podium, but singing it sweet and soulfully from womanly blues chambers of an American night. It is, perhaps, the presence of a long/black song that inspires confidence and lifts the spirit to continue in the face of events like Malcolm's assassination. In any case, Malcolm's death is redeemed in *Home Coming* in the poem "for unborn malcolms," where cold-blooded resolution seems to guarantee a legitimate black self-defense that will enable the Muslim leader's revolutionary spirit to have future effects. Further, there are in *Home Coming* playful erotic poems that suggest that when the womanly blues singer laments an absence or a failure of possibility of "nights" that "run soft with hands" she knows precisely what she is talking about. The reason for lamenting such failure, lack, or absence is because black love—when it is present—is *so* sweet:

> magic
>   my man
> is you
>   turning
> my body into
> a thousand
> smiles.
>   black
> magic is your
> touch
>   making
> me breathe (12–13).

Black magic/music/blues come together in a vision of sweet bonding. Sonia Sanchez, thus, appears before us, even in a first published collection, in a traditional guise for which she is fully qualified: The Lady sings the blues. It is scarcely surprising that one of her most inspiring volumes is entitled *A Blues Book For Blue Black Magical Women* (1974).[13]

While *A Blues Book* extends the autobiographical impulse of a personal/confessional category of *Home Coming* and suggests a revolutionary bonding of black women under the aegis of Elijah Muhammed and the Nation of Islam, *We A BaddDD People* (1970)[14] aggressively extends the category of running it down. We can contrast the *sounds* of the two works by first listening to *BaddDD People*'s "blk/chant":

we programmed for death/
die/en
  each day the man/
      boy
plans our death
  with short/bread
for short/sighted/minds
with junk to paralyze our
blk/limbs from leapen on the
wite/mutha/fucka/
    laughen at us
from his wite/castles/of
    respectability (33).

The poem—like the volume as a whole—continues by condemning black intraracial treachery and conflict, drug addiction, alcoholism, and low seriousness. It also lays waste the mad and murderous intentions and acts of a white world. Ceaselessly, *BadDD People* breaks old typographical rhythms and meaningless codes of manners. Its tone is an outraged didacticism. On its back cover, the author wears an expression that combines contempt, amusement, and, perhaps, outraged disgust. The Afro hairdo seems even more refulgent (the photo is a close-up) for the poet is truly "in our faces," running down hard truths to make us/keep us alive.

By contrast, her *Blues Book* shows the calm face of a woman whose head (in Muslim fashion) is covered and whose two children look out with curiosity and bemusement. The sound of *A Blues Book* is as follows:

This woman vomiting her
hunger over the world
this melancholy woman forgotten
before memory came
this yellow movement bursting forth like
coltrane's melodies all mouth
buttocks moving like palm trees,
this honeycoatedalabamianwoman
raining rhythms of blue/black/smiles
this yellow woman carrying beneath her breasts
pleasures without tongues

this woman whose body weaves
desert patterns,
this woman, wet with wandering,
reviving the beauty of forests and winds
is telling you secrets
gather up your odors and listen
as she sings the mold from memory (41).

The blues voice of *Blues Book* is vastly different from the *baddDD* phonics of its predecessor volume. The blues voice is one of wisdom achieved through self-examination. This wisdom is shared out of a deep sense of communal love. It is the wisdom, love, and personal expansion of vision of *A Blues Book*, as well as of *Love Poems* (1973),[15] that lead most directly to the voice of *Homegirls and Handgrenades*.[16]

In "Norma," a prose portrait from Part Two of *Homegirls*, a childhood moment is recorded as follows:

A sound from the back of the class made me turn around. It was the "people"—the "people" who sat in the back and talked when they wanted to, ate their lunches when they wanted to, and paid attention when they wanted to. They were paying attention to Mr. Cator and me. And I shook. I always wanted to be inconspicuous around the "people" (19).

"Just Don't Never Give Up on Love" from *Homegirls'* Part One begins:

Feeling tired that day, I came to the park with the children. I saw her as I rounded the corner, sitting old as stale beer on the bench, ruminating on some uneventful past. And I thought, "Hell. No rap from the roots today. I need the present. On this day. This Monday. This July day buckling me under her summer wings. I need more than old words for my body to squeeze into" (10).

"Travelling on an Amtrak Train Could Humanize You" commences with the following lines:

I saw him enter the train. His walk announced a hipster for all seasons; his clothing said doorways, hunger and

brawls. A lifetime of insults. I immediately put my large
brown bag on the seat next to mine, lowered my eyes,
turned my head to peer out at the figures rushing to
catch the train to NYC (50).

In each instance, the speaker assumes a posture of avoidance.
Her avoidance, however, is not rejection, but rather a self-
deprecatory resistance meant to be both contrastive and instructive. The "people" are, in fact, her captivating subject,
and her self-deprecation derives from her instinctual response
to "difference." Her instinct is to avoid the wretched of the
earth because they speak of "doorways, hunger, brawls" and
their various deprivations make them, again in the poet's
words, "men and women keloiding before us with pain" (52).
Hence, the writer as self-possessed observer and chronicler of
experience stands in contrast to "the people" who live and
define *experience* in its prototypical *black* form. The performative
strategy involved in this contrast is one of subtle blues; the
sound of the people insinuates itself insistently into the writer's private spaces, transforming her bourgeois, college-bred
posture as observer into a stance as singer and motivator of
global revolution. Lines from "MIA's," the final poem in
Homegirls, project the new singer as follows:

so i plant myself in the middle
of my biography
of dying drinking working dancing people
their tongues swollen with slavery
waiting and i say
yebo madola [come on men]
yebo bafazi [come on women]

* * * * *

let there be everywhere our actions.
breathing hope and victory
into their unspoken questions
summoning the dead to life again
to the hereafter of freedom.
comon. men. women.
i want to be free (76–77).

Planting herself in the middle of a mass "biography" is precisely what the poet accomplishes in *Homegirls and Handgrenades*. The volume's most moving and effective efforts are devoted to such figures as Mrs. Rosalie Johnson (the woman in the park who enjoins the poet to "never give up on love"), Norma (the class genius who becomes a drug addict), Herbert of the razor hands (who rides AMTRAK and, like Langston Hughes's mass philosophers, deconstructs the world of the worldrunners), Bubba (who "gave his genius up to the temper of the times"), and the almost Baudelairean bag-woman of Manhattan who "sits still as a Siamese" and is sarcastically aware of her iconic role in urban geographies: "Here I am, her smile announces, in the upper sanctum of Manhattan. A black Siamese for these modern monuments. Let those who would worship at my shrine come now or forever hold their peace. Hee. Hee. Hee" (41). The care with which the poet etches these figures is extraordinary. The language, personality, and wisdom she bestows upon figures like Norma and Herbert transform mere space into enduring *character*. The careful detailing that characterizes her sketch of the bag-woman as a modern instance of the selectivity of "rights" sounds as follows:

I watched her out of the corner of my eyes as I washed and dried my hands. What did she remind me of? This cracked body full of ghosts. This beached black whale. This multilayered body gathering dust.

Whose mother are you? Whose daughter were you for so many years? What grandchild is standing still in your eyes? What is your name, old black woman of bathrooms and streets?

She opened her dirty sheet of belongings and brought out an old plastic bowl. She looked up and signaled to me.

"Hey you. There. Yeah. You. Miss. Could you put some water in this here bowl for me please? It's kinda hard for me to climb back up once I sits down here for the night."

I took the bowl and filled it with water. There was no hot water, only cold. I handed it to her, and she turned the bowl up to her mouth and drank some of the water. Then she began the slow act of taking off her slippers

and socks. The socks numbered six. They were all old
and dirty. But her feet. A leper's feet. Cracked. Ulcer-
ated. Peeling with dirt and age (40).

Clearly, what the British once called "out door relief" will
be of little help in the face of such disaster, and momentary
charity (the donation of five dollars to a "harridan mumbling
pieces of a dead dream") can accomplish almost nothing.
Only a fundamental, earth-shaking change in the very conception of rights and of *the* right will alter conditions that
leave "bluebirds" (women who are beautiful and full of potential in their youth) "used up" and homeless, "watching the
whirl of people pass by." Similarly, only a revolutionary shift
in American axiology will save the Bubbas of this world.
Bubba, who was a stunning figure of the poet's girlhood—a
princely, black walker and dreamer in the Harlem universe—
runs out of options early in his American development, becoming the father of two and a wage-laborer in a fickle economy.
He is a visionary trapped in the permanent black underclass
(the economic castaways of postindustrialism) that gives way,
like Bubba, to devastating escapes. Like Norma, Bubba suc-
cumbs to drug addiction:

Bubba. If you hadn't fallen off of that roof in '57, you
would have loved the '60s. Bubba you would have loved
Malcolm. You would have plucked the light from his
eyes and finally seen the world in focus (58).

"Focus" is surely an appropriate word to describe *Homegirls'*
achievements; there is a far broader and sharper focus in
Homegirls than in Ms. Sanchez's earlier works. Rather than
chanting in and about claustral spaces marked by the individual (first-person) "I's," alienation and ennui, the transformed
singer of *Homegirls* speaks of a global "power of love" and
realizes that expressivity and weaponry must be coextensive—
"blues is bullets." The task at hand is to foster a general awareness of inequities and insanities that keep power in the hands
of "nuclear generals . . . nuclear presidents . . . nuclear scientists, who spread human and nuclear waste over the world"
(67). The necessity for all of us, according to Sanchez, is to move

"beyond the fallout" of despair and apathy that accompany our perception of "the horror."

> The artist . . . has to have the vision of political power . . .
> the vision of writing politically so that it will stir people.

"MIA's," the poem cited earlier, turns its attention to such world trouble spots as El Salvador and South Africa, enjoining the participation of all in the creation of a new peace. An expenditure of energy and an awareness of depths of oppression (signaled by the wasted lives and lost potential of *Homegirls'* prose sketches) are required to effect change—"Grenades Are Not Free." But their purchase is rewarded by an altered sensibility.

> If you are not really talking as a black artist about effecting change, where are you?

It is the expressive force—a nearly concussive jolt to consciousness—of the poet's grenadelike words that prompts our empathetic relationship to the "people." Under her urging and tutelage, we join in a reconceptualization of the world as a place that can be cleanly, peacefully, and equitably inhabited. We envision a universe in which there will be home for all, and in which we will all be *at home.* The poet's unequivocal dedication to rectification of the conditions of the dispossessed—the homeless—fully entitle her status as a "homegirl."

In the vernacular, we envision "street people" saluting her: "Yo, Home!" In a "poetics of space," we envision *Homegirls and Handgrenades* (and its creator) as a "poetic image," a habitable space and point of transmission for a black song of liberation. And in blue/black secular and spiritual vocabularies Sonia Sanchez is a rocking home in a weary land. A performer who can sing the blues, she also jolts consciousness and celebrates such African exemplars as Margaret Walker, Ezekiel Mphahlele, and Dr. Martin Luther King.

> I celebrate in my poem for Martin, people who have had
> a sense of loudness about freedom.

She commits herself to a new world in lines such as the following:

> As long as I have hands to write; as long as I have eyes that see; as long as I can bear your name against silence; I shall never forget our last talk Bubba . . . Bubba. Your footsteps sing around my waist each day. I will not let the country settle into the sleep of the innocent (57–58).

She is, however, also capable of a serene lyricism that allows us to infer her capacity for simple beauty:

> i saw you
> vincent van
> gogh perched
> on those pennsylvania
> cornfields communing
> amid secret black
> bird societies. yes.
> i'm sure that was
> you exploding your
> fantastic delirium
> while in the
> distance
> red indian
> hills beckoned (46).

The secret of successful performance and transformed consciousness is a combination of unequivocal commitment and simple beauty. Soniz Sanchez's awareness of this "secret" makes her not only an authentic "homegirl," but also Our Lady singing the blues. What is empowering about her sound—as those who saluted her on June 5, 1985, knew—is its ubiquity among the "people." The poet's benefit performances, volunteer community readings, workshops at prisons, public schools, YMCAs, churches, political rallies, and elsewhere, make her a people's poet in a very special sense. She offers the possibility of "renaissance" because she assumes responsibility for the condition of a world in which she is a "homegirl." (The gap, space, or stutter between "coming" and "home" is mightily bridged by her current sound.) She seeks her audience and effects among people who recognize and respond to her sound. She moves, chants, sings for a black mass audience in the manner of a blues artist bellowing down bullies. But she also ballasts lyrically the wretched of the earth, enjoining: "yebo madola / yebo bafazi."

If the notion of a black renaissance may be assumed to imply communal leadership and a response among black people themselves—a self-direction, selection, and empowerment that do not recreate bourgeois forms for private gain and white acknowledgment—then Sonia Sanchez and her audience clearly mark a new, postmodern, and dynamically sounding *renaissancism*.

There may well be more celebrated Afro-American women writers, but Sonia Sanchez helps bring an enduring spirit of *black* renaissancism to contemporary effectiveness. Her name is legion; it subsumes the world's dispossessed as referent. Nobody performs like Sonia Sanchez; nobody brings quintessential black cultural rituals to the high note she achieves. Words that she wrote to Zeke Mphahlele seem appropriate as concluding reflections on her own status in a world where some receive more kudos, but few (very, very few) do as much (Afro-American) cultural *work* as she. She writes:

> i talked to my sons as the car chased the long-legged rain running before us. i told them that men and women are measured by their acts not by their swaggering speech or walk, or the money they have stashed between their legs. i talked to my sons about bravery outside of bruce lee grunts and jabs, outside of star wars' knights fertilizing america's green youth into continued fantasies while reality explodes underground in neutron boldness (63).

The "acts" by which Sonia Sanchez will be measured are, I believe, ones of "renaissancism" par excellence. For she has formed a blue/black sound and transmitted it to the "people" to make us free.

> You can't have relationships with other people until you give birth to yourself.

NOTES

1. The words in italics in the present essay are drawn from interviews (some eight hours of good talk) that I conducted with Sonia Sanchez on September 9, 1985 and October 14, 1985. I am extremely grateful to Ms. Sanchez for the abundance of time she granted for these interviews.

2. In *When Harlem Was in Vogue*, David Levering Lewis describes the first dinner held to award literary prizes in *Opportunity* magazine's first literary competition as follows: "Three hundred sixteen people came to the elegant dinner at The Fifth Avenue Restaurant . . . As much as he [Charles Johnson] wanted to foster the arts, what he really wanted was to cement an alliance between the movers and shakers of the white and black communities in New York and beyond. How well . . . [his] strategy was succeeding was evident when he was able to announce at the end of the flawless evening, that funds for a second annual *Opportunity* contest were already in hand, promised by Casper Holstein—'business man' . . . 'It was not a spasm of emotion,' Johnson said later. 'It was intended as the beginning of something, and so it was' " (New York: Alfred Knopf, 1981), 113-115.

3. In *Negro Thought in America 1880-1915*, August Meier notes: "The phrase 'New Negro' was used at least as early as 1895. The Cleveland *Gazette* on June 28, 1895, commenting on the success crowning efforts to secure a New York civil rights law, editorialized about 'a class of colored people, the "New Negro," who have arisen since the war, with education, refinement and money' " (Ann Arbor: University of Michigan Press, 1963), 258.

4. For a discussion and elaboration of the "economics of slavery" and the blues, see Houston A. Baker, *Blues, Ideology, and Afro-American Literature: A Vernacular Theory* (Chicago: University of Chicago Press, 1984).

5. Langston Hughes:

> I, too, sing America.
> I am the darker brother
> They send me to eat in the kitchen
> When company comes,
> But I laugh,
> And eat well,
> And grow strong.
>
> Tomorrow,
> I'll be at the table
> When company comes.
> Nobody'll dare
> Say to me,
> "Eat in the kitchen,"
> Then.
>
> Besides,
> They'll see how beautiful I am
> And be ashamed—
>
> I, too, am America.

From *Selected Poems* (New York: Alfred Knopf, 1969), 275.

6. The twenties' point of view vis-à-vis "revaluation" can easily be inferred from Alain Locke's formulations in *The New Negro*, particularly his remarks in the collection's "Introduction."

7. "Of course, looking at the phenomenon of race records from a more practical point of view, as I am certain the owners of Okeh [Record Company that recorded *Crazy Blues*] must have done, Mamie Smith's records proved dramatically the existence of a not yet exploited market. *Crazy Blues* sold for months at a rate of 8,000 records a week. Victoria Spivey's first record, *Black Snake Blues*, recorded six years later, sold 150,000 copies in one year . . . Race records swiftly became big business." Quoted from LeRoi Jones, *Blues People* (New York: Morrow, 1963), 100.

8. The perspective here paraphrases Baldwin's well-known assertion that Richard Wright's protagonist Bigger Thomas felt "compelled" to battle for his "humanity." Baldwin suggests (with what now, thirty years later, appears charming naïveté) in his classic essay "Many Thousands Gone," in *Notes of a Native Son* (Boston: Beacon, 1955), 24–45, that Bigger needed only to "accept" his humanity.

9. "The bright ideals of the past—physical freedom, political power, the training of brains and the training of hands—all these in turn have waxed and waned, until even the last grows dim and overcast." Quoted from "The Souls of Black Folk," in John Hope Franklin, ed., *Three Negro Classics* (New York: Avon, 1969), 219.

10. For a more elaborate assessment of The Black Aesthetic, see Houston A. Baker, *The Journey Back: Issues in Black Literature and Criticism* (Chicago: University of Chicago Press, 1980).

11. Sonia Sanchez, *Home Coming* (Detroit: Broadside Press, 1969), 16. All citations refer to this edition and are hereafter marked by page numbers in parentheses.

12. Sonia Sanchez, *I've Been A Woman* (Chicago: Third World Press, 1978).

13. Sonia Sanchez, *A Blues Book For Blue Black Magical Women* (Detroit: Broadside Press, 1974).

14. Sonia Sanchez, *We A BaddDD People* (Detroit: Broadside Press, 1970).

15. Sonia Sanchez, *Love Poems* (New York: The Third Press, 1973).

16. Sonia Sanchez, *Homegirls and Handgrenades* (New York: Thunder's Mouth Press, 1984).

Gloria Naylor's Geography:

Community, Class, and Patriarchy in
The Women of Brewster Place and *Linden Hills*

Barbara Christian

I

Like Toni Morrison, Gloria Naylor is intrigued by the effect of place on character. Perhaps African-American writers have been particularly interested in setting, because displacement, first from Africa and then through migrations from South to North, has been so much a part of our history. Because of the consistency of forced displacement in our collective experience, we know how critical our location is to the character of our social creations, of how place helps to tell us a great deal about who we are, and who we can become. Perhaps place is even more critical to African-American women writers. For women within the African-American community have functioned both inside and outside the home, have been conservers of tradition (if only because we are mothers), while we have had to respond to the *nuances* of a changed environment. How we negotiate the relationship between the past, as it has helped to form us, and the present, as we must experience it, is often a grave dilemma for us.

The setting of *Linden Hills*, Naylor's second novel, makes it clear that she is creating a geographical fictional world similar to or in the manner of Faulkner's Yoknapatawpha county. Her first novel is set in Brewster Place, her second in Linden Hills. Brewster Place and Linden Hills are geographically in the same area; both are inhabited by blacks, and in both novels, characters refer to each of these places as proximate neighborhoods, though quite different in their orientation. Linden Hills is a posh upper–middle-class settlement, Brewster Place the last stop on the road to the bottom in American society, where you live when you can't live anywhere else. The outside world perceives Linden Hills as a symbol of black achievement while Brewster Place is seen as a manifestation of failure. Ironically, through her two novels' respective characters and structure, Naylor portrays Brewster Place as a black community (though flawed and vulnerable) held together primarily by women, while Linden Hills is characterized as a group of houses that never becomes a community, a showplace precariously kept in place by the machinations of one wealthy black patriarchal family.

A single writer's juxtaposition of two African-American neighborhoods, different in values, separated by class distinctions yet located in the same geographical area, is an unusual one in African-American literature. African-American writers have tended to portray black communities as distinct from white society. There have, of course, been novels about upper–middle-class African-Americans, such as the works of early twentieth-century writer Jessie Fauset, or more recently Andrea Lee's *Sarah Phillips* (1984). But when contrasts in class are discussed in these novels, they are usually in relation to the white world. There have been many novels about urban ghetto blacks, such as *The Street* by 1940s writer Ann Petry. Again, class distinctions are usually presented in relation to white society. There have been novels about small-town blacks, such as Toni Morrison's *The Bluest Eye* (1970), which indicate through their variety of characters that class distinctions among blacks do exist. But these characters are presented in relatively few situations. And there have been works about rural southern blacks, such as Alice Walker's *The Third Life of Grange Copeland* (1970) and *The Color Purple* (1982). But in these novels, the primary point of contrast in terms of class is decidedly the white world that tragically imposes its values on black people as a race.

Most African-American writers have tended to focus either on middle-class blacks or poor blacks, and have tended to feature their protagonists as belonging to a black community that is distinct, if only because of the threat of a racist white society. When class distinctions are commented on, as they are in Zora Neale Hurston's portrayal of Jody Starks in *Their Eyes Were Watching God* (1937), Paule Marshall's portrayal of Jay Johnson in *Praisesong for the Widow* (1982), and Toni Morrison's portrayal of Macon Dead in *Song of Solomon* (1977), they are located in the conflict between that one character and others, and on the price he pays for social mobility, or sometimes, as in Grier Brown of Shange's *Betsy Brown* (1984) in that character's allegiance to his less fortunate brethren. Even when the novel is decidedly about class distinctions, as in Morrison's *Tar Baby* (1980), conflict is gauged by individuals, in this case between the upwardly mobile Jadine and the underclass, Son. Neither is presented as having viable communities to which they belong. Marshall's monumental *Chosen Place, Timeless People* (1969) does present a black world in which class distinctions are extensively explored but this society is emphatically Caribbean.

Gloria Naylor's two novels, when looked at as the developing opus of a single writer, are unique in that together they offer us a graphic depictment of African-American groups, physically close, yet so distant because of their class differences. However, as my overview of recent African-American women novels indicates, Naylor's novels have been preceded in recent years by an increasing concern among these writers—Morrison in *Song of Solomon* and *Tar Baby*, Marshall in *Praisesong for the Widow*, Andrea Lee in *Sarah Phillips*, and Shange in *Betsy Brown*—on the issue of a distinct African-American middle class and on the implications of such a dimension in the African-American world view. As such, Naylor both participates in this concern of other African-American women writers even as she extends their analysis.

II

In the geographical world Naylor is creating, Brewster Place and Linden Hills coexist and persons from each place have attitudes about the other. So touched is she by the revolutionary fervor of the 1960s that Melanie Browne of Linden Hills changes her name to Kiswana and goes down to live with "the people" in Brewster Place, much as some whites in the sixties went to live in black communities. The people of Brewster Place wonder what this privileged black woman is doing living in their midst, even as Melanie's family in Linden Hills is hurt, for they have made sacrifices so that she would never have to be associated with the kind of people who live in Brewster Place. The class distinctions between the people of Brewster Place and those of Linden Hills are clearly perceived by each group and make for a great distance between them even as they both are black.

That is not to say that Gloria Naylor is unconcerned with race as a determining factor in her geographical world. It is precisely the fact that Naylor's two neighborhoods *are* black that causes them to perceive so clearly their difference. Importantly, Naylor locates their similarities and differences in a historical process. Both Brewster Place and Linden Hills have been created by racism, or more precisely, as a result of the effects of racism on their founders. Linden Hills is literally carved out of a seemingly worthless soil by an ex-slave, Luther Nedeed, who in the 1820s had the secret dream of developing "an ebony jewel," a community of successful blacks who could stave off the racism of America and exhibit through their fine houses that members of the race can be powerful. In contrast, Brewster Place is "the bastard child of clandestine meetings" between local white politicians, at first to satisfy expected protests from the Irish community over the undeserved dismissal of their too-honest police chief. Later, Brewster Place becomes the neighborhood of successive waves of European immigrants, unwanted Americans who finally become, over time, the black poor.

The origin of communities and their historical development are as critical to the structure of Naylor's novels as they are to Marshall's and Morrison's. These two writers—Marshall particularly in *Brown Girl, Brownstones,* Morrison particularly in *Sula*—begin their narrative not with the introduction of their characters but with the history of their characters' natal communities. In many ways, Naylor's recounting of the immigrant waves that precede the coming of blacks to Brewster Place echoes Marshall's rendition of the history of the Brooklyn brownstones. And Naylor's chronicle of the history of Linden Hills is similar to Morrison's tale of the Bottom on the top, for both communities are originated by ex-slaves in the nineteenth century. The differences between these authors' respective treatments, however, is instructive, for Marshall's West Indian immigrants see their brownstones as places they can eventually own, as a step up, while Naylor's blacks of Brewster Place are at a dead end. Morrison's ex-slave earns his "bottom" as payment from his ex-master and is cheated in the process, for he is given the worst land in the area. But Naylor's Nedeed carefully *chooses* his site, outwitting everyone who sees his plateau as having no value.

Although Naylor characterizes one neighborhood as held together by women and the other as controlled by a family, she stresses that both are started by men for the purpose of consolidating power. The intentions of these men are evident in the geographical choices they make. Nedeed's choice of "a V-shaped section of land," "the northern face of a worthless plateau" indicates his direction. Not only is his site so clearly visible; even more important, its V-shape allows his land to be self-enclosed yet situated in the world. And since Nedeed lives on the lowest level of "the hills," he stands as a sentry to his private development. The shape of Brewster Place too is self-enclosed, for a wall is put up, separating it from other neighborhoods and making it a dead end. Ironically, what is positive in one context is negative in another, depending on who has power. For black Nedeed uses his enclosed V-shape to select those who will be allowed to live near him, while the people of Brewster Place have a wall imposed on them by white city officials who want them separated from more "respectable" folk.

Although the wealthy Luther Nedeed appears to have power and the residents of Brewster Place do not, they are both immeasurably affected by their race, if only because they are separated from other Americans. The physical separation of Brewster Place and Linden Hills from the surrounding areas— one imposed, the other chosen—is itself symbolic of African-Americans' dilemma in the United States. Race and class distinctions are intertwined in Naylor's geography, for in attempting to transcend the racial separations on streets like Brewster Place, her middle class separates itself from less fortunate blacks. They shut themselves in, so that they might not be shut out from the possibility of achieving power in white America. And as Naylor's narrative in *Linden Hills* suggests, they also separate themselves from each other and are not able to become a community.

In keeping with the contours of this geography, Naylor uses quite different forms in her two novels, forms that demonstrate the relationship between the shapes of her two neighborhoods and the ways in which power relations affect them. Because women usually have little access to power in the larger society, it is not surprising that black women, doubly affected by their racial and gender status, are the central characters in poverty-stricken Brewster Place, while the apparently powerful Luther Nedeed is the kernel character in Linden Hills. Yet in dramatizing the stories of the women in Brewster Place, who seem to be in control but are not, and in analyzing the precarious position of Luther Nedeed, Naylor shows the inaccuracy of such terms as *matriarch* or *patriarch* as they apply to African-Americans.

The Women of Brewster Place begins with an introduction about the history of that street, which is followed by a series of stories, each about a particular woman who lives there. The novel concludes with Mattie Michaels's dream-story about a block party in which all the women appear, as well as a coda which announces the death of the street. Created by city officials, it is destroyed by them. Although each of their narratives could be called a short story, the novel consists of the interrelationship of the stories, as a pattern evolves, not only because the characters all live in Brewster Place but also because they are connected to one another. With the exception of the lesbians in "The Two" (a point to which I will return), Naylor emphasizes the distinctiveness of each story by naming it after the specific woman on whom she is focusing, even as she might include that woman in another's story. By using this form, one that heightens the individuality of her characters so that they are not merely seen as faceless "female heads of households," while stressing their interrelationships, Naylor establishes Brewster Place as a community in spite of its history of transients—a community with its own mores, strengths, and weaknesses. Even when that specific Brewster Place is destroyed, its characteristics remain, for most of its inhabitants must move to a similar street. Brewster Place, then, stands for both itself and other places like it.

Linden Hills also begins with its history, which is really the history of the Nedeed men, for they *are* Linden Hills. That history is followed by sections headed not by names but by dates, December nineteenth to the twenty-fourth—in spite of the many residents of Linden Hills we meet in the course of the novel. Ostensibly, the story line is the "winding of Lester," a recalcitrant Linden Hills resident, and Willie, his street friend from the nearby poor community of Putney Wayne, through the affluent neighborhood of Linden Hills, as they do odd jobs to make some money for the holidays, which ironically commemorate giving.

Although we meet many Linden Hills people, at the center of the story is Luther Nedeed himself, for he has power over the individuals who live in this settlement. His story includes within it the story of his wife, and the wives of the Nedeed men who precede him. For his story is all of their stories, the present Mrs. Nedeed, the story of all the Mrs. Nedeeds who preceded her, except that this Mr. and Mrs. Nedeed will be the last of their kind. What Naylor presents is the hidden history and herstory that has made Linden Hills possible, at least as it now exists. Hence, in contrast to *Brewster Place*, the process of time, rather than the character of distinct personalities, is the formal structural element of Linden Hills.

What is interesting to me is how many layers of stories Naylor attempts to weave together in Linden Hills, layers that finally do not hold together. For although the persons focused on in stories within the story overlap, they never connect with one another. Like *The Women of Brewster Place*, *Linden Hills* does conclude with a scene in which all the residents appear, signaling the end of this place as we have known it. But while the residents of Brewster Place are getting together to have a block party, the residents of Linden Hills unilaterally ignore the burning down of the Nedeed house by putting out their lights. Hence, the wall that separates Brewster Place from the outer world becomes their mark of community as well as their stigma, while the houses of Linden Hills are critical to the concluding section of that novel precisely because they are the measuring stick of both their owners' wealth and their own unwillingness to interact with one another. Only Lester and Willie, outcasts from Linden Hills, are "hand anchored to hand" in those last days of the year.

III

While Linden Hills destroys itself from within, Brewster Place is ostensibly destroyed from without. But Naylor's stories of the women there, usually characterized as strong, matriarchal, enduring by media, scholarship, and government policy, emphasize their powerlessness. Most of her central women characters, Mattie Michaels, Etta Mae Johnson, Lucielia Louise Turner, and Cora Lee live in Brewster Place because they must. Their possibility for controlling their own lives has been blocked by societal mores about women's sexuality and their individual responses to these restrictions. So although poverty is a condition that they all share, they have been condemned to that state because of society's view of them as women, and their response to that view.

These four women—Mattie Michaels, Etta Mae Johnson, Lucielia Louise Turner, and Cora Lee—are presented as sets of counterpoint, so that Naylor can demonstrate how individual personality is not the determining factor that brings them to this street. Both Mattie Michaels and Etta Mae Johnson come from the same southern community. But while Mattie is a sweet girl, domestic in her orientation, Etta Mae Johnson is rebellious, yearning for adventure. Still, both women are wounded by the fact that they *are* women. Mattie Michaels is "ruined" by a single sexual encounter; her pregnancy results in her estrangement from her doting, then enraged father who feels she has betrayed him. Mattie makes up for that loss by doting on her son Basil, only to receive from God what she prayed for, "a little boy who would always need her." The son's betrayal of his aging mother depletes her savings and precipitates the necessity for her move to Brewster Place. Etta Mae, too, is estranged from her community. Whites force her to leave because she is too uppity. She, however, lives primarily through hitching her wagon to a "rising black star," to a succession of men; she too never discovers that she can live through herself. Naylor's comment on the effect of sexism and racism on her is astute:

> Even if someone had bothered to stop and tell her that the universe had expanded for her, just an inch, she wouldn't have known how to shine alone.[1]

Although they have had opportunities to avoid a dead-end street like Brewster Place, both Mattie and Etta Mae end up there because of their concept of themselves as women. Mattie sacrifices herself to her son. Etta Mae will not put up with the nonsense that men bring with them, but neither is she able to see that she can make up her own life. As a result, the sweet Mattie and the adventurous Etta Mae arrive at a certain period in their lives without sufficient economic or psychological resources.

Both these middle-aged women live through others, but this is also true of the younger Lucielia and Cora Lee. Their lives complement Mattie's and Etta Mae's. For Lucielia will do practically anything to maintain her relationship with her husband, while Cora Lee is obsessed with having babies. Their stories are counterpoint to each other in that Lucielia's relationship with her husband is damaged because she does get pregnant while Cora Lee does not care about men except to get pregnant. Lucielia's husband sees her womanhood as a trap: "With two kids and you on my back, I ain't never gonna have nothing." Children for him are a liability, since he is a poor man. When Ciel aborts her second child only to lose her first while she is pleading with her husband to stay with her, she almost loses all sense of herself. On the other hand, encouraged by adults in her childhood to desire baby dolls, Cora Lee wants nothing more than to take care of babies. No longer concerned with her children when they naturally grow beyond babyhood, Cora Lee lives in a fantasy world, interrupted only by the growing demands of the human beings she has birthed.

Because of their lack of economic resources, these four women *must* live in Brewster Place. However, Kiswana Browne and "the two" choose to live there for different reasons. Kiswana feels repressed, both communally and sexually, in her natal home, Linden Hills. She sees her sojourn in Brewster Place as bonding with her true people, black people. As well, her interaction with her mother, the major event in her story, demonstrates quite clearly that Kiswana sees Linden Hills morality as hypocritical and narrow minded. Her prim mother characterizes African sculpture, the heritage Kiswana proudly displays, as obscene, too blatantly sexual. Yet these two women have much in common in that they both enjoy their sensuality, the younger quite openly (at least in Brewster Place), the older more covertly. Naylor's use of their adornment of their feet, a part of the female body that is usually hidden and which is not considered particularly sexual, is an indication of their own pleasure in themselves. But finally it is Mrs. Browne's willingness to visit Kiswana in Brewster Place, the fact that she is concerned about her daughter's welfare despite their disagreements, that is an indication of the strength of their bond. Like the daughter in Carolyn Rodgers' poem, "the bridge that is my back," Kiswana understands that "irregardless," *her* mother is there for her.

Kiswana's meeting with her mother is an amplification of a major chord sounded throughout this novel, for Brewster Place women mother one another. Perhaps these women are sometimes labeled "matriarchs" because together they are able to endure so much. There is no question that their stories in this novel are interconnected because of the caring bond they assume for one another—a bond that does not, however, preclude disagreements, falling outs, even ineffectiveness.

So although Mattie's mother is ineffectual in her dealings with her father, it is she who, through threatened violence, prevents him from beating the pregnant girl to a pulp. And it is a stranger, Miss Eva, who mothers Mattie and her son, giving them a secure and happy home. Miss Eva may, as she says, be partial to men, but in the novel it is Mattie she treats like kin. The same attitude is evident in Mattie's friendship with Etta Mae Johnson. First mothered by Billie Holiday's music, which articulates her spirit for her, Etta Mae believes that men are her means to success. But it is to Mattie that she perennially returns for renewal. Just as Kiswana is mothered, she also mothers. She takes Cora Lee and her children to see Shakespeare in the park and it is on that occasion that this lover of babies begins to think about possibilities for her children who are no longer babies. Ciel, as well, mothers her child Serena and in turn is mothered by Mattie. In one of the most moving scenes in the novel, Mattie bathes the numb, grief-stricken Ciel, bringing her from death into life as she reawakens her senses in a ritual of shared womanhood much like Rosalee's bathing of Avey Johnson in Marshall's *Praisesong For The Widow*, a ritual derived from African religions and still practiced in voodoo.

Women mothering other women is consistent throughout
this novel as they hold each other in survival. Such mothering, though, does not extend to "the two," the lesbians who
for most Brewster Place residents do not even have specific
names. The community of women in Brewster Place cannot
approach even the thought of sexual love between women,
partly because so many of them have had such close relations
with each other. As always, Mattie puts the community's
fears into words. When Etta Mae says how different Lorraine
and Theresa's love must be from the love so many of them
share, Mattie responds:

> Maybe it's not so different . . . maybe that's why some
> women get so riled up about it 'cause they know deep
> down it's not so different after all . . . it kinda gives you a
> funny feeling when you think about it that way, though.[2]

Unlike Celie and Shug in *The Color Purple*, Lorraine has no
community and very much wants one. It is her tragedy that
she believes that because she is black, she is in the same boat
as the other residents of Brewster Place. She learns too late
that the effects of racism on this community exacerbates the
homophobia so rampant in the outer world. Although she is
killed by men, the women of Brewster Place too share the
blame for her death. They do not mother her; rather, they
reject her.

Ben, the wino who had lost his crippled daughter, is the
only one who befriends Lorraine. Ironically, it is Ben who
Lorraine kills in her frenzied effort to defend herself from her
attackers. Ben is the first black resident of Brewster Place, and
his death at the wall is a sign of Brewster Place's death as a
community, of its inability to hold together much longer.
Even as the women in the final scene of the novel chip away
at the wall that imprisons them, we are aware that this is
someone's dream, for such an act would be the prelude to a
community rebellion, a step that these nurturing, restricted
women cannot take if they are to survive as they have. Before
such a route can be explored, Brewster Place is condemned by
politicians, forcing its people to disperse. As nurturing as
Brewster Place "Afric women" may be, the community cannot
withstand the power of those in high places. So Brewster

Place residents are displaced again, just as they had been before. They are as powerless as they were when they first came to Brewster Place.

IV

While Brewster Place is a community of transients, Linden Hills is a secure settlement with a long history. And unlike the people of Brewster Place, Luther Nedeed has access to people with power. In fact, because of careful planning and sacrifice, his family becomes one of those with power, at least in relation to Linden Hills. The Nedeed men caress, cultivate their dream of an ebony jewel community as if it were a woman they are wooing. Naylor's use of a V-shaped piece of land suggests the female body even as Nedeed's house, situated at the entry, suggests the male who wishes to take possession. The land is, for succeeding generations of Nedeed men, their love. They carefully select the families who are allowed to live on it. For *their* people

> are to reflect the Nedeeds in a hundred facets and then the Nedeeds could take these splintered mirrors and form a *mirage of power* to torment a world that dared to think them stupid—or worse totally impotent.[3]

But even the Nedeeds, gods that they are, cannot live forever. It is necessary that they have heirs in order to continue to cultivate their dream. Wives, then, are necessary to their plan, the choice of a wife critical. Naylor gives us the outlines of a developing patriarchy in her description of the way the pursuit of power affects the relations between men and women. In order to serve the dream, the women must be malleable (grateful to be the wife of a Nedeed); they must look like a prize (hence their light skin), but not be demanding beauties. They must bear a son as close in nature as possible to their father, and, of course, they must submerge their lives in the lives of their husbands.

It is this flaw in their century-old plan, critical to the development and maintenance of Linden Hills, that generates the novel. For the present Mrs. Nedeed does not give birth to a

Nedeed boy who resembles his paternal ancestors. Nature triumphs over planning, for this son harkens back to his maternal ancestors, as the too-long-submerged blood of the Nedeed women finally manifests itself. Unwilling to believe that this could happen, that his father's genes could be superseded by his mother's, Luther Nedeed convinces himself that his wife has been unfaithful for he will not recognize even his own mother's face in his son's features.

At the very core of patriarchal myth, as Naylor presents it, is the idea that the son must duplicate the father, and that he must be separated from the mother. In an attempt to restore order in the world he has created, Nedeed imprisons his wife and child in the cellar, causing the death of his motherlike son, hence ending the heretofore unbroken line of descent. He also precipitates his wife's discovery of the Nedeed women who preceded her, the final blow to his kingdom. In refusing to accept a variation in the pattern his father had decreed, Luther Nedeed destroys all that his forebears had set in motion.

But of course it is not only this individual Nedeed who causes the destruction of this artificial world; for years, Linden Hills has been rotting from the inside, as Nature refuses to succumb indefinitely to Luther's family's iron will. The imprisoned Mrs. Nedeed remembers *her* real name because she discovers the records left by her predecessors, letters, recipes, photographs—as the mothers cry out to be heard, to be reckoned with, to exist. As Willa Prescott Nedeed relives the herstory so carefully exhumed from the Nedeeds official records, we realize how the experiences of the women are a serious threat to the men's kingdom.

Naylor's rendition of this herstory emphasizes one element— that once these women have produced one male, once they have carried out their function for patriarchy, they are isolated from life until they no longer exist. They do, however, leave some record of their presence, their lives, in their own individual feminine forms. Through letters to herself, the first Mrs. Nedeed, the slave Luwana Packerville, tells us how she is silenced to death; through her recipes, Evelyn Creton demonstrates how she had eaten herself to death; and through the family photograph album, Patricia Maguire graphically displays that she is gradually disappearing. In an act of defiance, in the last photo of the album she scrawls the word "me" in the place where her face should be.

None of these women can fight back effectively, for at first they do not know what is being done to them. When they do begin to discover that *they* are not wrong—that they are being erased not because they have lost their charm or do not fix the right meals—it is too late. Since she has been systematically isolated from the world, no one questions the absence of the present Mrs. Nedeed, for no one knows her well enough to realize that she has not gone away for the holidays. By emphasizing the Nedeed women's ignorance of their own herstory, Naylor shows how the repression of women's herstory is necessary to the maintenance of patriarchy, and why it is that history is so exclusively male.

Naylor does not present Willa Prescott Nedeed's meditation on her dead child and on the herstory she discovers in a straight line. Rather she juxtaposes it with her presentation of other Linden Hills residents who also must erase essential parts of themselves if they are to stay in this jewel neighborhood. Most of these characters are men: the lawyer, Wynston Alcott; the businessmen, Xavier Donnell and Maxwell Smyth; the Rev. Hollis; the historian, Braithwaite; and one woman, Laurel. Each of their lives has been damaged by the pursuit of wealth and power that Nedeed embodies, though some do not even know it. They distort their natural inclinations, introducing death into their lives, even as the Nedeeds, who make their money as funeral parlor directors, have distorted their families in order to create Linden Hills.

Naylor shows us the different currencies in which these characters pay for their ascent to Linden Hills—usually it is their deepest natural pleasures that they give up in order to "make it." So Wynston Alcott gives up his lover David and marries, for homosexuality is not allowed in Linden Hills. Xavier Donnell gives up his idea of marrying Roxanne, a black woman who lives in Linden Hills, because she is so much herself that she might drain him of the energy necessary to reach the top. Maxwell Smyth becomes totally artificial. Everything—his diet, his clothes, the temperature in his house, sexuality—is regulated so as to eliminate any funk. The pressures of his fraudulent job leave Rev. Hollis without the wife he loves and he becomes an alcoholic. Laurel puts everything into becoming a successful businesswoman, sacrificing her relationship with her friends, her love of music and of swimming, even her concern for the grandmother who brought her up. Her relationship with her husband is described as an ascent up "two staircases, that weren't strictly parallel," and whose steps "slanted until even one free hand could not touch the other's." She finally breaks into a million pieces.

Important among Linden Hills folk is Braithwaite, the historian who separates himself from life in order to chronicle the comings and goings of the Nedeeds. His view of historiography is that of detachment and disinvolvement for only then, he thinks, can he be objective. He believes that he cannot participate in life if he is to observe it. As a result, he does not get to know history's cunning passages—the letters, recipes, photographs of the Mrs. Nedeeds—since only interest and concern could lead him to them. Through this character, Naylor critiques the intellectual version of Linden Hills, where official history making and an obsession with objectivity means that men like Braithwaite are not concerned with human life.

What Braithwaite does not know and does not wish to know are the very things that cause destruction of Linden Hills. On December twenty-fourth, the final day of the book, Nedeed insists on carrying out the family tradition of decorating the tree. He pays those Linden Hills handymen, Lester and Willie, to help him, for his family is supposedly away. By refusing to vary tradition one iota, Nedeed continues to effect his own downfall. He must have the homemade ornaments his family has always used. The closet door is left open so that Willa Nedeed Prescott can ascend, her dead child in hand, the *net* and *veil* of her predecessors encircling her, to make her own order. The final struggle between Luther and Willa will unite them and their child in a circle of fire: "They breathed as one, moved as one and one body lurched against the fireplace."

Nedeed is not only destroyed by his suppression of his mothers, he is destroyed as well by the Linden Hills residents whom he presumed to create. In an act that reveals their hatred for him as their controller as well as the disinvolvement he has always demanded of them, his neighbors let him and his house burn down. Only Willie from Putney Wayne is willing to try to save the Nedeeds, who after all are only flesh and blood to him. Finally, as if asserting *her* order, Nature immediately reclaims the Nedeed house. The lake, which served as the barrier between the Nedeeds and the world, pulls the century-old house into itself in one single stroke. The Nedeed tradition is extinguished forever.

I think it is important that Willie, the poet from Putney Wayne, and Lester, a descendent of Grammy Tilson, the only one who did not bend to the first Luther Nedeed's will, are the witnesses to this story of Linden Hills. Too, Naylor may be signaling, through Willie's importance in the novel as well as through the story of Wayne Avenue residents Ruth and Norm, that Putney Wayne, a working class neighborhood, may be the setting of her next novel.* If it is, these Putney Wayne characters have learned much about the folly of trying to be a god. They have learned, too, that those who place wealth above human beings cannot create a community that endures.

V

In *The Women of Brewster Place* and *Linden Hills*, Gloria Naylor's portrayal of her two neighborhoods demonstrates the effects of class distinctions on the African-American community and how these distinctions are gender oriented. As well, when read together, her two novels present "solutions" idealized during the last decade by important powerless American groups, solutions which are characterized by Naylor, finally, as ineffectual routes to empowerment.

By creating a tapestry of nurturing women in her first novel, Naylor emphasizes how female values derived from mothering— nurturing, communality, concern with human feeling—are central to Brewster Place's survival. Published in 1982, *The Women of Brewster Place* was preceded by a decade of American feminist writing that responded to patriarchal society's devaluation of women by revalorizing female principles.[4] In reaction to the Western patriarchal emphasis on the individual; on the splitting of human beings into mind and body; and on competition, conquest, and power, these writers saw the necessity of

---

*This essay was written before Gloria Naylor published her third novel, *Mama Day* (1987).

honoring female values. If women were to become empowered, it was necessary for them to perceive their own primacy, their centrality to their society, as well as to analyze how dangerous patriarchal values were to a harmonious social order.

Because of their origins and history, African-American women could lay claim to a viable tradition in which they had been strong central persons in their families and communities, not solely because of their relationship to men, but because they themselves had bonded together to ensure survival of their children, their communities, the race. Partly because of the matricentric orientation of African peoples from whom they were descended, partly because of the nature of American slavery, African-American women have had to bond with each other in order to survive. African-Americans as a race could not have survived without the "female values" of communality, sharing and nurturing.

At the same time, the centrality of African-American women in their communities was in such great contrast to the American norm of woman's subordination in the nuclear family that Afro-American women were denigrated both in black and white society. The African-American mother was punished and maligned for being too strong, too central in her family, for being a "matriarch," a vortex of attitudes that culminated in white American government policy, such as the Moynihan Report, and in black cultural nationalist rhetoric of the 1960s.

African-American women writers of the 1970s responded to black and white society's denigration of the black mother and of female values by showing how such a position was sexist, was based on a false definition of woman as ineffectual, secondary, weak. Marshall in *Brown Girl, Brownstones*, and Morrison in *Sula* present women who are strong, who believe in their own primacy, and who are effective in some ways. But these writers also presented another view—that African-American women who internalize the dominant society's definition of women are courting self-destruction. So Morrison's Pauline and Pecola Breedlove in *The Bluest Eye*, and Walker's Margaret and Mem Copeland in *The Third Life of Grange Copeland*, are destroyed by their inability to resist society's false definitions of man and woman. It is important to note, as well, that these novels demonstrate not only how these specific women fall prey to sexist ideology but also that they do so partly because black communities themselves are sexist. Thus Morrison in *Sula* and Walker in *Meridian* critique motherhood as the black community's primary definition of woman.

Naylor's rendition of her women's lives in the community of Brewster Place indicates that she is intensely knowledgeable of the literature of her sisters and that the thought of African-American women during the seventies is one means by which she both celebrates and critiques women-centered communities.

The obvious characteristic that her women share, with the exception of Kiswana and the "two," is that they *must* live in streets like Brewster Place—that is, that they are displaced persons. Naylor is not the first African-American woman writer to present a black community that is *where* it is because of socioeconomic factors. Marshall's Barbadian-American community in *Brown Girl, Brownstones* is in Brooklyn because Barbados offers them little opportunity for advancement; Morrison's southern folk in *The Bluest Eye* migrate to Lorain, Ohio, because they need jobs. Each of these communities is attempting to forge a new tradition based on the old but related to the new circumstances in which they find themselves. But while they still have some belief in being able to improve their lives, the women who live in Brewster Place are caught in a cycle of never-ending displacement. Thus Brewster Place has a tradition of mores long before Mattie Michaels or Etta Mae Johnson ever get there. Naylor, then, presents a small urban community of black women who are outcasts precisely because they are poor black women, a type of community that has been a part of black life in the United States for many generations. While the urban Selina of *Brown Girl, Brownstones* and the small-town Claudia of *The Bluest Eye* can look back at their story of growing up as an education, the women of Brewster Place are in a static landscape. They were here yesterday and unless there is some catastrophic change in society, they will be here tomorrow.

The culture of sharing and nurturing in Brewster Place is based on a black tradition in this country that hearkens back to slavery. Important contemporary novels written by African-Americans have presented women characters who are mutually supportive of one another. Margaret Walker's *Jubilee* (1966) reminds us that it was such values that allowed the ordinary

slave to survive. Paule Marshall's *Brown Girl*, Brownstones provides us with vivid scenes of Silla and her women friends
around the kitchen table as they defend themselves against
their men as well as against white society. Toni Morrison
gives us a lyrical account of southern women, like her Aunt
Jimmy in *The Bluest Eye*, who created communities in their
own image, as well as a stunning description of the Peace's
matrifocal house in *Sula*. In these novels, as in *The Women of
Brewster Place*, women share such common concerns as the
raising of children, and as in Brewster Place, these women-
communities are defenses against sexism and racism, against
the abuses that are inflicted on black women. But while these
women may be independent, it is an independence forged
from the necessity of having to fend off attack; in fact, some of
the women would prefer not to have this independence that
they have not chosen. And in all of these novels, the women
do not or cannot change their condition, so much as they cope
with it as best they can.

So neither the feistiness of Eva Peace nor the persistence of
Silla Boyce prevents the destruction of the Bottom nor the
tearing down of the Brooklyn brownstones. What does occur
in these novels is that someone understands something about
her relationship to her community. But Naylor is not only
concerned with this relationship. While stressing, through the
form of her novel, that her women have strong bonds with
one another, she emphasizes as well that these relationships
do not substantively change their lives. Her novel ends not
with Nel missing Sula nor with Selina understanding her
mother, but with the movement of these women to yet another such street, where they no doubt will relive this pattern
as "Brewster Place still waits to die."

By presenting a community in which strong women-bonds
do not break the cycle of powerlessness in which so many
poor black women are imprisoned, Naylor points to a theoretical dilemma with which feminist thinkers have been wres-
tling. For while the values of nurturing and communality are
central to a just society, they often preclude the type of behavior necessary to achieve power in this world, behavior such as
competitiveness, extreme individualism, the desire to con-
quer. How does one break the cycle of powerlessness without
giving up the values of caring so necessary to the achievement

of a just society? Doesn't powerlessness itself breed internalization of self-destructive societal values? How does one achieve
the primacy of self without becoming ego centered? Further,
since the values of these women are necessary to their survival, wouldn't they change if their socioeconomic conditions
changed? Isn't it the very fact that these women do cope
through these values that precludes their destruction of the
wall that entraps them? How does one fight power without
taking on the values of those who have power?

Two elements in the novel suggest other avenues. One is
Mattie's dream at the end of the story, in which the women
learn that they have participated in the destruction of Lorraine, one of their sisters, and can redeem themselves only if
they protest her death—in other words that their internalization of societal values helps to keep them powerless. Having
learned this, the anger of the women erupts against their real
enemy, the wall that shuts them in. But Mattie awakens
from this dream to a gloriously sunny day on which the community is to have a block party, an event which will take
away the pain, at least for a short time, of Brewster Place's
inhabitants.

The other element in the novel is Naylor's portrayal of the
character Kiswana. Although she is presented as lacking the
grit and humor of the other women who have endured more
and lived more deeply, she is nevertheless the only one who
attempts to help the community see itself as a political force
that can fight the landlords and demand its rights. Still, she
can leave Brewster Place when she wishes. She does not risk
survival, as the others would if they rebelled; nor has she yet
been worn down by the unceasing cycle of displacement that
the others have experienced. And she has a sense of how
power operates *precisely* because she comes from Linden Hills,
a place she leaves *precisely* because it is so focused on money
and power.

Naylor's inclusion of Kiswana as a pivotal character in *The
Women of Brewster Place* indicates the great distance between
women who *must* live in women-centered communities and
those who have the option to live in them. For Kiswana's
choice to live in Brewster Place is already a sign that, in
relation to the other women, she has some privilege in the
society. She is an "exception," while they are the majority.

And her privilege comes from the fact that she was raised in a wealthy community.

Kiswana is, in fact, the link between Naylor's first novel and her second, *Linden Hills*, in which the pursuit of money and power is a central issue. Given the nature of the power in this society, many powerless groups have experienced the ineffectiveness of sharing and nurturing communities as a means to liberation. They therefore have often idealized another solution in their search for autonomy—taking on the values of the powerful. In *Linden Hills*, Naylor analyzes the effects of the drive for power, a drive that originally emanates from Nedeed's desire to elevate black people's status in America.

Just as *The Women of Brewster Place* was preceded by a decade of writing about female values, *Linden Hills*, published in 1985, was preceded by a decade that marked the rise of a more distinctly visible black middle class than had ever existed before in this country.[5] This period was, as well, a time when the goal of women was often portrayed as "making it" in the system. Media events, such as *Newsweek*'s 1987 article on the black underclass and ABC's program on the women's movement, emphasize this orientation. What these analyses often omit, however, is that the rise of the money/power solution amongst powerless groups in the 1970s has much to do with the character of African-American and women's mass movements of the sixties and early seventies, when political goals were difficult to achieve, not because they were not vigorously fought for but because of the system's successful resistance to meaningful change. In the seventies, the emphasis on material gain that characterized so much of the media's presentation of these groups' desires is actually a return to an old strategy that has never worked. But since so few of us are aware of our history, it is not surprising that the swing from mass political movements to an emphasis on individual gain as a route to empowerment would occur.

In critiquing the solution of money and status as a means to empowerment, Naylor stresses that it too is part of African-American tradition. Unlike Morrison's Macon Dead of *Song of Solomon*, who begins his rise in the 1920s, Luther Nedeed's plan originated in the 1820s, when slavery was very much alive. By charting the Nedeed generations, Naylor reminds us that a black upper-middle class has existed for some time, and that the drive to liberate the race through the creation of an elite group is not unique to the 1970s. Also, in portraying the original Nedeed plan, Naylor points up an abiding element of this "solution," for in choosing those who will be allowed to become a part of this class, Nedeed recognizes that they must deny their history of shared oppression, lest they see structural changes, rather than a duplication of the existing structure, as their goal.

What also distinguishes Naylor's presentation of the black upper-middle class is her analysis of its patriarchal position. All the Nedeed men clearly grasp the fact that the subordination of the female to the male is an essential element in becoming a powerful people in America. The first Nedeed buys his wife, a slave, and never frees her, and successive Nedeed men imprison their wives through isolating them. As well, the subordination of female to male is, in Naylor's narrative, interwoven with the Nedeeds' emphasis on a fixed hierarchy as a necessary characteristic of their domain. So what level one lives on in the "hills" is a sure indication of one's status, and absolutely adhered-to traditions determine even the Nedeed men's behavior, as they attempt, through the control of community mores, to obliterate change.

In selecting her essential elements of a developing patriarchy, Naylor has learned much from contemporary African-American women's literature, for it has provided her with clues about the dangers to which the creation of a black elite might lead. So Linden Hills is not so much hill as plateau, in much the same way that in *Sula* Morrison's Bottom is actually the top. One means by which the powerless are kept powerless is through the distortion of words, of naming, that is imposed on them. Like Morrison, Naylor emphasizes then how language, in this case the language of one of the powerless, is distorted to camouflage truth. And, like Morrison, Naylor also uses dates to name her chapters, as if the march of time were the determining factor in her narrative. Naylor's dates are not only ironic in that they are the days of giving and of peace, but they also emphasize the Christian and therefore Western orientation of Linden Hills. So while Morrison's chapters emphasize that time for the folk is not so much chronology as it is significant action, Naylor's chapters are a means by which we discover the tension between Nedeed's

Western patriarchal orientation toward time and the difficulties such rigidity imposes on even his most willing residents. As has been true of so many monarchs, his inability to change is one major cause of his downfall in those last days of the year.

Naylor also revises Morrison by having Luther Nedeed, her ex-slave, become financially successful because he, unlike Morrison's nameless ex-slave, excludes from his settlement those blacks who refer to a collective history. While Morrison's Bottom, then, is a distinctly African-American community with a distinct African-American culture, Linden Hills residents reject black culture. It is no wonder that Luther Nedeed sees that his ancestors' plan has failed. For though Linden Hills residents have money and status, they are no longer black. They have lost their identity, the identity which was the source of Linden Hills's origins. They therefore cannot create a community, and worse, they hate their controller, Nedeed himself, who has conditioned them to be interested only in individual gain. By placing the pursuit of money and power above all else, the Nedeeds fragment the black community and destroy the goal for which they have sacrificed family feeling, love, fraternity, pleasure—the very qualities that make life worth living, qualities central to liberation and empowerment.

Ironically, not only have Linden Hills residents lost their identity, neither have they gained power. Nedeed perceives how his showplace is threatened by the proliferation of Brewster Places, those who have been excluded from money and status. To the larger world, Linden Hills's image is affected by Brewster Place's image, just as the status of the black upper-middle class today is affected by the fact that during the seventies there was a corresponding rise in poor blacks, particularly poor black women. The creation of an elite class has not empowered the race, nor has it resulted in the existence of a group of blacks unaffected by racism. The distance between Linden Hills and Brewster Place, then, is not as great as it might appear to be, and Nedeed is not so much a patriarch as a manager, who must hold to rules that are actually determined by whites.

Naylor recalls, as well, Marshall's depiction of her Barbadian-American community in *Brown Girl, Brownstones* by demonstrating that group's desire for property and status as a bulwark against failure. But while Marshall's Silla belongs to a distinct woman-community and passes on some of its values to her daughter, Selina, the Nedeed women are isolated from other women as all traces of female values or of a distinct woman-community are erased from Linden Hills. Like Marshall's Avey in *Praisesong for the Widow*, the Nedeed women lose their identity and sense of community. But while Avey is able to retrieve her true name because of her experience with her maternal ancestors, the Nedeed women are cut off from their own herstory and have no daughters to whom they can bequeath their personal experience. By emphasizing these women's ignorance of their herstory as well as their sons' separation from them, Naylor revises Marshall's emphasis in all of her novels of the continuity of community values, of "female values," among New World blacks. Naylor suggests then that such values can be obliterated by the predominant class distinctions inherent in the urge to develop a patriarchy.

In many ways, the Nedeed women more resemble Jadine of Morrison's *Tar Baby*, in that they themselves believe in the primacy of material success and place little value on the ancient women—properties of sharing and nurturing. But Jadine does sense, through her obsession with the African woman in the yellow dress and her dream in Eloe of her maternal ancestors, that she may be giving up something of incalculable value. However, the Nedeed women, as well as Laurel, the successful businesswoman of Linden Hills, do not sense this until it is much too late. Like the tragic mulattas of nineteenth and early twentieth-century literature, they are trapped, without being aware of it, by their own adherence to class values that demean them as women. Unlike Hurston's Janie Starks, who too experiences the trap of ladydom, they find, too late, the language to give a name to their condition. Nor, given the lack of a community with a tradition of pleasure as an important value, do they encounter a woman friend, as Walker's Celie does, who might enable them to challenge the Nedeed patriarchy.

What is also interesting about Naylor's account of Linden Hills, as opposed to recent African-American women's literature, is her presentation of central male characters. In her development of Nedeed's character, she gives us not only their attempt to develop their patriarchy but their failure as well. That failure is due to their inability to create a community, which Naylor suggests must be the source of any route African-Americans take to empowerment. A community does not exist if it is rigidly controlled; nor can it exist without a shared history or shared values. But Naylor also presents male characters who experience the restrictions of Nedeed's vision. Like Son in Morrison's *Tar Baby*, Willie in *Linden Hills* values fraternity above money, but significantly unlike Morrison's refugee, Willie is still a viable part of a working-class community, Putney Wayne. While her first novel focuses on friendships among women, *Linden Hills* emphasizes the friendship between men, Willie and Lester. And in contrast to one other such friendship in contemporary African-American women's fiction, the friendship between Morrison's Milkman and Guitar in *Song of Solomon*, Naylor's Willie and Lester are not opposed to each other's values. In so tenderly portraying the relationship of these two, Naylor may be suggesting that genuine friendship between men who share similar values, as well as friendship between women, is critical to the African-American community's search for empowerment.

Like Kiswana, who is the transitional character between *The Women of Brewster Place* and *Linden Hills*, Willie may be the transitional figure between Linden Hills and Naylor's next novel. Like Kiswana, he is interested in and knowledgeable about the history and literature of African-Americans. But he is also educated in one respect that she is not. He comes from a living working-class African-American community with a deep cultural past that is as old as Linden Hills. Through his friendship with Lester, he learns about Linden Hills from the inside and thus knows that the solution of the creation of an elite class fragments and destroys community. As a person intensely involved in the direction of his folk's future, then, he is not as likely to repeat, as some upwardly mobile working-class men have done, Nedeed's error.

What he and others like him can do to empower their communities is not solved for us in either of these novels. For Naylor does not so much give us solutions as she uses her knowledge of African-American women's literature to show how complex the conditions of powerless groups are. She may be the first African-American woman writer to have such access to her tradition. And the complexity of her two novels indicates how valuable such knowledge can be. In doing her own black feminist reading of her literary tradition so as to dramatize the convoluted hierarchy of class, race, and gender distinctions in America today, she has begun to create a geographical world in her fiction, as varied and complex as the structure of our society.

NOTES

1. Gloria Naylor, *The Women of Brewster Place* (New York: Penguin Contemporary American Fiction Series, 1982), 60.
2. *Ibid.*, 141.
3. Gloria Naylor, *Linden Hills* (New York: Tucknor and Fields, 1985), 141.
4. Marilyn French's *Beyond Power* and Bell Hooks's *Feminist Theory: From Margin to Center* both summarize this orientation and suggest theoretical dilemmas that result from it.
5. William Wilson's *The Declining Significance of Race* and Thomas Sowell's *Ethnic America* discuss this phenomena from different points of view.

Segregated Lives:

Rita Dove's *Thomas and Beulah*

John Shoptaw

At the beginning of Rita Dove's arresting new volume of poetry, we are given directions for reading that turn out to be true but impossible to follow: "These poems tell two sides of a story and are meant to be read in sequence." The impossibility is not physical, as in the instructions prefacing John Ashbery's long double-columned poem, *Litany*, which tell us that the columns "are meant to be read as simultaneous but independent monologues"; rather, the impossibility in reading the two sides of Rita Dove's book—Thomas's side (I. "Mandolin," 23 poems) followed by Beulah's side (II. "Canary in Bloom," 21 poems)—is biographical and historical. The lives of Thomas and Beulah, whether considered together or individually, lack what would integrate them into a single story. The events in *Thomas and Beulah* are narrated in strict chronological order, which is detailed in the appended chronology. The subjection of story time to historical time, unusual in modern narratives, gives Dove's sequence a tragic linearity, a growing sense that what is done cannot be undone and that what is not done but only regretted or deferred cannot be redeemed in the telling. The narrative runs from Thomas's riverboat life (1919) to his arrival in Akron (1921) and marriage to Beulah (1924), to their children's births, his jobs at Goodyear, his stroke (1960) and death (1963). Then the narrative begins again with Beulah: her father's flirtations, Thomas's flirtations and courtship (1923), their marriage (1924), a pregnancy (1931), her millinery work (1950), a family reunion (1964), and her death (1969). In the background, the Depression and the March on Washington mark respectively the trials of the couple's and their children's generations.

The sequence of *Thomas and Beulah* resembles fiction more than it does a poetic sequence—Faulkner's family chronicles in particular. Dove's modernist narrator stands back paring her fingernails like an unobtrusive master or God. The cover shows a snapshot, of Thomas and Beulah presumably, and the volume may be considered as a photo album, or two albums, with only the date and place printed underneath each picture. Thomas and Beulah are probably Rita Dove's grandparents; the book is dedicated to her mother, Elvira Elizabeth, and the third child born to Thomas and Beulah is identified in the chronology as Liza. But whether the couple is actually Rita Dove's grandparents is less important than the fact that all evidence of their relation has been removed. Any choice of genre involves an economy of gains and losses. Objective, dramatic narration—showing rather than telling—has the advantage of letting the events speak for themselves and the disadvantage of dispensing with the problematics of narrative distortion and a camera-eye or God's-eye view. *Thomas and Beulah* tells it like it is and assumes it is like it tells us.

The most surprising thing about *Thomas and Beulah* is the severance not between narrator and story but between story and story. In "Wingfoot Lake," Beulah's in-laws take the widow to a segregated Goodyear picnic: "white families on one side and them/on the other, unpacking the same/squeeze bottles of Heinz, the same/waxy beef patties and Salem potato chip bags." The "two sides of a story" are similarly segregated in Dove's volume, cordoned off by the roman numerals I and II. *Thomas and Beulah* tells no joyous love story, as we might expect, nor even a tragedy of love lost. The lives of Thomas and Beulah rarely intersect: There are few common events in their stories and no Faulknerian climax in which their worlds collide. They rarely think about each other (Beulah's name does not even appear in Thomas's side); and when they do, it is with an absentminded fondness. Their lives' desires lie elsewhere. The love of Thomas's life is Lem, who dies in the volume's brilliant inaugural poem, "The Event." The easygoing cadences of the opening stanzas obscure the irony that this is not the honeymooning couple we expected:

Ever since they'd left the Tennessee ridge
with nothing to boast of
but good looks and a mandolin,

the two Negroes leaning
on the rail of a riverboat
were inseparable: Lem plucked

to Thomas' silver falsetto.

On Thomas's drunken dare, Lem dives into the water toward
an island mirage, which sinks into the river like Atlantis along
with Lem. All Lem leaves Thomas is "a stinking circle of
rags,/the half-shell of a mandolin." The commonest images,
circles and lines, are the most capable of variation. One of the
signs of Dove's poetic power is the changes she rings on that
Orphic half-shell, the surviving Aristophanic hemisphere of
their round of love. The other half rises to heaven, becoming
the blue vault of the sky. A Zeppelin disaster in 1931 merely
replays Thomas's own tragedy. In a wonderfully interlaced
poem, "Nothing Down," Thomas and Beulah pick out a "Sky
blue Chandler," while in the alternating italicized stanzas,
Thomas combines the memories of a blue flower overhead
and a young Lem in a tree into a prophetic, ghostly gesture of
forgiveness. But the car, as we learn from the chronology
(which adds its own silent ironies to the volume), is repos-
sessed during the Depression. The sense of guilt and loss
stemming from the 1919 disaster drives Thomas for the next
half century to his death. Thomas spends his wedding night
playing Lem's mandolin; his disappointment over not having
any sons stems from his not making another Lem; the parable
of the possum playing dead recalls Lem; even his stroke is
Lem's doing:

he knows it was Lem all along:
Lem's knuckles tapping his chest in passing,
Lem's heart, for safekeeping,
he shores up in his arms.

The closest relative of Thomas's elegiac side of the story turns out to be Tennyson's *In Memoriam*, in which the poet deals with the death of his friend Arthur Hallem.

The bifurcations and divisions in *Thomas and Beulah* extend to the very grammar of its sentences, which are marked by the frequent appearance of free modifiers and absolute phrases. These constructions, uncommon in modern poetry and fiction (Faulkner, again, uses them more than any American writer, though less often than Dove), consist of a participial phrase (free modifier) or of a noun and a participial phrase (absolute), which are syntactically separated from the main clause or noun they modify. Both Thomas's sequence ("as the keys swung, ticking") and Beulah's ("the walls exploding with shabby tutus") end on these constructions. A stanza may employ several in a disjunctive series, as in "Courtship" when Thomas asks Beulah's father for her hand:

> Then the parlor festooned
> like a ship and Thomas
> twirling his hat in his hands
> wondering how did I get here.
> China pugs guarding a fringed settee
> where a father, half-Cherokee,
> smokes and frowns.
> *I'll give her a good life—*
> what was he doing,
> selling all for a song?
> His heart fluttering shut
> then slowly opening.

This pronounced style can tell us much about *Thomas and Beulah*. Since their verbs are subordinated and nominalized, such constructions tend to fragment action into a series of still shots. Although there is persistent imagery of a bomb ticking and finally exploding ("the walls exploding in shabby tutus"), *Thomas and Beulah* is in fact a drama devoid of suspense, in which nothing ever happens, or in which "The Event," Lem's drowning, sets the narrative aftermath in motion. There is no Faulknerian passion or war or rape or murder or incest. Like most of us, Thomas and Beulah meet and marry and work and have kids and die without much intention or commotion. The book is realist, not in the obvious sense of treating the sordid and grim elements of experience, but in the essential sense of privileging ordinary experience over the strange. If the strange was the dark continent of the South, the ordinary is the undiscovered country of the Midwest.

Free modifiers and absolute phrases function in an additive syntax like a cinematic closeup. As we can see in the following passages from Dove's book, the focus is usually upon parts of the body or clothing: "his wingtips balanced/on a scuffed linoleum square" (33), "the cigars crackling/in cellophane"(20), "Lem's knuckles tapping his chest in passing" (39), "storm door clipping her heel on the way in" (40), "white arms jutting into the chevrons of high society"(72). Since they are set off from their main clauses, these trailers can displace in a synecdochal flourish the sentences they supplement: "the cut-out magazine cloud taped to the pane"(65), "the white picket fence marching up the hill"(62), "the pale eyes bright as salt"(54), "cold drawing the yellow out"(47), "a pod set to sea,/a kiss unpuckering"(43), "white tongues of remorse/sinking into the earth"(30), "The canary courting its effigy./The girls fragrant in their beds"(28). These unbound phrases contain the most striking poetry in Dove's book, set off like mirage islands from the syntactical mainland where the prosaic lives of Thomas and Beulah are lived. It is a region both inviolable and unreachable.

There is no loss in Beulah's side of the story equivalent to the loss of Lem; her side consequently lacks the haunting pathos of Thomas's. Because it is not a relic, Beulah's canary makes insignificant music when compared to Thomas's man-dolin. The gap in Beulah's side is not an unrecovered loss but an unfulfilled promise. Beulah misses what she never knew; her never-never mirage island keeps its distance. An absence, however, is inevitably understood or felt as a loss. What we miss we must have had, and all empty names are markers. Dove dramatizes the positing of a loss in place of a fundamental absence in "Dusting," the best poem in the second half of *Thomas and Beulah*:

Every day a wilderness—no
shade in sight. Beulah
patient among knicknacks,
the solarium a rage
of light, a grainstorm
as her gray cloth brings
dark wood to life.

Under her hand scrolls
and crests gleam
darker still. What
was his name, that
silly boy at the fair with
the rifle booth? And his kiss and
the clear bowl with one bright
fish, rippling
wound!

Not Michael—
something finer. Each dust
stroke a deep breath and
the canary in bloom.
Wavery memory: home
from a dance, the front door
blown open and the parlor
in snow, she rushed
the bowl to the stove, watched
as the locket of ice
dissolved and he
swam free.

That was years before
Father gave her up
with her name, years before
her name grew to mean
Promise, then
Desert-in-Peace.
Long before the shadow and
sun's accomplice, the tree.

Maurice.

Strong poems omit their linkages. That remembering is like unearthing (dusting), or diving for, or thawing out memories is just what "Dusting" must leave unsaid for its details to resonate. Beulah's memory of freeing her fish from its "locket of ice" ("locked in ice") is itself an allegory of remembering. Beulah's dusting stirs up a "grainstorm" of memories—a nonce word gathering "brainstorm," "rainstorm," and "dust storm." The "wavery" wood grain with its "crests" has its own depths to fathom. Diving into the past is in fact the characteristic activity of this volume, as the opening poem's buried signature attests ("*Them's chestnuts,/I believe.* Dove"). The forgotten name, Maurice, surfaces in its own final stanza but begins to sound earlier in "ice," "Promise," and "accomplice." The name Maurice itself echoes and marks all her unrecovered memories as the name beginning with *M* ("Not Michael") on the tip of Beulah's tongue ("M-Maurice," "memories").

But there is another name, appearing for the first time in "Dusting," whose face or landscape cannot be remembered because it has not yet been discovered: Beulah. Coined first in *Isaiah* and most famously in *The Pilgrim's Progress*, Beulah names the Promised Land. In Hebrew, "Beulah" means "married." As Thomas is separated from Lem, Beulah is divorced from Beulah. Beulah's heart is set on Beulah-Land, which goes by several names. In "Magic," a giant Eiffel Tower appears in the sky as "a sign/she would make it to Paris one day." In "Pomade," a friend's fragrance "always put her/in mind of Turkish minarets against/a sky wrenched blue." From "The House on Bishop Street" it was nameless but nearly visible: "If she leaned out she could glimpse/the faintest of mauve—no more than an idea—/growing just behind the last houses." It appears last, and for what it is, in "The Oriental Ballerina," as daylight comes to Beulah's deathbed. Beulah's last moments are accompanied by a mechanical ballerina, a paltry Angel of Death, pirouetting on her jewelbox to "the wheeze of the old/rugged cross" on her radio. Ironic juxtapositions of the exotic and the homely, the beautiful and the vulgar, organize the poem. What finally dawns on Beulah is not a Beulah-Land but an unbridgeable nothing that the name has hidden:

The head on the pillow sees nothing
else, though it feels the sun warming

its cheeks. *There is no China,*
no cross, just the papery kiss
of a kleenex above the stink of camphor,
the walls exploding with shabby tutus. . . .

This uncompromising, Shakespearean renunciation explodes
Beulah's myths of Beulah. There is no China, no Promised
Land, no LandLord. Beulah also explodes the fiction of her
own story by denying the existence of the omniscient, absen-
tee Narrator who relates it—the rest is ellipsis. In "One Volume Missing," Thomas buys a used encyclopedia: "for five
bucks/no zebras, no Virginia,/no wars." And no Zion, as in
the "A.M.E. Zion Church," which sold it. *Thomas and Beulah*—
with its gaps, divisions, and deletions—comes also as an incomplete set. But that is Dove's bargain. For us to read any of
her fragmentary alphabet, the never-never Volume that would
integrate the Goodyear Picnic, Thomas and Lem, Thomas and
Beulah, the main clauses and their absolutes, Beulah and
Beulah, the narrator and her stories, must remain missing.

Autoethnography:

The An-Archic Style of
Dust Tracks on a Road

Françoise Lionnet

One is an artist at the cost of regarding that which all non-artists call "form" as content, as "the matter itself." To be sure, then one belongs in a topsy-turvy world: for henceforth content becomes something merely formal—our life included.
—Nietzsche, 1888

The words do not count . . . The tune is the unity of the thing.
—Zora Neale Hurston, 1942

The greatness of a man is to be found not in his acts but in his style.
—Frantz Fanon, 1952

One need only glance at the table of contents of Hurston's autobiography to notice that it presents itself as a set of inter-active thematic *topoi* superimposed on a loosely chronological framework. The seemingly linear progression from "My Birth-place" to "Looking Things Over" is more deceptive in that regard than truly indicative of a narrator's psychological de-velopment, quest for recognition, or journey from innocence to experience as traditionally represented in confessional auto-biographies. The chapter titled "Seeing the World as It Is," with which Hurston originally meant to conclude the book,[1] is a philosophical essay on power, politics, and human relations on a planetary scale. It is the radical testament of a writer who rejects *ressentiment* and, refusing to align herself with any "party," explains that it is because she does "not have much of a herd instinct" (344–345). Rather than recounting the events of her life, Hurston is more interested in showing us who she is—or, to be more precise, how she has become what she is—an individual who ostensibly values her independence more than any kind of political commitment to a cause, especially the cause of "Race Solidarity," as she puts it (327). Hers is a controversial and genealogical enterprise that has been much criticized, charged with accommodationism (xxxviii) and with disappointing the expectations of "frankness" and "truthfulness" which are all too often unquestioningly linked to this genre of self-writing.[2] Openly critical of Dust Tracks in his Introduction to the second edition, her biographer, Robert Hemenway, puts it thus: "Style . . . becomes a kind of camouflage, an escape from articulating the paradoxes of her personality" (xxxviii and see xxxiv–xxxv, for example).

AN-ARCHY AND COMMUNITY

In light of the skepticism with which contemporary literary theory has taught us to view any effort of self-representation in language, I would like to propose a different approach to the issue of Hurston's presumed insincerity and untrustworthiness.[3] It may perhaps be more useful to reconsider Dust Tracks on a Road not as autobiography but rather as self-portrait, in the sense redefined by Michel Beaujour—"texts which are self-contained rather than being the representation of past actions"[4]—and to try to elaborate a conceptual framework that would not conflict with Hurston's own avowed methodology as essayist and anthropologist. Indeed, what I would like to suggest here is that Dust Tracks amounts to autoethnography, that is, the defining of one's subjective ethnicity as mediated through language, history, and ethnographical analysis; in short, that the book amounts to a kind of "figural anthropology" of the self.[5]

In a recent essay, James Clifford refers to the "allegory of salvage," which generally tended to dominate the representational practice of field-workers in the era of Boasian anthropology. For these field-workers, says Clifford, the preservation of disappearing cultures and vanishing lore was seen as the vital "redemption" of the "otherness" of primitive cultures from a global entropy: "The other is lost, in disintegrating time and place, but saved in the text."[6] This textualization of the object of representation incorporated a move from the oral–discursive field experience of the collector of folklore to his or her written version of that initial intersubjective moment—a transcription that is also a way of speaking *for* the other culture, a kind of ventriloquism. Having been trained under Boas, Hurston was supposed to be going in the field to do just that: to salvage her own "vanishing" Negro culture. Her position of fundamental liminality—being at once a participant in and an observer of her culture—would bring home to her the distorting effects of that problematic shift from orality to fixed, rigid texuality and thus would reinforce her skepticism about the anthropological project, in her assigned role as detached, objective interpreter and translator. Having shared in that rural culture during her childhood in Eatonville, she could not adopt the nostalgic pose common to those western ethnographies that implicitly lament the loss of an Edenic, and preindustrial past. Instead, her skepticism about the writing of culture would permeate the writing of the self, the autobiography, turning it into the allegory of an ethnographic project that self-consciously moves from the general (the history of Eatonville) to the particular (Zora's life, her family and friends) and back to the general (religion, culture, and world politics in the 1940s). Unlike black spiritual autobiographies, which exhibit a similar three-fold pattern of death, conversion, and rebirth, as well as a strong sense of transcendent purpose, *Dust Tracks* does not seek to legitimate itself through appeal to what William L. Andrews has called a "powerful source of authorization," such as religion or another organized system of belief.[7] It is in that sense that *Dust Tracks* is a powerfully an-archic work, not anchored in any original and originating story of racial or sexual difference.

The tone of the work and its rhetorical strategy of exaggeration draw attention to its style and away from what it directly denotes. For example, the statement "There were no discrete nuances of life on Joe Clarke's porch . . . all emotions were naked and nakedly arrived at" (62) describes the men's reactions to instances of adultery (a folksy topic), but it also carries historical implications about the pioneer spirit in general, as the sentence that follows it makes clear: "This was the spirit of that whole new part of the state at the time, as it always is where men settle new lands" (62). Similarly, when Zora talks about her unhappy love affair, it is through vivid images that convey, with some irony, the universality of pain rather than deep personal anguish: "I freely admit that everywhere I set my feet down, there were tracks of blood. Blood from the very middle of my heart" (260). Regretting the "halcyon days" of childhood, she bemoans the gravity that pervades adulthood and makes us unable to "fly with the unseen things that soar" (78). And when she is discussing race, her denial—"No, instead of Race Pride being a virtue, it is a sapping vice" (325)—implicates us directly in that seemingly volatile statement instead of pointing us to the obvious historical context of the moment, that is, the rise of fascism, World War II, colonialism, the hypocrisy and self-satisfaction of "the blond brother" (343), and the preponderance of "instances of human self-bias" (281). Clearly, *Dust Tracks* does not gesture toward a coherent tradition of introspective self-examination with soul-baring displays of emotion.

Paradoxically, despite its rich cultural content, the work does not authorize unproblematic recourse to culturally grounded interpretations. It is an orphan text that attempts to create its own genealogy by simultaneously appealing to and debunking the cultural traditions it helps to redefine. Hurston's chosen objects of study, for example, the folktales that come alive during the storytelling, or "lying," sessions she observes, are indeed never "fixed." Their content is not rigid and unchanging but varies according to the tale-telling situation. It is the contextual frame of reference, the situation of the telling, that determines how a tale is reinterpreted by each new teller; hence, for the anthropologist, there is no "essential" quality to be isolated in the content of those tales, but there is a formal structure that can and must be recognized if she is to make sense of, and do justice to, the data gathered. The chapter titled "Research" puts the matter clearly and succinctly:

> I enjoyed collecting the folk-tales and I believe the people from whom I collected them enjoyed the telling of them, just as much as I did the hearing. Once they got started, the "lies" just rolled and story-tellers fought for a chance to talk. It was the same with the songs. *The one thing to be guarded against, in the interest of truth, was over-enthusiasm. For instance, if the song was going good, and the material*

ran out, the singer was apt to interpolate pieces of other songs into it. The only way you can know when that happens, is to know your material so well that you can sense the violation. Even if you do not know the song that is being used for padding, you can tell the change in rhythm and tempo. *The words do not count. The subject matter in Negro folk-songs. can be anything* and go from love to work, to travel, to food, to weather, to fight, to demanding the return of a wig by a woman who has turned unfaithful. *The tune is the unity of the thing.* And you have to know what you are doing when you begin to pass on that, because Negroes can fit in more words and leave out more and still keep the tune better than anyone I can think of (197–198). [Emphasis mine.]

The whole issue of form and content, style and message is astutely condensed here. "Truth" is clearly a matter of degree and can easily be distorted by the over-enthusiasm of the performer. If *over-enthusiasm* can be seen as another word for hyperbole, then Hurston the writer is hereby cautioning her own reader to defer judgment about the explicit referentiality of her text. Why come to it with preconceived notions of autobiographical truth when the tendency to make hyperbolic and over-enthusiastic statements about her subject matter is part of her "style" as a writer? Couldn't we see in this passage Hurston's own implicit theory of reading and thus use it to derive our interpretive practice from the text itself, instead of judging the work according to Procrustean notions of autobiographical form?

Hurston is fully aware of the gaps and discrepancies that can exist between intention and execution, reality and representation, reason and imagination, in short, between the words (or subject matter) and the tune, which is the source of unity for the singers on the porch. For her, too, the flow of creative energy is an imaginative transfiguration of literal truth/content through rhetorical procedures. The resulting text/performance thus transcends pedestrian notions of referentiality, for the staging of the event is part of the process of "passing on," of elaborating cultural forms, which are not static and inviolable but dynamically involved in the creation of culture itself. It is thus not surprising that Hurston should view the self, and especially the "racial self," as a fluid and changing concept, an arbitrary signifier with which she had better dispense if it is meant to inhibit (as any kind of reductive labeling might) the inherent plasticity of individuals.[8] Viewed from such an angle, *Dust Tracks*, far from being a "camouflage" and an "escape," does indeed *exemplify* the "paradoxes of her personality" by revealing a fluid and multidimensional self that refuses to allow itself to be framed and packaged for the benefit of those human, all-too-human mortals, "both black and white who [claim] special blessings on the basis of race" (235).

Indeed, in the case of the folkloric forms she studies, the plasticity of the "subject matter" of songs and tales is corroborated by her research experience in the field; if we can be justified in seeing the "subject" of the autobiography and the "subject matter" of folklore as homologous structures or *topoi* that reflect and mirror each other, then the dialogue between these homologies shapes the autobiographical text while revealing the paradoxes of the genre. This dialogue serves to illuminate Hurston's combined identities as anthropologist and writer as these simultaneously begin to emerge and to converge in *Dust Tracks*. In the process of articulating their differences, she actually establishes their inescapable similarities, prefiguring the practice of such theorists as Clifford Geertz or Victor Turner. As Hemenway rightly points out, "Zora never became a professional academic folklorist because such a vocation was alien to her exuberant sense of self, to her admittedly artistic, sometimes erratic temperament, and to her awareness of the esthetic content of black folklore."[9] But this psychologizing approach does not suffice to clarify the work and to explain Hurston's liminal position, her confident straddling of "high" (academic) and "low" (folk) cultures, the ease with which she brings to the theoretical enterprise of the academic collector of lore the insights and perceptivity of the teller of tales. What makes the autobiography interesting is that it unfolds the structures of meaning—the cultural "topics" that are discussed chapter by chapter (history, geography, mythology, kinship, education, work, travel, friendship, love, religion, politics, philosophy, and so on—through which the creative artist gives shape to her personal experiences as seen through the "spy-glass" of anthropology.[10]

Moving away from what might be the sterile analyses of a field-worker to the inspirational language of an artist, Hurston involves herself and her reader in a transformative process. She does not just record, describe, and represent; she transforms and is transformed by her autobiographical performance. To look at life from an aesthetic point of view and to celebrate her ethnic heritage are thus two complementary projects for her. Life is an aesthetic experience, a staged performance, reflected in the autobiography as well as the fictional writings, and literature is a means of recording with what Hemenway identifies as "a studied antiscientific approach" the lives and subjective realities of a particular people in a specific time and place.[11] It is this apparently antagonistic movement between life and literature, reality and its representation, orality and literacy, which informs the structural coherence of Dust Tracks, rather than the simply linear progression through the lived life. What the text puts in motion is a strategy of displacement regarding the expectations governing two modes of discourse: The "objective" exteriority is that of the autobiographer whose "inside search" does not bear out its promise of introspection, and the "intimate" tone is that of the anthropologist who implicates herself in her "research" by delving into Hoodoo, by performing initiation rites, and in an ironic and clever reversal of the ventriloquism of ethnography, by letting her informants inform us about Zora's persona in the field. As Big Sweet puts it, "You ain't like me. You don't even sleep with no mens . . . I think it's nice for you to be like that. You just keep on writing down them lies" (189).

So, if Hurston sometimes seems to be aspiring toward some kind of "raceless ideal," it is not because she is interested in the "universality" of human experiences. Quite the contrary, she wants to expose, as Hemenway explains, "the inadequacy of sterile reason to deal with the phenomena of living."[12] And "race" in that context is but a reasonable, pseudoscientific category for dealing with a basically fluid, diverse, and multifarious reality: "The stuff of my being is matter, ever changing, ever moving, but never lost" (279). Her philosophical position in Dust Tracks is in fact echoed more than twenty years later by Frantz Fanon in The Wretched of the Earth: "This historical necessity in which the men of African culture find themselves, that is, the necessity to racialize their claims and to speak more of African culture, than of national culture, will lead them up a blind alley." Warning that the undefined and vague entity "African culture" was a creation of European colonialism, Fanon chose to emphasize local historically and geographically specific contingencies, rather than "race" as a general and abstract concept: "And it is also true that those who are most responsible for this racialization of thought—or at least of our patterns of thought—are and remain those Europeans who have never ceased to set up white culture over and against all other so-called non-cultures [d'opposer la culture blanche aux autres incultures]."[13] Similarly, Hurston's interest in the folk communities of Eatonville, Polk County, Mobile, New Orleans, Nassau, Jamaica, and Haiti stemmed from the belief that the universal can only be known through the specific and that knowledge grounded in first-hand experience can yield more insights into the human condition and into the processes of acculturation, differentiation, and historicization to which human beings are subjected. I would thus argue that her unstated aim is identical to Fanon's later formulation: to destroy the white stereotype of black *inculture* not by privileging "blackness" as an oppositional category to "whiteness" in culture but by unequivocally showing the vitality and diversity of nonwhite cultures around the Caribbean and the coastal areas of the South, thereby dispensing completely with "white" as a concept and a point of reference. Unlike the proponents of the negritude movement, whose initial thrust was against white racism and prejudice, Hurston assumes the supremely confident posture of the anthropologist who need not *justify* the validity of her enterprise but can simply *affirm* by her study the existence of richly varied black cultures, thus delineating the semiotics of spaces where, in Houston Baker's words, "white culture's representations are squeezed to zero volume, producing a new expressive order."[14]

What must not be overlooked, therefore, in the passage I quoted from "Research," is the emphasis Hurston puts on contextual considerations and the implicit distinctions she then draws between her own position as anthropologist observing the event and the role of the singers directly involved in the performance. For example, it is important for the anthropologist —and for the literary critic attempting to model her approach on Hurston's—to know the "material," that is, to be steeped in the historical, geographical, and vernacular contexts of the "songs" in order to be able to determine where "pieces of other songs" are "interpolated" and used as "padding" when the original material "ran out." Does Hurston imply that there is a certain autonomy of the original text which is violated by the interpolation of fragments of other songs? It would seem, rather, that as an anthropologist she feels that it is important to make those kinds of distinctions; yet she recognizes that for the singers the question is unimportant. The song goes on; the participants collectively "keep the tune" and do not worry about the singularity or inviolability of a given text or song. In other words, the question of intertextuality or of hybridization of content is not significant for the artists (they do not see it as a transgression of rules of identity), however important it may be for the observer who wants to be able to determine where one particular song ends and the next one starts. The question of boundaries is thus raised and examined by the anthropologist while the artist in her recognizes both the futility of such conceptual distinctions and how severely limiting it is to try to establish the "true" identity and originality of the subject matter—or of authorial subjectivity, permeated as it is by the polyphonic voices of the community, which resonate throughout the text and thereby reflect different narrative stances, different points of view on life and on Zora herself.[15] Indeed, since "no two moments are any more alike than two snowflakes" (264), there is no inconsistency in presenting a multitude of personae and being nonetheless sincere. As a folk aphorism puts it, "Li'l flakes make de deepest snow," or what appears to be homogeneous is in fact a complicated layering of vastly disparate elements.

The chapter "Seeing the World as It Is" emphasizes Hurston's intentions and method: "I do not wish to close the frontiers of life upon my own self. I do not wish to deny myself the expansion of seeking into individual capabilities and depths by living in a space whose boundaries are race and nation" (330). Clearly, race and nation are singled out here as colonizing signs produced by an essentializing and controlling power ("Race Pride" 324–328) external to the inner self and bent on denying her access to "spaces" other than the ones to which she ostensibly belongs by virtue of her concrete situation. Her free-spirited call for "less race consciousness" (326) is to be understood in the context of her unabashed denunciation of "democracy" as just another name for selfish profiteering by the West at the expense of those "others" who live far away from the so-called democratic nations of Europe and America (338). These subversive and politically anarchic statements— which provoked the Procrustean editing of the autobiography— are the logical consequence of the ethnographer's skepticism. Because she remains radically *critical* without proposing positive and totalizing alternatives, she exemplifies a truly philosophical sensibility.[16] Her urge to ask questions rather than to propose solutions invites and provokes her readers to think beyond the commonplaces and received ideas of our cultures, beyond those proverbial voices of the community, the vox populi, *ouï-dire*, Heideggerian *Gerede*, or Barthesian *bêtise*— always rendered in free indirect speech—which enunciate the webs of beliefs that structure local consciousness of self.[17] Reporting those quotidian voices, she establishes cultural context, but by her skeptical detachment, she undermines the gregarious values of the group, whether it is the folk community (involved in "specifying" [186, 304], in "adult double talk" [62], and whose verbal creativity is nonetheless celebrated) or the social consensus that articulates interdictions and contradictions of all sorts ("This book-reading business was a hold-back and an unrelieved evil" [117]; "Not only is the scholastic rating at Howard high, but tea is poured in the manner!" [156]; "If it was so honorable and glorious to be black, why was it the yellow-skinned people among us had so much prestige?" [226]). These "common" values are now made available for parody. She thus opens up a space of resistance between the individual (*auto-*) and the collective (*-ethno-*) where the writing (*-graphy*) of singularity cannot be foreclosed.

Yet, a nagging question remains: How can Hurston's historical, embodied self, subject to the determinants of time and place—an Afro-American woman confronting racism and a world war—represent the site of a privileged resistance to those webs of belief that might encourage resentment and fixation on an unjust and painful past? As she puts it: "To me, bitterness is the under-arm odor of wishful weakness. It is the graceless acknowledgment of defeat" (280). Since both the perpetrators and the immediate victims of slavery are long dead and since she has "no personal memory of those times, and no responsibility for them" (282), she affirms that she would rather "turn all [her] thoughts and energies on the present" (284). This affirmation of life against "the clutching hand of Time" (284) is a creative release from the imposition of origin and the prison of history. Zora becomes a joyful Zarathustra, whose world is no longer limited and bound by the reality principle and who advocates deliverance from the spirit of revenge. But can this visionary posture of the self-portraitist allow for a positive involvement in the shaping of reality, present and future? How can it be reconciled with the anthropological claim to locally specific knowledge and with the historical novelist's success in drawing the suggestive allegorical fresco of a mythic Afro-Mediterranean past in *Moses, Man of the Mountain?*

Since Fanon, too, denounced revenge and fixation on the past as "a crystallization of guilt" (BSWM 228), perhaps he can provide some answer to the questions we ask of Hurston. If resentment is the essence of negative potentiality for the self, it is clear why Hurston rejects it outright. She wants the utmost freedom in "seeking into individual capabilities." Her refusal to adopt the "herd" mentality for the sake of solidarity actually places her in a long tradition of thinkers—Heraclitus, Montaigne, Nietzsche, Walter Benjamin, Frantz Fanon, and Roland Barthes—all essayists or masters of hyperbolic aphorisms. Fanon, in particular, was well aware of the peculiarly *racial* dilemma facing the children of the colonialist diaspora: Their marginality could not simply be articulated in terms of binary categories of black versus white. Fanon's plea against racialist attitudes thus echoes Hurston's reformulation of freedom and responsibility on a planetary scale:

> I as a man of color do not have the right to hope that in the white man there will be a crystallization of guilt toward the past of my race (228).

> I find myself—I, a man—in a world where words wrap themselves in silence; in a world where the other endlessly hardens himself . . .
> I am not a prisoner of history. I should not seek there for the meaning of my destiny.

I should constantly remind myself that the real *leap* consists in introducing invention into existence (229).

It is through the effort *to recapture the self and to scrutinize the self*, it is through the lasting tension of their freedom that men will be able to create the ideal conditions of existence for a human world (231). [Emphasis mine.]

The wish to "create . . . ideal conditions of existence" is synonymous here with the fight against all petit bourgeois mental habits that tend to favor manifestations of closure. Fanon wants to demythologize history and to prevent it from being used as the source of "reactional" behavior because, as "Nietzsche had already pointed out" and as he himself elaborates, "there is always resentment in a *reaction*" (BSWM 222). While severely criticizing his fellow colonized intellectuals for simply reproducing the values of the colonizer in adopting racialist thinking, Fanon did not hesitate to state that the quest for disalienation must be mediated by the refusal to accept the "Tower of the Past" (BSWM 226) and the problems of the present as definitive, in other words, by the belief that only the poetry of the future can move and inspire human beings to action and to revolution. Unlike Fanon, Hurston did not develop the visionary perspective into a revolutionary one, but her mystical desire to be one with the universe stems from a similar utopian need for a "waking dream"[18] of the possible that might inspire us to see beyond the constraints of the here and now to the idealized vision of a perfect future, albeit, in *Dust Tracks*, a life after death in which the substance of her being is again "part and parcel of the world" and "one with the infinite" (279). Both Fanon and Hurston suggest that we urgently need to retrieve those past traditions that can become the source of reconciliation and wholeness, for it is more important to learn from those traditions than to dwell on pain and injustice.

For Hurston, "the effort to recapture . . . and to scrutinize the self" is a project grounded in the quicksand of linguistic performance and thus inseparable from what Beaujour has called "a type of memory, both very archaic and very modern, by which the events of an individual life are eclipsed by the recollection of an entire culture." As Michael M. J. Fischer has stressed, ethnic memory is not only past- but future-oriented, and the dynamics of interpersonal knowledge within the intercultural strands of memory are inseparable from Hurston's project of self-portraiture, since to recapture the past is literally to create a new field of knowledge within her academic discipline: "If science ever gets to the bottom of Voodoo in Haiti and Africa, it will be found that some important medical secrets, still unknown to medical science, give it its power, rather than the gestures of ceremony" (205).[19] By suggesting historically valid mythological connections between ancient deities and prophets such as Isis and Persephone, on the one hand, and Damballah, Thoth, and Moses, on the other, and between those figures and the "two-headed" magicians of Hoodoo (191), who knows the creative power of words, Hurston leaves the door open for a historical revision both of Hoodoo religion and of antiquity, implying "two-headed" Egyptian and Greek origins for both Euro- and Afro-Americans. Because such a thesis would have been rejected by contemporary scholars, who then followed the "Aryan model" of antiquity, Hurston can only allude to it through literature.[20]

A comparison of the thematic similarities in Hurston's work does show that she was quite consciously using those ancient "personae" as multiple facets of her own self and of her own Afro-Mediterranean genealogy. One of her first published stories, "Drenched in Light," tells the story of Isis Watts, a protagonist who is clearly autobiographical, as is Isis Potts of *Jonah's Gourd Vine*.[21] This same persona is reintroduced in *Dust Tracks* under the name Persephone. The similarity of the protagonists suggests that the three narratives form a triptych: it is only by taking into consideration the mythological background of the protagonists' names that we can accurately understand the process of self-discovery through self-invention that characterizes Hurston's method. Tellingly, this process is a search for familial and maternal connections, for "mirrors" that can reflect positive aspects of the past instead of alienating images of subaltern faces.

HISTORY AND MEMORY

It is thus significant that the only events of her "private" life on which Hurston dwells in *Dust Tracks* are those that have deep symbolic and cultural value: The death of the mother and subsequent dispersion of the siblings echo the collective memory of her people's separation from Africa-as-mother and their ineluctable diaspora. That is why Kossola/Cudjo Lewis's story is an emblem of her own sense of bereavement and deprivation: "After seventy-five years, he still had that tragic sense of loss. That yearning for blood and cultural ties. That sense of mutilation. It gave me something to feel about" (204). Coming at the end of the "Research" chapter, the embedded narrative of Kossola's life serves as a powerful counterpoint to Zora's own story of strife and reconciliation with her brothers (172–173). It is thanks to her research and professional travels that she becomes, like the legendary Isis of Egyptian mythology, the link that reunites, reconnects the dispersed siblings, who can now "touch each other in the spirit if not in the flesh." The imagery that describes the disintegration of the family unit is a clear reminder of the historical conditions of the Middle Passage:

> I felt the warm embrace of kin and kind for the first time since the night after my mother's funeral, when we had huddled about the organ all sodden and bewildered, with the walls of our home suddenly blown down. On September 18th, that house had been a hovering home. September 19th, it had turned into a bleak place of desolation with unknown dangers creeping upon us from unseen quarters that made of us a whimpering huddle, though then we could not see why. But now, that was all over (173).

As private experiences echo collective ones and punctuate the deployment of the self-portrait, a picture of the field-worker as keeper of important knowledge, as go-between whose role is to facilitate the articulation of collective memory, emerges. By foregrounding the field research as the causal link to an empowering reunion with her scattered siblings, Hurston deploys much broader implications for the social lives of Afro-

Americans. She implies that connections to the past must not be severed if we are to regain a sense of what it is like to "touch each other in the spirit" and also that a sense of history must not be allowed to degenerate into the remembrance of paralyzing images. That is why she also remarks that "any religion that satisfies the individual urge is valid for that person" (205). Since ancient traditions such as Hoodoo contain, as Hemenway says, "the old, old mysticism of the world in African terms," they are useful to a "thick description" of cultural nuances, and they help demarcate the historical context relevant to the study of folklore.[22]

Hurston's aim is to maintain the integrity of black culture without diluting it and to celebrate its values while remaining critical of those pressures from within the "family" that can mutilate individual aspirations—as her eldest brother Bob had been guilty of doing to her when she went to live with him, hoping that he would help put her through school, only to find herself playing the role of maid to his wife. It is this de facto lack of solidarity among "brothers" that Hurston observes and that forms the basis for her critique of a blanket endorsement of simpleminded, universal "Race Solidarity" (327) or of the pan-Africanism that in the thirties and forties must have sounded disturbingly like pan-Germanism, whose evil historical consequences were well understood. The text of *Dust Tracks* thus shuttles between appreciation and opprobrium, finding its impetus in the joyful affirmation of its contradictions. To recall the past in order to transcend it, Fanon will also point out, is the only emancipatory stance we can confidently adopt without risk of falling prey to reactionary forces.

Thus, the chapter titled "Religion" reveals Hurston's total indifference to the "consolation" traditional religion affords: "I am one with the infinite and need no other assurance" (279). Her style subverts the need for "organized creeds," which are but "collections of words around a wish" (278) and which Fanon will denounce as the motor of a "closed society . . . in which ideas and people are in a state of decay" (BSWM 224).[23] Comfortable in the knowledge that the whole world exists in a Heraclitean flux of becoming, Hurston affirms a principle of eternal change based on her observation of the radical fluidity of inorganic, organic, social, and cultural forces:

I have achieved a certain peace within myself, but perhaps the seeking after the inner heart of truth will never
cease in me . . .

So, having looked at the subject from many sides,
studied beliefs by word of mouth and then *as they fit into
great rigid forms, I find I know a great deal about form, but
little or nothing about the mysteries I sought as a child* . . .

But certain things have seemed to me to be true as I
heard the tongues of those who had speech, and listened
at the lips of books (277).

The springing of the yellow line of morning out of the
misty deep of dawn, is glory enough for me. I know that
nothing is destructible; things merely change forms (279).
[Emphasis mine.][24]

Poetic speech has now replaced the folk idiom, the artist,
the anthropologist. The distinction between form and content
("mysteries") is made again but then put under erasure: "Things
merely change forms," and content is never lost; yet knowledge of content is determined by the "great rigid forms" that
structure the universe while veiling the motley appearance of
"matter." These allegories of death and rebirth, change and
permanence, temporality and eternity, retroactively map the
territory of the autobiographical text and the life it attempts to
represent. By retracing those ephemeral "dust tracks" whose
trajectory the table of contents surveys, Hurston seems to
spiral out into infinity and the cosmos: "The cosmic Zora
emerges," as she writes in "How It Feels to Be Colored Me"
(ILM 155). Her journey, like that of the storytellers who never
leave the porch, is an itinerary through language, "a journeying by way of narrating," as Alexander Gelley puts it. That is
why it is impossible to make, on a theoretical level, "any
clear-cut division between theme and form, between journey
as geography and journey as narrative."[25] The "curve in the
road" at which Hurston sees her first "vision" (93) is a mythical point of departure for the global adventure during which
she will learn to take distance from the "tight chemise" and
the "crib of negroism" (MM 3) that have shaped her. Distance
alone can enable her to recognize and assemble the fragments
of her changing folk culture in the New World, and because

she is dealing with familiar territory, she does not run the risk of subjugating the "other" to her self, of making her subjects into marionettes for the benefit of those patrons who are only interested in the static, "primitive" aspects of her research. Engaged in a truly dialogical enterprise and not in the delusions of Boasian "pure objectivity" to which she alludes ironically (174), she can negotiate the terms of her insertion within and without the ethnographic field and can even parody popular beliefs with impunity: the jokes come naturally with the territory of storytelling.

Similarly, the discursive enterprise of self-portraiture is a process of collecting and gathering, of assembling images and metaphors to portray a figural self, always already caught in entropy and in permanent danger of returning to "dust," of becoming again "part and parcel" of the universe. In what follows, then, I would like to examine briefly the textual mechanism that generates the journey of ethnic self-scrutiny, the slippage between particular and universal, individual and collective, daughter and mother(s), the self and its mythologies. In describing these displacements, I want to show how the collective functions as a silverless mirror, capable of absorbing the self into a duplicitous game in which one code, singularity, is set aslant by another, syncretic unity with the universe, thus preventing narrative closure.[26] The tensions at work in *Dust Tracks* between these two sets of expectations (local versus universal knowledge) are not simply resolvable through (ethnographic) narrative. They constitute what Stephen Tyler has called the proper domain of "post-modern ethnography," neither "the upward spiral into the Platonic . . . realm of conscious thought and faceless abstraction" nor the "descent 'beneath the surface' into the Plutonic 'other of separation.' " Hurston's approach to the study of culture indeed prefigures the future trend of the discipline as outlined by Tyler: "The ethnographic text will thus achieve its purposes not by revealing them, but by making purposes possible. It will be a text of the physical, the spoken, and the performed, an evocation of quotidian experience, a palpable reality that uses everyday speech to suggest what is ineffable, not through abstraction, but by means of the concrete. It will be a text to read not with the eyes alone, but with the ears in order to hear 'the voices of the pages.' "[27]

Hurston, too, captures the voices of the people and relays them through the "lips of books," which do not "announce" their purpose but braid "palpable reality" with the incommensurable, the quotidian with the ineffable. She makes it possible to envisage purposive, enabling, and empowering structures of meaning that do not coerce the subject into historically and Eurocentrically determined racial metaphors of the self. She succeeds in tracing a map of her territory—a symbolic geography —by using the same accommodating principles that governed the expedient building of roads over the winding footpath between Orlando and Maitland: the metaphor of the road that curves effortlessly around "the numerous big pine trees and oaks" (7) reinforces a principle of flexibility, a respect for nature rather than the need to dominate it, a pliability connoting the plasticity of human forms, the capacity to undergo mutations, to endure and survive hardships in that middle passage from birth to death, from mud to dust.

The allegory of the voyage that is only a return to one's point of departure is already present in the first chapter, "My Birthplace." The "three frontier-seekers" who embark for Brazil only to return to the United States prefigure Hurston, who journeys through black folklore in order to rediscover the "geography . . . within" (115), the lost community of her childhood in "A pure Negro town!" (9). Her search for an originary plenitude is the universal biblical "return to dust" at the end of the road of life—not the romantic nostalgia for a prelapsarian time of innocence. In that respect, the death of her mother represents the first moment in a chain of destabilizing experiences that forever undermine her sense of belonging to a specific place: "That hour began my wanderings. Not so much in geography, but in time. Then not so much in time as in spirit. Mama died at sundown and changed a world. That is, the world which had been built out of her body and her heart. Even the physical aspects fell apart with a suddenness that was startling" (89). The death scene of the speechless mother becomes the motivation for writing, for the effort of self-fashioning, which is also an effort to stave off death. Hurston's wandering phase will be the result of this experience of absence and loss, which is repeated on different levels throughout the next chapters. The narrator attempts to fill the void of death by journeying *and* by narrating.

That is why it is interesting to note that the description of
the mother's death in *Dust Tracks* closely parallels the fictional
rendering of that scene in *Jonah's Gourd Vine*. Telling details
are repeated almost word for word: "I could see the huge
drop of sweat collected in the hollow at Mama's elbow and it
hurt me so" (DT 88) and "Isis saw a pool of sweat standing in
a hollow at the elbow" (ILM 195); "I thought that she looked
to me (DT 86) . . . I think she was trying to say something,
and I think she was trying to speak to me" (DT 88) and "Isis
thought her mother's eyes followed her and she strained her
ears to catch her words" (ILM 195). Isis is indeed the fictional
alter ego Hurston chooses for herself, the name of an ancient
Egyptian goddess who wandered the world in search of her
dismembered brother, a mythical representation of interiority
as experience of death. In Egyptian mythology, her brother,
Osiris, is both the god of fertility (like Demeter/Ceres in the
Greco-Roman myth) and the king and judge of the dead. He
is also the companion of Thoth, god of death and of writing,
who presides with him in the underworld. Hurston thus makes
an implicit connection between the Osirian mysteries, which
were tied to the cult of the dead and of which Isis was the
high priestess, and the occult practices of Hoodoo, of which
Hurston herself became an initiate. Having flippantly named
herself the "queen of the niggerati" in one of her histrionic
moments among her New York friends,[28] Hurston then pro-
ceeded to develop (in the autobiographical triptych) in a mythically accurate and artistically sensible manner the theme of a life
lived in the shadow of Isis/Persephone, queens of the underworld, of the "dark realm" of otherness. The persona Isis—
both the goddess and the fictional daughter of Lucy Potts—is
like the mirror that figures prominently in the mother's death
scene. She is an image of memory and interiority, an "other"
who focuses, crystallizes, and gives sharp contours to the
project of self-invention. She is an important thread in the
process of re-membering one's past and one's own mortality
as one pays homage to the dead and departed. Here, the folk
custom of veiling the mirror (so that the dead may rest in
peace and not trouble the living) is implicitly criticized: the
dying mother suggests that the mirror should not be veiled if
the past and the faces of our mothers in it are to leave their
imprint on the memory of the living so that *we* may live in

peace with history and be thus able to "think back through our mothers," as Virginia Woolf believed it was important for women to be able to do.[29]

What the death scene allegorizes, then, is Hurston's subtle and complex view of the relationship of individuals to culture and history: some elements of culture, because they are unexamined traditions, "village custom" (86), "mores" (89) upheld by the voices of patriarchy (the "village dames," or phallic women, and the father, who together prevent her from fulfilling her mother's wishes), are destructive and stultifying. The child's (Isis' and Zora's) experience of anxiety and guilt is the result of those unexamined cultural myths that thwart the mother's desire to remain imprinted on the daughter's memory. As Adrienne Rich has put it, "The loss of the daughter to the mother, the mother to the daughter, is the essential female tragedy."[30] The loss brought about by the patriarchal customs of the "village" is a painful enactment of separation and fragmentation, of lost connections to the mother as symbol of a veiled and occulted historical past. Albert Memmi and Frantz Fanon will both point out that our problem as colonized people (or gender) is that we all suffer from collective amnesia. The self-portrait Hurston draws in *Dust Tracks* is an anamnesis: not self-contemplation but a painstaking effort to be the voice of that occluded past, to fill the void of collective memory.

Indeed, Zora feels that her mother "depended on [her] for a voice" (87), and in *Dust Tracks* she chooses the mythical Persephone as alter ego. The Greek word for voice is *phone* and the scene of the mother's death is symbolic of the daughter's responsibility to articulate her story, to exhume it from the rubble of patriarchal obfuscation. Martin Bernal has pointed out that the Eleusinian story of Demeter searching for Persephone has its roots in the Egyptian myth of Isis and Osiris.[31] By identifying with Persephone in *Dust Tracks*, Hurston makes a brilliant and sophisticated rapprochement between the two myths—a connection, says Bernal, that classicists who follow the "Aryan model" of antiquity have studiously avoided. Hurston approaches Afro-Mediterranean antiquity with the intuitions of the anthropologist who sees connections where traditional classical scholarship had not.

The displacement from Isis to Persephone as objective per-

sona is significant in helping us understand Hurston's feeling
of being an orphan, of being cut off from her origins, or *arche*.
"Isis" is the wanderer who conducts her research, establishes
spatiotemporal connections among the children of the diaspora, and re-members the scattered body of folk material so
that siblings can again "touch each other." "Persephone," on
the other hand, is not a rescuer but rather a lost daughter
whose mother searches for her with passion. She is an ambiguous figure "with her loving and hellish aspects."[32] Ironically,
it is Zora's reading of the Greco-Roman myth ("one of [her]
favorites" [48]) during the visit of two white women at her
school that attracts attention to her brilliance and configures
her later "rescue" by other white mentors, friends who become surrogate mothers (like Helen in "Drenched in Light").
If, as Ronnie Scharfman has noted, "mirroring" and "mothering" are twin terms for defining the reciprocal nurturing bonds
a female subject needs in order to feel anchored in the tradition linking her to her mother(s), then Zora's vain efforts to
prevent the veiling of the mirror in the mother's room must be
understood as an allegorical attempt to look into the mirror of
her mother's soul, to retain severed connections, to recapture
and to "read" the dark face of the mother in the silverless
mirror of the past, and to become the voice that bridges
generations.[33] Those efforts also prefigure her professional
predicament as an adult. Persephone was the queen of Pluto's
dark realm of the dead, but she also traveled back and forth
between the underworld and "the sunlit earth" (49), like
Hurston, who retrieves the voices of her black culture in order
to call her readers, in Karla Holloway's words, "back to primal
ground." Caught between the upper and the lower realms,
the black and the white world, life and death, she bridges the
tragic gap of separation by writing. As Beaujour has explained,
"the self-portrait tries to reunite two separate worlds, that of
the living and that of the dead."[34]

Her description of a ceremony in New Orleans in which she
participates draws the obvious parallels: "I had to sit at the
crossroads at midnight in complete darkness and meet the
devil, and make a compact. There was a long, long hour as I
sat flat on the ground there alone and invited the King of
Hell" (192). Since we also know that fasting was an essential
part of her initiation, the parellel with Persephone is even

more convincing, for Persephone's fate was to be Pluto's queen for three months of each year because "she had bitten the pomegranate" (49). Cleansing by fasting is, of course, a common part of initiatory practices in many religions and underscores Hurston's philosophy of the universal oneness of religious symbols.

When the child's experience of absence in *Dust Tracks* becomes specifically racial, a new and negative dimension is added to the metaphor of the mirror. As Hurston puts it, "Jacksonville made me know that I was a little colored girl" (94). This discovery of the ethnic self as mirrored by the other, the white culture of Jacksonville, functions in the text as another moment of an-archic self-discovery. The image reflected in the mirror of white culture is like the photograph in which Janie, in *Their Eyes Were Watching God*, cannot recognize herself because she does not yet know that she is colored, that for the white family who calls her "Alphabet," she is different because she symbolizes namelessness, darkness, absence, and lack.[35] This is Janie's first experience of difference, seeing her face as a bad photograph, as a "negative" and a flaw in the developed picture she holds in her hand. This scene of nonrecognition, like the deathbed scene, is the primal motivation for the journey of self-discovery through language. Isis, Persephone, Thoth, and Osiris are thus the four poles that mark the perimeter of Hurston's cultural mythology of the self. Thoth's gift links writing to death and to immortality; here the threads of memory and narrative allow Janie to "[pull] in her horizon like a great fish-net" (TE 286) in which the fragments of a faceless past are reassembled and given new names, new origins.

When we look at the allegory of the veiling of the mirror in *Dust Tracks* in the context of those similar scenes in the novels, a strong statement about the self and its enabling and distorting mirrors emerges. The idea that a mirror can be the vehicle of a negative self-image (depersonalization and loss) seems to be tied to two cultural myths perceived as destructive and debilitating by the child: the patriarchal folk belief about mirrors and death and the white culture's myths about blackness as radical otherness and absence. In both cases, reflections are void, absent, or distorted because they emanate from a reductionist context: the realities of a culture's myths about death

and otherness become a burden and a distortion of the historical metaphors by which women must learn to live if we are to
recapture the faces of our mothers in the mirrors of the past. It
is by uncovering those mirrors that we can begin to articulate
connections to ancient and empowering symbols of femaleness. Hence the anguish of the child at not being able to fend
off the voices of white and black patriarchy, which rob her
forever of the peace that comes from seeing the face(s)—and
knowing the mythical name(s)—that connect her to a cultural
tradition not grounded only in darkness and silence. Again
Beaujour's formulation is valid: "The self-portrait is constructed
around an empty center: vanished places and disrupted
harmonies."[36] The experience of death generates the writing
of a self-portrait through which appears, pentimento, the mother's lost face.

The child who leaves Eatonville after her mother's death
experiences alterity and dislocation, distances herself forever
from the illusory possibility of an unexamined and unmediated participation in the network of relations which constitutes culture. In effect, her avocation as anthropologist starts
right then and there: Her exile from Eatonville is the first step
on the nomadic road of lore collecting, a road on which "the
individual looks for soul-mates while simultaneously affirming [her] absolute difference from all others," Beaujour says.
That is why the collective voice is so often relayed with irony
and pathos: the self-portrait is the medium of subversion par
excellence, which relativizes the fetishistic recourse to a foundational world beyond its discourse. It evokes the ethnic reality of which it partakes but, in so doing, puts into question
the mimetic principles of description and classification that
inform its writing. It thus simultaneously demystifies the writing of both the self (auto) and the culture (ethno) because it
involves the self and its cultural contexts in a dialogue that
transcends all possibility of reducing one to the other. Michel
Beaujour expresses it thus: "Mirror of the subject and mirror
of the world, mirror of the 'I' searching for a reflection of its
self through the mirror of the universe: what might first appear as a simple correspondence, or a convenient analogy,
proves under close scrutiny to be a homologous relation war-
ranted by the rhetorical tradition and the history of literature."[37]
Beaujour's formulation can be applied to Dust Tracks with an

important modification: it is not the medieval rhetorical tradition that furnishes the topics of mimesis but the anthropological essay with its system of categories, which locate culture at the nexus of history and geography, religion and myth. What this formulation means for the "self-portrait," according to Beaujour, is that writing is engendered primarily by the *impossibility* of self-presence, by the realization that realist narratives are functionally distorting and that myths are more appropriately evocative and suggestive of a subject's liminal position in the world of discursive representation.

Here, a myth of ancient Afro-Mediterranean folklore establishes the parameters according to which Hurston will go on performing the role of daughter after her mother's death and until they can both be syncretically reunited. The faceless woman encountered on a porch in Jacksonville during a school walk, "who looked at a distance like Mama" (96), prefigures the last of her twelve "visions": the two women, one young (herself?), one old (the mother?), whose faces are averted as they are "arranging some queer-shaped flowers such as [she] had never seen" (58). This indirect allusion to the funeral flower—the white narcissus—is also the figure of the self reflected in the pool of language, the dark ("miroirs d'encre: mirrors of ink") medium of self-knowledge, the white symbol of death's attraction. It is an unformulated, unnamed, but richly suggestive allusion to the desire for the absent mother, which will be reenacted both in the bonds of female friendships (the visitors at the school, Big Sweet, Fannie Hurst, Ethel Waters, the Dahoman Amazons) and in those of hatred or rivalry with other women (her stepmother and knife-toting "Lucy").[38] At once Persephone and Narcissus, the autobiographical narrator attempts to recapture the (m)other in the self and the self through the (m)other:[39]

> Once or twice I saw the old faceless woman standing outdoors beside a tall plant with that same off-shape white flower. She turned suddenly from it to welcome me. I knew what was going on in the house without going in, it was all so familiar to me.
>
> I never told anyone around me about these strange things. It was too different. They would laugh me off as a story-teller. Besides, I had a feeling of difference from

my fellow men, and I did not want it to be found out
(58–59).

Her experiences of singularity and difference are intimately
connected to her visions of death. Not surprisingly, the reference to "Pluto's dark realm" (48) and to the temporary reunifi-
cation of Persephone with her mother turns the circumstances
of her life upside down and transforms the past by reorienting
it toward an unlived future in which the lost potentialities of
love and daughterhood are given a second chance, and an
elusive possibility of peace and transfiguration: "I stood in a
world of vanished communion with my kind, which is worse
than if it had never been. Nothing is so desolate as a place
where life has been and gone. I stood on a soundless island in
a tideless sea. Time was to prove the truth of my visions . . .
bringing me nearer to the big house, with the kind women
and the strange white flowers"(59).

If the mother is a figure for the "lost" potentialities of
history and for the "dark" continent of Africa, it is not surprising that images of death and decay begin to pervade the
daughter's self-recollection during those years of loneliness
and wandering in which she feels "haunted" (116). Just like
"Lazarus after his resurrection," she cannot experience her
own self in a unified way, past and present, mind and body
can never coincide completely: "I walked by my corpse. I
smelt it and felt it. I smelt the corpses of those among whom I
must live, though they did not. They were as much at home
with theirs as death in a tomb" (117). Like the Zombies she
will later study, she is one of the living dead whose childhood
memories of that time—between ten and fourteen years of
age—are the undeveloped photographic negative of the singular images of blankness which will keep recurring in later
chapters. For instance, her first love affair, although it provides the closeness and warmth she had sorely missed ever
since her mother's death, turns into an oppressive relationship that imprisons her in feelings of doubt and unreality that
cannot be shared with the husband: "Somebody had turned a
hose on the sun. What I had taken for eternity turned out to
be a moment walking in its sleep. . . . A wind full of memories blew out of the past and brought a chilling fog" (251).

Numbed by the impossibility to communicate, drained of

life, she buries herself in her work. The next time she falls in love, the pattern seems to repeat itself. She is thwarted by the conflicts caused by her career, the man's possessiveness, and his complaints that her "real self had escaped him." She is not permitted to have a life of her own, is restrained by limiting circumstances, "caught in a fiendish trap" (259). Love is never experienced as an empowering force—unlike friendship, this "mysterious and ocean-bottom thing" (321) without which life is not worth much: "To live without friends is like milking a bear to get cream for your morning coffee. It is a whole lot of trouble, and then not worth much after you get it" (248). In contrast to the flatness of her love life, her affective landscape is peopled with many picturesque and vivid portrayals of friends. The topic of "friendship" is a much richer and more satisfying one than "love," and the treatment it receives in *Dust Tracks* bears testimony to the importance self-portraitists have accorded to the interface with an other whose ambivalent companionship may be the spur that compels a writer to articulate the potentialities of his or her vision.[40] "Conversation is the ceremony of companionship" (248), Ethel Waters says to Zora and Zora's self-portrait is this conversation with the past, a ceremony for the dead mother(s), but one that simultaneously empowers the living.

The narrator also experiences singularity as separation from the realm of nature. After her departure to Jacksonville, her introduction to formal education goes together with another deprivation which adds to her grief and mourning: "the loving pine, the lakes, the wild violets in the woods and the animals [she] used to know" (95) are no longer part of her daily life. Orphaned for a second time when her father asks the school to "adopt" her and she is nonetheless sent home on the riverboat, she experiences a thrilling form of rebirth because she is again part and parcel of nature: "The water life, the smothering foliage that draped the river banks, the miles of purple hyacinths, all thrilled me anew. The wild thing was back in the jungle. The curtain of trees along the river shut out the world so that it seemed that the river and the chugging boat was all that there was, and that pleased me a lot" (109). The floating boat and the trees that "shut out the world" are like the protective layers of a womb; the boat's chugging motor connotes a maternal heartbeat, a reassuring companion that spells the return to an earlier form of peace and harmony. These layered allusions to the archaic times of a prenatal life and to the historical moments of preslavery days in Africa again configurate the mother as the sheltering presence whose disappearance generates the nomadic search for collective meanings that will establish a system of resonance between seemingly heterogeneous entities or "topics," such as daughterhood, friendship, nature, and antiquity—all of which can be seen as so many inaugurating moments of similarity within difference, of self-absorption in an enigmatic mirror, which can be contrasted and paralled with death itself, the "face that reflects the face of all things, but neither changes itself, nor is mirrored anywhere" (DT 87).

Later on, working as a maid for the soprano of the traveling opera company, Zora becomes a kind of mascot for the whole company, and her writing career gets started: "I got a scrapbook . . . and wrote comments under each picture . . . Then I got another idea. I would comment on daily doings and post the sheets on the call-board . . . The result stayed strictly mine less than a week because members of the cast began to call me aside and tell me things to put in about others . . . It was just my handwriting, mostly" (138–139). She becomes the repository of other people's words, a kind of transparent mind or ghostwriter. She experiences another form of Zombiehood, mediated by the acquisition of language, by the absorption of other voices, just like all that "early reading," which had given her "great anguish through all [her] childhood and adolescence" because, as she puts it, "My soul was with the gods and my body in the village. People just would not act like gods" (56). Her experiences at school in Baltimore follow the same pattern: "And here I was, with my face looking like it had been chopped out of a knot of pine wood with a hatchet on somebody's off day, sitting up in the middle of all this pretty" (150–151). Undefined features, "a woman half in shadow," the self-portraitist draws a picture of herself which remains "a figure in bas relief," an intaglio, "the weaving of anthropology with thanatography."[41]

These echoing patterns of disfiguration and death give an improvisational rhythm to the text, the ebb and flow of musical counterpoint, and suspend meaning between suggestive similarities the reader is free to associate or not. One subtle parallel the text thus draws is between two gruesome events: the decapitation of Cousin Jimmie, "mother's favorite nephew" (85), unintentionally shot by a white man, who covered up the accident by making it look as though a train had killed him, and the similar fate that had befallen the son of Kossola/ Cudjo, David, who was actually beheaded in a train accident. In both cases, it is the grief of the parental figures that reso- nates in the text, rather than a hypothetical repetition of real-life events. Indeed, framing as they do Hurston's vision of the two faceless women and Kossola's stories of famed Dahoman Amazons who sack cities and carry "clusters of human heads at their belts," the stories underscore a singu- larly repetitive pattern that would seem to point not to refer- ents beyond the text but to the allegorical disfiguring of generation upon generation of black individuals whose plight is ignored or covered up, except in the memory of those who grieve for them, as Cudjo's Takkoi King, beheaded by the Amazons, is mourned by his people (compare with 201).

The emphemeral quality of collective memory itself is re- flected in the transient nature of Hurston's "first publication": "On the blackboard . . . I decided to write an allegory using the faculty members as characters" (153). The "allegory" is the source of much entertainment and laughter for her school- mates, a successful rehearsal for her future tale telling and an important metaphoric hyphen between the immediacy of oral performance and the permanence of the written words. Like these allegorical portraits, which will be erased once they have served their purpose, her twelve visions, which were initially meant to structure the deployment of the autobiography, are soon forgotten because they do not need to be used. The tale teller dynamically reshapes her material as she goes along, the content of the visions becoming irrelevant since the essayistic form of the latter chapters ("My People! My People!" "Look- ing Things Over," "The Inside Light,") spontaneously gener- ates a framework through which to communicate her philosophy.

As she ironically suggests about the experiences told by the religious congregation: "These visions are traditional. I knew them by heart as did the rest of the congregation, but still it was exciting to see *how the converts would handle them. Some of them made up new details. Some of them would forget a part and improvise clumsily or fill up the gap with shouting.* The audience knew, but everybody acted as if every word of it was new" (272). [Emphasis mine.] Inconsistencies are inherent to the performance of traditional cultural forms: it is precisely in the way they individually diverge from the set norms that the converts excite interest in the audience. The "origin" of the tradition must be acknowledged, but acknowledgment does not sanction simple repetition: Each new performer "signifies" upon that origin by transforming it, and by allowing for infinite possibilities of permutations.[42] To approach a form genealogically, then, is to attempt to retrace its transformations back to an origin—*arche*— that will always prove elusive since every discrete manifestation is the interpellation of a previous one, which sets the stage for the next one, and so on ad infinitum. A particular form acquires value not from its timeless origin or essential qualities but because it is related to practices that inform a mode of life while dynamically shaping reality. Whether Hurston's twelve visions signify upon a particular religious tradition or the vernacular ritual of the "dozens" (compare with 187, 217) or both is of no importance since, in any case, she can make vicarious use of the cliches, parody some of them, ignore the rest, and "tell a story the way [she] wanted, or rather the way the story told itself to [her]" (206). Since "playing the dozens" or "specifying" is a form of invective and name calling that points genealogically to a fictitious origin—"they proceed to 'specify' until the tip-top branch of your family tree has been given a reading" (217)—we can readily infer that this "self-affirming form of discourse"[43] does not require foundational support in reality. It is by virtue of its perlocutionary function that it affirms the underlying gutsiness and creativity of the agent of discourse, drawing a portrait of the self as capable of enduring, diverging, and surviving because it adheres to the formal aspects of a dynamic and improvisational cultural tradition that allows the storyteller to "keep the tune" for the benefit of the collectivity, to lift the veil on the mirror of a different history, to be a "keeper of our memories" (Moses 350). Hurston's "exuberant sense of self"[44] allows her to adopt a thoroughly Nietzschean perspective on this "topsy-turvy world" of hers, and to value memory as a viable alternative to oppressive history.

In *Dust Tracks*, we have a powerful example of the braiding, or *métissage*, of cultural forms, since Persephone figures both as the voice of the dead mother and as the boundary crosser who links up two different worlds. Turning the mythical relation between Ceres and her daughter upside down, Hurston invents her own reading of the tradition, "signifying" upon that tradition in a specifically "black" way, diverging from the Greco-Roman text in the only way possible for the Afro-American self-portraitist. To rejoin her mother, Zora/Persephone must travel back to the underworld, to the "dark realm" of her own people, to the friendship with Big Sweet, in order to learn to say what her dying mother could not, in order to name the chain of legendary female figures who can teach her to re-member and to speak the past.

NOTES

1. See Robert Hemenway's comments in Appendix to Zora Neale Hurston, *Dust Tracks on a Road*, ed. Hemenway, 2d ed. (Urbana: University of Illinois Press, 1984), 288. All references will be included in the text and flagged DT when necessary.
2. By *genealogical* I mean the reconstruction of the self through interpretations that integrate as many aspects of the past as are deemed *significant* by the agent of the narrative discourse. It is clear that Hurston considers cultural forms more significant than specific events. Thus, the self she fashions through language is not a fixed essence, partaking of an immutable and originary racial substance. Rather, it is a *process* of active self-discovery through self-invention by means of the folk narratives of ethnic interest. For a recent thorough and definitive analysis of these Nietzschean questions, see Alexander Nehamas, *Nietzsche: Life as Literature* (Cambridge: Harvard University Press, 1986). David Hoy has done an excellent and useful review of this book; see "Different Stories" in *London Review of Books*, 8 January 1987, pp. 15–17. In the Afro-American context, genealogical revisionism is of course a common theme of literature. See Kimberly W. Benston, " 'I Yam What I Yam': Naming and Unnaming in Afro-American Literature," *Black American Literature Forum 16* (Spring 1982); as well as Jahnheinz Jahn, *Muntu: An Outline of the New African Culture* (New York: Grove Press, 1961), 125.
3. For an overview of contemporary theories of autobiography, see Paul John Eakin, *Fictions in Autobiography: Studies in the Art of Self-Invention* (Princeton: Princeton University Press, 1985), Chapter 4 in particular.
4. Michel Beaujour, *Miroirs d'encre* (Paris: Seuil, 1980), 348. All translations are mine.
5. This phrase is used by Michel Serres in *The Parasite*, trans. Lawrence R. Schehr (Baltimore: Johns Hopkins University Press, 1982), 6. The French phrase is "une anthropologie figurée." See *Le Parasite* (Paris: Grasset, 1980), 13. See also Alexander Gelley, *Narrative Crossings: Theory and Pragmatics of Prose Fiction* (Baltimore: Johns Hopkins University Press, 1987), 79–100, for a useful discussion of "parasitic talk" and narrative agency, cultural norms, and quotidian talk applied to Melville's *Confidence-Man*.
6. James Clifford, "On Ethnographic Allegory,"in Clifford and George E Marcus, ed., *Writing Culture: The Poetics and Politics of Ethnography* (Berkeley: University of California Press, 1986), 98–121 (112).
7. See William L. Andrews, ed. *Sisters of the Spirit: Three Black Women's Autobiographies in the Nineteenth Century* (Bloomington: Indiana University Press, 1986), 13. To say that Hurston is not interested in *organized* resistance to patterns of social injustice is not to imply that she is not strongly critical of injustice. See pp. 336–345.

8. This is not the place to engage in a detailed analysis of the methods and assumptions of Hurston's great teacher and mentor, "Papa" Franz Boas. Suffice it to say that as an anthropologist he was a firm believer in "the plasticity of human types": His research for his book *Changes in Bodily Forms of Descendants of Immigrants*, published in 1911, served to convince him that physical and mental characteristics were not simply inherited but profoundly modified by time and environment. Furthermore, the views expressed in his essay "The Race Problem in Modern Society," published in a work that was to be widely influential and of fundamental importance to the field of anthropology, *The Mind of Primitive Man*, (1911) reprinted in Ashley Montagu, *Frontiers of Anthropology* (New York: Putnam's, 1974), could not fail to influence Zora Neale Hurston's own attitudes about the race problem in America, to reinforce her personal tendency toward individualism, and to strengthen her belief that human beings are infinitely variable and not classifiable into distinctive national or racial categories. As Boas puts it, "Our tendency to evaluate an individual according to the picture that we form of the class to which we assign him, although he may not feel any inner connection with that class, is a survival of primitive forms of thought. The characteristics of the members of the class are highly variable and the type that we construct from the most frequent characteristics supposed to belong to the class is never more than an abstraction hardly ever realized in a single individual, often not even a result of observation, but an often-heard tradition that determines our judgment" (344). Boas recognizes the role played by "tradition" and ideology in our construction of the world, and his work paves the way for what I would call Hurston's dynamic and contextual approach to culture and to private forms of behavior.
9. Robert Hemenway, *Zora Neale Hurston: A Literary Biography* (Urbana: University of Illinois Press, 1977), 213.
10. See Zora Neale Hurston, *Mules and Men* (Bloomington: Indiana University Press 1978), 3, hereafter referred to as MM; and Barbara Johnson, "Thresholds of Difference: Structures of Address in Zora Neale Hurston," in Henry L. Gates, Jr., ed, *"Race," Writing, and Difference* (Chicago: University of Chicago Press, 1985), 317–328.
11. Hemenway, *Zora Neale Hurston*, 213.
12. Ibid.
13. Frantz Fanon, *The Wretched of the Earth*, trans. Constance Farrington (New York: Grove Press, 1968), 214. (I have modified the translation of both quotations.) *Les Damnés de la terre* (Paris: Maspéro, 1968), 146. The word *inculture* is practically untranslatable into English.
14. See Houston A. Baker, Jr., *Blues, Ideology, and Afro-American Literature: A Vernacular Theory* (Chicago: University of Chicago Press, 1984), 152.
15. See Claudine Raynaud, *"Dust Tracks on a Road:* Autobiography as a 'Lying' Session," in Joe Weixlmann and Houston A. Baker, Jr., eds., *Studies in Black American Literature*, Vol. III (Greenwood: Penkevill Publishing, 1988). Whereas Raynaud tends to see the autobiography as founding the self in a gesture of appropriation of the perennial proverbs and sayings of the community, I prefer to see in the text a continuing tension between philosophical skepticism about communal values and visionary creation.
16. It might perhaps be appropriate to add here that Hurston shows a truly "metaphysical" turn of mind on top of her properly "exegetical" talents! See a reference to the debate between Robert Penn Warren and Sterling Brown in Henry L. Gates, Jr., *Figures in Black: Words, Signs, and the "Racial" Self* (New York: Oxford University Press, 1987), xix. And indeed, Fanon takes up the same relay: the last words of *Black Skin, White Masks*, trans. Charles L. Markmann (London: Pluto Press, 1986), (hereafter referred to as BSWM) are "O my body, make me always a man who questions!" (232). It is not likely that Fanon either knew or read Hurston, although he was familiar with the work of Langston Hughes, but their accomplishments in *Dust Tracks on a Road* and *Black Skin, White Masks* derive from a parallel need to shake off the totalizing traps of historical determinism, and to do so in a style that is its own message, narrative, and aphoristic in order to subvert the cultural commonplaces they both abhor. See also Chester J. Fontenot's study of Fanon and his useful discussion of form and content in *Black Skin, White Masks*, "Visionaries, Mystics and Revolutionaries: Narrative Postures

in Black Fiction," in Joe Weixlmann and Chester J. Fontenot, eds., *Studies in Black American Literature* (Greenwood: Penkevill Annuals, 1983), 1:63–87.

17. For a detailed discussion of the philosophical and linguistic implications of the "discours indirect libre," see Gilles Deleuze and Félix Guattari, *Mille plateaux* (Paris: Minuit, 1980), 95–109.

18. The phrase is Ernst Bloch's. See Anson Rabinbach, "Unclaimed Heritage: Ernst Bloch's *Heritage of Our Times* and the Theory of Fascism," *New German Critique* 11 (Spring 1977), 7. Hurston was familiar with the German philosophical tradition of utopian thinking. She mentions Spinoza, for example, DT 285. See also my comments in Note 24.

19. Beaujour, *Miroirs d'encre*, 26; see Michael M. J. Fischer, "Ethnicity and the Post-Modern Arts of Memory," in Clifford and Marcus, *Writing Culture*, 194–233 (201). Fischer uses "ethnic" autobiographical narrative as a means of allowing "multiple sets of voices to speak for themselves" thus effectively marginalizing his anthropological commentary on the ethnic group he studies.

20. See Martin Bernal's revision of that model in *Black Athena: The Afroasiatic Roots of Classical Civilization* (London: Free Association Books, 1987). For Hurston's use of Damballah, Moses, and Thoth as facets of the same mythological persona, see her *Moses, Man of the Mountain* (Urbana: University of Illinois Press, 1984). See also Karla F. C. Holloway, *The Character of the Word* (New York: Greenwood Press, 1987), Chapter 3, for a useful discussion of those figures.

21. For the passages of *Jonah's Gourd Vine* that are useful here, I shall be quoting from *I Love Myself When I Am Laughing: A Zora Neale Hurston Reader*, ed. Alice Walker (New York: Feminist Press, 1979), 189–96, hereafter referred to as ILM. "Drenched in Light" is reprinted as "Isis" in *Spunk: The Selected Stories of Zora Neale Hurston* (Berkeley: Turtle Island Foundation, 1985), 9–18.

22. Hemenway, *Hurston*, 249. I use the phrase "thick description" after Clifford Geertz, *The Interpretation of Cultures* (New York: Basic Books, 1973), Chapter 1.

23. See Fontenot, *Black Skin*, 84 for a discussion of "open" and "closed" society as defined by Fanon. I have modified the translation of BSWM.

24. Hurston's Spinozist philosophy is evident here. See Benedict de Spinoza, *Ethics* (n.p.: Joseph Simon, 1981), Part 1, Proposition 8: "Every substance is necessarily infinite" (32). As SPR Charter puts it in the introduction to this edition, "Spinoza attempted to unite the mind/body complexity and the realities of existence with the all-embracing actuality of Nature, and to do so organically—that is, without the imposition of man-made religious structures" (3).

25. Gelley, *Narrative Crossings*, 31.

26. What I call the silverless mirror here is to some extent assimilable to what Houston A. Baker, Jr., associates with the term "black (w)hole": "a *singularly* black route of escape" (155). By analogy, it refers also to the covered looking-glass in the room of the dying mother (DT 88), to which I will return.

27. See Stephen Tyler, "Post-Modern Ethnography: From Document of the Occult to Occult Document," in Clifford and Marcus, *Writing Culture*, 133, 136.

28. Holloway, *Character of the Word*, 24.

29. See Jane Marcus, ed., "Thinking Back through Our Mothers," in *New Feminist Essays on Virginia Woolf* (Lincoln: University of Nebraska Press, 1981), 1–30.

30. Adrienne Rich, *Of Woman Born: Motherhood as Experience and Institution* (New York: Norton, 1976), 237. As Sandra M. Gilbert and Susan Gubar have amply demonstrated, the lack of a female tradition in which to insert her own words is the source of a great "anxiety of authorship" for the woman writer. See their *The Madwoman in the Attic: The Woman Writer and the Nineteenth-Century Literary Imagination* (New Haven: Yale University Press, 1979), 45–92.

31. Bernal, *Black Athena*, 69–73.

32. The words Bernal uses to describe Persephone in *Black Athena*, 70.

33. See Ronnie Scharfman, "Mirroring and Mothering in Simone Schwarz-Bart's *Pluie et vent sur Télumée Miracle*, and Jean Rhys's *Wide Sargasso Sea*," *Yale French Studies* 62 (1981), 88–106. Scharfman discusses psychoanalytic object-relation theorists. My purpose here is to relate those issues to the larger historical and ethnographical contexts within which I situate *Dust Tracks*.

34. Holloway, *Character of the Word*, 113; *Miroirs d'encre*, Beaujour, 161.

35. Zora Neale Hurston, *Their Eyes Were Watching God* (Urbana: University of Illinois Press, 1978), 21, hereafter referred to as TE.

37. Ibid., 15, 31.

38. For an analysis of the "thematic consistency . . . found in these echoing episodes of female strength," see Raynaud, "Autobiography as Lying." On this aspect of the text, I am in complete agreement with Raynaud.

39. See Beaujour, *Miroirs d'encre*, for an informative discussion of the associations between Demeter, Persephone, and Narcissus in Greek mythology and the connections between these divinities and death. His argument is that narcissism as commonly understood in psychoanalytic terminology is a distorted and reductive interpretation of the myth and that far from being "narcissistic" in that sense, "the self-portrait tries to reunite two separate worlds, that of the living and that of the dead. . . . Through anamnesis, Narcissus . . . performs a poetic invention of 'childhood memories' that recreates a timeless paradise, at once personal treasure trove and cultural topic" (161). See especially 156–162.

40. Augustine, Montaigne (O un amy!), Gertrude Stein, Christopher Isherwood, Roland Barthes, to name but a few. See Réda Bensmaïa, *The Barthes Effect: The Essay as Reflective Text* (Minneapolis: University of Minnesota Press, 1987), pp.62–89 especially.

41. The first two phrases are Fannie Hurst's in "A Personality Sketch," reprinted in *Zora Neale Hurston*, ed. Harold Bloom (New York: Chelsea House, 1986), 24, 23; the third is Michel Beaujour's, *Miroirs d'encre*, p. 13. The first one is also the title of Mary Helen Washington's introduction to ILM.

42. I am using the word *signifies* in the black traditional sense discussed in particular by Henry L. Gates, Jr., "The Blackness of Blackness: A Critique of the Sign and the Signifying Monkey," *Black Literature and Literary Theory* (New York: Methuen, 1984), 285–321.

43. See Susan Willis, *Specifying: Black Women Writing the American Experience* (Madison: University of Wisconsin Press, 1987), 31.

44. The phrase is Hemenway's in *Hurston*, 213.

Maternal Narratives:

"Cruel Enough to Stop the Blood"

Marianne Hirsch

In 1976, Adrienne Rich wrote that the "cathexis between mother and daughter—essential, distorted, misused—is the great unwritten story."[1] Since that time, feminist writing and scholarship has explored motherhood and mother–daughter relationships from a variety of personal and disciplinary perspectives. Yet nearly all of those perspectives have belonged to daughters. Even now, at the end of the 1980's, the "great unwritten story" remains the story of the mother herself, told in her own voice. Feminist writing and scholarship, continuing in large part to adopt a daughterly perspective, could be said to collude with patriarchy in placing the mother into the position of object and thereby keeping mothering outside of representation and maternal discourse a theoretical impossibility.

In this essay, I propose to illustrate the relationship between feminism and the maternal through a brief look at the tradition of contemporary black women's writing that defines itself as a daughterly tradition in relation to a complicated maternal past. In particular, I shall trace the confrontation and interaction of maternal and daughterly voices in Toni Morrison's *Sula*. Indeed, black women's writing of the 1960s, 1970s, and 1980s is one tradition among the various feminisms that have developed in these last decades where the mother is prominently featured in complex and multiple ways. As a generation of female/feminist writing just in the process of defining itself in relation to a maternal, largely oral past, it can provide a useful locus for the exploration of maternal discourse and points of resistance to it.

Unlike so many contemporary white women writers who define their artistic identity as separate from or in opposition to their mothers, black writers have recently been insisting on what Mary Helen Washington identifies as the "connection between the black woman writer's sense of herself as part of a link in generations of women, and her decision to write."[2] Alice Walker's "In Search of Our Mothers' Gardens" and "Saving the Life That Is Your Own,"[3] Paule Marshall's "Shaping the World of My Art"[4] and "From the Poets in the Kitchen"[5] are conscious and public attempts, as Mary Helen Washington puts it, to "piece together the story of a viable female culture, one in which there is generational continuity, in which one's mother serves as the female precursor who passes on the authority of authorship to her daughter and provides a model for the black woman's literary presence in this society" (147). Marshall and Walker explain that in their families theirs is the first generation to be college educated, the first generation engaged in writing down the stories handed down orally by their matrilineal heritage. Even though they sometimes choose middle-aged or older protagonists, I would argue that, for the most part, Marshall, Walker, Morrison, West, and Shange, write as daughters, and not as mothers.[6] Much more than white women writers, they find it necessary, however, to "think back through their mothers" in order to assume what Sandra Gilbert and Susan Gubar have called the "authority of authorship" and to define themselves identifiably in their own voices as subjects. Their public celebration of maternal presence and influence and their portrayals of strong and powerful mothers, on the one hand, combined with the relative absence of fathers, on the other, makes this uniquely female tradition a particularly interesting one in which to explore issues of maternal presence and absence, speech and silence. If maternal discourse can emerge in one particular feminist tradition, it may not be surprising that it should be one that is in itself marginal—or, to borrow a term from Rachel Blau du Plessis, "ambiguously (non-)hegemonic"—and therefore more ready to bond with mothers and daughters, and to let go of paternal, fraternal, or filial approval.[7]

Thus the issues of connection and separation that pervade

this body of writing have political as well as psychological dimensions. We need to keep in mind the complicated feelings that shape the portraits of mothers, and the tremendously powerful need to present to the public a positive image of black womanhood. E. Frances White writes in her recent "Listening to the Voices of Black Feminism": "How dare we admit the psychological battles that need to be fought with the very women who taught us to survive in this racist and sexist world? We would feel like ungrateful traitors."[8] This pressure explains, perhaps, the disturbing disjunction between the celebration of mothers in the essays of black women writers and the much more ambivalent portrayals in their novels. Although mothers are present, even dominant, in the texts of black women writers, maternal discourse suffers from important and symptomatic limitations and constraints. The daughter-writer often has to define herself in opposition to and not in imitation of the maternal figure. Thus, even while Paule Marshall publically presents herself as the *griot* (Mary Helen Washington's term), preserving the stories she heard and absorbed in her mother's kitchen as she was growing up, she admits privately in an interview that "my mother never directly encouraged me to write. What I absorbed from her was more a reaction to her negativity . . . she disapproved of all my ambitions."[9] Both Marshall and Walker, in fact, situate themselves between three maternal traditions, the black oral invisible lineage in which their own mothers were artistic—storytellers and gardeners—the black written tradition of Phillis Wheatley, Harriet Jacobs, and Zora Neale Hurston, among others, and the white written tradition of Virginia Woolf's *A Room of One's Own*, which does describe the contradiction of the woman writer, but must be revised to include the different story of the black writer. Alice Walker asks: "What did it mean for a black woman to be an artist in our grandmothers' time? In our great-grandmothers' day? It is a question with an answer cruel enough to stop the blood."[10]

These ambivalences and contradictions illuminate Toni Morrison's *Sula*,[11]—the complicated interaction of maternal and daughterly voices in this text, and, in particular, the mediated status of maternal discourse. The stories that the mothers in this novel tell are indeed "cruel enough to stop the blood." I would like to look closely at what happens when the mothers speak in this novel, at how the mothers' stories inform both the text that is structured around them, and the lives of the protagonist daughters. I should add that this reading of *Sula*, far from attempting to be totalizing, is my own experiment with bringing a maternal perspective to bear on a text that itself puts such a perspective into play.

Set between 1919 and 1965, *Sula* is clearly located in the generation of Morrison's mother and grandmother and not in her own. Thus, the novel's very structure depends upon its ambivalent relation to the past. The text presents the lives of the two protagonists, Sula and Nel, as they move from adolescence to old age. Sula and Nel are presented as members of a new generation of black women, eager to construct new lives and new stories for themselves. Yet their development and their friendship, and the text itself, revolve around their relationships to the powerful maternal figures who come to represent a female past, and around their attitude to maternity itself. Although the novel is clearly not written from the perspective of the mother, its generational structure allows it to serve as an emblem for the relation of an emerging feminism (new generation of women) to the maternal (oral tradition of the past).[12]

The novel begins not with these powerful women, however, but with the story of a young man, Shadrack. In the process of a symbolic birth into a violent and racist culture, Shadrack, an army private at the end of World War I, gains his sense of self by facing his mirror image in a toilet bowl: "There in the toilet water he saw a grave black face. A black so definite, so unequivocal, it astonished him" (11). Shadrack knows he is real because he is black, but, as a result of the war, and of his underprivileged social status, he has been dispossessed of everything, including his sense of bodily limits. Through the figure of Shadrack, and of the communal rituals he invents to survive his utter inadequacy, the community needs to confront the male impotence that defines it, represented later by Eva's son Plum. Shadrack's birth is motherless, just as Plum's death is caused by his mother: Mothers have ceased to be able to care for sons in the increasingly feminized, though clearly sexual, culture Morrison constructs. Even Ajax's mother, the "conjure woman," cannot keep her son from abandoning her and Sula.[13]

The dominating maternal presence in the novel is, of course, the matriarch Eva, who rules over the enormous house in which Sula and Nel spend a great deal of their childhood. Ironically, Eva's powerful presence is defined by lack—her amputated leg, which becomes the means of her survival and the mark of her distinction from the other poor and abandoned mothers in Medallion. Eva insists on flaunting her missing leg by wearing calf-length skirts that display and call attention to the beauty of her other leg. I would argue that Eva's missing leg is the mark of maternal discourse in the novel and the key to its (thematized) ambivalence toward it.

The absent leg functions as a gap in the center of the text, a gap around which Sula and Nel's stories begin to take shape. Following the account of Eva's abandonment by BoyBoy, of her miserable winter attempting to care for three children with no money at all, and of her night in the freezing outhouse helping baby Plum loosen his bowels, there is an ellipsis in the text, a silence surrounding Eva's eighteen-months' absence from Medallion. This gap gives rise to numerous tales, some told by Eva herself to amuse the children ("how the leg got up by itself one day and walked off"), others invented by the townspeople in their effort to explain her return without one leg, but with a new black pocketbook full of money. The tales are clearly apocryphal: The mother's (self-)mutilation in the service of her own and her children's survival remains, to the end of the novel, unnarrated, and perhaps unnarratable, but the source of endless narration. Maternal speech is sparse in this novel: Mothers and daughters never quite succeed in addressing each other directly; mothers fail to communicate the stories they wish to tell. This pattern of missed communication begins when Nel and her mother Helene undertake an exhausting journey south to attend the funeral of Nel's great-grandmother. Here, in the place of maternal origin, Nel cannot understand the Creole she hears her grandmother speak. Barely exchanging a few words with her mother, Helene later admits that she also does not know Creole. As Nel returns home and remembers the painful moments of the trip—her mother's profound humiliation by the white conductor and by the black men in the train, the disgust on her great-grandmother's dead face, and the coldness between her mother and grandmother, she looks into the mirror and begins a new life: "I'm

me. I'm not their daughter. I'm not Nel. I'm me"(24). Helene
Wright, the mother, emerges as wrong in many ways, wrong
in her adoption of middle-class values, wrong in her manipulative control of her daughter's life and in the foolish smile she
flashes at the train conductor who has just insulted her, wrong
too because she severed the connection with her own mother
and failed to learn her mother tongue. Nel's image of her
mother as formless custard barely contained by her heavy
velvet dress, makes it imperative that she identify herself as
separate, different from her maternal heritage, as a very definite "me." Filled with "power joy and fear" at this moment of
self-creation, she cannot sustain this self-definition alone, but
needs a friend to complete her, a friend who can offer reflection and support but who will be free of the heavy suitcases
and the orderly house, of the history that encumbers Helene
Wright. This friend is the much less conventional Sula.

Sula's family, although more communicative, succeeds no
better in bridging the distance between the lives and the
perspectives of the three generations. An important exchange
occurs between Sula's mother Hannah and her mother Eva:
Although Hannah is herself a mother, her discourse is circumscribed by her daughterly relation to Eva and by conventional
and clearly inapplicable conceptions of motherhood and maternal love. "Mamma, did you ever love us? . . . No." Eva
answers, "I don't reckon I did. Not the way you thinkin' "(58).
Hannah cannot bear to listen to what Eva has to tell: "I didn't
mean that, Mamma. I know you fed us and all. I was talkin'
'bout something else. Like. Like. Playin' with us . . . I know
'bout them beets, Mamma. You told us that a million times
. . . They had to be some time when you wasn't thinkin'
'bout . . ."(58–60). In response, Eva comes back with the same
old stories about the three remaining beets, about the sores in
the children's mouths, about their shitting worms, stories that
clearly fail to fit into the mythology of motherhood to which
Hannah wants to subscribe.

This exchange radically challenges this mythology, especially when Hannah asks Eva why she set fire to her adult son
Plum. Eva's response, an interior monologue followed by the
longest speech she makes in the novel, contains hurt and
pain, anger and love, but fails adequately to explain her in-
conceivable act. Eva's relation to Plum is so obscenely inti-

mate, it has to be described in the third person: "The last food staple in the house she had rammed up her baby's behind to keep from hurting him too much when she opened up his bowels to pull the stools out. He had been screaming fit to kill, but when she found his hole at last and stuck her finger up in it, the shock was so great he was suddenly quiet" (61). In her own voice Eva continues to articulate what she sees as Plum's inadequacy as an adult male ruined by the war, his passivity, his efforts to "crawl back in my womb . . . I had room enough in my heart," she insists, "but not in my womb, not no more"(62). The mutual penetration of bodies signals, perhaps, the limits of what any relationship can sustain, and demonstrates the ambiguous status of the mother, whose body has already been penetrated so that this child might be produced. In trying to explain to Hannah an act that is so obviously beyond comprehension, Eva dwells on an intense need for self-protection, a clear drawing of her own boundaries, a definitive expression of the limits of what she has to give, and she insists as well on Plum's boundaries, which, as a mother, she was forced to violate.

The double voice with which Eva delivers her painful explanation—"like two people were talking at the same time, saying the same thing, one a fraction of a second behind the other"(61)—suggests her double identity, as an individual subject and as a mother, signaling perhaps the self-division that by necessity characterizes and distinguishes maternal discourse. The text acts out this double voice, as it combines third- with first-person narration, free indirect discourse with dialogue. The message too is of course double; love is mixed with anger, pain with pride, sadness with tenderness, as Eva adds her afterthought: "But I held him close first. Real close. Sweet Plum. My baby boy" (62). This scene between Eva and Hannah, one of the few moments in the novel where mothers speak as mothers, enacts the difficulty of telling and of hearing her story. Later on, of course, Sula will send the grandmother away to an old-age home so as to silence her more completely: "Don't talk to me about how much you gave me, Big Mama, and how much I owe you or none of that" (79).

In her conversation with her mother, Hannah, like everyone else, refrains from addressing the central question of the missing leg, although the questions she asks, however awkwardly, revolve around this untold tale. Like Hannah's, Sula and Nel's very development is determined by it, because the leg becomes for them a very graphic representation of sexual (and perhaps racial) difference, seen as lack.[14] Interpreters of the novel have seen Eva as a kind of phallic mother who assumes Godlike powers of control over naming, creation, and destruction.[15] For example, she calls three different boys by the same name, Dewey, and quickly they become indistinguishable. But the story Eva tells reveals a mixture of power and powerlessness that calls the very notion of phallic mother into question. The phallic mother can exist only as a child's projection. If Eva chooses to flaunt her castration, to assume the logic of the lack that is essential to the male posture, in order thereby to gain a semblance of male power, she can only reveal how much *that* power depends on a masquerade. With this term I refer to Lacan's definition of femininity as masquerade, as constructed in reference to male desire.[16] Eva's strategy demonstrates, I think, that the male phallic position is also a sham, resting on conventional constructions that are easily overturned. Thus Morrison challenges phallocentrism, even as she shows Eva's manipulation of and complicity with the phallic order.

Sula adopts Eva's powerful strategy; her first act in the novel repeats Eva's gesture of (self)-mutilation in the service of survival and her denial of her powerlessness.[17] Threatened by some boys on the way home from school, Sula takes a knife and slices off part of her finger, frightening the boys with "If I can do that to myself, what do you suppose I'll do to you?"(47). This act is Sula's own moment of self-recognition, of her affiliation with Eva and the world of her maternal ancestors. Although Sula possesses her birthmark, a stemmed rose, ambiguously phallic and vaginal—a mark of plenitude that distinguishes her from other women—she is forced to recognize the vulnerability she shares with Eva, a vulnerability her act of self-injury, like Eva's, can disguise but cannot change. It is this recognition that causes Sula's continued and determined rebellion against a traditional womanhood defined for her by maternity and enslavement to the family.

Like Hannah and Eva, Sula and Hannah also share a pivotal moment of (indirect) confrontation around the subject of maternal love. Sula overhears Hannah and her friends discussing their children: " 'Well, Hester grown now and I can't say love is exactly what I feel.' 'Sure you do. You love her, like I love Sula. I just don't like her. That's the difference.' 'Guess so. Likin' them is another thing' " (48,49). This transgressive maternal speech determines the novel's structural progression: This scene is immediately followed by the drowning of Chicken Little. After overhearing what she takes as her mother's rejection, Sula runs off with Nel and, in a vaguely homo-erotic moment of tenderness in the grass as well as in their symbolic acting out of heterosexual play with sticks in the ground, they begin to discover their own sexuality. The appearance at this point of Chicken Little, the little boy in whom both girls take a maternal interest ("Your mama tole you to stop eatin' snot, Chicken"), focuses for Sula the conjunction of maternal rejection with her budding sexuality. I read Chicken's death—he quietly slips into the river and the girls don't try to save him—as a signal of Sula's and Nel's rebellious, if as yet unconscious, refusal of adult heterosexuality and mother-hood as they perceive it. In the novel's terms, however, this is but one in a series of murders, significantly parallel to Eva's murder of Plum.

Sula and Nel's reaction of *looking* or watching Chicken disappear in the water, instead of attempting to save him, is later repeated when Sula watches her mother's accidental death by burning, thrilled and wanting "her to keep on jerking like that, to keep on dancing." This contrasts sharply with Eva's unsuccessful attempt to save her daughter: "Eva knew there was time for nothing in this world other than the time it took to get there and cover her daughter's body with her own" (65). Ironically, of course, it is her original maternal act of self-mutilation, her missing leg, that prevents her from succeeding, but not from participating bodily in Hannah's painful death—she jumps out the window, drags herself across the lawn, and finally has to be taken to the hospital together with her dying daughter. Sula's complicity in her mother's death is only suggested in the text—she acted crazy on that day, distracting Eva and Hannah from interpreting the dream that foreshadowed the accident; she did not try to save Hannah, and she clearly failed to hear her mother's dying words: "Help me, y'all" (66).

Eva's own complicity, even more disguised, complicates the oppositions Sula constructs, between watching and helping, oppositions which underlie her unconditional refusal of a maternal role. As she emphatically declares, silencing Eva's suggestion that she needs babies, "I don't want to make somebody else. I want to make myself" (79). Here Sula conceives of herself as artist, as inventor of alternate plots and bodies for women. As she does so, however, she reinforces another irreconcilable dichotomy—that of mother and artist, a difference she equates with that between saving someone from dying and of watching her die. What looks at first like two contrasting reactions—Eva's and Sula's—emerges, however, more and more as equal complicity and ambivalence, the mark of maternal discourse in the novel, a discourse from which Sula tries to but cannot escape.

In the economy of this text, Sula's rejection of maternity means an assumption of male freedom. In several published interviews, Morrison has admitted fascination with Sula's choice, although it represents the ultimate evil for a woman as far as the community is concerned. "I guess I'm not supposed to say that. But the fact that they [men] would split in a minute just delights me . . . that has always been to me one of the most attractive features about black male life."[18] With characters like Sula, and later with Jadine in *Tar Baby*, Morrison invents a female character who will not be maternal, but will try to get beyond an ideology that identifies woman with nurturing and caretaking. Yet, Nel's warning is prophetic: "You *can't* do it all. You a woman and a colored woman at that. You can't act like a man" (123). Having children represents for Nel the crucial distinction between the male and the female position. Women, as Eva succeeds in demonstrating, can *act* like men, but in this novel, they cannot leave their children and get away with it. Yet when Sula contemplates the women who stay with their children, she is confronted with emptiness and desperation: "Those with men had had the sweetness sucked from their breath by ovens and steam kettles. Their children were like distant but exposed wounds whose aches were no less intimate because separate from their flesh. They had looked at the world and back at their children, back at the world and back again at their children, and Sula knew that one clear young eye was all that kept the knife away from the throat's curve" (105). Until her death, Sula is haunted by the fears of the destruction domesticity brings: Witness her dream about the baking powder girl who disintegrates into a pile of dust. Whereas for Sula motherhood constitutes a threat of disintegration, for Nel it comes to mean an immutable, inescapable, desperate fusion: "They [her children] were all she would ever know of love. But it was a love that, like a pan of syrup kept too long on the stove, had cooked out, leaving only its odor and a hard, sweet sludge, impossible to scrape off"(142).

The novel proposes female friendship as an alternative relationship to the maternal, but it does not do so unquestioningly. Might her friendship with Nel have saved Sula from the slow erosion that kills her? And who is to be blamed for endangering and impairing this friendship when Sula sleeps with Nel's husband? Other—truly artistic—possibilities of expression are unavailable to Sula in her world and, suffering from an "idle imagination," she remains "an artist with no art form." Although she can assert at the end of her life that she has indeed created herself ("I got my mind. And what goes on in it. Which is to say, I got me" [123]), her lack of attachments robs her of the food for her imagination and creativity. *"I have sung all the songs there are,"* she repeats. Yet even as she retreats totally into the utter aloneness of her head and slips from life to death, Sula longs to speak to Nel, to tell her about what death feels like. But Sula's repudiation of motherhood and attachment does not enable an alternate career as an artist. Whether under different economic and social conditions it could have, the text leaves unanswered.

The novel's conclusion—Nel's epiphanic recognition that it is her friend Sula she has missed all these years and not her husband Jude, her return to the fantasy of a perfect sisterhood— reasserts the perspective the text proposes as an alternate form of discourse to the maternal.[19] Nel's cry contrasts sharply with the literal stories told by Eva or Helene: "It was a fine cry—loud and long—but it had no bottom and no top, just circles and circles of sorrow." In her discussion of this cry, Margaret Homans presents it as an assertion of separatism, of a specifically female expression in language: "What finally expresses her woman-identified self is of necessity nonrepresentational."[20] It is perhaps understandable that such a moment should lead back to childhood, to a pre-oedipal, preseparational female past, as yet uncontaminated by social institutions. The fusion of Sula and Nel, affirmed in the last scene by the ancient Eva, who refuses to distinguish between them, offers a privileged if dangerous mode of relation and expression, one that in the economy of this novel could never be shared in by the mother. No such fusion or confusion exists between generations in this text; the roles and the voices of mother and daughter in the novel are forciby separated, even within the characters of Hannah, Helene, and Nel, who are each both mother and daughter. The novel's short circuit, its ultimate return to its own beginnings, only reinforces the two protagonists' inability to transcend the fate of their mothers, *as well as* their inability to repeat it. For women who reject unconditionally the lives and the stories of their mothers, there is nowhere to go. The novel both suggests and, in its own unfocused second part, actually acts out this lack of direction. Holding on to a pervasive belief in the danger of the maternal, and reiterating that danger not only in the deaths of Chicken Little and of Plum, but also in the death of a large part of the town in the half-built, womblike tunnel at the end of the novel, the text demonstrates the trap that lies within the attempt to escape from the maternal.[21]

The mother's discourse, *when it can be voiced at all*, is always repetitive, literal, hopelessly representational. It is rooted in the body that shivers, hurts, bleeds, suffers, burns, rather than in the eyes, or in the voice, which can utter its cries of pain. It is rooted in Eva's fierce bodily love for Hannah, as well as in her anger, aggression, her violence, not in the unspoken hostility, eventually overcome, between Nel and Sula. The ancient Eva in the old-age home, with her aggressive tone and her direct questions, is still a threat to Nel, whose polite visit cannot accommodate the vehement anger that keeps Eva alive. Maternal discourse, the story Eva never tells as well as the stories she repeats obsessively, remains both absent and present in the novel, a mark of difference that provides the novel with its momentum, but must to a degree remain unspoken in order to do so. Is the novel suggesting, then, that the mother's story can provide only the point of departure for the text but not its content, that art is, *in fact*, primarily based on the child's drama in relation to the mother?

Could it be that maternal discourse can exist in the text only on the condition that it remain fragmentary, incomplete, and mediated through the perspective of the daughter-writer? Could it be that the novel to some degree depends on maternal silence? Adrienne Rich says, "For me, poetry was where I lived as no-one's mother, where I existed as myself,"[22] provoking Helen Vendler to ask: "Is there something about the relation with children, in contrast to relations with adults, which makes it unavailable to the writer?"

Sula, I believe, thematizes some of the ambivalences about maternal discourse more broadly present in today's European and American feminist writing. It suggests that an acknowledgement of the specificity of maternal experience could offer a perspective crucial to feminist discourse. Until feminists can find ways to speak as mothers, feminism as an intellectual movement will be unable to account for important experiential differences among women.

Inasmuch as the mother is simultaneously a daughter and a mother, a woman and a mother, in the house and in the world, powerful and powerless, nurturing and nurtured, dependent and depended upon, maternal discourse is necessarily plural, divided. And, as *Sula* demonstrates, maternal discourse is intimately tied to and tied up in social and political reality as well as psychological structures. Maternal knowledge, moreover, if it could be voiced, could enlarge a feminist analysis and reverse traditional conceptions of love and anger, of power and knowledge, of self in relation to other, of femininity and maturity, of sexuality and nurturance. Mothers who must work to raise children to be acceptable members of their society can reveal a great deal about the functioning of ideology and the processes of assimilation and interpellation. Most of all, if feminists don't want to "stop the blood" flowing from one generation to the next, we need to find ways of hearing and telling the stories of mothers—to politicize motherhood from within feminism—even if those stories are "cruel enough to stop [our] blood."

Further consistent exploration of maternal discourse—whether in theoretical, fictional, or autobiographical writing—would reveal, I believe, notions of identity and subjectivity that correspond neither to the unified ego of ego-psychology, nor to the fluid boundaries of object-relations theory, nor to a subjectivity split against itself, as outlined by Lacanian psychoanalysis. What model or definition of subjectivity might be derived from a theory that begins with mothers rather than with children? Can we conceive of development as other than a process of separation from a neutral, either nurturing or hostile, but ultimately self-effacing "holding" background? I would suggest that if we start our study of the subject with *mothers* rather than with *children*, a different conception of subjectivity might emerge. Although it might be difficult to define, we might try to envision a culturally variable form of interconnection between one body and another, one person and another, existing as social and legal as well as psychological subjects.

Toni Morrison's *Beloved* explores just such a maternal voice.[23] Although the novel reiterates that Sethe's story is "not a story to pass on," *Beloved* is the story of the mother, and the novel's dominant voice and narrative is hers. Sethe's story—her life under slavery, the conception and care of her children in the most dire conditions, her escape and liberation, and her desperately violent and loving act of infanticide—provides, in a sense, the background for the story of Eva. *Beloved* explains Eva's anger, an anger handed down through generations of mothers who could have no control over their children's lives, no voice in their upbringing. And *Beloved* suggests why that anger may have to remain unspeakable, and how it might nevertheless be spoken. In fact, the mother-daughter conversations that do occur in *Beloved* are conversations from beyond the grave; if Sethe is to explain her incomprehensible act, she has to do so to a ghost.

Beloved provides some of the insights into mothers and women that *Sula* begins to adumbrate, and it does so all the more intensely for telling the story of a mother who is a slave. The economy of slavery circumscribes not only the process of individuation and subject formation, but also heightens and intensifies the experience of motherhood—of connection and separation. It raises questions about what it means to have a self, and to give that self away. It raises questions about what *family* means. If mothers cannot "own" their children or themselves, they experience separation and loss all the more intensely.

At the end of the novel, the doubly bereaved Sethe, who

has lost her daughter twice, is nursed back to life by her other daughter Denver and by her lover, Paul D. To her self-effacing "she was my best thing," he insists, "You your best thing, Sethe. You are." Holding her fingers, he enables Sethe for the first time to see herself as subject, as mother and subject both: "Me? Me?" she says tentatively, and thus enables the mother's voice and subjectivity to emerge, allowing herself to question, at least for a moment, the hierarchy of motherhood and selfhood on which her life, until that moment, had rested. However, she can do so only in the context of another human bond; she can do so only because Paul D. is holding her hand. Is this a reversion to oedipal mediations and triangulations, or is it an affirmation of a subjectivity that, even when it is maternal, can only emerge in and through human interconnection? Sethe's story is "not a story to pass on," yet this novel, more than Morrison's earlier works, does let the mother speak for herself. It allows her to recognize both her love for Beloved and her love for herself. With this novel, Toni Morrison has done more than to shift the direction of her own work and of feminist theorizing: Along with writers like Grace Paley and Tillie Olsen, she has opened the space for maternal narrative in feminist fiction. That narrative is surely "cruel enough to stop the blood."[24]

NOTES

1. Adrienne Rich, *Of Woman Born: Motherhood as Experience and Institution* (New York: Norton, 1976), 225.
2. Mary Helen Washington, "I Sign my Mother's Name: Alice Walker, Dorothy West, Paule Marshall," in Ruth Perry and Martine Watson Brownly, eds., *Mothering the Mind* (New York: Holmes and Meier, 1984), 161.
3. Both in Alice Walker, *In Search of Our Mothers' Gardens* (New York: Harcourt Brace Jovanovich, 1983).
4. Paule Marshall, "Shaping the World of My Art," *New Letters* 40 (Autumn 1973), 105.
5. Paule Marshall, "From the Poets in the Kitchen," *New York Times Book Review* (9 January 1983), 3, 34–5.
6. Alice Walker's "Everyday Use," in *In Love & Trouble: Stories of Black Women* (New York: Harcourt Brace Jovanovich, 1973) offers one counterexample, as does the story of Mattie Michael in Gloria Naylor's *The Women of Brewster Place* (New York: Penguin Books, 1983).
7. See "For the Etruscans," in Alice Jardine and Hester Eistenstein, eds., *The Future of Difference* (Boston: G.K.Hall, 1979).
8. E. Frances White, "Listening to the Voices of Black Feminism," *Radical America* 18, Nos. 2–3 (Spring 1985). Mary Helen Washington pointed out to me that contemporary black women writers are responding to a powerful tradition of maternal praise going

back to the times of slavery and the celebration of the resilience of the slave mother. For recent explorations of mother/daughter relationships in Afro-American culture, see Gloria I. Joseph and Jill Lewis, *Common Differences: Conflicts in Black and White Feminist Perspectives* (New York: Doubleday, 1981) and a special issue on mothers and daughters of *Sage: A Scholarly Journal on Black Women* 1, No. 2 (Fall 1984).

9. Cited by Washington, "I Sign My Mother's Name," 156.

10. Walker, "In Search of Our Mothers' Gardens," 233.

11. Toni Morrison, *Sula* (New York: Bantam, 1973).

12. Hortense J. Spillers, in "A Hateful Passion, A Lost Love," *Feminist Studies* 9, No. 2 (Summer 1983), 293–323, stresses the radical departure of *Sula* in relation to the tradition of black female writing. In its novelty *Sula* is representative of its generation, she says: "The black woman as artist, as an intellectual spokesperson for her own cultural apprenticeship, has not existed before, for anyone" (297).

13. For a different view of the novel's relation to heterosexual relations, see Houston A. Baker, Jr., "When Lindbergh Sleeps with Bessie Smith: The Writing of Place in Toni Morrison's *Sula*," Colloquium Paper, School of Criticism and Theory, Dartmouth College, 1987.

14. For an interesting discussion of lack as a figure for the experience of racial otherness, see Susan Willis, "Eruptions of Funk: Historicizing Toni Morrison," in Henry Louis Gates, ed., *Black Literature and Literary Theory* (New York: Methuen, 1984).

15. Mary Helen Washington, in *Midnight Birds: Stories of Contemporary Black Women Writers* (New York: Doubleday, 1980), 153–155, calls Eva the "creator and sovereign" who "gives and takes life." Hortense Spillers says that "Eva behaves as though she were herself the sole instrument of divine inscrutable will" (314).

16. See Jacques Lacan, "The Meaning of the Phallus," in Juliet Mitchell and Jacqueline Rose, eds., *Feminine Sexuality: Jacques Lacan and the école freudienne* (New York: Norton, 1982), as well as "Introduction II" in the same volume, for a discussion of the notions of "phallic mother" and "masquerade." See also Joan Rivière, "Womanlines as Mascarade," *IJPA*, x (1929), 303–13 and Michèle Montrelay "An Inquiry into Femininity," *Semiotext(e)* 10, Vol. 4, 1(1981), 228–235.

17. See Susan Willis, "Eruptions of Funk," for a discussion of self-mutilation as a literary figure of black confrontation with white domination (277). Willis sees Sula's gesture as a more radical rebellion than I do.

18. Robert Stepto, " 'Intimate Things in Place': A Conversation with Toni Morrison," *The Massachusetts Review*, 487.

19. For a discussion of the implications of the novel's celebration of female friendship, see Elizabeth Abel,"(E)Merging Identities: The Dynamics of Female Friendship in Contemporary Fiction by Women," *Signs* 6, No.3 (Spring 1981), 413–435, and Judith Kegan Gardiner, "The (Us)es of (I)dentity: A Response to Abel on '(E)Merging Identities,' "*Signs* 6, No. 3 (Spring 1981), 436–444.

20." 'Her Very Own Howl': The Ambiguities of Representation in Recent Women's Fiction," *Signs* 9, No. 2 (Autumn 1983), 193.

21. Whereas critics like Hortense Spillers see in Sula's rejection of traditional woman-hood a "radical alternative" and a "radical freedom," I find that the novel thematizes a much more ambivalent attitude toward the maternal, showing both its dangers and the dangers of rejecting it.

22. Adrienne Rich, *Of Woman Born*, 31. See also Mary Gordon, "On Mothership and Authorhood," *The New York Times Book Review*, (19 February 1985), 1, 34–35.

23. Toni Morrison, *Beloved* (New York: Knopf, 1987).

24. This essay is part of a larger study, Marianne Hirsch's *The Mother/Daughter Plot: Narrative, Psychoanalysis, Feminism* (Bloomington: Indiana University Press, 1989).

Romance, Marginality, and Matrilineage:

The Color Purple and
Their Eyes Were Watching God

Molly Hite

The publication of *The Color Purple* transformed Alice Walker from an indubitably serious black writer whose fiction belonged to a tradition of gritty, if occasionally "magical," realism into a popular novelist, with all the perquisites and drawbacks attendant on that position. Unlike either *The Third Life of Grange Copeland* (1970) or *Meridian* (1976), *The Color Purple* gained immediate and widespread public acceptance, winning both the Pulitzer Prize and the American Book Award for 1982–1983. At the same time, however, it generated immediate and widespread critical unease over what appeared to be manifest flaws in its composition. Robert Towers, writing in the *New York Review of Books,* concluded that on the evidence of *The Color Purple* "Alice Walker still has a lot to learn about plotting and structuring what is clearly intended to be a realistic novel," and his opinion was shared by many reviewers, who pointed out variously that in the last third of the book the narrator-protagonist Celie and her friends are propelled toward a fairy-tale happy ending with more velocity than credibility; that the letters from Nettie, with their disconcertingly literate depictions of life in an African village, intrude into the middle of the main action with little apparent motivation or warrant; and that the device of the letters to God is especially unrealistic inasmuch as it foregoes the concretizing details that traditionally have given the epistolary form its peculiar verisimilitude: the secret writing place, the cache, the

ruses to enable posting letters, and especially the letters received in return.[1]

Indeed, the violations of realist convention are so flagrant
that they might well call into question whether *The Color
Purple* "is clearly intended to be a realistic novel," especially
as there are indications that at least some of those aspects of
the novel discounted by reviewers as flaws may constitute its
links to modes of writing other than Anglo-American nineteenth-century realism. For example, Henry Louis Gates, Jr.,
has recently located the letters to God within an Afro-American
tradition deriving from slave narrative, a tradition in which
the act of writing is linked to a powerful deity who "speaks"
through scripture and bestows literacy as an act of grace.[2] For
Gates, the concern with finding a voice that he sees as the
defining feature of Afro-American literature becomes the context for the allusive affinities between Celie's letters and the
"free indirect 'narrative of division' " that characterizes the
acknowledged predecessor of *The Color Purple*, Zora Neale
Hurston's 1937 novel *Their Eyes Were Watching God*.[3]

Gates's paradigm suggests how misleading it may be to
assume that mainstream realist criteria are appropriate for
evaluating *The Color Purple*. But the Afro-American preoccupation with voice as a primary element unifying both the speaking subject and the text as a whole does not deal with many of
the more disquieting structural features of Walker's novel. For
instance, while the letters from Nettie clearly illustrate Nettie's
parallel acquisition of her own voice, a process that enables
her to arrive at conclusions very like Celie's under very different circumstances, the Afro-American tradition sheds little
light on the central *place* that these letters occupy in the narrative or on why the plot takes this sudden jump into geographically and culturally removed surroundings. And Gates's subtle
explication of the ramifications of "voice" once Walker has
reconstrued the term to designate a *written* discourse does not
attempt to address the problematic ending, in which the disparate members of Celie's extended family come together, as
if drawn by a cosmic magnet—and as if in defiance of the
most minimal demands of narrative probability.

The example of *Their Eyes Were Watching God* tends to compound these problems rather than provide a precedent that
helps explain them, for Hurston's most famous novel has also

been judged flawed, and for many of the same reasons. To a certain extent, placing *Their Eyes* in the context of an Afro-American tradition that Hurston herself did much to document[4] reveals how central the act of storytelling is in this book, to the point where Janie's discovery and use of her narrating voice emerges as the major action.[5] This context helps explain the tendency of the story *about* storytelling to usurp the ostensible main plot of Janie's quest for happiness with a man—for example, the apparently disproportionate emphasis given to the digressive "co-talkin' " of such minor characters as Hicks and Coker in Eatonville,[6] or to the rhetoric of the "skin games" played by Ed Dockery, Bootyny and Sop-de-Bottom on the muck (200–202). It also helps to explain the exuberant fabulation that so completely takes over Chapter 6 that the story of the mule "freed" at Janie's instigation turns completely away from realism and becomes a beast fable, with buzzards as parsons, and the congregation chanting a parodic litany over the carrion (81–97).

But once again the Afro-American paradigm leaves untouched some of the most problematic structural elements of this novel, elements that according to many critics constitute lapses or flaws in its composition. Dianne Sadoff makes the case most persuasively and sympathetically, inasmuch as she discerns "marks, fissures, and traces of 'inferiorization' "[7] that amount to "scars of disguise or concealment because [Hurston] is black and female—doubly alienated from a white and partriarchal mainstream literature."[8] Sadoff views *Their Eyes Were Watching God* as a celebration of heterosexual love that is undercut by Hurston's own ambivalence over the compatibility of marriage and the creative "voice" that produces fiction. The ambivalence is figured most acutely in the misogynistic attitudes and behavior that Hurston tacitly ascribes to Janie's third husband and great love, Tea Cake, and in the action of the scene where, according to the covert logic of the narrative if not the overt logic of explication, Janie murders Tea Cake, just as she has murdered her previous husband, Jody Starks. As Sadoff observes, "Hurston has motivated her narrative, perhaps unconsciously, to act out her rage against male domination and to free Janie, a figure for herself, from all men."[9]

In making the "marks" and "scars" that she perceives in Hurston's novel the inevitable consequence of Hurston's dou-

bly marginalized social position, Sadoff employs a version of
the Gilbert and Gubar "anxiety of authorship" model pio-
neered in *The Madwoman in the Attic*.[10] In the process, however,
she underscores problems with this model's presumption that
apparent inconsistencies in the narrative are due to unin-
tended eruptions of repressed biographical material into the
text. While Sadoff is more thorough and more sympathetic in
her treatment of *Their Eyes Were Watching God* than, say, Robert Towers is in his treatment of *The Color Purple*, she pre-
sumes, as Towers does, that the author has inadvertently
written something other than what she intended, and that
what the author intended was an unironic and unambiguous
realism—in the case of Hurston, specifically, the realism of the
heterosexual romance plot that structured so many European
and American novels about women in the eighteenth and
nineteenth centuries.[11] Neither critic entertains the possibility
that certain ostensible violations may be calculated subver-
sions of conventions that the authors regarded as permeated
with white, masculinist values, or that other ostensible violations may arise from the fact that the authors were writing not
realism but romance—perhaps in part because, unlike the
genre of realism, the genre of romance is recognized as highly
conventional, so that its ideological implications are easier
both to underscore and to undermine.[12]

"Romance" is a term with a wide range of applications,
especially when contrasted to "realism,"[13] but it also has a
more delimited technical sense that turns out to be surprisingly relevant to *The Color Purple*, and it illuminates certain
analogous aspects of *Their Eyes Were Watching God*. Such late
plays of Shakespeare as *The Tempest* and—especially—*The Winter's Tale*, which draw on the pastoral for a number of their
governing premises but go on to use these premises as means
to develop a tragicomic plot, have striking affinities with the
narrative strategies created by Walker and Hurston. Shakespearean romance can in certain respects serve as a structural
paradigm for these two novels without necessarily standing in
a relationship of direct influence to them[14] or absorbing them
into its own network of assumptions about how the world is
structured and how human beings fit into it. Indeed, the
romance paradigm seems most important in this context precisely because it formally encodes a system of hierarchical

relations that have ideological repercussions—and because this recognizably conventional system of hierarchical relations is also the ideology of racism and patriarchy that the two novels expose and, ultimately, invert.

I

In his introduction to the New Arden edition of *The Tempest*, Frank Kermode advances "pastoral tragicomedy" as a more precise, if more cumbersome, designation for the late plays of Shakespeare more commonly termed romances.[15] The phrase is useful insofar as it invokes the tradition of the pastoral and thus a set of conventions celebrating a rural, "natural" community often explicitly identified with the nonwhite inhabitants of Africa or the New World and constituted in implicit opposition to a dominant urban community.[16] *The Color Purple* is clearly pastoral in these respects, for in it Walker makes a group of black farmers the central social unit, and uses this community as a vantage point from which to deliver a blistering critique of the surrounding white culture. The denunciation is sometimes overt, as when Sofia fulminates,[17]

> They have the nerve to try to make us think slavery fell through because of us . . . Like us didn't have sense enough to handle it. All the time breaking hoe handles and letting the mules loose in the wheat. But how anything they build can last a day is a wonder to me. They backward . . . Clumsy, and unlucky.[18]

More frequently, however, the white society figures as profoundly unnecessary, invisible for most of the action and appearing only as explosions of violence and insanity that sporadically intrude into the relatively intelligible world of the protagonists, as when the Mayor's wife asks Sofia to be her maid and precipitates the beating, jailing, and domestic servitude of Sofia and the rape of Squeak, or as when the English engineers casually eradicate the Olinka village in the process of turning the jungle into a rubber plantation.

The point of view of the pastoral is conventionally simple, artless, and naive—values rendered, of course, by means that are complex, subtle, and sophisticated—and can become the locus of a sustained attack on the mores of the mainstream society.[19] Walker's protagonist, Celie (whose name by various etymologies means "holy," "healing," and "heavenly"), is in these respects an exemplary pastoral protagonist, for her defining quality, and thus the defining quality of the narrative, is innocence. If this innocence subjects her to violation at the outset of the story, it also figures as a capacity for wonder and thus for experience. Celie learns, and as she learns her pastoral community develops, in a movement that implicitly restores a submerged Edenic ideal of harmony between individual human beings and between humanity and the natural order.

It is this development that makes *The Color Purple* a narrative—tragicomedy as well as pastoral—and provides striking affinities with the late Shakespearean romances. Kermode has defined romance as "a mode of exhibiting the action of magical and moral laws in a version of human life so selective as to obscure, for the special purpose of concentrating attention on these laws, the fact that in reality their force is intermittent and only fitfully glimpsed."[20] Certainly the moral laws of Walker's novel, subtitled in the original hardcover edition *A Moral Tale*, have magical power, producing consequences that are not in naturalistic terms remotely credible. Nettie, Samuel, and the children miraculously return from the sea after their ship is reported missing, to provide a conclusion that brings together all the far-flung characters in a celebration that is part family reunion, part assertion of a new social order that will supplant the old (the celebration takes place on the Fourth of July, a date on which, as Harpo explains to a representative of the younger generation, white people are busy "celebrating they independence from England" and consequently black people "can spend the day celebrating each other" [250]). Shortly before this climactic juncture, Shug returns from her last heterosexual fling to find Celie and Albert reconciled and living in platonic harmony, a reversal prompted by Albert's recognition that "meanness kill" (201). Shortly before *this* development Celie inherits a house, a store, and the information that her children are not the product of incest. And this last windfall comes after the success of Celie's company, Folkspants, Ltd., an enterprise purveying androgyny to Depression-era black sharecroppers. The comic impetus of Walker's story

is so powerful that it absorbs questions of probability and motivation. As Northrop Frye has noted of analogous Shakespeare
plots, "What emerges at the end is not a logical consequence
of the preceding action, as in tragedy, but something more
like a metamorphosis."[21]

In Shakespearean romance the metamorphosis is both social
and metaphysical. It is social in that it involves a redemptive
conclusion absorbing all the principal characters, whether or
not they seem to deserve redemption. Moreover, as J. H. P.
Pafford observes in the context of *The Winter's Tale*, the element of tragedy in romances derives from the suffering that
characters must undergo because of the misbehavior of a
powerful male figure, a figure who, however, "always shares
to the full in the final blessings, and, however guilty and
responsible for the sufferings of others, he is ultimately absolved by facile excuse, if any is needed at all."[22] In *The Color
Purple* the most important agent of suffering is also a (relatively) powerful male figure, Celie's husband Mr.———, whose
unarticulated name, in the manner of epistolary fictions
since Richardson's *Pamela*, suggests fearful effacement of an
identity too dangerous to reveal, and whose transformation is
signaled by a renaming that at once diminishes and humanizes.[23]
In this case, the gratuitous absolution is also a conversion that
affects descendents, for both Mr.——— (who is transformed
into a little man given to collecting shells and called merely
Albert) and his son, Harpo, are absolved by becoming integrated into a female-defined value community, "finding themselves" at last in the traditionally female roles of seamstress
and housekeeper.

The metamorphoses of romance are not limited to the social
order, and they have an analogous metaphysical dimension in
The Color Purple, where Celie's progress also serves to redefine
the proper relation between human beings and the natural
world they inhabit. Shug's disquisitions on religion and on
the behavior that a redefined God requires are consonant with
the pastoral's characteristic fusion of reverence and hedonism,
and with a long tradition that uses pastoral convention to
attack the excesses and misconceptions of established religious practice.[24] "God love all them [sexual] feelings," Shug
assures a scandalized Celie. "That's some of the best stuff
God did." She goes on to maintain, "God love admiration . . .

Not vain, just wanting to share a good thing" (178). In the ensuing critique of prevailing religious beliefs, this undemanding God emerges as not only sexless—an "it" rather than a "he"—but also radically decentered: not one but many, and in fact, according to Shug, "Everything that is or ever was or ever will be. And when you can feel that, and be happy to feel that, you've found It" (178). Like the value systems governing traditional romances, the nurturing pantheism that this novel affirms as an ideal also figures implicitly as a preexisting state or Edenic norm that must be restored before human beings can attain social equilibrium. Celie only embraces it completely in the greeting of her last letter, which describes the celebratory reunion of all the principal characters: "Dear God. Dear stars, dear trees, dear sky, dear peoples. Dear Everything. Dear God" (249).[25]

Finally, Shakespearean romances provide precedent and rationale for an aspect of *The Color Purple* that readers have found particularly anomalous, the "Africa" passages that in effect disrupt the American action for some forty pages, when a whole cache of withheld letters from Nettie is suddenly revealed. These letters detail the story of Nettie's adoption by a missionary family and her subsequent travels to New York, England, Senegal, Liberia, and, finally, to the unnamed country of the Olinka. In the Olinka village she recapitulates Celie's discoveries, decrying the irrationality of the sex-gender system, becoming increasingly committed to the nonhuman, asexual God, and achieving a heterosexual version of Celie's stable, loving relationship. The function of the "Africa" section is clearly to provide analogies and contrasts to the dominant action. In this function, as in its seeming violation of realist conventions, it parallels scenes in the romances taking place in what Frye has called the "green world," a pastoral landscape that serves as a "symbol of natural society, the word natural referring to the original human society which is the proper home of man," and that is "associated with things which in the context of the ordinary world seem unnatural, but which are in fact attributes of nature as a miraculous and irresistible reviving power."[26] This "green world" is "particularly the world in which the heroine . . . dies and comes back to life,"[27] and as such it is the locus of Nettie's reincarnation as correspondent and co-narrator.

The village of the Olinka, with its organically round huts, its roof-leaf religion, its restorative myths of black hegemony, and its simple, agrarian economy, is in some respects, and especially initially, an idyllic counter to the world that Celie must dismantle and remake. In its geographical distance from the world of the main action, in the length of time the daughter-heroine spends there (as missing and presumed dead), in its structural function of healing old wounds through a marriage and the founding of a family, and in its operation of recapitulating major themes of the containing drama, this generic "Africa" most resembles the Bohemia of *The Winter's Tale*—with one signal difference. Whereas Perdita in *The Winter's Tale* learns from the pastoral Bohemia, which in many respects remains an ideal, Nettie in *The Color Purple* ends up criticizing the Olinka society, which she first perceives as a natural and self-determining black community but soon finds sexist and vulnerable to incursions by the encompassing white empire. By contrast, Celie's world becomes more woman centered and more self-sufficient as it develops, finally containing and assimilating even elements of the white community in the person of Sofia's former charge, Miss Eleanor Jane, who leaves her own home to work for Sofia.

But this one difference in many ways completely inverts the emphasis of the romance, suggesting the extent to which Walker unsettles this structural paradigm in the process of applying it. As a marginal and marginalizing work, *The Color Purple* not only reveals the central preoccupations of the tradition within which it locates itself but succeeds in turning a number of these preoccupations inside out, at once exposing the ideology that informs them and insinuating the alternative meanings that, by insisting on its own centrality, the paradigm has suppressed.

II

One of the chief preoccupations of romance as a genre is the relation between men and women. *The Winter's Tale*, which in this, as in other respects, is the closest structural analogue to *The Color Purple*, deals with the unmotivated jealousy and cruelty of a man who is also a ruler, his loss of his wife and daughter for a period of sixteen years, and their restoration—both had been preserved in "green worlds"[28]—after he atones and comes to terms with his own misdeeds. The restoration is bittersweet: On the one hand, time has elapsed and many opportunities are gone for good; on the other hand, a young central couple restores the succession and suggests a more humane and rational future, both for this family and for the state that they govern.

Allowing for the fact that in *The Color Purple* the female roles of mother, daughter, wife, and lover are slippery to the point of being interchangeable, the plot of *The Winter's Tale* has clear affinities with the plot of *The Color Purple*—and a very different focus. As the sketch above should indicate, despite the attention given to the main female characters, the play is *about* the father and ruler, Leontes, about his crime, his punishment, and his eventual, though partial, restitution. By analogy *The Color Purple* ought to be about Mr.———, about *his* crime, punishment, and eventual restitution. And of course Mr.——— goes through all these stages, emerging at the conclusion as an integral part of the new society embodied in the family that surrounds him. But *The Color Purple* is not his story.

This point is especially important in view of the fact that Steven Spielberg seized on the underlying romance structure of Walker's novel when he made it into a film, and in the process reinscribed Mr.——— (whom he renamed simply Mister, so that the title of authority became this character's identity) at the center of the story, making his change of heart the turning point of the action and involving him in supplementary scenes that show him coming to reembrace his estranged family. Even more strikingly, Spielberg went on to reinscribe the law of the father exactly where Walker had effaced it, by providing Shug with a textually gratuitous "daddy" who is also a preacher and thus the representative of the Christian white father-God explicitly repudiated in the passage that gives the book its title.[29] This father asserts his power by refusing to *speak* to Shug until she and all the inhabitants of the evolving new society who have gathered in the alternative structure of the juke joint are themselves assimilated to the Christian church and give *voice* to Christian hymns. Spielberg's restorative instinct here was unerring, for Walker uses the Afro-American motif of "finding a voice" primarily to decenter patriarchal authority, giving speech to hitherto muted women, who change meanings in the process of articulating and thus appropriating the dominant discourse. Speilberg replaced this entire narrative tendency with its reverse, not only restoring voice to the father but making paternal words uniquely efficacious: The film's Mister is shown visiting Washington, talking to bureaucrats, and in substance becoming the agent of the climactic reunion between Celie and Nettie.[30]

In the novel, on the other hand, the emphasis is skewed away from this male discovery of identity. If Albert and Harpo "find themelves," it is within a context of redefinition that not only denies male privilege but ultimately denies that the designations "male" and "female" are meaningful bases for demarcating difference. In a fictional universe governed by the written "dialect" of Celie and initially conditioned by the paternal injunction *"You better not tell nobody but God. It'd kill your mammy"* (11), speech among women turns out to be revivifying rather than death dealing, especially inasmuch as such speech has the potential to bring about romance's characteristic reconstitution of society.

The reconstitution of society is largely a matter of redefinition. For example, in the notorious "little button" passage in which Shug introduces Celie to her own sexuality, Shug replaces conventional terminology for the female genitals, shifting emphasis from the lack or hole of patriarchal representation to a "little button" that "git hotter and hotter and then it melt"—a mixed metaphor from the point of view of the dominant discursive practice, which of course has only recently begun to acknowledge the existence of buttons that behave in this way. The consequence is immediately clear to Celie: If the important organ is not a hole but a button, then stimulation can come from such androgynous appendages as "finger and tongue," and intercourse is not only insufficient but unnecessary for female sexual pleasure. Shug's redefinition of the word "virgin" in this passage is equally threatening to patriarchal control over women's bodies, in that it places priority not on penetration, and thus on the social mechanism for guaranteeing ownership of children, but on enjoyment, making the woman's own response the index of her "experience" (79).

In the development of the story Celie, along with the appositely named Squeak, acquires a voice and becomes a producer of meanings, while Shug and Sofia, articulate all along, increase their authority until it is evident that female voices have the power to dismantle hierarchical oppositions that ultimately oppress everyone, and to create a new order in which timeworn theories about male and female "natures" vanish because they are useless for describing the qualities of people. Near the conclusion, the transformed Mr.————, now happily calling himself only Albert, tries to explain his admiration for Shug: "To tell the truth, Shug act more manly than most men. I mean she upright, honest. Speak her mind and the devil take the hindmost." But Celie takes issue with these categories. "Harpo not like this, I tell him. You not like this. What Shug got is womanly it seem like to me. Specially since she and Sofia the ones got it." Albert continues to worry the problem—"Sofia and Shug not like men . . . but they not like women either"—until Celie makes the relevant distinction: "You mean they not like you or me" (236). On the basis of such redrawn lines the entire immediate society reconstitutes itself, in the manner of Shakespearean romance, around a central couple. This couple is not only black, it is aging and lesbian. Yet clearly Celie and Shug are intended to suggest the nucleus of a new and self-sustaining society: The triply marginalized become center and source.

III

The issue of voice—and especially of voice as a way of appropriating discourse and remaking meanings—returns this discussion to the writer whom Walker has repeatedly claimed as her "foremother," Zora Neale Hurston, and to *Their Eyes Were Watching God*, in which the protagonist, Janie, discovers her voice and uses it to assert her own authority in a world full of speechmakers and tale-tellers. Janie's voice, first muted by the pathos of her Nanny's stories, emerges to threaten her first husband but then is subsumed to the "big voice" of Jody Starks until the moment of the signifying that by the logic of the narrative kills him: "Humph! Talkin' 'bout *me* lookin' old! When you pull down yo' britches, you look lak de change uh life" (123). Janie's relationship with Tea Cake reinforces the association of language and sexual potency—"He done taught me de maiden language all over," Janie tells her best friend Pheoby (173)—and finally raises her to a level of equality that is to some extent both sexual and narrative, for in "the muck," the fertile Florida bottom land where Tea Cake takes her, "she could listen and laugh and even talk some herself if she wanted to. She got so she could tell big stories herself from listening to the rest" (200).

"The muck" in this novel plays the role of a "green world" in Shakespearean romance: It is a magical, somehow "more natural" realm that shapes both the outside world and the conclusion toward which the narrative tends. Tea Cake describes it in unmistakably pastoral terms: "Folks don't do nothin' down dere but make money and fun and foolishness" (192). The narrator elaborates,

> Pianos living three lifetimes in one. Blues made and used right on the spot. Dancing, fighting, singing, crying, laughing, winning and losing love every hour. Work all day for money, fight all night for love. The rich black earth clinging to bodies and biting the skin like ants (197).

Precisely because "the muck" is a "green world," however, it represents a transitory stage in Janie's passage toward achieving her own identity, a passage that the romance paradigm further implies will lead to achieving the basis for a reconstituted society. The heterosexual idyll with Tea Cake is thus not the culmination of the plot, but a transformative moment that leads to the culmination. In other words, the theme of finding a voice does not supplement the heterosexual romance plot of *Their Eyes Were Watching God* but supplants that plot, just as the story of Janie's *telling* her story frames, and in framing displaces, the ostensible main story of Janie's quest for heterosexual love.

The action of *Their Eyes Were Watching God* begins with a homecoming, but against the evidence that the Eatonville residents eagerly collect—the "overhalls" that Janie wears[31] and her manifestly mateless state—this is a triumphal return. The whole of the ensuing narrative aims to establish that triumph, displayed especially in the significance of Janie's ability to tell her own story. The capacity to tell this story rests on two conditions. The first is that there be a story to tell: a plot, a completed action in Aristotle's terms. But because a completed action is one that has ended, the quest for heterosexual love must terminate in order to be appropriated by discourse, and the only terminus that will preserve the fulfillment of the quest while imposing closure on it is the apparently tragic one of Tea Cake's death. Rather paradoxically, then, the killing of Tea Cake becomes part of the larger *comic* impetus that establishes Janie's voice and gives him a fictional "life" that she can possess wholly:

> Of course he wasn't dead. He could never be dead until she herself had finished feeling and thinking. The kiss of his memory made pictures of love and light against the wall. Here was peace (286).

The appropriative move goes further. In appropriating Tea Cake in the form of her story, Janie brings the "horizons" so important in the development of her aspirations—she undertook her "journey to the horizons in search of *people*" (138)—back to Eatonville, the black community that functions as the locus of black storytelling in this novel. "Ah done been tuh de horizon and back and now Ah kin sit heah in mah house and live by comparisons," she tells Pheoby (284), but the closing image of the narrative affirms that the horizon has come with her:

> She pulled in her horizon like a great fish-net. Pulled it from around the waist of the world and draped it over her shoulder. So much of life in its meshes! She called in her soul to come and see (286).

And this looping, "netting" action also contains the novel, which begins at the end of Janie's story and comes back to it, drawing the whole "life" of the plot in its meshes.[32]

The central action of *Their Eyes Were Watching God* is thus Janie's telling of her story, and the climax of this central action is the pulling in of the horizon, a dramatization of the fact of closure that establishes Janie as an accomplished storyteller. If one condition of this action is a completed story that can be told, a second condition is an audience capable of hearing it.

Janie's privileged listener is her best friend Pheoby, whose credentials as audience are her empathy and equality with the narrator—to the point of being at least potentially interchangeable with her. "You can tell 'em what Ah say if you wants to," Janie assures her. "Dat's just same as me 'cause mah tongue is in mah friend's mouf" (17). The image implies that the relation of female narrator to female audience is nonhegemonic and reversible. But like so many of the images associated with storytelling in this book, it is also highly sexual, suggesting further that the narratorial couple composed of Janie and Pheoby has displaced the heterosexual couple as the desired union that motivates and finally terminates the action. The commencement of Janie's "conscious life" dates from a revelation in which the spectacle of bees fertilizing the blossoms of a pear tree led to the conclusion, "So this was a marriage!" (23–24), but Janie's subsequent three marriages somewhat miraculously produce no children.[33] The real fertilization seems to occur when Janie combines with Pheoby to give birth to her story after she has returned to Eatonville, the town of tale-tellers. This story addresses the values governing her community, its misplaced emphasis on possession, status, class, and sexual hierarchy, all legacies of its founder, Jody Starks. In narrating, Janie moves to renovate the society that she has rejoined, transforming it at last into a female speech community embracing the playful, nonhierarchical values that constitute the lesson she draws from her experience— an *Eden*ville.[34]

Walker clearly picks up on these implications in her own revision of *Their Eyes Were Watching God*. In *The Color Purple* a homosexual romance plot replaces the heterosexual one, with the appetizing Tea Cake ("So you sweet as all dat?" Janie inquires when she learns his name [149]) transformed into Celie's lover and mentor, Sugar Avery. Moreover, the drama of Celie's epistolary self-creation revolves around the discovery of a female audience that finally fulfills the ideal of correspondence. Celie initially writes to God as an alternative to speech. The process of finding her speaking voice is a process of finding her audience, first in Sofia, then in Shug. But she is not able to deliver the Old Testament-style curse that in turn delivers her from bondage until she is assured of the existence of Nettie, her ideal audience, who also tells a story leading to identical conclusions about the nature of spiritual and social reality—as if her sister's tongue were in her mouth.

IV

Thus in *Their Eyes Were Watching God*, Hurston's ostensible frame-tale decenters what it appears to comprehend, shifting the story of heterosexual love to marginal status even as it contains and completes that story. It behaves, that is, like the frame or margin that Jacques Derrida has discussed under the rubric of the *parergon*. Conventionally extrinsic, supplementary, or inessential to that which it borders, a parergon is simultaneously intrinsic and essential, inasmuch as the priority of the center depends entirely on the oppositional relation of center to margin.[35] Yet to call attention to this margin is to destroy its marginal status, for the parergon is what it is by virtue of "disappearing, sinking in, obliterating itself, dissolving just as it expends its greatest energy."[36] To call attention to the margin is to render it no longer marginal, and consequently to collapse the center in a general unsettling of oppositional hierarchies.

This turning of attention to what is not conventionally in the center—most obviously to conventionally marginal characters—is of course a characteristic activity of conventionally marginal writers: black women, for example. And, of course, to give voice to marginality—to let the margins *speak*—is to mix a metaphor intolerably, for a speaking margin cannot be a margin at all, and in fact threatens to marginalize what has hitherto been perceived as the center.[37] Or, rather, such a phenomenon tends to destabilize precisely the hierarchical oppositions that give "margin" and "center" clearly demarcated meanings.

Such hierarchical oppositions are the basis of traditional genres. In the paradigm of the Shakespearean romance they guarantee the distinction between major and minor characters; between dominant and peripheral lines of action; and between classes, sexes, and generations—all of which may become confused during the development of the plot, but which must be sorted out so as to fall into place in a conclusion that at once reconciles apparently conflicting elements and confirms their inherent differences: the ritual marriage. This conclusion makes its model of unity the patriarchal family and its model of continuity the order of succession in which power passes from father to son. Distinctions of class, gender, and generation coincide with distinctions between major and minor, dominant and peripheral, on the levels of character and plot. These distinctions are unalterable, a premise that becomes the basis for both the tragic and the comic aspects of pastoral tragicomedy.

But these distinctions are destabilized in *Their Eyes Were Watching God* and *The Color Purple*, novels that Rachel Blau du Plessis has identified as employing a "narrative strategy of the multiple individual," in which the female hero "encompasses opposites and can represent both sociological debate and a psychic interplay between boundaries and boundlessness" and who eventually "fuses with a complex and contradictory group; her power is articulated in and continued through a community that is formed in direct answer to the claims of love and romance."[38] Not only is the traditional heterosexual couple supplanted as emphasis of the action, but it is replaced by interchangeable versions of the same-sex couple: mother and daughter, sisters, lovers, narrator and audience. The roles of the characters have become slippery and permeable.

Perhaps most significantly, the mother–daughter relation is continuously transformed. Dianne Sadoff observes the extent to which both novels suppress or overtly repudiate traditional mothering—Janie hates her Nanny and produces a story with Pheoby rather than children in any of her three marriages; Celie loses her children, and their foster mother subsequently dies—and suggests that such suppressions or repudiations "question anxiety-free matrilineage."[39] The issue is particularly important in light of the role of literary foremother that Walker has assigned to Hurston, and Sadoff uses what she perceives as an unacknowledged theme of failed mothering within the two novels to bolster readings that discern "ruptures" within *Their Eyes* and "scars of concealment" within *The Color Purple*, with its imbedded claims of unproblematic descent from the mother tale.

But the preceding discussion of the two novels might suggest, rather, that the issue is less one of the failure of mothering than of a redefinition, in which mothering is presented as a wholly relational activity. In *The Color Purple*, children create mothers by circulating among women who in other contexts are daughters, sisters, friends, wives, and lovers. Celie's children pass first to Corrine, then to Nettie. Squeak takes on Sofia's children when Sofia goes to jail, and Sofia later mothers Squeak's daughter Suzie Q and—with exasperated acknowledgement that even unwilling nurture can engender filial affection—the white girl Eleanor Jane. And Celie's love affair with Shug begins from an erotic exchange that is poignantly figured as a mutual reparenting: "Then I feels something real soft and wet on my breast, feel like one of my little lost babies mouth. Way after while, I act like a little lost baby too" (109).

In *Their Eyes Were Watching God*, mothering is intimately allied with production of a powerful narrative that enjoins a world view and a series of prescriptions about how to live. Nanny's story of Janie's lineage, which begins from what appears to be a piece of maternal wisdom—"De nigger woman is de mule uh de world so fur as Ah can see" (29)—concludes with the demand that Janie marry the man who, in Hurston's wonderfully apt conflation of social class and phallic power, owns "de onliest organ in town" (41). While Janie ultimately repudiates this version of her story as unlivable, her repudiation is explicitly dissociated from an agonistic oedipal model in which the child kills the parental figure in order to revise this parent's master narrative.[40] If the narrative logic by which an ensuing action is figured as a consequent action[41] indicates that Janie is responsible for the death of two husbands, the same logic makes Nanny's death the consequence of her own story, for Nanny's acknowledgement that she is dying ("Put me down easy, Janie, Ah'm a cracked plate") occurs at the end of the narrative in which she coerces Janie into marrying Logan Killicks (37). In replacing Nanny's story about sexual oppression with an alternative story about sexual love that paradoxically enables her to live independently and alone—"by comparisons" (284)—Janie in effect takes on the maternal function, in company of course with her listener, Pheoby. She becomes author of her own story, both source and subject of maternal wisdom, in effect giving birth to herself.

Clearly in Walker's and Hurston's novels mothers are no

guarantors of succession or legitimacy, and mothering is a slippery and even reversible relationship. Furthermore, Walker has suggested that the same sort of observation holds for literary motherhood among black women writers. Indeed, in her essay, "In Search of Our Mothers' Gardens," she elides the distinction between biological and literary motherhood in the same way that in *The Color Purple* she elides the distinction between mothering and other, conventionally contrary, female functions. Mothers are artists, artistic precursors are mothers, and in either case the mother's creation may be inseparable from the daughter's: Perhaps Phillis Wheatley's mother "herself was a poet—though only her daughter's name is signed to the poems we know."[42] This collaborative model of maternal influence suggests a subversively extended family romance, in which the mother as co-creator is simultaneously parent of the writer and her lover or spouse. Most disruptively for the absolute status of all these role definitions, she may even become the daughter of her own daughter. Du Plessis has suggested that in fulfilling or completing her biological mother's work, the twentieth-century woman writer is inclined to dramatize her mother's situation, recreating her mother as a character and revising her destiny by reinscribing it in the fiction.[43] Alice Walker, who gave birth to her step-grandmother when she created Celie,[44] also uses *The Color Purple* to revise her relation to the woman she has elsewhere called her foremother. Gates points out that the photograph of Hurston parenthetically described in Walker's essay, "Zora Neale Hurston: A Cautionary Tale and a Partisan View" ("I have a photograph of her in pants, boots, and broadbrim that was given to me by her brother, Everette. She has her foot up on the running board of a car—presumably hers, and bright red—and looks racy") is in essence the photograph of Shug Avery that fascinates Celie in *The Color Purple*: "I see her there in furs. Her face rouge. Her hair like somethin tail. She grinning with her foot up on somebody motocar" (16).[45] In recreating her relationship to Hurston as a reciprocal and interactive one, Walker dramatizes Hurston's literary role as the undoer of inessential and divisive hierarchies. In casting Hurston as Shug, she revises theories of influence as they apply to black women.

What is finally at stake in readings of the two novels is the

centrality of the paradigms and values informing what mainstream Western society chooses to call literature. To invoke these
paradigms and values as if they exhausted the possibilities, and
to castigate Walker and Hurston for failure to realize them is
to judge according to assumptions rather like those of the
white community that Sofia ridicules in *The Color Purple*: It is
like maintaining that slavery failed because blacks didn't have
sense enough to handle it. This essay has suggested that on
the contrary, by treating the marginal as central and thereby
unsettling the hierarchical relations that structure "mainstream"
genres, Walker and Hurston manage to handle very well the
conventions that threaten to enslave them in a system of
representation not of their own making.

NOTES

1. Robert Towers, review of *The Color Purple*, by Alice Walker, *The New York Review of
Books*, 12 August 1982, 36. Adam Gussow notes the "sudden swerve" into Nettie's
letters and calls it "one of the novel's few weaknesses" in *Chicago Review*, 34, No. 1
(1983), 125. Maria K. Mootry-Ikerionwu, in *"The Color Purple: A Moral Tale," CLA
Journal*, 27, No. 3 [1984], 347, opposes Walker's ideas to her "craft," "which doesn't
quite carry off her vision," and finds the letters to God as improbable as Celie's
passivity. Tamar Katz elegantly points out the ways in which *The Color Purple* refrains
from exploiting many of the most characteristic conventions of the epistolary form
in " 'Show me how to do like you': Didacticism and Epistolary Form in Alice
Walker's *The Color Purple*," unpublished paper, Cornell University, 8. Significantly, it
is a Renaissance scholar, Ruth El Saffar, who suggests the genre with which I believe
the novel is most closely allied; in a review of *The Color Purple* in the *International
Fiction Review* 12, no. 1 (1985), 15, she writes, "the discovery of 'Pa's' usurpation
affects the novel itself, turning it from history, with all its emphasis on power and
control, to romance, whose main focus is love and redemption."
2. These motifs are summed up succinctly in a quotation of Rebecca Cox Jackson that
serves as a headnote to Gates's Walker chapter, "I am only a pen in His hand." Henry
Louis Gates, Jr., "Color Me Zora: Alice Walker's (Re)writing of the Speakerly Text,"
in his *The Signifying Monkey: A Theory of Afro-American Literary Criticism* (New York:
Oxford University Press, 1988), 239.
3. Gates maintains that the letters to God thus represent a further turn on Hurston's
own invention of a discourse accommodating both "dialect" and standard English:
"Celie's written voice to God, her reader, tropes the written yet never uttered voice
of free indirect discourse which is the predominant vehicle of narrative commentary
in Hurston's novel" (243).
4. Hurston trained as an anthropologist at Barnard with Franz Boas. Her book-
length study of black folklore, *Mules and Men* (1935; Bloomington, Indiana: University
of Indiana Press, 1978), serves as a useful thematic and rhetorical source for *Their Eyes
Were Watching God*. See especially Barbara Johnson, "Thresholds of Difference: Structures of Address in Zora Neale Hurston," *Critical Inquiry*, 12 (Autumn 1985), 278–289.
5. In *Reading Zora: Discourse and Rhetoric in "Their Eyes Were Watching God"* (unpublished manuscript, Yale University), Henry Louis Gates, Jr., and Barbara Johnson
maintain, "the very subject of this text would seem to be not primarily Janie's quest,
but the emulation of the phonetic, grammatical, and lexical structures of actual speech."
(33). Elizabeth Meese places a more overtly feminist construction on the role of voice

in "Orality and Textuality in Zora Neale Hurston's *Their Eyes Were Watching God*," in her *Crossing the Double-Cross: The Practice of Feminist Criticism* (Chapel Hill, N.C.: University of North Carolina Press, 1986), 41–53.

6. Zora Neale Hurston, *Their Eyes Were Watching God* (Urbana: University of Illinois Press, 1978), 58–59; future page references to this novel appear in parentheses in the text.

7. Dianne Sadoff, "Black Matrilineage: The Case of Alice Walker and Zora Neale Hurston," *Signs: A Journal of Women in Culture and Society*, 11, No. 1 (1985), 4.

8. Sadoff, "Black Matrilineage," 18.

9. Sadoff, "Black Matrilineage," 22.

10. Sandra M. Gilbert and Susan Gubar, *The Madwoman In the Attic: The Woman Writer and the Nineteenth-Century Literary Imagination* (New Haven and London: Yale University Press, 1979); see especially 46–53.

11. Nancy Miller coined the phrase "heroines' texts" for such novels; see her *The Heroine's Text: Readings In the French and English Novel, 1722–1782* (New York: Columbia University Press, 1980). Rachel Blau DuPlessis summarizes Miller's argument in her *Writing Beyond the Ending: Narrative Strategies of Twentieth-Century Women Writers* (Bloomington: Indiana University Press, 1985), 15: " 'Story' for women has typically meant plots of seduction, courtship, the energies of quest deflected into sexual downfall, the choice of a marriage partner, the melodramas of beginning, middle, and end, the trajectories of sexual arousal and release." DuPlessis contends that twentieth-century narratives by women deliberately "rupture" traditional sequence or syntax in order to evade the closure imposed by such plots.

12. The critical responses already mentioned suggest one reason that a writer concerned with revising encoded ideologies might have for avoiding realism. Despite the existence of a great deal of narrative theory establishing that the realist novel is as conventional in its premises and methods as the sonnet, the epic, or such "genre" novels as the detective story or the gothic—see, for example, David Lodge, *The Modes of Modern Fiction: Metaphor, Metonymy, and the Typology of Modern Literature* (Ithaca: Cornell University Press, 1977), especially 22–41—realism is such a dominant form that its tacit claim to mirror reality is often difficult to question. More significantly, the assumption that the realist novel is "like life" tends to imply that the rules governing this sort of novel come from a repository of dicta called "reality" and carry moral as well as metaphysical weight. Thus to call a fictional outcome—say, a conclusion that redraws racial or gender boundaries—"unrealistic" is to suggest not only that things don't happen this way "in reality" (which may amount on examination to the observation that things have never happened this way before) but that the rules of "reality" do not *allow* such developments, and therefore that they *ought* not to occur. In this way the mode of fictional realism becomes an arena for prescriptions based on a reading of ethics presumptively enjoined by something like a natural order.

13. Richard Chase, in his classic study *The American Novel and Its Tradition* (Garden City, N.Y.: Doubleday/Anchor, 1957), distinguishes between "the romance, or romance-novel, and the novel proper," the former category including "that freer, daring, more brilliant fiction that contrasts with the solid moral inclusiveness and massive equability of the [nineteenth-century] English novel" (vii–viii).

14. Walker graduated from Sarah Lawrence College; Hurston, from Barnard College. Both read widely in several traditions. There is no reason to believe that either writer's desire to claim her black heritage precluded a canny reappropriation through re-vision of the white, patriarchal canon.

15. Introduction to William Shakespeare, *The Tempest* (New York: Random House, 1964), liv.

16. Kermode, *English Pastoral Poetry: From the Beginnings to Marvell* (London: George G. Harrap and Co., 1952), 19, 40.

17. All of Sofia's dialogue is of course comprehended in the written "dialect" of Celie's letters to God, a point that Gates makes in "Color Me Zora," as he observes, "In the speeches of her characters, Celie's voice and a character's merge into one, almost exactly as we saw happen in *Their Eyes* when Janie and her narrator speak in the merged voice of free indirect discourse. In these passages from *The Color Purple*, the

distinction between mimesis and digesis is apparently obliterated: the opposition between them has collapsed" (249).

18. Alice Walker, *The Color Purple* (New York: Washington Square Press, 1982), 100. All future page references to this novel will appear in the body of the essay.

19. In his *English Pastoral Poetry* (New York: Norton, 1938), William Empson observes "This indeed is one of the assumptions of pastoral, that you can say everything about complex people by a complete consideration of simple people" (137).

20. Introduction to Shakespeare, *The Tempest*, liv.

21. Northop Frye, *A Natural Perspective: The Development of Shakespearean Comedy and Romance* (New York: Columbia University Press, 1965), 123–124.

22. Introduction to Arden Shakespeare Edition of William Shakespeare, *The Winter's Tale* (London: Methuen, 1968), lxii.

23. Frye, in *A Natural Perspective*, notes that the comic drive is essentially directed toward identity. Insofar as this drive toward identity is an individual matter (rather than involving a whole society) it takes the form of "an awakening to self-knowledge, which is typically a release from a humor or a mechanical form of behavior" (118). It is interesting in this context to note that masculine brutality appears to be a "humor or mechanical form of behavior" in *The Color Purple*.

24. The most famous attack on religious excesses and misconceptions in the English pastoral occurs in Milton's "Lycidas." In *The Oaten Flute: Essays on Pastoral Poetry and the Pastoral Ideal* (Cambridge: Harvard University Press, 1975), Renato Poggioli suggests that even in its most orthodox Christian manifestations the pastoral ideal is based on "a double longing after innocence and happiness" and ultimately "stands at the opposite pole from the Christian one, even if it believes with the latter that the lowly will be exalted and that the only bad shepherds are the shepherds of men" (1). Kermode, in *English Pastoral Poetry*, points to the Renaissance pastoral as a site where neoplatonism could systematize "the relation between spiritual and physical love and beauty" and the *Song of Solomon* "provided all the necessary authority for expressing mystical love in erotic imagery" (35).

25. Poggioli, in *The Oaten Flute*, remarks that utopias constitute "after all . . . the idyll of the future," the pastoral Eden made the terminus of the narrative instead of the origin (28–29). Frye, in *A Natural Perspective*, similarly argues that in Shakespearean romance the return to Eden or a Golden Age is "a vision of something never seen or experienced, and hence, when it is presented as something we return to, it is a genuinely new vision" (132–133).

26. Frye, *A Natural Perspective*, 142–143.

27. Frye, *A Natural Perspective*, 145.

28. Frye identifies Paulina's chapel, where Hermione hides for an unimaginable sixteen years, as the corollary to Perdita's Bohemia. It is worth noting that if this is the case, the pastoral quality of this particular "green world" derives largely from the fact that all its inhabitants are female.

29. "Then she tell me this old white man is the same God she used to see when she prayed. If you wait to find God in church, Celie, she say, that's who is bound to show up, cause that's where he live . . . Cause that's the one that's in the white folks' bible" (177).

30. Scott McMillin reminds me that, paradoxically, Spielberg's additions are often powerful precisely inasmuch as they make patriarchal speech a *visual* phenomenon: Mister's plot-advancing words are not *heard*, but are presented in a series of dumb-show vignettes. Furthermore, Mister does not speak at the concluding celebration; his Jaques-like self-exclusion from the reunion (which requires him to occupy a separate frame, as he stands alone in the middle of a sunset-stained field) evokes instead the American icon of isolate and taciturn masculinity, withdrawing from the din of female society to light out for the territories or ride off into that sunset. Walker's own character, Albert, is unremarkable at the conclusion of the novel because he belongs— he is *absorbed* into the buzzing, blooming female community.

31. Miriam Amihai has pointed out to me that the fact that Hurston chose to introduce a female hero who is not only wearing the pants (and very proletarian pants at that) but looking sexy in them (to the Eatonville onlookers Janie looks as if she has two grapefruits in her hip pockets) doubtless inspired Walker to base Celie's

economic independence on the cottage industry that produces unisex, but provocatively sexual, trousers.

32. Fishing is also one of the activities asserting Janie's egalitarian relation to Tea Cake: Pheoby announces at the end of Janie's story, "Ah means tuh make Sam take me fishin' wid him after this" (284). And fishing itself is an exemplary pastoral activity (for "piscatory" as a subgenre of the pastoral see Poggioli, *The Oaten Flute*, 7).

33. A point underscored in the version developed by *The Color Purple*, where the consequence of heterosexual activity for women is almost invariably "getting big."

34. Eatonville is a real community, founded by (among others) Hurston's own father; see Alice Walker, "Zora Neale Hurston: A Cautionary Tale and a Partisan View" in *In Search of Our Mothers' Gardens: Womanist Prose* (New York: Harvest/HBJ, 1983), 85. But even the names of real towns are sometimes the product of just this sort of highly literary slippage—for example Pysht, in the state of Washington, which was christened out of a postal clerk's misreading: The town was to have been called Psyche, and to have been companion to a town that did receive its intended name, Sappho. Minority communities, like minority texts, appear particularly subject to mainstream misreadings.

35. Derrida, "The Parergon," *October*, 9 (Summer 1979), 35. See also Marian Hobson, "Derrida's Scroll-Work," *Oxford Literary Review*, 4, No. 3 (1981), 94–102.

36. Derrida, 26.

37. Philip Brian Harper aligns the parergonal positing of the margin as essential with the decentering of the postmodern subject, and suggests "the supposed postmodernist 'decentering of the subject' [is] merely a symptom of the recentering of subjectivities which have traditionally been relegated to the borders—of texts, of works of art in general, of societies—as mere parerga to the dominant subjectivity whose hegemony itself has so long skewed our view of the relation between center and margin." "The Recentered Subject: *Pale Fire* and the Question of Marginality," unpublished paper, Cornell University, 2–3.

38. DuPlessis, *Writing Beyond the Ending*, 142.

39. Sadoff, "Black Matrilineage," 25.

40. This is of course the (masculine) model of influence introduced by Harold Bloom in *The Anxiety of Influence* (New York: Oxford University Press, 1973).

41. Narrative tends to insinuate more causal links than we are allowed to infer from sequences in daily life; to construe "the king died and then the queen died" as "the queen died *because* the king had died" is both an informal fallacy and an orthodox reader response that makes a plot out of mere sequence. In narrative, *post hoc* is likely to be *propter hoc*, unless the causal interpretation is expressly ruled out.

42. Walker, *In Search of Our Mothers' Gardens*, 243.

43. Du Plessis, *Writing Beyond the Ending*, 93–94.

44. She has captioned a photograph in *The Alice Walker Calendar For 1986* (New York: Harvest/HBJ, 1985): "My mother, 'Miss Mary,' my stepmother Rachel ("Celie"), and my mother's mother Nettie"(unpaginated). And Gates cites a personal letter from Walker reporting "All names in *Purple* are *family* or Eatonton, Georgia, community names . . . The germ for Celie is Rachel, my stepmother: she of the poem 'Burial' in *Revolutionary Petunias*" in Gates, "Color Me Zora," 551–552, Note 13.

45. In Walker, *In Search of Our Mothers' Gardens*, 88. Gates compares the passages in "Color Me Zora," 254.

Writing the Subject:

Reading *The Color Purple*

Bell Hooks

The Color Purple broadens the scope of literary discourse, asserting its primacy in the realm of academic thought while simultaneously stirring the reflective consciousness of a mass audience. Unlike most novels by any writer it is read across race, class, gender, and cultural boundaries. It is truly a popular work—a book of the people—a work that has many different meanings for many different readers. Often the meanings are not interesting, contained as they are within a critical discourse that does not resist the urge to simplify, to overshadow, to make this work by a contemporary African-American writer mere sociological treatise on black life or radical feminist tract. To say even as some critics do that it is a modern day "slave narrative" or to simply place the work within the literary tradition of epistolary sentimental novels is also a way to contain, restrict, control. Categorizing in this way implies that the text neither demands nor challenges, rather, that it can be adequately and fully discussed within an accepted critical discourse, one that remains firmly within the boundaries of conservative academic aesthetic intentionality. While such discourse may illuminate aspects of the novel, it also obscures, suppresses, silences. Michel Foucault's comments on discourse in *The History of Sexuality* serve as a useful reminder that critical vision need not be fixed or static, that "discourse can be both an instrument and an effect of power, but also a hindrance, a stumbling block, a point of resistance and a starting point for an opposing strategy."

To critically approach *The Color Purple* from an oppositional perspective, it is useful to identify gaps—spaces between the text and conventional critical points of departure. That the novel's form is epistolary is most obvious, so apparent even that it is possible to overlook the fact that it begins not with a letter but an opening statement, a threatening command— speaker unidentified. "You better not never tell nobody but God. It'd kill your mammy." Straightaway Celie's letter writing to God is placed in a context of domination; she is obeying orders. Her very first letter reveals that the secret that can be told to no one but God has to do with sexuality, with sexual morality, with a male parent's sexual abuse of a female child. In form and content the declared subject carries traces of the sentimental novel with its focus on female characters and most importantly the female as potential victim of exploitative male sexual desire, but this serves only as a background for deviation, for subversion.

Significantly, *The Color Purple* is a narrative of "sexual confession." Statements like: "First he put his thing up gainst my hip and sort of wiggle it around. Then he grab hold my titties. Then he push his thing inside my pussy" refer solely to sexual encounters. Throughout *The Color Purple*, sexuality is graphically and explicitly discussed. Though a key narrative pattern in the novel, it is usually ignored. As readers approaching this novel in the context of a white supremacist patriarchal society wherein black women have been and continue to be stereotyped as sexually loose, a black woman writer imagining a black female character who writes about sexuality in letters to God, using graphic and explicit language, may not seem unusual or even interesting, particularly since graphic descriptions of sexual encounters conform to a current trend in women's writing. But this is most unlikely, as it is the culture's fascination with sexual autobiography that has led to a burgeoning of fiction and true-life stories focusing on sexual encounters. This trend is especially evident in popular women-centered novels. Attracting mass audiences in similar ways as their nineteenth-century predecessors, these new works captivate readers not by covert reference to sexual matters but by explicit exposure and revelation. They completely invert the values of the Victorian novel. While the nineteenth-century female protagonist as innocent had no language with which to speak sexual desire, the contemporary heroine in the woman-centered novel is not only the speaking sex, the desiring sex; she is talking sex.

Celie's life is presented in reference to her sexual history. Rosalind Coward's witty essay, "The True Story of How I Became My Own Person," in her collection *Female Desires*, warns against the reproduction of an ideology where female identity is constructed solely in relationship to sexuality, where sexual experience becomes the way in which a woman learns self-knowledge.

> There's a danger that such structures reproduce the Victorian ideology that sexuality is somehow outside social relationships. The idea that a woman could become her own person just through sexual experiences and the discovery of sexual needs and dislikes again establishes sexual relations as somehow separate from social structures.

Walker reproduces this ideology in *The Color Purple*. Patriarchy is exposed and denounced as a social structure supporting and condoning male domination of women, specifically represented as black male domination of black females, yet it does not influence and control sexual desire and sexual expression. While Mr.———, dominating male authority figure, can become enraged at the possibility that his wife will be present at a jukejoint, he has no difficulty accepting her sexual desire for another female. Homophobia does not exist in the novel. Celie's sexual desire for women and her sexual encounter with Shug is never a controversial issue even though it is the catalyst for her resistance to male domination, for her coming to power. Walker makes the powerful suggestion that sexual desire can disrupt and subvert oppressive social structure because it does not necessarily conform to social prescription, yet this realization is undermined by the refusal to acknowledge it as threatening—dangerous.

Sexual desire, initially evoked in the novel as a subversive transformative force, one that enables folk to break radically with convention (Mr.———'s passion for Shug transcends marriage vows; Celie's acceptance and fulfillment of her desire for a female leads her to reject heterosexuality; Shug's free-floating lust shared with many partners, each different from the other, challenges the notion of monogamous coupling) is suppressed and finally absent—a means to an end but not an end in itself. Celie may realize she desires women, express that longing in a passionate encounter with Shug, but just as the signifier lesbian does not exist to name and affirm her experience, no social reality exists so that she can express that desire in ongoing sexual practice. She is seduced and betrayed. Seduced by the promise of an erotic vocation wherein sexual fulfillment is deemed essential to self-recovery and self-realization, she must deny the primacy of this sexual awakening and the pain of sexual rejection.

Ironically, Shug's rejection serves as a catalyst enabling Celie and Albert to renew and transform their heterosexual bonding. Walker upholds the promise of an intact heterosexual bond with a relational scenario wherein the point of intimate connection between coupled male and female is not the acting out of mutual sexual desire for one another, but the displacement of that desire onto a shared object—in this case, Shug. Given such a revised framework for the establishment of heterosexual bonds, sex between Shug and Celie does not threaten male-female bonding or affirm the possibility that women can be fulfilled in a life that does not include intimate relationships with men. As Mariana Valverde emphasizes in *Sex, Power, and Pleasure:*

> Lesbianism is thus robbed of its radical potential because it is portrayed as compatible with heterosexuality, or rather as part of heterosexuality itself. The contradictions that our society creates between hetero- and homosexuality are wished away and social oppression is ignored.

Wedded by their mutual desire for Shug, their shared rejection, Celie and Albert are joined in a sustained committed relationship. Reunited, they stand together, "two old fools left over from love, keeping each other company under the stars."

Shug, whose very name suggests that she has the power to generate excitement without the ability to provide substantive nourishment, must also give up sexual pleasure. Betrayed by the sexual desire that has been the source of her power, Shug's lust for a young man is not depicted as an expression of sexual liberation, of longing for a new and different sexual pleasure, instead it is a disempowering force, one that exposes her vulnerability and weakness. Placed within a stereotypical heterosexist framework wherein woman is denied access to ongoing sexual pleasure which she seeks and initiates, as the novel progresses Shug is depicted as an aging female seducer who fears the loss of her ability to use sex as a means to attract and control men, as a way to power. Until this turning point, sex has been for Shug a necessary and vital source of pleasure. As object of intense sexual desire, she has had power to shape and influence the actions of others but always in the direction of a higher good.

Ultimately, Walker constructs an ideal world of true love and commitment where there is no erotic tension—where there is no sexual desire or sexual pleasure. Just as the reader's perception of Shug is dramatically altered towards the end of the novel, so is the way we see and understand Celie's sexual history; her sexual confession changes when it is revealed that she has not been raped by her real father. The tragedy and trauma of incest, so graphically and poignantly portrayed, both in terms of the incest-rape and Celie's sexual healing which begins when she tells Shug what happened, is trivialized as the novel progresses. Presented in retrospect as though it was all an absurd drama, the horror of Celie's early sexual experience and the pleasure of her sexual awakening assume the quality of spectacle, of exaggerated show. A curious tale told in part as a strategy to engage and excite the reader's imagination before attention is diverted towards more important revelations. Given the fascination in this culture with sex and violence, with race and sex, with sexual deviance, a fascination which is recognized and represented most often in pornography, Walker's subject has immediate appeal. Readers are placed in the position of voyeurs who witness Celie's torment as victim of incest-rape, as victim of sexual violence in a sadistic master-slave relationship; who watch her sexual exploration of her body and experience vicarious pleasure at her sexual awakening as she experiences her first sexual encounter with Shug. Ironically, pornographic fiction consumed by a mass audience is a genre which has always included narratives describing women engaged in sexual acts with one another, observed by powerful others—usually men. Walker subverts this pattern. As readers we represent the powerful other. Her intent is not to titillate sexually, but to arouse disgust, outrage, and anger at male sexual exploitation of females and to encourage appreciation and acceptance of same-sex female sexual pleasure.

To achieve this end, which is fundamentally anti-male domination, Walker relies on similar narrative strategies and preoccupations as those utilized in the pornographic narrative. Annette Kuhn's essay on representation and sexuality which focuses on pornography's "Lawless seeing" points to the connection between pornographic fiction and other simple narratives:

> In pornographic stories, literary as well as visual, characters are never very strongly developed or psychologically rounded human beings. They perform function, they take on roles already fixed within the commonplace fantasies that porn constructs—the sexually active woman, the Peeping Tom, the plumber out on his rounds. In porn, characters are what they do, and given a minimal amount of familiarity with the genre, the reader needs little by way of explanation in order to understand what is going on. Pornography has a good deal in common with other simple forms of narrative, stories in which characters are no more than what they do and the reader has some general idea, as soon as the story begins, of who is going to do what to whom and with what outcome . . . In many respects, pornographic stories work like fairy tales.

Characters are very much what they do in *The Color Purple*. Mr.——— is brute, Lucious the rapist, Harpo the buffoon, Celie the sexual victim, Shug the sexual temptress. Many of the characters perform roles that correspond with racial stereotypes. The image of "the black male rapist" resonates in both racial and sexual stereotypes; Walker's characterization cannot be viewed in a vacuum, as though it does not participate in these discourses which have been primarily used to reinforce domination, both racial and sexual.

Pornography participates in and promotes a discourse that exploits and aesthetizes domination. Kuhn asserts that pornography insists on sexual difference, that sexual violence in master-slave scenarios reduces this difference to relations of power. Feminists who focus almost exclusively on male violence against women as the central signifier of male domination also view sexual difference as solely a relation of power. Within pornography, Kuhn states, there is

> an obsession with the otherness of femininity, which in common with many forms of otherness seems to contain a threat to the onlooker. Curiosity turns to terror, investigation to torture, the final affirmation of the objecthood of the other. The feminine here represents a threat to the masculine, a threat which demands containment. Sexually violent pornography of this kind concretises this wish for containment in representations which address the spectator as masculine and place the masculine on the side of container of the threat. It insists that sexuality and power are inseparable.

Walker inverts this paradigm. Presuming a female spectator (women and specifically white women from privileged classes as the primary audience for women-centered novels), she constructs a fiction in which it is the masculine threat, represented by black masculinity, that must be contained, controlled, and ultimately transformed. Her most radical re-visioning of the oppressive patriarchal social order is her insistence on the transformation of Mr.————. He moves from male oppressor to enlightened being, willingly surrendering his attachment to the phallocentric social order reinforced by the sexual oppression of women. His transformation begins when Celie threatens his existence, when her curse disempowers him. Since sexuality and power are so closely linked to politics of domination, Mr.———— must be completely desexualized as part of the transformative process.

Unable to reconcile sexuality and power, Walker replaces the longing for sexual pleasure with an erotic metaphysic animated by a vision of the unity of all things, by the convergence of erotic and mystical experience. This is ritually enacted as Shug initiates Celie into a spiritual awakening wherein belief in God as white male authority figure, who gives orders and punishes, is supplanted by the vision of a loving God who wants believer to celebrate life, to experience pleasure, a God who is annoyed, "if you walk by the color purple in a field somewhere but don't notice it." In *The Color Purple* Christianity and patriarchy are oppressive social structures which promote anhedonia. Celie and Albert, as oppressed and oppressor, must as part of their personal transformation learn to feel pleasure and develop a capacity to experience happiness. Concurrently, Nettie and Samuel, laboring as missionaries in Africa, develop a critical consciousness that allows them to see the connections between Western cultural imperialism and Christianity; and this enables them to see God in a new way. Nettie writes to Celie, "God is different to us now, after all these years in Africa. More spirit than ever before, and more internal." Though critical of religious beliefs which reinforce sexist and racist domination, Shug insists on the primacy of a spiritual life, constructing a vision of spirituality which echoes the teachings of religious mystics who speak of healing alienation through recognition of the unity in all life.

Spiritual quest is connected with the effort of characters in *The Color Purple* to be more fully self-realized. This effort merges in an unproblematic way with a materialist ethic which links acquisition of goods with the capacity to experience emotional well-being. Traditionally mystical experience is informed by radical critique and renunciation of materialism. Walker positively links the two. Even though her pronounced critique of patriarchy includes an implicit indictment of perverse individualism which encourages exploitation (Albert is transformed in part by his rejection of isolation and self-sufficiency for connection and interdependency), Celie's shift from underclass victim to capitalist entrepreneur has only positive signification. Albert, in his role as oppressor, forces Celie and Harpo to work in the fields, exploiting their labor for his gain. Their exploitation as workers must cease before domination ends and transformation begins. Yet Celie's progression from exploited black woman, as woman, as sexual victim, is aided by her entrance into the economy as property owner, manager of a small business, storekeeper—in short, capitalist entrepreneur. No attention is accorded aspects of this enterprise that might reinforce domination: attention is focused on how useful Celie's pants are for family and friends; on the way Sofia as worker in her store will treat black customers with respect and consideration. Embedded in the construction of sexual difference as it is characterized in *The Color*

Purple is the implicit assumption that women are innately less inclined to oppress and dominate than men; that women are not easily corrupted.

Rewarded with economic prosperity for her patient endurance of suffering, Celie never fully develops capacities for sustained self-assertion. Placed on a moral pedestal which allows no one to see her as a threat, she is always a potential victim. By contrast, Sofia's self-affirmation, her refusal to see herself as victim, is not rewarded. She is consistently punished. Sadly, as readers witness Celie's triumph, her successful effort to resist male domination which takes place solely in a private familial context, we also bear witness to Sofia's tragic fate, as she resists sexist and racist oppression in private and public spheres. Unlike Celie or Shug, she is regarded as a serious threat to the social order and is violently attacked, brutalized, and subdued. Always a revolutionary, Sofia has never been victimized or complicit in her own oppression. Tortured and persecuted by the State, treated as though she is a political prisoner, Sofia's spirit is systematically crushed. Unlike Celie, she cannot easily escape and there is no love strong enough to engender her self-recovery. Her suffering cannot be easily mitigated, as it would require radical transformation of society. Given all the spectacular changes in *The Color Purple*, it is not without grave and serious import that the character who most radically challenges sexism and racism is a tragic figure who is only partially rescued—restored to only a semblance of sanity. Like the lobotomized Native American Indian in *One Flew Over the Cuckoo's Nest*, Sofia's courageous spirit evokes affirmation, even as her fate strikes fear and trepidation in the hearts and minds of those who would actively resist oppression.

Described as a large woman with a powerful presence, Sofia's vacant position in the kinship network is assumed by Squeak, a thin petite woman, who gains presence only when she acts to free Sofia, passively enduring rape to fulfill her mission. This rape of a black woman by a white man does not have grievous traumatic negative consequences, even though it acts to reinforce sexist domination of females and racist exploitation. Instead, it is a catalyst for positive change—Sofia's release, Squeak asserting her identity as Mary Agnes. Such a benevolent portrayal of the consequences of rape contrasts sharply with the images of black male rapists, images which highlight the violence and brutality of their acts. That the text graphically emphasizes the horror and pain of black male sexist exploitation of black females while de-emphasizing the horror and pain of racist exploitation of black women by white men that involves sexual violence is an unresolved contradiction if Walker's intent is to expose the evils of sexist domination. These contrasting depictions of rape dangerously risk reinforcing racist stereotypes that perpetuate the notion that black men are more capable of brutal sexist domination than other groups of men.

Throughout *The Color Purple* exposures of the evils of patriarchal domination are undercut by the suggestion that this form of domination is not necessarily linked to race and class exploitation. Celie and Albert are able to eradicate sexism in their relationship. The threat of masculine domination ceases when Albert forgoes phallic privilege and serves as a helpmate to Celie, assuming a "feminine" presence. However, the phallocentric social order which exists outside the domain of private relationships remains intact. As symbolic representation of masculine otherness, the phallus continues to assert a powerful presence via the making of pants that both women and men will wear. This is not a radical re-visioning of gender. It is a vision of inclusion that enables women to access power via symbolic phallic representation. As French feminist Antoinette Fougue reminds us:

> Inversion does not facilitate the passage to another kind of structure. The difference between the sexes is not whether or not one does or doesn't have a penis, it is whether or not one is an integral part of a phallic masculine economy.

Within *The Color Purple* the economy Celie enters as entrepreneur and landowner is almost completely divorced from structures of domination. Immersed in the ethics of a narcissistic new-age spiritualism wherein economic prosperity indicates that one is chosen—blessed, Celie never reflects critically on the changes in her status. She writes to Nettie, "I am so happy. I got love. I got work. I got money, friends and time."

Indeed the magic of *The Color Purple* is that it is so much a book of our times, imaginatively evoking the promise of a world in which one can have it all; a world in which sexual exploitation can be easily overcome; a world of unlimited access to material well-being; a world where the evils of racism are tempered by the positive gestures of concerned and caring white folks; a world where sexual boundaries can be transgressed at will without negative consequences; a world where spiritual salvation is the lot of the elect. This illusory magic is sustained by Walker's literary technique, the skillful combining of social realism and fantasy, the fairy tale and the fictionalized autobiographical narrative.

As the fictive autobiography of an oppressed black woman's journey from sexual slavery to freedom, *The Color Purple* parodies those primary texts of autobiographical writing which have shaped and influenced the direction of African-American fiction—the "slave narrative." With the publication of slave autobiographies, oppressed African-American slaves moved from object to subject, from silence into speech, creating a revolutionary literature—one that changed the nature and direction of African-American history; that laid the groundwork for the development of a distinct African-American literary tradition. Slave autobiographies worked to convey as accurately as possible the true story of slavery as experienced and interpreted by slaves, without apology or exaggeration. The emphasis on truth had a twofold purpose, the presentation of reliable sources, and, most importantly, the creation of a radical discourse on slavery that served as a corrective and a challenge to the dominant culture's hegemonic perspective. Although Walker conceived of *The Color Purple* as a historical novel, her emphasis is less on historical accuracy and more on an insistence that history has more to do with the interpersonal details of everyday life at a given historical moment than with significant dates, events, or important persons. Relying on historical referents only insofar as they lend an aura of credibility to that which is improbable and even fantastic, Walker mocks the notion of historical truth, suggesting that it is subordinate to myth, that the mythic has far more impact on consciousness. This is most evident in the letters from Africa. Historical documents, letters, journals, articles, provide autobiographical testimony of the experience and attitudes of nineteenth-century black missionaries in Africa, yet

Walker is not as concerned with a correspondence between the basic historical fact that black missionaries did travel to Africa than providing the reader with a fictive account of those travels that is plausible. Walker uses the basic historical fact as a frame to enhance the social realism of her text while superimposing a decidedly contemporary perspective. Historical accuracy is altered to serve didactic purposes—to teach the reader history not as it was but as it should have been.

A revolutionary literature has as its central goal the education for critical consciousness, creating awareness of the forces that oppress and recognition of the way those forces might be transformed. One important aspect of the slave narrative as revolutionary text was the insistence that the plight of the individual narrator be linked to the oppressed plight of all black people so as to arouse support for organized political effort for social changes. Walker appropriates this form to legitimize and render authentic Celie's quest without reflecting this radical agenda. Celie's plight is not representative; it is not linked to collective effort to effect radical social change. While she is a victim of male domination, Shug is not. While she has allowed patriarchal ideology to inform her sense of self, Sofia has not. By de-emphasizing the collective plight of black people, or even black women, and focusing on the individual's quest for freedom as separate and distinct, Walker makes a crucial break with that revolutionary African-American literary tradition which informs her earlier work, placing this novel outside that framework. Parodying the slave narrative's focus on racial oppression, Walker's emphasis on sexual oppression acts to delegitimize the historical specificity and power of this form. Appropriating the slave narrative in this way, she invalidates both the historical context and the racial agenda. Furthermore, by linking this form to the sentimental novel as though they served similar functions, Walker strips the slave narrative of its revolutionary ideological intent and content, connecting it to Eurocentral bourgeois literary traditions in such a way as to suggest it was merely derivative and in no way distinct.

Slave narratives are a powerful record of the particular unique struggle of African-American people to write history—to make literature—to be a self-defining people. Unlike Celie, the slave who recorded her or his story was not following the oppressors' orders, was not working within a context of domination. Fundamentally, this writing was a challenge, a resistance affirming that the movement of the oppressed from silence into speech is a liberatory gesture. Literacy is upheld in the slave narrative as essential to the practice of freedom. Celie writes not as a gesture of affirmation or liberation but as a gesture of shame. Nettie recalls, "I remember one time you said your life made you feel so ashamed you couldn't even talk about it to God. You had to write it." Writing then is not a process which enables Celie to make herself subject, it allows distance, objectification. She does not understand writing as an act of power, or self-legitimation. She is empowered not by the written word but by the spoken word—by telling her story to Shug. Later, after she has made the shift from object to subject she ceases to write to God and addresses Nettie, which is an act of self-affirmation.

Taken at face value, Celie's letter writing appears to be a simple matter-of-fact gesture when it is really one of the most fantastical happenings in *The Color Purple*. Oppressed, exploited as laborer in the field, as worker in the domestic household, as sexual servant, Celie finds time to write—this is truly incredible. There is no description of Celie with pen in hand, no discussion of where and when she writes. She must remain invisible so as not to expose this essential contradiction—that as dehumanized object she projects a self in the act of writing even as she records her inability to be self-defining. Celie as writer is a fiction. Walker, as writing subject, oversees her creation, constructing a narrative that purports to be a space where the voice of an oppressed black female can be heard even though the valorization of writing and the use of the epistolary form suppress and silence that voice.

Writing in a manner that reads as though she is speaking, talking in the voice of a black folk idiom, Celie, as poor and exploited black female, appears to enter a discourse from which she has been excluded—the act of writing, the production of story as commodity. In actuality, her voice remains that of appropriated other—interpreted—translated—represented as authentic unspoiled innocent. Walker provides Celie a writing self, one that serves as a perfect foil for her creator. Continually asserting her authorial presence in *The Color Purple*, she speaks through characters sharing her thoughts and values. Masquerading as just plain folks, Celie, Nettie, Shug, and Albert are the mediums for the presentation of her didactic voice. Through fictive recognition and acknowledgement, Walker pays tribute to the impact of black folk experience as a force that channels and shapes her imaginative work, yet her insistent authorial presence detracts from this representation.

Traces of traditional African-American folk expression as manifest in language and modes of storytelling are evident in Celie's letters, though they cannot be fully voiced and expressed in the epistolary form. There they are contained and subsumed. Commenting on the use of the epistolary form in *Seduction and Betrayal: Women and Literature*, Elizabeth Hardwick suggests,

> A letter is not a dialogue or even an omniscient exposition. It is a fabric of surfaces, a mask, a form as well suited to affectations as to the affection. The letter is, by its natural shape, self-justifying; it is one's own evidence, deposition, a self-serving testimony. In a letter the writer holds all the cards, controls everything.

That Celie and Nettie's letters are basically self-serving is evident when it is revealed that there has never been a true correspondence. And if readers are to assume that Celie is barely able to read and write as her letters suggest, she would not have been able to comprehend Nettie's words. Not only is the inner life of the characters modified by the use of the epistolary form, but the absence of correspondence restricts information, and enables the letters to serve both the interest of the writers, and the interests of an embedded didactic narrative. Functioning as a screen, the letters keep the reader at a distance, creating the illusion of intimacy where there is none. The reader is always voyeur, outsider looking in, passively awaiting the latest news.

Celie and Nettie's letters testify, we as readers bear witness. They are an explanation of being, which asserts that understanding the self is the precondition for transformation, for radical change. Narrating aspects of their personal history, they engage in an ongoing process of demythologizing that makes new awareness and change possible. They recollect to recover and restore. They seek to affirm and sustain the initial bond of care and connection experienced with one another in their oppressive male-dominated family. Since the mother is bonded with the father, supporting and protecting his interests, mothers and daughters within this fictive patriarchy suffer a wound of separation and abandonment; they have no context for unity. Mothers prove their allegiance to fathers by betraying daughters; it is only a vision of sisterhood that makes woman bonding possible. By eschewing the identity of Mother, black women in *The Color Purple*, like Shug and Sofia, rebelliously place themselves outside the context of patriarchal family norms, revisioning mothering so that it becomes a task any willing female can perform, irrespective of whether or not she has given birth. Displacing motherhood as central signifier for female being, and emphasizing sisterhood, Walker posits a relational basis for self-definition that valorizes and affirms woman bonding. It is the recognition of self in the other, of unity, and not self in relationship to the production of children that enables women to connect with one another.

The values expressed in woman bonding—mutuality, respect, shared power, and unconditional love—become guiding principles shaping the new community in *The Color Purple*, which includes everyone, women and men, family and kin. Reconstructed black males, Harpo and Albert are active participants expanding the circle of care. Together this extended kin network affirms the primacy of a revitalized spirituality in which everything that exists is informed by godliness, in which love as a force that affirms connection and intersubjective communion makes an erotic metaphysic possible. Forgiveness and compassion enable individuals who were estranged and alienated to nurture one another's growth. The message conveyed in the novel that relationships no matter how seriously impaired can be restored is compelling. Distinct from the promise of a happy ending, it allows for the recognition of conflict and pain, for the possibility of reconciliation.

Radical didactic messages add depth and complexity to *The Color Purple* without resolving the contradictions between radicalism—the vision of revolutionary transformation, and conservatism—the perpetuation of bourgeois ideology. When the novel concludes, Celie has everything her oppressor has wanted and more—relationships with chosen loved ones; land ownership; material wealth; control over the labor of others.

She is happy. In a *Newsweek* interview, Walker makes the revealing statement, "I liberated Celie from her own history. I wanted her to be happy." Happiness is not subject to revision, radicalization. The terms are familiar, absence of conflict, pain, and struggle; a fantasy of every desire fulfilled. Given these terms, Walker creates a fiction wherein an oppressed black woman can experience self-recovery without a dialectical process; without collective political effort; without radical change in society. To make Celie happy she creates a fiction where struggle—the arduous and painful process by which the oppressed work for liberation—has no place. This fantasy of change without effort is a dangerous one for both oppressed and oppressor. It is a brand of false consciousness that keeps everyone in place and oppressive structures intact. It is just this distortion of reality that Walker warns against in her essay "If the Present Looks Like the Past":

> In any case, the duty of the writer is not to be tricked, seduced, or goaded into verifying by imitation or even rebuttal, other people's fantasies. In an oppressive society it may well be that *all* fantasies indulged in by the oppressor are destructive to the oppressed. To become involved in them in any way at all is, at the very least, to lose time defining yourself.

For oppressed and oppressor the process of liberation—individual self-realization and revolutionary transformation of society—requires confrontation with reality, the letting go of fantasy. Speaking of his loathing for fantasy Gabriel García Márquez explains:

> I believe the imagination is just an instrument for producing reality and that the source of creation is always, in the last instance, reality. Fantasy, in the sense of pure and simple Walt Disney-style invention without any basis in reality, is the most loathsome thing of all . . . Children don't like fantasy either. What they do like is imagination. The difference between the one and the other is the same as between a human being and a ventriloquist's dummy.

The Future of Female:

Octavia Butler's Mother Lode

Dorothy Allison

I love Octavia Butler's women even when they make me want to scream with frustration. The problem is not their feminism; her characters are always independent, stubborn, difficult, and insistent on trying to control their own lives. What drives me crazy is their attitude: the decisions they make, the things they do in order to protect and nurture their children—and the assumption that children and family always come first.

Butler's nine books are exceptional not only because she is that rarity, a black woman writing science fiction, but because she advocates motherhood as the humanizing element in society (not a notion I have ever taken too seriously). But even though the lives she creates for her women characters make me impatient, I cannot stop reading her. I buy her new books, look for her short stories, and hunt down her old paperbacks for friends. While acknowledging the imbalances and injustices inherent in traditional family systems, Butler goes on writing books with female characters who heroically adjust to family life and through example, largeness of spirit, and resistance to domination make the lives of those children better—even though this means sacrificing personal freedom. But she humanizes her dark vision of women's possibilities by making sure that the contradictions and grief her women experience are as powerfully rendered as their decision to sacrifice autonomy. Within the genre of science fiction, Butler is a realist, writing the most detailed social criticism and creating some of the most fascinating female characters in the genre. For me, it's like reading about my mother, my aunts, my sisters. Even when I'm gnashing my teeth, I go on believing in them.

Butler creates dystopias, landscapes in which the hard edge of cruelty, violence, and domination is described in stark detail. Her work addresses the issues of survival and adaptation, in which resistance, defeat, and compromise are the vital elements. Like Samuel Delaney's *The Bridge of Lost Desire* and *Stars in My Pocket Like Grains of Sand,* Butler's most recent work, the Xenogenesis series (*Dawn*, *Adulthood Rites*, and *Imago*), radically reexamines human sexual relations and what it means to be other.

Homosexuality, incest, and multiple sexual pairings turn up in almost all her books, usually insisted on by the patriarchal or alien characters and resisted by the heroines, who eventually give in. Her women are always in some form of bondage, captives of domineering male mutants or religious fanatics or aliens who want to impregnate them. Though the men in Butler's novels are often equally oppressed, none is forced so painfully to confront the difference between surrender and adjustment. Women who surrender die; those who resist, struggle, adjust, compromise, and live by their own ethical standards survive to mother the next generation—literally to make the next world. Maybe if this world were not so hard a place, Butler might be writing less painful fiction.

The circumstances of Butler's life have shaped her fiction. Her father died when she was two and her mother supported the family by working as a maid. Butler grew up on the stories of her maternal grandmother, a woman who raised seven children alone in Louisiana and died a property owner in Pasadena, California, where Octavia was born in 1947. Echoes of Butler's grandmother turn up in all her books, from *Patternmaster* (1976) to *Imago* (1989). *Patternmaster*, like most first novels, lays out her concerns. The men in this book, as in all that follow, begin with sexist assumptions about women. Amber, a small, sturdy, practical black woman, is a prototypical Butler heroine. Her response to Teray, the domineering hero, when he offers her power and prestige as his "lead wife," is to ask him, "How interested would you be in becoming my lead husband?" Butler makes it clear that Teray cannot rule his world until he accepts Amber's independence; she pledges to bear his children but only so long as she has her own household, her own life, and her female lovers.

None of Butler's heroines ever again manages that much autonomy, though the nearly egalitarian relationship that Teray and Amber finally arrange is the ideal each of her women aims for. Though Butler designates the mother as the civilizing force in human society—the one who teaches both men and children compassion and empathy—she also shows it is not a role that women easily or willingly take on. She also carefully shows how mothering can mimic paternalistic domination. When Mary, the telepathic black heroine of *Mind of My Mind*, defeats her father, Doro, she becomes a tyrant herself, though a more benevolent one.

Butler's Patternist novels, a series that includes *Patternmaster*, *Wild Seed*, *Mind of My Mind*, *Survivor*, and *Clay's Ark*, cover a period from the 1600s through a far future in which disease has decimated Earth's population. The series reworks one of science fiction's traditional motifs: mutants who are hated and endangered until they gain control of their talents. Butler's mutants are self-destructive, immature characters deliberately bred for their psychic skills by Doro, a 4,000-year-old psychic vampire and patriarch, who never frees them to grow up and live independently. In the early books (*Wild Seed*, *Patternmaster*, *Mind of My Mind*), ordinary people, known as nontelepaths or "latents," are cast as the racial inferiors to the psychically gifted humans. The latents are also known as "mutes"; when Doro explains that the term means "ordinary people," his wife Emma tells him, "I know what it means, Doro. I knew the first time I heard Mary use it. It means nigger!" Butler's use of the term nigger is as deliberate as her matter-of-fact handling of racism in the everyday lives of her characters. By portraying the "ordinary" ones as lesser people who are treated with contempt, bred like animals (or slaves) for desirable genetic material, and murdered as if they were not fully human, Butler is commenting on the underlying structure of racism.

But those on top are also on the bottom. The telepaths cannot function in normal human society; they are prone to violence, madness, and unreasoning hatred. Many are also black. In the early novels they are enslaved, victimized, assaulted, and killed. In the later, they enslave, victimize, assault, and kill normal humans. The nigger, Butler suggests, is the one who's made slave/child/victim. It is the concept of nigger, the need for a victim, and the desire to profit by the abuse or misuse of others that corrupts and destroys.

Butler's best known and most successful novel, *Kindred*, first published in 1979 and reprinted by Beacon Press in 1988, is a recreation of plantation life rather than a symbolic examination of slavery. In the introduction to the Beacon edition, Butler called *Kindred* a "grim fantasy"—an accurate description. *Kindred*'s heroine, Dana, is an articulate young black writer who works for a temporary agency, which she calls "a slave market," a reference that takes on new meaning when she finds herself on an antebellum plantation where the everyday horrors of slavery are no metaphor. Like all Butler's works, *Kindred* concentrates on the psychological, here the emotional impact of slavery on Dana as she is continually transported back in time to save the life of Rufus, her abusive, slave-owning, white great-grandfather. The novel doesn't explain the mechanism of her time travels, suggesting only that she is pulled back whenever Rufus's life is threatened and can return to 1976 L.A. only when her own life is threatened.

Kindred reads like a historical slave narrative, a horror tale of the real. Violence is not passed over quickly. When Dana witnesses a slave being beaten by nightriders it's not from a safe distance.

> I could literally smell his sweat, hear every ragged breath, every cry, every cut of the whip. I could see his body jerking, convulsing, straining against the rope as his screaming went on and on. My stomach heaved, and I had to force myself to stay where I was and keep quiet. . .
>
> I shut my eyes and tensed my muscles against an urge to vomit.
>
> I had seen people beaten on television and in the movies. I had seen the too-red blood substitute streaked across their backs and heard their well-rehearsed screams. But I hadn't lain nearby and smelled their sweat or heard them pleading and praying, shamed before their families and themselves.

Dana's attitudes, language, and beliefs about herself are those of a black woman in 1976. She objects indignantly to

being called "nigger" by Rufus, is contemptuous of the ignorant white masters, and thinks at first that she will just write
herself a pass and flee north. But nothing she thinks she
knows about slavery prepares her for suddenly being property in 1800s Maryland. Rufus's father thinks her an "uppity
nigger" and whips her for teaching a slave boy to read. At the
same time, the plantation slaves accuse her of being "more
like white folks than some white folks." Alice, Dana's great-
great-grandmother, tells her, "They be calling you mammy in
a few years." In this world, compromise is a close cousin to
betrayal, but refusing to compromise means risking not only
your own life but the lives of family and friends. Each slave is
hostage to the others, Dana realizes, and the choices are all
deadly. When Rufus tells Dana she must help him persuade
the slave Alice to accept him as a lover, she is horrified but
unable to refuse. She can't "refuse to help the girl—help her
avoid at least some pain." Alice "wouldn't think much of me
for helping her this way," Dana tells herself. "I didn't think
much of myself." This is not a simple or easy decision, but it is
the one Butler's heroines invariably make. From Anyanwu of
Wild Seed to Lilith in *Dawn*, Butler's women submit and bear
children rather than die or murder the rapists/masters/aliens.

Kindred is the only one of Butler's books in which the woman
refuses to submit, and even here Butler emphasizes the internal struggle resistance prompts. Early in the book, Dana realizes she is "the worst possible guardian for [Rufus]—a black
to watch over him in a society that considered blacks subhu-
man, a woman to watch over him in a society that considered
women perennial children." But still she hopes to "plant a
few ideas in his mind that would help both me and the people
who would be his slaves in the years to come." She gives up
this illusion only with grief and difficulty. When Rufus tries to
rape Dana, she hesitates, unable for a moment to use the
knife she has hidden in her hand. While he sees her only as a
female animal and his by right, she feels a link to him as kin.
But when she looks at herself from Rufus's perspective, she
realizes that if she submits to him she will become the slave
he believes her to be. "And Rufus was Rufus—erratic, alternately generous and vicious. I could accept him as my ancestor, my younger brother, my friend, but not as my master,

and not as my lover." In horror, Dana kills him—the boy she has saved so many times.

Other than the death of Rufus, Butler offers no resolutions at the end of *Kindred*. Dana is left wounded and unsure even of her own sanity. Just as we never learn the mechanism of her time travel, we do not know what will become of her marriage to Kevin, a white man. More important, neither we nor Dana know what has become of Hagar, Dana's great-grandmother and the girl child of Alice, the slave woman Dana persuaded to submit to Rufus. Dana, Alice, and Hagar remind us of all the women in Butler's work, the victims and survivors she envisions not as dispassionate historical constructs, overlaid with political slogans and psychological reinterpretations, but as real women caught in impossible situations.

In her most recent books, the Xenogenesis trilogy, Butler portrays a world in which the worst has happened. Nuclear winter and disease have killed off most of the people who were not killed in the initial nuclear conflict, and only the intervention of the alien Oankali has kept anyone alive at all. The Oankali blame the catastrophe on humanity's obsession with conflict and hierarchy. Butler clearly believes that these human characteristics must be overcome if society is to survive, but *Dawn* offers little reason to believe this is possible.

Lilith, another of Butler's black female mother figures, has been kept in suspended animation for 250 years. Like Dana in *Kindred* and Anyanwu in *Wild Seed*, Lilith compromises in order to save lives and ease pain. The Oankali teach her first to tolerate and then to join an Oankali family, and then to "mother" a group of human survivors until they too have adjusted. In *Imago* and *Adulthood Rites* Lilith's Oankali/human children triumph and survive, reclaiming Earth and forcing the Oankali to free the remaining humans.

Unfortunately, these last two books do not provide the vivid sense of alien encounter that is so strong in *Dawn*. The savage humans abandon their resistance to the aliens too easily; their hatred seems more stubbornness than xenophobia. It is a hopeful vision, but not very convincing—as if Butler has tried to demonstrate where her philosophy of mother-nurturance leads. But her reasonable humans are nowhere near as captivating as the rebellious mothers and complex villains of her earlier books, and Butler seems to lose interest in their story even before we do.

What continues to hold her interest and ours are many-layered and extensive explorations of male/female relationships, resistance to traditional moral teachings, women's responsibility to bear and raise children, and the fine line between compromise and betrayal. The alien Oankali have some slavemaster attitudes toward humans, but they also introduce new and positive variations on traditional sexual relationships.

Since the sexual abuse of women and women's desire for autonomy are central themes in all of Butler's books, the Oankali's benign attitude toward sex and sexual variation is vitally important in understanding what Butler sees as the answer to sexual violence—not abstinence or enforced celibacy, but a redefinition of sex and a rapprochement between the genders. Without the human need to impose a hierarchical male dominant/female submissive structure on sexuality, the Oankali approach the act with a genuine sense of joy equally shared. Nothing is sinful, nothing is forced. Everything is permitted except violence. After all, traditional male and female role expectations cannot be rigidly imposed on a people whose gender is mutable and unspecified until the onset of adolescence. And incest, a continuing obsession for Butler, is not a meaningful concept among the Oankali, whose third sex, the ooloi, literally construct genetic material, sorting for healthy and useful attributes. Sex among the Oankali is seen as both an act of blissful biological exchange (sperm for egg) and a euphoric ritual that lovingly bonds participants—the family bond that Butler invariably emphasizes. The Oankali represent Butler's solution to the sexual horrors she details in every novel—a people who honor the act of procreation so greatly they are incapable of rape, and who enjoy sex so much they treat all sexual acts with matter-of-fact honesty, an approach that appalls the kidnapped humans.

Much of *Dawn* concentrates on the cultural shock the humans experience when they marry Oankali. The men feel as if they have lost authority (they have); the women feel as if they are being bred like animals (they are); and all feel some horror of what might be hidden homosexual desires—after all, there is no way to be sure an ooloi is a man or a woman. Humans feel a deep psychochemical attraction to ooloi, almost a compulsion. It is as if the slavemasters had gotten under their skins, and humans no longer control their own desires. The Oankali sound authentically alien, sexy, and terrifying. They are also completely family-centered. All of them are mothers, nurturers, healers—traditional Butler heroines in new forms. But they are also tyrants, with the same tendency to infantilize, to make choices for the child's "own good."

At the end of the trilogy, Lilith's son thinks about how humans and aliens treat each other, how they struggle and resist chaos by clinging together. "The whole business was like Lilith's rounded black cloud of hair," he thinks. "Every strand seemed to go its own different way, bending, twisting, spiraling, angling. Yet together they formed a symmetrical, recognizable shape, and all were attached to the same head." This is the dream of an ideal family, the mother making possible her children's lives and freeing them to choose their own destinies—the essential vision of Octavia Butler.

INTERVIEWS

An Interview with Rita Dove

Helen Vendler *

We're talking today, Rita Dove and I—I'm Helen Vendler—
about her poetry and her prose and her work this year at the
National Humanities Center. I'd like to say first that Rita Dove
is the author of three extraordinary books of poetry: *The Yellow
House on the Corner* (1980), *Museum* (1983), and *Thomas and
Beulah* (1986). She has also written a book of stories called *Fifth
Sunday* that came out in 1985. I knew nothing about Rita Dove
when I first saw a group of her poems in the *Ohio Review* some
years ago, and I'd like to begin by asking her now the questions I would have liked to ask then: Who are you? Where did
you come from? What did you read? Where were you educated? How old are you?—all those questions that readers
want to ask when they see extraordinary works on the page.
Maybe you could tell us something about yourself.

Dove: Well, let's see, which one to begin with. I was born in
1952 in Akron, Ohio, the oldest daughter of a family of four
children, an older brother, two younger sisters. My mother is
a housekeeper, my father was the first black chemist at the
Goodyear Tire and Rubber Company in Akron. Rubber is *the*
industry in Akron. And that, I think, did have an influence on
me because we were a first-generation middle-class family.
My grandparents were lower class on both sides, and we were
upwardly mobile with all the insecurities and sense of privilege I think that can give someone. That's where I came from
and in the spirit of that kind of newly educated and upwardly

*The national Humanities Center, January 16, 1989.

mobile family, I was encouraged to read a lot. So I did read practically anything I could get my hands on and in the beginning with very little discrimination. I just ate it up. So that I read everything from comic books to Louis Untermeyer's *Treasury of Best Loved Poems*, and I loved them all.

Vendler: That was a book I read, and I think I loved all the poems in it, too. You went on to Miami University and then from there to Tübingen on a Fulbright.

Dove: Yes. I did an English degree at Miami University in Ohio, went to Tübingen on a Fulbright to study modern European literature. Actually, I just wanted to get to Europe. And that was a way of doing it. After that year at Tübingen, I went to the University of Iowa to do an MFA in creative writing.

Vendler: Could I stop for a minute? You had learned German in college, I heard, before you went to Tübingen. Was that the case or did you really learn it in Germany?

Dove: I had learned it before. I started German when I was in seventh grade; it was one of the three languages offered if you were in the college prep slot, and you had a choice between French, Spanish, and German. Spanish was discouraged, as I believe it was often. They said it was too easy, which is, I think, regrettable. It certainly isn't that easy. Everyone else wanted to take French, so I took German out of spite—out of reaction, let's say. And also because my father had German books in the house. When he had been in the war he had studied Italian and German, "to know the language of the enemy," as he told us. So I saw these books that I could not read shelved among all the books that I had devoured. I saw these two or three books I could not read but wanted to. So that's why I took German and kept taking it. It was fascinating to think that people could exist in other languages.

Vendler: What did you study at Tübingen actually?

Dove: I studied drama, expressionist drama, and I studied Rilke and Paul Celan.

Vendler: That's interesting. I hadn't known exactly what you did there. And then you came back and took your MFA in Iowa—was *The Yellow House on the Corner* your thesis for the MFA?

Dove: Well, the thesis was the basis for that. I graduated from Iowa in 1977 and revised the manuscript extensively, actually, before it came out.

Vendler: One of the experiments that interested me in *The Yellow House on the Corner* is your imitating the language of a past era. I'm thinking of some poems like "The Slave's Critique of Practical Reason" or another poem called "David Walker, 1785–1830" or "The Transport of Slaves from Maryland to Mississippi." These were poems with a specifically historical focus and in some cases the use of historically accurate language—things people might have said in the nineteenth century. And I wondered whether this was an experiment that you wanted to continue or whether it was something you tried but then decided to drop. How do you feel about that attempt to write semi-archaic language?

Dove: Well, the attempt to do that was spun by the sense of the language—what it could say and its restraint. In fact you could incorporate horrific things within a language of this strength because the slave narratives are related in a so-called "civilized" language that makes the events to my mind actually more horrible—the telling of it was not more horrible than the events, but you could sense in the silences just how horrific it was. And that was the original impulse, the edge I was exploring. I can't really tell you if I'm going to do it again. It's not something I've abandoned as being untenable. I think more that it hasn't come up again yet. In the poems that I'm writing now, in some of the poems which have to do with Albrecht Dürer, the sense of another language is coming in again.

Vendler: Is that an archaic language or the alternative language, German?

Dove: It's both. German, obviously, is constructed syntactically so differently from English and I've always professionally seen differences in effect and certainly the different thought processes you have when you're in German. Put the verb on the end of a sentence and you've got to suspend everything until then and then revelation comes in a rush. Epiphany is really easy in German. And that fascinates me on the one hand. On the other hand, the language that Dürer spoke in fifteenth-century and sixteenth-century Germany is radically different in its pacing from modern German and modern English and that fascinates me too.

Vendler: Have you been reading Dürer's letters and notebooks, or what have you been doing to prepare for the Dürer work?

Dove: I've been reading a little bit of everything and very haphazardly, as I felt the need for it. I've been reading his letters, his diary, his treatises—he had several treatises, such as his manual for young painters in which he tries to explain to them what a point is, what a line is, what a spiral is. And there's no language for it even in medieval German, so he's inventing it. That spirit of inquiry, that kind of . . .

Vendler: Theorizing?

Dove: Yes, that kind of theorizing, that need to try to invent a language for what you need is also fascinating to me. But I am immersing myself in a certain way in that German and trying to find an equivalent in English which is not too strange to the ear.

Vendler: You've done this with Berlioz a little, too. You've written a poem about Berlioz, and I wonder whether you might be able to say something about what draws you to particular historical characters. After all, there's a large tradition of art in Germany and Dürer is not the only artist any more than Berlioz is the only French composer. Why Berlioz and not Debussy? Why Dürer and not Altdorfer, or whatever?

Dove: I don't know. Particularly in the case of Berlioz, I can't say. I can't articulate why Berlioz instead of someone else. It was the particular story in that poem, I guess. As for Dürer, I can say that for me he was one of the most interesting examples of an inquisitive mind. He was an artist really poised, I think, between two eras, who sensed that the Renaissance was happening and that Germany was somehow behind and that the dark kind of iconic representations in medieval German art were going to change. He didn't know what was coming after that but he was willing to move outside of art, in his case, and go into philosophy and mathematics. He was willing to move out of his cultural frame and try to figure out, to stretch himself. That of course is one of the things that always interests me when an historical character occurs to me, but I have no rules for choosing them; they choose me.

Vendler: Can we go back a little to your work in *Museum*? I wanted to ask you about the differences among the titles of your three volumes. First, *The Yellow House on the Corner*, which seems to be a domestic title; then *Museum*, which seems to be a different sort of title; and finally, *Thomas and Beulah*, where the title characters seem to be in some way modeled on your grandparents. That's an interesting double sequence, one sequence belonging to Thomas, the man, one sequence belonging to Beulah, the woman, with the story of a marriage told through two coordinate sequences, Thomas's and Beulah's. I don't know if these titles represent stages in your own conceptualizing in your art—the titles are so very different that I wanted to ask you about them.

Dove: Looking back at them now, there was a counter-impulse after *The Yellow House on the Corner*, which I did conceive as a very domestic title, but one on the edge of domesticity. I mean, the house is on the corner and there's a sense of something beyond that—outside of that boundary there is something else. But after that I wanted another kind of title—first of all, I wanted it shorter. The poems in *Museum* are concerned with matters of art, matters of, I think, artifacts: How do you retain culture and make it available to another generation; what gets chosen and what doesn't? I suppose if compared to cinematographic techniques, it's the wide angle, the zoom back—the lens pulling back to take in a larger picture. *Thomas and Beulah*—obviously the title gives the names of the two characters in the book, and I chose to list them in that order because it sounds better than Beulah and Thomas; also because Thomas's section occurs first, and because the name "Beulah" contains much more longing and resonance than "Thomas." It's a lingering tone. What's interesting is that I had originally intended to have a section dealing with Thomas, a section dealing with his wife Beulah, and then a section dealing with the town they lived in, Akron. I started some of those Akron poems but aborted the section. I realized that the town would have to emerge through them or not at all. Looking back on it, I can see that though the first two books are of places and areas of containment, these already have been subsumed in *Thomas and Beulah*.

Vendler: And now you're doing a book called *Grace Notes*. Is that a pun?

Dove: Of course! Since the book has just been finished, it's very hard to talk about. With *Grace Notes* I had several things in mind: every possible meaning of grace, and of notes, and of grace notes, and also a little added riff. In a sense, I am trying to counter the heavy weight of *Thomas and Beulah*, which had such a big scope.

Vendler: Well, I'll just have to wait and see.

Dove: Yes, that would be best.

Vendler: What has interested me most about your poetry, I think, is its extraordinary concision. You say so much with so few words and everything is condensed into a very pregnant set of images. I know you've done some collaborative work with a colleague in photography; and when you mentioned cinematography just now, I wondered whether that concision comes to you as images which crystallize in a certain way. I'm thinking of images in the poems about adolescence, or the single image in "Parsley" about the parrot, or the single image of the painting in the title poem of *Museum*. In *Thomas and Beulah*, the image of the mandolin hanging on the wall begins to stand for the abandoned earlier life of Thomas, and the image of the ballerina dancing on the little jewel box—in the last poem about Beulah—begins to sum up all Beulah's longing.

These things seem to focus the poems very strongly, and enable you to be as concise as you are.

Dove: It's true that at various points in the composition of *Thomas and Beulah*, I was conscious of the fact that I had toeholds—that as I was working through a poem I would go back to the mandolin. Even if it didn't appear in the next poem, it stood there as—I don't want to say an image or a totem, which suggests that it's impenetrable, but almost like an oracle, something I could ask questions of and so explore further. I also do kind of photographic takes. But the composition depends just as much on the way that language can be telescoped to contain much more. Sometimes I find myself moving through the syntax as well.

Vendler: That's true. Your syntax is as compressed as your language. Do you make poems that are longer and then cut them down, or do they start out as very small and get added to?

Dove: It depends on the poem. I tend to write in fragments, and I tend to work on several poems at once. Very often a poem will exist only as a line or two and there will be several other poems like that, and then they get added to bit by bit. I think there is a lot of editing done. My poems don't start out as five-page rambling things which then are whittled down to one page. It doesn't work that way.

Vendler: So far, you've been a writer of lyrics and short stories. You mentioned that you're now writing a novel, and this is a large departure for you in scale. Is it coming in bits—are you working on several chapters at once, or is it going in a sequential way, or does it have an overarching form into which you are putting the writing, or how is that going?

Dove: It's terrifying. It's not coming in little bits; it's coming in scenes and I'm not doing it sequentially, either—though I have the idea, I know basically what it's about. I'm sure that's going to change as I go along. I had started writing the novel several years ago; put it away, took it out and started to revise it, then left it alone again. And now I'm coming back. I'm writing the novel mainly because it's a story I've wanted to tell; it wouldn't leave me alone. But another part of me—the dutiful daughter or something—was always told that if you don't understand something you should study it until you can understand it. You try, you don't run away from it. I just feel that if as a writer I have the idea for a novel and also the desire to write it, I should try it. No reason to turn back. I'm not sure I'm going to be good at it, but I'm going to try.

Vendler: Poets' novels have an interest all their own; they're a subgenre in the history of the novel. I think the exploration of particular forms always has benefits and byproducts in some larger-scale exploration of form in general that you are engaged in.

I wonder if any of the labels that could be attached to you— that you're a woman writer, that you're a black writer, that you're an American writer, that you're a contemporary writer— have meaning for you and to what extent your work comes out of these sociological grids into which you might be said to fit.

Dove: I could answer: all the above. Certainly I come out of all those and they impinge on my writing at all times, in a way. First and foremost is just the language that is my clay and my primary interest. I try not to think about it, certainly not when I'm writing. But I am also positive that the fact that I am a woman, that I am black, that I am an American, and that I'm living in the time that I'm living in now has an enormous impact on my writing. And probably not only on the content, but certainly on the way it's presented or what I feel impelled to write about. For instance, the fact that, when I was growing up, I could not find anything written about what it was like to grow up as a black woman, or woman-child, was important—I wanted to read that book, so I try to write those poems. Obviously I can't force them, but it's a hole that I'm trying to fill. In terms of labels, though, in terms of whether I want to be called one thing or another—I want to be called a poet. I'm also a black poet, I'm a woman poet. If that means that my books get filed in the women's study section or the black history section, and not cross-listed in the general literature section, then I say no. But that's someone else's problem.

Vendler: That's true, and I think you will be found in many sections. One of the things that interests me in your poetry is specifically what you have just mentioned, the bringing into visibility of many things that were hitherto invisible. I find that very strongly in your poems about adolescence—"Hully Gully," and the two "Adolescence" ones, and so on. In them there were experiences that had never been articulated before, and often when I've taught those poems students are just astonished—especially about the sealmen in the bathroom in "Adolescence"—astonished that such things can be brought into visibility. Students were shocked at having things made visible that they had thought should be kept under wraps, so to speak. And this is true also of the poems about your grandparents, in so far as they are your grandparents. There's a photo, I gather of your grandparents, on the cover of *Thomas and Beulah*, and in that sequence there's a life that might not have been recorded that has been brought into visibility, including public things like the Goodyear picnic for the workers, and including private things like Beulah's reminiscences when she's dusting. These poems, especially "Dusting," have already become very well known. Is there any sense in which as you bring certain things into visibility that other things occur to you that need to be brought into visibility, too? Do you have a sense of maternity that needs to be brought into visibility?

Dove: The question is fascinating for me as a writer because it really gets into how writers continue, how they build on what they've done before, on what others have done and what has been satisfied for the time being, and what still gnaws. And I believe, in bringing certain things to light in *Thomas and Beulah*, I discovered other things beneath them. One of the things that happened in writing *Thomas and Beulah*, particularly with Beulah's section, was that the whole notion of children and motherhood began to come to light; I realized that I was in fact feeding some of my own experiences as a young mother into Beulah and I was feeling incredibly uncomfortable about it until I realized that I was harboring an unspoken notion that poems about children and mothers are mushy and you just don't write those things. Once I became aware of that, I realized that what I had to do is to write these poems and that I was covering up a part of my own life that was very important. Technically, that meant that I had to work with poems which were much closer to my present state, which was also good for me, I think. So, in fact, in my next book, *Grace Notes*, there are some poems about motherhood.

Vendler: Those, I think, are the hardest poems to write. I've often been struck by the fact that someone like, say Adrienne Rich, who did have three children, has represented motherhood almost not at all in her poetry, as though it were an unrepresentable part of her experience, although her experience with men and women and love and friendship and her experience with her parents and grandparents have all been brought into representation. The one thing that seems to have escaped is the representation of motherhood, except, interestingly enough, in her prose book *Of Woman Born*, which is not a specifically personal memoir, but talks about motherhood in general. One of the things I'm interested in is how things are brought into lyric treatment, and you did it, as you said, by going through Beulah in one instance. Presumably the later poems in your new book are more directly first-person. Are they?

Dove: They are first-person, and they were brought into view because of a project that I had started with a woman photographer at Arizona State University. We wanted to work together to create images and poems; we started out not knowing what we were going to do—no preconceived notions—and we wandered around until we found a space we could work in, which turned out to be my backyard. So we started to write about and photograph that backyard. Then children started coming into it, so it became absolutely necessary to talk about that aspect of domesticity.

Vendler: That's another backyard to add to A. R. Ammons's Ithaca backyard. His backyard doesn't have too many children in it. Can you tell me, do you feel generationally accompanied in your work and your exploration of language? You were in a cohort in Iowa, and there is a cohort of young writers that you probably know in Germany as well as in America. Is there any sense of what your generation is up to that you can convey to us?

Dove: My generation is so diverse in the United States; I can't speak for any other country. What's very interesting lately is this drive toward narrative that has come up, which is, I think, a response to a very heady kind of disembodied lyric. I'm not sure where we're heading. I don't feel particularly accompanied by anyone in my generation, though there are people whose work I admire and follow; I think we're all kind of stumbling along. I feel accompanied by earlier generations. Rilke accompanies me. Derek Walcott accompanies me in a funny kind of way, and Toni Morrison does, and Heinrich Heine does, and that kind of list goes on—

Vendler: Anybody from England?

Dove: Oh, from England! Well, Shakespeare, of course, but I'm trying to think if there's anyone else. No, I guess not.

Vendler: That's interesting in itself. It shows something about the present cohort of poets here who are much more likely to be influenced by Rilke, Neruda, or Milosz, than by someone in England. It's a kind of colonial insolence in American literature against its English background that other Americans and foreigners are one's cohort, rather than the English. That's an interesting piece of testimony.

I wonder if you could say what you find hardest and most rewarding about writing. What is it that makes you look at a blank page day after day after day after day? Is there something that is more of a block than anything else so that you find overcoming it more of a joy than anything else?

Dove: I think that it's constantly changing. That in the end I am in a dialogue with myself and also with the entire culture that I am immersed in, but I find different things hardest all the time. Sometimes it's simply putting down the first word, and sometimes it's having a fairly written poem in front of me that has no gut at all, but different things keep rearing their heads as impossible at that moment.

Vendler: That's a good answer. Thank you.

An Interview with Jamaica Kincaid

Donna Perry

With the appearance of her first collection of stories, *At the Bottom of the River* (Random House, 1983), Jamaica Kincaid was praised as an important new voice in contemporary fiction. In these stories and in those collected in her widely acclaimed autobiographical first novel, *Annie John* (Farrar Straus Giroux, 1985), Kincaid writes from her experiences as a child and adolescent on the island of Antigua, growing up in the shadow of a loving but domineering mother while learning proper British etiquette at colonial schools. What impressed reviewers at the time, and still does, was the honesty, lyrical beauty, and richness of detail in her prose.

The political awareness only hinted at in *Annie John* became clearer in her controversial nonfiction work, *A Small Place* (Farrar Straus Giroux, 1988). Again drawing on firsthand experience, Kincaid explores the underside of colonial life in Antigua and the failure of freedom once the country gained its independence. In this book of many moods—at times lyrical, sardonic, accusatory—Kincaid demonstrates that she is not a writer to be neatly categorized. She isn't interested in playing it safe.

I interviewed Jamaica Kincaid on April 18, 1990, in North Bennington, Vermont, where she lives with her husband, Allen Shawn, a composer and faculty member at nearby Bennington College, and her two children, Annie, 5, and Harold, 1½. In the course of the three hours we spent together, she discussed her development in style and subject matter from the early stories to the most recent ones, which will appear, collected, in a novel entitled *Lucy* (Farrar Straus Giroux, Fall 1990). And she discussed other things: the writing process; her growing radicalization; the relationship between autobiography and fiction; world politics; the significance of family life.

Kincaid left her own family at an early age. Shortly after her sixteenth birthday, in 1965, she left Antigua and her parents for the United States. Once here, she worked as an *au pair*, a receptionist, and a magazine writer; she studied photography at New York's New School for Social Research and spent over a year at Franconia College in New Hampshire before settling in New York. Her first published piece was an interview with Gloria Steinem that appeared in *Ingenue* in 1973.

The turning point for Kincaid came when she became friends with George W. S. Trow, a writer for *The New Yorker*, who started writing "Talk of the Town" pieces about her. Soon she met the editor, William Shawn, who began publishing her stories.

The stories collected in *Lucy*, like those in *Annie John*, appeared originally in *The New Yorker*. They represent yet another departure for Kincaid: sharper-edged than the earlier stories; more indirect than *A Small Place*. These stories chart the experiences of a young woman from the islands who is an *au pair* to a couple and their four daughters. Disaster strikes—the marriage fails—but this domestic tragedy, like everything else in the stories, is filtered through the crystalline consciousness of the cultural outsider who lives among them. She is the person we care about, ultimately.

Kincaid's parents named her Elaine Potter Richardson, but she took the name Jamaica Kincaid when she started writing—the first name because it evoked the West Indies; the second simply because it seemed to go well with the first. The same independent spirit that led her to change home and name characterizes everything this writer does. During the interview she said of her writing, "When people say you're charming you are in deep trouble." As charming as she is in person, no one will call Jamaica Kincaid's work charming any more.

Perry: Could we start by talking a bit about *Annie John*, your first novel? I know that the situation is autobiographical. How do you translate what has happened in your life into fiction?

Kincaid: A lot of what happens in *Annie John* were things that actually happened to me. But one of the things that I seem to do in writing is, I often take a lot of disparate events and, I don't know how, but sometimes they make a kind of psychological sense that I couldn't have foreseen or I can't see until I'm writing. I would say that everything in *Annie John* happened—every feeling in it happened—but not necessarily in the order they appear. But it very much expresses the life I had. There isn't anything in it that is a lie, I would say.

For instance, the story of the long rain and the girl's illness. Both really happened—I had whooping cough when I was about eight or nine—but in the book the girl is older, about fifteen. These feelings and some of the things that happened—like the bathing of the pictures—happened when I was about 9.

Perry: Why did you choose to write fiction instead of autobiography?

Kincaid: Because autobiography is the truth and fiction is, well, fiction. In an autobiography, for instance, I could not have had the long rain coincide with the girl's illness. One of the things I found when I began to write was that writing exactly what happened had a limited amount of power for me. To say exactly what happened was less than what I knew happened. Mr. Shawn used to say I was a terrible reporter. I like the idea that when something happens it has a more powerful meaning than the moment in which it actually happens. When I started to write these autobiographical things I was told, "Oh, why don't you write a sort of autobiographical reminiscence about life?" but I wanted something more than that. I could see that if you put it in a sort of straightforward memoir that it would have a sort of bitterness that I didn't want—that wasn't the point. The point wasn't the truth and yet the point was the truth. And I don't know how to explain that.

Perry: So you were after something more universal?

Kincaid: More universal. Yes. But at the time I did not know that and I now make it a point not to know that.

Perry: Would you ever write a story about something that hasn't happened to you?

Kincaid: I don't know how to do that, no. I read sometimes that a writer says, "Oh, I overheard a snippet of conversation and I went from there." I can't do that. If I overhear something I have to completely internalize it. I can only find the thing inside me. If it's not there, then I'm not able to figure things out. It's not that I couldn't write about something that didn't happen to me, but I would have to find the emotion somewhere inside myself.

Perry: I gave the book to a young woman from Jamaica who enjoyed it, but she didn't like the ending because Annie leaves home. Have you heard that reaction before?

Kincaid: That's happened a lot among West Indian girls who have read the book. Many teachers have told me that. One teacher in Queens said that the class split over it: the West Indian girls said it didn't have a happy ending, the other students—not West Indian—disagreed. I don't know if it is but I have noticed that black people don't like unhappy endings. Perhaps we have too many. This reality of life is perhaps hard for us to face. Another reality is that life is ambiguous; it has many meanings and many endings. Most endings in life, I have noticed, are not happy. Death, of course, is the most common one.

I wonder why it is that Africans like a one-party state. Even when they are not communists, they insist on one party. They can't stand the idea of many opinions, where the one that is most popularly expressed is the one that will go, but that the other differences are accommodated also. It's as if we must all think alike or nothing, and we must all think happily. And this idea that it must be happy and it must be the same means that there is deception all the time. So, yes, the reality of the ending of *Annie John* is very disturbing.

Perry: I see the central character in *Annie John* as in some ways an outsider. Did you think of yourself as an outsider then?

Kinkaid: I didn't think of myself as an outsider because of my race because, for one thing, where I grew up I was the same race as almost everyone else. And I did not feel I was an outsider because of my sex. Many people were the same sex as me also. But still I did feel that I was an outsider.

It is true that I noticed things that no one else seemed to notice. And I think only people who are outsiders do this. I must have felt very different from everybody. When I tell people there now how I felt then, they look at me with pity. For instance, I have a friend now who is a little bit older than I am who grew up in the same area I did. Our families were not acquainted—her parents are practically aristocrats, my parents are peasants. But she and I have now become friends and I can tell her all of these things that I noticed about her. But at the time I was little and observing her I wasn't observing her for any reason I knew of. I mean, some of the people I knew were, like her, from a different class—they had land and money—and most of the people I knew were like me, just from working people.

So why did I notice her? I remember an incredible number of things about her and it was just from seeing her come and go. We weren't friends. We never spoke to each other. She has two sisters and a brother and I can even tell her what they were like. I just knew the kind of people they were then.

Perry: Would you say that you grew up with a consciousness of class difference?

Kincaid: No. Not really. I noticed things that came under that heading but I noticed other things also. I just noticed things, a lot of things. I had all this information about everybody. I can just imagine that if it had not worked out this way I would have been someone who would have caused enormous mischief, because I knew so much about everyone that I would either have spread rumors or engineered catastrophes, including the catastrophe of my own life, I'm sure.

Perry: Getting back to something you said earlier about drawing from experiences in your own life, did the "Columbus in Chains" episode really happen to you—the incident in *Annie John* when you write under the picture of an enslaved Columbus the words your mother spoke about her father: "The Great Man Can No Longer Just Get Up and Go"?

Kincaid: Yes, but my mother had really said, "The great man can't shit." I had written that and it wouldn't go in *The New Yorker*, so I changed it. Then I left it that way for the book because I realized that it had a more profound meaning, and now I can't exactly remember why. But I thought about it for a long time—I had a long conversation with my editor at the time because *shit* was not a word that appeared in *The New Yorker* then—appropriately, I have now come to feel.

The two incidents happened separately in real life.

Perry: That section seems to be the part of *Annie John* that most clearly reveals a political consciousness. Do you agree?

Kincaid: I think that's the first place I began to know how to express it. I think in the things I just wrote [in 1988 and 1989], it becomes clearer and it becomes clearer, also, to me, how to express it. But the typical reality of someone like myself in a place like Antigua is that the political situation became so normal that we no longer noticed it. The better people were English and that was life. I can't say that I came from a culture that felt alienated from England—Europe. We were beyond alienation.

It was amazing that I could notice the politics the way I did, because most of those who took notice did so in some sort of world context, like the man who became prime minister. But I took notice of it in a personal way and I didn't place it within the context of political action. I almost made a style out of it.

Perry: Speaking of political consciousness, why did you write *A Small Place*? That's a very political book.

Kincaid: I really wrote it as a piece for *The New Yorker*. Mr. Shawn, the former editor, loved it and bought it; then Bob Gottlieb, the present editor, hated it. He said it was very angry. Not badly written. Angry. I now consider anger a badge of honor. It had a sort of traumatic history because it was so intimate. It was written for the readers of *The New Yorker*, whom I had come to think of as friends in some peculiar way. And then it was very much loathed by the new people.

I don't know how it is for most people—other writers—but I

feel that I am sort of lucky or privileged to get to do this thing called writing, in which basically all I am doing is discovering my own mind. I'm very grateful that I am able to make a living at it, but that's all it is, discovering my own mind. I mean, I didn't know that I thought those things. I didn't go around saying them to myself. But then, somehow, once I had the opportunity to think them, I just did. I went to Antigua and I began to see things again about it and they turned into this article. So when *The New Yorker* didn't buy it, Mr. Shawn thought it should be presented as a book, all by itself. He was right of course, as usual.

Perry: I felt when I read *A Small Place* as though it was a kind of turning point in your writing, a growth in political awareness in some way, and that your works to follow would be different. Is that so?

Kincaid: Yes. I thought it was a turning point in me. I wrote with a kind of recklessness in that book. I didn't know what I would say ahead of time. Once I wrote it I felt very radicalized by it. I would have just thought of myself as a liberal person until I wrote it, and now I feel that liberal is as far right as I can go.

Perry: There's a lot of anger in it.

Kincaid: Yes, that's right, and I've really come to love anger. And I liked it even more when a lot of reviews said it's so angry. *The New York Times* said that the book didn't have the "charm" of *Annie John*. Really, when people say you're charming you are in deep trouble. I realized in writing that book that the first step to claiming yourself is anger. You get mad. And you can't do anything before you get angry. And I recommend getting very angry to everyone, anyone.

As I wrote it I realized that I had all this feeling and that it was anger. I wanted it to be crude and impolite—and all the other things that civilized people are not supposed to be. I no longer wanted to be a civilized person. Really, for me, writing is like going to a psychiatrist. I just discover things about myself.

I can see that *At the Bottom of the River* was, for instance, a very unangry, decent, civilized book and it represents sort of this successful attempt by English people to make their version of a human being or their version of a person out of me. It amazes me now that I did that then. I would never write like that again, I don't think. I might go back to it, but I'm not very interested in that sort of expression any more. Now, for instance, I've become very interested in writing about sex, or smells. I'm interested in being not a decent person.

Perry: You said earlier that if you hadn't become a writer you might have caused a lot of mischief because of what you knew. Did *A Small Place* cause mischief? Were there repercussions in Antigua?

Kincaid: Not really. I think people thought it would and they talked about it. There's a section of the book that very much describes the reaction of Antiguans to the book. It was sort of a great event, and now it's just part of what happened that someone wrote this book and said these things that we—they—all know happened. There wasn't anything in it anyone learned, except that someone would make an attempt to tell the world about them. They have always seen themselves—we see ourselves—as little, insignificant people that great things happen to: slavery, America, the British, whatever. They never really thought that any of us could just stand up and say to the world the things that we know about ourselves.

So the world looking at them has become part of their everyday life. And I think the government was a little afraid that it would hurt them at first, so they sort of banned it, but then they were reelected by an overwhelming majority.

One thing Antiguans said about *A Small Place* is: "It's true, but did she have to say it?" No one says that it's a lie; the disagreement is did I have to say it.

Perry: In the book you mention that the library was closed. Has it been reopened?

Kincaid: No. But you know, yesterday I was reading an article about a newspaperman in Zambia who writes satirical articles about his government and he said that there isn't one bookstore in Zambia. There isn't a library or anything. So there is

this incredible, almost conspiratorial effort on the part of the
people who rule in the black third world to keep any institution of learning out of their country. Mobutu, apparently,
simply closed the universities when the students protested
against him.

Perry: Do you see this as similar to what happened in China?

Kincaid: To some extent, but the Chinese want their students
to be educated—in their own way. It's quite a big difference;
the Chinese don't mean to do away with education. The
Africans and the West Indians don't make that fine a distinction. They just don't want any opposition. The fact is that a
lot of the things that are considered essential to having a
nation are not in existence in Black Africa or in the West
Indies. We had better health and education under colonialism.

Perry: The saddest part of *A Small Place* is that after colonialism many things in Antigua seem worse than they were
under the British.

Kincaid: It's absolutely true; it's not an exaggeration. In the
hospital in Antigua—the children's ward—most of the children are there because they suffer from malnutrition. And
Antigua has the highest standard of living in the eastern
Caribbean—I have no idea, by the way, what that means, but
that's what they say. You do see people with a lot of things.
Everyone has a car, everyone has a television. They have
cable television, and they get something like thirty channels
from North America. It has all of what looks like prosperity.
My mother, who lives in a tiny house, has a refrigerator and a
better television set than we do. It's really quite remarkable.

Perry: Could you talk about "Ovando," a short story of yours
that appeared in *Conjunctions* [vol. 14, 1989]? As an allegorical
portrait of the horrors of colonialism, that work seems to
continue this concern with domination.

Kincaid: I can only say that story is something that I stopped
because I realized I didn't know enough to go on. As I go
around the world I understand it better and better. I think in

some way I am very interested in domination. I suppose we all are. I feel that, in particular, my own history is so much about dominion; in fact we were called "the dominion," and all the colonies were "the dominions." So when I started to write "Ovando" I thought I was going to write a grand work about the question of dominion.

The other insight I have into history is that it's a bit like musical chairs. When the music stops some people are standing up and some people are sitting down, but at any moment you don't know if you will be among the stand-ups or the sit-downs. I feel as though if I am among the people sitting down I always will identify with the people who are standing up—that my knowledge of my history tells me that I have to always make room on the chair for the people standing up. In writing "Ovando," I was trying to understand how for some people who found themselves sitting down it would become important to try to remove the apparatus for the game to continue—so that they would never again be standing up.

Perry: Do you see this as the situation of the colonizing countries like Europe and the United States?

Kincaid: Yes. On the other hand, we know that every relief also bears its own prison. If you remove the apparatus for the game to go on, then permanently sitting down is its own prison.

I realized that in order for me to finish "Ovando," I would have to understand more about the reality of someone like Christopher Columbus than I know now. His journals are in Seville and you can go and read them. I really need to know more about these explorers themselves. I need to be older.

All these people are very admirable when you think of what they did—these "great men." People thought the world was flat. A very poetic idea.

In some ways, these explorations to the New World were very touching. I realize that one of the things that is bound up in this horrible thing that happened (slavery—the domination) is the great curiosity in every human being. I mean making maps, building a boat—there's something really extraordinary about it, very moving, when you think of these people just going somewhere without knowing what really they would find. It's not like going to the moon at all, which has this incredible support. It had an individual element that was admirable and inspiring.

But, of course, by the time they made their discoveries, everything admirable about them becomes lost.

Perry: They became the conquerors?

Kincaid: Yes.

Perry: At the end of "Ovando," you say that "A true and just sentence would be imbued with love for Ovando." That suggests that you think it would take a great-hearted person to understand Ovando.

Kincaid: It's a funny thing. I grew to understand that, too.

Perry: "Ovando" seems very medieval. I kept thinking of Barbara Tuchman's *A Distant Mirror* and the cult of the Black Death. Were you suggesting parallels with the medieval period?

Kincaid: Yes. When you read the history of what the Europeans left behind, it is a record of disease and incredible suffering, poverty.

When I hear people talking about "The Great Western Tradition," I think, wait a minute, what are they talking about here? All I see is a tradition of incredible cruelty and suffering and injustice—not to mention murder, complete erasing of whole groups of people. Everybody is always looking for a way out. And what was their way out? The New World. Start fresh. But of course you can't. There's no such thing as a fresh start.

Perry: I'm struck by the parallels with contemporary American politics and policies. This imperialism seems so characteristic of the Bush-Quayle administration. What do you think?

Kincaid: I don't find Quayle so distressing. My theory about Quayle is that it's time the United States suffered the way it's made other people suffer. And I think Quayle would make Americans suffer.

Perry: We have had other presidents who were disasters. I'm thinking of Harding or Hoover, for example.

Kincaid: But this is really serious. Americans are not on the upswing.

Perry: To return to your fiction, can you talk a little about your writing process? How do you write?

Kincaid: I read about writers who have routines. They write at certain times of the day. I can't do that. I'm always writing— but in my head. I just finished writing a book about a month ago. I started it when Harold was three months and then I finished it when he was a year and six months. It will be published in the fall. It will be some stories that have appeared in *The New Yorker*. I don't know how I did it. I wrote in between things. I have to figure out how things will go—what we will have for dinner, how the children's lives will be, Allen's life, my life. I sort of expect that I'll figure it out.

I think I have to have a great deal of domestic activity to write. I am essentially a person very interested in domestic life and very interested in things that we think of, either in a good way or a bad way, as women's things. I know a woman and she comes to see me in the morning and we sit at the kitchen table. We just sit and talk. That's not how I write, but in a way it is. I sit with this woman and we sort of arrange the world. We talk about Bush. We talk about the Russians. We talk about Nicaragua. We talk about the homeless. We sort of settle the day—the world. Then, at about eleven o'clock, I say, "Well, goodbye," and I go off to my office—a room at home. And I do whatever I do.

I may do absolutely nothing but read the newspaper and then for fifteen minutes I write a paragraph or maybe a sentence or a page. I can't tell how it may go. But that's how I write. I sort of think about it as part of my domestic life. In fact, I think I reduce everything to a domestic situation. I wouldn't be very interested in putting the world in the way the world is actually arranged. If I actually ran the world, I'd do it from the kitchen. It's not anything deliberate or a statement or anything, that's just how I understand things. It's arranged along informal lines. I don't like formality. I realize, for instance, that I would never live in a house with a dining room. I couldn't stand a room in which you only ate. If I ran the world I would do it from the kitchen.

When I was little I had this great mind for history. And I never really understood it until I realized that the reason I liked history is that I always reduced it to domestic activity. History was what people did. It was organized along the lines of who said what and who did what, not really unlike how the society in which I grew up was organized. The idea that things are impersonal occurrences is very alien to me. I personalize everything.

Perry: That personalizing is what enabled you to make the connection between Columbus and your grandfather.

Kincaid: That's right. You see, I reduce everything to a domestic connection. It's all the great men who have been humbled. Finally.

Perry: What difference have your children made in your life? You described the domestic arrangements that make writing possible, but I get the sense that motherhood takes a lot of time.

Kincaid: Absolutely. I have two children: Annie, who is named after my mother and Allen's grandmother, and Harold, who is named after Allen's father's brother. Annie is five and Harold is a year and a half.

I don't mean to be one of those people who says everything happens for the best, because when you hear someone say that you are listening to a defeated person. But I have these two children and yet I wrote one book in a year and three months. There was a long period after I had Annie that I didn't write at all. I don't know if I didn't have time to write or if I was gathering. You know there is a fallow period that one gets frightened of. You think, "Maybe I'll never write again." I never felt that way. As long as I can have some way of earning a living or doing something, I don't worry too much about it. I think, "Well, I haven't quite figured out how to say what I want to say."

That was true after I wrote *Annie John*. I wanted to say

something but I didn't know what, and it turned out to be *A Small Place*. And then I planned to write a book after that, but I got pregnant and couldn't write. Then I had Harold. And then, just to earn some money, I started to write the first story of this new book. I didn't mean to write the whole book at all. And then within a year and three months I finished it.

Perry: Is it harder to write now that you have children?

Kincaid: It's hard to write now but it was hard to write before. I feel incredibly free—I feel I could have more children, I feel that I can write. I don't feel writing is cut off for me because I don't feel having experience is cut off from me. I think somehow if I didn't have the children I might feel that way. But, you see, being so interested in domestic activity, having children can only add to my feeling of domestic life. I am beginning to see their life as going out into the world, whatever it is. But I can only see that from the kitchen table.

Perry: When do you let other people read your work? Does your husband read what you have written when you think it is ready?

Kincaid: He reads it daily [laughter]. Probably I couldn't be a writer without Allen. When I'm writing, every night before he goes to sleep, he reads. It's not quite a joint project, but I really depend on him as a reader.

The way I wrote *Annie John* was that I would get up every day and I would say to him, "Well now, today I'm going to do . . ." and I would say pages and pages of how I would write. And he would say, "Oh, that sounds good" or "Well, but what happens when this . . . ?" And I would say, "Oh, but this . . ." Then, just as I told him, I would go into my room and write, and later I would show him what I had written.

He's not a writer, but he is very interested in writing and very interested in me, I must say. He's great fun to be married to. It's wonderful to have this great companion, in every way.

The terrible thing about traveling is that he doesn't like to travel, and so I travel alone. It is a great loss because I have all these experiences and usually when we have these experiences we just chatter, chatter, chatter all the time. And when I'm alone there's no one to talk to. So then we just have these huge phone bills.

Perry: Based on the stories that have run in *The New Yorker* so far, your new book seems harder-edged than *Annie John*.

Kincaid: I think they are more frank. I think that after writing *A Small Place* and seeing the reaction to it, I realized that people couldn't stand a certain sort of frankness. But I knew that what I wanted to be, more and more as a writer, was frank about what the lives I wrote about were really like, as frank as I could express or as I could know. I didn't know if that would be possible, but that was what I wanted.

In the context of that, I'm still very conscious of art, of making something, and I'm always very interested in the right word. I want to use the word that would best express something. But yet I wanted to be very frank and to be unlikable within the story. To be even unpopular. In the last two stories I wanted to risk more.

As I go on writing, I feel less and less interested in the approval of the First World, and I never had the approval of the world I came from, so now I don't know where I am. I've exiled myself yet again. In fact, the world that comforted me and made me a writer is now the world where I don't care about their approval: *The New Yorker*. I used to care about *The New Yorker*. I used to feel I had a personal stake in it. Now it's just another thing owned by someone with a billion dollars. Like everything else in the world.

Perry: Yet they are still publishing your stories, aren't they?

Kincaid: Yes. I'm shocked. They bought all of them.

Perry: This couple whom you describe in your last stories—Lewis and Mariah—seem like readers of *The New Yorker*, actually: white, upper-middle-class, politically left of center, city dwellers. But they also seem somewhat vapid to me. Is this your idea?

Kincaid: Yes. Well, you have to read the other two to come because the couple divorce. I really was an *au pair*, but I was writing about my own experience. The other people are incidental; they are not anyone I actually knew. I went out of my way to make the other characters not like people I actually knew.

Perry: On a recent trip to the Bronx Botanical Garden I found a place called "Daffodil Hill," a hill covered with daffodils that reminded me of the garden where the wife takes the narrator in the story "Mariah." Was that the place you had in mind?

Kincaid: No. I had never been to a specific garden; I just imagined it. This story of the daffodils did not really happen. But it is amazing to me that there is such a place and so it could have happened.

Perry: Were you really forced to memorize Wordsworth's "I Wandered Lonely as a Cloud," the poem where he praises the daffodils?

Kincaid: Every colonial child has to do that. It's a two-edged thing because I wouldn't have known how to write and how to think if I hadn't read those things. I wouldn't have known my idea of justice if I hadn't read *Paradise Lost*, if I hadn't been given parts of *Paradise Lost* to memorize. It was given to me because I was supposed to be Satan. The last chapter of the book I have written has a lot of things about that. The book is called *Lucy*, short for Lucifer.

Perry: So in this work, as in *Annie John*, there is some of what really happened and some manipulation of what really happened.

Kincaid: Like *Annie John*, everything happened but not necessarily in this way. I want the truth. I begin to understand this thing about the mind, and I'm sure it's not just true of me. I'm always shocked to see that things are more neatly connected than we think. I really manipulate the facts, but within the manipulation there is no lie. I believe I can safely say that— that in everything I say there is the truth.

I arrange things in a way that I can understand them, but it isn't completely fiction; it is, in fact, not in my imagination. I have no imagination when it comes to that. It's as if you were given a broken plate and you rearranged it into a pitcher. The rearrangement wouldn't deny the fact that the plate and the pitcher are made of the same stuff. I use the same material but I make it into a different thing, something new.

In these stories, the place and the girl herself aren't named. It is New York, but it could be anywhere. I didn't want to specify because I didn't want any preconceptions about the place. She doesn't even name the island she comes from.

Perry: Your stories seem seamless—both these new ones and the parts of *Annie John*. How do you account for the particular shape they take?

Kincaid: I just write and things come to a crest and that's how it is. My mind works in this way—it's sort of like a puzzle. I know where the pieces are, but I don't want to fit them for myself or for the reader. I just write.

Perry: It sounds like *Lucy* has an unhappy ending, too.

Kincaid: Yes. The last two stories are very painful, even for Allen.

Perry: What contemporary fiction writers do you read? Your comments about domestic matters made me think of Paule Marshall's essay, "The Making of a Writer: From the Poets in the Kitchen" [*New York Times Book Review*, January 9, 1983]. Is she one of the people you read?

Kincaid: Do you know any of the French West Indian writers? They are amazing. There is a collection of Caribbean women's writing, *Her True-True Name*, that is amazing [Pamela Mordecai and Betty Wilson, eds., Heinemann, 1989]. The French writers are much more frank, much more exciting. You can see the French influence in *Wide Sargasso Sea* (Jean Rhys) and *The Orchid House* (Phyllis Shand Allfrey). *The Orchid House* is very good. I can understand if someone would think it was deeply flawed if they don't know the story, but I think it's very good.

If you don't know something intimately, you might not know if it is good. I'm supposed to write an introduction to a work by Zora Neale Hurston, but I don't know what to say. I think that I do not appreciate her as some people do because I have not had a certain kind of experience. The language makes assumptions about things that I just don't understand.

These French writers are also unbelievably bold about sex, and of course, sex is everything. The world starts at the crotch, essentially. And it's not that people are a slave to the crotch, but they are a bit. I once read an article about AIDS in Africa and the writer said that the reason AIDS is spreading so fast there is that Africans are sex-positive. I thought this was a wonderful phrase. For instance, prostitution was not known in Africa until Europeans came. An African woman would have many lovers, but there was no money exchanged. A man would bring a gift, but it wasn't in exchange for the sex. It was to show affection. And I think there's something like that where I come from, and so almost all the most basic arrangements are made on that basis: no exchange, just a gift.

I'm just about to get to this in my own fiction, this commodification of relationships. The commodifying of things is what I wanted to discuss in "Ovando."

Perry: Before we end, I want to ask you about the role *The New Yorker* has played in your development as a writer. How important was it?

Kincaid: I don't think I would have become a writer if it wasn't for *The New Yorker*—the old *New Yorker*, that is. Not the thing that still calls itself *The New Yorker*. It was writing for them—for Mr. Shawn, really—that helped me learn how to write. I'm very grateful to him for that.

Notes on Contributors

Born in Greenville, South Carolina, **Dorothy Allison** now lives in San Francisco, where she is an editor of *Out/Look*, the national lesbian and gay quarterly. She is the author of *The Women Who Hate Me* and *Trash*, which won the 1988 Lambda Literary Awards for Lesbian Fiction and Lesbian Small Press Book. Her novel, *A Bastard Out Of Carolina*, will be published by New American Library/Dutton.

Houston A. Baker, Jr., is Director of the Center for the Study of Black Literature and Culture at the University of Pennsylvania. He is the author of seven critical studies of Afro-American literature, including *Modernism and the Harlem Renaissance*, and is a practicing poet.

Hazel V. Carby is a professor of English and African American Studies at Yale University. The author of *Reconstructing Womanhood: The Emergence of the Afro-American Woman Novelist*, published by Oxford University Press in 1987, she is currently finishing a book on black women in the culture industry in the United States.

Barbara Christian is a professor of Afro-American Studies at the University of California at Berkeley. She is the author of *Black Women Novelists: The Development of a Tradition—1892–1976*, published by Greenwood Press in 1980, of *Teaching Guide to Black Foremothers*, published by Feminist Press in 1980 and of *Black Feminist Criticism: Perspectives on Black Women Writers*, published by Pergamon Press in 1985. She is an editor at *Feminist Studies* and *Black American Literature Forum*. In 1988, she published a monograph on Alice Walker and *The Color Purple*. Her essays on black women writers have appeared in many literary and academic journals.

Selwyn R. Cudjoe, an associate professor of Black Studies at Wellesley College, is the author of *V. S. Naipaul: A Materialist Reading* (1988), *Movement of the People* (1983), and *Resistance and Caribbean Literature* (1980). His articles have appeared in *The New York Times*, the *Boston Globe*, *Harvard Educational Review*, and many other publications.

Rita Dove, born in 1952 in Akron, Ohio, graduated from Miami University in Oxford, Ohio, and received an M.F.A. in creative writing from the Iowa Writers Workshop. Her first collection of poems, *The Yellow House on the Corner*, was published in 1980, followed by *Museum* (1983) and *Thomas and Beulah* (1986), for which she won the Pulitzer Prize. In 1985, her collection of short stories, *Fifth Sunday*, appeared. Ms. Dove has been awarded fellowships from the National Endowment for the Arts and the Guggenheim Foundation. Her most recent book is *Grace Notes*. She is now a professor of English at the University of Virginia.

Elizabeth Fox-Genovese is the Eleonore Raoul Professor of the Humanities and Director of Women's Studies at Emory University, where she is also a member of the History department and an associate member of the English department. Her publications include *Within the Plantation Household: Black and White Women of the Old South* (1988) and *Feminism Without Illusion: A Critique of Individualism* (forthcoming).

Henry Louis Gates, Jr., is the author of *Figures in Black* and *The Signifying Monkey*. He has edited several works, including *Our Nig*, by Harriet Wilson, and the thirty-volume *Schomburg Library of Nineteenth-Century Black Women's Writings*. He recently edited *The Works of Zora Neale Hurston*. He is the John Spencer Bassett Professor of English at Duke University, and has won several awards, including the American Book Award and the Anisfield-Wolf Book Award for Race Relations.

Jewelle L. Gomez is the author of *Flamingoes and Bears*, a collection of poetry, and *The Gilda Stories*, a forthcoming novel. She is a black, lesbian/feminist activist and lives in Brooklyn, N.Y. Her literary reviews have appeared in *The New York Times, The Village Voice, The Nation, Gay Community News,* and *Belle Lettres*. She is coeditor of poetry for *Outlook Magazine*.

Mae Gwendolyn Henderson is an associate professor in the African American World Studies program and the Department of English at the University of Iowa. She is the editor of the five-volume *Anti-Slavery Newspapers and Periodicals: An Annotated Index of Letters, 1817–1871,* and her book on Black expatriate writers will be published soon. She is at work on a Black feminist theory of writing.

Marianne Hirsch is a professor of French and chair of the comparative literature program at Dartmouth College. Her most recent book is *The Mother/Daughter Plot: Narrative, Psychoanalysis, Feminism*. She is currently editing, with Evelyn Fox Keller, a collection of essays on *Conflicts in Feminism*.

Molly Hite is a member of the English department faculty at Cornell University. She is the author of *Ideas of Order in the Novels of Thomas Pynchon*, published by Ohio State University Press in 1983, of the novel *Class Porn* published by Crossing Press in 1983, and of *The Other Side of the Story: Structures and Strategies of Contemporary Feminist Narrative*, published by Cornell University Press in 1989.

Bell Hooks is a writer and teacher who speaks widely on issues of race, class, and gender. Her previous books are *Ain't I a Woman: Black Women and Feminism; Feminist Theory from Margin to Center;* and *Talking Back: Thinking Feminist, Thinking Black*. She is a professor of English at Oberlin College, and writes a monthly column for *Zeta* magazine.

Zora Neale Hurston, 1891–1960, was the author of seven books, including *Their Eyes Were Watching God* (1937), the most frequently taught book by a black woman in the American college curriculum today. In addition, she was an anthropologist, and studied with Franz Boas at Columbia. She received two Guggenheim Fellowships, and the Anisfield-Wolf Book Award in Race Relations for her autobiography, *Dust Tracks on a Road*.

Barbara E. Johnson is a professor of English and Comparative Literature at Harvard University. She is author of *Défigurations du langage poétique; The Critical Difference;* and *A World of Difference.* She is translator of Jacques Derrida's *Dissemination,* and editor of *The Pedagogical Imperative: Teaching as a Literary Genre.* With Jonathan Arac, she is editor of *Some Consequences of Theory.*

Stetson Kennedy, like Zora Neale Hurston, is a Floridian and a folklorist. He worked with Hurston on the WPA Florida Writers Project during the thirties, and utilized some of the lore they collected in his first book, *Palmetto Country,* published in 1942 and reprinted in 1989. In the post–World War II period, Kennedy infiltrated the KKK and a score of other racist-terrorist bands, reporting on his findings in three other books, *The Klan Unmasked; Jim Crow Guide;* and *Southern Exposure.* His most recent work is a history of Reconstruction, *After Appamatox,* scheduled for publication in 1990.

Jamaica Kincaid is the author of two novels, *At the Bottom of the River* and *Annie John,* and of *A Small Place,* a critical essay on her native Antigua. She is a frequent contributor to *The New Yorker* and has won the Norton Dauwen Zabel award for fiction.

Françoise Lionnet teaches French and comparative literature and theory at Northwestern University. She is the author of *Autobiographical Voices: Race, Gender, Self-Portraiture,* published by Cornell University Press in 1989.

Deborah E. McDowell is an associate professor of English at the University of Virginia. She is coeditor, with Arnold Rampersad, of *Slavery and the Literary Imagination,* the author of numerous essays on fiction by blacks and women, and editor of the Beacon Press, Black Women Writers series.

Nellie Y. McKay is a professor of English and Afro-American Literature at the University of Wisconsin, Madison. She is the author of *Jean Toomer, Artist: A Study of His Literary Work and Life;* editor of *Critical Essays on Toni Morrison,* and of essays on topics in American and Afro-American literature in anthologies and journals. Currently, she is working on a study of the autobiographies of twentieth-century Afro-American women.

Timothy Murray teaches in the English department at Cornell University. He is the author of *Theatrical Legitimation: Allegories of Genius in Seventeenth-Century England and France,* published by Oxford University Press in 1987, *Subliminal Libraries: Writing the Death Drive of Vision,* forthcoming from Routledge, and is editor of *Positioning Representation: French Poststructuralism and Theatre,* forthcoming from Routledge. He served as editor of *Theatre Journal* from 1984 through 1987, and has published widely in the areas of critical theory, theatre, visual studies, and Renaissance studies.

Donna Perry, Associate Professor of English at William Paterson College, received a New Jersey Governor's Fellowship in the humanities for 1989–90 to complete a study of contemporary women writers who are outside the mainstream. She has conducted workshops on transforming the curriculum to include race, class, and gender concerns and published essays in *Teaching Writing: Pedagogy, Gender, and Equity* (State University of New York Press, 1987), *Gender/Body/Knowledge: Feminist Reconstructions of Being and Knowing* (Rutgers University Press, 1989), and several journals.

John Shoptaw is an assistant professor at Princeton University. He is writing two books: *Living Within The System: The Poetry of John Ashbery* and *American Sentimental Discourse.*

Valerie Smith is an associate professor of English at the University of California, Los Angeles. She is the author of several articles on Afro-American literature, black feminist criticism, and black women filmmakers, and has written *Self-Discovery and Authority in Afro-American Narrative*, published by Harvard University Press in 1987. She is currently at work on studies of slavery and recent Afro-American fiction and of black feminist literary and cultural theory.

Hortense Spillers is a professor of English at Cornell University. She has previously taught at Wellesley College, the University of Nebraska, Lincoln, and Haverford College. She has written numerous essays, reviews, and short stories, appearing widely in various journals, including *Diacritics*, *The American Quarterly*, and *English Institute Essays*. With Marjorie Pryse, she coedited *Conjuring: Black Women, Fiction, and Literary Tradition* published by Indiana in 1985. Her *In the Flesh: A Situation for Feminist Inquiry* is forthcoming.

Helen Vendler is Kenan Professor of English literature at Harvard University and poetry critic of *The New Yorker*. She is the author of books on Yeats, Stevens, Herbert, and Keats. Her essays on modern American poetry have been collected in *Part of Nature, Part of Us: Modern American Poets*, which won the National Book Critics' Circle Prize in 1980. Her most recent book is *The Music of What Happens* (1988). She reviews contemporary poetry for many journals, and has edited *The Harvard Book of Contemporary American Poetry* and *Voices and Visions: The Poet in America* (1987).

Michele Wallace, a faculty member of the Center for Workers' Education in New York, is the author of *Black Macho and the Myth of the Superwoman*.

Mary Helen Washington has published three collections of writings by African-American women, including *Midnight Birds*; *Black-Eyed Susans*; and *Invented Lives*. One of the pioneering figures in the Black women's literary movement, she has published several essays about the Black women's literary tradition. Most recently, she has published a new edition of Zora Neale Hurston's classic work, *Their Eyes Were Watching God*. She is a professor of English at the University of Massachusetts in Boston.

Sherley Anne Williams is a teacher and writer who teaches and lives in California. She is the author of a critical study of African-American literature, *Give Birth to Blackness*, and a novel, *Dessa Rose*. She is a professor of literature at the University of California at San Diego.

Index